COMPARATIVE FINANCIAL REGULATION

RESEARCH HANDBOOKS IN COMPARATIVE LAW

Series Editors: Francesco Parisi, *Oppenheimer Wolff and Donnelly Professor of Law, University of Minnesota, USA and Professor of Economics, University of Bologna, Italy* and Tom Ginsburg, *Professor of Law, University of Chicago, USA*

The volumes in this series offer high-level discussion and analysis on particular aspects of legal systems and the law. Well-known scholars edit each *Research Handbook* and bring together accessible yet sophisticated contributions from an international cast of top researchers. The first series of its kind to cover a wide range of comparative issues so comprehensively, this is an indispensable resource for students and scholars alike.

For a full list of Edward Elgar published titles, including the titles in this series, visit our website at www.e-elgar.com.

Comparative Financial Regulation

Edited by

Alessio M. Pacces

Professor of Law & Finance, Amsterdam Center for Law & Economics, University of Amsterdam, the Netherlands

Edoardo D. Martino

Assistant Professor of Law & Finance, Amsterdam Center for Law & Economics, University of Amsterdam, the Netherlands

Hossein Nabilou

Assistant Professor of Law & Finance, Amsterdam Center for Law & Economics, University of Amsterdam, the Netherlands

RESEARCH HANDBOOKS IN COMPARATIVE LAW

Edward Elgar PUBLISHING

Cheltenham, UK • Northampton, MA, USA

Published by
Edward Elgar Publishing Limited
The Lypiatts
15 Lansdown Road
Cheltenham
Glos GL50 2JA
UK

Edward Elgar Publishing, Inc.
William Pratt House
9 Dewey Court
Northampton
Massachusetts 01060
USA

Authorised representative in the EU for GPSR queries only: Easy Access System Europe – Mustamäe tee 50, 10621 Tallinn, Estonia, gpsr.requests@easproject.com

A catalogue record for this book
is available from the British Library

Library of Congress Control Number: 2024951106

This book is available electronically in the **Elgar**online
Law subject collection
https://doi.org/10.4337/9781035306473

MIX
Paper | Supporting responsible forestry
FSC® C013604

ISBN 978 1 0353 0646 6 (cased)
ISBN 978 1 0353 0647 3 (eBook)

Printed and bound by CPI Group (UK) Ltd, Croydon, CR0 4YY

Contents

Contributors

Luca Amorello is currently a Director and Head of Recovery and Resolution Planning at Citibank Europe Plc, London, UK. He has previously worked as a legal counsel for the Bank of New York Mellon, Cleary Gottlieb Steen Hamilton LLP, the European Central Bank and Bank of Italy. He holds an LLM from Harvard Law School and a PhD in Law and Economics of Money and Finance from Goethe University of Frankfurt. He graduated *magna cum laude* at the University of Trieste Law School. He has authored a number of publications on macroprudential policy and regulations, including his book titled *Macroprudential Banking Supervision & Monetary Policy: Legal Interaction in the European Union.*

Phoebus L. Athanassiou is Senior Lead Legal Counsel with the Financial Law Division of the European Central Bank, Frankfurt, Germany, a member of the Faculty of the Institute of Law & Finance at Frankfurt University, Germany and a Fellow of the European Law Institute, Vienna, Austria. He holds a PhD in Law, from King's College, London, and he is a qualified lawyer. He has published extensively on financial services, capital markets regulation, and EMU-related issues. He is the author of several monographs, including, more recently, *Digital Innovation in Financial Services – Legal Challenges and Regulatory Policy Issues* (Kluwer, 2018), and *The European Sovereign Debt Crisis: Breaking the Vicious Circle Between Sovereigns and Banks* (Routledge, 2022; with A. Vouldis).

Iris H.-Y. Chiu is Professor of Corporate Law and Financial Regulation at the Faculty of Laws, University College London, UK. She joined the Faculty in 2009. She was Director of the UCL Centre of Ethics and Law (2016–2024) and advances the public and stakeholder engagement of the Centre's agenda in relation to a wide range of issues in relation to law, regulation, governance and ethics in business and finance. She has published extensively in the areas of corporate governance and financial regulation, including *The Foundations and Anatomy of Shareholder Activism* (2010), *Investment Management and Corporate Governance* (2017), *The Legal Framework for Internal Control in Banks and Financial Institutions* (2015) and *Banking Law and Regulation* (2019). She has interests in financial regulation and governance, law and technology, corporate law and governance and the law and policy for business and finance generally. She is a Research Member of the European Corporate Governance Institute, and most recently, a Senior Scholar at the European Central Bank's Legal Research Programme.

Lucrezia Cipriani is a PhD student at Ca' Foscari University of Venice, Italy, where she is doing research on the European framework on crypto-assets, focusing on the 'dialogue' between substantive law (MiCAR) and anti-money laundering regulation. She graduated in Law from Sapienza University of Rome and completed a second-level Master's degree in 'Regulation of Financial Activities and Markets'. In 2017, she studied for a semester at Suffolk Law School, Boston and in 2023 she conducted research at CBS Law, Copenhagen. She qualified to practice law in 2022 and interned as 'legal expert' at the Italian Competition Authority. Currently, she serves as an officer at the Italian Supreme Court.

Matteo Gargantini is Assistant Professor (tenure-track) of Business Law at the University of Genoa, Italy. He has been Assistant Professor of European Economic Law at the University of Utrecht and, previously, Senior Research Fellow at the Max Planck Institute Luxembourg for Procedural Law. Before joining the academia, Matteo served at Consob, the Italian Securities and Exchange Commission. He is a member of the Consultative Working Group for Corporate Finance of ESMA's Issuers. He holds the Italian National Academic Qualification as Full Professor of Business Law and as Associate Professor of Law and Economics and Financial Markets Law.

Sergio Gilotta is Associate Professor in Business Law at the University of Bologna, Italy, where he teaches business law and financial markets regulation. He holds a PhD in Corporate Law and Financial Markets Regulation from the University of Bologna and an LLM from Harvard Law School. Before joining the Bologna Law School in 2012, he taught international commercial law at the School of Economics of the University of Bologna and was a Research Fellow at the University of Florence. His research interests range from comparative corporate law and governance to financial market regulation, and include topics such as corporate disclosure, company groups, financial derivatives, insider trading, takeover law and sustainable finance. He is the author of three books and of numerous articles on these and other topics in the fields of corporate law and financial market regulation. He is a member of the Italian bar.

Seraina Grünewald is Professor of International Economic Law and Finance Law at the University of St. Gallen, Switzerland and a part-time Professor at the European University Institute in Florence, Italy. Before joining the University of St. Gallen in 2024, she held the chair for European and Comparative Financial Law at Radboud University Nijmegen in the Netherlands. She is also a member of the Academic Board of the European Banking Institute, an academic fellow with the Jean Monnet Centre of Excellence at the University of Genoa and a member of the Committee on International Monetary Law of the International Law Association. Her expertise includes areas such as sustainable finance, central banking, and the digitalization of money as well as bank resolution and she is frequently commissioned by national, European and international institutions and authorities.

Shuai Guo is Assistant Professor at the School of International Law, China University of Political Science and Law. He holds a doctoral degree from Leiden University. He serves as a consultant for the International Institute for the Unification of Private Law (UNIDROIT), a consultant for the Economic Research Institute for ASEAN and East Asia/United Nations Conference on Trade and Development (UNCTAD), as well as a working group member for the United Nations Economic and Social Commission for Asia and Pacific. He was a visiting scholar at the University of Texas at Austin. He is the author of four books and has published in leading international journals such as *International Insolvency Review*, *Asia Pacific Law Review*, *International Corporate Rescue*, *Norton Journal of Bankruptcy Law and Practice*, etc. He sits on the board of several international associations such as the International Insolvency Institute Academic Committee and INSOL International Early Researcher Academics, and is a Conferee at the Conference on European Restructuring and Insolvency Law. In 2022, he was recognized in the Global Restructuring Review 40 Under 40.

Rosa Lastra is the Sir John Lubbock Chair in Banking Law at the Centre for Commercial Law Studies, Queen Mary University of London, UK. She is Director of the Banking and Finance Institute, Co-director of the Sovereign Debt Forum, Co-director of the UNIDROIT-QMUL

Institute of Transnational Law, Vice-Chair of MOCOMILA, Research Associate of the Financial Markets Group of the London School of Economics, member of the European Shadow Financial Regulatory Committee, European Banking Institute, European Law Institute and PRIME. She is a renowned author in her areas of expertise and has consulted for the International Monetary Fund, European Central Bank, World Bank, Bank for International, Settlements, Bank of England, Asian Development Bank, United Nations (UNCTAD), Federal Reserve Bank of New York and the European Parliament (Monetary Panel and Banking Union Panel). She has also acted as Specialist Adviser to the House of Lords in 2009, 2021 and 2023.

Lauren Yu-Hsin Lin is an Associate Professor at City University of Hong Kong and Associate Director of the Center for Chinese and Comparative Law. Professor Lin is a leading scholar in comparative corporate law and governance. Using empirical methodologies, her work provides profound insights into the impacts of various governance regulations and practices. Professor Lin's scholarly work has been published in top academic journals such as the *Journal of Legal Studies* and the *Journal of Empirical Legal Studies*. Her work has also garnered significant attention in major media outlets, including the *Wall Street Journal*, *The Economist* and *Bloomberg*. She currently serves as the Associate Editor of the *International Review of Law and Economics* and is a Research Member of the European Corporate Governance Institute. Professor Lin has held visiting positions in Washington University in St Louis, Reichman University, Israel and Academia Sinica, Taiwan. Her research has been cited by the Delaware Court of Chancery, the US Securities and Exchange Commission, and the US–China Economic and Security Review Commission. She holds a JSD degree from Stanford Law School.

Eugenia Macchiavello (PhD, 2011; LLM, 2010, NYU) is Associate Professor in Economic Law at the University of Genoa, Academic Fellow and co-manager of the Jean Monnet Centre of Excellence in Sustainable Finance (EuSFIL) and Academic Fellow of the Genoa Centre for Law and Finance–CEDIF as well as certified attorney-at-law in Italy. Eugenia is also an Academic Board member and supervisor of PhD candidates in the area of sustainable finance regulation within the transdisciplinary national PhD course in Sustainable Development and Climate Change (IUSS Pavia and other Italian universities) and Academic Board member of the transdisciplinary PhD Course in Security, Risk and Vulnerability (University of Genoa). She is a member of the Italian Association of Professors in Economic Law and of the Associated Researchers Group of the European Banking Institute as well as former participant to the Italian Financial Markets Authority (Consob) Expert Working Group on FinTech and former visiting Fellow at the NYU Center of Financial Institution. She is an expert in the regulation of alternative finance and fintech, author of a book on microfinance regulation in Europe from a comparative law and multi-disciplinary perspective, and editor of the recent international commentary published by Edward Elgar Publishing: *Regulation on European Crowdfunding Service Providers for Business: A Commentary*.

Ugo Malvagna is an Associate Professor, with qualifications as a Full Professor, in Economic and Financial Markets Law at the Law School of the University of Trento, Italy, where he also serves as deputy director of the PhD School of Comparative and European Legal Studies. He is a corresponding member of the Italian Society of Professors of Law and Economics and the Italian Society of Civil Law Scholars, where he sits on the Financial Law commission. Additionally, he is a fellow of the European Law Institute, Vienna and a member of the

Associated Researchers Group at the European Banking Institute, Frankfurt. He is a member of the Editorial Board of the legal journal *Banca Borsa Titoli di Credito* and editor-in-chief of the *Rivista di Diritto Bancario* (*Banking Law Review*). He serves as an Arbitrator for Financial Controversies and as the financial ombudsman for the Italian Financial Markets Authority (Consob). Appointed by the Italian Minister of Economy and Finance, he has served on the Technical Commission of the Italian Savers' Indemnification Fund (Fondo Indennizzo Risparmiatori). He has authored two monographs on risk allocation in payment services and on the use of benchmarks in asset management undertakings. His extensive publications cover bank resolution, investor protection, banking contracts, consumer credit, and various topics related to corporate and contract law.

Menelaos Markakis is Associate Professor of International and European Union Law at Erasmus University Rotterdam, the Netherlands and Scientific Coordinator of the Erasmus Center for Economic and Financial Governance. He also lectures on EU law at Worcester College, Oxford. His main areas of research are public law and EU law. His core expertise is in the Economic and Monetary Union and the European Banking Union. He has published his research in prestigious edited volumes and peer-reviewed journals, including the *Common Market Law Review*, the *European Law Review*, the *European Constitutional Law Review*, *Public Law*, the *Review of European Administrative Law* and the *Journal of International Economic Law*. His monograph, entitled *Accountability in the Economic and Monetary Union: Foundations, Policy, and Governance*, was published in 2020 by Oxford University Press and won the 2022 European Court of Auditors publication award. He has also obtained funding for his research from the Academy of Athens, the Oxford Law Faculty, the Modern Law Review award, the EUR Fellowship, the Erasmus Trustfonds and the European Social Fund.

Edoardo D. Martino is Assistant Professor of Law & Finance at the University of Amsterdam, the Netherlands and a Research Associate at the European Banking Institute, Germany. He is Program Director of the Master in Law and Finance at the University of Amsterdam. He engages in research and teaching activities in the broad field of law and finance. His research focuses on financial regulation, corporate governance and fintech. On these topics, he has published book chapters with publishers such as Routledge and Edward Elgar Publishing, as well as articles in journals such as the *European Business Organization Law Review*, the *Journal of Corporate Law Studies* and the *European Company and Financial Law Review*. He is a guest contributor to, among others, the Oxford Business Law Blog and the Columbia Blue Sky Blog. He has been a visiting researcher in several universities, such as Oxford University, the University of Hamburg, the University of Bologna and Goethe University Frankfurt.

Andrea Minto is an Associate Professor of Law at Ca' Foscari University of Venice, Italy. He is Full Professor of Law at the University of Stavanger Business School and holds the Chair in Digitalisation in EU Financial Law Studies (EUDIFIN), financed by the European Commission. Andrea works as Of Counsel at Annunziata&Conso Law Firm in Milan. In addition, he cooperates with several financial supervisory authorities and central banks on a wide array of regulatory topics.

Katrien Morbee is a Senior Lecturer in Banking and Finance Law at the Centre for Commercial Law Studies, Queen Mary University of London, UK. Her teaching and research interests focus on corporate governance, systemic risk and sustainability, exploring how to design, finance and regulate corporations to align their incentives with sustainability considerations. She regularly publishes articles on these topics. Katrien completed her DPhil in Law and Finance at the University of Oxford. She holds an LLB and LLM from Ghent University, Belgium and an LLM from Yale University, USA.

Hossein Nabilou is an Assistant Professor of Law & Finance at the University of Amsterdam (UvA) Law School, the Netherlands. Prior to joining UvA, Hossein was UNIDROIT-Bank of Italy Chair at the International Institute for the Unification of Private Law (UNIDROIT). His research focuses on monetary and banking law, shadow banking, financial market infrastructures, financial contracting, alternative investment funds and legal issues of fintech, payments and crypto-assets. He teaches European banking law, financial contracting, fintech: law and policy, and law and economics.

Alessio M. Pacces is Professor of Law & Finance at the Amsterdam Law School and the Amsterdam Business School, the Netherlands and the Director of the Amsterdam Center for Law & Economics. He is a Research Member of the European Corporate Governance Institute and a Fellow Academic Member of the European Banking Institute. He has published over 50 pieces of scholarship as books, chapters, and articles in journals such as *Harvard Business Law Review*, *Journal of Corporate Law Studies*, *International Review of Law and Economics* and *American Business Law Journal*, among others, and with publishing houses such as Edward Elgar Publishing, Routledge, Cambridge University Press and Oxford University Press, among others. Alessio has been invited to speak at several universities in Europe, Asia, Israel, and the USA and at policymakers such as the European Commission, the Organisation for Economic Co-operation and Development, the International Monetary Fund, and the European Central Bank. He has had visiting positions at UC Berkeley, Columbia Law School, University of Haifa, LUISS University in Rome and Stanford University.

Katarzyna Parchimowicz is Assistant Professor at the Academic Excellence Hub – Digital Justice Center, University of Wrocław, Poland and Associate Researcher at the European Banking Institute, Germany. She holds a Master's degree in Law from University of Wrocław, a Master's degree in Law and Finance (LLM Finance) from the Institute for Law and Finance (Goethe University Frankfurt) and a PhD in Law from the University of Wrocław. She conducted research as a Visiting Scholar at the University of Oxford, Duke Law School (sponsored by Kosciuszko Foundation) and Amsterdam Law School. She is the author of *The Regulation of Megabanks. Legal Frameworks of the USA and EU* (Routledge, 2023), an awardee of the ECB Legal Research Programme 2022 and recipient of the Foundation for Polish Science START award.

Youcef Rahmani is currently a DPhil in Law candidate at the University of Oxford, UK, where he is pursuing research at the intersection of sustainability and financial regulation. He leads the Sustainable Law and Finance Working Group of Droit & Croissance, a Paris-based European think-do tank. He is also an active member of the Oxford Sustainable Law Programme. Youcef received his Bachelor of Arts in Philosophy and Middle-Eastern Studies from McGill University, a Master's in Economic Law from Sciences Po and an MSc in Law and Finance from the University of Oxford.

Paolo Saguato is Professor of Law and Founder and Executive Director of the Program on Financial Markets at Antonin Scalia Law School, George Mason University, USA. Paolo's teaching and research interests focus on international, US and EU financial regulation. He focuses on the regulation of banks, securities and derivatives markets, and financial market infrastructures; financial innovation and technology; and corporate law and theory. Paolo serves on the Consultative Working Group of the European Securities and Markets Authority's Central Counterparty (CCP) Policy Committee and on the CCP Risk and Governance Subcommittee of the Commodity Futures Trading Commission's Market Risk Advisory Committee. His research has been featured in publications including the *Yale Journal on Regulation*, the *Stanford Journal of Law, Business and Finance*, the *Columbia Business Law Review*, the *Journal of Corporate Law Studies* and the *Oxford Handbook of Financial Regulation*. Paolo is a co-editor of one of the leading books on financial market infrastructures, *Financial Market Infrastructures: Law and Regulation* (Oxford University Press, 2022) and the co-author of *Business Associations: A Modern Approach* (Foundation Press, 2023). Professor Saguato graduated *summa cum laude* from the University of Genoa Law School, Italy and earned a PhD in Private, Business and International Law at the same university. In addition, he holds an LLM from Yale Law School, which he attended as a Fulbright Scholar.

Ana Taleska is Affiliated Lecturer at the Faculty of Law, University of Cambridge, UK and a Bye-fellow and Director of Studies at Wolfson College, University of Cambridge. Previously, Dr Taleska was the Slaughter and May Lecturer in Corporate Law and Corporate Finance at the University of Cambridge. She is a practising Corporate/M&A attorney at Loyens & Loeff.

Preface

Reflecting the growing importance of finance in the economy, financial regulation is becoming ubiquitous. However, while finance flows globally, regulation remains national or at least regional. This observation motivates this book on comparative financial regulation.

We have collected contributions from worldwide experts in financial regulation, namely from the European continent, the UK, the USA and Asia. We asked them to engage in a functional comparison of different areas of financial regulation in several jurisdictions. Because opinions of reasonable minds may differ about the function of financial regulation, we introduce this book with an analytical framework for comparison. On the one hand, we point out the functions of different parts of the financial system and how regulation addresses market failures therein. On the other, we ask the overarching question: 'What drives convergence and divergence of financial regulation?'

We asked all contributors to answer this question. The answer is manifold and differs considerably depending on the area of financial regulation. Reflecting a longstanding distinction in financial economics, we have divided the regulatory analysis into two macro areas: financial markets (Part II) and financial institutions (Part III). Because financial innovation makes this distinction even more blurred than it traditionally was, we have collected the latest cross-cutting regulatory developments in Part IV ('Frontiers'). The three parts are preceded by Part I ('Introduction'), including chapters on the analytical framework, the history of financial regulation, and its institutional architecture.

We discussed the first version of each chapter in a meeting with our authors in Amsterdam on 20 April 2023. Every contribution had a discussant and received additional comments from the other authors. Somewhat unusually for a collection of book chapters, every revised version underwent rigorous and anonymous peer-review. The third version has been professionally edited and finally reviewed by the editors.

This refined collection of articles aims at a broad readership, including but not limited to policymakers, graduate students, and academics. A globe-spanning group of contributors, coupled with the functional approach, provides the reader with a broad overview of how financial regulation converges (or not) towards common standards in key jurisdictions. More importantly, the book provides the analytical tools to understand and interpret financial regulation from a comparative perspective, even in jurisdictions not directly covered. As this book is research-driven, we hope that it will raise more questions than it answers.

Edoardo D. Martino
Hossein Nabilou
Alessio M. Pacces

Amsterdam, July 2024

Acknowledgements

This book is the result of the effort and dedication of many people. We owe sincere thanks to the anonymous reviewers for generously giving their time in refereeing the chapters of this book and ensuring high academic standards. We can now (collectively) reveal their identity. We thank Dan Awrey, Nik de Boer, Alper Demir, Gabriella Gimigliano, Jens van 't Klooster, Marleen Och, Tom Vos, Jeffrey Zhang and many of the book's contributors for their comments on several chapters.

Thanks to Ernst & Young Amsterdam for hosting the meeting with our contributing authors in April 2023 and to the Amsterdam Center for Law & Economics for sponsoring the event and the time of the editors. A special thank you to Emily Ross and Robert Hoek for their invaluable support in the organization and warm welcome.

Finally, we are grateful to Yannick Roos for his invaluable help in the editing phase.

Abbreviations

AFS	Australian Financial Service
AIF	Alternative Investment Fund
AIFMD	Alternative Investment Fund Managers Directive
AMEX	American Stock Exchange
AML	Anti Money Laundering
AMLD	Anti Money Laundering Directive
API	Application Programming Interface
ART	Asset Referenced Token
ASIC	Australian Securities and Investments Commission
ASPSP	Account Service Payment Service Provider
AUM	Assets under Management
BCBS	Basel Committee on Banking Supervision
BIS	Bank for International Settlements
BoE	Bank of England
BPF	Brown Penalising Factor
BRRD	Bank Recovery and Resolution Directive
BSA	Banking Secrecy Act
CAPM	Capital Asset Price Model
CBDC	Central Bank Digital Currency
CBIRC	China Banking and Insurance Regulatory Commission
CBOE	Chicago Board Options Exchange
CBRC	China Banking Regulatory Commission
CCB	Capital Conservation Buffer
CCCB	Countercyclical Capital Buffer
CCP	Central Counter Party
CDD	Costumer Due Diligence
CDIC	Canada Deposit Insurance Corporation
CDICA	Canada Deposit Insurance Corporation Act
CET1	Common Equity Tier 1
CFPB	Consumer Financial Protection Bureau
CFT	Combating Financing Terrorism
CFTC	Commodity Future Trading Commission
CIS	Collective Investment Scheme
CISA	Collective Investment Schemes Act
CME	Chicago Mercantile Exchange

CMS	Capital Markets Services
CoB	Conduct of Business
COBS	Conduct of Business Sourcebook
CONC	Consumer Credit sourcebook
COODCI	Cabinet Office Ordinance on Disclosure of Corporate Information
CPSS	Committee on Payment and Settlement Systems
CPMI	Committee on Payments and Market Infrastructures
CRA	Credit Rating Agency
CRD	Capital Requirement Directive
CRFR	Climate-related Financial Risk
CRR	Capital Requirement Regulation
CSA	Credit Support Annex
CSD	Central Securities Depositories
CSP	Crowdfunding Service Provider
CSR	Corporate Social Responsibility
CSRC	China Securities Regulatory Commission
CSRD	Corporate Sustainability Reporting Directive
C&S	Clearing and Settlement
DAO	Decentralised Autonomous Organization
DCS	Dual Class Shares
DLT	Distributed Ledger Technology
DORA	Digital Operational Resilience Act
DSA	Digital Settlement Assets
DSTI	Debt Service-To-Income
DTC	Depository Trust Corporation
DTCC	Depository Trust & Clearing Corporation
DvP	Delivery versus Payment
EBA	European Banking Authority
EBC	Equity Based Crowdfunding
ECB	European Central Bank
ECMH	Efficient Capital Market Hypothesis
ECSPR	European Crowdfunding Service Providers Regulation
EEA	European Economic Area
EFRAG	European Financial Reporting Advisory Group
EIOPA	European Insurance and Occupational Pensions Authority
ELMI	Electronic Money Institution
EMD	Electronic Money Directive
EMI	Electronic Money Institution
EMIR	European Financial Market Infrastructure Regulation

EMR	Electronic Money Regulation
EPC	European Payments Council
ERPB	Euro Retail Payments Board
ESCB	European System of Central Banks
ESG	Environmental, Social, Governance
ESMA	European Securities and Market Authority
ESRB	European Systemic Risk Board
ESRS	European Sustainability Reporting Standards
ETF	Exchange Traded Funds
EU	European Union
EUPR	European Union Prospectus Regulation
FAFT	Financial Action Task Force
FCA	Financial Conduct Authority
FCA	Financial Choice Act
FASB	Financial Accounting Standards Board
FCD	Financial Collateral Directive
FCM	Futures Commission Merchants
FD	(Regulation) Fair Disclosure
FDIC	Federal Deposit Insurance Corporation
FED	Federal Reserve
FHC	Financial Holding Company
FICC	Fixed Income Clearing Corporation
FINMA	(Swiss) Financial Market Supervisory Authority
FINRA	Financial Industry Regulatory Authority
FIRO	Financial Institutions Resolution Ordinance
FMI	Financial Market Infrastructure
FPC	Financial Policy Committee
FRB	Board of Governors of the Federal Reserve System
FRC	Financial-return Crowdfunding
FSA	Financial Services Authority
FSB	Financial Stability Board
FSMA	Financial Services and Markets Act
FSMB	Financial Services and Markets Bill
FSOC	Financial Stability Oversight Council
G-SIBs	Globally Systemically Important Banks
GAAP	Generally Accepted Accounting Principles
GDP	Gross Domestic Product
GFC	Global Financial Crisis
GFIT	Green Finance Industry Taskforce

GMRA	Global Master Repurchase Agreements
GMSLA	Global Master Securities Lending Agreements
GSF	Green Supporting Factor
GSII	Globally Systemic Important Institutions
HFCAA	Holding Foreign Companies Accountable Act
HKSE	Hong Kong Stock Exchange
HMT	His Majesty's Treasury
HNWI	High Net Worth Individuals
HQLA	High Quality Liquid Assets
IAIS	International Association of Insurance Supervisors
IAS	International Accounting Standards
IASB	International Accounting Standards Board
IBC	Investment-based Crowdfunding
ICMA	International Capital Market Association
ICO	Initial Coin Offering
IFD/IFR	Investment Firms Directive/Regulation
IFRS	International Financial Reporting Standards
IMF	International Monetary Fund
IOSCO	International Organization of Securities Commissions
IP	Instant Payment
IPCC	Intergovernmental Panel on Climate Change
IPO	Initial Public Offering
ISDA	International Swaps and Derivatives Association
ISLA	International Securities Lending Association
ISSB	International Sustainability Standards Board
ITASA	Innovative Technological Arrangements and Services Act
ITPA	Insider Trading Prohibition Act
JFIEA	Japanese Financial Instrument and Exchange Act
KA	Key Attributes (of Effective Resolution Regimes for Financial Institutions)
KID	Key Investor Documents
KIID	Key Investor Information Document
KIIS	Key Investor Information Sheet
LAAP	Liquidity Adequacy Assessment Process
LBC	Loan-based Crowdfunding
LCH	London Clearing House
LCR	Liquidity Coverage Ratio
LGD	Loss Given Default
LSEG	London Stock Exchange Group
LTD	Loan to Deposit

LTI	Loan to Income
LTV	Loan to Value
MAR	Market Abuse Regulation
MAS	Monetary Authority of Singapore
MASA	Monetary Authority of Singapore Act
MiCAR	Market in Crypto Asset Regulation
MiFID	Market in Financial Instruments Directive
MiFIR	Market in Financial Instruments Regulation
MIS	Managed Investment Scheme
MMF	Money Market Funds
MREL	Minimum Requirement for Own Funds and Eligible Liabilities
MSP	Major Swap Participant
NAAFMII	National Association of Financial Market Institutional Investors
NASD	National Association of Securities Dealers
NAV	Net Asset Value
NBFI	Non-bank Financial Intermediation
NFRD	Non-financial Reporting Directive
NGFS	Network for Greening the Financial System
NSCC	National Securities Clearing Corporation
NSFR	Net Stable Funding Ratio
NYSE	New Your Stock Exchange
OCC	Office of the Comptroller of the Currency
OCC	Options Clearing Corporation
OECD	Organisation for Economic Co-operation and Development
OTC	Over the counter
P2P	Peer to peer
PBOC	People's Bank of China
PCAOB	Public Company Accounting Oversight Board
PD	Probability of Default
PFMI	Principles for Financial Market Infrastructures
PRA	Prudential Regulation Authority
PRI	Principles of Responsible Investment
PRIIPs	Packaged Retail and Insurance-based Investment Product
PSD	Payment Service Directive
PSP	Payment Service Provides
PSR	Payment Services Regulations
PSU	Payment Service Users
QAT	Qualitative Asset Transformation
QE	Quantitative Easing

QFC	Qualified Financial Contracts
RBI	Regulation Best Interest
RCAP	Regulatory Consistency Assessment Programme
RRP	Recovery and Resolution Plans
RWA	Risk Weighted Assets
SCT	SEPA Credit Transfer
SDD	SEPA Direct Debit
SDR	Sustainability Disclosure Requirements
SEC	Securities and Exchange Commission
SEPA	Single Euro Payments Area
SFA	Singapore's Securities and Futures Act
SFCA	Security Financial Collateral Arrangement
SFD	Settlement Finality Directive
SFTR	Securities Financing Transactions Regulation
SGX	Singapoore Stock Exchange
SIFMA	Securities Industry and Financial Markets Association
SME	Small or medium-sized enterprise
SNB	Swiss National Bank
SPAC	Special Purpose Acquisition Vehicle
SPE	Single Point of Entry
SPV	Special Purpose Vehicle
SREP	Supervisory Review and Evaluation Process
SRMR	Single Resolution Mechanism Regulation
SRO	Self-regulatory Organizations
SSFA	Securities and Futures Act
SSM	Single Supervisory Mechanism
SSS	Securities Settlement Systems
SVB	Silicon Valley Bank
TARGET	Trans-European Automated Real-time Gross Settlement Express Transfer
TCFD	Task Force on Climate-related Financial Disclosures
TFEU	Treaty on the Functioning of the European Union
TIPS	TARGET Instant Payment Settlement
TLAC	Total Loss Absorbing Capacity
TPP	Third Party Provider
TTCA	Title-transfer Financial Collateral Arrangement
UCC	Uniform Commercial Code
UCITS	Undertakings for the Collective Investment in Transferable Securities
UK	United Kingdom
UMSA	Uniform Money Services Act

UNIDROIT	International Institute for the Unification of Private Law
URD	Universal Registration Document
US	United States
USSA	United States Securities Act
USSEA	United States Securities Exchange Act
VaR	Value at Risk
VFAA	Virtual Financial Assets Act
WKSI	Well-known Seasoned Issuers
WWI	World War I
WWII	World War II

PART I

INTRODUCTION

1. An analytical framework

Edoardo D. Martino, Hossein Nabilou and Alessio M. Pacces

1. INTRODUCTION

Financial markets are essential for society. The development of financial markets is an important aspect of the development of modern institutions.[1] While the relevance of financial markets is a constant throughout history,[2] in modern economies they are ubiquitous and shape economic decisions of private and public actors like never before.[3] This is an inherently global phenomenon. However, financial law remains national or regional despite the forces toward global convergence.

In this chapter, we develop an analytical framework to study the role of law in finance and how to approach financial regulation from a comparative perspective, identifying the drivers of convergence and divergence in different jurisdictions. The comparative exercise is relevant along several dimensions. First, it helps understand the different preferences of policymakers across time and space. For instance, if Country A tightly regulates banks compared with Country B or compared with what country A used to do in previous years, this reveals a specific set of social, economic, and political preferences that result in financial regulation. Second, a comparative approach to financial regulation helps detect the underlying forces of convergence and divergence shaping regulation in different areas of finance and different jurisdictions. Third, a comparative approach to financial regulation can also provide insights into the desirable legal tools and level of harmonization for the new challenges posed by an ever-evolving financial system, such as financial transactions happening in the blockchain or the growing interest in sustainable finance. This chapter does not aim to identify the efficient degree of harmonization. However, it provides some guiding principles.[4]

We first discuss the micro-foundation of financial markets and look at the theory of financial intermediation, showing that intermediation is inherent to financial transactions.[5] We move on to explain why financial intermediation is prone to market failures. We then explore

---

1 Franklin Allen and Douglas Gale, *Comparing Financial Systems* (MIT Press 2001) 25.

2 See, for instance, Peter Temin, 'Financial Intermediation in the Early Roman Empire' (2004) 64 The Journal of Economic History 705.

3 A process called 'financialization', see Gerald A Epstein (ed.), *Financialization and the World Economy* (Edward Elgar Publishing 2005).

4 On the promises and limitation of comparative law and economics methodology, see Nuno Garoupa and Thomas S Ulen, 'Comparative Law and Economics: Aspirations and Hard Realities' (2021) 69 The American Journal of Comparative Law 664.

5 On the tension between financial intermediation and the hype on financial disintermediation, see Fatjon Kaja, Edoardo D Martino and Alessio M Pacces, 'FinTech and the Law and Economics of Disintermediation', in Iris Chiu and Gudula Deipenbrock (eds), *Routledge Handbook of Financial Technology and Law* (Routledge 2021).

the role of the law. Having observed that financial markets are legally constructed, in Section 2 we discuss how the law can correct market failures. In Section 3, we categorize the drivers of convergence and divergence in four groups. First, the underlying national private laws, in particular property and contract law, provide the legal basis for financial contracts and for financial entities to carry out financial transactions. Second, different regulators may pursue different policy goals or use different legal tools while pursuing the same goal. Third, financial regulators must account for the different structure and degree of integration of financial markets. Fourth, regulators are exposed to a set of other, heterogeneous forces shaping their policymaking. Based on the economic rationales and the drivers of convergence and divergence, we apply our comparative framework to the capital markets, banking and the hybrid sectors of the financial system in Section 4. We conclude in Section 5.

2. FROM FINANCIAL MARKETS TO FINANCIAL REGULATION

2.1 Financial Markets and Financial Intermediaries

Financial markets are the institutions allowing a society to mobilize capital. Financial markets facilitate exchanges through the payment system, mobilize savings of fund givers and select projects of fund takers. In so doing, financial markets manage and allocate financial resources and risks across the economy.[6] Ideally, financial regulation copes with market failures in mobilizing savings and allocating scarce capital to the projects that generate the highest social welfare. We call this goal allocative efficiency.

Capital allocation requires some form of intermediation. We define intermediation broadly, as any subject, institution or technology that facilitates the interaction between fund takers and fund givers employing some degree of centralization. To understand why intermediation is pivotal, imagine an economy where only spot transactions are possible. A potential fund taker needs finance for her project, but potential fund givers cannot observe if it is a 'good' or a 'bad' project. This informational asymmetry prevents uninformed fund givers from pricing their risk correctly and they are forced to average the risk of high- and low-quality projects. Hence, low-quality projects dominate the market because they are the only ones willing to accept a higher cost of capital. This phenomenon is called adverse selection.[7] Both fund givers and fund takers could produce, at a cost, information about the quality of the projects. However, the information may not be reliable.[8] Moreover, if an agent could produce reliable information, which could be used by other agents free of charge, no agent would have incentive to produce information because of free riding.[9] The result of this completely disin-

---

6 John Armour and others, *Principles of Financial Regulation* (Oxford University Press 2016) 24–26.

7 On the detrimental effects of adverse selection in finance, see Stephen Morris and Hyun Song Shin, 'Contagious Adverse Selection' (2012) 4 American Economic Journal: Macroeconomics 1.

8 Jack Hirshleifer, 'The Private and Social Value of Information and the Reward to Inventive Activity' (1971) 61 American Economic Review 561.

9 Sanford J Grossman and Joseph E Stiglitz, 'On the Impossibility of Informationally Efficient Markets' (1980) 70 The American Economic Review 393.

termediated financial market defies the goal of allocative efficiency. Financial intermediation has emerged to address asymmetric information and allow intermediaries to profit from the generation of reliable information.[10]

While the forms of financial intermediation vary over time and across jurisdictions, intermediation is inherent to finance. Intermediary-based financial markets are the result of the inability of spot market transactions to efficiently allocate capital in complex societies. In this framework, the disintermediation debate can be understood as a process of designing new, often technologically enabled and hopefully more efficient, intermediation mechanisms performed by new agents such as algorithms (or their coders) and data analysts.

The traditional distinction of financial intermediaries is between financial institutions and capital markets participants. Such a distinction is simplistic in many respects because there are overlaps. However, it remains conceptually useful because institutions and markets employ different strategies to generate information about the efficient allocation of funds and to generate trust among agents. This is best understood by looking at the two extreme cases: on the one hand, banks performing 'heavy' intermediation; on the other, the securities market, where arm's length transactions are supported by 'light' intermediaries, such as broker-dealers, guaranteeing the quality of information available to agents.

Banks engage in 'Qualitative Asset Transformation' whereby they borrow short-term, liquid and riskless funds, such as insured deposits or repos, and use the borrowed funds to finance long-term, illiquid and risky projects.[11] This results in a mismatch between the maturity, liquidity and risk profiles of assets and liabilities of the banks. This construction, albeit inherently fragile, provides key services to society. In normal times, a bank can withstand this fragile construction acting as delegated monitor.[12] Since fund givers are unwilling to generate information about the creditworthiness of borrowers, banks attract them by doing the monitoring on their behalf while promising safety and liquidity. Moreover, banks specialize in generating superior, non-public information to minimize credit risk, pooling together a diversified portfolio of loans and mortgages.

The key to supporting the business model of a bank is to safeguard the borrowers' trust in bank solvency.[13] To achieve this result, bank debt should be information insensitive, meaning that bank borrowers, mainly depositors, have no incentives to acquire private information about the solvency of the borrowing bank.[14] For depositors, deposit insurance is the paradigmatic device to ensure information insensitivity. This device allows banks to borrow cheaply and lend at higher rates to support the delegated monitoring and screening activities.

On the other side of the spectrum, capital markets generate information on which market players can rely for their saving and investment decisions. While the agents and transactions of

---

[10] For a formalization of this intuition, see John H Boyd and Edward C Prescott, 'Financial Intermediary-coalitions' (1986) 38 Journal of Economic theory 211.

[11] Anjan V Thakor, 'Financial Intermediation and the Market for Credit' (1995) 9 Handbooks in Operations Research and Management Science 1073.

[12] Douglas W Diamond, 'Financial Intermediation and Delegated Monitoring' (1984) 51 The Review of Economic Studies 393.

[13] Douglas W Diamond and Philip H Dybvig, 'Bank Runs, Deposit Insurance, and Liquidity' (1983) 91 Journal of Political Economy 401.

[14] Tri Vi Dang, Gary Gorton and Bengt Holmström, 'The Information View of Financial Crises' (2020) 12 Annual Review of Financial Economics 39.

the capital markets are heterogenous, they all aim to match fund givers and fund takers. Again, this matching does not arise spontaneously but requires intermediaries. Stock exchanges, clearing houses, custodians and other participants allow the market to function. Other intermediaries support fund takers and fund givers in their activities, such as underwriters, brokers, and financial advisors.

Capital market intermediaries generate and disseminate reliable information on the quality of the investment projects, under the assumption that such information will be unbiasedly incorporated in the securities price.[15] These intermediaries appropriate the gains from generating information, for instance, via brokerage fees and the bid-ask spreads from securities trading. In principle, the price determined by capital markets should guide the efficient allocation of funds between borrowers and lenders.

2.2 Intermediaries, Market Failures and Financial Regulation

Financial intermediaries arise to cope with the failures of spot market transactions. However, the existence of intermediaries does not eliminate all market failures. On the contrary, financial intermediaries may generate new market failures. In turn, financial regulation aims to address these further failures in the process of efficiently allocating capital.

There are two related but conceptually different rationales for financial regulation. First, regulation underpins financial markets and supports the reliability of key intermediaries.[16] Second, regulation counters abusive and inefficient behaviors of these intermediaries. These rationales are related insofar as the same legal tool may address both. Sometimes, however, legal tools aiming at increasing the intermediaries' reliability generate additional inefficiencies which we label regulatory failure. Two examples, one from banking and the other from capital markets, will clarify this mechanism.

As said, financial intermediaries emerge to cope with adverse selection. However, intermediaries may run into the same problem if the information they produce is not reliable. In this situation, the law should support intermediaries to foster efficient capital allocation, for instance providing deposit insurance to maintain information insensitivity. Commercial banks raise capital by 'transforming' short-term liquid liabilities into long-term illiquid assets. The promise of short-term liquidity is only sustainable for private institutions in 'good times'. In contrast, during crises, depositors would 'run' in case of adverse perception of a bank's solvency. Deposit insurance supports the promise of short-term liquidity provided by banks in any circumstance. The downside of deposit insurance is that banks, facing no risk of runs, tend to take excessive risks and externalize the potential losses on taxpayers.[17] This, in turn, calls for further regulation, such as capital and liquidity requirements, resolution regimes, and other regulatory measures.[18]

---

[15] The so-called Efficient Capital Market Hypothesis, Eugene F Fama, 'Efficient Capital Markets: A Review of Theory and Empirical Work' (1970) 25 The Journal of Finance 383.

[16] Katharina Pistor, 'A Legal Theory of Finance' (2013) 41 Journal of Comparative Economics 315.

[17] Franklin Allen and others, 'Moral Hazard and Government Guarantees in the Banking Industry' (2015) 1 Journal of Financial Regulation 30.

[18] Mathias Dewatripont and Jean Tirole, *The Prudential Regulation of Banks* (MIT Press 1994).

In capital markets, intermediaries may be unable to signal their trustworthiness to overcome the adverse selection problem. A typical example of a legal tool supporting intermediaries' trustworthiness is licensing. The government screens and certifies the trustworthiness of capital market agents and includes them in the 'club' of agents that are allowed to carry out a certain activity, such as asset management.[19] A license signals the trustworthiness of the advisor to potential investors. Investors will value the signal and trust the licensed asset management. Licensing works as signal if the requirements are costly enough to disallow mimicking by untrustworthy agents. For instance, to be licensed as financial advisor one must meet several requirements in terms of professional expertise and personal reputation.

Licensing as a legal tool is not only useful as a signal to investors, but also plays a crucial role in regulating intermediaries. First, regulation usually targets licensed entities – the so-called entity-based regulation. For instance, licensed asset managers must truthfully disclose the information about the risk profile of the investment and must guarantee the suitability of the investment for the client. Imposing the same duties on any agent who carries out the activity of asset manager – so-called activity-based regulation – might not be as effective because monitoring a function is costlier for regulators than monitoring an entity. However, licensing creates a barrier to entry. If only licensed entities can compete in the market for asset managers, competition is restricted and efficiency is undermined.[20]

These examples highlight a tradeoff between different goals: in the first example, promoting bank stability, on the one hand, and fostering moral hazard on the other; and in the second example, promoting competition, on the one hand, and limiting other market failures on the other. The sources of market failure in capital markets differ from those of banking. Whereas in capital markets information asymmetry is the main source of market failure, in banking the main problem is negative (systemic) externalities.[21] Again, overlaps exists but this distinction remains useful to explain the different tradeoffs in the two contexts.

In capital markets, regulators are mainly concerned with information asymmetries between investors and their agents.[22] The paramount example in this regard is the prohibition of insider trading, whereby the agents – the inside management – cannot profit from non-public information they possess at the expense of the principals, namely the investors who only have access to public information. The prohibition of insider trading supports pricing based on unbiased, public information, attracting investors to liquid capital markets that allocate their capital efficiently.[23] However, the prohibition of insiders trading also reduces the speed with which information is incorporated in prices.[24]

In banking, regulators focus on the negative externalities from Qualitative Asset Transformation, which is a welfare-increasing way to overcome information asymmetries.

---

[19] Licenses and entity-based regulation are employed also with banks; here the reference is specific to capital markets only for the sake of the example.

[20] Harold Demsetz, 'Barriers to Entry' (1982) 72 The American Economic Review 47.

[21] Text to notes 35–36.

[22] Anat R Admati and Paul Pfleiderer, 'Selling and Trading on Information in Financial Markets' (1988) 78 The American Economic Review 96.

[23] Zohar Goshen and Gideon Parchomovsky, 'The Essential Role of Securities Regulation' (2005) 55 Duke LJ 711.

[24] Henry G Manne, 'Insider Trading and the Administrative Process' (1966) 35 Geo. Wash. L. Rev. 473.

The negative externalities of Qualitative Asset Transformation are potentially systemic because they can affect the whole economic system.[25] Banks pose systemic risks to the financial system because of their size, leverage, interconnectedness and importance to the overall economy. Therefore, banks rely on governments implicitly guaranteeing their solvency which, in turn, generates moral hazard. Moral hazard means taking excessive risk because the downside is borne by someone else, in this case the governments which guarantee solvency. The consequences of moral hazard vary depending on the credit cycle. A bank takes excessive risks in periods of economic booms but forgoes profitable investments in times of crisis. This leads to credit crunch and, when it concerns the entire banking system, may result in a severe contraction of the economy.[26] In the aftermath of the 2007–2008 Global Financial Crisis (GFC), policymakers worldwide established 'macro-prudential' regulation to curb Qualitative Asset Transformation in good times and reduce the probability and impact of systemic crises in bad times.[27]

The relationship between finance and regulation is not unidirectional, from the developments of financial intermediation to regulatory responses. On the contrary, the relationship is bidirectional because regulation can also drive the development of finance, shaping the way financial markets emerge and evolve.[28] A paradigmatic example is the peculiar structure of banks in the US characterized by holding companies controlling commercial banks. This arrangement derives from the structural separation of commercial and investment banking in the US established by the Glass–Steagall Act of 1932 and the Bank Holding Company Act of 1956.[29] This regulatory-driven development proved sticky: it did not disappear after the repeal of the Glass–Steagall in the 1990s. Consequently, a new version of structural regulation after the GFC was easier to implement in the US than in Europe. In the US, the Volcker Rule – prohibiting proprietary trading and banking entities' investment in and sponsorship of private funds – was part of the post-crisis Dodd–Frank legislation. In contrast, in the EU, such a structural reform was proposed and widely debated, but never adopted, despite the adoption of certain variations of it at the Member State level.

Profit-seeking market players participate in the production of regulation. They look for regulatory loopholes as opportunities for arbitrage.[30] Regulatory arbitrage can promote innovation and more efficient regulations but also, if used opportunistically, may allow market

---

25 Steven L Schwarcz, 'Systemic Risk' (2008) 97 Geo. LJ 193.

26 For a formal explanation of such a counterintuitive risk incentive, see Stewart C Myers, 'Determinants of Corporate Borrowing' (1977) 5 Journal of Financial Economics 147.

27 Daniel K Tarullo, 'Macroprudential Regulation' (2014) 31 Yale J. on Reg. 505.

28 Dan Awrey, 'Toward a Supply-side Theory of Financial Innovation' (2013) 41 Journal of Comparative Economics 401, 413.

29 Dafna Avraham, Patricia Selvaggi and James I Vickery, 'A Structural View of US Bank Holding Companies' (2012) 18 Economic Policy Review 65, 3.

30 Arbitrage is 'the exploitation of a price difference between two goods that are essentially the same'. See Andreas Engert, 'Transnational Hedge Fund Regulation' (2010) 11 European Business Organization Law Review 329, 357. Regulatory arbitrage, broadly defined, refers to shifting activities from a heavily regulated financial sector to an unregulated or lightly regulated financial sector with the aim of maximizing profits by taking advantage of regulatory differentials. In essence, 'regulatory arbitrage exploits the gap between the economic substance of a transaction and its legal or regulatory treatment'. See Victor Fleischer, 'Regulatory Arbitrage' (2010) 89 Tex. L. Rev. 227, 229.

participants to benefit financially while externalizing risks to society and undermining the overall quality of regulation.[31]

Finally, beyond the distinction between banking and capital market, hybrid areas exist. Areas such as derivatives, clearing and settlements, and market infrastructures are part of the capital market infrastructure, but include functional elements of banking. Several chapters of this book compare regulatory approaches in these hybrid areas along the lines sketched out above. This bird's eye view shows that financial markets need regulation. Moreover, there are many legal tools to regulate finance. However, whereas standard legal tools are employed to address comparable market failures, financial regulation is not easy to standardize. On the contrary, the chapters of this book will introduce and discuss the varying forces of convergence and divergence in financial regulation. For instance, we have mentioned the tradeoffs in addressing different market failures. Different jurisdictions may solve these tradeoffs differently. This introduction to financial markets and regulation frames the analysis of convergence and divergence in different areas of financial regulation.

Studying convergence and divergence is important because finance is cross-border in nature, and the allocation of capital transcends geographical borders. Therefore, the interplay between regulations of different jurisdictions affects the efficient allocation of capital. This has two implications. First, national law is relevant because financial transactions are based on private law, mainly property and contract law.[32] Second, depending on the different forms of intermediation and market failure, some areas require more regulatory coordination and convergence across different jurisdictions than others.

3. WHAT DRIVES CONVERGENCE AND DIVERGENCE?

In this section, we propose four drivers of convergence and divergence in financial regulation. First, national private laws provide the legal basis for financial transactions; therefore, they are of primary relevance to financial regulators. Second, regulators may pursue different policy objectives or use different legal tools while pursuing the same objective. Third, financial regulators must account for the different structure and degree of integration of financial markets. Fourth, regulators are exposed to a set of other, heterogeneous, forces shaping their policymaking.

3.1 Private Law Underpinnings

The private law provisions relevant for finance are the rules concerning the allocation of resources among private parties, such as property and contract law (notably including bankruptcy).[33] These are key aspects in people's everyday lives and touch upon their fundamental

---

[31] Charles AE Goodhart and Rosa M Lastra, 'Border Problems' (2010) 13 Journal of International Economic Law 705.

[32] Pistor (n 16) 317.

[33] The literature has identified five key aspects where private laws diverge in the field of finance: (1) the availability of insolvency set-off; (2) the availability and scope of security interest; (3) the availability of commercial trust; (4) the marketability of contracts, receivables and claims; and (5) the availability of tracing delinquent money on the insolvency of the final holder. Philip R

rights. Therefore, private law is entrenched in the national legal systems and resistant to convergence, despite the increasing globalization of finance. The analysis of divergent private laws in finance is beyond the scope of this chapter because we focus on regulation. However, existing private law arrangements are the baseline for regulating finance. Two examples illustrate this point.

First, consider the creation of a security interest which rests on (diverging) property law provisions. Different ways to create such interests would decrease the liquidity of financial markets by reducing the fungibility of the financial collateral. This increase in transaction cost led to considerable harmonization at international level during the liberalization wave of the 1990s, eliminating all formal requirements for establishing security interests on financial collateral.[34] This example shows how divergent private laws converge to foster the efficiency of financial transactions.

Second, consider the different regimes of repurchase agreements (repos) in Europe and in the US. In Europe, repos operate through a true sale of the collateral. In contrast, in the US, transferring the title to collateral would be impractical under New York State law, so the collateral is pledged, realizing a fictitious sale.[35] These two arrangements are functionally equivalent but have different legal bases. Consequently, in regulating repo transactions, EU and US regulators must employ different legal tools.

3.2 Policy Goals and Regulatory Tools

Beyond private law, a second driver of convergence or divergence depends on the regulatory preferences in pursuing social welfare.[36] In financial markets, this means addressing three key market failures:

1. *Externalities* – the allocation of funds to a specific activity may generate negative externalities, namely costs that are borne by non-contracting parties and the society at large. In this case, the activity is overproduced. An example is the excessive subprime mortgage lending that generated the housing market bubbles leading to the GFC in 2007.
2. *Information asymmetry* – contracting parties have different information so that the least informed party cannot correctly price financial assets while the informed party can extract a rent from her informational advantage, resulting in fund misallocation. An example is insider trading.[37]
3. *Imperfect competition* – the price of financial services or the cost of credit is higher than optimal because of barriers to entry and other restrictions of competition. This results in misallocation of financial resources too. An example is the existence of systemically

---

Wood, *Law and Practice of International Finance, University Edition* (Sweet & Maxwell 2019) 18–21.

[34] Luc Thévenoz, 'Intermediated Securities, Legal Risk, and the International Harmonization of Commercial Law' (2007) 13 Stan. JL Bus. & Fin. 284.

[35] For a more detailed analysis, see Songjiwen Wu and Hossein Nabilou, 'Repo Markets across the Atlantic: Similar but Unalike' (2018) 30 European Business Law Review 513.

[36] Richard J Herring and Robert E Litan, *Financial Regulation in the Global Economy* (Brookings Institution 1995).

[37] Text to note 20.

important banks that can attract cheaper funds due to economies of scale and engage in moral hazard because they are too big to fail.[38]

Financial regulation should aim to correct such market failures and ensure efficient allocation of funds. In so doing, regulators pursue goals such as financial stability, investor protection, capital market efficiency and competition.[39] These goals sometime conflict with one another and the regulator must balance them. Consequently, regulation converges or diverges, in form and in substance, depending on how different regulators balance conflicting policy goals.

For example, the existence of some form of deposit insurance to protect financial stability is uncontested in modern banking regulation.[40] However, as we have seen, deposit insurance generates moral hazard, reducing market efficiency. Therefore, the design of deposit insurance varies across jurisdictions depending on how these conflicting goals are balanced. Before the GFC, the UK regulator believed that deposit insurance should be capped so that depositors would have some skin in the game and retain incentives to monitor their bank. Therefore, deposits were insured only up to 90% of their value. Such deposit insurance was insufficient to stop bank runs and to protect financial stability. While regulators have learned their lesson, the way in which the UK balanced conflicting policy goals resulted in considerable regulatory divergence with tangible implications in terms of bank runs.[41]

Divergence of financial regulation across jurisdictions also depends on different styles of public law. For example, some jurisdictions may opt for principles-based regulation while others may choose rules-based regulation. Moreover, regulation may be based on financial market entities or participants (entity-based regulation), the instrument traded in such markets (instrument-based regulation) or particular financial activities (functional or activity-based regulation). These varying approaches also create divergence. For instance, a functional approach may carry considerable benefits in terms of regulatory consistence, limiting the room for arbitrage; however, the persistence of entity-based approaches in many jurisdictions reflects the difficulty of defining financial intermediation in the face of technological innovation and regulatory arbitrage.

The existence of many regulatory strategies foreshadows variety and divergence in financial regulation, justifying the need for comparative studies in financial regulation. Given the sources of divergence in public law and private law, the call for harmonization has been palpable in global financial markets.

3.3 Structure and Integration of Financial Markets

The third factor explaining convergence and divergence of financial regulation relates to the differences in financial markets. Financial markets can vary along several dimensions, we briefly consider their structure and their degree of integration.

---

38 Franklin Allen and Douglas Gale, 'Competition and Financial Stability' (2004) 36 Journal of Money, Credit and Banking 453.

39 Armour and others (n 6) 73.

40 Diamond and Dybvig (n 13).

41 Hyun Song Shin, 'Reflections on Northern Rock: The Bank Run That Heralded the Global Financial Crisis' (2009) 23 Journal of Economic Perspectives 101.

Financial systems are usually categorized as 'bank-based' or 'market-based'.[42] This dichotomous distinction is a simplification because a comprehensive analysis of the differences in global financial markets is beyond the scope of this chapter. However, stylized differences between bank-based and market-based financial systems help understand divergence of financial regulation.

The three largest economic and financial actors in the world, the US, the EU and China, have radically different ways of promoting fund allocation. In the US, it is common for companies to access the equity market or the debt market. Accordingly, capital market regulation was developed earlier than anywhere else. On the other hand, banks play a more prominent role in the European financial system: fund takers access capital mainly through the intermediation of credit institutions, which play a prominent role in EU rulemaking. China represents yet another case, where both banking and capital markets have grown quickly in the past few decades under the close control and direction of the government.[43]

Financial systems differ not only in their structure across jurisdictions or regions, but also in their degree of cross-border integration. Some parts of the financial systems are inherently cross-border and have a global reach, such as the derivative markets. Others tend to be more national and less interconnected with other financial systems, such as the stock market or the market for insurance products. This creates momentum toward convergence and divergence of financial regulation. Regulatory divergence in highly internationally interconnected sectors implies considerable transactions costs for market operators. Therefore, industry initiatives in these areas, such as those pioneered by the International Capital Market Association, the International Organization of Securities Commissions and the International Swaps and Derivatives Association have pushed toward a considerable degree of harmonization through self-regulation[44] or lobbying.[45]

Moreover, market failures stemming from financial intermediation can have extra-territorial and systemic reach. This is another driver of convergence in global financial regulation. An example is the harmonization of bank capital regulation. During the liberalization of the banking industry in the 1980s, it became clear that banking activities (and crises) could have a global impact. In the absence of harmonization, a single jurisdiction would have limited incentives to account for the adverse effects of the banking activities in other countries (cross-border externalities). Therefore, the Basel Committee on Banking Supervision, established in 1974, became the global standard-setter for the prudential regulation of banks with the so-called 'Basel Accords', whose first version was published in 1988.

---

[42] See, for instance, Ross Levine, 'Bank-based or Market-based Financial Systems: Which Is Better?' (2002) 11 Journal of Financial Intermediation 398.

[43] Franklin Allen, Jun 'QJ' Qian, and Xian Gu, 'An Overview of China's Financial System' (2017) 9 Annual Review of Financial Economics 191.

[44] Saule T Omarova, 'Rethinking the Future of Self-Regulation in the Financial Industry' (2010) 35 Brook. J. Int'l L. 665.

[45] For the lobbying of the financial industry to reach the harmonization bankruptcy safe-harbor for financial assets, see Philipp Paech, 'The Value of Financial Market Insolvency Safe Harbours' (2016) 36 Oxford Journal of Legal Studies 855, 868. On lobbying and financial regulation in general, see later text to note 48.

3.4 Other Shaping Forces

The fourth driver relates to other, heterogeneous forces shaping financial regulation. We focus on regulatory competition, other political considerations, lobbying and technological innovation.

Divergence of financial regulation may not only depend on different regulatory preferences or financial systems. Divergence can also arise because of regulatory competition. Regulatory competition describes the actions of regulators in response to other regulators, to generate or counter competitive pressure.[46] A competitive financial regulation is considered a key ingredient for economic growth.[47] Moreover, a competitive financial regulation can attract financial flows, increasing tax revenues and employment in financial services as well as the investment opportunities for domestic firms. The long-lasting debate about regulatory competition focuses on whether this competition gives rise to a 'race-to-the-bottom' or a 'race-to-the-top'. Race-to-the-bottom means that regulatory competition undermines the quality of regulation to attract financial firms towards a more favorable, but hardly more efficient regime. Race-to-the-top means that competition between financial regulators incentivizes innovation and experimentation, eventually resulting in more efficient regimes. A welfare analysis of regulatory competition in financial regulation would be very complex, and touches on politically sensitive matters beyond the scope of this chapter. Whether a race-to-the-top or a race-to-the-bottom emerges is context dependent and the analysis should be limited to specific cases. Yet the mere existence of regulatory competition partly explains convergence and divergence of financial regulation.

Regulatory competition is not the only political force shaping financial regulation. Wider political agendas can also influence convergence and divergence. For instance, in the aftermath of the World War II, the political project to facilitate the integration of western European countries, which resulted in the European Union (EU), required establishing an internal market based on the free movement of capital, among other features. This agenda is not directly related to the objective to attract financial flows. However, it has influenced convergence of financial regulation in Europe, so much so that the EU is currently considered as an almost unitary jurisdiction, despite the continuing divergence of national laws.

An opposite trend of regulatory divergence can be observed in the case of Brexit.[48] The UK is currently in the final stages of approval of the Financial Services and Markets Bill, which is centered around the repeal of a large share of EU-based financial regulation.[49] This approach

---

46 Katrin Gödker and Lars Hornuf, 'Regulatory Competition', *Encyclopedia of Law and Economics, Volume 3 (OZ)* (Springer 2019).

47 This is the basic intuition in Rafael La Porta and others, 'Law and Finance' (1998) 106 Journal of Political Economy 1113. Beyond such intuition, the legal origin approach to comparative law, especially in the field of finance, has been largely disproven. See Mathias M Siems, 'Legal Origins: Reconciling Law & Finance and Comparative Law' (2007) 52 McGill LJ 55.

48 David Howarth and Lucia Quaglia, 'Brexit and the Battle for Financial Services' (2018) 25 Journal of European Public Policy 1118.

49 The text and related documents are available at <https://bills.parliament.uk/bills/3326> accessed 25 May 2023.

can be framed as regulatory competition, but at least partly, reflects also the independent political wish to implement a 'hard' Brexit.[50]

Another source of divergence currently driven by different political agendas is the integration of sustainability in financial regulation. The need to transition toward more sustainable finance is not, or at least should not be, a political issue. However, whether and to what extent to tweak financial regulation to facilitate such a transition remains a politically sensitive topic, with the EU leading the global discourse and the US lagging behind.[51]

So far, the analysis of convergent and divergent paths of financial regulation has rested on the assumption that regulators make choices in the public interest. However, there are also private interest theories of regulation.[52] Pressure from stakeholders, for instance lobbying, is also a driver of convergence and divergence of financial regulation. Lobbying is ubiquitous in the financial sector and plays an important role in conveying different preferences to the regulators. However, lobbyists only consider the private costs and benefits for their specific constituencies, overlooking social costs and benefits. Therefore, if one specific constituency is powerful enough to capture the regulator, the resulting policy will allow such constituency to extract a rent from the new policy but will not necessarily pursue allocative efficiency.[53]

Lobbying activities can lead to convergence or divergence. For instance, the wave of financial deregulation of the 1990s and the early 2000s was the result of an intense lobbying activity by the financial industry.[54] Conversely, the industry can also lobby for fragmenting a harmonized regulatory landscape, earning a preferential treatment compared with foreign competitors.

The financial industry is not the only stakeholder to influence the production of regulation. Especially in good times, the financial industry has more resources and expertise. In the aftermath of crises or scandals, however, other interest groups – including the investors hit by the scandal or the crisis – can influence regulation.[55] Lobbying is not an independent driver of convergence or divergence. Rather, it amplifies or dampens other drivers, supporting the status quo or regulatory reform depending on the external circumstances.

Finally, technological innovation drives changes in financial regulation. The application of new technologies to finance is inherent to the history and development of financial systems. Yet the recent pace of technological innovation in finance has been unprecedented because of significant developments in information technology, availability and computation of data, the rise of the blockchain technology, and the sudden increase of artificial intelligence. This recent wave of innovation is called 'Fintech.'

---

[50] John Armour, 'Brexit and Financial Services' (2017) 33 Oxford Review of Economic Policy S54, S59.

[51] John Armour, Luca Enriques, and Thom Wetzer, 'Mandatory Corporate Climate Disclosures: Now, but How?' (2021) Colum. Bus. L. Rev. 1085, 1095.

[52] Johan den Hertog, 'Economic Theories of Regulation', in Roger van den Bergh and Alessio M. Pacces (eds), *Regulation and Economics* (Edward Elgar Publishing 2012).

[53] George J Stigler, 'The Theory of Economic Regulation' (1971) 2 The Bell Journal of Economics and Management Science 3.

[54] See, for instance, Deniz Igan and Prachi Mishra, 'Wall Street, Capitol Hill, and k Street: Political Influence and Financial Regulation' (2014) 57 The Journal of Law and Economics 1063.

[55] Pepper D Culpepper, *Quiet Politics and Business Power* (Cambridge University Press 2011).

Financial innovation brings about new, more advanced forms of intermediation. New forms of intermediation create more room for divergence. Some regulators may act fast, enjoy the first mover advantage and lead the debate. Other regulators may adopt a 'wait and see' approach, letting the innovation develop free from specific regulatory constraints. This allows jurisdictions to experiment with different legal tools and determine which one(s) better fit their system and their regulatory preferences. In facing novel financial transactions, the probability of making erroneous decisions is high and a harmonized solution is often unwarranted.[56]

An example in this regard is the regulation of the crypto economy. The regulatory spectrum is incredibly wide. It ranges from the ban on crypto activities in China to the recognition of Bitcoin as legal tender in El Salvador, passing through the new, encompassing European Market in Crypto Asset Regulation, the light and pro-competitive approach of the UK legislator in the Financial Service and Market Bill and the enforcement-driven approach in the US.[57]

From a different perspective, financial innovation is related to regulatory arbitrage because the possibility of profiting from arbitrage opportunities stimulates innovation.[58] The examples are countless and beyond the scope of this chapter. Suffice it to say that the shadow banking system has emerged from several opportunities for regulatory arbitrage.[59]

4. PATHS OF CONVERGENCE AND DIVERGENCE: APPLICATIONS

In this section, we apply the framework developed in the previous sections to the regulation of capital markets, banking and sectors falling in between capital markets and banking, such as financial market infrastructures (FMIs) including payment, securities custody and settlement systems, and central clearing counterparties and other hybrid sectors. The aim is to set the stage, in a stylized fashion, for the comparative analysis of these fields and subfields.

4.1 Capital Markets

Capital markets are populated by heterogeneous intermediaries, such as stock markets, asset managers and financial advisors. The function of these intermediaries is to generate information to support saving and investment decisions. This does not eliminate asymmetric information and market failure stemming from it.[60] Therefore, capital market regulation mainly deals with asymmetric information. Despite the unicity of the goal, significant divergence remains.

---

56 Roberta Romano, 'Against Financial Regulation Harmonization: A Comment' (2010) 414 Yale Law & Economics Research Paper 17.

57 Edoardo D Martino, 'Cryptocurrencies and Stablecoin Regulation: A Framework for a Functional Comparative Analysis', *Research Handbook in Comparative Financial Regulation* (Edward Elgar Publishing forthcoming).

58 Peter Tufano, 'Financial Innovation' in Geroge Constantinides, Milton Harris and René Stulz (eds), *Handbook of the Economics of Finance* (Elsevier 2003) 307, 318.

59 Hossein Nabilou and Alessio M Pacces, 'The Law and Economics of Shadow Banking', in Iris Chiu & Iain MacNeil (eds), *Research Handbook on Shadow Banking* (Edward Elgar Publishing 2018) 22.

60 Armour and others (n 6) 216–218.

First, the private law underpinnings are important in capital markets because investor protection is still based on the regulation of contractual provisions and the liability of capital market intermediaries.[61] Although many of these protections have been moved to command-and-control regulation, the historic link with private law is a source of divergence, for instance in the context of doctrinal bases for bank liability.[62]

In terms of goals, jurisdictions may diverge if regulators have different views of the tradeoffs in fostering efficient allocation of capital. On the one hand, some jurisdictions may impose a considerable regulatory burden on capital market players to adequately protect investors. On the other hand, other jurisdictions may focus on alleviating the regulatory burden on capital market players to incentivize more services to investors.

The different structure and degree of integration of financial markets also play a role in divergence. The territorial reach of market failure is limited because capital markets do not necessarily have systemic implications. This weakens the case for harmonization. Moreover, regulatory competition is a powerful driver of divergence in capital markets. For instance, less burdensome capital market regulation subsidizes domestic fund takers (public companies, small and medium enterprises, etc.) and attracts financial flows.

Despite the incentive to engage in regulatory competition, wider political goals may push toward convergence. The most spectacular example of this convergence is the EU: the establishment of an internal (capital) market is essential to pursuing the goal of creating a political, economic and social union. Therefore, the last decades witnessed an unprecedented level of harmonization in the EU capital markets law, so much so that – from a comparative perspective – the EU can almost be considered as a unitary jurisdiction.

The political agenda of different jurisdictions also converges after financial scandals. For example, the accounting scandals of the early 2000s involved many companies on both sides of the Atlantic. These scandals resulted in new auditing and disclosure rules in Europe and in the US.[63]

4.2 Banking

Differently from capital markets, banks allocate capital through Qualitative Asset Transformation,[64] which leads to systemic risk.[65] Because banking greatly contributes to

61 For an application to crowdfunding and contractual protection of investors, see John Armour and Luca Enriques, 'The Promise and Perils of Crowdfunding: Between Corporate Finance and Consumer Contracts' (2018) 81 The Modern Law Review 51.

62 Ross Cranston and others, *Principles of Banking Law* (3rd edn, Oxford University Press 2017) ch 10.

63 For a comparative analysis, see Luca Enriques, 'Bad Apples, Bad Oranges: A Comment from Old Europe on Post-Enron Corporate Governance Reforms' (2003) 38 Wake Forest L. Rev. 911. For a critical take on these reforms, see Roberta Romano, 'The Sarbanes–Oxley Act and the Making of Quack Corporate Governance' (2004) 114 Yale LJ 1521.

64 Text to notes 11–12.

65 Text to note 25. For a wider discussion of market failures in banking see Armour and others (n 6) ch 13.

systemic risk, regulatory harmonization – such as the Basel Accords – is needed to avoid cross-border externalities.[66]

Harmonization of prudential requirements comes at a cost. First, globally harmonized requirements may increase the impact of regulatory arbitrage by (shadow) banks as they may induce similar strategies for regulatory arbitrage.[67] Second, harmonization amplifies the impact of regulatory mistakes.[68]

Despite considerable convergence, some divergence remains in the implementation of the Basel Accords.[69] Three aspects are worth mentioning. First, different jurisdictions diverge on the timing of implementation. The global standard setter usually provides a preferred timing; however, some jurisdiction may fully implement the new requirements before the deadlines while others can extend such deadlines, generating *de facto* divergence.

Second, some jurisdictions may decide to impose stricter requirements than the global standard. For instance, the leverage ratio requirement for US systemically important banks is that equity be at least 5% of the assets, whereas the minimum equity requirement in the Basel Accords is 3%, which corresponds with the EU requirement.

Third, different jurisdictions may set different thresholds for the full application of the prudential requirements. The comparison between the US and the EU regime is still enlightening. In the US, full-fledged prudential requirements are imposed only on the eight largest, systemically important banks, with over $250 billion in assets. The regime for other 'smaller' banks is lighter and does not include the compliance with liquidity requirements or the annual supervisory review and evaluation. The EU adopts a similar two-tier approach with the notable difference that the threshold below which the lighter regime applies is €30 billion in assets. This example illustrates a big regulatory divergence, which played an important role in the recent failure of regional, mid-sized US banks.[70]

4.3 Hybrid Sectors

The distinction between banking and capital markets is useful for explanatory purposes but does not entirely capture the reality of modern finance, where several overlaps and grey areas exists. Areas such as derivatives, clearing and settlements, market infrastructures and the shadow banking system are paramount examples. These sectors are quite heterogenous. An individual discussion of each of them falls beyond the scope of this chapter. However, these hybrid sectors share two functional characteristics. First, hybrid sectors display features of

66 Text to note 38.

67 Guillaume Plantin, 'Shadow Banking and Bank Capital Regulation' (2015) 28 The Review of Financial Studies 146.

68 Romano (n 56) 17.

69 Beyond prudential requirements, other considerable divergences persist in other aspects of banking regulation, such as bank governance and bank resolution. See, for instance, Jeffrey N Gordon and Wolf-Georg Ringe, 'Bank Resolution in the European Banking Union: A Transatlantic Perspective on What It Would Take' (2015) 115 Colum. L. Rev. 1297.

70 Enrico Perotti, 'Learning from Silicon Valley Bank's Uninsured Deposit Run' (*VoxEU*, 5 May 2023) <https://cepr.org/voxeu/columns/learning-silicon-valley-banks-uninsured-deposit-run> accessed 29 May 2023.

both capital markets and banking. Second, their territorial reach is large, often global, and as wide as the scope of their market failures.

From a comparative perspective, this means that the regulation of these sectors has mixed features of convergence and divergence, some typical of capital markets, others typical of banking. Moreover, the private law underpinnings are particularly relevant. For example, one significant friction in FMIs stems from varying private law regimes of custody of securities. Despite the recent waves of harmonization in financial regulation, such differences persist and have contributed to inefficient fragmentation of financial markets.[71] In addition, how securities are held and transferred varies considerably across jurisdictions. At least five different models for holding and transferring securities can be identified; they include the trust model (England and Wales), the 'securities entitlement' model (US & Canada), undivided property interest to the investors (France), pooled holding (Germany, Austria and Japan) and the transparent approach (Nordic countries, Greece, Poland, Spain, China and Brazil).[72] These different approaches are a major source of friction in international finance. The same security could be subject to different private law rules of holding and transferring securities, depending on how and where it is custodied.[73]

Coupled with the inherent cross-border reach of these markets, the result has been a considerable push toward private law harmonization coming from the industry, with the aim of reducing transaction costs. This has been achieved through lobbying, self-regulation or standardization of international commercial and financial practices, including a massive recourse to the choice of law clause in derivatives, repurchase agreements and securities lending contracts.[74]

5. CONCLUSION

This chapter provides an analytical framework to study comparative financial regulation. Such a conceptual framework is predicated on understanding the main functions of finance,

---

[71] See Philipp Paech, 'Shadow Banking: Legal Issues of Collateral Assets and Insolvency Law' (European Parliamentary Research Service 2013) <https://policycommons.net/artifacts/1332897/shadow-banking/> accessed 29 May 2023.

[72] Philipp Paech, 'Market Needs as Paradigm: Breaking up the Thinking on EU Securities Law' in Conac, Pierre-Henri, Segna, Ulrich and Thévenoz, Luc (eds), *Intermediated Securities: The Impact of the Geneva Securities Convention and the Future European Legislation* (Cambridge University Press 2013).

[73] For example, in the EU, the law of relevant intermediary approach (PRIMA) has been adopted to reduce the legal uncertainly about the law applicable to intermediates securities. *See* Art. 9, Directive 2002/47/EC of the European Parliament and of the Council of 6 June 2002 on financial collateral arrangements *OJ L 168*, and Art. 9(2) Directive 98/26/EC of the European Parliament and of the Council of 19 May 1998 on settlement finality in payment and securities settlement systems *OJ L 166*.

[74] These contracts, which play an important role in the well-functioning of financial markets, are entered into under various master agreements such as ISDA Master Agreements, Global Master Repurchase Agreements or Global Master Securities Lending Agreements drafted by the relevant industry associations. All these master agreements provide for choice of law clauses. The most popular jurisdictions are New York and England.

its instruments and its participants. The main function of finance is to channel funds from fund givers to fund takers. However, market failures are ubiquitous regardless of whether financial intermediation is undertaken by banks or capital markets. Having studied the main market failures in banking and capital markets with a view to how these market failures are addressed by regulation, this chapter identifies and aims to conceptually categorize significant patterns of divergence in financial regulation despite similar market failures in banking, capital markets and financial market infrastructures. The sources of such divergences are in the private law underpinnings of financial markets, diverging policy objectives and regulatory goals and the varying structure of financial markets.

Despite such divergences, significant convergence and harmonization of financial regulation has occurred globally in the past decades. Two main drivers of such convergence have been the push by industry associations to reduce transaction costs, particularly in cross-border financial transactions such as derivatives, and the harmonization of financial regulation to address risk spillovers and prevent potential race-to-the-bottom from regulatory arbitrage. By investigating the drivers of convergence and divergence in financial regulation at the global level, this chapter sets out an analytical framework for the other chapters in this book, which will investigate several topics in financial regulation from a comparative perspective.

2. History and convergence of financial regulation

Katarzyna Parchimowicz[1]

1. INTRODUCTION

Financial regulation is a complex legal phenomenon of unparalleled impact. It can either contribute to preventing or mitigating potential crises or 'become a wolf in sheep's clothing' by limiting competition and stymieing growth, as Henry Paulson warned.[2] Financial regulation can be understood broadly, as an overarching concept, encompassing all sorts of legal norms, originating both with legislative bodies and regulatory agencies.[3] It is tightly linked to administrative law, to the extent that some perceive it as 'a form of administrative governance'.[4] The administrative element is reflected in the 'regulation' component. Yet, the distinction between law and regulation is not clear also in this context.[5] For instance in the USA, regulation refers to a set of rules adopted by the agencies of federal government, whereas laws are passed by Congress.[6] On the other hand, financial regulation can be defined based on the character of the provisions, as they refer only to the public aspect of financial institutions, with their risk and potential externalities, excluding the private commercial component covered by the concept of financial law.[7] Further, forms of financial regulation can vary, from more general and flexible

---

1 This chapter is a result of the research project No 2020/37/N/HS5/00119 funded by the Polish National Science Centre. It came about within the framework of Academic Excellence Hub – Digital Justice Center carried out under the Initiative of Excellence – Research University at the University of Wrocław.

2 Famous quote by Henry Paulson. Marcus Baram, 'Henry Paulson Memoir "On The Brink" Exclusive: Strongly Defends TARP, AIG Bailout, Praises Bush, Slams Palin' (*Huffpost*, 29 March 2010) <https://www.huffpost.com/entry/henry-paulson-memoir-on-t_n_438545> accessed 17 November 2022.

3 The concept is represented in this chapter.

4 Gillian E. Metzger, 'Through the Looking Glass to a Shared Reflection: The Evolving Relationship between Administrative Law and Financial Regulation' (2015) 78 Law & Contemporary Problems 129, 129. Alternatively as a governance of market process – see Martin Ricketts, 'Economic Regulation: Principles, History and Methods' in Michael Crew, David Parker (eds) *International Handbook on Economic Regulation* (Edward Elgar Publishing 2006), 34, 35, 52.

5 For general analysis of this distinction, see Nir Kosti, David Levi-Faur and Guy Mor, 'Legislation and Regulation: Three Analytical Distinctions' (2019) 7 The Theory and Practice of Legislation, 169.

6 University of Colorado Boulder, 'Laws and Regulations' (University Libraries website) <https://libguides.colorado.edu/lawsandregs> accessed 26 April 2024.

7 Iris H-Y Chiu and Joanna Wilson, *Banking Law and Regulation* (OUP 2019) 1.

principles-based approach (followed in the UK) to detailed rules-based strategy providing legal certainty (practiced in the USA).[8]

In spite of the complexity of the mere concept of financial regulation, it indisputably achieved a level of global convergence unprecedented for rules of originally domestic character. Even though national regimes still differ in various aspects, there are many significant legal solutions based on uniform global standards, contributing to certainty and fairness of financial regulation worldwide. Such harmonization helps eliminate regulatory arbitrage and boosts competition by removing potential national advantages.

The main focus of this chapter is on banking regulation (although not exclusively), as it provides a valuable perspective for grasping the trends of convergence and divergence in financial regulation. It follows the bumpy road toward said convergence and aims to demonstrate that it stems mostly from financial turmoil sending cross-border shockwaves, but tends to be omitted when major non-financial events take over the global scene.

In the first part of the chapter the period up to World War II is described in order to outline major developments in financial regulation, that were mostly of domestic character at that time. This section also encompasses post-WWII desire for unity and peace, that was reflected in some steps toward regulatory convergence, but at more general, not strictly financial level. The second part of this chapter analyzes the second half of the 20th century, when financial events triggered a wave of reforms, many of them coordinated at the international level, providing for a certain boom in the area of regulatory convergence concerning finance. The third section turns to the recent global events, such as the pandemic, climate change and the technological boom that seem to draw the attention away from financial regulation and contribute to its growing divergence across the country lines. The final section concludes.

The analysis is conducted both from domestic and global perspectives depending on the significance of regulatory developments.[9] When it comes to regional provisions the focus is placed mostly on the US and European regimes, as they are leaders in adopting novel regulatory solutions applying to financial services and broader geographical analysis is not possible owing to the word limit restrictions.

2. NATIONAL FOCUS: THREE WARS AND A CRISIS

Financial regulation has been developing for centuries now. It accompanied evolution of payment, investment and trade systems. However, even though some relevant regulatory actions were undertaken as early as in the 17th century,[10] the first developments toward the

---

8 CFTC, 'Release Number 8183-20' (CFTC website) <https://www.cftc.gov/PressRoom/PressReleases/8183-20> accessed 26 January 2023; Pascal Frantz and Norvald Instefjord, 'Rules vs Principles Based Financial Regulation' (25 November 2014) <https://ssrn.com/abstract=2561370> accessed 26 January 2023.

9 For more on globalization of regulation see Peter Drahos and John Braithwaite, 'The Globalisation of Regulation' (2001) 9 Journal of Political Philosophy 103.

10 For instance the world's first securities law and ban on short-selling in the Netherlands. See Lodewijk Petram, 'Contract Enforcement on the World's First Stock Exchange' in Piet Clement, Harold James and Herman Van der Wee (eds), *Financial Regulation, Innovation and Crises in History* (Pickering & Chatto 2014) 13.

financial regulation we know today took place in the 19th and 20th centuries. They resulted from four major events: the American Civil War, World War I, the Great Depression and World War II. Despite the global character of three out of those four crises, regulatory changes remained prevailingly domestic.

2.1 Civil War

The example of the Civil War demonstrates that early history of financial regulation is actually history of banking regulation.[11] The need to fund the war and inadequacy of Independent Treasury System in that regard prompted Congress to establish a new regime.[12] The National Banking Acts of 1863 and 1864 constituted the origins of one of the most characteristic features of the US financial system. Namely, they created a dual banking system by adding national banks to the state-oriented landscape. Exclusive state control was over, as banking became possible also at the federal level. The duality persists to this day, even though state banks remain in a numerical majority.[13]

The rift between different states, vividly reflected in Civil War atrocities, was visible also in the context of branching. Southern state banks had branches, even if limited in numbers, but there was no branching practice in the Northeast and only loose networks of banks functioned in the Midwest.[14] The Civil War and the National Banking Acts further worsened the branching landscape, as Southern banks were destroyed and replaced by national banks that were not allowed to branch. The need to transfer money cross-border was addressed in a risky and inefficient way – by means of transporting money physically from one bank to another.[15] In order to tackle this situation, banks started holding deposit accounts with each other. This practice constituted the beginning of correspondent banking, so vital for the subsequent development of global banking system.

As an exception to prevailing banking aspects of finance, insurance regulation was vastly developed only after the Civil War. State regulators focused on protecting the insured and the Supreme Court long treated insurance business as strictly state business.[16] The regulatory prevalence of states in this context remains crucial in the US financial system.[17]

All these changes to the financial regulatory landscape were of a domestic character. No convergence-leading tendencies were visible at that time. This is understandable, as the Civil War constituted a domestic conflict. However, nationally oriented developments of financial regulation could be spotted also in the context of global military conflicts and a worldwide economic crisis.

---

[11] Stephen J. Friedman and Connie M. Friesen, 'A New Paradigm for Financial Regulation: Getting from Here to There' (1984) 43 Md L Rev 413, 416.

[12] Richard Carnell, Jonathan Macey, Geoffrey Miller, *The Law of Financial Institutions* (Wolters Kluwer 2017) 10.

[13] Michael Barr, Howell Jackson, Margaret Tahyar, *Financial Regulation: Law and Policy* (Foundation Press, 2018) 41.

[14] Carnell, Macey, Miller (n 12) 12.

[15] Barr, Jackson, Tahyar (n 13) 42.

[16] *Paul v. Virginia* 75 US 168 (1869).

[17] Carnell, Macey, Miller (n 12) 15.

2.2 World War I

World War I had an impact on financial regulation even before it started owing to geopolitical tensions often reflected by financial systems. The US banking panic of 1907 revealed two major issues with the American financial system – it was lacking an elastic currency supply and a lender of last resort.[18] This prompted discussions about creating a US central bank analogous to the Bank of England.[19] As international tensions were rising, with Britain dominating trade finance and Germany becoming one of the industrial powers, financial regulatory reforms followed a nationally oriented path. Even the name of the new US central bank – the Federal Reserve, that started operating in 1914 – was a reminder of military or naval reserves that are of mostly national character.[20] Another example of domestic regulatory reform was visible in Germany. Cooperation between the central bank, Reichsbank, and the financial sector developed and laid the foundations for so-called 'corporatist regulation', an approach persistent even after World War I.[21] Germany also tried to compete with the UK for the leading place in the financial markets.

The first global military conflict constituted an important test for national financial systems and for the nascent global one. It deepened the fragmentation of financial landscape. The Federal Reserve emerged as the war financier and at the same time gained independence from the Treasury.[22] The City of London lost its privileged position to Wall Street. New financial centers in Europe, such as Amsterdam and Zurich, emerged. Short-term lending to sovereigns became an essential activity of banks.[23]

In the aftermath of the war, countries needed to face their post-war debts and, as with war funding, they approached it in various ways.[24] The need to administer reparations drove the only international effort in the area of financial regulation. Namely, in 1930, the Bank of International Settlements (BIS), the first international institution focused on banking, was established. Its main role at that time was to collect and distribute war reparations from defeated Germany.

Importantly for the subsequent events of this century, the position of the US at the global arena changed. From a beginner in terms of industrial development it became the 'world bank-

---

18 Barr, Jackson, Tahyar (n 13) 47.

19 Harold James, 'Lessons from the Financial Preparations in the Lead-up to the First World War' (*VOXEU/CEPR*, 9 July 2014) <https://cepr.org/voxeu/columns/lessons-financial-preparations-lead-first-world-war> accessed 26 January 2023.

20 ibid.

21 Niels Krieghoff, 'Banking Regulation in a Federal System: Lessons from American and German Banking History' (LSE Doctoral Thesis, 2013) 70–71.

22 Phil Davies, 'The Federal Reserve's Role During WWI' (*Federal Reserve History*, 22 November 2013) <https://www.federalreservehistory.org/essays/feds-role-during-wwi> accessed 26 January 2023.

23 Nicholas Mulder, 'War Finance' (International Encyclopedia of the First World War, 8 February 2018) <https://encyclopedia.1914-1918-online.net/article/war_finance> accessed 26 January 2023.

24 ibid.

er'.[25] And so, after the war, the US financial system entered a decade of prosperity. The dollar became a go-to international currency and investing in the stock market gained popularity.[26]

2.3 The Great Depression

The Great Depression put an end to American prosperity and drastically worsened the economic situation in Europe. The financial shock also did not contribute to the internationalization of financial regulation. On the contrary, as each country's experience with this crisis was unique and required a national approach, it further cemented the regulatory differences between individual countries, deepening the domestic character of financial regulation.

Even though 24 October 1929 (Black Thursday) marks the beginning of this downturn in the US, the following banking panics of the 1930s triggered the most prominent reforms. After US banking system collapsed in 1933, which prompted newly elected President Roosevelt to announce an unprecedented nationwide bank holiday, there was no time to waste. As bank runs stem from 'fear itself',[27] that very fear had to be addressed. Thus, the Banking Act of 1933 created federal deposit insurance up to the amount of $2500 and established Federal Deposit Insurance Corporation (FDIC) to administer these funds.[28]

The same legal Act effectively separated investment and commercial activities. The ability to provide investment services stemmed from the duality of American banking systems (state banks were allowed to provide those, national banks were not) and World War I financing needs (when national banks were allowed to sell bonds issued by the federal government). When regulators wanted to encourage state banks to join the Federal Reserve System, they allowed them to pursue their investment activities. The same privilege had to be granted to national banks to avoid creating a competitive advantage.[29] The dire consequences of these decisions materialized during Great Depression, as it turned out that banks engaged in speculative and risky activities. The Banking Act of 1933 in this context, better known as the Glass–Steagall Act, banned depository institutions from engaging in investment activities.[30]

The stock market plunge also led to the first regulation of securities. The Securities Act of 1933 established new disclosure requirements forcing issuers to comprehensively inform investors.[31] One year later, the Security Exchange Act was adopted and created first capital markets regulator – the Securities and Exchange Commission.

The Great Depression had a different impact on European economies and their regulatory choices. It battered not only investors who had joined the US stock market boom,

---

[25] Patricia Clavin, *The Great Depression in Europe, 1929–1939* (Macmillan Press 2000) 19.

[26] Barr, Jackson, Tahyar (n 13) 49.

[27] Roosevelt in his inauguration speech adequately commented ongoing banking panics saying that 'the only thing we have to fear is fear itself'. See White House, 'Franklin D. Roosevelt' (White House website) <https://www.whitehouse.gov/about-the-white-house/presidents/franklin-d-roosevelt/> accessed 26 January 2023. It described metaphorically the mechanism of bank runs. See Charles Calomiris and Gary Gorton, 'The Origins of Banking Panics: Models, Facts, and Bank Regulation' in Robbert Hubbard (ed.) *Financial Markets and Financial Crises* (NBER 1991).

[28] The amount was increased over the years up to 250 000 USD today.

[29] Friedman, Friesen (n 11) 422.

[30] Barr, Jackson, Tahyar (n 13) 51.

[31] Carnell, Macey, Miller (n 12) 21.

but also European farmers and primary producers when prices started falling drastically.[32] Additionally, even within Europe the impact was not equal – some European banking sectors (even those that were agricultural) survived without bankruptcies.[33]

As for financial regulation, the Great Depression prompted reforms, but different from American ones. For instance, the Italian Banking Act of 1936 only seemingly resembled the Glass–Steagall Act and the separation of commercial and investment banking. Its main aim was not to curb investment activities of commercial banks, but to 'address the problems caused by the long-term debt and equity stakes in industrial firms held by Italian commercial banks'.[34] Consequently banks needed regulatory approval to be active on capital markets, but the activity was not banned (as it was in the case of the USA). In Germany, regulators focused on establishing a centralized system of oversight for banking sector, with competences to set capital and liquidity ratios.[35] The concepts of both deposit insurance and regulation of financial markets materialized only after World War II.

2.4 World War II

World War II was a horrendous tragedy and a turning point for the history of the world. The atrocities of this time and the long-lasting trauma awakened a common motivation to achieve unity, peace and harmony. However, the impact of World War II on financial regulation was more complex and can be analyzed from the perspective of individual countries or internationally.

As for the former, the post-war economic situation was shaped differently in each country involved. For instance, in Germany the rationale for reforms was linked to the role that finance had played in building their national military potential. The victorious allies focused on decentralization of the German financial sector. They transferred the regulatory and supervisory powers to state level and deprived central banks both at state and national levels of their non-monetary competences.[36] The reasoning behind these changes was clear – Germany should not be able to turn into a military power in the future. The fragmentation of financial regulation achieved by granting regulatory powers to state governments deepened its national character and drew it further away from international convergence.

Further, in the case of the USA, regulatory developments were shaped by the post-war prosperity. The growth of personal wealth and income triggered a wave of new home projects. The services of thrift institutions that focused primarily on financing home ownership were suddenly in high demand. Soon these entities were subjected to Regulation Q provisions, including a limit on deposit interest rates.[37]

---

[32] Clavin (n 25), 100.

[33] For instance the Netherlands. See Joke Mooij, 'Co-operative Banking in the Netherlands in Pre-second World War Crises' in Piet Clement, Harold James and Herman Van der Wee (eds), *Financial Regulation, Innovation and Crises in History* (Pickering & Chatto 2014) 37.

[34] Piet Clement, Harold James and Herman Van der Wee, 'Financial Innovation, Regulation and Crises: A Historical View' in Piet Clement, Harold James and Herman Van der Wee (eds), *Financial Regulation, Innovation and Crises in History* (Pickering & Chatto 2014) 10.

[35] Krieghoff (n 21) 87.

[36] ibid 109–113.

[37] Carnell, Macey, Miller (n 12) 23.

As for the international perspective, the domestic character of financial regulation constituted one of the cornerstones of the post-war Bretton Woods system.[38] Exchange controls discouraged any internationalization of banking and consequently vastly contributed to the regulatory fragmentation along country lines.[39] The only internationalized elements in this new order included trade and the establishment of international bodies, such as the International Monetary Fund, the World Bank and the International Trade Organization. None of these organizations was meant to deal with financial regulation, though.

3. TOWARD CONVERGENCE: LESSONS LEARNED FROM FINANCIAL EVENTS

The tendency to keep financial regulation strictly national began to fade in the 1960s. Several factors played an important role in this shift. Importantly, as Roberta Romano pointed out, 'most significant financial regulation is adopted in response to financial crises'.[40] In the second half of the 20th century world witnessed several problematic financial events. Not all of them turned into fully fledged crises, but each one triggered relevant financial reforms, many of which were agreed on at the international level. The Great Depression could have constituted the first such an event but regardless of the scale of this crisis, regulatory changes remained domestic. This situation changed in the 1960s when regulation in all areas was giving in to the general trend of globalization, which fueled the wave also for financial standards. Further, the public interest theory of financial regulation positioning it as a measure securing social welfare and protecting from market failures was slowly replaced by private interest theory stressing the motivations of regulatory institutions, that sometimes are not aligned with public interest and are shaped by the private goals of regulators or lobbyists.[41] As the assumption that regulatory authorities act in their self-interest is much more universal than the notion of serving public (usually nationally oriented) interest, this transformation of regulatory mentality was also crucial for slowly developing the international convergence of financial regulation.

Consequently, the international financial regulatory process, 'a process that is likely to be a foremost achievement of international cooperation in the twenty-first century',[42] was set in motion by an array of financial events with international impact.

---

[38] Rolf H Weber and Douglas W Arner, 'Toward a New Design for International Financial Regulation' (2007) 29 U Pa J Int'l L 391, 391.

[39] Charles Goodhart, 'From National Toward European/Global Financial Regulation' in Morten Balling and Ernest Gnan (eds), *50 Years of Money and Finance: Lessons and Challenges* (SUERF – The European Money and Finance Forum 2013) 229.

[40] Roberta Romano, 'Regulating in the Dark and a Postscript Assessment of the Iron Law of Financial Regulation' (2014) 43 Hofstra L Rev 25, 28.

[41] Sophie Harnay and Laurence Scialom, 'The Influence of the Economic Approaches to Regulation on Banking Regulations: A Short History of Banking Regulations' (2016) 40 Cambridge Journal of Economics 401.

[42] David T Zaring, 'Finding Legal Principle in Global Financial Regulation' (2012) 52 Va J Int'l L 683, 686.

3.1 Herstatt Bank

The end of Bretton Woods system, i.e. the pegging of the US dollar to gold reserves and the other currencies to the dollar, constituted a true beginning of the internationalization of finance. Countries could freely choose their exchange system, with the major economies selecting floating exchange rates.[43]

Between 1973 and 1974, during the final years of Bretton Woods, the dollar was very volatile. Its volatility had a great impact on a relatively small German bank – Herstatt Bank – that had been active in the foreign exchange markets. Namely, the bank incurred heavy losses from its bets on the dollar and had to be closed by the supervision authority. Internationalization of financial regulation, flawed risk management, auditing and misplaced supervisory efforts all contributed to this failure.[44] Crucially, its demise had cross-border consequences, with many foreign banks trembling owing to interbank ties.

Herstatt's collapse gave the final impulse to establish arguably most important international body in the context of global harmonization of financial regulation – the Basel Committee on Banking Supervision (BCBS). It was founded by heads of central banks and supervisory authorities of G10 countries. In 1975 its first document was published. The Basel Concordat outlined the path for the supervision of internationally active banks. Nevertheless, as there is a tendency 'to discount any international arrangement that is not accompanied by a treaty and a court',[45] the BCBS remained an informal international body. However, its standards, even if non-binding, have shaped financial regulation for decades now, slowly creating a novel phenomenon of global financial regulation.

Apart from the international level, a leaning toward harmonization was visible also regionally. The failure of Herstatt Bank motivated European regulators to address supervisory omissions exposed by it and they adopted the First Banking Directive.[46] The aim of this legal act was to create a uniform system of licensing and supervision of banks pursuing cross-border operations.

3.2 Savings and Loan Crisis

The next financial crisis that contributed to the further increase of global regulatory convergence originated in the USA. The savings and loan crisis (S&L crisis) unfolded slowly in the 1980s, as thrift institutions started to become insolvent owing to the pressure from high interest rates, their inability to compete with unregulated money market funds and their own

---

43 IMF, 'The end of the Bretton Woods System (1972–81)' (IMF website) <https://www.imf.org/external/about/histend.htm> accessed 26 January 2023.

44 Christoph Kaserer, 'Fifty Years of Financial Regulation in Germany' in Alexis Drach, Youssef Cassis (eds), *Financial Deregulation: A Historical Perspective* (OUP 2021) 108.

45 Zaring (n 42) 684.

46 First Council Directive 77/780/EEC of 12 December 1977 on the coordination of the laws, regulations and administrative provisions relating to the taking up and pursuit of the business of credit institutions [1977] OJ L 322.

overwhelming maturity mismatch.[47] In total 1284 thrift entities failed with their total assets reaching USD 615 billion.[48]

As a result, US regulators tightened and harmonized capital requirements among various credit institutions (mostly thrifts, but also FDIC-insured banks). However, they did not wish to leave US international banks at a disadvantage, so they pursued a global agenda of uniform capital rules using BCBS as a forum.[49] In 1988, BCBS members, also motivated to act by the Latin American debt crisis, published the first Basel Capital Accord, dubbed Basel I.[50] It outlined a simple system of risk weights for various assets and introduced minimum capital requirement of 8% (Tier 1 and Tier 2). Even though this document did not have a binding character, all BCBS member countries implemented these rules nationally and later also non-member countries followed suit. Eventually, it was adopted in more than 100 jurisdictions.[51] Its revision of 2004, dubbed Basel II, broadened the scope of this act, encompassing standards not only on capital (Pillar 1), but also on supervision and compliance with capital framework (Pillar 2), as well as on disclosure (Pillar 3).[52]

The post-S&L crisis move toward convergence of financial regulation went beyond capital requirements. It brought regulatory attention back to the issue of deposit insurance. US regulators first made FDIC responsible for the thrift insurance and later enacted the FDIC Improvement Act, strengthening the framework and FDIC's powers to act preventively. European authorities soon agreed on a harmonized level of insured deposits.[53] Deposit insurance started to become a global standard.

3.3 Asian Financial Crisis

In the late 1990s, the IMF's and World Bank's lack of mandate in the area of financial regulation turned out to be problematic. As their main roles revolved around monetary and fiscal policy, regulatory flaws concerning finance in emerging economies escaped their attention. Consequently, the Asian financial crisis stemmed from unregulated currency exposures of local banks (mostly in Thailand and Indonesia) and triggered discussions about the need for a World Financial Authority equipped with enforcement powers.[54] In the end, the Financial Stability Forum was established by G7 finance ministers and central bank governors. It gath-

---

[47] For details, see Lawrence White, 'The United States Savings and Loan Debacle: Some Lessons for the Regulation of Financial Institutions' in Dimitri Vittas (ed.) *Financial Regulation Changing the Rules of the Game* (EDI Development Studies 1992).

[48] Carnell, Macey, Miller (n 12) 26.

[49] Stéphane Rottier and Nicholas Véron, 'Not All Financial Regulation Is Global' (2010) 22 PIIE Policy Brief 1.

[50] BCBS, International convergence of capital measurement and capital standards (15 July 1988).

[51] Stefan Hohl, Maria Cynthia Sison, Tomas Stastny, Raihan Zamil, 'The Basel Framework in 100 Jurisdictions: Implementation Status and Proportionality Practices' (2018) 11 *FSI Insights*.

[52] BCBS, Basel II: International Convergence of Capital Measurement and Capital Standards: a Revised Framework (10 June 2004).

[53] Directive 94/19/EC of the European Parliament and of the Council of 30 May 1994 on dcposit-guarantcc schcmcs [1994] OJ L 135.

[54] Howard Davies and David Green, Global Financial Regulation (Polity Press 2008) 110ff.

ered not only national representatives, but also members of international financial bodies, both general such as the IMF, World Bank and BIS and specialized ones such as BCBS, IOSCO and IAIS.[55] Its mandate was relatively broad, with coordination of financial supervision at the forefront. It constituted the first international entity dealing with the entirety of financial regulation, not just one sector.

Simultaneously, in the aftermath of the Asian crisis, the IMF and the World Bank jointly established a Financial Sector Assessment Program aimed at evaluation of national financial systems and preemptive reaction to potential vulnerabilities.[56] Participating in such an assessment exercise conducted by centralized international institutions naturally contributed to bringing financial systems closer.

In the European Union, the European Commission issued the Financial Services Action Plan, with the aim of finalizing a single financial market and facilitating future harmonization of global financial standards.[57]

3.4 Global Financial Crisis

The Global Financial Crisis (GFC) inspired reforms establishing the global financial regulatory system that we know today. The GFC exposed the flaws of the self-regulation strategy and started a rapid turn toward reregulation.[58] Policymakers stopped shying away from intervention and putting constraints on the financial industry. Also politicians became much more involved in the process of creating and enforcing financial regulation.[59] For the first time reforms originating at international level went beyond banking regulation and also addressed issues linked to other entities of finance industry.

3.4.1 Banking regulation

In the area of banking, the two most prominent sets of standards were adopted by the BCBS and Financial Stability Board (FSB), a successor of Financial Stability Forum. The Basel III accord encompassed various measures aiming at preserving financial stability, 'promoting a more resilient banking sector'[60] and remedying the deficiencies of Basel II exposed by the GFC.[61] It strengthened the capital framework, by increasing the required amount of common equity capital, adding new buffers (countercyclical and capital conservation buffers) and

---

55 Financial Stability Forum, Background Information on the Financial Stability Forum For the IAASB Consultative Advisory Group (March 2008).

56 See IMF, Financial Sector Assessment Program <https://www.imf.org/en/About/Factsheets/Sheets/2023/financial-sector-assessment-program-FSAP> accessed 26 January 2023.

57 European Commission, Commission Communication of 11 May 1999 entitled 'Implementing the Framework for financial Markets: Action Plan', COM(1999) 232 final – not published in the Official Journal.

58 Rottier, Véron (n 49) 3.

59 For more, see Stavros Gadinis, 'From Independence to Politics in Financial Regulation' (2013) 101 Calif L Rev 327.

60 BCBS, Basel III: A Global Regulatory Framework for More Resilient Banks and Banking Systems (December 2010) 1.

61 John F. Rosato, 'Down the Road to Perdition: How the Flaws of Basel II Led to the Collapse of Bear Stearns and Lehman Brothers' (2010) 17 Conn Ins LJ 475.

a non-risk-dependent leverage ratio. Improvements to capital calculation methods were introduced gradually.[62] Also, Basel III included liquidity-oriented standards – the liquidity coverage ratio and the net stable funding ratio. In order to mitigate systemic risk, it also established an entire set of requirements applicable solely to systemically important banks, designated as such on the basis of a methodology created by BCBS and FSB.[63] As for the pre-existing frameworks, the BCBS and the International Association of Deposit Insurers co-issued new set of rules regarding deposit insurance.[64] Finally, BCBS laid the foundations for the FSB's framework on resolution by issuing its recommendations.[65]

The Financial Stability Board has a broad mandate, as its main role is the coordination of actions of more specialized standard-setters (such as BCBS or IOSCO). However, the FSB has been active in two banking-related regulatory areas. First, it published its Key Attributes of Effective Resolution Regimes, thereby creating a regulatory environment for internationally convergent resolution strategies.[66] Second, the FSB started publishing a list of global systemically important banks (G-SIBs), designated on the basis of BCBS's methodology. This designation method was implemented in national legal regimes, and as a result the FSB's list reflects the true status of G-SIBs. Finally, combining these two, it also published G-SIB-specific recapitalization rules.[67]

3.4.2 Beyond banking regulation

Before the GFC, international financial standards revolved primarily around banking. Only the broad scope of financial damage incurred during this downturn pointed toward omissions in another areas. First, regulatory attention was turned toward OTC derivatives. The lack of common rules applicable to these instruments and the ominous situation of America Insurance Group caused by lack of collateral held against their OTC positions incentivized policymakers to promote international standardization and central clearing. For that purpose, OTC Derivatives Regulators' Forum was established and later the G20 published principles regarding OTC derivatives markets.[68] It advocated for reporting to trade repositories and for clearing through central counterparties. The FSB was tasked with monitoring national reform efforts.[69]

Also novel financial institutions were subject to post-crisis reform. The FSB along with other standard-setters (mainly IOSCO) published recommendations on the regulation of

---

62 Also during subsequent revisions of the framework.

63 Katarzyna M Parchimowicz, *The Regulation of Megabanks: Legal frameworks of the USA and EU* (Routledge 2022).

64 BCBS, IADI, Core Principles for Effective Deposit Insurance Systems (June 2009).

65 BCBS, Report and Recommendations of the Cross-border Bank Resolution Group (March 2010).

66 FSB, Key Attributes of Effective Resolution Regimes for Financial Institutions (October 2014).

67 FSB, Principles on Loss-absorbing and Recapitalisation Capacity of G-SIBs in Resolution. Total Loss-absorbing Capacity (TLAC) Term Sheet (November 2015).

68 The G20 Toronto Summit Declaration, Annex II 24–29 (27 June 2010) <http://www.g20.utoronto.ca/2010/to-communique.html#annex2> accessed 26 January 2023.

69 FSB, *Making Derivatives Markets Safer* <https://www.fsb.org/work-of-the-fsb/market-and-institutional-resilience/post-2008-financial-crisis-reforms/making-derivatives-markets-safer/> accessed 26 January 2023.

non-bank entities extending credit, the so-called shadow banking system.[70] Also credit rating agencies were put under extensive scrutiny, with FSB releasing Principles for Reducing Reliance on CRAs[71] and IOSCO updating a CRA-specific Code of Conduct.[72]

The main regulatory goal was to create incentives for firms to conduct internal assessments and due diligence instead of relying solely on CRAs' ratings. Regulators also wanted to establish a framework of oversight over these entities and for that purpose IOSCO provided a note on 'international cooperation in oversight'.[73]

3.4.3 The true power of implementation

The standards issued by the BCBS, FSB and IOCSO should be implemented by the members of these bodies. These should be considered as minimum standards and national implementation can be more stringent. However, in the pursuit of international convergence of financial regulation the prevailing regulatory tendency is that not only members adopt these standards, but also non-members join in the implementation efforts.[74] For them such actions constitute an opportunity to prepare their financial systems for smooth international cooperation. As for the implementation status in the biggest world economies,[75] the USA, Japan and the UK stand out in their implementation activities with the majority of the standards already implemented.[76] The giants lagging behind are China and India. However, given the scale and complexity of this endeavor, it is an enormous success of FSB and international standard-setters, that they literally coordinate a global harmonization of financial regulation.

4. BACK TO NATIONAL FOCUS: THE PANDEMIC, CLIMATE AND TECHNOLOGICAL INNOVATION

Fragmented regulatory responses are noticeable in the area of finance when non-financial events are plaguing the world. As shown above, in the aftermath of the Civil War, World War I and World War II, a nationalistic approach to financial regulation prevailed. Even the financial character of Great Depression did not alter this tendency. It took several major financial events to trigger the process of global harmonization of financial regulation. Finally, it is

---

70 FSB, *FSB publishes Recommendations to Strengthen Oversight and Regulation of Shadow Banking* (29 August 2013) <https://www.fsb.org/2013/08/pr_130829a/> accessed 26 January 2023.

71 FSB, *Reducing Reliance on Credit Ratings* <https://www.fsb.org/work-of-the-fsb/market-and-institutional-resilience/post-2008-financial-crisis-reforms/reducing-reliance-on-credit-ratings/> accessed 26 January 2023.

72 IOSCO, Code of Conduct Fundamentals for Credit Rating Agencies Final Report (March 2015).

73 IOSCO, International Cooperation in Oversight of Credit Rating Agencies (March 2009).

74 Hohl, Sison, Stastny, Zamil (n 51).

75 Business Insider India, 'Top Largest Economies in the World' (7 November 2022) <https://www.businessinsider.in/top-10-largest-economies-in-the-world/articleshow/70547252.cms> accessed 26 January 2023.

76 FSB, *Promoting Global Financial Stability Annual Report 2022 – Annex II* (16 November 2022) <https://www.fsb.org/wp-content/uploads/P161122.pdf#page=35> accessed 26 January 2023; BIS, *RCAP Implementation Dashboards* (30 September 2022) <https://www.bis.org/bcbs/implementation/rcap_reports.htm> accessed 26 January 2023.

underway. It seems, though, that an array of significant global issues could change this course of regulatory action. Regulators differ in their reactions to the COVID pandemic, the challenge of the climate change and technological progress.

4.1 The Pandemic

In the context of the responses to the COVID pandemic, no coordinated international action was undertaken. The G20 issued relatively vague statements setting fairly obvious goals of 'protecting lives' and 'minimizing disruptions'.[77] Even though 'coordination on public health and financial measures' was mentioned there, it was not reflected in the course of action.[78] Similarly, the FSB published several broadly formulated principles mainly warning against giving up on introduced reforms.[79] The only truly impactful response of these international standard-setters was to postpone implementation deadlines for several of their previously adopted rules. The BCBS,[80] IAIS[81] and IOSCO[82] delayed their work schedules and extended implementation timelines.

Regulatory responses to COVID were primarily domestic and uncoordinated. In the EU, in order to maintain financial stability and simultaneously boost lending, regulators introduced an array of different solutions. The Single Resolution Board took action, providing operational relief and an easing resolution planning process and promising to reflect the unprecedented circumstances in its MREL decisions.[83] The ECB intervened also in its supervisory capacity. It provided comprehensive capital relief by allowing entities to go below Pillar 2 Guidance,

---

[77] Extraordinary G20 Leaders' Summit: Statement on COVID-19 (26 March 2020) <http://www.g20.utoronto.ca/2020/2020-g20-statement-0326.html> accessed 26 January 2023.

[78] ibid.

[79] FSB, *FSB Publishes a Report on International Cooperation to Address the Financial Stability Implications of COVID-19* (15 April 2020) <https://www.fsb.org/2020/04/fsb-publishes-report-on-international-cooperation-to-address-the-financial-stability-implications-of-covid-19> accessed 26 January 2023.

[80] BIS, Governors and Heads of Supervision Announce Deferral of Basel III Implementation to Increase Operational Capacity of Banks and Supervisors to Respond to Covid-19 (27 March 2020) <http://www.bis.org/press/p200327.htm> accessed 26 January 2023; BCBS, IOSCO, Basel Committee and IOSCO Announce Deferral of Financial Implementation Phases of the Margin Requirements for Non-centrally Cleared Derivatives (3 April 2020) <https://www.bis.org/press/p200403a.htm> accessed 26 January 2023.

[81] IAIS, *IAIS Executive Committee Takes Steps to Address Impact of COVID-19 on the Insurance Sector* (27 March 2020) <https://www.ivass.it/media/avviso/iais-covid/?com.dotmarketing.htmlpage.language=3&dotcache=refresh> accessed 26 January 2023.

[82] IOSCO, IOSCO Reprioritizes its Work Program to Address Impact of COVID-19 (8 April 2020) <https://www.consob.it/documents/1912911/1926395/IOSCONEWS562.pdf> accessed 26 January 2023; BCBS, IOSCO, Basel Committee and IOSCO Announce Deferral of Financial Implementation Phases of the Margin Requirements for Non-centrally Cleared Derivatives (3 April 2020) <https://www.bis.org/press/p200403a.htm> accessed 26 January 2023.

[83] Elke König, 'An Extraordinary Challenge: SRB Actions to Support Efforts to Mitigate the Economic Impact of the COVID-19 Outbreak' (*The SRB Blog*, 1 April 2020) <https://www.srb.europa.eu/en/content/extraordinary-challenge-srb-actions-support-efforts-mitigate-economic-impact-covid-19> accessed 26 January 2023.

the capital conservation buffer and liquidity coverage ratio and by altering the CET1 definition for the purposes of Pillar 2 Requirements.[84] In fear of future losses, the ECB asked banks to temporarily stop share buybacks and dividend payments.[85] Some measures required legislative intervention and so in the quickly adopted regulation implementation of IFRS 9 was extended, application of the leverage ratio buffer for G-SIIs was moved and the rules on non-performing loans were loosened.[86] In order to better monitor capital markets in these unprecedented times the European Securities and Markets Authority adjusted its reporting requirements.[87] Several national regulators went one step further and imposed a short-selling ban.[88] This difference, although legitimate – highlights that the EU regulatory response was fragmented. First, divergence stems from the fact that not all Member States participate in the Banking Union. Second, in the Single Supervisory Mechanism significant powers, for instance those related to macro-prudential tool, remained at the national level and so the domestic authorities often made regulatory choices independently.

The UK financial regulators followed a different path in comparison with their EU counterparts. For instance, banks were strongly discouraged from increasing dividends and bonuses, not prohibited from paying them out.[89] Also regarding short-selling the UK stance differed. The Financial Conduct Authority did not decide to impose a temporary ban on such activity, but preferred to keep markets open. Finally, in the area of capital relief, it decided to reduce some of the buffers to 0%, not only to allow operation under required levels.[90]

The situation was more complex in the US, where the application of enhanced prudential standards was limited only to the largest banks (minimum asset threshold of $250 billion) in 2019, months before the COVID outbreak. This turned out to be crucial in the aftermath of

---

84 ECB, 'ECB Banking Supervision Provides Temporary Capital and Operational Relief in Reaction to Coronavirus' (12 March 2020) <https://www.ecb.europa.eu/press/pr/date/2020/html/ecb.pr200312~45417d8643.en.html> accessed 27 January 2023.

85 ECB, 'ECB Asks Banks not to Pay Dividends until at least October 2020' (27 March 2020) <https://www.bankingsupervision.europa.eu/press/pr/date/2020/html/ssm.pr200327~d4d8f81a53.en.html> accessed 27 January 2023.

86 Regulation (EU) 2020/873 of the European Parliament and of the Council of 24 June 2020 amending Regulations (EU) No 575/2013 and (EU) 2019/876 as regards certain adjustments in response to the COVID-19 pandemic [2020] OJ L 204; See more Christos Gortsos, 'The Response of the European Central Bank to the Current Pandemic Crisis: Monetary Policy and Prudential Banking Supervision Decisions' (2020) 17 European Company and Financial Law Review 231, 252.

87 ESMA, ESMA decision of 16 March 2020, ESMA70-155-9546.

88 Danny Busch, 'Is the European Union Going to Help us Overcome the COVID-19 Crisis?' in Christos V Gortsos, Wolf-Georg Ringe (eds) *Pandemic Crisis and Financial Stability* (EBI 2020) 32. This decision was controversial see Luca Enriques, and Marco Pagano, 'Emergency Measures for Equity Trading: The Case Against Short-selling and Stock Exchange Shutdowns' in Christos V Gortsos. and Wolf-Georg Ringe (eds) *Pandemic Crisis and Financial Stability* (EBI 2020).

89 Stephen Morris, David Crow and Chris Giles, 'British Lenders Suspend Dividends after BoE Pressure' *Financial Times* (London, 1 April 2020) <https://www.ft.com/content/c13d3d21-b6f3-4449-a916-2ba4271818e4> accessed 29 April 2024.

90 Mohammad Bitar and Amine Tarazi, 'A Note on Regulatory Responses to COVID-19 Pandemic: Balancing Banks' Solvency and Contribution to Recovery' (2022) 60 Journal of Financial Stability 1, 4, 7.

COVID pandemic and later during the 2023 banking turmoil, as several objectively significant institutions suffered from the wave of monetary expansion.

The US COVID-related prudential strategy was based on easing the supplementary leverage ratio and TLAC requirements.[91] The authorities took advantage of institutional diversification of the US banking system and reduced the leverage ratio for community banks only.[92] They decided to conduct extended stress-testing exercise but without publishing its results.[93] Finally, the regulators used the characteristic link between capital buffers and dividend distributions in order to allow banks to build up their capital conservation buffers more easily.[94]

It could be argued that many of abovementioned regulatory actions are similar in principle – they aim at easing capital restrictions and incentivizing financial entities to support real economy without sacrificing financial stability. However, the specific measures selected to achieve this goal vary. In the context of capital-related interventions, the UK basically removed some of the buffers, the EU allowed credit institutions to operate below them, while the US altered the calculation method crucial for the build-up of capital conservation buffers. Such differences mirrored persisting discrepancies in national regulatory strategies when it comes to stabilizing national financial systems and the tendency to prioritize domestic stability over global stability. None of these actions were coordinated internationally and importantly, they can produce different results and have an adverse impact on economy in the medium term.[95]

4.2 Climate

The wave of regulatory changes triggered by the pandemic constituted a perfect opportunity to acknowledge the need to include climate-related aspects in financial regulation. However, these actions again are not as coordinated as they should be and the need for a comprehensive

---

[91] Board of Governors of the Federal Reserve System, 'Federal Reserve Board Announces Technical Change to Support the U.S. Economy and Allow Banks to Continue Lending to Creditworthy Households and Businesses' (23 March 2020) <https://www.federalreserve.gov/news events/ pressreleases/ bcreg20200323a .htm> accessed 27 January 2023; Board of Governors of the Federal Reserve System, 'Federal Reserve Board Announces Temporary Change to its Supplementary Leverage Ratio Rule to Ease Strains in the Treasury Market Resulting from the Coronavirus and Increase Banking Organizations' Ability to Provide Credit to Households and Businesses' (1 April 2020) <https://www.federalreserve.gov/newsevents/pressreleases/bcreg 20200401a.htm> accessed 27 January 2023.

[92] Board of Governors of the Federal Reserve System, 'Agencies Announce Changes to the Community Bank Leverage Ratio' (6 April 2020) <https://www.federalreserve.gov/newsevents/ pressreleases/bcreg20200406a.htm> accessed 27 January 2023.

[93] Board of Governors of the Federal Reserve System, 'Federal Reserve Board Releases Results of Stress Tests for 2020 and Additional Sensitivity Analyses Conducted in Light of the Coronavirus Event' (25 June 2020) <https://www.federalreserve.gov/newsevents/pressreleases/bc reg20200625c.htm> accessed 27 January 2023.

[94] 85 FR 15909 – Regulatory Capital Rule: Eligible Retained Income; OCC Bulletin 2020-87 (8 October 2020).

[95] Bitar, Tarazi (n 90) 16.

climate-related regulatory framework is largely omitted.[96] Also, the lack of convergence in the context of climate-related financial regulation reaches far beyond regulatory reactions to pandemic.

Even though climate change is not a war, its disastrous impact on the environment and on our lives turns it into an event that can be compared with the most gruesome conflicts in history.[97] As in these past cases, regulatory reactions follow. Even though 'making finance flows consistent with a pathway toward low greenhouse gas emissions and climate-resilient development' constitutes one of the goals of Paris Agreement,[98] the G20 remains deeply divided on that matter.[99] Geopolitical tensions persist regardless of the increasing climate threat.[100] A ray of hope appeared when in 2017 central banks and supervisors created the Network for Greening the Financial System. However, its goals were not reflected in the 2017 update to Basel III that did not encompass climate-related measures.[101] Only recently did BCBS move in the right direction – in 2020 it established Task Force for Climate-related Financial Risks. In 2022 it published the 'Principles for the effective management and supervision of climate-related financial risks'[102] and some guidance on how the existing framework could be used to take into account such risks.[103] The FSB also set up a task force on climate-related financial disclosures.[104] Regulatory measures *sensu stricto* are necessary to achieve some level of harmonization in this area.[105] Meanwhile, individual countries/legal regimes keep pursuing distinct strategies in the area of climate financial regulation.[106]

---

96 Paola D'Orazio, 'Towards a Post-pandemic Policy Framework to Manage Climate-related Financial Risks and Resilience, Climate Policy' (2021) 21 Climate Policy 1368.

97 Bill McKibben, 'A World at War' (*The New Republic*, 15 August 2016) <https://newrepublic.com/article/135684/declare-war-climate-change-mobilize-wwii> accessed 27 January 2023.

98 Article 2(1)(c) of Paris Agreement, UN 2015.

99 Michel Cardona and Maria Eduarda Berenguer, 'What Role for Financial Regulation to Help the Low-carbon Transition?' (2020) Institute for Climate Economics 1, 37; Robin Harding, Alex Barker, Demetri Sevastopulo, 'G20 Deeply Divided on Trade and Climate Change' *Financial Times* (Osaka, 29 June 2019).

100 Dominic Evans, Aidan Lewis, Jake Spring, 'COP27 negotiators still far apart on strong climate deal' (*Reuters,* 16 November 2022) <https://www.reuters.com/business/cop/cop27-climate-talks-get-boost-g20-declaration-2022-11-16/> accessed 29 April 2024.

101 BCBS, Basel III: Finalising Post Crisis Reforms (7 December 2017).

102 BCBS, Principles for the Effective Management and Supervision of Climate-related Financial Risks (15 June 2022).

103 BCBS, 'Basel Committee Clarifies How Climate-related Financial Risks May Be Captured in the Existing Basel Framework' (8 December 2022).

104 Task Force on Climate-Related Financial Disclosures, 2022 Status Report (October 2022) <https://assets.bbhub.io/company/sites/60/2022/10/2022-TCFD-Status-Report.pdf> accessed 27 January 2023.

105 And even those measures partially based on international standards diverge vastly and create chaos in the context of compliance. See Dirk A Zetzsche, Marco Bodellini, Roberta Consiglio, 'The EU Sustainable Finance Framework in Light of International Standards' (2022) 25 Journal of International Economic Law 659.

106 Stephen Kim Park, 'Legal Strategy Disrupted: Managing Climate Change and Regulatory Transformation' (2021) 58 American Business Law Journal 711, 732.

For instance, in the context of climate risk and climate-sensitive stress testing, the EU started in 2020 with ECB's Guide on Climate-related and Environmental Risks[107] and continued efforts in this matter regardless of pandemic and macroeconomic conditions. Soon afterwards, the ECB decided to include climate risks in the Supervisory Review and Evaluation Process methodology[108] and the world's first launch of a climate stress test was announced.[109]

The USA for years has lagged behind on the agenda for climate-related financial regulation.[110] Also in the context of climate risk and stress testing it became slightly more active only recently. The first climate-focused stress testing exercise was announced in September 2022 and will apply to six largest banks only.[111] In general, only the SEC is making real progress in the context of climate-oriented financial regulation.[112] The rest of the US regulators, apart from acknowledging that climate risk constitutes a systemic threat and preparing the pilot stress testing exercise, did not produce substantial regulatory outcomes.[113]

Generally, reports from various jurisdictions show divergence in the pace and scope of climate-related regulatory actions.[114] These tendencies are also confirmed by the market movements. Recent research[115] has shown, that both 'sustainable' and 'non-sustainable' firms could expect a value boost after the passage of REPowerEU plan[116] and US Inflation Reduction Act.[117] Even though these findings refer to broader economy, they could be indic-

---

107 ECB, Guide on Climate-related and Environmental Risks. Supervisory Expectations Relating to Risk Management and Disclosure (November 2020).

108 ECB, 'Banks must Accelerate Efforts to Tackle Climate Risks, ECB Supervisory Assessment Shows' (22 November 2021) <https:// www .bankingsupervision .europa .eu/ press/ pr/ date/ 2021/ html/ssm.pr211122~6984de0ae5.en.html> accessed 27 January 2023.

109 ECB, 'ECB Banking Supervision Launches 2022 Climate Risk Stress Test' (27 January 2022) <https://www.bankingsupervision.europa.eu/press/pr/date/2022/html/ssm.pr220127~bd20df4d3a .en.html> accessed 27 January 2023.

110 Park (n 106) 733.

111 Board of Governors of the Federal Reserve System, 'Federal Reserve Board Announces that Six of the Nation's Largest Banks will Participate in a Pilot Climate Scenario Analysis Exercise Designed to Enhance the Ability of Supervisors and Firms to Measure and Manage Climate-related Financial Risks' (29 September 2022) <https://www.federalreserve.gov/newsevents/pressreleases/ other20220929a.htm> accessed 27 January 2023.

112 SEC, 'SEC Proposes Rules to Enhance and Standardize Climate-Related Disclosures for Investors' (21 March 2022) <https://www.sec.gov/news/press-release/2022-46> accessed 27 January 2023.

113 CERES, 2022 Climate Risk Scoreboard <https://ceres.org/accelerator/regulation/scorecard? _ga=2.138638837.793384190.1674056087-1388955393.1674056086> accessed 27 January 2023.

114 Net Zero Knowledge Hub, 'Overview of Select Climate-related Regulatory and Sustainability Initiatives' <https://www.net-zero-hub.com/regulations/climate-regulations-for-the-financial-sec tor/> accessed 27 January 2023.

115 Ming Deng, Markus Leippold, Alexander Wagner, Qian Wang, 'The Net-Zero Transition and Firm Value: Insights from the Russia–Ukraine War, REPowerEU, and the US Inflation Reduction Act' (2022) CEPR Discussion Paper DP17207.

116 Communication from the Commission to the European Parliament, the European Council, the Council, the European Economic and Social Committee and the Committee of the Regions REPowerEU Plan, COM/2022/230 final.

117 H.R.5376 – Inflation Reduction Act of 2022.

ative regarding financial regulation, indicating that both action and non-action could turn out to be beneficial.

4.3 Technological Innovation

The divergence noticed in the context of COVID pandemic and climate change also appears with regards to major technological developments. It can be especially expected in view of regulatory competition and geopolitical considerations. As analyzing all technological novelties is beyond the scope of this contribution, only two examples will be used: cryptocurrencies and Big Tech.

In contrast to climate aspects, a lot has been agreed on internationally regarding technology in finance. In the case of cryptocurrencies, most of the international bodies recently adopted relevant standards.[118] Regardless, national regulators choose different strategies to regulate this asset class. For instance, China is taking a very radical stance regulating crypto-assets as property only for the purposes of inheritance, but simultaneously banning crypto-exchanges. In the end, China prohibited mining and trading in crypto.[119] In contrast, in the UK, crypto-exchanges ought to be registered with Financial Conduct Authority, but not much more regulatory attention is given to these assets. In the EU, however, a comprehensive regulation on the matter has just been passed into law.[120]

Financial regulation of Big Tech companies is even more problematic, because these giants do not belong in their entirety to the world of finance. Any regulatory attempt addresses a trade-off between financial stability/market integrity, efficiency and competition, or data privacy and consumer protection.[121] Regardless of this challenge, regulatory coordination both at international and national levels is crucial, given the cross-border character of Big Tech's presence[122] and the need to combine entity- and activity-based approaches.[123]

Unfortunately, not much has been done internationally in this context. Most likely national interests prevail especially in case of the Big Tech home jurisdictions – the USA and China.

---

118 FSB, 'FSB Proposes Framework for the International Regulation of Crypto-asset Activities' (11 October 2022) <https://www.fsb.org/2022/10/fsb-proposes-framework-for-the-international-regulation-of-crypto-asset-activities/> accessed 27 January 2023; BCBS, *Prudential treatment of cryptoasset exposures* (16 December 2022); IOSCO, 'IOSCO Published its Crypto-Asset Roadmap for 2022–2023' (7 July 2022) <https://www.iosco.org/news/pdf/IOSCONEWS649.pdf> accessed 27 January 2023.

119 Alun John, Samuel Shen, Tom Wilson, 'China's Top Regulators Ban Crypto Trading and Mining, Sending Bitcoin Tumbling' (*Reuters*, 24 September 2021) <https://www.reuters.com/world/china/china-central-bank-vows-crackdown-cryptocurrency-trading-2021-09-24/> accessed 30 April 2024.

120 Regulation of the European Parliament and of the Council on Markets in Crypto-assets, and amending Directive (EU) 2019/1937 (MiCA), final text as announced by the Council 2020/0265 (COD).

121 Matthew Saal, Harish Natarajan, Jon Frost, Leonardo Gambacorta, Erik Feyen, 'A Policy Triangle for Big Techs in Finance' (VOXEU/CEPR, 23 October 2021) <https://cepr.org/voxeu/columns/policy-triangle-big-techs-finance> accessed 27 January 2023.

122 ibid.

123 Parma Bains, Nobuyasu Sugimoto, and Christopher Wilson, 'BigTech in Financial Services: Regulatory Approaches and Architecture' (2022) 2 IMF FinTech Notes.

The BIS in its bulletin only stressed the need for hybrid approach focusing simultaneously on individual entities and types of activities.[124] The FSB published a report on the financial role of Big Tech in emerging markets and developing economies,[125] but no standards aiming at international harmonization were adopted. This is especially surprising as BIS acknowledged the dire need for consistency.[126]

National regulatory approaches to Big Tech differ in all relevant aspects, probably reflecting the most beneficial approach for the country in question. For instance, in terms of operational resilience EU is the most advanced jurisdiction with its adopted Digital Operational Resilience Act (DORA) regulation establishing an entire detailed framework applicable to Big Tech.[127] China simply included such firms in their financial holding companies' (FHC) regime. In turn, the US regulatory solutions are rather limited in this regard – the 'Bank Service Company Act' provides banking regulators with authority to examine and regulate third-party vendors that provide services to banks.[128] Consequently most of the regulatory attention is focused on Big Tech firms providing cloud services. In the area of financial stability, China is slightly ahead with its FHC framework covering this aspect.[129] In the EU no stability-oriented initiatives have been undertaken and the DORA framework's indirect effects are the only regulatory steps in this regard. In the USA, the Financial Stability Oversight Council could designate one of the Big Techs as systemically important, but it has not been done yet.[130]

5. CONCLUSION

The global regulatory harmonization in finance, so desired after the Global Financial Crisis, seems to have lost momentum. This may be because of tightening tendencies – harmonization around light regulation can be easier.[131] Also financial multipolarity and the fragmentation of the financial power across the globe can hinder the process of creating international standards.[132]

---

[124] Agustín Carstens, Stijn Claessens, Fernando Restoy and Hyun Song Shin, 'Regulating Big Techs in Finance' (2021) 45 BIS Bulletin.

[125] FSB, Report: BigTech Firms in Finance in Emerging Market and Developing Economies (12 October 2020).

[126] Juan Carlos Crisanto, Johannes Ehrentraud, Aidan Lawson, Fernando Restoy, 'Big Tech Regulation: What is Going on?' (2021) 36 FSI Insights 18.

[127] Regulation (EU) 2022/2554 of the European Parliament and of the Council of 14 December 2022 on Digital Operational Resilience for the Financial Sector and Amending Regulations (EC) No 1060/2009, (EU) No 648/2012, (EU) No 600/2014, (EU) No 909/2014 and (EU) 2016/1011 [2022] OJ L 333.

[128] Paul Tierno, 'Big Tech in Financial Services' (Congressional Research Service No R47104, 29 July 2022) 19.

[129] Crisanto, Ehrentraud, Lawson, Restoy (n 126) 15–16.

[130] US Department of Treasury, Designations website as of 27 January 2023 <https://home.treasury.gov/policy-issues/financial-markets-financial-institutions-and-fiscal-service/fsoc/designations> accessed 27 January 2023; Gina Chon, 'Big Tech in Finance? There's a Regulator for That' *Reuters* (1 August 2022).

[131] Rottier, Véron (n 49) 4.

[132] ibid.

However, the current path of divergence can be also explained from historical perspective. International convergence in financial regulation, especially banking regulation, has been achieved in waves. As shown in this chapter, it has mostly developed after financial crises or financially troublesome events, and this progress has halted (regulation of domestic character prevailed) after non-financial occurrences.[133] So, in the aftermath of the regional and global wars of the 19th and 20th century, financial regulation remained a national matter. Only after the array of financial downturns in the second half of the 20th century did movement toward harmonization seem like an unstoppable force. Yet nowadays financial crises have been replaced by the global pandemic, climate destruction and unlimited technological boom. Regulatory reactions to these events have confirmed that regulators think domestically when a crisis is not of a financial character. These shifts between global harmonization and national focus depending on the character of a given event could simply stem from complex differences between countries. The impact of financial downturns may vary in terms of severity, but the core consequences remain more or less similar in different countries, and so universal rules addressing issues are easier to draft. In contrast, the impact of a pandemic, a global war or climate change depends on many geopolitical aspects unrelated to finance that may trigger a preference to protect individual, domestic interests.

[133] One exception is Great Depression, see section 2.3.

3. The institutional architecture of financial regulation and supervision

Menelaos Markakis

1. INTRODUCTION

Financial regulation and supervision are of fundamental importance, in their economic, social and political dimensions, all of which have increasingly come under scrutiny, notably since the Global Financial Crisis (GFC). The institutional structures which support rulemaking and the supervision of financial system participants and activities have undergone substantial reforms, with several initiatives launched at domestic, regional and international levels so as to strengthen the regulation and supervision of the financial sector and to reduce the likelihood of another financial crisis.[1]

This chapter looks at the institutional architecture of financial regulation and supervision from a theoretical and comparative perspective. It is structured as follows. The discussion begins with the significance of institutional design, the 'fit' between supervisory models and the existing supervisory structures, and the circumstances in which one structure may work better than others (Section 2). The focus then shifts to the main supervisory models and the manner in which they allocate functions to one or more authorities (Section 3). It will be seen that the choice of financial supervisory model is influenced by various factors, and that it entails, in principle, different benefits and challenges. We then turn to consider the role accorded to central banks in financial supervision, which is a key feature of any financial supervisory architecture (Section 4), as well as other functions for supervisory authorities, whether these are accorded to central banks or separate supervisory agencies (Section 5). The penultimate section of this chapter focuses on the accountability of financial supervisors, which is very much affected by the institutional choices adumbrated above (Section 6). It will be concluded that, although there is no 'silver bullet' for an ideal architecture of financial sector oversight, institutional design matters – even if only to an extent – to supervisory efficiency, effectiveness and accountability (Section 7).

2. THE SIGNIFICANCE OF INSTITUTIONAL DESIGN, THE RELEVANT FACTORS IN DESIGNING SUPERVISORY SYSTEMS AND THE 'FIT' WITH REAL-WORLD SYSTEMS

Before we set out the different institutional structures of financial regulation and supervision, a number of introductory observations are warranted on the (relative) significance of institutional design. These observations are distinct, albeit interrelated.

---

[1] See also Niamh Moloney, Eilís Ferran and Jennifer Payne, 'Introduction' in Niamh Moloney, Eilís Ferran and Jennifer Payne (eds), *The Oxford Handbook of Financial Regulation* (OUP 2015).

First of all, we know that institutions matter, and that the institutional architecture of financial regulation and supervision matters. And indeed, following the GFC, many countries revised their institutional structures for financial regulation and supervision. However, in what follows, there should be no assumption that institutional design is the sole (or perhaps even the main) determinant of the effectiveness of financial regulation and supervision. John Armour et al. observe that 'none of the various models of regulatory architecture fared particularly well in the financial crisis' and that it is therefore 'hard to resist the inference that the choice of regulatory architecture, at least insofar as the question was framed before the crisis, made little difference for financial stability'.[2] However, they readily admit that 'the strength of this inference should not be overstated' and that '[i]t can only be drawn as respects models that were actually in operation prior to the crisis'.[3] In similar vein, Eilís Ferran argues that 'there is good reason to regard the organizational structure of financial supervision as a second-order problem rather than a fundamental concern: a good institutional model will not neutralize weak supervisory policies and practices, but, on the other hand, dedicated, high-quality supervisory personnel and sensible working practices and arrangements for cooperation can compensate for limitations in the formal institutional arrangements'.[4] Over and above the financial supervisory structure opted for, it is important that financial supervisors possess the requisite powers as well as adequate resources to deploy those effectively in the pursuit of their goals.[5] Eventually, however, the regulatory regime would need to be updated and modernized so as to keep pace with the evolution of financial markets and institutions, where appropriate.[6]

Second, the institutional architecture of financial regulation and supervision in the jurisdictions commonly examined does not neatly correspond to the institutional models examined below, and vice versa. These models are, as Eilís Ferran writes, 'over-simplifications of real-world financial supervisory systems'.[7] This point should be kept well in mind whilst going through them. In turn, existing systems 'tend to be the somewhat messy product of an incremental and often accidental process in which institutional "stickiness" resulting from path dependencies competes with forces militating for change, and ideas for radical overhaul often give way to more pragmatic adaptations'.[8] 'No "pure" example of any model may actually exist, and blurring between approaches is prevalent'.[9] As such, various systems can be difficult to categorize. They can combine elements of more than one model or be difficult to assign to

---

2 John Armour, Dan Awrey, Paul Davies, Luca Enriques, Jeffrey N Gordon, Colin Mayer and Jennifer Payne, *Principles of Financial Regulation* (OUP 2016) 597.

3 ibid 597.

4 Eilís Ferran, 'Institutional Design: The Choices for National Systems' in Niamh Moloney, Eilís Ferran and Jennifer Payne (eds), *The Oxford Handbook of Financial Regulation* (OUP 2015) 98–99.

5 ibid 99.

6 See also Group of Thirty, *The Structure of Financial Supervision: Approaches and Challenges in a Global Marketplace* (Group of Thirty 2008), available at: <https://group30.org/images/uploads/publications/G30_StructureFinancialSupervision2008.pdf> accessed 19 January 2023, 13.

7 Eilís Ferran (n 4) 100.

8 ibid 100.

9 Group of Thirty (n 6) 23.

any of these models. In this connection, Evan Gibson notes, primarily with reference to Hong Kong's financial regulatory design but also more generally, that:

> Defining a supervisory model in accordance with a strict definition is problematic because the design evolves with market developments, financial crises, and policies that are inherent to a jurisdiction. ... Attempts to label a supervisory model are usually a best-fit description rather than an exact fit. Designating a type of model to a financial system involves identifying the most common characteristics that reflect that model.[10]

Third, in what follows, there will be no suggestion, either explicit or implicit, that one model, system or institutional design is superior to the others, in line with Eilís Ferran, who argues that: 'There is no single "right" or "wrong" institutional model for financial supervision. Strong (and weak) financial supervision can come in a variety of packages'.[11] Although there will be no preoccupation in this chapter with which structure is the most effective and efficient,[12] we will highlight, as we go through the various models, their respective benefits and drawbacks, from a theoretical – and, where appropriate, an empirical – standpoint. This is meant to illustrate the implications of adopting each model and the design choices facing national systems. 'Ultimately, of course, the success of any regulatory approach must be measured by the ability of regulators to achieve the policy goals of regulation in real world contexts rather than by simply tallying theoretical pros and cons'.[13] Schooner and Taylor rightly note that:

> Most commentators conclude that there is no such thing as the single best structure for financial services regulation. Different structural approaches will work best in different sets of circumstances, and whichever structure is chosen, events will always create opportunities for criticism. Instead of looking for an ideal institutional structure, perhaps a consideration of the circumstances in which one structure works better than another is more appropriate.[14]

Fourth, in designing regulatory systems, context matters.[15] Reviewing 17 major national supervisory systems, the Group of Thirty observes that 'while dealing with similar problems and challenges, such systems are fashioned through a process that includes a myriad of political, cultural, economic, and financial influences'.[16] The same study notes that 'the United States is a prime example of the role that historical precedent, politics and culture have played

---

[10] Evan Gibson, *A Regulatory Design for Financial Stability in Hong Kong* (CUP 2022) 51. For a historic account of Hong Kong's financial regulatory design, see ibid, chs 2 and 3.

[11] Eilís Ferran (n 4) 124.

[12] See John Armour and others (n 2) ch 27, who consider questions of regulatory architecture from a normative perspective.

[13] Group of Thirty (n 6) 34.

[14] Heidi Schooner and Michael Taylor, *Global Bank Regulation: Principles and Policies* (Elsevier 2010) 275.

[15] On the factors that drive convergence and divergence in financial regulation more generally, see Introduction by Edoardo Martino, Hossein Nabilou and Alessio Pacces.

[16] Group of Thirty (n 6) 7, reviewing China, Hong Kong, Mexico, Brazil, France, Italy, Spain, Canada, Germany, Japan, Qatar, Singapore, Switzerland, the UK, Australia, the Netherlands and the US.

in the regulatory structure'.[17] In addition, the way we think about these supervisory models and about financial regulation more generally can significantly change over time, especially following crisis episodes.[18] Ultimately, '[c]hoosing the optimum supervisory model to manage financial stability requires a consideration of country-specific preferences based on the level of market development and the configuration of the financial system'.[19] In terms of the relevant factors to be taken into account, Eilís Ferran notes that:

> What works in a less-developed economy with a relatively unsophisticated financial market is likely to be inadequate for a mature economy with a large financial sector, and even among developed economies what works for one may be quite unsuitable for another because of country-specific factors, including whether the system of government is federal, confederal, or unitary; whether the economy is bank-based or market-based; prevalent business structures and corporate governance norms; the character of the legal, administrative, and judicial system; historical accidents; and cultural influences.[20]

Notwithstanding the force of the preceding arguments, it is fair to observe that 'institutional and functional models are coming under strain'.[21] This is because, as will be seen below, traditional sectoral boundaries and demarcations have collapsed.[22] There has been 'a marked shift from domestic firms engaged in distinct banking, securities and insurance businesses to more integrated financial services conglomerates offering a broad range of financial products across the globe', and many financial products nowadays have elements of banking, insurance and securities products.[23]

Relatedly to the previous point, 'the design of national supervisory architecture rarely, if ever, takes place with policymakers proceeding from a blank slate. Instead, regulatory structures evolve as a result of particular national debates, events, and economic crises that may prompt a reappraisal of existing frameworks'.[24] In what follows, it should be borne in mind that writing on a blank sheet of paper (or computer screen) is a luxury unavailable to those directly engaged in imagining the future architecture of financial regulation and supervision.[25] What is more, it should be borne in mind that a reform process may (ideally) lead to a better structure, but that it can also create costs and burdens in itself.[26]

---

17 ibid 14. On the US system, see further, among many others, Eric Pan, 'Organizing Regional Systems: The US Example' in Niamh Moloney, Eilís Ferran and Jennifer Payne (eds), *The Oxford Handbook of Financial Regulation* (OUP 2015) ch 7, with further references.

18 See also John Armour and others (n 2) 597.

19 Evan Gibson (n 10) 51.

20 Eilís Ferran (n 4) 100–101. See also Group of Thirty (n 6) 23–24.

21 Eilís Ferran (n 4) 101.

22 ibid 101.

23 Group of Thirty (n 6) 19–21.

24 ibid 13.

25 This phrase is partly borrowed from Stephen Weatherill, *Law and Values in the European Union* (OUP 2016) 299–300.

26 Group of Thirty (n 6) 50.

3. SUPERVISORY MODELS

There is a voluminous bibliography on the institutional choices facing different jurisdictions with respect to financial regulation and supervision.[27] The nomenclature invariably differs between different authors. In what follows, we will distinguish between four main supervisory models: institutional; functional; objectives- or goal-based; and unified or integrated.[28] These models concern the allocation of subject-matter jurisdiction, namely the way in which regulatory power is allocated between one or more authorities.[29]

The institutional model allocates jurisdiction to different regulatory and supervisory authorities on the basis of the financial institution being supervised and regulated, whereas the functional model concentrates on the financial activity being supervised and regulated.[30] John Armour et al. helpfully explain that:

> The institutional model allocates regulatory responsibility on the basis of distinctions between different types of regulated *financial institutions* – that is, banks, securities dealers, insurance companies – irrespective of the nature of the activities undertaken by these firms. The functional model, conversely, contemplates the allocation of responsibility on the basis of the nature of the *financial activity*, regardless of institutional type.[31]

Seen in this light, the identity of the supervisor is determined under the *institutional model* by the legal status of the institution (viz. bank, insurance company, securities firm, or pos-

---

[27] See, among many others, Richard K Abrams and Michael W Taylor, 'Issues in the Unification of Financial Sector Supervision' (2000) IMF Working Paper 00/213 <https://www.imf.org/external/pubs/ft/wp/2000/wp00213.pdf> accessed 19 January 2023; Charles A E Goodhart, 'The Organisational Structure of Banking Supervision' (2000) Financial Stability Institute FSI Occasional Paper 1 <https://www.bis.org/fsi/fsipapers01.pdf> accessed 27 February 2023; Jeroen J M Kremers, Dirk Schoenmaker and Peter J Wierts, 'Cross-Sector Supervision: Which Model?' in Robert E Litan and Richard J Herring (eds), *Brookings–Wharton Papers on Financial Services 2003* (Brookings Institution Press 2003) 225–243; Jeffrey Carmichael, Alexander Fleming and David T Llewellyn (eds), *Aligning Financial Supervision Structures with Country Needs* (World Bank 2004); Martin Čihák and Richard Podpiera, 'Is One Watchdog Better Than Three? International Experience with Integrated Financial Sector Supervision' (2006) IMF Working Paper 06/57 <https://www.imf.org/external/pubs/ft/wp/2006/wp0657.pdf> accessed 19 January 2023; David T Llewellyn, 'Institutional Structure of Financial Regulation and Supervision: The Basic Issues' (2006) <https://www.researchgate.net/publication/255585648_Institutional_structure_of_financial_regulation_and_supervision_the_basic_issues> accessed 19 January 2023; Group of Thirty (n 6); Heidi Schooner and Michael Taylor (n 14) ch 15; Eilís Ferran (n 4); John Armour and others (n 2) chs 24, 27; Daniel Calvo, Juan Carlos Crisanto, Stefan Hohl and Oscar Pascual Gutiérrez, 'Financial Supervisory Architecture: What Has Changed After the Crisis?' (2018) Financial Stability Institute Insights on policy implementation 8 <https://www.bis.org/fsi/publ/insights8.htm> accessed 27 February 2023; Evan Gibson (n 10) chs 4 and 5.

[28] We will principally follow the terminology used and the distinctions made by John Armour and others (n 2) and Eilís Ferran (n 4), as well as the Group of Thirty (n 6).

[29] John Armour and others (n 2) 597.

[30] The introductory chapter to this volume also speaks of entity-based and activity-based regulation.

[31] John Armour and others (n 2) 615 fn 4.

sibly pension fund).[32] The supervisor, which possesses expertise with respect to the relevant activities, is responsible for both prudential (safety and soundness) and conduct of business oversight of the institution. This model works neatly in a world where commercial banks issue debt, securities firms deal in securities and insurance companies offer insurance products and services. Historically, the institutional architecture of financial regulation and supervision reflects the structure of the domestic financial services industry and the financial sector's own institutional boundaries. However, as this structure begins to change and the financial system becomes more interconnected and complex, various challenges begin to emerge for supervisors. When the regulatory environment so permits, financial institutions often engage in activities outside these traditional demarcations, and different institutions, falling in principle under the remit of different supervisors, can offer functionally equivalent financial products.[33] This also affects the nature and distribution of risk in the financial system concerned. 'Banks are no longer as insulated from securities market risks and insurance risks as they had been in the past, whereas securities firms and insurance companies are exposed to risks that had been more characteristic of the banking system'.[34]

If the institution concerned engages in additional lines of business which are ancillary to its main business, these, too, will be supervised by the same supervisor, which may or may not possess the requisite expertise in those additional fields.[35] In principle, no institutional regulator will have a holistic overview of the regulated entity's business or of the relevant market as a whole. It is possible that different regulators will apply rules and regulations in an inconsistent manner and that coordination between those agencies/authorities will present challenges. What is more, the regulators concerned may differ in their tools and approach. This opens up the possibility of regulatory arbitrage, which can occur when multiple regulators interpret and enforce the same, or perhaps even inconsistent, rules in different ways.[36]

Under a *functional model*, different supervisors are responsible for different lines of business, regardless of the type of institution engaging in those lines of business. The identity of the supervisor is determined by the business that is being transacted by the entity, without

---

32 For example, the European System of Financial Supervision, which comprises, *inter alia*, the European Banking Authority, the European Securities and Markets Authority, and the European Insurance and Occupational Pensions Authority, largely reflects an institutional model: John Armour and others (n 2) 87, 542–545. On the EU system, see generally Eilís Ferran, 'Understanding the New Institutional Architecture of EU Financial Market Supervision' in Eddie Wymeersch, Klaus Hoopt and Guido Ferrarini (eds), *Financial Regulation and Supervision: A Post-Crisis Analysis* (OUP 2012) ch 5; Niamh Moloney, *EU Securities and Financial Markets Regulation* (3rd edn, OUP 2014) ch XI; Brigitte Haar, 'Organizing Regional Systems: The EU Example' in Niamh Moloney, Eilís Ferran and Jennifer Payne (eds), *The Oxford Handbook of Financial Regulation* (OUP 2015) ch 6; Gianni Lo Schiavo and Alexander Türk, 'The Institutional Architecture of EU Financial Regulation: The Case of the European Supervisory Authorities in the Aftermath of the European Crisis' in Leila Simona Talani (ed.), *Europe in Crisis: A Structural Analysis* (Palgrave Macmillan 2016) 89–121; and Nathan de Arriba-Sellier, 'Go Big or Go Home: The Home State Supervision Principle in the European System of Financial Supervision' (PhD thesis, Erasmus University Rotterdam 2023) ch 2, all with further references.

33 See also Evan Gibson (n 10) 52; John Armour and others (n 2) 87.

34 Heidi Schooner and Michael Taylor (n 14) 260.

35 Eilís Ferran (n 4) 99; John Armour and others (n 2) 87–88.

36 Group of Thirty (n 6) 34; John Armour and others (n 2) 87–88.

regard to its legal status. In other words, activities are regulated along functional, as opposed to legal entity, lines. There will typically be one supervisor for each of the three traditional business functions, viz. banking, insurance, and securities.[37] This means that, at least in principle, a single, technically expert regulator will apply consistent rules to the same activity, regardless of the entity in which it is conducted, thereby addressing the risk of regulatory arbitrage that was highlighted above.[38] However, if a financial institution is licensed to engage in various lines of business, it will in principle come under the remit of multiple supervisors, which can lead, *inter alia*, to disputes over which regulator/supervisor has jurisdiction over a certain activity and to duplication of efforts.[39] It is further possible, in cases of disagreement, that different regulators may adopt different positions with respect to the same activity.[40] They may even compete with one another to expand their jurisdiction in ways that benefit the firms they oversee, thereby leading to a 'race to the bottom' and rendering them vulnerable to regulatory capture. Furthermore, in the absence of a dedicated macroprudential authority, no functional regulator will have sufficient information on all the activities of a particular entity (or entities), which has important implications for monitoring and addressing systemic risk.[41]

We have already noted above that no pure example of a particular model may exist, and that blurring between different approaches is prevalent. In similar vein, existing systems could be said to possess both institutional and functional elements.[42] For example, a functional

---

37 Group of Thirty (n 6) 13–14, 34–35; Eilís Ferran (n 4) 99.

38 Group of Thirty (n 6) 35.

39 An example is furnished by the treatment of Wirecard, which combined banking and non-banking activities, by the German Federal Financial Supervisory Authority (BaFin). The events that unfolded led to the adoption of the Act to Strengthen Financial Market Integrity, which confers more powers on BaFin. See further BaFin, 'After Wirecard: More Powers for BaFin' (Bafin, 4 August 2021) <https://www.bafin.de/SharedDocs/Veroeffentlichungen/EN/Fachartikel/2021/fa_bj_2106_FISG_en.html> accessed 18 July 2023. I am grateful to Katarzyna Parchimowicz and Edoardo Martino for providing this example. It should be noted that BaFin brings together under one roof the supervision of banks and financial services providers, insurance undertakings, and securities trading.

40 By way of example, over and above supervisory models, the Commodity Futures Trading Commission (CFTC) and the Securities and Exchange Commission (SEC) are engaged in a turf war over which agency should regulate cryptocurrencies. While the CFTC regulates futures and derivatives trading of cryptocurrencies, the SEC has asserted its authority to regulate initial coin offerings and decentralized finance platforms. I am grateful to Katarzyna Parchimowicz and Edoardo Martino for providing this example. See further Taylor Anne Moffett, 'CFTC & SEC: The Wild West of Cryptocurrency Regulation' (2023) 57 University of Richmond Law Review 713, esp. 715–736; Soumen Datta, 'SEC vs. CFTC: Inside the Battle for Control of the Crypto Landscape' (16 May 2023) <https://www.bsc.news/post/sec-vs-cftc-inside-the-battle-for-control-of-the-crypto-landscape> accessed 18 July 2023. On the regulation of cryptocurrencies, including in the US, see also Chapter 20 by Edoardo Martino in this volume. It should be noted that the US system is characterized as 'both a functional and a consolidated regulatory system': Group of Thirty (n 6) 215. See also Eilís Ferran (n 4) 100 fn 7, who cites 'The Department of the Treasury Blueprint for a Modernized Financial Regulatory Structure' (Treasury Department 2008) <https://home.treasury.gov/system/files/136/archive-documents/Blueprint.pdf> accessed 18 July 2023, 139, which speaks of an 'institutionally based functional system'.

41 Group of Thirty (n 6) 35.

42 See also Evan Gibson (n 10) 52.

approach may be used to regulate the firms' sales practices, whereas an institutional approach to ensure the firms' safety and soundness. Examples of systems that blend institutional and functional regulation include the system introduced in the US by the Gramm–Leach–Bliley Act in 1999 and the British regulatory system prior to 1997.[43]

A further option is to adopt an *integrated model* (also known as single, consolidated, or unified, depending on the author(s) concerned), in order to respond to the above-mentioned challenges facing supervisors in an interconnected financial system. A single universal regulator conducts both safety and soundness oversight and conduct-of-business regulation for all sectors.[44] The 'most visible and complete manifestation' of this model was the Financial Services Authority (FSA) in the UK.[45] Prior to that, the integrated model was adopted in Singapore, as well as in Norway, Denmark and Sweden. In the fullest form of this model, one supervisor has full consolidated responsibility for all institutions and functions. All banking, securities and insurance regulation becomes the responsibility of a single authority.[46] However, it is also possible to opt for less than full consolidation, for example by assigning responsibility for the banking and insurance sectors to one authority and setting up a separate authority for the securities sector.[47] Institutional frameworks based on the integrated model can vary significantly across jurisdictions, with one of the main dividing lines being the relationship between the integrated regulator and the central bank. The former could be subsumed within the latter, or the two could be separate from one another.[48]

On the positive side, the integrated approach should lead to 'a streamlined focus on regulation and supervision without confusion or conflict over jurisdiction lines that are possible under both the Institutional Approach and the Functional Approach'.[49] It facilitates the oversight of financial institutions that are involved in multiple areas of business. Moreover, other things being equal, an integrated supervisor should have a more comprehensive, panoramic view of the regulated entity's business, given that it is allowed to look holistically at an entity. It should be able to consistently apply the relevant rules to firms.[50] The integrated approach can be effective and efficient in smaller markets, where oversight of the broad spectrum of financial services can be successfully conducted by one regulator, or in larger, complex markets, where it is viewed as a flexible and streamlined approach to regulation.[51]

On the negative side, however, this approach 'may create the risk of a single point of regulatory failure'.[52] If the integrated supervisor fails to spot an issue, there is no other agency/authority to compensate for that. 'Concerns have grown that the model can ask too much of

---

[43] Heidi Schooner and Michael Taylor (n 14) 262–265. Closer to the present volume, the chapter by Edoardo Martino discusses how an activity-based approach may be taken to cryptocurrency regulation, combined with an entity-based regulation of gatekeepers such as trading platforms (also with respect to the EU's Markets in Crypto-Assets Regulation).

[44] Group of Thirty (n 6) 13.

[45] ibid 24.

[46] Heidi Schooner and Michael Taylor (n 14) 260.

[47] Eilís Ferran (n 4) 99; Evan Gibson (n 10) 71.

[48] John Armour and others (n 2) 615 fn 11.

[49] Group of Thirty (n 6) 36.

[50] ibid 36.

[51] ibid 14.

[52] ibid 14.

a single authority, that some objectives may be prioritized at the expense of others, and also that it can result in central banks being unwisely side-lined from financial supervision.'[53] For example, the UK FSA prioritized consumer protection concerns over prudential matters.[54] What is more, coordination and communication challenges may arise even when the integrated approach is adopted, because the integrated regulator will almost always be organized internally along sectoral or functional lines. There is no guarantee that different divisions or units will communicate effectively with one another.[55] Various such issues were highlighted in the UK with respect to the supervision of Northern Rock by the FSA.[56]

Last but not least, there is the *objectives-* or *goal-based model* (also known as 'twin peaks'), pursuant to which supervisory responsibility is allocated according to regulatory objectives. Supervisory responsibilities are distributed between (typically) two supervisors: one authority is responsible primarily for prudential objectives and the other authority primarily for conduct of business objectives. Subsidiary objectives, such as the promotion of competition, may also be present. As such, different institutions and activities may be supervised by more than one authority, and these authorities will pursue different goals or objectives.[57] This model was initially conceived as a *'twin peaks' model*, a form of regulation by objective in which there is a separation of regulatory functions between two authorities: one that performs the safety and soundness supervision function and the other that focuses on conduct-of-business regulation.[58] It was 'designed to garner many of the benefits and efficiencies of the Integrated Approach, while at the same time addressing the inherent conflicts that may arise from time to time between the objectives of safety and soundness regulation and consumer protection and transparency'.[59] It also 'takes advantage of potential synergies arising in the prudential or

---

[53] Eilís Ferran (n 4) 101. See further Michael W Taylor, 'The Road from "Twin Peaks" – and the Way Back' (2009) 16 Connecticut Insurance Law Journal 61.

[54] See further Eilís Ferran, 'The Break-up of the Financial Services Authority' (2011) 31 OJLS 455.

[55] Group of Thirty (n 6) 36–37. See, for example, with respect to communication between different teams within BaFin: European Securities and Markets Authority, 'Fast Track Peer Review Report – Wirecard' (3 November 2020) <https://www.esma.europa.eu/document/fast-track-peer-review-report-wirecard> accessed 19 July 2023.

[56] See FSA Internal Audit Division, 'The Supervision of Northern Rock: A Lessons Learned Review' (March 2008) <https://www.fca.org.uk/publication/corporate/fsa-nr-report.pdf> accessed 20 January 2023.

[57] Eilís Ferran (n 4) 100; John Armour and others (n 2) 598–599. In fact, there may be more than two (main) objectives. Charles A E Goodhart, Philipp Hartmann, David T Llewellyn, Liliana Rojas-Suarez and Steven Weisbrod, *Financial Regulation: Why, How, and Where Now?* (Routledge 1998) advance a version of this model structured around six objectives: systemic risk, non-systemic prudential, retail conduct of business, wholesale conduct of business, financial exchange and competition regulation.

[58] Group of Thirty (n 6) 14. See further Michael Taylor, *Twin Peaks: A Regulatory Structure for the New Century* (Centre for the Study of Financial Innovation 1995); Michael Taylor, 'Regulatory Reform after the Financial Crisis: *Twin Peaks* Revisited' in Robin Hui Huang and Dirk Schoenmaker (eds), *Institutional Structure of Financial Regulation: Theories and International Experiences* (Routledge 2015) ch 1; Andrew Godwin and Andrew Schmulow (eds), *The Cambridge Handbook of Twin Peaks Financial Regulation* (CUP 2021).

[59] Group of Thirty (n 6) 14, 37.

the business conduct supervision of different types of financial institution'.[60] Potential drawbacks of this model include the risk of jurisdictional conflicts and/or regulatory duplication and overlap between the two agencies/authorities.[61] The twin peaks system has been adopted *inter alia* in Australia, New Zealand and South Africa.[62] Within the European Union (EU), the model is also employed in the Netherlands and Belgium. The establishment of macroprudential authorities in various jurisdictions could also be seen as implementing 'a partial version of the objective-based model', in the sense that an authority is set up with the goal of managing systemic risk.[63] Macroprudential supervision may be combined with microprudential supervision in one authority, or may be assigned to a different authority.[64]

As noted above, other authors may use slightly different terminology than the one employed in this chapter. For example, Daniel Calvo et al. refer to the sectoral model, the integrated model, and the partially integrated model, with the latter encompassing the twin peaks and two agency models. The sectoral model consists of three separate authorities that are responsible for the prudential and conduct of business supervision of the banking, insurance and securities sectors, respectively. In the integrated model, one authority is responsible for all oversight functions in all three sectors. Partially integrated models group responsibilities according to supervisory objectives or sectors. Twin peaks is an example of the former, as two separate authorities are responsible for the prudential monitoring and the conduct of business oversight for all types of financial institutions, respectively. The two-agency model is an example of the latter, as one authority is responsible for the prudential and conduct of business supervision of the banking and insurance sectors, and another authority is responsible for securities firms and markets.[65] Evan Gibson distinguishes between the institutional model, which supervises and regulates based on the type of institution; and the sectoral model, which supervises and regulates the business being transacted or the financial sector. He further treats the integrated model as a stand-alone design, which encapsulates, in his view, the 'twin peaks' and functional models.[66] Both these models consist of agencies which are underpinned by a supervisory function or objective.[67]

Based on a survey covering 82 jurisdictions, Daniel Calvo et al. find that the sectoral model is used in about half of the jurisdictions studied, and that it remains the most commonly used institutional design for financial sector supervision in all regions of the world except Europe. The integrated model is employed in about one third of jurisdictions and is most prominent in Europe, where about half of the jurisdictions apply it. They also find that certain jurisdictions operating with a single supervisory authority are relatively small in terms of population or GDP. Partially integrated models, viz. twin peaks and two agency models, have been adopted by around a fifth of the jurisdictions, including some with large financial systems.[68]

---

60 Daniel Calvo and others (n 27) 5.

61 Heidi Schooner and Michael Taylor (n 14) 275; Eilís Ferran (n 4) 102.

62 See further Andrew Godwin and Andrew Schmulow (n 58).

63 John Armour and others (n 2) 89.

64 See also Eilís Ferran (n 4) 100.

65 Daniel Calvo and others (n 27) 1, 4–6.

66 Evan Gibson (n 10) 51–52.

67 ibid 71–72. For more examples, see Eilís Ferran (n 4) 99–110 fn 6, with further references.

68 Daniel Calvo and others (n 27) 2, 7–9, 26–27, reviewing – as classified in the study itself – Angola, Botswana, Egypt, Mauritius, Morocco, South Africa, Tunisia, Sudan, Zambia, Argentina,

4. THE ROLE OF THE CENTRAL BANK IN FINANCIAL SUPERVISION

A related matter is whether the central bank should be involved in financial supervision or whether this role should best be accorded to another agency or authority.[69] Those who support locating responsibility for supervision within central banks claim that they bring significant expertise to the function which could be compromised if the role were accorded to another authority. They argue that central banks have a supervisory competitive edge owing to their superior knowledge of market conditions and the depth of their staff's expertise. A (nascent) supervisory authority could benefit from tapping into the credibility – and independence – of a central bank. It is further claimed that, by virtue of their supervisory function, central banks would be better equipped to perform their other roles with respect to monetary policy, financial stability, and oversight of payment systems. Any potential conflicts between those mandates would be better managed, according to the argument, if one entity (*in casu*, the central bank) were in charge of balancing various objectives against one another. Furthermore, the division of responsibilities between the central bank and other authorities could impair the efficiency of emergency liquidity provision in a crisis setting. It can be very difficult for a central bank to promptly act as lender of last resort without timely and complete information over the situation of ailing banks.

Those who oppose assigning supervisory functions to central banks argue that, by centralizing so much responsibility and authority in a single entity, the central bank may become too powerful and omnipresent in financial matters, but that it may also become overwhelmed by juggling its monetary policy and supervisory mandates. Supervision requires specialist skills that, according to the argument, may not usually be associated with central banks. Moreover, the type of independence and accountability arrangements commonly associated with central banks may be inappropriate for banking supervision, given its interference with bank businesses and its impact on individual rights. Furthermore, there could be conflicts of interest between the monetary policy and supervisory functions. For example, a central bank may not wish to raise or lower interest rates, even though this is mandated by monetary policy considerations, if it knows that this would negatively affect the financial position of banks, of which it is the supervisor. What is more, if the central bank performs poorly as a supervisor, this could also hurt its credibility as a monetary policy authority.

---

the Bahamas, Belize, Brazil, Canada, Chile, Colombia, the Dominican Republic, Ecuador, El Salvador, Guatemala, Mexico, Panama, Paraguay, Peru, Trinidad and Tobago, Uruguay, Australia, Bangladesh, Hong Kong, India, Japan, Korea, the Kyrgyz Republic, Malaysia, New Zealand, Pakistan, the Philippines, Russia, Singapore, Thailand, Timor–Leste, Vietnam, Albania, Austria, Belgium, Bosnia and Herzegovina, Bulgaria, Cyprus, the Czech Republic, Denmark, Estonia, Finland, France, Georgia, Germany, Greece, Hungary, Iceland, Ireland, Italy, Latvia, Luxembourg, the Former Yugoslav Republic of Macedonia, the Netherlands, Norway, Poland, Portugal, San Marino, Serbia, Slovakia, Slovenia, Spain, Sweden, Switzerland, Ukraine, the UK, Bahrain, Israel, Kuwait, Lebanon, Saudi Arabia and Turkey.

[69] The arguments presented in this section in favour of and against assigning supervisory functions to central banks are taken from the Group of Thirty (n 6) 39–41; Heidi Schooner and Michael Taylor (n 14) 271–273; and Eilís Ferran (n 4) 113–115, with further references. On the law of central banking, see also Chapter 17 by Rosa M Lastra in this volume.

All supervisory models that were examined above are compatible with different degrees of central bank involvement in financial sector oversight.[70] In the study mentioned above, Daniel Calvo et al. find that central banks are responsible for microprudential banking supervision in two thirds of the jurisdictions surveyed. Since the GFC, central banks have gained more microprudential responsibility for banks and insurance firms, as well as new macroprudential and resolution functions. The latter are examined in more detail in the following section. Insurance firms continue to be mostly supervised by separate supervisory agencies (in two-thirds of the jurisdictions). The securities business and firms are predominantly supervised by separate supervisory agencies as well (in slightly more than 80% of jurisdictions). Moreover, those jurisdictions surveyed that changed their supervisory model in the aftermath of the GFC have tended to give more supervisory powers to their central banks.[71]

5. OTHER FUNCTIONS FOR FINANCIAL SECTOR AUTHORITIES

After the GFC, some jurisdictions changed their financial supervisory models, whereas most jurisdictions implemented incremental changes in their models. These reforms include, *inter alia*, new macroprudential and resolution frameworks. These two functions were assigned either to new or existing authorities. They will now be discussed in turn.

Whereas microprudential supervision is concerned with the safety and soundness of individual institutions, macroprudential supervision focuses on the safety and soundness of the financial system as a whole.[72] In the aftermath of the GFC, most jurisdictions have modified their legislation to adopt new macroprudential tools. These frameworks give authorities tasked with macroprudential supervision the mandate to activate these policies or to issue recommendations for other authorities to act. Daniel Calvo et al. report that central banks are the leading authority for macroprudential policy in the largest number of jurisdictions surveyed. This is more likely to be the case when the central bank is also responsible for the microprudential supervision of banks. In other cases, responsibility for macroprudential policy is assigned to the supervisory agency which is the microprudential bank supervisor, or to a dedicated inter-agency committee which comprises central bank officials, supervisors and government representatives. In keeping with the theme of synergies with and potential conflicts between different financial oversight functions, it should be noted that 'the integration of both macro- and microprudential responsibilities within the same agency can facilitate an integrated approach to financial stability assessment and coordinated action' but that 'the risk arises that macroprudential policies, with their typically longer time horizon, could become subordinated to microprudential priorities, which are more short-term'.[73] Overall, most jurisdictions surveyed have sought to strengthen their frameworks for monitoring financial stability, typically

70 Daniel Calvo and others (n 27) 6.

71 ibid 2, 10, 11–13.

72 Rosa M Lastra, 'Systemic Risk and Macro-Prudential Supervision' in Niamh Moloney, Eilís Ferran and Jennifer Payne (eds), *The Oxford Handbook of Financial Regulation* (OUP 2015) 315–317.

73 Daniel Calvo and others (n 27) 6.

by setting up a specific coordination body or committee.[74] It is particularly noteworthy that in the case of the European Banking Union, the European Central Bank directly supervises the 'significant' (i.e. larger) banks of the participating countries and ensures a consistent approach in the supervision of 'less significant' (i.e. small and medium-sized) banks by the national authorities, but it is mainly responsible for assessing macroprudential measures adopted by the national authorities in the Member States participating in the Banking Union. If deemed necessary to address risks to financial stability, the European Central Bank also has the power to apply more stringent measures than those adopted nationally.[75]

As regards resolution regimes, their objective is to render feasible the resolution of financial institutions without severe systemic disruption and without exposing taxpayers to losses, while protecting vital economic functions through mechanisms which make it possible for shareholders and creditors of the institution concerned to absorb losses. According to the Financial Stability Board's *Key Attributes of Effective Resolution Regimes for Financial Institutions*, jurisdictions should have in place a resolution regime that provides the resolution authority with a broad range of powers and options to resolve a firm that is no longer viable and has no reasonable prospect of becoming so.[76] The primary resolution authority is typically located within the authority responsible for the microprudential supervision of banks, especially when the latter is the central bank. This 'may facilitate the achievement of well-coordinated arrangements for crisis prevention and resolution', but it 'could also encourage supervisory forbearance, as the prudential authority may have an incentive to delay resolution in order to protect its credibility or to avoid a potential spill-over to other institutions'.[77] In a number of jurisdictions (such as in the EU), bank resolution requires the involvement of more than one authority, and central banks are usually involved in the resolution process even when they are not the single resolution authority.[78]

6. ACCOUNTABILITY OF FINANCIAL SUPERVISORS

The institutional choices adumbrated above also influence the extent to which a financial supervisory or regulatory authority can be held effectively to account for the exercise of its tasks. Accountability connotes 'a relationship between an actor and a forum, in which the actor has an obligation to explain and to justify his or her conduct, the forum can pose questions

---

74 ibid 17–19. See further Rosa M Lastra (n 72), with further references; and the chapter by Luca Amorello in this volume.

75 I am grateful to Edoardo Martino for this observation. See further Menelaos Markakis and Diane Fromage, 'The Accountability of the European Central Bank: New Frontiers, New Challenges' (2023) 30 MJ 359, 360, 374.

76 Financial Stability Board, 'Key Attributes of Effective Resolution Regimes for Financial Institutions' (15 October 2014) <https://www.fsb.org/wp-content/uploads/r_141015.pdf> accessed 2 March 2023, 3–4. See further John Armour, 'Making Bank Resolution Credible' in Niamh Moloney, Eilís Ferran and Jennifer Payne (eds), *The Oxford Handbook of Financial Regulation* (OUP 2015) ch 15, with further references; and the chapter by Shuai Guo in this volume.

77 Daniel Calvo and others (n 27) 6.

78 ibid 20–21.

and pass judgement, and the actor may face consequences'.[79] Accountability is important from a democratic and constitutional perspective, namely for providing a democratic means to monitor and control those holding public office and for preventing and curtailing abuses of power, respectively. It is also important from a learning perspective, namely as a tool to enhance the learning capacity and effectiveness of governments, agencies and individual officials in delivering on their promises.[80] Furthermore, the answers to the basic questions of accountability – who is the actor that should render account; to whom account is to be rendered; what is the aspect of the conduct that account should be rendered for; and what is the nature of the obligation of the actor to render account to the forum[81] – are very much influenced by the design of financial regulatory and supervisory systems. For example, when different (regulatory or supervisory) functions are dispersed between a number of agencies/authorities, it can be particularly difficult to unravel who has contributed and in what way to a policy outcome or failure.

In evaluating the accountability arrangements for financial regulatory and supervisory authorities, the distinction between *preconditions* (or requirements) and *instruments* of accountability is crucial.[82] This analytical framework serves to frame the inquiry on the accountability of the financial authority concerned, but ultimately much depends on the institutional context or system within which the authority concerned is embedded and/or the function(s) it performs.[83] For example, '[a]n agency only entrusted with supervisory tasks and thus, with the execution of a predetermined legal framework may call for fewer mechanisms than a unified financial regulator, which combines supervisory with regulatory tasks'.[84] Getting the balance right, also in light of the trade-off between independence and accountability, is notoriously difficult.[85]

The existence of clear objectives or standards against which to assess the performance of the actor concerned constitutes one of the preconditions for an effective accountability regime.[86] It is rightly noted that 'the more complex the activity that is entrusted to an agency is, the more difficult it is to identify specific goals and standards and the more evasive accountability becomes' and that 'this problem is particularly acute in the context of financial regulatory

---

79 Mark Bovens, 'Analysing and Assessing Accountability: A Conceptual Framework' (2007) 13 ELJ 447, 450.

80 ibid 462–467.

81 See also ibid 454–462.

82 As regards central banks, see Fabian Amtenbrink, *The Democratic Accountability of Central Banks: A Comparative Study of the European Central Bank* (Hart Publishing 1999) 334–359. This analytical framework may also be applied with respect to financial regulatory agencies: Fabian Amtenbrink and Rosa M Lastra, 'Securing Democratic Accountability of Financial Regulatory Agencies – A Theoretical Framework' in Richard V de Mulder (ed.), *Mitigating Risk in the Context of Safety and Security. – How Relevant Is a Rational Approach?* (OMV 2008) 115–132. For its application to bank supervisors, see Fabian Amtenbrink and Menelaos Markakis, 'Towards a Meaningful Prudential Supervision Dialogue in the Euro Area? A Study of the Interaction between the European Parliament and the European Central Bank in the Single Supervisory Mechanism' (2019) 44 EL Rev. 3.

83 See also Fabian Amtenbrink and Rosa M Lastra (n 82) 124.

84 ibid 124.

85 I am grateful to Hossein Nabilou for this observation.

86 Fabian Amtenbrink and Rosa M Lastra (n 82) 124–127; Fabian Amtenbrink (n 82) 335–339.

agencies'.[87] 'Performance accountability is facilitated when: there is one objective, rather than multiple objectives; when that objective is narrowly defined rather than formulated in broad terms; if there are multiple objectives, a clear and unambiguous ranking is better than no ranking at all.'[88] Another precondition for an effective accountability regime is the provision of information on the execution of the actor's tasks, which should include 'an explanation or justification of the agency's actions or decisions'.[89] As such, transparency is not equated with accountability – and accountability should not be reduced to transparency – but is rather seen as a prerequisite for robust accountability arrangements.[90] However, it can be difficult to strike a balance between the need for confidentiality and the need for information to be publicized.[91]

There should also be instruments placed in the hands of the accountability holder (or forum) through which the latter may assign consequences to its judgment of the performance of the actor concerned. More specifically, the accountability holder may opt, if so empowered, to amend (or even repeal) the enabling statute so as to sanction the actor concerned for the performance of its tasks, thereby adding rules, responsibilities or conditions thereto, changing its independent status or the composition of its bodies, or even abolishing it altogether. An institution's involvement in adopting the respective legislation in the first place constitutes a form of *ex ante* accountability and is arguably very important from the standpoint of democratic legitimacy. However, it does not constitute a means of judging the performance of the actor concerned (*ex post* accountability). Moreover, appointment, reappointment and dismissal procedures may contribute to the accountability of an actor, especially if performance-based dismissal is permitted, although, realistically, the government and parliament would be involved in such procedures only as regards the heads or high-ranking members of such supervisory and regulatory agencies. What is more, reappointment and dismissal may be legally excluded (at least in most cases), so as to safeguard the independence of the actor concerned. Moreover, the relevant rules may provide for an override mechanism which would allow the accountability holder to postpone the adoption of a decision by the actor concerned or, as the case may be, to amend or overrule it, under the conditions set out in those rules. Such mechanisms may, however, run counter to or diminish the independence of the actor concerned. Furthermore, budgetary accountability may include the power conferred on the accountability holder to approve the budget of the actor concerned, as well as the possibility of audits. However, the actor concerned may have its own budget, which does not have to be approved by another body, and audits could be either restricted in scope or excluded altogether, so as to protect the actor's budgetary independence. Last but definitely not least, existing avenues of judicial

---

87 Fabian Amtenbrink and Rosa M Lastra (n 82) 125. The authors invoke the example of the UK FSA in ibid 125–127.

88 ibid 125.

89 ibid 127–129; Fabian Amtenbrink (n 82) 335–346.

90 Fabian Amtenbrink and Rosa M Lastra (n 82) 127–128; Menelaos Markakis, *Accountability in the Economic and Monetary Union: Foundations, Policy, and Governance* (OUP 2020) 15.

91 Fabian Amtenbrink and Rosa M Lastra (n 82) 128. See also Charles A E Goodhart, 'Regulating the Regulator – An Economist's Perspective on Accountability and Control' in Eilís Ferran and Charles A E Goodhart (eds), *Regulating Financial Services and Markets in the 21st Century* (Hart Publishing 2001) ch 11; Luca Enriques and Gerard Hertig, 'Improving the Governance of Financial Supervisors' (2011) 12 EBOR 357, esp. 372ff; Menelaos Markakis (n 90) 182–186, with further references.

review, including actions for damages, to the extent that such avenues are available and/or not severely circumscribed, are also an important instrument of accountability. Restrictive rules on standing, high standards of review, extremely light touch review, or even the lack of an effective remedy altogether, allude to the lack of legal accountability of a given actor.[92]

7. CONCLUSIONS

This chapter examined the institutional architecture of financial regulation and supervision. We have noted that the blurring of lines between different financial sectors and businesses has led to an evolution of supervisory and regulatory approaches. The various financial supervisory structures may be categorized under the four main supervisory models we discussed above: institutional; functional; objectives- or goal-based; and unified or integrated. These models present different benefits and challenges for policymakers. This chapter has sought to illustrate the various implications flowing from adopting one or another of the four principal models of supervisory oversight. Moreover, we have seen that, while dealing with similar problems and challenges, the existing supervisory systems can look quite different from one another. Their design is influenced by factors that are as diverse as they are context-specific. Whichever the approach taken to financial supervision in a particular jurisdiction, effective coordination and information-sharing arrangements among supervisory agencies, central banks, finance ministries and so on are of cardinal importance. Such information-sharing (and decision-making) linkages are also important between the central bank and other agencies, whether the former is involved in financial supervision or not. We have further seen that the reforms implemented in various jurisdictions after the GFC included the adoption of macroprudential policy and resolution frameworks, which can involve both the central bank as well as separate supervisory agencies. Furthermore, the institutional choices adumbrated above also have consequences for the accountability of the financial authorities in a given jurisdiction, in the manner explained above. Overall, '[t]here seems to be no "silver bullet" for an ideal architecture of the organization for financial supervision' but 'fit-for-purpose arrangements to facilitate information flows, adequate coordination across relevant parties and a good structure of incentives for responsible authorities do matter'.[93] Supervisory structures matter, even if only to an extent, to economic outcomes and to supervisory efficiency, effectiveness, and accountability.[94]

---

92 Fabian Amtenbrink and Rosa M Lastra (n 82) 129–132; Menelaos Markakis (n 90) 15–17.
93 Daniel Calvo and others (n 27) 22–23.
94 Eilís Ferran (n 4) 99.

PART II

REGULATION OF FINANCIAL MARKETS

4. Mandatory disclosure

Matteo Gargantini

1. INTRODUCTION: THE RATIONALE OF MANDATORY DISCLOSURE

All major jurisdictions around the world require firms that approach – or have approached – a significant number of investors to disclose material information to their counterparty or, more often, to the public at large. This chapter compares the most significant regulatory approaches to mandatory disclosure in some selected jurisdictions.

Mandatory disclosure is traditionally considered a remedy to market failures such as asymmetric information, which leads to adverse selection and moral hazard, externalities and agency problems.[1] In a nutshell, the rationale underlying the rules analysed in this chapter is that, without sufficient information on the securities and the issuing firms, potential investors will discount the risk of 'lemons' from the price they are willing to pay, thus preventing transactions on high-quality market segments (or potentially, on *any* market segments). A similar reasoning applies to ongoing disclosure that occurs once the investment is done, because the lack of a credible commitment by the investee firms to provide information in the future creates the same uncertainty for investors. Absent ongoing disclosure, issuers could exploit their information advantage to the detriment of investors, because these cannot easily monitor the use of the resources they have invested.

Remarkably, investors and issuers may share a common interest in bridging the gap of asymmetric information. Investors are eager to know as precisely as possible what risks they are taking on, and firms that credibly display the good quality of their business will reduce investor uncertainty and their cost of capital. Moreover, in the case of equity securities, investors appoint companies' directors, who are responsible for disclosure, and could bind them to disseminate material information through ad hoc provisions in the articles of association.

However, market forces alone may not be able to lead parties to share the optimal level of information.[2] First, such incentives are weak for negative information, which issuers are unlikely to disclose spontaneously. Issuers may be reluctant to share positive information, as well, when they fear that disclosure could benefit their competitors. This is particularly problematic because it leads to missing a positive externality, as those who invest in such competitors will lose their ability to compare the performance of their company against that of the issuer whose information is missing.[3] Second, commitments based on private bargaining

---

1 For an overview, see Thomas A Lambert, *How to Regulate. A Guide for Policymakers* (CUP 2017) 91, 185.

2 For an analysis, see John Armour and others, *Principles of Financial Regulation* (OUP 2016) 160.

3 Frank A Easterbrook and Daniel R Fischel, 'Mandatory Disclosure and the Protection of Investors' (1984) 70 Virginia Law Review 669, 685–686; Luca Enriques and Sergio Gilotta,

may not be sufficiently credible for indefinite periods of time.[4] By making themselves subject to mandatory disclosure and the supervision that accompanies it, the party in the possession of information addresses all these problems at once.

Just like any other regulatory measure, mandatory disclosure has its drawbacks as well. The most obvious one is that drafting documents is expensive in terms of time and efforts and leads to compliance risk in case of unintentional violations. Most importantly, information is an asset. Mandating disclosure is tantamount to defining negative propriety rights on such an asset and, therefore, results in an expropriation. One the one hand, the disclosing entity loses its ability to take advantage of that information; on the other hand, as we have seen, competitors can exploit it to their own benefit, although information originating from such competitors (when these are subject to the same duties) may compensate this effect to some degree. Moreover, the standardized nature of mandatory disclosure inevitably makes it simultaneously over- and under-inclusive compared with the preferences of some issuers and investors.

The remainder of the chapter analyses a selection of the most salient provisions on mandatory disclosure in major jurisdictions worldwide. It highlights how policymakers try to strike the right balance between the aim to ensure investor confidence and market integrity and the need to not make the regulatory framework so expensive that it may discourage firms from going public in the first place.

2. THE SCOPE OF APPLICATION OF MANDATORY CORPORATE DISCLOSURE: PRIMARY AND SECONDARY MARKETS

Mandatory disclosure kicks in for the first time in the life of a public company at the very moment that company goes public. Access to financial markets is accompanied in all major jurisdictions by the publication of a document, often a rather complex one, that displays the main features of the company to the benefit of prospective investors. With some exceptions,[5] this duty therefore pertains in principle to primary market transactions, as the requirement typically applies to the issuance of new securities offered for subscription or, when it involves securities that have already been issued, it normally supports the formation of prices with mechanisms that are distinct from the ordinary trading practice in terms of amounts involved and methods adopted to determine the price. For instance, a public offering may involve a book-building procedure, as opposed to direct individual bargaining or a continuous auction in an order-driven trading system.

In most jurisdictions, a general rule bans securities offerings or the admission to trading on a security exchange, or both, without prior publication of an information document most often labelled as 'prospectus'. Offerings normally trigger disclosure duties of this kind when they involve a sufficiently large number of addressees. In the US, for instance, a federal provision[6]

'Disclosure and Financial Market Regulation' in Eilís Ferran, Niamh Moloney, and Jennifer Payne (eds), *The Oxford Handbook of Financial Regulation* (OUP 2017) 521–532.

4 ibid., 511, 523.

5 See, e.g. below, on the definition of 'public offer of securities' in the EU.

6 This chapter does not address state legislation on securities offerings (often referred to as 'Blue Sky Laws').

prohibits any offering of securities through any means of communication unless such securities are registered with the Securities and Exchange Commission (SEC).[7]

In a similar manner, the EU prospectus regime applies to any 'communication to persons in any form and by any means, presenting sufficient information on the terms of the offer and the securities to be offered, so as to enable an investor to decide to purchase or subscribe for those securities'.[8] Similar provisions exist in the UK[9] and Singapore.[10] These definitions are deliberately broad enough to encompass any form of collection of orders, regardless of their legal qualification under private law.[11] Therefore, there typically is no need for the communication to display the features of a contractual proposal open for acceptance. To the contrary, even generic invitations to submit contractual proposals are included.

Prospectuses are normally required, as well, when issuers tap capital markets by getting their securities admitted to trading on a regulated exchange.[12] This may be combined with an offering, but it may also occur without any contextual underwriting or transfer of securities.

In any event, mandatory disclosure applies to listed companies well beyond the moment when they first tap financial markets through primary market offerings and initial listing. Listed companies remain subject to disclosure duties also once their securities have been admitted to trading on a securities exchange. The main disclosure duty issuers are subject to in secondary markets is the publication of periodic reports on their financial and economic conditions. This is a subject that lies at the boundary between company law and financial law, as financial law often builds upon company law with additional requirements. Such requirements are everywhere attached to the admission of securities to trading on a regulated exchange but, in some cases, they also apply to companies that have a widespread basis of shareholders. This is the case in the US, where periodic disclosure under the US Securities Exchange Act is also due by issuers with total assets above 10 million dollars and more than either 500 'unaccredited shareholders' or 2000 total shareholders, including both accredited and unaccredited ones.[13]

Currently, all major jurisdictions require issuers to publish their financial reports at least on a yearly basis and, typically, on a semi-annual basis as well.[14] In some countries, and most

---

7 Section 5(a), (b) and (c) Securities Act 1933 (USSA).

8 Council Regulation (EC) 2017/1129 of 14 June 2017 on the prospectus to be published when securities are offered to the public or admitted to trading on a regulated market, and repealing Directive 2003/71/EC [2017] OJ L168/12, Art. 2(d) [hereinafter EUPR].

9 Financial Services and Markets Act 2000 (FSMA 2000), s 85(1). The proposed new UK regime in the post-Brexit scenario ('Edinburgh Reforms') confirms the approach (Sections 8 and 11 Draft Financial Services and Markets Act 2000 (Public Offers and Admissions to Trading) Regulations 2023).

10 Securities and Futures Act 2001 (SSFA), s 240.

11 See, e.g. Thomas Lee Hazen and David L. Ratner, *Securities Regulations. Cases and Materials* (Thomson West 2003), 130 (US).

12 Section 12 Securities Exchange Act 1934 (USSEA); FSMA 2000, s 85(2).

13 Sec. 12(g) USSEA. Accredited shareholders are investors satisfying requirements that demonstrate their reduced need of protection (such requirements concern, among the others, their income, net worth, asset size or professional experience: SEC Rule 230.501 – Regulation D).

14 Sections 13 and 15(d) USSEA (for annual reports – Form 10-K); Council Directive 2004/109/EC of 15 December 2004 on the harmonization of transparency requirements in relation to information about issuers whose securities are admitted to trading on a regulated market and amending Directive 2001/34/EC [2004] OJ L 390/38 [hereinafter Transparency Directive] Arts

notably in the US, the law also mandates quarterly reports.[15] The frequency of disclosure has politically sensitive implications because the short time span elapsing between periodic reports (and quarterly reports in particular) has been regarded as a reason for market short-termism,[16] although the actual relevance of this problem remains debated.[17]

According to the pessimistic view on corporate short-termism, frequent mandatory disclosure duties deliver unintended consequences that exceed their benefits. Therefore, in countries other than the US, the law tends to be more flexible for quarterly reports, but as a matter of fact these will often be required by the competent authority or by listing rules of the stock exchange, whether in general (as is the case in China[18]) or where the issuer shows signs of financial distress (as is the case in Singapore[19]). EU laws mandates yearly and half-yearly reports, but allows Member States to introduce quarterly reports after running a cost–benefit analysis demonstrating that this does not lead to an excessive burden (particularly for SMEs) and does not entail an excessive focus on the issuers' short-term results.[20] What is noteworthy, however, is that investors seem to appreciate quarterly reports, to the point that demand may drive supply and lead companies to voluntary produce such information, absent mandatory disclosure.[21]

3. MANDATORY DISCLOSURE AND STANDARDIZATION

One of the main reasons why mandatory disclosure can be more efficient than voluntary disclosure lies with its ability to force the adoption of common standards for the selection and the presentation of information. Indeed, disclosure better performs its function when it produces comparable data. This function is of such relevance that prospectus schemes and accounting principles have been regarded as rules for which uniformity is key and trumps the

---

4 and 5 (for annual and half-yearly reports); Sec. 394 UK Companies Act and Sec. 4.2.2 FCA Disclosure Guidance and Transparency Rules Sourcebook (DTR) (for annual and half yearly reports respectively); Art. 201 Singapore Companies Act (annual and half-yearly reports); Art. 145 Chinese Company Law (annual and half-yearly reports); see also Weiping He, *The Regulation of Securities Markets in China* (Palgrave Macmillan 2018) 83.

15 Sections 13 and 15(d) USSEA (Form 10-Q).

16 John Kay, *The Kay Review of UK Equity Markets and Long-Term Decision Making. Final Report* (2012) 73–74 <www.gov.uk> accessed 20 June 2023.

17 Mark Roe, Missing the Target: Why Stock-market Short-termism is not the Problem (OUP 2022) 45–46, 132–135.

18 Shanghai Stock Exchange (Section 2.12 Listing Rules; Weiping He, *The Regulation of Securities Markets in China* (Palgrave Macmillan 2018), 89, 114).

19 Singapore Stock Exchange (Section 705 SGX Rulebook Mainboard Rules), requiring more frequent periodic reports by issuers whose auditors have not released an unqualified positive opinion.

20 Transparency Directive Art. 3(1a).

21 On the determinants of such decision, see Asheq Rahman and others, 'Quarterly Reporting in a Voluntary Disclosure Environment: Its Benefits, Drawbacks and Determinants' (2007) 42 The International Journal of Accounting 416.

relevance of the content ('focal point rules').[22] To be sure, private bodies can define standards that may become dominant if they meet market needs, but mandatory provisions are often buttressing these efforts either by supporting privately defined standards (as is often the case with secondary market disclosure) or by creating their own (which is typical of primary market transparency, instead).

As to primary markets, the content of prospectuses and other similar documents is specified in different jurisdictions with variable levels of detail. The common regulatory strategy seems to rely on multiple tiers of regulation, often including: (i) a general statement on the purpose of mandatory disclosure, such as the need to provide 'all the information that investors and their professional advisers would reasonably require to make an informed assessment' of the main features of the issuers and its securities or 'the necessary information which is material to an investor for making an informed assessment of' the financial and economic condition of the issuer, as well as of the rights attaching to the securities;[23] (ii) some high-level indications of prospectus contents, such as the rights attached to a security and the issuers' overall financial conditions;[24] and (iii) detailed schedules fleshing out the information items prospectuses should include, often adopted by regulators upon delegation. The first movers were the US, which after the Great Depression introduced the registration statement as the key document for primary market transactions and IPOs.[25] The main component of the registration document, intended for publication, is the prospectus.[26] Based on the power to integrate the high-level indications in Schedule A SEA,[27] the US SEC has specified the information items to include in prospectuses through Regulation S-K (for qualitative information) and Regulation S-X (for financial information).

Moving now to secondary markets, the most traditional distinction among countries in the realm of periodic disclosure refers to the accounting standards adopted. This is an area where the trade-off between flexibility and comparability that standardization brings along can be seen particularly clearly. Principle-based rules leave room for discretion and therefore may reduce uniformity in mandatory disclosure. At the same time, excessively detailed rules on financial reports lend themselves to circumvention when they do not capture functionally equivalent but legally different transactions.[28]

---

[22] David Charny, 'Competition Among Jurisdictions in Formulating Corporate Law Rules: An American Perspective on the "Race to the Bottom" in the European Communities' (1991) 32 Harvard International Law Journal 423, 442.

[23] Section 243(1)(a) SSFA (Singapore) and EUPR Art. 6, respectively.

[24] Section 243(3) SSFA (Singapore) and EUPR annex I, respectively.

[25] Sections 2(8) and 6 USSA; Section 12 USSEA. Securities registration typically occurs via specific unified SEC forms (such as S-1, S-2 and S-3, depending on issuers' previous registration history) that apply to registrations under either the USSA, the USSEA, or both (on the development of the system see Hazen and Ratner (n 11), 156–157).

[26] Sections 2(10) and 10 USSA.

[27] Section 7 USSEA.

[28] Dirk Beerbaum, Maciej Piechocki, and Christoph Weber, 'Is There a Conflict Between Principles-based Standard Setting and Structured Electronic Reporting with XBRL?' (2017) 12 European Financial and Accounting Journal 33, 35.

With some simplifications,[29] the big divide in this regard is between the US GAAPs prepared by the FASB and the IAS/IFRS prepared by the IASB. While the relevance of the former set of standards is mostly related to the US markets, IFRS are more widely spread at international level and are progressively being adopted by countries that were previously only relying on national accounting principles. Among the jurisdictions that have made this move are the EU, China, India, Brazil, South Korea and Indonesia.[30] The evidence on the net benefits of IFRS vis-à-vis national GAAPs is mixed, and the attempts to approximate the two systems have not always led to material changes in the accounting practice.[31] This may show that legal transplants in accounting matters may be only superficial, with traditional interpretations and approaches remaining active below the surface to reflect underlying differences in key factors such as legal origins, corporate governance, securities regulation and litigation risks.[32]

In any event, the distance between national GAAPs and IFRS can be material in crucial matters. A case in point among the many possible example is the notion of 'control', which is the basis for a number of accounting rules – chief among them the preparation of consolidated accounts. While the IFRS define that concept through principles, the US GAAPs follow their traditional rule-based approach.[33] Empirical evidence shows that US GAAPs lead to more consistent interpretations, while the IFRS are more prone to divergent readings and leave broader room for national variations.[34]

The role of standardization in periodic reporting can be appreciated by looking at the current lack of shared standards on non-financial information. Owing to its relatively young development, the market for sustainable products cannot yet rely on a (few) dominant set(s) of reporting principles, a situation that is believed to prevent comparability.[35] The EU is develop-

---

29 The US FASB has adopted a relatively more principle-based approach ever since the Enron scandal. For an account and a criticism, see George J Benston, Michael Bromwich and Alfred Wagenhofer, 'Principles-versus rules-based Accounting Standards: The FASB's Standard Setting Strategy' (2006) 42 ABACUS 165.

30 See IFRS, *Who uses IFRS Accounting Standards?* <www.ifrs.org> accessed 20 June 2023.

31 See, e.g. Nina Franzen and Barbara E Weißenberger, 'Capital Market Effects of Mandatory IFRS 8 Adoption: An Empirical Analysis of German Firms' (2018) 31 Journal of International Accounting, Auditing and Taxation 1.

32 Lawrence A Cunningham, 'Accounting and Financial Reporting. Global Aspirations, Local Realities', in Jeffrey N Gordon and Wolf-Georg Ringe (eds), *The Oxford Handbook of Corporate Law and Governance* (OUP 2018), 489, 495–504.

33 See FASB, 'Consolidation (Topic 810)' (2018) Accounting Standards Update No 2018-17 <www.fasb.org> accessed 20 June 2023 (control usually occurs when the reporting entity owns more than 50 percent of the outstanding voting shares of another entity. The power to control may also exist with a lesser percentage of ownership); IASB, *IFRS 10 – Consolidated Financial Statements* (2021) <www.ifrs.org> accessed 20 June 2023 (control exists when the consolidating entity has power over the investee, has right to variable returns from its investment and can use its power to affect the amount of the investor's returns).

34 Jenice Prather-Kinsey, Scott Boyar and Anthony C Hood, 'Implications for IFRS Principles-based and US GAAP Rules-based Applications: Are Accountants' Decisions Affected by Work Location and Core Self-evaluations?' (2018) 32 Journal of International Accounting, Auditing and Taxation 61, 62.

35 Sebastian Steuer and Tobias H Tröger, 'The Role of Disclosure in Green Finance' (2022) 8 Journal of Financial Regulation 1, 9.

ing its own set of non-financial reporting standards with the support of the European Financial Reporting Advisory Group, although at the risk of adding an additional layer of complexity to the current system.[36]

4. MANDATING DISCLOSURE WHEN IT IS NEEDED: MATERIALITY TESTS

Disclosure is expensive, so it should be mandated only when its benefits exceed its costs. Not only are the costs of preparing disclosure documents unjustified when information is irrelevant, but investors can also suffer from information overload when they receive more data than they need. One way to achieve a reasonable balance is to make sure transparency only applies to transactions and information that are sufficiently relevant in light of their features, including their size.

As to primary markets, all major jurisdictions require the involvement of a material number of prospective investors as a precondition for the duty to publish a prospectus.[37] The legal techniques may range from embedding the requirement in the definition of the relevant offerings (for instance by specifying that these shall be made 'to the public'[38]) to setting an exemption for private placements[39] – or a combination of the two.[40] The same applies to the value of the offering, which normally needs to cross pre-determined amounts to trigger the duty to publish a prospectus.[41] The analytical framework sketched out in Section 1 above helps explain these regulatory choices as an attempt to strike a balance between the benefits of disclosure in terms of reduced adverse selection, on the one hand, and the costs of drawing up complex documents such as prospectuses.[42]

---

36 Gaia Balp and Giovanni Strampelli, 'Institutional Investors as the Primary Users of Sustainability Reporting', in Kern Alexander, Michele Siri and Matteo Gargantini (eds), *The Cambridge Handbook of EU Sustainable Finance: Regulation, Supervision and Governance* (forthcoming CUP 2025). For sustainability-related disclosure, see Chapter 18 in this book.

37 In the specific case of offerings of fund units – which we do not further consider here – such limits may not attach to the requirement to publish a prospectus, but to the requirement that the fund gathers collective investments and therefore, by definition, gather s plurality of investors (for the EU see, e.g. Council Directive 2009/65/EC of 13 July 2009 on the coordination of laws, regulations and administrative provisions relating to undertakings for collective investment in transferable securities [2009] OJ L23/203 [hereinafter UCITS] Art. 68).

38 EUPR Art. 2(d).

39 Section 4(2) USSA.

40 EUPR Art. 1(4)(b), which sets a numerical threshold by exempting offerings addressing 'fewer than 150 natural or legal persons per Member State, other than qualified investors'.

41 See, e.g. Section 4(6) USSA.

42 Spotting the right materiality threshold is a difficult task. In the EU, for instance, the threshold is not perfectly harmonized, despite the repeated attempts to reduce national discretion in this regard. In its last version, the law sets a threshold of 12 million euros calculated over a period of 12 months, but Member States can lower the figure to 5 million euros. See European Parliament, *Increasing the attractiveness of public capital markets and facilitating access to capital for SMEs – amending certain Regulations European Parliament legislative resolution of 24 April 2024 on the proposal for a regulation of the European Parliament and of the Council amending Regulations*

The need to select relevant information also characterizes periodic secondary market disclosure. In this case, the selection does not involve the need to make documents public: periodic disclosure is always due, and even the absence of material developments would be material. However, the selection is meant to determine which information deserves inclusion in periodic documents and, most importantly, when an omission or misstatement violates the accounting rules. The typical criterion is that of materiality, which applies to both the US GAAP and the IAS/IFRS spheres. As to the former, the SEC stated that information is material 'if there is a substantial likelihood that a reasonable person would consider it important'.[43] According to FASB, this means that materiality occurs when 'the magnitude of the item is such that it is probable that the judgment of a reasonable person relying upon the report would have been changed or influenced by the inclusion or correction of the item'.[44] In the IAS/IFRS system, information is material when it 'could [...] influence the economic decisions of users taken on the basis of the financial statement', depending on the size and nature of the information. A user is supposed 'to have a reasonable knowledge of business and economic activities and accounting and a willingness to study the information with reasonable diligence'.[45]

4.1 Event-Based Information Duties

Materiality tests play a particularly pervasive role in the realm of ongoing disclosure duties. In most jurisdictions, listed companies are subject to the duty to disseminate information concerning major developments that can affect the market price of the securities they have issued. As opposed to periodic disclosure duties, this kind of disclosure is event-driven and, therefore, requires publication of information on an ad hoc basis. In this field, the regulatory conundrum lies with the challenging balance between legal certainty for issuers, on the one hand, and support of price discovery mechanisms through conveyance of all material information, on the other hand. The ability of disclosure to prevent insider dealing plays a role in this trade-off, as well, because trading on inside information is, by definition, impossible when such information ceases to be confidential due to publication.

Regulatory choices on this matter vary across jurisdictions. Legal certainty is best achieved in jurisdictions where disclosure is due upon occurrence of certain events that are pre-determined by the law. This is the typical US approach to ongoing disclosure duties, which require issuers to publish 'on a rapid and current basis information concerning material changes in the financial condition or operations of the issuer'. The same provision delegates the SEC to determine when issuers shall disclose based on the need to protect investors and

---

(EU) 2017/1129, (EU) No 596/2014 and (EU) No 600/2014 to make public capital markets in the Union more attractive for companies and to facilitate access to capital for small and medium-sized enterprises (COM(2022)0762 – C9-0417/2022 – 2022/0411(COD)) (P9_TA(2024)0350) (hereinafter: 'Listing Act'), Art. 1(3).

[43] SEC, 'Materiality' Staff Accounting Bulletin No 99 (1999) <www.sec.gov> accessed 20 June 2023.

[44] FASB, *Conceptual Framework for Financial Reporting. Chapter 3, Qualitative Characteristics of Useful Financial Information* (2018), QC 11 <https://fasb.org> accessed 20 June 2023. According to SEC (n 43), this criterion is identical to the one adopted to assess materiality under the US case law on insider dealing (see Section 4.1).

[45] §§ 11 and 12 IAS 1 (see also § 5 IAS 8).

the public interest.[46] The SEC has developed a list of pre-defined facts the occurrence of which triggers disclosure (Form 8-K). For instance, publication is due when the entity 'has completed the acquisition or disposition of a significant amount of assets, otherwise than in the ordinary course of business', with the Form 8-K specifying what information is due to the market.[47] In a similar vein, Chinese law lists a series of material events, as well. These include the decision taken on major investments or asset purchase, as well as the involvement in major disputes.[48] A particularly detailed set of pre-defined relevant developments exists in Japan, where disclosure – through an 'extraordinary report' – is required in 'cases that are specified by Cabinet Office Order as necessary and appropriate in the public interest or for the protection of investors'.[49] In turn, the delegated regulation specifies the relevant events.[50]

In other countries, publication follows any event that can have a material impact on market prices. In this case, issuer discretion – and hence legal risk – is higher, as the interpretation of open-textured rules that define the boundaries of mandatory disclosure is inevitably prone to diverging interpretations. The most obvious example seems to be the EU, which requires dissemination of any inside information directly concerning issuers or their financial instruments.[51] This is not-yet-public information that simultaneously displays precision, specificity and price sensitivity. Precision occurs when information refers to events that have materialized or are reasonably likely to happen in the future. Specificity and price-sensitiveness are similar concepts that, in turn, require information to be sufficiently complete to support an understanding of its possible effect on market prices (specificity), and to lead to the conclusion that such effect will be material (price-sensitiveness).

Mandatory disclosure systems that rely on forward-looking assessments have the advantage of potentially reducing the scope for insider trading and of facilitating price accuracy. This may occasionally come at the cost of some higher volatility when the initial estimations prove wrong and the initial press release requires corrections. Another drawback is the need to ensure legal certainty through sufficiently clear guidance for issuers on the level of certainty that, based on the assessment of the current circumstances, issuers need to reach concerning the likely occurrence of a future event (precision test). EU law particularly stresses that even preliminary steps in protracted processes that might end up with a material development (such as an agreement-in-principle) are subject to disclosure duties. Typical examples here are negotiations that may be finalized in a contract or intermediate results in the R&D process that could lead to the synthesis of a new molecule. Overall, information concerning final events

---

46 Sections 13(l) USSEA.

47 Such information includes, for instance, the date of completion of the transaction, a brief description of the assets and the consideration paid or received (Item 2-10 Form 8-K).

48 Section 80 and 81 2020 Securities Law of the People's Republic of China.

49 Section 24-5(4) Japanese Financial Instrument and Exchange Act [hereinafter JFIEA].

50 Section 19 Cabinet Office Ordinance on Disclosure of Corporate Information [hereinafter COODCI].

51 Council Regulation 596/2014 of 16 April 2014 on market abuse (market abuse regulation) and repealing Directive 2003/6/EC of the European Parliament and of the Council and Commission Directives 2003/124/EC, 2003/125/EC and 2004/72/EC [2014] OJ L 173/1 [hereinafter MAR] Arts 7 and 17. The same regime applies, for the time being, to the UK, as per the European Union (Withdrawal) Act 2018: Section 2.2.1A FCA DTR (Disclosure of inside information).

(and even intermediate steps) is precise when there is a realistic prospect that these occur, without a high probability of occurrence being needed.[52]

As disclosure of preliminary steps may be detrimental to listed companies, EU law allows these to defer publication when delay can protect their legitimate interests, as long as confidentiality is maintained and postponing dissemination would not mislead investors. However, the conditions issuers must meet to delay dissemination do not always lead to straightforward interpretations,[53] and the uncertainties surrounding the need to disclose future events remain, as the decision to delay publication requires formalization and is subject to disclosure towards supervisors.[54] All in all, event-based mandatory disclosure in the EU is often perceived as burdensome, so that EU policymakers have recently agreed to confine it to final events of protracted process.[55]

What makes event-based disclosure a complex matter to handle in most jurisdictions is, however, the uncertainty surrounding the materiality filter. Only developments that can significantly affect market prices should be disclosed, but once again the assessment involves some level of discretion. In the US, an event is deemed material when a reasonable investor would either consider it important or view its omitted disclosure as a significant alteration of the overall available information.[56] The absence of a similar guiding criterion reportedly reduces legal certainty in the Chinese system, which also involves a materiality test within event-based mandatory disclosure.[57]

The materiality test boils down to a reasonable investor test in the EU, as well, as issuers must consider whether such kind of investor would use the relevant information 'as part of the basis of his or her investment decisions'.[58] In the EU, the precision and the materiality tests run separately, because a higher potential impact of the event on market prices cannot compensate for a lower level of probability that that event will occur (and vice-versa), although the recent amendment allowing for disclosure only after the final event of protracted process will probably simplify this kind of assessment. There is no need, instead, to predict the direction of price movements.[59] Hence, material events that may lead to either an increase or a decrease in market prices require disclosure in spite of this uncertainty – the typical example being that of an issuer launching a takeover.

In the EU, the same disconnection between precision and materiality applies to the determination as to whether a person perpetrates insider dealing, as opposed to the US system where, for this purpose only, the assessment is done by balancing out the probability that the event

---

[52] Case C-19/11 *Geltl v Daimler* [2012] ECR I- 397. For a comment, see Carmine Di Noia and Matteo Gargantini, 'Issuers at Midstream: Disclosure of Multistage Events in the Current and in the Proposed EU Market Abuse Regime' (2012) 9 European Company and Financial Law Review 484.

[53] MAR Art. 17(4). See also Listing Act (n 42), Art. 2(6)(c), replacing the requirement that delay is not misleading with a reference to the need that the new information does not contradict previous issuer statements.

[54] MAR Art. 17(4).

[55] Listing Act (n 42), Art. 2(6)(a).

[56] *TSC v. Northway*, 426 US 438 (1976), 449; *Basic Inc. v. Levinson*, 426 U.S. 224 (1998).

[57] He (n 18), 84–85.

[58] MAR Art. 7.

[59] C-628/13 *Lafonta v. Autorité des marches financiers* [2015] ECLI:EU:C:2015:162.

will occur and the anticipated magnitude of the event (probability/magnitude test).[60] As the US law predefines a set of events that require publication, this test applies to mandatory disclosure only in specific circumstances. The most important triggers of mandatory disclosure in the US other than the completion of a Form 8-K event are based on the general rule that prevents market frauds (SEC Rule 10b–5). The US case law has interpreted this general provision as requiring disclosure when a decision is taken to trade when in possession of inside information ('disclose or abstain')[61] or when issuers receive a question on such information (unless they decide to release a 'no comment' statement).[62] In these contexts, information concerning future developments may be relevant in the US, as well.[63]

In the realm of event-driven disclosure, one can spot a slight tendency to increase legal certainty by specifying issuer disclosure duties through lists of pre-determined events. Even in the EU, lawmakers have recently agreed that a list of events requiring disclosure shall be part of the regulatory framework. However, this does not suffice for the EU to abandon its standard-based approach requiring publication of any material events. Pre-defined events will be non-exhaustive, indeed, so that relevant developments not included in the list may still require disclosure.[64]

Japan provides, instead, a remarkable example of rule-based assessment of materiality in the context of ongoing disclosure. The Cabinet Office Order that specifies the events requiring disclosure equally sets forth – when relevant for the enlisted events – a materiality threshold. For instance, an extraordinary report is due when a serious disaster affects the reporting company, which means 'a disaster in which the book value of the assets of the reporting company that have been damaged [is equivalent to] 3 percent or more of the amount of net assets'.[65]

Finally, securities exchanges listing rules may add additional requirements on top of those defined in the law. For instance, the Rulebook of the Singapore Stock Exchange mandates disclosure of information which is necessary to avoid the establishment of a false market or which would be likely to materially affect the price or value of securities,[66] and similar provisions also appear in the NYSE and the NASDAQ rules. However, the enforcement of such requirements is reportedly scant.[67]

5. ADDRESSING UNSOPHISTICATED INVESTORS

The rationale for mandatory disclosure and the problems it entails are not identical for sophisticated and non-sophisticated investors. Sophisticated investors are more likely to be aware

---

60 *SEC v. Texas Gulf Sulphur Co.*, 401 F.2d 833 (2d Cir. 1968).

61 *Basic Inc. v. Levinson* (n 56), 1988.

62 ibid.

63 Hazen and Ratner (n 11), 223–235.

64 Listing Act (n 42), Art. 2(6)(f).

65 Art. 19(2)(v) COODCI.

66 Section 203 Singapore Securities and Futures Act; Section 702 SGX Rulebook Mainboard Rules.

67 Section 202.05 MYSE Listed Company Manual; Section 5250(b)(1) NASDAQ Stock Market LLC Rules; Gill North, 'National Company Disclosure Regulatory Frameworks: Superficially Similar but Substantively Different', (2015) 3 Global Markets Law Journal 187, 218.

of the information they need to assess the quality of the financial instruments involved, and normally have the bargaining power to obtain such information from the counterparty. In this case, the costs of mandatory disclosure are more likely to outweigh their benefits and, therefore, applicable laws waive some disclosure duties, especially on primary markets. This leads to an apparent paradox. Complex and bulky documents, as prospectuses normally are, have retail investors as their ideal addressees – so much so that if these investors are not involved in a sufficient number, no mandatory disclosure applies. At the same time, retail investors have little to no incentives to read these documents, because very few have the time and the skills required to understand them, let alone to assess whether the price of the security offer adequately reflects the information conveyed.

Most jurisdictions have tried to tackle this conundrum by making prospectuses easier to read for unsophisticated investors. One strategy is to require issuers to prepare additional documents that convey only the essential information in a better structured format. The most striking example is the EU, where prospectuses for equity and debt instruments, including those for closed-end funds, comprise a summary that reports the key information investors may want to consult when deciding whether it is worth analysing the rest of the document. The information provided in the summary includes the data that are necessary to understand the nature and the risks of the issuer.[68] Open-ended investment funds are subject to a similar requirement when they qualify for the UCITS label, which identifies mutual funds subject to liquidity and risk diversification requirements that make them eligible for an EU-wide passport for retail investors.[69] While only the offerings of UCITS used to require the publication of a 'key investor information document' (KIID), today a 'key investor document' (KID) accompanies all retail financial and insurance products whose payoff varies because of exposure to assets not directly purchased by the retail investor ('packaged retail and insurance-based investment product' – PRIIPs).[70] Despite the similar acronyms, KIDs follow a different disclosure philosophy compared with KIIDs. While KIIDs (and prospectus summaries) rely on the selection of the most relevant information, KIDs pay more attention to the way information is conveyed. KIDs include standardized charts displaying the level of risk (on a scale from 1 to 7) and four different performance scenarios that show how different contexts affect the products' payoff.[71]

Another strategy to make information more accessible relies on mandating the use of plain language that an average retail investor can understand. In the US, this means that issuers must present information in a clear, concise and understandable manner, including by using short and explanatory sentences that avoid legal and technical business terminology and by relying

---

68 EUPR recital 28 and Art. 7.

69 UCITS Arts 78–82 and 94.

70 Council Regulation 1286/2014 of 26 November 2014 on key information documents for packaged retail and insurance-based investment products [2014] OJ L 352/1 [hereinafter PRIIPS] Arts 4(3) and 5. PRIIPs KIDs can replace prospectus summaries and UCITS KIIDs to simplify disclosure requirement (see EUPR Art. 7(7) and UCITS Art. 82a, respectively).

71 See Delegated Regulation 2017/653 of 8 March 2017 supplementing Regulation (EU) No 1286/2014 of the European Parliament and of the Council on key information documents for packaged retail and insurance-based investment products (PRIIPs) by laying down regulatory technical standards with regard to the presentation, content, review and revision of key information documents and the conditions for fulfilling the requirement to provide such documents [2017] OJ L 100/1 annexes III and IV Regulation.

on bullet lists. Moreover, the prospectus summary and the risk factors should use 'everyday words' and active verbal voices with no multiple negatives.[72] Similar rules on clarity also exist in the EU and China.[73]

6. REDUCING THE COSTS OF MANDATORY DISCLOSURE

Striking the right balance between the costs and benefits of forcing publication of information is traditionally at the heart of regulatory concerns surrounding mandatory disclosure. The most illustrative examples of measures that try to facilitate access to capital markets while retaining a sufficient level of information relate to prospectuses. In particular, incorporation by reference and shelf registration systems are well-established devices that address some of the most relevant drawbacks of primary market mandatory disclosure. First, the success of an offer may depend on the ability of the issuer to take advantage of quickly changing price conditions, but tapping capital markets with the required swiftness may prove impossible when it involves a prospectus approval procedure for securities that have not yet been registered. This need for speed arises with regard to any security, but is particularly intense for bond markets. Second, for issuers that are already subject to periodic and ad hoc disclosure obligations, the need to republish in a prospectus information that is already available to investors – and that prices are already reflecting – would result in an additional burden with little added value.

The US has paved the way in deploying a broad array of tools to alleviate the burden of red tape upon issuers. Ever since the adoption of the Securities Act (and the Securities Exchange Act), issuers have been allowed to refer, in their prospectuses (as well as in other mandatory disclosure documents, respectively), to information previously filed with the SEC to fulfil a disclosure obligation.[74] A similar option is available in most jurisdictions, including the EU, Singapore, Australia, Japan, and Switzerland.[75] In combination with incorporation by reference, another tool devised in the US is the shelf registration, which enables issuers to register their securities in advance and to run their offer within a maximum period of three years after registration.[76] For primary offerings, the regime graduates the advantages of shelf registrations depending on certain eligibility requirements. In their maximum extension, these benefits

---

72 SEC Rule 17 CFR § 230.421.

73 Commission Delegated Regulation 2019/980 of 14 March 2019 supplementing Regulation (EU) 2017/1129 of the European Parliament and of the Council as regards the format, content, scrutiny and approval of the prospectus to be published when securities are offered to the public or admitted to trading on a regulated market, and repealing Commission Regulation (EC) No 809/2004 [2019] OJ L 166/26 Art. 37; He (n 18), 87 (China).

74 See SEC, *FAST Act Modernization and Simplification of Regulation S-K* (Release No 33-10618; 34-85381) (2019), 69 <www.sec.gov> accessed 20 June 2023 (also streamlining the provisions for the publication and retrieval of information incorporated by reference).

75 See, e.g. EUPR Art. 19 (also excluding the prospectus summary from this option, to increase readability: Art. 7(11)); Sec. 239(2) SSFA (Singapore). For a comparative assessment Paola Leocani, 'Omission of Information, Incorporation by Reference, Publication, and Language of the Prospectus' in Danny Busch et al. (eds), *Prospectus Regulation and Prospectus Liability* (OUP 2020), 333, 337.

76 SEC Rule 17 CFR § 230.415.

are only accessible to 'well-known seasoned issuers' (WKSI)[77] and include the option to file automatic shelf registration statements, which makes the registration automatically effective upon filing, and omit some information.[78]

In the attempt to satisfy similar issuer needs, other jurisdictions have developed comparable tools. A country where shelf registration seems to play a material role is Japan, which allows issuers to file their 'shelf registration statement' for equity and non-equity securities and to rely on it for a period of up to two years for future offerings.[79] At the moment of issuance, a supplement is filed with the supervisor that integrates the shelf registration statement, thus allowing capital markets to be tapped more quickly – an option that appears to be particularly suitable to non-equity financial instruments.[80]

The EU system appears more convoluted, which shows the struggle it underwent to reduce the regulatory burden on equity and non-equity capital raising. In the EU, issuers can prepare their prospectuses in a tripartite format, which splits it into a registration document (containing the information on the issuer), a securities note (containing the information in the financial instruments) and a summary.[81] The registration document has a validity of one year from approval,[82] so that only the securities note and the summary are submitted for a separate approval. Moreover, the length of the administrative scrutiny at offering time is reduced (from ten to five days) when the registration document takes the form of 'universal registration document' (URD), which also satisfies the requirements of periodical information (annual and half-yearly financial reports) and is therefore continuously available to the public.[83] After having received approval of the URD for two consecutive financial years (a time span soon to be reduced to one year only), the issuer qualifies as 'frequent issuer' and may file the URD with the supervisor without prior approval.[84] Approval will be required at issuance, in the shorter timeframe mentioned above, but the supervisor can scrutinize the URD upon its own motion and ask for amendments at any time.

In general, the EU URD system is therefore less efficient than the US shelf-registration, which does not require approval for supplementation of documents 'on the shelf'.[85] Only for non-equity securities does EU law provide for the opportunity of tapping capital markets based on previously approved documents and without the need for further scrutiny. Base prospectuses report, to this end, all the information that is available on the issuers and the securities that will be offered and allows the offer to be opened with the publication of final terms that

---

77 SEC Rule 17 CFR § 230.405.

78 Among the information that can be omitted are the amount of the different types of securities to register, the plans of distributions and a description of the securities, which can be limited to generic labels such as 'debt' or 'common stock'. See also SEC Form S-3.

79 Section 23-3 JFIEA.

80 Section 23-8 JFIEA. Kozo Sasaki and Kosuke Miyashita, 'Requirements for a public offering of bonds in Japan and recent developments', Practical Law (2016) <https://uk.practicallaw.thomsonreuters.com> accessed 20 June 2023.

81 EUPR Art. 10.

82 EUPR Art. 12.

83 EUPR Art. 9(12).

84 The Listing Act (n 42), Art. 1(8) (amending EUPR Art. 9).

85 Dorothee Fischer-Appelt, 'Reforming EU Securities Laws: The New EU Prospectus Regulation' (2019) 18 Journal of Investment Compliance 53, 57.

are not subject to supervisory approval – as long as the prospectus has been kept up to date through supplements approved by the supervisor.[86]

Other more recent developments aimed at calibrating the costs of disclosure based on the size of the issuing companies, under the understanding that SMEs are relatively more prone to the costs of disclosure due to their largely fixed nature. These costs are perceived to be among the main reasons for the decline in corporate listings in the Western world.[87] It is of little surprise, therefore, that initiatives to simplify offerings by SMEs were particularly salient in this part of the world. In the US, for instance, the 2012 JOBS Act introduced the definition of 'emerging growth company',[88] and granted issuers falling into its scope a series of regulatory simplifications, such as exemptions from the rules on market sounding ('test-the-waters' communications) and a lighter regime for narrative disclosure and auditing requirements at registration.[89] Smaller reporting companies are subject to a lighter regime, as well.[90] In the EU, a lighter document is available for SMEs and other firms traded on SMEs growth markets ('EU Growth Prospectus', soon to be subject to further simplifications in its contents and be relabelled as 'EU Growth Issuance Prospectus').[91]

Are these measures delivering on their expectations? The answer to this question is mixed, and shows one of the most striking features of prospectuses, namely the relative low correlation between variations in the legal framework for mandatory disclosure on primary markets, on the one hand, and the law in action in the same field, on the other hand. For instance, countries within the European Union are subject to a perfectly harmonized legal framework on prospectuses and to an integrated supervisory system. As to the law, directly applicable rules define both the overarching principles and the detailed information items prospectuses should include.[92] As to supervisors, the European Securities and Markets Authority (ESMA) plays a coordination role and fosters convergence through guidance, recommendations, Q&A documents and peer review exercises.[93] Despite this perfectly aligned system, experience shows that prospectuses can still look very different across EU member states, if only because of their

---

86 EUPR Arts 8 and 23.

87 For data comparing the decline in listed companies in the US and the EU with the increasing figures in Asian markets, see Oxera, *Primary and Secondary Equity Markets in the EU* (Publications Office of the European Union 2020), 25–28 <https://op.europa.eu> accessed 20 June 2023.

88 The definition includes entities that have never offered common equity securities through a registration document and whose gross revenues are below a certain threshold (Sec. 2(a)(19) USSA).

89 Sec. 5(d) and 7(2) USSA.

90 SEC Rules § 229.10(f)(1) Regulation S-K and § 210.8 Regulation S-X.

91 See respectively EUPR Art. 15 (on EU Growth Prospectus) and Listing Act (n 42), Art. 1(14), repealing EUPR Art. 15 and introducing the new EUPR Art. 15a (on EU Growth Issuance Prospectus).

92 These are defined in the EUPR and, respectively, in the Annexes to Commission Delegated Reg 2019/980.

93 See Council Regulation of 24 November 2010 1095/2010 establishing a European Supervisory Authority (European Securities and Markets Authority), amending Decision No 716/2009/EC and repealing Commission Decision 2009/77/EC [2010] OJ L 331/84 Art. 8.

length.[94] Divergent supervisory styles are the ideal culprit for these differences, as the empirical evidence – available only for the US – shows a direct correlation between the comments received by the competent supervisor after the filing of the draft prospectuses and the length of the final version of such documents.[95]

Even the simplification measures described above had an uneven success in the EU. Issuers have made recourse to universal registration documents, which were inspired by the French experience, mostly in France.[96] By the same token, the relative success of EU growth prospectuses mainly depends on their widespread adoption in Sweden.[97] This shows how very similar rules can deliver very different results depending on the legal and economic context, including the supervisory style of competent authorities.

7. CONCLUSIONS

This chapter has shown that the regulatory strategies for mandatory disclosure display remarkable similarities across jurisdictions. In more detail, some level of convergence seems to characterize the overall development of financial regulation, with the US continuing playing a leading role in this regard. Clear examples in this direction are certain strategies to facilitate primary market information for frequent issuers as well as the simplification of ongoing disclosure duties through the pre-defined lists of material events.

At the same time, however, the chapter has also highlighted that resemblance in the law on the books is not necessary a good proxy for the actual level of convergence, and vice-versa. While similar rules may lead to divergent outcomes depending on the legal context and the supervisory styles, as is the case with prospectuses, regulatory strategies that are far apart may not involve equally divergent approaches in practice, as is the case with accounting principles.

These dynamics are hardly surprising if one considers that, on the one hand, capital markets integration inevitably pushes towards uniformity of rules and, on the other hand, factors such as legal traditions, supervisory practices and specific market features cannot be deleted with a stroke of the pen.

Where all main jurisdictions seem to converge is rather in their common quest for the right balance in the delineation of disclosure duties. Identifying a single point of equilibrium

---

94 ESMA, *Peer Review of the Scrutiny and Approval Procedures of Prospectuses by Competent Authorities. Peer Review Report* (ESMA42-111-7170) (2022) 31-7 <https://www.esma.europa.eu> accessed 20 June 2023. To curb the size of documents, the Listing Act (n 42), Art. 1(6)(c), has recently introduced a cap of 300 pages for prospectuses relating to shares.

95 Michelle Lowry, Roni Michaely and Ekaterina Volkova 'Information Revealed Through the Regulatory Process: Interactions Between the SEC and Companies Ahead of their IPO' (2020) 33 Review of Financial Studies 5510, 5519–5521. In the EU, policymakers are aware that divergent approaches to requests for additional information may be at the origin of the different average sizes of prospectuses across Member States. Hence, the Listing Act (n 42) has recently empowered the Commission to define the circumstances that allow national supervisors to ask for additional information, as well as the contents of such information (see Art. 1(28), replacing EUPR Art. 20(11)).

96 ESMA, *Report. EEA Prospectus Activity and Sanctions in 2020* (ESMA32-382-1153) (2021) 21 <https://www.esma.europa.eu> accessed 20 June 2023.

97 ibid, 19.

between the preferences of issuers and those of investors is indeed a challenging task, if not an impossible one. This leads to some common dynamics. One of such dynamics is the swing of pendulum between the adoption of rules mandating a high level of transparency and the attempts to reduce the costs of those duties. Another example is the increasing fragmentation of disclosure duties based on the nature of the recipient or the supplier of capital, as Sections 5 and 6 have shown. Both forms of fragmentation are an attempt to define multiple regulatory points of equilibrium that approximate the optimum level of disclosure based on the features of market participants.

These regulatory efforts are a difficult exercise, partially owing to the complexity of the dynamics through which mandatory disclosure reveals its costs and benefits. Regulatory costs are often neglected when it comes to transparency, as this is often invoked as a catch-all solution to most market failures, while its drawbacks are seldom pointed out in the public debate. Simultaneously, the benefits of transparency may come through indirect mechanisms that are hardly quantifiable. For instance, even though not all investors have the skills required to understand prospectuses, the mechanisms of price discovery, which mostly rely on larger and more sophisticated market participants, also protect retail investors because they support the accuracy of market prices under the paradigm of informational efficiency. By free riding on the activity of their larger peers, retail investors can reasonably trust that they are not overpaying the financial instruments they purchase. At the same time, even though information that unsophisticated investors do not read is not entirely wasted, the question remains whether the positive externalities of professional investors' trading activity could still develop without mandatory disclosure. After all, sophisticated market participants will probably ask for and obtain the information they need even in the absence of any issuer duty to publish a prospectus, but in that case they will do so without the risk of including superfluous information that standardization brings along.

5. Conduct of business rules

Sergio Gilotta

1. INTRODUCTION

Conduct of business (CoB) rules are the set of rules governing investment firms' behavior when dealing with (i.e., offering financial services to) their customers.[1] This chapter provides a comparative analysis of CoB rules in the EU and the US.

The primary goal of CoB rules is to offer enhanced protection to a class of investors – the 'retail investors' – considered, for various good reasons, particularly vulnerable when it comes to making investment decisions.[2] To address this vulnerability, the law imposes a number of duties and obligations on investment firms vis-à-vis their clients.

First, investment firms are required to minimize – via a number of organizational and disclosure requirements – the potential negative impact of conflicts of interest on their clients.[3] Second, they must offer them 'suitable' financial products (namely, products that match the client's needs and objectives)[4] and screen their investment decisions to check whether they are 'appropriate' (that is, whether they are consistent with the client's knowledge and experience of financial investing).[5] Finally, investment firms are required to seek the best possible market conditions for the execution of their clients' investment choices.[6]

---

1 In EU law, retail clients are those clients of an investment firm that may not be qualified as professional or 'institutional' clients. See European Parliament and Council Directive (EU) 2014/65 on markets in financial instruments and amending Directive 2002/92/EC and Directive 2011/61/EU (recast) [2004] OJ L 173/349 [hereinafter MiFID II] art 4, para 1(11). Note, however, that key CoB rules, such as the suitability rule, also apply (albeit not in full) to professional clients. See n 71 and accompanying text.

2 For the most part, retail investors are inexperienced, unsophisticated investors who lack the skills and knowledge required to make sound investment decisions. They suffer from numerous cognitive limitations and behavioral biases impairing their ability to make correct financial choices (i.e., financial choices that maximize their own utility) (see, e.g., Hooman Estelami, 'Cognitive Drivers of Suboptimal Financial Decisions: Implications for Financial Literacy Campaigns' (2009) 13 J. Fin. Serv. Marketing 273). Furthermore, also because of these limitations and biases, retail investors are unable to absorb and properly process large amounts of information, a limit that undermines the efficacy of regulatory strategies aimed at protecting investors via disclosure (see, e.g., Troy A Paredes, 'Blinded by the Light: Information Overload and its Consequences for Securities Regulation' (2003) 81 Wash. U. L. Q. 417; Omri Ben-Shahar & Carl E Schneider, 'The Failure of Mandated Disclosure' (2011) 159 U. Pa. L. Rev. 647). These features of retail investors' behavior increase the likelihood that they will make wrong financial decisions and expose them to the risk of opportunism on the part of their (more sophisticated) counterparties. See n 7.

3 See Section 2.

4 See Section 3.1.

5 See Section 3.2.

6 See Section 4.

On the offer side, the goal of CoB rules is to prevent 'mis-selling', namely the distribution of unsuitable financial products that may harm the investor and frustrate his or her investment goals.[7] On the demand side, the goal is to minimize the risk of retail investors making unsound financial decisions on their own.[8]

Conduct of business rules are present in both EU and US securities regulations. In the EU, they are a fairly homogeneous and well-defined piece of legislation. They are included in the MiFID II directive and its delegated acts.[9] These regulations provide a harmonized regulatory framework for the market for financial services in the EU. In addition to establishing the set of duties that investment firms owe to their clients, they identify the financial services to which they apply, establish the conditions under which investment firms may offer these services and set out the circumstances under which CoB rules do not apply in part or in full.

In the US, the regulatory framework is more fragmented. There, financial services are offered by two different intermediaries, broker-dealers and investment advisers, subject to different sets of rules. Broker-dealers are subject to the specific anti-fraud provisions of the 1934 Securities Exchange Act and to the relevant SEC implementing rules.[10] Investment advisers are subject to the federal rules included in the Investment Advisers Act of 1940.[11] The client–intermediary relationship has also a different nature. Investment advisers are qualified as fiduciaries of their clients[12] and therefore owe them the typical duties of a fiduciary: most notably, they must always serve their clients' best interests.[13]

Broker-dealers, instead, are not generally regarded as fiduciaries of their clients[14] and therefore are held to a less demanding standard of conduct. The core duty to which they are subject is to 'deal fairly' with their customers,[15] a duty that encompasses the obligation to make suitable investment recommendations to them.[16]

There is a substantial overlap between the services offered by broker-dealers and investment advisers. Most notably, broker-dealers are allowed to offer investment advice to their clients, provided that the advice is 'solely incidental' to the other services offered and that no special

---

7 Mis-selling may be caused by negligence or by investment firms' pursuit of their own conflicting interests. The latter is a typical manifestation of agency problems and is exacerbated by the limited financial knowledge of retail investors and the resulting inability to effectively monitor the behavior of their (more knowledgeable and sophisticated) counterparty.

8 This could be due to one or more of the limitations and biases recalled in n 2.

9 See Commission Delegated Regulation (EU) 2017/565 supplementing Directive 2014/65/EU of the European Parliament and of the Council as regards organisational requirements and operating conditions for investment firms and defined terms for the purposes of that Directive [2017] OJ L 87/1 [hereinafter 'Delegated Regulation no. 565'].

10 See Securities Exchange Act of 1934 [1988] 15 U.S.C. § 78o(c), sec 15(c).

11 15 U.S.C. § 80b-1 [hereinafter 'Advisers Act'].

12 See *SEC v. Capital Gains Res. Bureau, Inc.*, 375 U.S. 180, 191 (1963).

13 See, e.g., SEC, 'Study on Investment Advisers and Broker-Dealers' (2011), iii.

14 Id at iv.

15 This duty arises from case law and has its doctrinal underpinnings is the so-called 'shingle theory'. See James D. Cox and others, 'Securities Regulation' (10th edn, Aspen 2022), 943. See also Roberta S. Karmel, 'Is the Shingle Theory Dead' (1995) 52 Wash & Lee L Rev 1271 (for a comprehensive account and a critical discussion of the theory).

16 SEC, 'Study on Investment Advisers and Broker-Dealers' (2011), at iv. See also Section 3.1 below.

compensation is received for it.[17] The consequence is that when it comes to offering financial advice in conjunction with other investment services, at least from the retail client's perspective the services offered by broker-dealers and investment advisers often appear indistinguishable.[18] This has made the existence of different standards of conduct a potentially harmful source of confusion for the retail investor.[19] The SEC put an end to this state of affairs in 2019 with the introduction of the Regulation Best Interest (RBI). By establishing that broker-dealers, when offering investment advice to retail clients, must act in their clients' best interest, RBI largely aligned the standard of conduct of broker-dealers to that of investment advisers.[20]

Overall, the EU and US CoB regimes show remarkable convergence regarding the substantive content of CoB duties: both contain a fairly similar regulation of conflict of interests, suitability obligations applying to services involving financial advice and 'best execution' duties aimed at ensuring the best terms for clients' transactions. This is somehow striking in light of the deeply different general architectures of the two regimes and the different legal construction of some of their key principles (most notably, the suitability principle).[21] One of the reasons for this convergence may be that EU CoB rules are younger than US ones: it is thus likely that EU policymakers drew on the substantive content of US rules when designing their own CoB regime.

The roadmap of the chapter is as follows: Section 2 provides a description and a critical analysis of the regulation of conflict of interests, focusing on the deficiencies that both EU and US rules show in this area. Section 3 offers a discussion of the suitability principle, highlighting its different articulation in EU and the US, its relationship with regulatory paternalism and its role in curbing systemic risk. Section 4 discusses the best execution duties, underscoring their importance for investor protection in contexts of market fragmentation. Section 5 focuses on what appears to be today's most visible difference in the substantive content of EU and US CoB rules: EU investment firms' sustainability-related duties. Section 6 concludes offering some reflections on the future trajectory of the two regimes.

---

[17] See Advisers Act, Sec. 202(a)(11)(c).

[18] See, e.g., Arthur B Laby, 'Fiduciary Obligations of Broker-Dealers and Investment Advisers' (2010) 55 Vill L Rev 701, 702 ('retail customers today see little difference between a broker and an adviser').

[19] See John Armour and others, 'Principles of Financial Regulation' (OUP 2016), 235.

[20] See also n 47 and accompanying text. EU investment firms are also subject to an overarching duty to act 'fairly and [...] in accordance with the best interests of [their] clients'. See MiFID II, art 24(1). Differently from the US, however, this duty is not limited to the provision of investment advice but applies to all investment services. The prescriptive content of this all-encompassing obligation is in many respects unclear. See Veerle Colaert, 'Investor Protection in The Capital Markets Union', in Danny Busch, Emilios Avgouleas and Guido Ferrarini (eds) 'Capital Markets Union in Europe' (OUP 2018), 353 (stressing the multifaceted nature of the principle). Furthermore, its broad scope of application appears 'quite difficult to reconcile with services characterized by arms'-length relationships between the investment firm and the client' (Luca Enriques and Matteo Gargantini, 'The Expanding Boundaries of MiFID's Duty to Act in the Client's Best Interest: The Italian Case', (2017) 3 Ital. L.J. 485, 485).

[21] In the US, investment advisers' suitability obligations are a corollary of their fiduciary obligations, while the same cannot be said for those of broker-dealers. See n 13–16 and accompanying text. In the EU, the suitability duty has instead a unitary nature. See Section 3.1.

2. CONFLICTS OF INTEREST

Conflicts of interest in the investment services market are common, if not pervasive. They arise from an array of different sources, including the remuneration structure of the investment firm and that of its employees, and (especially in the EU) from its multi-business model.[22]

Conflicts of interest are perhaps the greatest challenge to retail investor protection.[23] Their presence may harm the investor by leading the investment firm to suggest or engage in investment strategies that do not pursue his or her best interests. Common manifestations of conflict of interest are the sale of unsuitable financial products to gain the commissions, fees or other benefits ('inducements', in EU policymakers' terminology) offered by the product issuer or manufacturer, 'churning', namely the excessive trading of the investor portfolio to increase management fees, the sale of unsuitable proprietary products, such as those that the firm creates in its capacity as a 'manufacturer' of financial products or (even worse) those that the firm – as a public or private corporation – issues to finance its operations,[24] and the sale of unsuitable financial products to reduce the exposure that the investment firm – in its capacity as a lender or equity capital provider – has in a given issuer.[25]

Conflicts of interest in investment services are obviously regulated in both the EU and the US, and the relevant rules contribute to define the standard of conduct of investment firms in their relationships with clients.

However, both in the EU and the US conflict of interest regulation is surprisingly indulgent.[26] In the EU the approach is mostly based on disclosure and the imposition of organizational requirements aimed at minimizing the negative impact of conflicts of interest. Investment firms are required 'to take all appropriate steps to identify and to prevent or manage conflicts

---

22 This is often dubbed the 'financial supermarket' model, an expression referring to the fact that financial intermediaries are allowed to operate in a number of different sectors of the financial intermediation landscape (e.g., as both commercial banks and financial services providers).

23 See Niamh Moloney, 'Regulating the Retail Markets', in Niamh Moloney, Eilís Ferran, and Jennifer Payne (eds), 'The Oxford Handbook of Financial Regulation' (OUP, 2015) ('remuneration-based conflict-of-interest risk poses the greatest threat to good investor outcomes [footnote omitted] and is the most significant driver of mis-selling and poor-quality advice internationally').

24 The conflict of interest arising from the sale of the firm's own securities can be particularly acute (and therefore harmful for the client) when the investment firm is in financial distress. The urgency to raise capital may induce the firm to exploit its sales network to systematically place its securities among its customers, leading to widespread mis-selling.

25 The Cirio and Parmalat scandals in the early 2000 provide an emblematic example of the mis-selling risks arising from this type of conflict of interest. See Veerle Colaert and Thomas Incalza, 'Conflicts of Interest and Inducements in the Financial Sector', in Veerle Colaert, Danny Busch, Thomas Incalza, 'European Financial Regulation' (Hart 2019), 377.

26 See John Armour and others, 'Principles of Financial Regulation' (OUP 2016), 240 for similar observations. But see Stefan Grundmann and Philipp Hacker, 'Conflicts of Interest', in Danny Busch and Guido Ferrarini (eds), 'Regulation of the EU Financial Markets' (OUP 2017), 168, arguing that 'conflicts of interest are treated [...] more intensively in the area of financial services than other parts of contract law or private law more generally, or at least with more emphasis on a strict rule to have clients' interests prevail'.

of interest'[27] that may arise between them and their clients. To this end, they must have in place 'organizational or administrative arrangements [...] to prevent conflicts of interest from adversely affecting the interest of its client'.[28] Firms must also disclose to clients the presence of conflicts of interest. However, disclosure is conditional upon the firm's (self-assessed) inability to ensure that the conflict does not adversely affect the client's interests. So long as the firm considers its organizational measures capable of avoiding that the conflict of interest harms the client, it may not disclose it to the latter.[29]

In the US, broker-dealers and investment advisers are subject to an obligation to disclose material conflicts of interests to their clients.[30] Apparently, this disclosure obligation is not subject to the condition that the firm's internal organizational measures are able to prevent the conflict of interest from harming the client, as it is in the EU. This feature seemingly makes the US regime stricter than the EU one. It must also be noticed that broker-dealers' disclosure obligations have traditionally been more limited than those of investment advisers,[31] a difference that can be traced back to the fact that broker-dealers are not considered fiduciaries of their clients.[32] However, the recently enacted Regulation Best Interest has probably tightened up broker-dealers disclosure obligations, bringing them closer to those of investment advisers.[33]

The EU and US approaches to the regulation of conflicts of interest show some significant limitations. First, the firm's self-assessment about its ability to properly manage the conflict and ensure that it does not harm the client, required by EU CoB rules, may itself be biased by the very presence of the conflict, leading the firm to systematically overstate its ability to properly manage conflicts of interest. The consequence will be that the existence of the conflict will not be disclosed also when there is a real risk that it may harm the investor. This, in turn, will prevent the investor from reacting *ex ante* to the presence of the conflict (e.g., by discounting the advice received or by switching to another investment firm)[34] and thus from possibly avoiding its negative consequences.[35]

---

27 MiFID II art 23(1).

28 MiFID II art 23(2).

29 MiFID II art 23(2).

30 As a general rule, broker-dealers must disclose the existence of control relationships with the issuer of the securities being sold or recommended to clients (FINRA rule 2262) and their participation or interest in the primary or secondary distributions of the securities being sold or recommended (FINRA rule 2269). Following the enactment of Regulation Best Interest, broker-dealers providing investment advice to retail customers must disclose 'all material facts relating to conflicts of interest that are associated with the recommendation'. See SEC, 'Regulation Best Interest' <https://www.sec.gov/info/smallbus/secg/regulation-best-interest> accessed 3 May 2024. Regarding investment advisers see *SEC v. Capital Gains Research Bureau, Inc.* – 375 U.S. 180, 84 S. Ct. 275 (1963), 201.

31 See, e.g., *Shivangi v. Dean Witter Reynolds, Inc.*, 825 F.2d 885.

32 See Section 1.

33 See n 30.

34 However, doubts can be cast on retail investors' ability to properly react to the existence of conflicts of interest. See n 36 and accompanying text.

35 To be sure, the investor may always challenge *ex post* in a lawsuit the correctness of the firm's self-assessment. However, this is a costly option compared to the possibility of avoiding harm *ex ante* via proper disclosure of the conflict on the part of the investment firm.

Second, and more fundamentally, disclosure appears an especially weak regulatory strategy when it comes to addressing conflict of interest problems. On the one hand, also when the conflict is properly disclosed to the client, it is far from warranted that the latter will be able to properly react to the information. Indeed, cognitive biases and other psychological factors may lead retail investors to systematically underestimate the conflict's negative effects on the quality of the service offered.[36] On the other hand, disclosure may have adverse consequences on the behavior of the investment firm. Research in the field suggests that disclosure may induce the firm to distort its behavior even more (i.e., to pursue the conflicting interest even more aggressively) because it alleviates the agent's phycological restraints in this respect (a phenomenon dubbed 'moral licensing'), and for other reasons.[37]

To be clear, as a legal matter, disclosure does not authorize the firm to pursue the conflicting interest to the detriment of the client. I already noticed that EU and US investment firms are subject to a general duty to deal fairly and honestly with their clients and to always pursue their best interests.[38] This duty prevents investment firms from pursuing any conflicting interest that may harm the client even if that conflict has been properly disclosed *ex ante*, and allows clients to seek redress *ex post* for the damage suffered in the case that duty has been violated.

Instead, what appears problematic is the lack of an abstention duty – a prohibition to recommend or undertake on behalf of the client investments in which the investment firm has a conflicting interest, unless the firm receives clear and explicit consent from the client – at least for the most acute conflicts, such as those arising from the distribution of the firm's own securities. A solution of this type would be more effective in protecting retail investors than the current one based on disclosure and the establishment of conflict-mitigating organizational measures.

3. SUITABILITY AND APPROPRIATENESS

As pointed out in Section 1, investment firms are subject to a suitability duty mandating them to propose investments that are consistent with their clients' objectives, needs, and financial situation. In the EU, a lighter version of the suitability duty, the appropriateness duty, applies to 'execution' services that do not entail financial advice or delegated management of the client's financial assets. Subsections 3.1 and 3.2 will examine these two duties. Subsections 3.3 and 3.4 will discuss their alleged paternalistic nature and their systemic effects.

---

[36] See Daylian M Cain, George Loewenstein and Don A Moore, 'Coming Clean but Playing Dirtier: The Shortcomings of Disclosure as a Solution to Conflicts of Interest' in Don A Moore and others (eds), 'Conflicts of Interest: Challenges and Solutions in Business, Law, Medicine, and Public Policy' (CUP 2005), 108–114.

[37] See Id at 114–116.

[38] Note 20 and accompanying text and n 13 and accompanying text, respectively.

3.1 Suitability

The suitability rule is in many respects CoB rules' key principle.[39] It mandates investment firms to make or recommend investments that are suitable for their clients. Traditionally, suitability is assessed against a threefold benchmark: (i) the client's financial situation; (ii) his or her investing experience and knowledge; and (iii) his or her investment goals.[40] An investment is unsuitable when inconsistent with any of these parameters. When this is the case, the investment firm may not recommend the investment or undertake it on behalf of the client.[41] A fourth benchmark, a client's sustainability preferences, has been recently added to the EU suitability rule. I will discuss it in Section 5.

The suitability duty is present in both EU and US CoB rules.[42] In the EU, it applies to financial advice and portfolio management. These two investment services have a common element: to a varying degree, the investor relies on the counterparty to realize his interests.[43] This feature, typical of fiduciary relationships in which one party entrusts the other with the task of taking care of its own interests and welfare, demands a high standard of conduct. In exercising its discretion in the choice of investments, the firm must act fairly and loyally toward the client and always pursue his or her interests.

As already noticed, in the US broker-dealers providing investment advice are subject to a suitability duty whose contents and features are largely similar to those of EU CoB rules.[44] Interestingly, however, in the US the suitability duty is viewed as a less demanding standard of conduct than the proper fiduciary standard to which investment advisers are held.[45] Indeed, the fiduciary duty of care that investment advisers owe to their clients requires them to propose not just 'suitable' investments (as broker-dealers are required to do), but 'investments that they believe are in the best interests of their client'.[46]

---

39 See, e.g., Filippo Annunziata, 'Towards a General Charter for the Protection of Investors and Consumers of Financial Products and Services in EU Financial Law', in R D'Ambrosio and S Montemaggi (eds) 'Private and Public Enforcement of EU Investor Protection Regulation' (Banca d'Italia Conference papers 2019), 36.

40 See MiFID II art 25(2); Delegated Regulation no. 565 art 54(2); SEC, General Information on the Regulation of Investment Advisers (2011).

41 See, e.g., Delegated Regulation no. 565 art 54(10).

42 See n 40.

43 Regarding investment advice, investor reliance is likely more intense when the service is provided upon request of the client than when it is provided at the initiative of the investment firm. The reason is that in the former case the client, by actively seeking the investment firm's support for his or her investment decisions, shows trust in the counterparty. This is not necessarily the case when he or she receives advice without having solicited it. However, also in this case a high standard of conduct appears justified. Indeed, the counterparty's professional character and superior experience and knowledge may easily induce the retail investor to rely on the advice received.

44 See FINRA rule 2111.

45 See, e.g., Howell E Jackson and Talia B Gillis, 'Fiduciary Law and Financial Regulation', in Evan J Criddle, Paul B Miller, and Robert H Sitkoff (eds), 'The Oxford Handbook of Fiduciary Law' (OUP 2019), 861.

46 Polina Demina, 'Broker-dealers and Investment Advisers: A Behavioral-economics Analysis of Competing Suggestions for Reform', (2014) 113 Mich. L. Rev. 429, p. 431.

Regardless of how wide this difference may be in practice, RBI has arguably greatly reduced it (if not eliminated it altogether) by requiring broker-dealers offering investment advice to act in the client's best interest – a higher standard of conduct that more closely, if not completely, aligns their obligations to those of investment advisers.[47]

The suitability duty has obvious importance in raising the quality of the services offered and thus in protecting the retail investor against the risk of poor investment decisions. However, the suitability duty has its own limitations. As already noticed,[48] in an important sense it is a *de minimis* standard that prevents the firm from offering 'bad' investments but falls short of requiring that it looks for and chooses the best ones for the client.[49]

3.2 Appropriateness

In the EU, a lighter version of the suitability rule – the appropriateness rule – applies to investment services other than financial advice and portfolio management. These services are usually execution services where the investment firm has the more limited task of implementing a client's (non-advised) investment decision. There, investment firms are required to assess whether the client has 'the necessary experience and knowledge in order to understand the [investment's] risks'.[50] In the case of a negative answer, the firm must warn the client that the investment is inappropriate.[51] However, the firm is not prevented from executing the relevant transaction in the case the client still wishes to make the investment.[52] It being a one-parameter test, the appropriateness test is simpler (and thus less costly to perform) than the suitability test.

This difference in investment firms' standard of conduct can easily be explained by the nature of the intermediary–client relationship. Absent advice, there is little if any fiduciary component to the relationship. The investor is not seeking guidance from the investment firm and thus is not relying on the latter for her investment decisions. She autonomously decided how to invest her money[53] and simply asks the counterparty to execute the transaction. This

---

47 But see Robert J Jackson Jr, 'Statement on Final Rules Governing Investment Advice', June 5, 2019, <https://www.sec.gov/news/public-statement/statement-jackson-060519-iabd> accessed 3 May 2024 (stressing the ambiguity of the standard and arguing, among other things, that it 'fails to require that investor interests come first').

48 Text to n 45.

49 See Iris H-Y Chiu, 'More Paternalism in the Regulation of Consumer Financial Investments? Private Sector Duties and Public Goods Analysis', (2021) 41 Legal Studies 657, 660.

50 Delegated Regulation no. 565 art 56(1).

51 MiFID II art 25(3), para. 2.

52 Similarly, the firm is not prevented from executing the transaction if the client does not provide information (or does not provide sufficient information) about his or her knowledge and experience. It must only warn the client that it will not be able to assess whether the investment is appropriate. See MiFID art 25(3), sub-para 3.

53 Although this decision may have been influenced by the investment firm, e.g., via the promotional materials it has made available to its customers. See John Armour and others, 'Principles of Financial Regulation' (OUP 2016), 242. Under EU law, this type of 'soft' influence does not amount to 'advice' (and therefore does not trigger the suitability duty), since advice involves the provision of personalized investment recommendations. See text to nn 68–70. The US, to the contrary, adopts a broader notion of advice encompassing also non-personalized investment recom-

lower reliance, and the related fact that the investment firm has no discretion in the choice of the investment, justify the adoption of a less demanding standard of conduct. Accordingly, the firm is not required to verify whether the investment is suitable for the client, but has the more limited task of preemptively checking whether the client has the ability to fully understand the features (and therefore the risks) of the financial product in which he wishes to invest.

The appropriateness test does not apply to 'execution only' services[54] concerning 'non-complex' financial instruments.[55] These are common, liquid and easy-to-understand financial instruments, such as shares and bonds of listed companies and shares in mutual funds.[56] When the service is provided at the initiative of the client, it may be offered without the need to perform the appropriateness test.[57] The firm must only inform the client that 'in the provision of that service [the firm] is not required to assess the appropriateness [of the investment]'.[58]

Thus, retail investment into non-complex financial instruments may take place without any regulatory 'safety net'. While this choice can be considered reasonable from many viewpoints,[59] there is no reasonable ground to assume that retail investors will be capable of systematically making optimal investment decisions with respect to this sub-group of financial instruments. Quite the opposite, they may still easily harm themselves by engaging in too much trading and/or suboptimal diversification, and by falling prey to heuristics and biases leading to wrong decisions.[60]

US CoB rules do not feature anything similar to the appropriateness duty of EU CoB rules. One reason for this difference may be that the notion of advice adopted by US CoB rules is broader than that adopted in EU law,[61] with the consequence that suitability obligations have a wider scope in the US than in the EU and may thus cover the area (or part of the area) that in the EU is covered by the lighter appropriateness standard.

---

mendations. See, e.g., Investment Advisers Act, Sec. 202(a)(11) (detailing the activities that qualify a person as an investment advisor, thus triggering registration requirements). Accordingly, the type of soft influence recalled above may fall into US law's notion of advice.

[54] These are the investment services 'that only consist of execution or reception and transmission of client orders': see MiFID II art 25(4).

[55] See MiFID II art 25(4).

[56] See MiFID II art 25(4)(a).

[57] See MiFID II art 25(4)(b). The firm must also comply with its obligations pertaining to conflicts of interest. See MiFID II art 25(4)(d).

[58] See MiFID II art 25(4)(c).

[59] To list the most intuitive reasons, extending the appropriateness test to execution-only services offered in connection with non-complex financial instruments (i) would have probably been an excess of precaution, since most investors may reasonably be expected to know the features of those instruments (or to be able to easily acquire knowledge of them), and for this reason (ii) it would have unduly increased the costs of financial services, ultimately to the detriment of retail investors.

[60] See n 2.

[61] See n 53.

3.3 Suitability as an Instance of Regulatory Paternalism?

Suitability duties are often viewed as the expression of an interventionist, paternalistic approach to the protection of retail investors.[62] This approach, especially characterizing the regulatory interventions that followed the 2008–2009 global financial crisis,[63] is inspired, among other things, by the goal of providing a stronger and more effective solution to retail investors' cognitive limitations and behavioral biases[64] and it is motivated, among other things, by the growing awareness that 'light-touch' regulatory strategies – such as those based on disclosure – are of limited effectiveness in protecting retail investors.[65]

Yet, upon closer look suitability duties strictly intended (i.e. the obligation to suggest – or make on behalf the client – suitable investments) do not appear an expression of regulatory paternalism, at least as it is commonly intended today, namely as a regulatory strategy that 'influenc[es] the choices of affected parties in a way that will make those parties better off'.[66] Rather, the suitability duty appears to be a quite straightforward corollary of general (and long-standing) private law and common law principles. More precisely, the suitability duty can be viewed as a corollary of the fiduciary or fiduciary-like nature of the relationship to which it applies.[67] It is the particular nature of the client–intermediary relationship – one in which the former entrusts the latter with the care of his or her financial interests – that commands the adoption of this standard of conduct. A hypothetical alternative (and laxer) regulatory choice allowing the investment firm to suggest (or make on behalf of the client) unsuitable investments would be inconsistent with the nature of that relationship. Consider EU CoB rules: the suitability duty appears inherent to the very notion of investment advice (one of the services to which the duty applies). Investment advice is defined as a 'personal recommendation',[68] in turn defined as a recommendation that is 'presented as suitable'[69] for the person to whom it is addressed or that is 'based on a consideration of the circumstances of that person'.[70] It is hard to imagine how an investment firm providing investment recommendations that are explicitly presented as suitable for the individual client (or otherwise as tailored to his or her specific needs and objectives) may then be allowed to suggest financial instruments that are not.

The idea that suitability obligations are not, or at least are not primarily, an instance of regulatory paternalism finds further support in the fact that they apply also to professional clients[71]

---

62 This is noticed also by John Armour and others, 'Principles of Financial Regulation' (OUP 2016), 238.

63 See generally Niamh Moloney, 'The Investor Model Underlying the EU's Investor Protection Regime: Consumers or Investors?' (2012) 13 EBOR 169.

64 See n 2.

65 See n 2.

66 See Cass R Sunstein and Richard H Thaler, 'Libertarian Paternalism', (2003) 93 Am. Econ. Rev. 175, 175. The two authors dub this regulatory strategy 'libertarian paternalism' because it does not entail coercion and thus does not restrict freedom of choice. Id.

67 See supra Section 3.1.

68 See MIFID II art 4(1)(4).

69 See Delegated Regulation no. 565 art 9, para 2.

70 See Delegated Regulation no. 565 art 9, para 2.

71 Under EU law, when the client is a professional one, the investment firm may only assume that it has the necessary experience and knowledge to understand the risks that the investment involves. See Delegated Regulation no. 565 art 54(3). Thus, the other two benchmarks of the suita-

– a choice that would be difficult to explain under a paternalistic view of suitability – and that they exist well before the ascent of behavioral finance – the main theoretical pillar of today's regulatory paternalism in financial regulation.[72]

Instead, what appears to be a more genuine manifestation of regulatory paternalism are the appropriateness obligations typical of EU CoB regulation. Appropriateness imposes on investment firms a screening obligation on the investment choices of the retail investor also when these choices are the result of the investor's autonomous determinations. With the important (but overall narrow) exception of non-complex financial instruments,[73] the law entrusts the intermediary in charge of executing the transaction with the task of checking whether the investor has sufficient knowledge and experience to fully understand the features (and thus the risks) of the financial product that he or she is willing to purchase. This is a clear instance of paternalism, based as it is on the assumption that retail investors are unlikely to make sound, let alone optimal, investment choices through the exercise of their autonomous judgement.[74]

Paternalistic or not, rules aimed at preventing that retail investors undertake or are otherwise induced into wrong investment decisions are even more important (and probably justified from an efficiency standpoint) in light of the fact that in many developed economies fundamental social welfare tasks once taken up by the state, such as the provision of retirement income, have increasingly been delegated to individual investors' financial choices.[75] This shift – leading not only to an increased responsibility of the single investor for his or her own future

---

bility assessment – whether the financial product meets the investor investment goals and whether it is consistent with its financial situation (and especially with its ability to bear losses) – fully apply to professional clients. Similar rules apply in the US: see, e.g., FINRA rule 2111(b).

[72] In the US, investment advisers' suitability obligations exist, in the form of the (more demanding) duty to propose investments that fit the client's best interest (text to n 46), at least since the enactment of the Investment Adviser Act of 1940. Broker-dealers' suitability obligations have existed at least since the mid-1960s, when the SEC proposed 'a shift in the standard of care that broker-dealers were subject to from a fiduciary obligation to one of suitability'. See Michael S Barr, Howell E Jackson and Margaret E Tahyar, 'Financial Regulation: Law and Policy' (Foundation Press, 3rd ed 2021), 495. Tellingly, their origin can be at least in part traced back to the professionalization of the securities dealers' industry, whereby broker-dealers increasingly identified themselves as (and marketed their services as those of) investment professionals who guide retail investors in their decisions, rather than as salesmen whose primary goal is to sell securities – a shift that encouraged reliance on the broker-dealer on the part of its clients. See Robert H Mundheim, 'Professional Responsibilities of Broker-Dealers: The Suitability Doctrine' (1965) 1965 Duke LJ 445, 446–450.

[73] Text to n 54–58.

[74] Product governance rules, namely the set of rules requiring intermediaries who create ('manufacture') and distribute financial instruments to identify a target market for them and sell them only within the boundaries of that target market, are another straightforward example of paternalism: see Veerle Colaert, 'Product Governance: Paternalism Outsourced to Financial Institutions?' (2020) 31 EBOR 977, 995–996.

[75] See Niamh Moloney, 'Regulating the Retail Markets', 742; Dimity Kingsford-Smith and Olivia Dixon, 'The Consumer Interest and the Financial Markets', in Niamh Moloney, Eilís Ferran, Jennifer Payne (eds), 'The Oxford Handbook of Financial Regulation', OUP 2015, 698.

financial welfare but also to a shift in risk from the state to the investor[76] – provides a further argument in support of interventionist approaches aimed at minimizing the risk of wrong investment decisions, given their potentially very high social costs.

3.4 Suitability's Systemic Effects

Suitability duties are not only an important tool for the protection of retail investors. They also have indirect beneficial effects at the macro level, contributing to strengthening financial stability. It has been argued that the US sub-prime mortgage crisis that triggered the 2008–2009 global financial crisis would have 'been avoided, or at least greatly mitigated', if the intermediaries marketing those mortgages had been subject to suitability obligations toward their clients, as those obligations would have limited the marketing of those mortgages.[77]

On a more general level, it can be argued that financial consumer protection measures may help curb systemic risk by reducing investors' excessive risk-taking and the consequent risk of investors' default[78] – a risk that may easily undermine the financial stability of many financial institutions.

4. BEST EXECUTION

Investment firms are not only required to offer suitable investment products to their clients[79] (and, in the EU, to screen for their appropriateness in the case of non-advised financial decisions).[80] Under both EU and US CoB rules, they are also required to seek the best possible terms for the execution of the relevant transactions.[81] As some commentators noted, this 'best execution' duty is not aimed at correcting investors' behavioral biases, but at addressing the agency problems characterizing the relationship between the investment firm and the client.[82] The rule's goal is to prevent the investment firm, exploiting retail investors' limited ability to monitor the counterparty's behavior at the execution stage, from choosing execution options that do not fit the client's interest.

Quite intuitively, the importance of the best execution duty in protecting investors is higher where securities markets are fragmented into a plurality of different trading venues competing for intermediaries' order flows. Although competition and arbitrage from professional traders

---

76 As Kingsford-Smith and Dixon put it, '[p]reviously, the state, following Marshall's social citizen idea [...], took the risk that consolidated revenue would not be sufficient to fund retirement and welfare needs of its citizens. In the last two decades, these risks have been shifted to the citizen investor, unless that investor is content with schemes like the old-age pension'. See Kingsford-Smith and Dixon (n 75) 698.

77 Jonathan R Macey and others, 'Helping Law Catch up to Markets: Applying Broker-Dealer Law to Subprime Mortgages' (2009) 33 J Corp L 789, 837–842.

78 See, e.g., Erik F Gerding, 'The Subprime Crisis and the Link between Consumer Financial Protection and Systemic Risk' (2009) 5 FIU L Rev 93.

79 See Section 3.1.

80 See Section 3.2.

81 See MiFID II art 27; Investment Advisers Act, Rule 206(3)–2(c); FINRA Rule 2320.

82 Armour and others, 'Principles of Financial Regulation' (OUP 2016), 243.

should limit the divergence in prices (and transaction terms more generally) among the various trading venues, the investment firm may still be induced to choose a trading venue that does not offer the best terms for the client because it pays a high price for the firm's order flow.

5. CONDUCT OF BUSINESS RULES AND SUSTAINABILITY

EU CoB rules have recently been amended to integrate sustainability factors and preferences into the duties of investment firms.[83] Among other things, EU investment firms are now required to (i) include 'sustainability factors'[84] in the selection process of financial instruments and provide clients, where relevant, with a description of these factors,[85] (ii) collect from clients information regarding their sustainability preferences (as part of the information that the firm has to collect about clients' investment objectives)[86] and (iii) assess an investment's suitability also against the client's sustainability preferences (if any).[87]

The chief goal of these rules is to align retail investors' choices not only to their financial objectives (as it was before their introduction), but also to their non-financial preferences.

The new EU rules on sustainability mark a significant divergence with the US CoB regime, where no similar reforms have been introduced. This is at least in part due to an overall more prudent approach to sustainability issues by US policymakers, which is probably driven, among other things, by a more diffused skepticism about the desirability of introducing non-financial considerations into the set of duties of financial intermediaries, especially when they act as clients' fiduciaries entrusted with the task of managing their money.[88]

The new EU 'sustainability duties' have been fully integrated into investment companies' duties toward their clients. The amended regime makes it clear that recommending or investing in products that reflect not only a client's financial goals but also his or her sustainability preferences is now part of investment firms' overarching duty to act in the client's best interest.[89] In line with this, an investment that matches the client's financial profile (i.e., that is suitable according to the standard financial benchmarks underpinning the suitability test also before the enactment of the new rules) but does not match the client's sustainability prefer-

---

[83] See Commission Delegated Regulation (EU) 2021/1253 amending Delegated Regulation (EU) 2017/565 as regards the integration of sustainability factors, risks and preferences into certain organisational requirements and operating conditions for investment firms [2021] OJ L 277/1 [hereinafter Delegated Regulation 2021/1253].

[84] 'Sustainability factors' are defined as environmental, social and employee matters, respect for human rights, anti-corruption and anti-bribery matters. See Commission Delegated Regulation (EU) 2017/565 as amended by the Commission Delegated Regulation (EU) 2021/1253 [hereinafter 'amended Regulation 2017/565'], art 2(8), and European Parliament and Council Regulation (EU) 2019/2088 on sustainability-related disclosures in the financial services sector [2019] OJ L 317/1, art 2(24), combined.

[85] See amended Regulation 2017/565, art 52(3)(c).

[86] See amended Regulation 2017/565, art 54(5).

[87] See amended Regulation 2017/565, art 54(2)(a).

[88] This skepticism helps explaining why US pension fund managers are allowed to consider ESG factors in their investment decisions only to the extent they are relevant 'to a risk and return analysis'. See 29 CFR § 2550.404a-1(b)(4).

[89] See Delegated Regulation 2021/1253, Preamble 5.

ences may not be considered suitable,[90] with the consequence that the investment firm must refrain from recommending it when offering financial advice and from making it on behalf of the client when offering portfolio management services. Relatedly, recommending or trading a financial instrument as meeting a client's sustainability preferences when in fact it does not now amounts to both an instance of mis-selling and a form of 'greenwashing'.[91]

The new regime is driven by the twofold (and largely commendable) objective of (i) steering retail investors' money toward sustainable investments, in an attempt to foster the transition of EU economies to more sustainable models, and (ii) ensuring that investment choices maximize retail investors' overall personal welfare by conforming also to their non-financial preferences.

However, the new rules create a tension with CoB rules' traditional goal of protecting investors against the risk of *financially* suboptimal decisions. This is due to the fact that sustainable investing and financial performance do not necessarily go hand in hand.

Sustainable investments carry their own risks. First, they are often related to novel, non-established technologies (e.g., green energy production technologies), and may thus be comparatively more volatile[92] (i.e., risky) than non-sustainable investments relating to more established, non-green technologies. Second, sustainable investments may be negatively affected by changes in public policies regarding sustainability in a way that is very similar to how non-sustainable activities may be affected (so called 'transition risk'). For example, a policymaker's decision to delay transition or the inclusion of technologies previously considered non-sustainable into the catalogue of sustainable activities may affect the value of sustainable investments.[93] Financial performance may be negatively affected if the price of sustainable financial assets does not adequately reflect these risks.

Furthermore, and perhaps more importantly, sustainability considerations may limit the range of investment opportunities, impeding the maximization of financial returns (since

---

90 See amended Regulation 2017/565, art 54(12) and Delegated Regulation 2021/1253, Preamble 5. See also Veerle Colaert, 'Integrating Sustainable Finance into the MiFID II and IDD Investor Protection Frameworks', in Danny Busch, Guido Ferrarini and Seraina Grünewald (eds), 'Sustainable Finance in Europe' (Springer 2021), 458 (similarly arguing that 'the inclusion of sustainability preferences into the "investment objectives" test means that a transaction can only be considered suitable for a client, if it complies both with the financial and sustainability preferences').

91 See Commission Delegated Regulation 2021/1254 of 21 April 2021 correcting Delegated Regulation (EU) 2017/565 supplementing Directive 2014/65/EU of the European Parliament and of the Council as regards organisational requirements and operating conditions for investment firms and defined terms for the purposes of that Directive [2021] OJ L 277/6 [hereinafter Delegated Regulation 2021/1254], Preambles 7 and 8.

92 For an early study finding that private investors perceive sustainable investments as highly volatile, see Falko Paetzold and Timo Busch, 'Unleashing the Powerful Few: Sustainable Investing Behaviour of Wealthy Private Investors', (2014) 27 Org. & Env. 347. However, ESG investment being much more mainstream today than when the study was conducted, this perception may well have changed.

93 See Andrea Perrone and Andrea Cardani, 'Servizi di investimento e finanza sostenibile. Le conseguenze non volute della recente disciplina europea', (2022) 2 Osservatorio Monetario 84, 86 (stressing how various exogenous factors, such as interest group pressures, adverse economic trends, and geopolitical tensions, may induce policymakers to hinder or delay transition).

a number of non-sustainable but highly profitable investments are forgone) and possibly also leading to suboptimal diversification (and therefore to an undue *increase* in risk). This problem appears particularly serious with respect to investors with strong sustainability preferences,[94] as those preferences may significantly limit the range of suitable investments.

EU regulators seem to be aware of the potential trade-offs between sustainability and financial performance and appear to prioritize investors' financial interests over their sustainability preferences by allowing investment firms to recommend 'financial instruments that are not eligible for individual sustainability preferences', provided that they are described as such (i.e., as not meeting those preferences) and that the client has adapted his or her preferences.[95]

However, what appears to be missing in the new regulatory framework is proper disclosure of these trade-offs. Retail investors must be fully aware of their existence at the time they express their sustainability preferences. They must know that sustainable investment may come at a price, in the form of lower returns and an increase in risk.

Yet the new rules do not require investment firms to alert retail investors of the costs of sustainable investment, notwithstanding it is highly likely that retail investors are unaware of them. It is important that they are informed of these costs before (or at least at the same time as) they express their sustainability preferences, since knowing of their existence is highly likely to affect those preferences. To this end, investment firms should not only ask retail investors about the nature and contents of their sustainability preferences, but also about whether (and in the affirmative, to what extent) the client would be willing to accept lower returns and/or suboptimal investment diversification (i.e. higher risk) in exchange for investment choices that conform to those preferences.

Such a 'strength test' on sustainability preferences appears particularly valuable, since it allows the intensity of those preferences to be measured, an elusive and difficult-to-capture element that nonetheless has key importance in understanding how deeply those preferences can be expected to influence the client's investment choices.

6. CONCLUSION

Conduct of business rules – the set of duties and obligations governing investment firms' behavior when offering financial services to their clients – play a fundamental role in the protection of unsophisticated investors. They defend them against the opportunism of their more sophisticated counterparties (a significant risk given the marked information asymmetry characterizing the relationship) and they protect them against their own unwise financial choices.

---

[94] This might be the case of investors willing to invest only in financial instruments with the highest ESG scores (e.g., shares or bonds of companies that have already reached their net zero emissions goals). These 'dark green' preferences may easily lead to the exclusion of entire industry sectors from the composition of a portfolio, leading to suboptimal diversification.

[95] See Delegated Regulation 2021/1254, Preamble 8; ESMA, 'Final Report: Guidelines on certain aspects of the MiFID II suitability requirements', pp. 60–61. The idea that sustainability considerations do not stand on the same ground as standard financial considerations is further supported by ESMA's view that the incorporation of sustainability preferences is a second-step task that must be performed after the 'standard' financial suitability assessment is made. See ESMA, 'Final Report', 60.

Conduct of business rules are present in both EU and US securities regulations and show significant similarities. As already noticed, one intuitive explanation for this high degree of convergence is that CoB rules were introduced in the US well before they were in the EU. EU policymakers, as latecomers, have probably largely drawn on US rules to design their own regulatory framework. However, the two regimes also show some significant differences. One concerns the different scope of the suitability and appropriateness duties: EU investment firms are subject to a broad screening obligation regarding the appropriateness of clients' investment decisions. Instead, a similarly broad appropriateness duty is seemingly missing in the US. One reason for this difference may be that suitability duties have a broader scope in the US and thus cover the area (or part of the area) that in the EU is covered by appropriateness obligations. Another significant difference concerns sustainability: following recent reforms, EU investment firms are required to collect retail investors' sustainability preferences and to suggest (or make on behalf of their clients) investments that are consistent with those preferences. The US does not have similar rules in place. Accordingly, in the US the suitability test remains based on purely financial parameters, whereas in the EU it now also accommodates non-financial considerations. As of today, this appears to be the most significant difference between the two regimes.

It is hard to predict the evolution of the two regulatory systems: whether it will be toward more convergence or whether the two will maintain or increase the existing differences. The global nature of financial markets and the high degree of integration, interconnectedness and interdependence between EU and US capital markets push toward greater regulatory convergence. However, the largely idiosyncratic nature of the two systems' structures and the different legal articulation of some of CoB rules' key principles may be a source of enduring divergence.

6. Market integrity and insider trading

Ana Taleska

1. INTRODUCTION

The differences in the theoretical and judicial approach to regulating insider trading in the US and the EU have been well documented in comparative legal scholarship.[1] The EU has traditionally adhered to the fairness (or parity-of-information) approach and the consequential disclose-or-abstain principle, thereby outlawing essentially any and all trading on inside information, unless falling within a narrow scope of exceptions set out in EU legislation. The inherent appeal of the fairness and equal access to information approach was also put forward by the US enforcement agencies (namely, the Securities and Exchange Commission) and even had a short-lived acceptance by the US courts[2] but it was soon rejected by the US Supreme Court, which had decided to apply the classical theory, and later on the misappropriation theory of insider trading.[3]

The main difference between parity-of-information on the one hand, and the classical and misappropriation theories, on the other, is that under each of these theories, a breach of a duty must occur before a finding of insider trading liability can be made. Namely, under the classical theory, a corporate insider breaches a duty towards the shareholders of the issuer of the securities by trading in such securities for personal gain on the basis of information conferred upon them in their capacity as corporate officer (insider), whereas the misappropriation theory was subsequently developed by US courts to cover breaches of duty of trust and confidence towards other sources of inside information. In the absence of a relevant duty (and breach of such duty), no insider trading liability attaches to persons trading on the basis of material non-public information. Under the parity-of-information approach, which is largely followed by the EU regulation of insider trading, any person in possession of inside information is deemed to be an insider, and trading in securities while in possession of such information constitutes insider trading.

This tale of divergence between the breach of a duty standard and the equal access to information standard, respectively in the US and the EU insider trading laws, in most cases would not lead to different outcomes. For example, the classical insider trading scenario in which a corporate insider trades on inside information acquired as a result of his/her position as insider (corporate officer) of the issuer of the securities would constitute a clear case of insider trading under both the US and the EU regimes.

---

1 See generally Marco Ventoruzzo, 'Comparing Insider Trading in the United States and in the European Union: History and Recent Developments' (2014) 11 *European Company and Financial Law Review* 554; Edward Greene and Olivia Schmid, 'Duty Free Insider Trading' (2013) 2013 *Columbia Business Law Review* 369; Sergio Gilotta, 'The Regulation of Outsider Trading in the EU and the US' (2016) 13 *European Company and Financial Law Review* 631.

2 See Section 2.

3 ibid.

The divergence in approach becomes more visible, for example, when the insider does not himself/herself trade on inside information but rather communicates inside information – without receiving any pecuniary or other benefit in return – to a securities analyst who then trades himself/herself on such inside information or advises his/her clients to buy or sell securities on the basis of the inside information it has obtained from the insider.[4] Under EU law, even if neither the insider nor the analyst have traded on inside information, they would both be liable for communicating (tipping) inside information to the analyst, provided that they did it intentionally. That is to say, a person qualifies as an insider if he/she knows or ought to know that the information it possesses is inside information.[5]

Under US law, the liability of the analyst (the tippee) is derivative of the liability of the tipper (the insider), and the latter would only be liable if it had personally benefited from communicating inside information to the tippee (the so-called 'personal benefit' test).[6] The elements of the personal benefit test were subject to different and at times conflicting interpretations by US courts leading to uncertainties as to when the personal benefit test is met and whether tippees of insiders that have disclosed inside information without receiving a pecuniary benefit in return are liable under insider trading laws.[7]

This chapter analyses in Section 2 the divergence in terms of the theoretical foundations, legal basis and substantive regulation of insider trading in the US and the EU. In Section 3 it discusses calls for codifying US insider trading laws and the introduction of recent bills to the US Congress amending the Exchange Act by way of introducing a definition of insider trading. Additionally, Section 3 critically assesses whether such bills would clarify and codify insider trading law and if they would be effective in reducing uncertainty and confusion in the application of insider trading law. After having discussed the current codification proposals in Section 3, Section 4 evaluates whether the convergence between the US and EU in terms of having a statutory basis for regulating insider trading would result in convergence between these two legal regimes also from a substantive standpoint, i.e. to what extent (if any) the definitions of – and possibly, the approach to regulating – insider trading, would converge. Section 5 concludes the chapter.

---

4 See n 17 et seq. and accompanying text for instances where this difference in (the EU/US) approach is particularly relevant, i.e. chains of tippees involving potential future exchange of informational gift or disclosure of inside information involving a fraud at the issuer of securities disclosed by an insider (as in the *Dirks* case).

5 MAR art 8(4).

6 See nn 18–22 et seq. and accompanying text.

7 For other instances where inside information was obtained through a criminal activity that does not involve deception or fraud (and as a result is not caught by the duty-based regime of insider trading in the US developed under Section 10(b) of the Exchange Act), please refer to Section 2 below. These instances of insider trading were another reason for the calls to codify insider trading law in the US.

2. INSIDER TRADING IN THE US AND THE EU – A STORY OF REGULATORY DIVERGENCE

Insider trading regulation typically aims to strike a balance between fairness and investor protection on securities markets, on the one hand, and efficiency of securities markets, on the other.[8] On this continuum, the insider trading regulation in the European Union has taken investor protection and equal access to information as the main regulatory principle for the insider trading rules as set out in the EU Market Abuse Regulation (EU MAR).[9] Under the EU MAR, any person in possession of non-public material information is considered to be an insider and is prohibited from trading on or communicating (tipping) such information. There are limited exceptions from these broad insider trading and tipping bans, typically subject to conditions intended to safeguard the (perception of) fairness on securities markets.[10]

The concept of fairness takes the perspective of an investor that executes a securities trade with a counterparty that is in possession of material non-public information. From such an investor's standpoint, these trades undermine the integrity of securities markets, leading to investors perceiving securities markets as rigged and unfair and ultimately, exiting securities

---

[8] See n 1 and accompanying text. See also, Ana Taleska, 'European Insider Trading Theory Revisited: The Limits of the Parity-of-Information Theory and the Application of the Property Rights in Information Theory to Activist Investments Strategies' (2020) 17(5) European Company and Financial Law Review 558 (arguing that even the EU approach towards insider trading (based primarily on the parity-of-information principle) includes rules that are aimed at preserving (in certain instances) market efficiencies and allowing market professionals to trade on proprietary inside information).

[9] Council Regulation (EU) No 596/2014 of the European Parliament and of the Council of 16 April 2014 on market abuse (market abuse regulation) and repealing Directive 2003/6/EC of the European Parliament and of the Council and Commission Directives 2003/124/EC, 2003/125/EC and 2004/72/EC [2014] OJ L 173/1. See MAR recital (24), providing that '[t]he question whether a person has infringed the prohibition on insider dealing or has attempted to commit insider dealing should be analysed in the light of the purpose of this Regulation, which is to protect the integrity of the financial market and to enhance investor confidence, which is based, in turn, on the assurance that investors will be placed on an equal footing and protected from the misuse of inside information.'

[10] MAR uses the broader concept of 'market abuse' which encompasses insider trading, unlawful disclosure of inside information (or tipping) and market manipulation. See MAR recital (7) and article 1. For the prohibition on insider trading and unlawful disclosure of insider information, see MAR art 14 (*Prohibition of insider dealing and unlawful disclosure of inside information*). For the conduct qualifying as legitimate behaviour, see MAR art 9 (*Legitimate behavior*). Examples of exceptions from the prohibition of unlawful disclosure of inside information are set out, for example, in (i) MAR art 10 (*Unlawful disclosure of inside information*) – which provides that disclosures made in the normal exercise of an employment, a profession or duties do not constitute unlawful disclosure of inside information and (ii) MAR art 11 (*Market soundings*) – which covers market soundings, i.e. communication of information to potential information before announcement of a transaction for the purpose of gauging the interest of potential investors in a possible transaction and the conditions relating thereto such as in respect of a potential size or pricing, provided the conditions set out in MAR art 11 are met and more generally, the provisions of MAR art 11 are complied with.

markets and/or avoiding to invest in securities altogether.[11] As a result, a regulatory policy centred on the concept of fairness would typically include a straightforward prohibition of trades executed while in possession of inside information as well as the communication of inside information.

Aside from the complexity of detecting insider trading, the general ban on insider trading and communication of inside information typical for insider trading regimes adhering to the fairness/parity-of-information approach makes the application of insider trading laws and their enforcement relatively straightforward. At the same time, it may stifle the incentives of investment professionals who may be reluctant to invest time and resources in researching companies (including by way of holding discussions with management) out of fear that the information developed as a result of, or exchanged during, such interactions may qualify as insider information and fall into the broad prohibitions on insider trading and communication of inside information.[12] Likewise, management of companies with listed equity may have very scripted conversions and limited engagement with investors out of fear of (inadvertently) disclosing inside information. Considering that the efficiency of securities markets and pricing of publicly listed securities critically depends on the work of investment professionals (primarily securities analysis), it has been argued that insider trading laws with broad scope of application may reduce informational efficiency of share prices and securities markets more generally.[13]

For these and other reasons further illustrated below in this section, the US insider trading case-law has rejected the fairness and the disclose-or-abstain approach. It has based itself not on the perspective of an investor that executes a trade with a counterparty with an informa-

---

[11] See for instance MAR recital (23) elaborating on the concept of fairness in securities markets by providing that 'the essential characteristic of insider dealing consists in an unfair advantage being obtained from inside information to the detriment of third parties who are unaware of such information and, consequently, the undermining of the integrity of financial markets and investor confidence. Consequently, the prohibition against insider dealing should apply where a person who is in possession of inside information takes unfair advantage of the benefit gained from that information'.

[12] See, e.g. the holding of the US Supreme Court in *Dirks* which provides that 'imposing a duty to disclose or abstain solely because a person knowingly receives material non-public information from an insider and trades on it could have an inhibiting influence on the role of market analysis, which the SEC itself recognizes is necessary to the preservation of a healthy market. It is commonplace for analysts to "ferret out" and analyse information and this often is done by meeting with and questioning corporate officers and others who are insiders. And information that the analysis obtain normally may be the basis for judgments as to the market worth of a corporation's securities. The analyst's judgment in this respect is made available in market letters or otherwise to clients of the firm. It is the nature of this type of information, and indeed of the markets themselves, that such information cannot be made simultaneously available to all of the corporation's stockholders or the public generally.'

[13] ibid. See also, Henry G Manne, 'Insider Trading and Property Rights in New Information' (1985) 3(4) Cato Journal 933, 935 (arguing that 'the effect of insider trading will always be to move a share's price towards the level correctly reflecting all the real facts about the company'). In contrast, EU MAR mentions market efficiency only in recital (19) providing that '[t]he Regulation is not intended to prohibit discussions of a general nature regarding the business and market developments between shareholders and management concerning an issuer. Such relationships are essential for the efficient functioning of markets and should not be prohibited by this Regulation.'

tional advantage (and perceives securities markets as unfair for not sanctioning such trades), but on property rights in the inside information itself. In doing so it essentially requires that an analysis is made in each case, whether a fiduciary or other duty of trust or confidence was breached by the trading counterparty in respect of the inside information such trading counterparty possessed at the time the trades were executed. The US Supreme Court has expressly rejected the fairness/disclose-or-abstain approach in *Chiarella* and stated that 'there is no general duty to disclose before trading on material information' and that 'such duty arises, rather, from the existence of a fiduciary relationship'.[14]

The requirement to show a breach of duty before imposing insider trading liability while basing insider trading cases as a violation of US anti-fraud statutes such as Section 10(b) and Rule 10(b)-5 of the Exchange Act of 1934, has made prosecution of inside traders more difficult and has led (expectedly) to important setbacks in the enforcement record of the US Securities and Exchange Commission (SEC).[15] In fact, from an enforcement and policy perspective, the position of the SEC in insider trading cases, has been akin to the disclose-or-abstain approach adopted in the EU, i.e. that parties with informational advantages amounting to inside information should abstain from trading or disclose the inside information prior to trading.[16] As Section 3 below illustrates, the SEC has in a few cases used its rule-making authority to adopt rules based on the fairness/disclose-or-abstain approach, without the need to establish a breach of any duty for an insider trading liability to apply (e.g. Rule 14e-3 and Regulation FD). However, these rules have a narrow scope and the duty-based approach to insider trading remains the foundation of the US insider trading regime.

The difficulty of establishing a breach of duty does not lie with the classical insider trading scenario where a corporate officer deals in the securities issued by the company on whose board he/she serves and as a result realizes a profit, but it is rather associated with the liabilities of tippees, in particular in instances when the corporate insider received no profits or other benefits in exchange for the disclosure of the inside information to the tippee. This brings us to the seminal case of the US Supreme Court in *Dirks*, where it was held that generally, the liability of the tippee is derivative of the liability of the tipper and with respect to the tipper that was an insider of the issuer of the securities, 'the test is whether the *insider personally will benefit, directly or indirectly, from his disclosure*.[17] Absent some personal gain, there has been no breach of duty to stockholders. And absent a breach by the insider, there is no derivative breach' (emphasis added).

This personal benefit test as developed in *Dirks* was also based on important market efficiency justifications put forward by the US Supreme Court. The court held that analysts such

---

[14] *Chiarella v. U.S.*, 445 U.S. 222 (1980).

[15] The Bharara Task Force on Insider Trading, 'Report of the Bharara Task Force on Insider Trading' (The Bahara Task Force on Insider Trading January 2020) <https://www.bhararataskforce.com/> accessed 23 September 2023; see also, Preet Bharara, 'Report on the Insider trading by the Bharara Task Force' (Harvard Law School Forum on Corporate Governance, 13 February 2020) <https://corpgov.law.harvard.edu/2020/02/13/report-on-insider-trading-by-the-bharara-task-force/> at 3–4 (discussing how the current regime has made it difficult for courts, prosecutors and defence counsels to pursue and discharge their competences in a consistent and efficient manner).

[16] See *Dirks*, 463 U.S. at 463 stating that 'the SEC's theory of tippee liability in both cases appears rooted in the idea that the antifraud provisions require equal information among all traders'.

[17] ibid 662.

as Raymond Dirks, who uncovered a major accounting fraud at an insurance company by speaking with insiders, should not be disallowed to 'ferret out' material non-public information. The rationale here was that such restriction, if imposed on analysists, would be detrimental to the important role they play in the informational efficiency and accuracy of securities prices in the US markets. The personal benefit test developed by the US Supreme Court therefore distinguishes between communications for legitimate corporate purposes (such those made between Raymond Dirks and the insiders) as opposed to disclosure of inside information (and trading) for personal gains.[18]

One of the most intriguing and hard to interpret aspects in *Dirks* was the circumstances when the personal benefit test would be met, i.e. what amounts to a personal benefit in an insider trading context. Here, the US Supreme Court held that the court 'should focus on objective criteria, i.e. whether the insider receives a direct or indirect personal benefit from the disclosure, such as *pecuniary gain or a reputational benefit that will translate into future earnings*' (emphasis added).[19] The Court also held that a gift from the insider to a trading relative or friend would also satisfy the personal benefit test.[20]

Yet, in the investment community, informational gifts can easily occur without immediate financial benefit. In fact, as Professor John Coffee has pointed out: 'Wall Street is a giant "favour bank"', and reciprocity in giving and owing (paying back) by way of favours is well established and operates outside of any specific (cash) payments taking place.[21] By having this aspect overlooked, chains of tippees composed primarily of institutional investors could freely trade on inside information they exchange in return for future favours (whether by reciprocal disclosure of inside information or otherwise) without being caught under the insider trading prohibition.

The difficulty in prosecuting tipping chains on the basis of the application of the personal benefit test was further reinforced by the more recent decision of the US Supreme Court in *Newman*.[22] In interpreting the personal benefit test, the US Supreme Court held that a 'proof of a meaningfully close personal relationship that generates an exchange that is objective, consequential, and represents at least a potential gain of a pecuniary or similarly valuable nature' has to be shown before insider trading liability attaches. Another condition for insider liability to arise was that 'the tippee knew of the tipper's breach, that is, he knew the information was confidential and divulged for personal benefit'.

The holding in *Newman* made prosecuting tipping cases even more challenging for the SEC. This was particularly the case when SEC was confronted with several levels of tippees in a tipping chain and/or where proving exchange of a pecuniary benefit and satisfying the knowledge standard on the part of the tippee (as articulated in *Newman*) would pose serious difficulties.

---

18 ibid 16.

19 ibid.

20 ibid.

21 See John C Coffee Jr, 'Congress and the Insider Trading Prohibition Act: "Can't Anybody Here Play this Game"' (Columbia Law School's Blog on Corporations and the Capital Markets, 25 May 2021) <https://clsbluesky.law.columbia.edu/2021/05/25/congress-and-the-insider-trading-prohibition-act-cant-anybody-here-play-this-game/> accessed 23 September 2023.

22 773 F.3d at 452.

Additionally, the advancement of information technology and rise of cybersecurity attacks in the last couple of decades exposed another weakness of the duty-based approach towards regulating insider trading. The current insider trading case-law based on an antifraud statute – Section 10(b) and Rule 10(b)-5 of the Exchange Act – required a showing of fraud or deceit.[23] While certain types of manipulations to gain access to information systems or outright theft of information would qualify as fraudulent or deceitful conduct within the scope of Section 10(b), trading on inside information obtained by way of hacking or otherwise exploiting weaknesses in information technology systems may not implicate any fraudulent or deceitful behaviour or breach any duty of trust and confidence and as a consequence, would fall out of the scope of the insider trading prohibition.[24] Thus, these types of acquisition of inside information by way of criminal activity were another incentive for legislators to take up initiatives of codification of insider trading so as to prescribe these cases as a clear violation of the insider trading prohibition.

3. CONVERGENCE TRENDS: TOWARDS A STATUTORY REGULATION OF INSIDER TRADING

As briefly mentioned in Section 2 above, insider trading in the European Union is regulated by the EU MAR – a regulation with direct application in the EU member states. The EU MAR sets out the definition of inside information and the prohibitions on trading and disclosing inside information based on the equal access to information and the disclose-or-abstain principles. The European Court of Justice has developed further case-law interpreting certain aspects of EU MAR and in that respect, complements the primary source of insider trading regulation, that is the EU MAR. In the UK, EU MAR was retained in UK law following the exit of the UK from the EU pursuant to the European Union Withdrawal Act 2018, as supplemented by the Market Abuse Amendment (EU Exit) Regulation 2019 (SI 2019/310).

In the US, the insider trading prohibition has been based on a broad judicial interpretation of the anti-fraud securities law statutes, namely Section 10(b)[25] of the Exchange Act and Rule

---

[23] Under Section 10(b) of the Exchange Act of 1934, 'it shall be unlawful for any person, directly or indirectly, by the use of any means or instrumentality of interstate commerce or of the mails, or of any facility of any national securities exchange to use of employ, in connection with the purchase or sale of any security registered on a national securities exchange or any security not so registered, or any securities-based swap agreement *any manipulative or deceptive device* or contrivance in contravention of such rules and regulations as the Commission may prescribe as necessary or appropriate in the public interest or for the protection of investors' [emphasis added]. Bharara Report (n 15) 2.

[24] See *SEC v Dorozhko*, 574 F.3d 42, 48–50 (2d Cir. 2009) (where the Second Circuit held that in the *Dorozhko* case there was no breach of any fiduciary duty and no obligation to disclose the information obtained via a Dorozhko's hack into the computer system of a company) and subsequently trading on that information for a profit. See also generally, Sean F Doyle, 'Simplifying the Analysis: The Second Circuit Lays Out a Straightforward Theory of Fraud in *SEC v. Dorozhko*' (2010) 89 North Carolina Law Review 357.

[25] Section 10(b) of the 134 Act, 48 Stat. 891, 15 U.S.C. § 78j, prohibits the use 'in connection with the purchase or sale of any security … [of] any manipulative or deceptive device or contrivance in contravention of such rules and regulations as the Commission may prescribe'.

10b-5[26] promulgated by the Securities and Exchange Commission under Section 10(b), which does not deal with insider trading but rather with fraud and deception generally. The development of a duty-based insider trading prohibition in the US – where a breach of a pre-existing duty must be established before insider trading liability can be imposed – has been argued to have occurred *inter alia* because of the anti-fraud nature of the statutory basis for the insider trading prosecution in the US, i.e. Section 10(b).

As a result, the judicial opinions of US courts have had decisive influence on the development of the insider trading practice and doctrine in the US, including the afore-mentioned classical and misappropriation theories of insider dealing as well as the personal benefit test. This approach, however, has created important uncertainties, confusion and at times, contradictions in US insider trading law and overall, a legal and regulatory environment that increasingly became difficult to navigate for all stakeholders – investors, analysts, issuers and enforcement agencies, i.e. Securities and Exchange Commission.[27]

Before elaborating on (recent) attempts to adopt a federal statute that for the first time will define the violation of insider trading, it is worth nothing that there are several rules and regulations that the SEC has adopted in order to bring clarity and certainty for investors, often after being prompted by a judicial opinion that contradicts or upends the established understanding of the insider trading violation as developed by the US Courts under Section 10(b).

First, SEC adopted Rule 14e-3(a) under Section 14(e) of the Exchange Act,[28] which prohibits any person from trading on inside information in respect of a pending tender offer. Rule 14e-3 was developed and adopted in response to the seminal case of the US Supreme Court in *Chiarella* that a breach of a duty towards the issuer shareholders must be established for insider trading liability to occur.[29] In *Chiarella*, the US Supreme Court found that Vincent Chiarella, a third-party employee of a copying company who came across non-public information of an upcoming takeover bid by copying tender offer materials, escaped insider trading liability as he had no relationship or any duty towards the companies implicated in the tender offer and as a result, did not breach any duty by trading on the inside information about the prospective tender offer. Rule 14e-3(a) adopted by the SEC in the aftermath of *Chiarella*,

---

26 Rule 10b-5 (*Employment of manipulative and deceptive devices*) of Securities and Exchange Act of 1934 provides that

> it shall be unlawful for any person, directly or indirectly, by the use of any means or instrumentality of interstate commerce, or of the mails or of any facility of any national securities exchange,
> (a) To employ any device, scheme, or artifice to defraud,
> (b) To make any untrue statement of a material fact or to omit to state a material fact necessary in order to make the statements made, in the light of the circumstances under which they were made, not misleading, or
> (c) To engage in any act, practice, or course of business which operates or would operate as a fraud or deceit upon any person, in connection with the purchase or sale of any security.

27 Bharara Report (n 15) 4.

28 17 CFR § 240.14e-3 (Transactions in securities on the basis of material, non-public information in the context of tender offers).

29 See Bharara Report (n 15) 9 (noting the from the perspective of the SEC, 'the *Chiarella* decision made the rule necessary, emphasizing the importance of protecting information relating to tender offers because of the detrimental impact such trading has on "tender offer practice, shareholder protection and the securities markets"').

applies the disclose-or-abstain principle to any person trading on non-public information about a tender offer, irrespective of the (non-)existence of a duty and/or a breach of such duty.

Another SEC attempt to regulate in the area of insider trading was Regulation Fair Disclosure (Regulation FD),[30] which was developed owing to material non-public informational advantages about the securities of an issuer being conferred to institutional investors at private meetings with insiders. Under Regulation FD, when insiders of issuers have (inadvertently) disclosed inside information to a market participant (probably, securities analysts or investors), issuers must without delay publicly disclose such information. Just as Rule 14e-3, Regulation FD is another example of SEC's rule-making that strongly resembles the equal access to information approach taken up by the EU – a similar obligation for issuers to disclose inside information that directly concerns the issuer is set out in article 17 of the EU MAR albeit under Regulation FD the obligation to disclose inside information arises for issuers in the event that selective disclosure of inside information has occurred, whereas under EU MAR there is an obligation to disclose inside information that directly concerns the issuer regardless of the whether a selective disclosure has already occurred.

Notwithstanding the foregoing SEC rule-making, the core insider trading prohibition remained over the decades shaped by judge-made opinions developed in the context of very specific sets of facts and that expanded or restricted the insider trading violation and each time an opinion was perceived to depart from the then-existing understanding of the scope of the insider trading prohibition, a new wave of legal uncertainty was created.

The efforts made to include a statutory definition of insider trading in the Exchange Act go back to the Insider Trading Proscription Act of 1987, which was proposed in the US Senate but never put for a vote. The most recent attempt is the Insider Trading Prohibition Act (ITPA),[31] which content-wise is another take up of the bill that the House of Representatives already passed in 2019 but which did not pass in the US Senate owing to insufficient support.[32] The ITPA was introduced in the House of Representatives in the beginning of 2021 and was passed with a bipartisan majority of 350 to 75. At the time of writing of this chapter, the ITPA is pending before the US Senate.

Before discussing the approach to defining the insider trading prohibition in the ITPA, it is worth noting that the passing of the ITPA in 2021 was not the only evidence of the momentum for a statute on insider trading gaining pace. In January 2020, the influential Bharara Task Force on Insider Trading was set up and composed of representatives of practitioners and academics in the field of insider trading, including Preet Bharara, the former US Attorney for the Southern District of New York, who personally led important insider trading cases against Wall Street professionals. The Bharara Task Force on Insider Trading produced a report (The Bharara Report) setting out the need for codification of US insider trading law in a bid to

---

30 17 C.F.R § 243, 2015.

31 H.R., 2655 – 117th Congress (2021–22), Text – H.R.2655 – 117th Congress (2021–2022): Insider Trading Prohibition Act | Congress.gov | Library of Congress (accessed 2 February 2024) (ITPA).

32 H.R.2534 – 116th Congress (2019–2020), Insider Trading Prohibition Act Actions – H.R.2534 – 116th Congress (2019–2020): Insider Trading Prohibition Act | Congress.gov | Library of Congress (accessed 2 February 2024).

introduce clarification and remove ambiguities arising from the current judge-made insider trading law in the US.[33]

The Bharara Report developed four principles that a legislation on insider trading should consider whether to: (i) to aim for clarity and simplicity; (ii) to focus on the broader concept of 'wrongful' use of material non-public information instead of relying solely on the anti-fraud concepts, as currently set out in Section 10(b) of the Securities and Exchange Act, i.e. such as deception, fraud or manipulation but to also encompass information obtained by way of breach of duty of trust and confidence and any agreements not to communicate information as well through criminal activities such as theft, misappropriation, 'hacks and other unauthorized means of accessing corporate secrets'; (iii) to remove the personal benefit test; and (iv) to introduce a separate intent for criminal and civil insider trading and a clear knowledge requirement for tippees. As the ITPA was based on a 2019 Insider Trading Prohibition Act, it does not take up all of the conclusions set out in the Bharara report, as further elaborated herein below.

To be sure, in spite of the momentum for adoption of a statutory definition of insider trading gaining pace (in particular after Newman), some legal commentators deem the adoption of the ITPA unnecessary and argue that with the jurisprudence developed over the decades by US courts, sufficient clarity on the interpretation and scope of the insider trading prohibition exists.[34] In this context, it has been further argued that even if one is of the opinion that a statutory definition would bring clarity and prevent conflicting opinions of the US courts, the ITPA would not remove such unclarity and that the uncertainties as they may be currently existing as it attempts to codify existing concepts without bringing any further clarifications. Furthermore, it does not explicitly provide that it is the exclusive legal basis for prosecuting insider trading cases and as a result, parties may still continue bringing cases under Section 10(b) and other criminal law statutes, where applicable.[35]

The ITPA effectively amends the Exchange Act by inserting Section 16A (*Prohibition on Insider Trading*) which for the first time would set forth a definition on the prohibition against insider trading in US law. More specifically, Section 16A(a) ITPA deals with the insider trading prohibition, i.e. it makes unlawful for any person, directly or indirectly, to trade into securities[36] while aware of material, non-public information relating to such security, that may have a material effect on the market price of any such security, if such person knows or recklessly disregards, that such information has been obtained *wrongfully*, or that such purchase or sale constitute a wrongful use of such information.

Section 16A(b) deals with the prohibition of communication (tipping) of insider information and provides that it is unlawful for any person whose own purchase or sale of a security would violate the insider trading prohibition (set out in Section 16A(a)) to *wrongfully* communicate material, non-public information relating to such security, that has, or would reasonably be expected to have, a material effect on the market price of any such security if such person trades in any securities to which the tip relates or tips that information to another person who trades in such information.

---

33 Bharara Report (n 15).

34 See Stephen M Bainbridge, 'A Critique of the Insider Trading Prohibition Act of 2021' (2021) 21 Law & Economics Research Paper University of Illinois law Review Online 231.

35 ibid 239–241.

36 See Section 16A(a) ITPA (the scope of Section 16A(a) expands also to security-based swaps or security-based swap agreements).

The concept of 'wrongful' use and communication of non-public material information is further defined in Section 16(A)(c)(1) and includes information that has been obtained by, or its further communication or use would constitute 'directly or indirectly (i) thefts, bribery, misrepresentation or espionage (ii) a violation of any Federal law protecting computer data or the intellectual property or privacy of computer users; (iii) conversion misappropriation or other unauthorized and deceptive taking of such information or (iv) a breach of any fiduciary duty, a breach of a confidentiality agreement, a breach of contract, of any code of conduct or ethics policy or any other personal or other relationship of trust and confidence *for a direct or indirect personal benefit (including pecuniary gain, reputational benefit, or a gift of confidential information to a trading relative or friend)*' [emphasis added].

Thus, the proposed Section 16A(c)(1) effectively provides a statutory basis for the duty-based approach under the classical and the misappropriation theories, as well as the broader violations based on deception, fraud and misrepresentation and hacks of computer data and systems and largely aligns with the Bharara Report's conclusions in respect of introducing a broader concept of 'wrongfully' obtain information to include the different ways and methods insider information could be obtained.

One could argue that since the ITPA marks a new beginning in insider trading regulation by setting out a separate independent statutory ground for insider trading violations, it could have departed altogether from the breach-of-duty standard and potentially, move towards adopting an equal access/parity-of-information principle and the related disclose-or-abstain principle. Yet, such major departure from the current approach would have not received a broad consensus between members of the US Congress. More generally, the goal of the ITPA and previous bills attempting to codify US insider trading law has been said to be not to overhaul the US approach towards regulating insider trading, but rather to codify existing case law and the doctrinal underpinnings thereof as developed from the application and interpretation of Section 10(b) and Rule 10b-5 by the US courts, and at the same time, eliminate the existing uncertainties, unclarities and confusion.[37]

One major departure of Section 16A(c)(1) ITPA from the proposals set out in the Bharara Report and indicated in the foregoing sections, a major cause of confusion and uncertainty in the US insider trading regime, is the retention of the personal benefit test in the ITPA. To be fair, the 2019 insider trading bill on which the ITPA is based, did not include the 'personal benefit' test in its initial draft, but this was changed at last minute owing to concerns that the bill would not have Republican support without the inclusion of the personal benefit test.[38]

The ITPA still aims to bring clarity or at least codify the current understanding of the personal benefit test by qualifying – in addition to pecuniary gains – reputational benefits and gifts of confidential information to relatives and family as personal benefits for the tippee. This wording represents return to the holding in *Dirks* as reiterated post-Newman by the US

---

[37] See statement of Representative Hill, 'Congressional Record House of Representatives' (2021) 167 Congressional Record H2461 <www.congress.gov/117/crec/2021/05/18/167/86/CREC-2021-05-18.pdf> accessed 2 February 2024.

[38] See H.Amdt.696 to H.R.2534 – Insider Trading Prohibition Act <https://www.congress.gov/amendment/116th-congress/house-amendment/696?s=a&r=2> accessed 2 February 2024 (providing that this amendment added the personal benefit text). The Act did not pass by a 231–196 vote (see: Roll Call 648, Bill Number H.R, 2533 <https://clerk.house.gov/Votes/2019648> accessed 2 February 2024).

Supreme Court in *Salman*, which explicitly provided that gifts to family and friends would satisfy the personal benefit test and is a departure of the Second Circuit holding in *Newman* which – as indicated in Section 2 above – required a 'proof of a meaningfully close personal relationship that generates an exchange that is objective, consequential, and represents at least a potential gain of pecuniary or similarly valuable nature'.

Some commentators have even argued that the personal benefit test as currently drafted in the ITPA may be interpreted by US Courts to apply not only in respect of 'other relationships of trust or confidence' but to the entire Section 16A(c)(1)(D), i.e. to also apply to contractual breaches, codes of conduct and ethics policies, or even to the instances where inside information was wrongfully obtained by engagement in criminal activity – which would clearly make the personal benefit test significantly wider in application than under the existing case-law.[39] Otherwise, i.e. in the absence of a statutory requirement of satisfaction of the personal benefit in respect of insider information obtained through criminal activity, these insider trading violations would be most accurately seen from a theoretical standpoint as reflecting the abstain-or-disclose principle. In other words, any trading while in possession of non-public material information or disclosure of information obtain through such criminal activities, would constitute violation of Section 16A ITPA, without the need to show a breach of any fiduciary or other duty of trust and confidence.

All in all, both commentators for and against statutory definition[40] of insider trading seem to agree that as long as the personal benefit test is imported in a US statute on insider trading, the interpretational difficulties, uncertainty and confusion associated with this test would persist, at least where the facts do not fall within any of the examples satisfying the personal benefit test set out in the ITPA (such as, for example, making a gift to a person that does not have a close family or friendly relationship and without clear motivation for making the gift[41]). As a result, the ITPA is unlikely to bring the much-needed clarity for market participants or the SEC and prosecution of tipping chains would remain challenging. Further, if adopted in its current form, the prosecution of insider trading violations under the ITPA may be circumvented by prosecutors in instances when action can be brought under an alternative statutory basis such as Title 18 (*Wire and securities fraud*) where no showing of 'personal benefit' for the tippee is required and the actual fraud, deceit or theft can be prosecuted in a straightforward manner.[42]

Further, the ITPA now introduces a knowledge requirement applicable to persons trading or communicating/tipping wrongfully obtained information and provides that it shall not be necessary for a person to know the specific means by which the information was obtained or communicated, or whether any personal benefit was paid or promised to any person in the

---

39 See John Coffee (n 21) (arguing how the current broad wording of Section 16A(c) could lead courts – in the fear of over-criminalization – to interpret this provision as if the personal benefit test applies also with respect to (i) thefts, bribery, misrepresentation or espionage (Section 16A(c)(1)(A)); (ii) a violation of any Federal law protecting computer data or the intellectual property or privacy of computer users (Section 16A(c)(1)(B)); and (iii) conversion misappropriation or other unauthorized and deceptive taking of such information.

40 See John Coffee (n 21) and Bainbridge (n 34).

41 Bharara Report (n 15).

42 18 U.S. Code § 1348. For further discussion on this point see Bharara (n 15) 8 and Coffee (n 21).

tipping chain, as long as the person trading or tipping inside information '*was aware, consciously avoided being aware, or recklessly disregarded that such information was wrongfully obtained, improperly used, or wrongfully communicated*'. Even though the broad knowledge requirement as set out in the ITPA is intended to make it easier for knowledge to be imparted on (remote) tippees, such broad wording – as pointed out in the Bharara Report – does not clearly distinguish between knowledge and intent requirements in civil and criminal cases and will inevitably lead to further interpretational issues to be solved by US courts.

4. WILL A STATUTE ON INSIDER TRADING IN THE US LEAD TO (SUBSTANTIVE) CONVERGENCE IN THE REGULATION OF INSIDER TRADING IN THE US AND THE EU?

The different attempts of the US legislator to adopt a statute on insider trading would lead (if such statute is adopted by the US Congress) to a clear statutory definition of insider trading in the US. As such, the US and the EU would converge in terms of both jurisdictions having set out the elements of the insider trading violation in legislation as a primary legal source dealing directly with the prohibition on insider dealing.

The extent to which such a statute – whether the ITPA (if adopted) or subsequent attempts to pass federal legislation on insider trading – would make the prosecution of insider trading cases straightforward and eliminate unclarity and confusion would largely depend on the goal of the legislator to be achieved by such statute. The US Congress could adopt insider trading legislation that overhauls the approach taken thus far by US courts, although, based on prior legislative attempts, this seems unlikely. Alternatively, by the example of the ITPA, it could simply codify existing jurisprudence and provide legal basis for certain cases of insider trading that may have escaped prosecution under Section 10(b) of the Exchange Act (e.g. thefts, bribery, espionage, violation of protecting data privacy, etc.). The proposed bills in the US Congress in the last 30 years were along the line of the latter approach, i.e. they were intended to codify, remove uncertainties and confusion and thereby, bring clarity for investors, analysts, enforcement agencies and courts but not depart from the classical and misappropriation theories of insider trading as developed by the US courts.

As set out in Section 3 above, the ITPA suggested the introduction of a definition of insider trading and tipping of inside information by reference to a novel concept of 'wrongfully' used (for trading purposes) and/or 'wrongfully' obtained material non-public information (in the context of tipping inside information). The introduction of such a catch-all concept encompassing instances that did not involve deceit or fraud and therefore, escaped prosecution on the basis of Section 10(b) even though there was no public policy interest in not prosecuting the cases (e.g. a hack of a corporate database), was welcomed by the Bharara Report. Yet the concept of wrongful trading and/or communication of inside information still revolves around misappropriation of information or breach of a fiduciary duty to shareholders of an issuer and additionally, retains the personal benefit test.

From this perspective, the EU and the US will continue to diverge in the theoretical and practical differences in terms of when liability for insider trading arises. Therefore, the ITPA or subsequent acts aimed at codifying existing insider trading law are unlikely to lead to further convergence of US and EU insider trading laws.

5. CONCLUSION

The goal of this chapter is twofold. First, it compares the different approaches in the regulation of insider trading in the US and in the EU from a theoretical and functional perspective. In doing so, it focuses on the effects of the differences in the respective US and EU regulatory insider trading approaches, on sanctioning and prosecuting tipping cases.

Second, it reviews recent proposals and reform initiatives in the US aimed at providing statutory basis for the insider trading prohibition. It investigates the extent to which such proposals – if adopted into law – will lead to convergence of the US and the EU insider trading regimes.

Focusing specifically on the proposed text of the Insider Trading Prohibition Act of 2021 and the conclusions of the Bharara Report, it finds that the potential adoption of a statute on insider trading in the US would lead to convergence with the EU (only) in terms of both jurisdictions having a statutory basis for prosecuting insider trading cases. Convergence of insider trading regulations between the US and the EU in substantive terms, for example by way of alignment of the US approach to insider trading with the EU disclose-or-abstain principle, however, is unlikely. The current attempts in the US aimed at adopting insider trading legislation revolve around codifying, and not (radically) departing from, the existing case-law on insider trading as already developed by the US Courts.

7. Securities markets regulation

Lauren Yu-Hsin Lin

1. INTRODUCTION

The capital market is vital for a country's economic development because it provides financial resources for firms to grow. The flourishing of a capital market hinges on a sound investor protection regulatory regime and an efficient private enforcement environment.[1] Securities regulation is a set of legal rules that regulates the information disclosure of public companies and the behavior of market participants in trading securities. The mandatory disclosure regime is the mainstream regulatory method in securities regulation in major capital markets. The regulatory rationale of mandatory disclosure is based on the efficient capital market hypothesis which posits that the market is generally efficient if the share price incorporates all information about the company. Mandatory disclosure facilitates the flow of information by reducing the cost of information sharing and making information available to the market in a timely fashion.

Scholars have long inquired about the ways to produce optimal level of disclosure and whether and to what extent government regulation of securities market is justified. Drawing on the successful competition story of corporate-law producing in the US, US scholars have advocated for a market-oriented competitive model for both domestic and global securities regulation.[2] Professor Romano argues that issuers subject to choices frequently disclose more information than required and the feedback mechanism of a market also allows for regulators to ascertain which rules are cost-effective.[3] Furthermore, providing issuers with a choice of regulatory regimes through a market mechanism is superior to a single national regulator or regulatory cartel of internationally harmonized regimes. This is because there will be a net flow of capital to firms operating under the regimes investors prefer, creating a feedback mechanism for regulators to ascertain which rules are cost-effective.

The major concern over the market-oriented competitive model is that such competition might lead to a 'race-to-the-bottom' where stock exchanges will loosen up the listing rules to attract more listings.[4] In particular, providers of regulation are insufficiently motivated to provide innovative and efficient regulatory schemes, and since managers choose where to list, the listing choice is subject to managerial agency problem.[5] Managers might choose a listing

---

[1] Rafael La Porta and others , 'Law and Finance' (1998) 106 Journal of Political Economy J1113; Rafael La Porta, Florencio Lopez-de-Silanes and Andrei Shleifer, 'What Works in Securities Laws?', 61 Journal of Finance 1.

[2] Roberta Romano, 'Empowering Investors: A Market Approach to Securities Regulation', 107 Yale Law Journal 2359.

[3] Roberta Romano, 'The Need for Competition in International Securities Regulation' (2001) 2 Theoretical Inquiries in Law 387.

[4] Robert A Prentice, 'Regulatory Competition in Securities Law: A Dream (That Should Be) Deferred' (2005) 66 Ohio St. LJ 1155, 1160–1161.

[5] Ibid 1160.

destination that provides loose corporate governance requirements at the cost of outside investors and hence drives down the regulatory standard in jurisdictions that are keen to attract foreign issuers.[6] Whether competition leads to a race-to-the-top or race-to-the-bottom is an empirical question that needs to be answered based on the evidence.

Drawing on the surge of cross-listing in the US market since the 1990s, Professor Coffee famously argues that cross-listing allows foreign issuers to 'bond' themselves to the higher disclosure standards and greater enforcement tensity in the US in exchange for a higher market valuation.[7] In that respect, cross-listing appears to produce a desirable form of regulatory competition. Similarly, Professors Jackson and Pan examine the impact of regulatory competition on international securities markets through evidence from Europe in 1999.[8] The interview findings presented in the paper with respect to intra-European capital-raising practices in 1999 offers some comfort to proponents of issuer choice and that the race in the quality of securities regulation seems to be headed upwards and not downwards. However, a more recent study on cross-listing between Israel and the US shows that the standard for disclosure of executive pay was lowered by both jurisdictions to attract more listings to the stock exchanges, suggesting that competition leads to a race-to-the-bottom in regulation.[9]

This chapter intends to revisit the theory of regulatory competition in the context of globalization and the resulting stock exchange competition. Globalization has led to a greater degree of integration in capital markets around the world. With the advancement of technology and internet, cross-listing can be completed at a much lower cost and subject to fewer barriers than 20 years ago when Professor Coffee proposed the famous legal bonding theory. This means that global stock exchanges are subject to more fierce and direct competition. I will use two recent examples to re-examine the debate over regulatory competition: the reform of dual-class share (DCS) listing and the special purpose acquisition company (SPAC).

Furthermore, it appears that the theory of regulatory competition does not seem to capture some of the more recent developments in the global securities regulation regime. Two new developments in global securities regulation will be discussed: international harmonization and geopolitics. The 2008 financial crisis has led people to question whether free competition would lead to regulatory arbitrage and intensify systemic risk for the entire global financial system.[10] In that regard, a centralized global securities regulator might be needed to prevent regulatory arbitrage by managers and promote a higher and uniform standard of regulation in the global securities market.[11] The force of international organizations in promoting corporate governance of public companies after the 1998 Asian financial crisis has been well recognized

---

6 Luigi Zingales, 'The Future of Securities Regulation' (2009) 47 Journal of Accounting Research 391, 401.

7 John C Coffee Jr, 'Racing Towards the Top: The Impact of Cross-listing and Stock Market Competition on International Corporate Governance' (2002) 102 Columbia Law Review 1757.

8 Howell E Jackson and Eric J Pan, 'Regulatory Competition in International Securities Markets: Evidence from Europe in 1999-Part I' (2000) 56 Business Lawyer 653.

9 Sharon Hannes and Ehud Kamar, 'The Teva Case: A Tale of a Race to the Bottom in Global Securities Regulation', in Sean J Griffith and others (eds), *Research Handbook on Representative Shareholder Litigation* (Edward Elgar Publishing 2018).

10 Eric C Chaffee, 'Finishing the Race to the Bottom: An Argument for the Harmonization and Centralization of International Securities Law' (2010) 40 Seton Hall Law Review 1581.

11 ibid 1584–1585.

in the literature.[12] In this chapter, I will discuss the harmonization of environmental, social, and governance (ESG) disclosure by international organizations in recent years and the backlashes from local politics in the US.

Finally, the impact of rising geopolitical risks on securities regulation will be examined. The rise of China as a global economic power and the tension between China and the US in recent years have posed greater geopolitical risk on the international equity financing activities. The rise of economic nationalism and protectionism expedited the speed of deglobalization especially after the COVID-19 pandemic. Such tension among different national securities markets caused sudden changes in the highly integrated global financial market leading to legal uncertainties in corporate financing activities. The examples of US–China audit oversight dispute and the delisting crisis of US-listed Chinese companies since 2020 will be used to illustrate the implication of geopolitics on securities regulation.

2. COMPETITION AMONG STOCK EXCHANGES

One major driving force for the changes in securities regulation in the past decades comes from the competition among global stock exchanges. To maintain competitiveness, stock exchanges need to ensure that their rules are friendly enough to attract new listings. Two examples illustrate how the force of market competition leads to changes in securities regulation: reforms in DCS and SPAC.

2.1 Dual-Class Share

The US is the major market where dual-class firms are listed. DCS is a type of common share where typically two classes of shares are issued: one with one vote per share and the other with multiple votes (usually 10 votes) per share. The DCS structure violates the principle of proportionality between economic rights and voting rights by granting disproportionate control to the owner of super-voting shares. In the past, DCS structure was more popular among family firms and media firms. Since Google's initial public offering (IPO) in 2003, the DCS structure has become a popular ownership structure for newly listed technology firms.

The super-voting shares are usually held by founders and are not available for trading in the stock market. From the corporate governance perspective, DCS structure is an anti-takeover measure that prevents the control rights of founders from being diluted in the going public process and shields controlling founders from the threat of hostile takeovers. Despite the concern over management entrenchment, DCS structure is said to be justified on the basis that the human capital of founders can be preserved and the idiosyncratic value arising therefrom can be fully utilized.[13] Such justification is widely accepted among investors of tech

---

[12] Mariana Pargendler, 'The Rise of International Corporate Law' (2021) 98 Washington University Law Review 1765.

[13] Jyh-An Lee and Lauren Yu-Hsin Lin, 'Legal Institutions of Human Capital: Property, Contract, and Organisation' (2022) 13 Journal of the Knowledge Economy 3326; Zohar Goshen and Assaf Hamdani, 'Corporate Control and Idiosyncratic Vision' (2016) 125 Yale Law Journal 560.

companies who believe in the idiosyncratic vision of founders for the future of technological development.

There is strong empirical evidence showing that DCS firms are associated with significantly lower firm valuation.[14] The lower valuation probably comes from the agency cost arising from management entrenchment and the pursuit of personal benefits by the management, such as higher CEO pay and conducting lower value acquisitions for empire building.[15] Such an entrenched governance structure is to the detriment of minority shareholders but to the private benefit of controllers. In the IPO process, the choice of listing location and governance structure is made by the founders and not by shareholders. This choice is subject to serious agency problems.[16] The globalization of capital markets and stock exchanges lowers the cost of cross-border listing. Founders of tech companies can easily choose among various listing jurisdictions by comparing the cost and benefit of different regulatory regimes with the advice of underwriters and lawyers. It is against this backdrop that, since Google's IPO in 2003, many newly listed technology companies have chosen to list their shares on the US stock exchanges and adopted the DCS structure. In 2003, 11.1% of non-tech IPO adopted the DCS structure while only 5.6% of tech IPO adopted such a structure. In 2022, the percentage of dual-class tech IPO rises to 50% while that of non-tech dual-class IPO only rises to 15.6%.[17]

However, DCS also faced strong criticism within the US, mainly from the Securities Exchange Commission (SEC), investor advocacy group and academics.[18] The final outcome of permitting DCS firms to list on US stock exchanges is the product of regulatory competition. The New York Stock Exchange (NYSE) allowed firms to recapitalize with multi-class shares in 1986 owing to the strong competition from the American Stock Exchange and NASDAQ, both of which allowed dual-class share firms to list. Twenty years later, the very same reason brought about regulatory changes in major capital markets outside the US, in both Europe and Asia.

The triggering event for changes among Asian stock exchanges was Alibaba's listing on NYSE on September 19, 2014. Alibaba's IPO was the largest IPO ever at that time, raising over $25 billion. Before listing on NYSE, Alibaba originally sought to list on Hong Kong Stock Exchange (HKSE). However, the securities authority in Hong Kong and HKSE rejected its application for the reason that Alibaba's ownership and control structure was in violation of the one-share-one-vote principle. Market participants in Hong Kong soon put pressure on the stock exchange to release the ban on dual-class share and other control-enhancing

---

14 Paul A Gompers, Joy L Ishii and Andrew Metrick, 'Extreme Governance: An Analysis of Dual-Class Firms in the United States' (2010) 23 Review of Financial Studies 1051; Karl V Lins, 'Equity ownership and firm value in emerging markets' (2003) 38 Journal of Fiancial and Quantitative Analysis 159; Stijn Claessens and others, 'Disentangling the Incentive and Entrenchment Effects of Large Shareholdings' (2002) 57 The Journal of Finance 2741.

15 Ronald W Masulis, Cong Wang and Fei Xie, 'Agency Problems at Dual-class Companies' (2009), 64 The Journal of Finance 1697.

16 Zingales (n 6).

17 Jay R Ritter, IPOs 2022 Dual Class <https://site.warrington.ufl.edu/ritter/ipo-data/> accessed 1 March 2023.

18 Congressional Research Service, 'Dual Class Stock: Background and Policy Debate' (*Congressional Research Service*, 8 December 2021) <https://crsreports.congress.gov/product/pdf/IF/IF11992/2> accessed 28 February 2023.

mechanisms with the fear of losing a whole generation of technology firms, particularly those from Mainland China. In the following four years, significant efforts have been made by the HKSE to persuade the Securities and Future Commission to relax the ban but to no avail until Singapore decided to join the game.

The shift in the regulatory attitude of Singaporean government was triggered by the decision of Manchester United to list its shares in the US in 2012, who originally sought listing in Singapore but decided to turn away owing to the delay in the final approval from the Singapore stock exchange.[19] To maintain the competitiveness in the global offering market, Singapore amended its company law to allow public companies to adopt the DCS structure in 2014. Later, in 2017, the Listing Advisory Committee of the Singapore Stock Exchange endorsed the listing of DCS firms predicated upon the introduction of corporate governance safeguards to contain the governance risks of DCS firms.[20] That was at a time when the HKSE still struggled with its securities authority for DCS listing. Both stock exchanges faced competition not only from the US but also from each other and raced to remove the regulatory obstacles to DCS listing.

The consultation timeline from the two sides gives us a clue to how fierce the competition was. In February 2018, the HKSE launched the third public consultation which addressed the governance concern over DCS structure by imposing a number of governance safeguards.[21] At around the same time, in March 2018, the Singapore stock exchange also launched another round of public consultation with similar governance safeguards hoping to finalize the proposal soon. To avoid losing the race, HKSE concluded the consultation in less than two months and announced the official adoption of DCS listing in April 2018. Soon after, Singapore also permitted DCS listing in June 2018.

Parallel to the reforms in Asia, stock exchanges and policymakers in Europe are also seeking ways to relax the restrictions over DCS in order to compete with the US and Asian stock exchanges. Policy consultations and regulatory reforms have been undertaken not only at the European Union level but also at the member state level. The turn toward relaxation and permissive use of DCS structure among listed companies in Europe provides further evidence over the force of regulatory competition in shaping international securities regulations.

Traditionally, unequal voting has been regarded as an appropriate tool to promote long-term decision-making in some continental European countries, particularly among the Nordic countries. More recently, France, Italy and Belgium introduced the 'loyalty shares' scheme that grants double voting rights to shares held by the same shareholder for at least two years. The Netherlands is also known for its permissive approach toward DCS, making it an attractive destination for listing. Italian companies like Campari and the Agnelli family's Exor holding company have in recent years left Italy to both register in the Netherlands and list on

[19] Zijing Wu and Lee Spears, 'Manchester United Said to Weigh IPO in U.S., Not Singapore' (Bloomberg, 14 June 2012) <https://www.bloomberg.com/news/articles/2012-06-13/manchester-united-said-to-weigh-u-s-ipo-instead-of-singapore#xj4y7vzkg> accessed 21 February 2023.

[20] Listings Advisory Committee: Fy 2016 Annual Report 13 (2017).

[21] Hong Kong Stock Exchange, 'Consultation Paper: A Listing Regime for Companies from Emerging and Innovative Sectors' (Hong Kong Stock Exchange, February 2018) <https://www.hkex.com.hk/-/media/HKEX-Market/News/Market-Consultations/2016-Present/February-2018-Emerging-and-Innovative-Sectors/Consultation-Paper/cp201802.pdf> accessed 28 April 2024.

Euronext Amsterdam for greater flexibility in corporate ownership and governance.[22] Owing to the competition from the Netherlands and other European countries, the Italian government submitted a draft bill for company law to the parliament in March 2023 and proposed raising the vote ratio from 3 to 10 times.[23] The bill was finally passed by the Italian parliament on 27 February 2024.[24]

The level of tolerance to DCS structure varies among European countries. In an attempt to harmonize regulation and attract more firms to list in the EU region, the European Commission proposed a new directive in December 2022 to allow firms that list on the small and medium-sized enterprises (SME) growth market to issue multiple-vote shares.[25] The EC proposal is an important move for the Commission itself given its long-standing commitment to the one-share one-vote principle. Such a change is clearly a response to the global competition from the US, Asia and UK in attracting innovative, high-tech companies to list in the EU region.[26]

UK also joins the game of competition over innovative tech firms. The London Stock Exchange (LSE) has traditionally discouraged the listing of DCS firms in adherence to the one-share-one-vote principle. In light of the global competition, the Financial Conduct Authority (FCA) revised the listing rules in 2021 to allow DCS companies to list on the Premier segment, albeit with several restrictions.[27] To stay competitive in the international capital market, the FCA further proposed relaxing most of the restrictions and revised the rules to provide a more flexible regime in December 2023.[28] The new regime gives more freedom to the listed companies to set terms that are suitable for themselves, including no mandated sunset rule. The move by UK FCA is clearly motivated by the competition among international stock exchanges in attracting tech firm listings and is a vivid example of regulatory competition.[29]

---

22 Francesca Landini, 'Italy's Campari to Move Registered Office to the Netherlands' (Reuters, 18 February 2020); Reuters, 'Agnelli's Exor to Move Listing to Amsterdam from Milan' (Reuters, 29 July 2022).

23 Giuseppe Fonte, 'Italy to Boost Multiple-Vote Shares to Support Milan Bourse, Sources Say' (Reuters, 9 March 2023) <https://www.reuters.com/markets/europe/italy-boost-multiple-vote-shares-support-milan-bourse-sources-say-2023-03-09/> accessed 28 April 2024.

24 Latham & Watkins, Italy Approves New Legislation to Support Listings on Euronext Milan (28 February 2024) <https://www.lw.com/admin/upload/SiteAttachments/Italy-Approves-New-Legislation-to-Support-Listings-on-Euronext-Milan.pdf> accessed 28 April 2024.

25 European Commission, Proposal for a Directive of The European Parliament and of The Council on multiple-vote share structures in companies that seek the admission to trading of their shares on an SME growth market 2022/0406 (COD) (2022) 761 final.

26 The European Company Law Experts Group, 'The European Proposal to Open Up Multiple-Vote Share Structures to Listing Companies: A Simplification In Trompe L'oeil' (Short Version, Oxford Business Law Blog 2023).

27 Bobby V Reddy, 'The UK and Dual-class Stock-lite – Is it Really Even Better Than the Real Thing?'(2023) 14 University of Cambridge Faculty of Law Research Paper 1, 5–6.

28 Cooley, 'FCA Consults Further on the New UK Listing Regime' (*Cooley*, 22 December 2023) <https://www.cooley.com/news/insight/2023/2023-12-22-fca-consults-further-on-the-new-uk-listing-regime> accessed 24 December 2023.

29 Tome Godwin, Richard Ho and Jennifer McCarthy, 'Why is the FCA Changing its Rules on Dual-Class Share Structures?' (Freshfields Bruckhaus Deringer, 1 June 2023) <https://transactions.freshfields.com/post/102ifbx/why-is-the-fca-changing-its-rules-on-dual-class-share-structures>

2.2 Reforms in SPAC

Another example of recent regulatory changes owing to competition among global stock exchanges is the listing of SPAC. SPAC emerged as a popular financial product of the Wall Street in 2020. The percentage of SPAC listing in the US in terms of total number of IPOs increased from 4% in 2010 to 55% in 2020 and peaked at 73% in 2022.[30] The popularity of SPAC as a novel fund raising tool draws the attention of other global stock exchanges seeking to attract more SPAC listings on their platforms. Hence, we have seen a trend of SPAC regulatory reforms among different stock exchanges around the world since 2020.

Similar to the dual-class share structure, SPAC listings have been subject to criticisms in the US. The most important governance risks in SPAC is the inherent conflict between the SPAC sponsors and the public shareholders.[31] With the free 20% sponsor's shares, the SPAC governance structure itself dilutes public investors' shares and provides conflicted incentives to the sponsors. In particular, in the post-IPO de-SPAC transaction where the SPAC will merge with the target company, it is possible that the sponsors will choose a target to complete the deal even though the de-SPAC transaction might not be beneficial to public shareholders. Recently, US scholars have critically pointed out the governance risks of SPAC and have taken SPAC companies to court alleging misstatements and breach of directors' fiduciary duties.[32] The US stock exchanges have been treating SPAC listings as regular IPOs with no specific regulatory requirements imposed thereon. The terms between sponsors and public shareholders were pretty much left to the market to decide. Research studies have shown that most SPAC investors were ending up suffering losses in the investment, casting doubt to the rigorousness of the regulatory regime in the US.[33]

Similar to the DCS reform, the need to grow market share and the fierce competition among global stock exchanges push other stock exchanges to design rules to attract SPAC listings outside the US despite the governance risks involved. Scholars have observed a trend in SPAC reforms among European stock exchanges since 2020 and have contributed such a wave of reform to regulatory competition.[34] To date, there is no uniform EU regulation on SPAC. The status quo of SPAC regulation in the EU is highly de-regulated, and the requirements for

---

accessed 28 April 2024; Bobby V Reddy, 'From Dual-class Shares-lite to Full Fat: The FCA's Potential About-turn on Dual-class Shares' (Oxford Business Law Blog, 20 June 2023) <https://blogs.law.ox.ac.uk/oblb/blog-post/2023/06/dual-class-shares-lite-full-fat-fcas-potential-about-turn-dual-class-shares> accessed 28 April 2024.

[30] SPAC Analytics, SPAC and US IPO Activity <https://www.spacanalytics.com/> accessed 27 February 2023.

[31] Michael Klausner, Michael Ohlrogge and Emily Ruan, 'A Sober Look at SPACs' (2022) 39 Yale Law on Regulation 228, 246–254.

[32] Roy Strom, 'Enemy of the SPAC: Law Professor Takes Deal Sponsors to Court' (Bloomberg 22 September 2022) <https://news.bloomberglaw.com/business-and-practice/enemy-of-the-spac-law-professor-takes-deal-sponsors-to-court> accessed 28 April 2024.

[33] Klausner, Michael Ohlrogge and Emily Ruan (n 31) 274–278.

[34] Daniele D'Alvia, 'From Darkness to Light: A Comparative Study of Special Purpose Acquisition Companies in the European Union, the UK, and the US' (2023) 24 Cambridge Yearbook of European Legal Studies 201.

SPAC listing are largely a matter of national laws.[35] At the EU level, the European Securities and Markets Authority (ESMA) published a statement on 15 July 2021 to unify the prospectus disclosure and investor protection in relation to SPAC listing.[36] The purpose of the statement is to harmonize the interpretation of prospectus regulations within the EU framework.[37] However, such a guideline is not binding. The SPAC regulation is mostly subject to national laws and such diversity invites competition among member states.

The leading SPAC listing jurisdiction is the Netherlands owing to its flexible and lenient corporate law regime. In 2021, 16 SPACs listed in Euronext Amsterdam, which accounted for 40% of EU SPAC IPOs.[38] Under the Dutch law, market participants can set their own rules with regard to the internal governance of SPACs and most of them adhere to the US practice.[39] In August 2021, the UK FCA implemented new SPAC rules to make the LSE a more attractive destination for SPAC listings.[40] The new rule will lift the previous suspension requirement should SPACs adopt additional investor protection measures.[41]

Similar competition has also been observed between Hong Kong and Singapore. Singapore initiated a public consultation on SPAC listing in March 2021 and published its final framework in September 2021 to allow SPAC listing.[42] Shortly after, Hong Kong also initiated a public consultation in September 2021 and concluded its final regulatory framework in December 2021.[43] The close timing of the reforms in these two jurisdictions attests to the fierce competition between the two exchanges in Asia and globally.

---

35 Daniele D'Alvia, 'The International Financial Regulation of SPACs' in Daniele D'Alvia (ed.) *Mergers, Acquisitions and International Financial Regulation: Analysing Special Purpose Acquisition Companies* (Routledge 2021) ch 4, 112.

36 European Securities and Markets Authority, 'SPACs: Prospectus Disclosure and Investor Protection Considerations' (ESMA 2021) <https://www.esma.europa.eu/sites/default/files/library/esma32-384-5209_esma_public_statement_spacs.pdf> accessed 28 April 2024.

37 ibid.

38 Netherlands Authority for the Financial Markets, 'Edition 5 – An Overview of the Dutch SPAC Market' (*AFM Market Watch*, 2022) <https://www.afm.nl/~/profmedia/files/onderwerpen/afm-market-watch/afm-market-watch-5-spacs.pdf?sc_lang=nl-nl&hash=A2FCBACDA570648 99361E1446327D826> accessed 28 April 2024.

39 D'Alvia (n 34) 20–21.

40 Financial Conduct Authority, 'PS21/10: Investor protection measures for special purpose acquisition companies: Changes to the Listing Rules' (*FCA*, 2022) <https://www.fca.org.uk/publications/policy-statements/ps21-10-investor-protection-measures-spacs-listing-rules> accessed 28 April 2024.

41 ibid.

42 Singapore Exchange, 'Consultation Paper on Proposed Listing Framework for Special Purpose Acquisition Companies' (*Singapore Exchange*, 31 March 2021) <https://cfasocietysingapore.org/wp-content/uploads/2021/10/Response-Paper-on-Proposed-Listing-Framework-for-Special-Purpose-Acquisition-Companies.pdf> accessed 28 April 2024; Singapore Exchange, 'Responses to Comments on Consultation Paper: Proposed Listing Framework for Special Purpose Acquisition Companies' (*Singapore Exchange*, 2 September 2021) <https://cfasocietysingapore.org/wp-content/uploads/2021/10/Response-Paper-on-Proposed-Listing-Framework-for-Special-Purpose-Acquisition-Companies.pdf> accessed 28 April 2024.

43 Hong Kong Stock Exchange, 'Consultation Paper: Special Purpose Acquisition Companies' (*Hong Kong Stock Exchange*, September 2021) <https://www.hkex.com.hk/-/media/HKEX-Market/News/Market-Consultations/2016-Present/September-2021-Special-Purpose-Acquisition

2.3 Analysis

The reform patterns in Asian and European stock exchanges with respect to DCS and SPAC are very similar. They initiated reforms to facilitate certain type of listing that was popular in the US market to catch the wave of listing at the time. However, did the regulatory competition result in the worrying race-to-the-bottom phenomenon? To answer this question, we need to assess the overall regulatory measures in these jurisdictions, including *ex ante* regulation and *ex post* enforcement. The US relies on the disclosure regime and imposes very light restrictions *ex ante* on the listing. Such a regulatory approach gives the market more flexibility to adapt to the financial needs at the moment and allows the US stock exchanges to be the first mover in catching new types of listings. If the market mechanism somehow fails to protect investors' interests when the listing was made, *ex post* enforcement will kick in to protect the investors. SPAC litigations that are currently filling up the docket of Delaware court are good examples.

While jurisdictions outside of US generally lack a strong *ex post* private enforcement environment, these foreign stock exchanges and government authorities sought to strengthen the *ex ante* regulation in the DCS reform. For example, both Hong Kong and Singapore only allow large firms to list with DCS structure by setting a much higher threshold on market capitalization.[44] They also both restrict the voting ratio to 1-to-10 while no restriction has been set in the US.[45] Overall, jurisdictions outside of US learned from the US experience and imposed *ex ante* regulations that sought to address the governance risks that were presented in the US market to compensate for the laxity in *ex post* enforcement. Hence, there is no clear evidence showing that competition has led to a race-to-the-bottom in the international capital markets. Perhaps there are other forces that constrain the behavior of stock exchanges – that is an international order in corporate governance and securities regulation, which we will discuss in the next section.

3. INTERNATIONAL HARMONIZATION AND LOCAL POLITICS

International organizations, like World Bank, IMF and OECD, have been influential in shaping global corporate governance since the 1997 Asian financial crisis.[46] These organizations serve as a standard setter for corporate governance internationally by publishing guidelines and conducting ratings for different jurisdictions. These efforts help to standardize

---

-Co/Consultation-Paper/cp202109.pdf> accessed 28 April 2024; Hong Kong Stock Exchange, 'Consultation Conclusions: Special Purpose Acquisition Companies' (Hong Kong Stock Exchange, December 2021) <https://www.hkex.com.hk/-/media/HKEX-Market/News/Market-Consultations/2016-Present/September-2021-Special-Purpose-Acquisition-Co/Conclusions-(Dec-2021)/cp202109cc.pdf> accessed 28 April 2024.

[44] The minimum market capitalization in NYSE is US$40 million while that in Singapore is US$214 million and that in Hong Kong is US$5.1 billion. *See* Hong Kong Stock Exchange, 'Research Report, Weighted Voting Rights: Angel or Evil to Investors?' (Hong Kong Stock Exchange,19 July 2019) 21.

[45] ibid.

[46] Pargendler (n 12) 1778–1793.

corporate governance practice around the world and facilitate cross-border investments by institutional investors.[47] However, the harmonization efforts in a way suppress regulatory innovation domestically and reduce regulatory competition among different nations.[48]

Similar trend has been observed in ESG and climate-related disclosure. The UN, International Organization of Securities Commissions (IOSCO), and the G20 Financial Stability Board (FSB) are the key players in promoting ESG disclosure. The standard setting in corporate governance rose as a response to prevent the next financial crisis and the resulting systemic risk to all nations around the world. Similarly, the call for ESG and climate-related disclosure is also an effort to prevent financial systemic risk that might arise if the pricing of financial assets does not fairly reflect the risk relating to sustainability.[49] The need for regulation is urgent and apparent given the imminent threat of climate change. The market being captured by the profit-oriented and short-termism corporate managers has failed to respond to such a need for change. Similarly, governments being captured by business and interest groups also failed to pass legislation to address the market failure. Therefore, international organizations step in to formulate consensus and put pressure on national governments to pass relevant regulation.

In 2006, the UN Global Compact and the United Nations Environment Programme Finance Initiative launched the Principles of Responsible Investment (PRI) addressing the need for institutional investors to consider ESG matters when making investment decisions. The UN-supported PRI played an essential role in fostering consensus in the international investment community about sustainable investment and such consensus among institutional investors further pushed national regulators to reform ESG disclosure requirements. Further to the UN's effort in regulating ESG disclosure and promoting sustainable finance, in 2015, the G20 FSB established the industry-led 'Task Force on Climate-Related Financial Disclosures' (TCFD) to develop recommendations on climate-related disclosures. The TCFD issued its recommendation in 2017 and has since become the international standard for climate-related

---

47 Zingales (n 6) 395.

48 Pargendler (n 12) 1776–1777.

49 'Ultimately, successful investment depends on a vibrant economy, which depends on a healthy civil society, which is ultimately dependent on a sustainable planet', The Global Compact, *Who Cares Wins: Connecting Financial Markets to a Changing World* (United Nations, 2004), 3. '[S]ystemic shocks are more likely when the prices of a wide variety of financial assets do not fully reflect climate-related physical and transition risks [because] when [these] risks are not fully priced in, market participants will accumulate larger exposures to risky assets than would otherwise be desirable. A sudden revision of market participants' perceptions about climate risk could trigger a disorderly repricing of assets, which could have cascading effects on portfolios and balance sheets and, therefore, systemic implications for financial stability', US Commodity Futures Trading Commission, *Managing Climate Risk in the U.S. Financial System* (2020), 26 <https://www.cftc.gov/sites/default/files/2020-09/9-9-20%20Report%20of%20the%20Subcommittee%20on%20Climate-Related%20Market%20Risk%20-%20Managing%20Climate%20Risk%20in%20the%20U.S.%20Financial%20System%20for%20posting.pdf> accessed 27 September 2024.

disclosure.[50] By October 2022, countries that align its regulatory framework with the TCFD recommendations included Brazil, Egypt, New Zealand, Singapore, Switzerland and the UK.[51]

These harmonization efforts, however, received pushbacks from national governments owing to the pressure from local politics and interest groups. In particular, the US has been resisting pressures from the UN, G20 FSB and IOSCO to enhance ESG disclosure requirements in the US.[52] The polarization of political views in the US in recent years has made it harder to move legislation forward. In particular, climate-related issues are controversial and deeply connected with the interests of public companies. While the US institutional investors have been embracing ESG and sustainable investments in the past decades, the pushback against such investments has escalated sharply in the Republican-led states since 2022. Some Republican-led states, like Florida, West Virginia and Texas, have barred the state from considering ESG factors in its investment management practices or blacklisted financial institutions, like BlackRock, for promoting ESG consideration in investments which is hostile to the fossil fuel industry.[53] In March 2023, the US Republican-controlled Senate passed a resolution to overturn a rule that allows retirement fund managers to consider ESG factors when making investment decisions.[54] Even though the resolution was vetoed by President Biden, reforms on ESG and climate-related disclosure are expected to encounter challenges under such a political climate.

On March 21, 2022, the US SEC proposed rules to require public companies to disclose extensive climate-related information.[55] The proposed regulatory framework in general follows the standards set by international organizations, like the TCFD recommendations for climate-related disclosure and the Greenhouse Gas Protocol Corporate Standard for greenhouse gas ('GHG') emissions reporting (the 'GHG Protocol'). However, the proposal caused great controversy, with more than 11,000 comments submitted. Even though most of the comments supported climate disclosure regulation in general, comments diverged significantly on the regulatory path and approach.[56] Some even called into question the SEC's authority in reg-

---

50 TCFD, 'Final Report: Recommendations of the Task Force on Climate-related Financial Disclosures' (TCFD, June 2017) <https://assets.bbhub.io/company/sites/60/2020/10/FINAL-2017-TCFD-Report-11052018.pdf> accessed 28 April 2024.

51 TCFD, 2022 Status Report 99 (TCFD, October 2022) <https://assets.bbhub.io/company/sites/60/2022/10/2022-TCFD-Status-Report.pdf> accessed 28 April 2024.

52 Pargendler (n 12) 1807.

53 Patrick Temple-West, 'US Republicans Pull $1bn from BlackRock over ESG Investing Concerns', *Financial Times* (10 October 2022) <https://www.ft.com/content/41de28af-a487-473e-bc17-5e8cb71f4ced> accessed 10 March 2023.

54 Evie Liu, 'The Senate Votes to Block ESG Retirement Rule from Biden Administration' (2023) *Barron's* (1 March 2023) <https://www.barrons.com/articles/esg-dol-biden-trump-congress-fbd75b0c> accessed 10 March 2023.

55 *See* Securities and Exchange Commission, 'Proposed Rule on the Enhancement and Standardization of Climate-Related Disclosures for Investors' (proposed 21 March 2022) 87 Federal Register 21334.

56 Subodh Mishra, 'SEC Climate Disclosure Comments Reveal Diversity of Views, Harvard Law School Forum on Corporate Governance' (31 August 2022) <https://corpgov.law.harvard.edu/2022/08/31/sec-climate-disclosure-comments-reveal-diversity-of-views/> accessed 27 February 2023.

ulating climate-related matters.[57] On March 6, 2024, almost two years into the first proposal, the SEC finally adopted climate-related disclosure rules.[58] The climate-related law-making experience in the US is a perfect example manifesting the limits of international organizations in shaping national securities regulation. The soft nature of international organization norm-setting is subject to nation-state sovereignty and democratic politics.[59] The recent trend of deglobalization and the rise of protectionism both in the US and China have heightened the geopolitical risks. In the next section, this chapter will explore the threat of rising geopolitical risks to the international equity financing market and related regulations.

4. GEOPOLITICAL RISKS

If globalization and international harmonization set the parameters for securities regulation in the past few decades, rising economic nationalism and protectionism, in particular after the 2008 financial crisis, marked a turn in globalization. The trend toward deglobalization accelerated during the COVID-19 pandemic which caused a sudden disruption in the global supply chain, trade and travel among countries.[60] The sudden disruption triggered countries to retreat from external reliance and reorient toward protectionism. In the US, such a concern coincides with the fear of the rise of China which challenges the leading economic position of the US since the cold war. The US–China trade war initiated by the Trump administration since 2018 addressed the concern by raising tariffs and setting other trade barriers on goods imported from China with the goal of forcing China to make changes in the alleged unfair trade practices that resulted in the US trade deficit.

On the other hand, the US also tries to encounter China's economic influence over US businesses by strengthening the scrutiny over cross-border acquisition transactions through national security review. The divest-or-ban law over TikTok, a popular social media owned by ByteDance, a Chinese company, illustrated the heightened concern over Chinese companies among US politicians.[61] Under such a hostile political climate, Chinese public companies that

---

57 Virginia E Harper Ho, 'Climate Disclosure Line-Drawing & Securities Regulation, (2023) 56 U.C.Davis Law Review (forthcoming) 1875, 1, 3.

58 SEC, *Press Release: SEC Adopts Rules to Enhance and Standardize Climate-Related Disclosures for Investors* (6 March 2024) <https://www.sec.gov/news/press-release/2024-31> accessed 28 April 2024. However, the newly adopted rules were temporarily put on hold by the Fifth Circuit on 16 March 2024 amid a pending litigation. *See* Andrew Ramonas, *SEC Climate Disclosure Regulations Paused by Fifth Circuit (2)*, Bloomberg Law (15 March 2024) <https://news.bloomberglaw.com/securities-law/sec-climate-disclosure-regulations-paused-by-fifth-circuit-court> accessed 28 April 2024.

59 Pargendler (n 12) 1814–1815.

60 Christian Keller and Renate Marold, 'World Economic Forum, Deglobalisation: What You Need to Know' (*World Economic Forum*, 17 January 2023) <https://www.weforum.org/agenda/2023/01/deglobalisation-what-you-need-to-know-wef23/#:~:text=Today%2C%20%22slowbalisation%22%20appears%20to,corporations%20to%20reconsider%20external%20dependencies> accessed 28 February 2023.

61 Hannah Murphy, Ryan McMorrow and Cristina Criddle, 'TikTok Chief Faces Hostile Congress in Bid to Fight off US Ban' *Financial Times* (24 March 2023) <https://www.ft.com/content/6f0b931f-10c3-4f85-9f30-5d9977aab459> accessed 25 March 2023.

relied on global financing for funding soon find themselves at the forefront of the conflict. The US government is exerting greater scrutiny over the financing activities of Chinese companies, including those listed on the US stock exchanges. The US–China audit oversight dispute and the resulting passage of the Holding Foreign Companies Accountable Act (HFCAA) is a vivid example.

Chinese companies have been listed on US stock exchanges since the 1990s, ranging from the more established state-owned enterprises in the early days to companies in the technology, media and telecom industry since the 2000s. The listing of Chinese companies on the US stock exchanges benefits both countries. First, the US securities market provides the financial funding that Chinese companies need in order to grow themselves into world-class enterprises. Such funding opportunities are not available to most private companies in a state-dominated economy like China. Second, the listing of Chinese companies in the US enables US investors to participate in and profit from the growth of Chinese economy. Third, the vast number of listings by Chinese companies in recent decades has contributed to the growth of the US stock exchanges. Statistic shows that foreign companies account for around 20% of all listed companies in the US and Chinese companies rank second in numbers among all foreign issuers.[62] Finally, the cross-listing strengthens the economic tie between the US and China and promotes the governance and legal compliance of Chinese companies to be more in line with the international standards.

However, deglobalization and the political concern over state influence on Chinese companies pose significant threat to the equity funding of Chinese companies in the US capital market. The long-standing US–China audit oversight dispute soon became the leverage that US government used to put pressure on China in the midst of a trade war. The audit dispute stems from the 2002 Sarbanes–Oxley Act which requires all auditors of US listed companies to be put under the supervision of a new oversight body – the Public Company Accounting Oversight Board (PCAOB). As the US was the first to establish an independent audit oversight body, the PCAOB encountered objections and questions about the extraterritorial reach of the PCAOB from foreign auditors and foreign government authorities in the beginning. Over time, the PCAOB worked out different models of oversight with foreign regulators to accommodate restrictions from local laws and regulations. However, the dispute with China was never resolved.[63]

The disputes arose from the objections of audit firms registered in China based on the restriction on transferring auditing documents to overseas parties, in particular for documents that might contain state secret according to the State Secrets Law and other related laws and regulations.[64] To resolve the dispute, the US SEC, which oversees the PCAOB, the China

---

62 Robin H Huang, 'The US-China Audit Oversight Dispute: Causes, Solutions, and Implications for Hong Kong' (2021) 54 The International Lawyer 151 <https://ssrn.com/abstract=3708068> accessed 28 April 2024.

63 ibid 11.

64 Law of the People's Republic of China on Guarding State Secrets (April 29, 2010) (State Secrets Law), art. 26. The CSRC 'Circular 29' re-iterates the legal restrictions on handing any documents that involve state secrets and national security issue over to foreign institutions. *See* CSRC, 'The Regulation on Strengthening Confidentiality and Archives Administration Relating to Overseas Issuance and Listing of Securities' (CSRC, 20 October 2009) (Circular 29). For other laws and regulations that impose restrictions on foreign access to audit documents, see ibid 13–16.

Securities Regulatory Commission (CSRC) and the Ministry of Finance first reached an agreement in 2013 through the signing of a Memorandum of Understanding on Enforcement Cooperation (2013 MoU), establishing a cooperative framework for the exchange of audit documents.[65] However, the 2013 MoU did not pave the way for inspecting audit firms resident in China as expected owing to the lack of willingness to cooperate on the side of Chinese authorities.[66]

With the worsening of relations between the two sides amid a trade war and the outbreak of the high-profile securities fraud of Luckin Coffee in 2020, the Trump administration decided to take a tough stand against China on the audit dispute that had hung unresolved for almost two decades. NASDAQ was the first stock exchange to bar new listings of companies that are not able to fulfil the audit oversight requirement. In May 2020, the US Senate followed by passing the HFCAA, requiring a listed company to disclose whether it employed a foreign audit firm that PCAOB is not able to inspect.[67] If so, the company will need to certify to the SEC that it is not 'owned or controlled by a foreign government'. If the PCAOB is unable to inspect the issuer's public accounting firm for three consecutive years, the issuer's securities are banned from trading on a national exchange or through other methods. The HFCAA was finally passed and signed into law by President Trump on December 18, 2020, followed by the SEC's release of the final implementation amendments on December 2, 2021.

The HFCAA served as a wake-up call for Chinese companies who used to rely on US capital market for financing. The passage of the HFCAA sent a message to the market that US listing and disclosure requirements have become a product of political negotiation rather than a market mechanism. The PCAOB inspection was intended to enhance investor protection; however, the triggering of recent enforcement action and the fact that the enforcement was dormant for 20 years suggest that, during political conflict, national security concern and political power struggle trumped the economic benefits brought about by cross-listings. The political concern can also be manifested in the China-specific elements in Section 3 of HFCAA which requires foreign issuers to disclose information related to any board members who are officials of the Chinese Communist Party, and whether the articles of incorporation of the issuer contain any charter of the Chinese Communist Party.[68] Section 3 of HFCAA further attests to the political nature of such act and the rising geopolitical risks of cross-border listings.

Even though the US–China audit dispute seemed to settle temporarily after the PCAOB successfully inspected and investigated audit records of US-listed Chinese companies in Hong Kong from September to November 2022,[69] the political conflict has put international

---

65 PCAOB, 'PCAOB Enters into Enforcement Cooperation Agreement with Chinese Regulators' (PCAOB, 23 May 2013) <https://pcaobus.org/news-events/news-releases/news-release-detail/pcaob-enters-into-enforcement-cooperation-agreement-with-chinese-regulators_430> accessed 23 February 2023.

66 Huang (n 62).

67 S.945 – 116th Congress (2019–2020): Holding Foreign Companies Accountable Act (HFCAA), Public Law No 116–222 (12/18/2020).

68 HFCAA, Section 3.

69 Enock Yiu, 'US inspectors arrive in PwC, KPMG offices in Hong Kong to Review Chinese Companies' Audit Records, Sources Say' *South China Morning Post* (19 September 2022) <https://www.scmp.com/business/article/3192982/us-inspectors-arrive-pwc-kpmg-offices-hong-kong-review-chinese-companies> accessed 27 February 2022).

financial order in turmoil. Five major Chinese state-owned enterprises announced voluntary delisting from the NYSE on August 12, 2022, ahead of the implementation of HFCAA.[70] Over 200 Chinese firms were put on the watch list of the SEC subject to huge de-listing risks during the course of the dispute.[71] Facing the threat of de-listing, US-listed Chinese firms had to seek alternative route for financing outside the US and most of them sought dual listing in Hong Kong. As of January 9, 2023, 31 US-listed Chinese companies have dual listing on the Hong Kong Stock Exchange, all of which have been previously listed as non-compliant with the HFCAA.[72]

5. CONCLUSION

Existing scholarly debate about the ways to produce optimal level of disclosure centers around regulatory competition. At the normative level, proponents of a market-based competitive model believe that market competition can produce the optimal level of disclosure without government intervention. Hence, a single national regulator or an internationally harmonized regime is not a superior regulatory model. Opponents of the competitive model fear that competition will lead to a 'race-to-the-bottom' because the listing choice is in the hands of the managers and the stock exchanges are generally profit-driven. Therefore, government intervention is necessary. However, on the empirical front, we see mixed evidence on the effect of regulatory competition.

In light of the increased competition among global stock exchanges owing to globalization and technological advancement, this chapter revisits the regulatory competition theory by reviewing two recent regulatory reforms in Asian and European stock exchanges – the listing of dual-class share firms and special purpose acquisition companies. The analysis shows that the enhanced competition among the global stock exchanges does not seem to lead to a 'race-to-the-bottom'. Even though the competition does open up more options for listing, foreign stock exchanges were cautious in crafting a locally suitable regulatory regime by imposing governance safeguards that are not presented in the US, the source of competition.

The theory of regulatory competition does not seem to capture some more recent developments in the global securities regulatory regime. This chapter further identifies two other forces that account for recent regulatory changes: international harmonization and geopolitics. The example of US reform on ESG and climate-related disclosure highlights the continued presence of international organizations in harmonizing differences and imposing specific agendas in the national securities regulation. The international harmonization efforts to some extent supplement the deficiencies in market competition and government intervention in generating an optimal level of regulation. However, the soft-law nature of international standards might face opposition from local politics.

---

[70] US–China Economic and Security Review Commission, 'Chinese Companies Listed on Major U.S. Stock Exchanges' (USCC, 9 January 2023) <https://www.uscc.gov/sites/default/files/2023-01/Chinese_Companies_Listed_on_US_Stock_Exchanges_01_2023.pdf> accessed 10 March 2023).

[71] SEC, 'Conclusive List of Issuers Identified under the HFCAA' (SEC, 10 March 2023) <https://www.sec.gov/hfcaa> accessed 10 March 2023.

[72] USCC (n 70) 5.

The other force that brings about change is geopolitics. This chapter points out that the tension between US and China since 2018 has heightened the geopolitical risks on international equity financing activities. The passage of Holding Foreign Companies Accountable Act in 2020 and the resulting de-listing risks for US-listed Chinese companies disrupted the order of international capital market. With the rise of protectionism and deglobalization, geopolitics is expected to play a more important role in global securities regulation.

8. Investment fund regulation

Ugo Malvagna

1. THE NOTION OF 'INVESTMENT FUND' FROM A FINANCIAL PERSPECTIVE: CATEGORIES OF INVESTMENT FUNDS

1.1 Collective Investment Schemes: Core Elements

In financial jargon, the phrase 'investment fund' designates a diverse and multifaceted phenomenon, which includes a vast range of vehicles aiming at pooling resources from different investors through which pursuing various forms of investment transactions. Such transactions may differ from each other with reference to the invested asset classes, the fund's size, the underlying financial 'logics' based on which the undertakings are carried out, the nature of the end investors which the fund's shares or unit are intended to be offered to, and the negotiability of the units or shares in the investment vehicle.

One may therefore wonder what the common denominator of such notion is, also to distinguish an investment fund from an 'ordinary' common enterprise carried out through a company or other arrangements. Indeed, the essence of investment funds can be found in some core elements, namely: (i) the existence of a *plurality of investors*, providing the financial resources to set up the fund through the purchase of a pool of assets; (ii) the *segregation* of the invested assets from investors' and managers' personal assets; (iii) the existence of a pre-determined *investment policy* for those assets, with the purpose of generating an aggregated yield for the investors' benefit; and (iv) the managers' autonomy in implementing the investment policy, with the subsequent investors' inability to influence the operational implementation of the investment policy or to modify it on their own initiative.

If the above captures the structural aspects of the phenomenon, one can fully understand the inherent nature of the different activities carried out by investment funds, as well as the specific risks each activity is associated with, only by breaking down the existing different categories of funds. Such categories should be based on the characteristics of the funds' investment policy (including the invested assets) and on the contents of the investors' rights *vis-à-vis* the fund (and, particularly, whether there is an implicit or explicit 'promise' of liquidity). These two parameters shape the specific features of the intermediation carried out through each type of investment fund.

All of the above is mirrored by the existing framework, where – in all major jurisdictions – a two-layer set of regulations exists, namely a general set of rules addressing regulatory needs which are common to all investment funds (insofar they are the consequence of an investment vehicle having the three features set out above) and specific sets of rules whose applicability depends on the relevant category the fund can be ascribed to.

In this regard, a fundamental distinction must be drawn between funds whose strategy is generally built on risk diversification (such as open-ended mutual funds, including money markets mutual funds, MMF, and exchanged-traded funds, ETFs) and funds which pursue a specialized strategy (closed-ended funds and hedge funds).[1]

1.2 Open-Ended Mutual Funds

The establishment of mutual funds as one core pillar of current financial markets[2] can be traced backed to the idea that benefits associated with risk diversification would be amplified by pooling single end-investors' financial portfolio into larger vehicles, which could leverage a higher diversification potential and reduced marginal transaction costs in pursuing investment policies, owing to economies of scale.

In terms of how investment strategies can be structured and implemented, there is in fact no significant difference between a collective vehicle and an individual portfolio management service provided by an advisor, investment firm or broker-dealer. In all cases, investments are generally managed in line with the assumptions underpinning Markowitz's 'modern portfolio theory', i.e. that a rational approach to financial investments should aim at maximizing risk-adjusted returns, meaning optimizing the relationship between the portfolio expected returns and its global riskiness, as measured by the portfolio volatility and correlation.[3] The latter is intended as the relationship between the increase/decrease of each single financial instrument's value and the increase/decrease of the overall value of the portfolio: the so-called 'beta' of the financial instrument.

Under this approach, the main driver to reduce the portfolio's riskiness without reducing expected returns (thus pursuing higher risk-adjusted returns) is to reach an appropriate level of diversification by setting up portfolios that consist of non-correlated or negatively correlated financial instruments, by way of the asset class and financial nature of the instrument, geographical area and relevant industry. If the returns of portfolio's securities show a perfectly positive correlation, then the increase or decrease in one security's price would be associated with an equal and identical change of other instruments in the portfolio. In that case, the riskiness (standard deviation) of the portfolio is in effect equal to the weighted average of the standard deviations of the securities in the portfolio.[4] Consequently, the positive or negative variations in a securities' price would be 'amplified', at the portfolio level, by an equal change

---

1 In the absence of a commonly acknowledge standard definition of what 'hedge funds' are, it can be said that their qualifying feature consist in their private nature, meaning that they are not intended to be offered (at least directly) to the general public of investors, but can be accessed only by accredited investors that are in possession of specific requirements in terms of their total assets, annual income and experience in the investment field.

2 See data reported on Financial Stability Board, 'Global Monitoring Report on Non-Bank Financial Intermediation' (Financial Stability Board 2023).

3 H.M. Markowitz, Portfolio Selection (March 1952) The Journal of Finance 77; idem, *Portfolio Selection. Efficient Diversification of Investments* (Yale University Press 1952), *passim*.

4 Assuming a two-securities portfolio (p) where the two securities have the same weight and there is maximum correlation between them, the formula for calculating its standard deviation would be: $\sigma_p = \sqrt{[(0.25 * \sigma_1^2) + (0.25 * \sigma_2^2) + (0.5 * \sigma_1 * \sigma_2)]}$, where σ_p = standard deviation of the portfolio; w_1, $w_2 = 0.5$ = weights of the two assets in the portfolio; σ_1, σ_2 = standard deviations of the two assets; and ρ_{12} = correlation between the returns of the two assets. Of course, as the two stocks are perfectly correlated, their correlation coefficient (ρ_{12}) is equal to 1; hence the notation is omitted in the equation.

in the other securities. If, however, this correlation was only weakly positive or even negative, then the situation would change significantly. Should this be the case, the impact on the performance of the overall portfolio of a decline in the value of one or more instruments would be 'mitigated' or, more appropriately, 'hedged' by the opposite performance of the other instruments. Consequently, diversification minimizes the portfolio's overall risk without necessarily sacrificing its expected returns (which continue to be represented by the weighted average of the expected returns of individual financial instruments).

In fact, a low aggregate 'beta' of the portfolio reaches the effect of eliminating, through diversification, idiosyncratic risks, meaning risks relating to the performance of single issuers, while the portfolio only remains exposed to systematic risk (to be intended as risks that would affect the market – ore some of its parts – as a whole). This also appears to be in line with the assumptions of Sharpe's capital asset price model (CAPM), according to which investors should and would only remunerate capital based on the size of the (non-diversifiable) systematic risk, while they would not remunerate (diversifiable) idiosyncratic risk.

One further pivotal element behind the success of mutual funds is efficient capital, the idea that, if the invested pool of assets is only composed of *liquid* securities (meaning securities having an active and deep secondary markets), then one can rely on the listing price for those instruments, without the need for engaging in fundamental and technical analysis of single securities. This assumption lies at the heart of the efficient capital markets hypothesis (ECMH), according to which all public information relating to the issuer and the security is promptly reflected in the security's price, provided that there is an active secondary market for the relevant security.

It can therefore be said that the coupling of the modern portfolio theory with the ECMH enabled the birth of mutual funds that would be 'open-ended'. This means that, on the one hand, the investor base can grow over time through periodical or continuous issuance of new units and, on the other hand, investors are legally entitled to withdraw their investment during the fund's lifetime and receive their share of the net asset value (NAV) of the fund.[5] As a matter of fact, such a model functions smoothly if the asset pool is mainly composed of securities that can be promptly liquidated at fair value, which is generally the case when the invested assets are liquid, low-risk securities (provided that markets are not in stressed conditions, when, instead, an incentive to 'run' – i.e. to redeem – may be generated, thus possibly affecting the fund's integrity: see *infra*, Section 2). However, it should be noted that, especially in recent times (owing to an extended period of exceptionally low interest rates), the asset management industry has been experiencing the growth of open-ended funds whose investment policy also involves financial instruments that are not liquid, low-risk securities. This can imply vulnerability in terms of the fund's ability to meet redemptions without affecting the post-redemption value of the fund, thus requiring specific regulatory response.

Against this backdrop, it is intuitive that mutual funds appear to be able to pursue the agreed investment policy in a more efficient way than individual portfolio management. This is true with reference to both 'passively' and 'actively' managed funds. The former means that the manager just seeks to track one or more pre-determined benchmarks through long-only strategic asset allocation (passive management), while the latter means that the manager aims at outperforming relevant indexes by taking a higher 'active share' based on tactical

---

5 This does not mean that open-ended funds are necessarily required to provide daily liquidity.

asset allocation decisions (active management). Different management styles imply different degrees of managerial discretion, thus affecting the assessment of the manager conduct from the perspective of its liability according to the duty of care.

Be the management style active or passive, either way the collective nature of the undertaking positively affects the cost-effectiveness of the collective investment scheme (hereinafter, also 'CIS'), *vis-à-vis* the alternative scenario of a series of autonomous portfolio management contracts between single end investors and the asset manager. On the one hand, the standardized nature of the undertakings (where investors are exposed to the same risks, stemming from a unitary strategy) reduces marginal costs relating to the implementation of investment strategies, including research costs for determining which tactical decisions to take. On the other hand, the higher amount of asset under management enables higher diversification and reduces transaction costs, both for tracking and for the acquisition of market information in order to assess whether to adopt an active share.

1.3 Closed-Ended Mutual Funds

Unlike the previous category, closed-ended funds do not come with the promise of liquidity through redeemability of their units, so that no asset–liability mismatch is implied in their business model. On the contrary, investments in the scheme/vehicle are collected through a fixed number of units at the fund's inception and cannot be pulled until the agreed term expires, so that the investment policy can be less concerned with concentration risk and can be oriented towards illiquid assets.

Closed-ended funds include, *inter alia*, real estate, art, debt financing to close unlisted companies in the form of loan origination or loan participation (private) and private equity. The rationale of such categories of funds is therefore partially different than that for open-ended, liquid ones. Provided that these funds are hardly ever market funds aiming at full-range diversification, their function lies in their ability to fractionalize investments in illiquid assets, thus enabling their accessibility. Besides, even if the investment policy is not oriented toward diversifying any idiosyncratic risk away, nevertheless a certain grade of diversification is granted by the risk-spreading principle that alternative investment funds also follow.

Furthermore, the very existence of an investment vehicle managed by asset managers ensures that the set-up of the investment policy, the selection of investments and the structuring of transactions is carried out by specialized professionals within an organized structure, who would also monitor investments on a continuous basis in order to maximize risk-adjusted return.

Delegation to fund's managers is therefore able to reduce transaction costs borne by investors, both with reference to investments' selection and execution phase and in terms of reducing monitoring and management.

2. FINANCIAL STABILITY AND INVESTOR PROTECTION IN THE INVESTMENT FUND'S INDUSTRY

2.1 Collective Investment Schemes and 'Shadow Banking'

The core characteristics set out above enable the very function of investment funds to be framed as part of the financial system. In this respect, it can be said that investment funds reflect a 'hybrid' intermediation model, insofar they combine features of indirect intermediation (that is, when funds recipients are in a direct legal relationship with a financial intermediary which is, in its turn, in a direct legal relationship with investors) and of direct intermediation (that is, when funds recipients and investors are in a direct legal relationship between themselves). With reference to the former, it is worth noting that the surplus and deficit units' contractual counterparty is not directly that of the deficit units, but instead the collective investment undertaking and/or its managers. With reference to the latter, invested assets are purchased on capital markets at least when the fund's investment policy requires it to mainly invest in liquid, low-risk securities. Therefore, funds do not only perform an intermediation function, but also are core market participants that can contribute to the liquidity of secondary markets for financial instruments, and, when they hold large equity stakes, even impact listed companies' governance.

The extreme flexibility of investment funds as vehicles through which investment transactions can be deployed is such that, based on the contents of the agreed investment policies and the units' features (above all, their being open-ended or closed-ended), their specific intermediation function can vary. So, for instance, on one side of the spectrum we can name unlisted closed-ended funds investing in equity stakes of closed companies (private equity funds) or other illiquid assets: such transactions perform an intermediation function but do not imply any kind of transformation (in the form of credit, maturity or liquidity). On the opposite side of the spectrum, open-ended loan origination funds perform maturity transformation in the very same way as commercial banks do. If we consider liquidity transformation, it has already been noted that money market mutual funds' units are generally treated as money-like instruments. With reference to credit transformation, pass-through securitization funds aim at financing the purchase of loan portfolios through the issuance of securities that are safer than the portfolios themselves.

All of the above suggests that if the activity of investment funds qualifies – generally speaking – as a form of 'non-bank financial intermediation', in various cases this intermediation can have features that epitomize the very notion of shadow banking, with all the regulatory challenges that this poses to the financial system. Indeed, after the great financial crisis, supervision and regulation of shadow banking (and non-bank financial Intermediation in general) have been put under the spotlight, especially from a financial stability perspective, that can be adversely affected both in case of the fund's inability to meet its obligations *vis-à-vis* investors upon redemption, especially when the fund performs maturity or liquidity transformation, and in case of the fund's default in financing contracts in place with external lenders and/or in derivative contracts.

Because the investment fund industry collects financial resources from many and extremely diversified investors, including banks, investment firms and other financial institutions, liquidity and leverage issues can be the source of systemic risk through different transmission channels. All this poses 'bank-like financial stability risks'[6] that lies at the heart of prudential regulation in this field (see *infra*, Sections 3 and 4). Besides, given the great importance that collective investment schemes (both market funds and alternative funds) have reached as market participants, massive sales of portfolio assets owing to the need to meet redemption requests or other payment obligations can significantly impair the market value of those assets, thus triggering contagion across asset classes.

2.2 Agency Issues Affecting the Relationship Between Investors and Managers

Having put in context the phenomenon of investment funds from a system-wide view point and assuming now an inner perspective on the relationships between managers and unitholders, as well as between unitholders themselves, it should be noted that, regardless of the legal form through which they are set up (meaning, through contractual arrangements, trusts or companies),[7] an investment fund's structure eventually comes down to a delegation on management powers over the fund's assets, from the investors 'as a whole' and the fund's managers.

In fact, the core element of collective asset management (as opposed to individual management) lies in the fact that each unit/shareholder finds itself in the very same position *vis-à-vis* the fund (since each unit represents a certain percentage of the entire fund's assets) and the managers (since the units' legal and financial features of units are standardized based on one or more 'classes').

From a functional perspective, this implies that an agency relationship is established between investors, considered as a group, and managers., The size and level of agency costs depends here on the actual degree of incompleteness that is inherent to the agreed investment policy: the higher the managerial discretion, the more likely it is that managers' behavior will not maximize investors' welfare, thus resulting in a market failure in respect of efficient allocation of financial resources. In this regard, it is worth noting that also in investment funds in which discretion appears to be absent, such as index funds and ETFs, some room for managerial discretion remains in the choice and implementation of the tracking methodology. Moreover, in several cases the index itself is structured and operated by benchmark providers

---

6 See Financial Stability Board, 'Global Monitoring Report on Non-Bank Financial Intermediation' (Financial Stability Board 2022).

7 The irrelevance, from a regulatory perspective, of the legal form through which funds are structured – provided that it is able to ring fence the funds' risks from different risks relating to managers and/or other funds – emerges clearly from relevant legal definitions. With reference to UCITS art 1(2) and AIFMD art 2(2). In Switzerland, see art 7 of the Collective Investment Schemes Act (CISA). UK legislation maintains the same structure as the EU: see FSMA Part XVII Collective Investment Schemes, sect. 235 ff., including the possibility to resort to different legal structures and arrangements in order to set up trusts. In Singapore, see Section 2 and Section 286 of the Securities and Futures Act 2001. In Hong Kong, see Schedule 1 of the Securities and Futures Ordinance, that would include both unit trusts and fund companies. In the US, investment funds regulation revolves around the 1940 Investment Company Act and SEC rule 4.80a–4. With reference to Australia, see Chapter 5C of the Corporations Act 2001 (Cth) (Corporations Act), on which see P. Hanrahan and I. Ramsay, Regulation of Mutual Funds in Australia, in William Birdthistle and John Morley (eds) *Research Handbook on Mutual Funds* (Edward Elgar Publishing 2017), 418.

in a discretionary way:[8] consequently, some sort of sub-delegation from the asset managers to the benchmark administrators occurs.

Against this background, the collective nature of such agency relationships (multiple investors *versus* one entity acting as manager) comes with collective action costs that – based on the number of unitholders – make it hard, if not impossible, for private contracting to manage such possible market failure through appropriate contractual arrangements (at the moment of the setup of the investment policy and the fund's regulation) and monitoring throughout the fund's life. When it comes to funds marketed to retail investors, such issues are exacerbated by the fact that collective action costs are added to significant investors' asymmetry of information and rational apathy. Funds' regulations and investment policies are not bargained by investors, that in any case would not be able to engage in such negotiations: therefore, managers and sponsors are incentivized to set up regulations that give them room for reducing accountability towards investors through limited transparency and high discretion (with reference, for instance, to investment limits, redemption timing and discretionary restrictions, applicable fees), as a precondition for enabling them to maximize their own welfare instead of that of the investors.

Beyond that, it is the very nature of collective investment schemes that requires separation between investors in the funds and managers,[9] with the consequence that the former, even if unanimous, are neither able to intervene in the implementation of the investment strategy by the latter, nor to modify it on their own initiative. This organizational feature is peculiar to all and only the investment funds and underpins their financial rationale, enabling them to pursue their function, that is to expose investors *exclusively* to the specific market risks that have been agreed upon in the fund's regulation and investment policy.[10] This outcome is reached by legally separating the fund (as an entity, trust unit or contractual arrangement)[11] from the managing entity ('asset partitioning'),[12] and by contractually entrusting managers with the exclusive power to manage the fund, which would grant them a significant autonomy in the pursuing of the investment undertaking. Without such separation and managers' autonomy, it would be impossible, on the one hand, to ring-fence each fund's risks from one another and, on the other, to ensure to investors that the fund would act accordingly to the agreed investment policy and would not change its features and risk profile over time. Consequently, it is fairly

---

8 Benchmarks often involve discretion on the side of entities contributing with input data and on the side of the administrator. Calculation methodologies can in fact change over time and may explicitly provide administrator with the power to make discretionary decisions with reference to the selection of the benchmarks' constituents and the elaboration of input data. On this topic, see Adriana Z. Robertson, Passive in Name Only: Delegated Management and 'Index' Investing (2019) 36 Yale Journal on Regulation 805 ff. In the EU, Regulation 2016/1011 is intended to provide a framework intended, among other policy objectives, to provide transparency in regard of relevant methodologies.

9 John D Morley, The Separation of Funds and Managers: A Theory of Investment Fund Structure and Regulation (2014) 123 Yale Law Journal 1118, 1228 ff.

10 ibid 1258.

11 The ability of the fund's legal structure to reach the outcome of an effective asset partitioning leverage on applicable private law. To this regard, it is importantly noted that jurisdictions that do not have trust as a legal tool, in contract-based investment funds the effect of 'asset separation' is granted by special legal provisions.

12 See again Morley (n 9), page 1258.

said that a certain amount of agency costs owing to the principals' lack of ability to control their agent is a necessary side-effect of this investment paradigm.

In the same line, one further aspect to be considered is that open-ended funds show a specific form of agency problems, affecting the relationships among investors themselves. In particular, provided that unitholders are entitled to pull their investment at any point in time and obtain the corresponding proportion of the fund's NAV, it can happen that – in period of stressed markets or financial turmoil – investors' concerns on losses that may be suffered by the fund generate positional externalities incentivizing strategic behaviour that results in amplifying losses, if not even generating a 'run' on the fund.

When the fund's liquidity and/or value is affected by market-wide or system-wide events, the first redemptions will be met through the fund's most liquid assets (including cash reserves), that can be liquidated without losses, while subsequent redemptions will require the fund's manager to liquidate assets whose market value has been already impaired or by less liquid assets, possibly forcing fire-sales that would adversely impact the fund's NAV, to the detriment of investors that have not pulled their investments. Consequently, investors that in theory would be willing to maintain their investments are pushed to redeem, only to avoid being negatively impacted by the others' behaviour. In their turn, such runs can trigger contagion through both unitholders and, when funds are leveraged, creditors according to financing contracts or derivatives.

Eventually, also leverage can itself become an issue from the investors' perspective. The reason for this lies in the fact that competition between funds is essentially driven by the track records of their performance. Therefore, as managers' incentive is to grow their AUMs (because their fees are generally structured as a percentage thereof), one way to make this happen is to show a consistent record of above-their-peers returns. In periods of bull markets, resorting to leverage contributes to bolstering performances every time the cost of debt is lower than the increase in portfolio returns. This produces a cyclical effect that exposes funds to liquidity and solvency issues in periods of bear markets. Apparently, competition cannot itself handle this issue, as investors tend to appreciate past performance more than they are able to factor-in the fund's leverage (so that an adverse selection dynamic kicks in). Besides, without regulatory intervention it is even more difficult for investors to monitor how the leverage ratio would evolve over time, owing – as discussed above – to the high discretion that asset managers grant themselves.

2.3 The Intertwining Between Financial Stability and Investor Protection

All the above enables me to set out some brief remarks on the existing relationship between financial stability and investor protection, as the two main policy goals underpinning the mutual funds industry's regulation.

As in any other field of the financial system, protection of funds' unitholders addresses potential market failures in the perspective of fostering allocation efficiency. As shown above, the need for protection is here rooted in agency problems and adverse selection investors may face owing to the separation between the fund and its managers,[13] and to agency-like problems occurring between investors themselves.

Considering the mutual funds industry from the perspective of financial stability, the most relevant vulnerabilities have been previously identified in the ability of liquidity and leverage issues affecting investment funds to work as systemic risk spreading channels onto the financial system and the real economy, through: (i) potential 'runs' from funds; (ii) defaults in financing contracts and derivatives; and (iii) impairment of the market value of asset classes held by the fund, owing to fire-sales forced by liquidity constraints.

It is worth noting that, owing to the specific financial structure of funds where all unitholders are 'residual claimants' *vis-à-vis* the fund, each phenomenon that can affect financial stability must have affected unitholders. Consequently, in the context of collective investment schemes the intertwining between investor protection and financial stability – namely, the former being instrumental to the latter – is even closer than in any other financial institution.

All this makes it useless to organize the analysis of the existing regulatory framework distinguishing between investor protection-oriented and financial-stability-oriented rules. Sound and prudent management aims essentially at avoiding 'runs' by unitholders during stressed market conditions or as a consequence of economic shocks, as this could trigger financial contagion in various forms. Prudential provisions are, above all, intended to protect investors. From this standpoint, it is no accident that regulatory convergence in this field is mainly by organizations whose mandate is financial stability,[14] with outcomes that essentially impinge on investor protection: in aiming at preventing financial instability as the consequence of ineffective risk management by funds' managers, the FSB's activity provides regulatory high-level frameworks that set standards for the entire industry as they are made applicable to all funds, regardless of their systemic importance.

It is also true that all of the most relevant jurisdictions show the existence of provisions that enable managers to temporarily restrict the exercise of investors' redemption rights in order to avoid financial instability phenomena. Based on what was set out before, it should however be clear that these are exceptional provisions for extraordinary cases affecting systemically important collective undertakings in situations of actual risk of severe contagion, and should always be perceived and treated as such.

---

[13] A different layer of problems regarding investors relates to the fact that funds are inevitably exposed to a certain measure of idiosyncratic risk, that should be addressed through diversification at the level of the investor's portfolio.

[14] Reference is made to the Financial Stability Board, see Policy Recommendations to Address Structural Vulnerabilities from Asset Management Activities, 12 January 2017; Assessment of the Effectiveness of the FSB's 2017 Recommendations on Liquidity Mismatch in Open-Ended Funds, 14 December 2022; Addressing Structural Vulnerabilities from Liquidity Mismatch in Open-Ended Funds – Revisions to the FSB's 2017 Policy Recommendations, Consultation report, 5 July 2023. Besides, IOSCO has also mainly approached funds regulation, especially liquidity-related issues, from the angle of systemic risk: see Recommendations for Liquidity Risk Management for Collective Investment Schemes – Final Report, February 2018.

3. THE SCOPE OF REGULATION: REGISTRATION REQUIREMENTS AND SUBJECTION TO PUBLIC SUPERVISION AND OVERSIGHT

It is an internationally long-established principle[15] that the set-up, marketing and operation of collective investment schemes shall be considered as a regulated activity, thus requiring that the fund's managers are registered before a competent authority, in charge of the supervising the collective investment schemes throughout its entire life.

Clearly, if registration or licensing requirements work by way of an *ex ante* public enforcement means, that is as an entry barrier intended to impose a previous scrutiny on the existence of statutory predetermined requirements, subjection to a public authority's oversight enables a continuous scrutiny on the permanence of those requirements over time. More generally, the competent authority is entrusted with the responsibility of supervising the asset managers' organization and conduct through the exercise of inspection, supervisory and sanctioning power. To this purpose, reporting duties are imposed on supervised entities, relating to the AUM's amount and types of assets, leverage, market and credit risk exposures, derivatives and internal policies.

With reference to registration, a distinction must be made between managers or advisors, on the one hand, and collective investment schemes, on the other. All relevant jurisdictions require entities that intend to sponsor and manage funds on a professional basis to be registered or licensed.[16] To obtain registration or licensing, information has to be provided on the legal status, internal governance and organizational arrangements, personnel and initial capital, together with a plan of activities that includes the nature of funds it intends to operate. The filing is then subject to evaluation, which may result in the licensing, a rejection or the proceeding's stay and the request for further information. The thoroughness and timing of the assessment, as the specific preconditions to take up business, vary significantly across jurisdictions.

Differences can also be noted in respect of the existence and content of a 'de minimis' exemption. In the US a full exemption from SEC-registration is provided (and State-level regulations may apply) for entities that advise for AUM that are under a certain threshold ($100 million);[17] above that threshold, the duty to be SEC-registered is triggered. Besides, a significant exemption from registration requirements was traditionally provided with reference to 'private advisers', meaning investment advisers having fewer than 15 clients. Before the Great Financial Crisis, this exemption was phrased and construed in such a way that each

---

15 See International Organization of Securities Commissions (IOSCO), 'Principles for the regulation of collective investment schemes' (International Organization of Securities Commissions October 1994).

16 With reference the US, see the Investment Advisers Act, Sec. 203. For the EU, see UCITS art 5 and AIFM art 6. In the UK, see Sec. 19 and FSMA Schedule 2. In Hong Kong, see Schedule V of the Securities and Futures Ordinance (Cap. 571). In Singapore, see Sec. 285 of the Securities and Futures Act 2001. In Australia, see Sec. 9 of the Corporations Act 2001.

17 Advisers with less than $25 million in AUM are barred from SEC-registration, while between $25 and 100 million SEC-registration is permitted when certain conditions are met.

fund would be considered as a client, regardless of the number of investors in the fund itself[18] and the AUM's size. This enabled systemically significant asset managers, and in particular hedge funds, to avoid SEC's oversight. Such a deficiency in the regulatory framework has then been fixed by the Dodd–Frank Act. Currently, according to Section 203(m) of the Investment Advisers Act, all advisers managing more than $100 million are required to be registered unless they '1 [act] solely as an investment adviser to one or more qualifying private funds; and 2 [manage] private fund assets of less than $150 million'; where a 'qualifying private fund' is a fund that neither intends to carry out public offerings of their units, nor deals with more than 100 'accredited investors'[19] [§ 275.203(m)-1 Private fund adviser exemption].[20]

Even after the Dodd–Frank Act, the US remains the jurisdiction with the largest room for benefiting from regulatory exemptions, if compared with the European Union and other relevant jurisdictions.[21] Exempted advisers are nevertheless subject to some reporting duties to the SEC through parts of the Form ADV.

A second and distinct layer of regulatory screening refers to the approval of the setup of collective investment schemes themselves.[22]

Differently from the authorization of advisers/managers, the approval of the fund's regulation instrument – in the form of a contract, a trust deed or a corporate bylaw, depending on the fund's legal form – is intended to work as a public *ex ante* means of enforcement of substantive statutory and regulatory provisions regarding the contents that funds' regulations must and must not have (see below, no. 4). Such a regulatory technique is intended to enhance the effectivity of those substantive provisions, thus creating market confidence as far as the compliance of funds with the applicable framework, and reducing transaction costs also in this respect.

The general trend of regulatory framework across the world is that each fund's prospectus should be approved by the competent authority before the fund can be marketed.[23] Furthermore, in several jurisdictions – including the EU, the UK and Switzerland – simplified authorization proceedings and light supervisory frameworks are provided, based on the fund's size and typology. In the US, 'private funds' benefit from an exemption from registration under Form N-1A (Registration form for open-end management investment companies) and Form 2 (Registration statement for closed-end management investment companies). However, they remain subject to reporting duties, to be complied with through Form PF (§ 275.204(b)-1).

---

18 See James Jalil in Andrew J. Donohue, Symposium: The Regulation of Investment Funds (2011) 16 Fordham Journal of Corporate & Financial Law 7ff.

19 See SEC's Rule 506 of Regulation D.

20 See Deborah A. DeMott and Arthur B. Laby, United States of America in Danny Busch and Deborah DeMott (eds) *Liability of Asset Managers* (OUP 2012), 416ff.

21 In Switzerland, a '*de minimis*' exemption exists, but managers are nevertheless required to be registered as individual portfolio managers.

22 In several jurisdictions, the fund's regulation is different than the offering prospectus, that needs to be set up and published, after approval of the competent authority, according to securities/financial instruments regulations. Like for all securities, exemption relating to private placement may apply.

23 Some jurisdictions, such as the UK (only when funds are set up in the form of unit trust) and Hong Kong, admit unauthorized funds when specific circumstances are met.

4. DISCLOSURE AND GOVERNANCE RULES

As explained above, the core structural feature of collective investment schemes is the separation of the fund and its managers, meaning that, on the one hand, the fund's assets are legally separated from investors' and the manager's personal assets, and, on the other, the fund's managers are entrusted with autonomy in carrying out the fund's investment activity. Consequently, contractual incompleteness generates agency problems that result in an investor's inability to appropriately select and monitor their investment and potentially in their failure to maximize their welfare and inefficient allocation of resources.

As competition is not able to entirely overcome this issue owing to asymmetry of information and rational apathy that affect non-institutional investors, all existing regulatory frameworks around the globe have developed a set of regulatory strategies that lay out the conditions for preventing market failures in the mutual fund's industry.

In this context, the fundamental and highest-level regulatory technique is for the law to treat the relationship between investors and manager as a trust-like situation, with the consequence that managers owe fiduciary duties (duty of loyalty and duty of care).[24] Obviously, such duties are principle-based and often rooted in each jurisdiction's private law system,[25] so that its enforcement is generally up to each state's Courts.

In addition to that, financial regulation has shaped over time a more detailed and comprehensive regulatory framework, that would foster effective investor protection. In this regard, the salient aspects to be considered are: (i) mandatory contract provisions governing the fund (company's bylaws, trust deeds and management/advisory contracts); (ii) governance rules, addressing the relationships between all interested parties, including the provision according to which an external depositary shall be appointed for safekeeping purposes; and (iii) provisions setting limits to portfolio composition.

As contractual incompleteness would hamper the investors' ability to take informed investment decisions and would incentivize managers to engage in self-serving behaviour, in order for the establishment of a new fund to be approved by the competent authority some specific contents have to be present in the offering documentation.

The law requires that the relevant documentation (the vehicle bylaws, trust instrument and fund's regulation) contain at a minimum information that would describe the most relevant features of the funds,[26] including the open-ended or close-ended nature, details on the redemp-

---

24 This implies a fiduciary duty to pursue the investors' best interest, which implies, in turn, that asset managers must comply with market-accepted sound financial methodologies. Provided that, at least as far as mutual funds are concerned, the manager's duty of care revolves around its ability to set up and maintain a portfolio that shows an adequate level of diversification, thus maximizing risk-adjusted returns, one core element of mutual funds regulation pertains to the understanding of the existing relationship between the funds managers' fiduciary duty and the indexes or benchmarks that are – and must be, according to basically all applicable laws and regulations – indicated as relevant in the transaction documents (especially, the fund's regulations).

25 Regulations dedicated to collective investment schemes reaffirm the existence of such duties, which per se would stem by the very nature of this relationship according to general private law.

26 See UCITS arts 68, 69 and 78 and AIFMD arts 22–24. In the US, see Form N-1A (Registration form for open-end management investment companies) and Form 2 (Registration statement for closed-end management investment companies). In the UK, see the Collective Investment Schemes

tion policy, characteristics of the investment policy, kinds of financial instruments the fund is authorized to deal with, fund's risk profile and past performance.

In the mutual fund industry, the fund's legal taxonomy significantly facilitates investors' understanding of the nature of the product. As mentioned before (Section 1), the variety of transactions that can be carried out through collective investment schemes justifies different legal 'labels' for each macro-category of funds, to provide a certain grade of standardization and immediately convey information to clients as to the type of investment that characterizes each collective fund. For instance, in the EU and in the UK, the notion of 'unit in collective undertakings in transferrable securities' (UCITS) includes in its scope open-end investment funds investing in liquid assets and managed according to the risk-spreading principle (see the modern portfolio theory introduced above, Section 1), while an 'alternative fund' refers to all other funds. Quite similarly, the US relies on two 'labels' that apply simultaneously, that is, open-ended *versus* close-ended and diversified *versus* non-diversified.

It should also be pointed out that rules mandating specific contents on the fund regulation/deed/bylaw aim not only at enhancing transparency, but also at imposing substantive rules to protect investors, also by shaping redemption rights (both in term of timing and unit's appraisal) or limiting costs and fees that can be charged to investors.[27]

4.1 Internal Governance Requirements

Alongside the above, existing regulations design a governance framework 'for the organization and operation of CIS that seeks to ensure that CIS are organized and operated efficiently and exclusively in the interests of CIS Investors, and not in the interests of CIS insiders'.[28]

It is worth noting that all relevant jurisdictions tend to converge on mandatory governance rules. These include, *inter alia*, internal governance requirements for management companies, in particular provisions aiming at ensuring sound and prudent management and mitigating conflicts of interests that may arise. In this context, remuneration policies play a relevant role in trying to reduce incentive misalignments between investors and managers.[29]

However, the pivotal elements around which all frameworks are built are that (i) funds' managers be subject to oversight by an independent body/entity, and that (ii) funds' assets be separated by the management company and the investment vehicle, and custodied by a qualified institution that is independent from both the managers and the body/entity in charge of oversight functions. In this regard the oversight function is arranged differently depending on the legal form of the CIS.

In corporate-based funds, the responsibility to carry out oversight on the fund's managers is generally on the board of the investment company or on an external depositary bank. When

---

Sourcebook 2021, coll 4.2.5. In Hong Kong, see the SFC Handbook for Unit Trusts and Mutual Funds, Investment-Linked Assurance Schemes, Chapter 6 (Disclosure requirements).

27 See for instance the Adviser Act, Sec. 205. [80b–5] (Investment Advisory Contracts), the Investment Company Act Sec. 15. [80a–15] (Investment Advisory and Underwriting Contracts), Sec. 22. [80a–22] (Distribution, Redemption, And Repurchase of Redeemable Securities) and Sec. 22. [80a–23] (Distribution and Repurchase of Securities: Closed-End Companies).

28 IOSCO, 'Examination of Governance for Collective Investment Schemes, Final Report – Part I' (International Organization of Securities Commissions June 2006), 3.

29 See UCITS arts 14a and 14b.

such functions are carried out by the investment company's board, member independence requirements *vis-à-vis* the fund's managers are set by statutory law. This is the case in the US, where the Investment Company Act [SEC. 10. 80a–10 (a)] dictates that 'no registered investment company shall have a board of directors more than 60 per centum of the members of which are persons who are interested persons of such registered company'.[30] Independence enables the board to effectively perform its oversight function, both when the fund enters into an advisory contract with the fund adviser and over time, through the exercise of monitoring on the adviser's carrying out of the undertaking. Other jurisdictions,[31] on the contrary, rely more heavily on regulation and supervision of the investment company's internal governance,[32] and therefore allow for internally managed companies.[33]

While in trust-based models the role of the investment company is performed by the trustee, in contract-based models the absence of the scheme's subjectivity (meaning that the fund itself does not have legal personality) implies that a different entity should be entrusted with oversight functions. More specifically, such an entity is generally identified by the law in the custodian/depositary bank, that – when entrusted with such function – is required to ensure that the undertaking is carried out accordingly to applicable law and the fund rules or instruments of incorporation.[34]

Regardless of whether the custodian is entrusted or not with an oversight role,[35] a common feature of existing regulatory frameworks is that such a custodian or depositary bank perform the function of assets safekeeping.[36] Third-party safekeeping serves two main purposes.

Firstly, there is a practical reason: because management companies are not part of payment and securities infrastructures, they must resort to banks to settle trades and payments. Secondly, safekeeping duties support rules mandating segregation of each fund's assets from the managers' personal assets and from other funds. However, a fully fledged 'ring-fencing' of mutual fund's assets can only be obtained insofar as they are protected from the depositary bank's failure and/or resolution procedure.[37] Consequently, one key attribute of the bank res-

---

30 More on detail on this topic, see Mohammed K. Alshaleel, *Regulation and Governance of Mutual Funds: United Kingdom and United States of America Perspectives on Investor Protection* (Routledge 2022), 139.

31 Such as the EU and the UK.

32 See AIFMD art 15.

33 See UCITS art 29 and AIFMD art 5; in the UK, see 6.6.25 of FCA's Collective Investment Schemes Sourcebook.

34 In the UK, see 6.6B.16 of the FCA's Collective Investment Schemes Sourcebook. In the EU, UCITS art 22 and AIFMD art 21. In Hong Kong, see SFC Handbook for Unit Trusts and Mutual Funds, Investment-Linked Assurance Schemes, Chapter 4 (Trustee/Custodian). In Singapore, see the Code on Collective Investment Schemes, page 8.

35 With reference to the US, see the Adviser Act, § 275.206(4)-2 Custody of funds or securities of clients by investment advisers.

36 In trust-based models a trustee bank may operate as a custodian/depositary.

37 See Technical Committee of The International Organization of Securities Commissions, 'Survey of Regimes for the Protection, Distribution and/or Transfer of Client Assets – Final Report' (The International Organization of Securities Commissions March 2011).

olution framework is that resolution tools, particularly the bail-in tool, may not apply to these assets and money.[38]

4.2 Constraints on the Fund's Composition

If the provisions considered above are intended to set the general operating conditions for mutual funds, regulatory frameworks across all jurisdictions show that specific set of rules exist, which are intended to constrain the managers' discretion in composing funds' investment portfolios and, more in general, in allocating funds' resources. These limits are primarily intended to address financial stability issues stemming from maturity, liquidity or credit risk transformation that collective investment schemes perform.

Such rules are at the crossroads between investor protection and financial stability regulation, insofar as their ultimate purpose is to avoid investors' 'runs' from open-end funds by removing any incentive to strategic behaviours (owing to the existence of a 'first-mover advantage') by unitholders.[39]

Given the impact that runs may have on the broader financial system (through the channels and drivers discussed above, Section 2), it is not by chance that, in respect of this topic, regulatory convergence is mainly driven by the policy-making activity of the Financial Stability Board[40] and of IOSCO.[41]

All relevant jurisdictions are aligned with these policy recommendations, which require both *pre-emptive* measures, such as limits on eligible assets and portfolio concentration for open-end funds,[42] provision of so-called swing prices (which tend to neutralize the 'first mover advantage')[43] and the set-up of sound internal arrangements and programmes for managing liquidity (together with reporting duties),[44] and *post-event measures* such as the

---

38 See FSB, 'Key Attributes of Effective Resolution Regimes for Financial Institutions' (FSB October 2014), app II–Annex 3.

39 See John Armour and others, *Principles of Financial Regulation* (OUP 2016), 478ff.; Financial Stability Board, 'Assessment of the Effectiveness of the FSB's 2017 Recommendations on Liquidity Mismatch in Open-Ended Funds' (Financial Stability Board December 2022); Michael Grill and others, 'Liquidity Transformation by Investment Funds: Structural Fault Line or Desirable Financial Transformation? A Systemic Perspective' (European Central Bank 2023) <https://www.ecb.europa.eu/pub/financial-stability/macroprudential-bulletin/html/ecb.mpbu202104_1~70b30f25c9.en.html>.

40 See Financial Stability board, 'Policy Recommendations to Address Structural Vulnerabilities from Asset Management Activities' (Financial Stability Board January 2017).

41 IOSCO, 'Recommendations for Liquidity Risk Management for Collective Investment Schemes Final Report' (International Organization of Securities Commissions February 2018).

42 Technical aspects of these rules vary across jurisdictions, provided that in all jurisdictions open-end funds promising to redeem at par value can only invest in liquid assets.

43 Importantly, in the US an amendment proposal to the Investment Company Act has been made, in order to better regulate 'swing prices': see SEC Document 87 FR 77172. Besides, alternative funds and hedge funds may have 'gates', that is minimum holding periods or other pre-determined limitations to redemptions.

44 See UCITS arts 50–53, AIFMD arts 16 and 25, § 270.22e-4 (Liquidity Risk Management Programs) of the Investment Company Act.

possibility to limit or freeze redemptions in exceptional circumstances, redemption in-kind or the resort to liquidity 'side-pockets'.

Similarly, as excessive leverage can adversely impact the fund's ability to meet its obligations *vis-à-vis* both investors and counterparties, it can be a potential source of creation or amplification of risks to the global financial system through several channels. Consequently, the fund's leverage is limited (to a lower or higher extent based on the nature of the fund) and subject to reporting requirements to competent authorities.

9. Investment platforms regulation

Eugenia Macchiavello

1. INVESTMENT-BASED CROWDFUNDING: MAIN CHARACTERISTICS UNDER A FUNCTIONAL APPROACH

Modern crowdfunding started in the early 2000s to facilitate donations and micro-loans but soon developed worldwide to occupy also credit and investment markets,[1] spurred on by the global financial crisis and its consequent banking credit crunch as well as distrust towards traditional finance. It now represents a market of nearly $114 billion worldwide, with North America leading the way by market size.[2]

This chapter focuses on financial-return crowdfunding ('FRC'), also called 'investment crowdfunding',[3] generally defined as an open call from entrepreneurs/consumers addressed to a multitude of internet users to receive small contributions (when individually considered) in the form of loans (lending-based crowdfunding, LBC) or investments (investment-based crowdfunding, IBC) in specific projects, usually through specialized online platforms.[4]

Business models deployed by crowdfunding service providers (CSPs) can vary too: under the basic model ('client-segregated account'), they facilitate the financing transaction between project owners and crowd-lenders/investors, putting them in contact through the publication of funding requests on an online platform. However, the CSPs can also pre-screen applicants, provide pricing and contractual templates, and handle money transfers. Most platforms also handle the contractual relationships between clients, including information flow, servicing and mandate to renegotiate and/or vote. Especially in LBC, CSPs might even adopt models allow-

---

1 Aki Kallio and Lasse Vuola, 'History of Crowdfunding in the Context of Ever-Changing Modern Financial Markets' in Rotem Shneor, Liang Zhao, Bjørn-Tore Flåten (eds), *Advances in Crowdfunding* (Palgrave Macmillan 2020). The author is grateful to Chiara Valenti for her valuable research assistance and to the participants of the authors' workshop (E&Y Amsterdam and ACLE, 20–21 April 2023) and referees for their insightful feedback. A pre-referee and longer version is available on SSRN.

2 The 2020 main market shares were: USA and Canada (65%), UK (11%), Europe (9%), Asia and Pacific (excluding China) (8%). Singapore and Australia were, respectively, the first and second country in Asia for equity crowdfunding: Taria Ziegler and others, 'The 2nd Global Alternative Finance Market Benchmarking Report' (2021) <https://www.jbs.cam.ac.uk/wp-content/uploads/2021/06/ccaf-2021-06-report-2nd-global-alternative-finance-benchmarking-study-report.pdf>.

3 On the regulation in Europe of non-financial/non-investment crowdfunding, please see Eugenia Macchiavello and Chiara Valenti, 'Beyond the ECSPR and Financial-return: The Regulation of Donation and Reward-based Crowdfunding in the EU' in Eugenia Macchiavello (ed.), *Regulation on European Crowdfunding Service Providers for Business: A Commentary* (Edward Elgar Publishing 2022) 619ff.

4 See Eugenia Macchiavello, 'Introduction to the Crowdfunding Regulation' and Rotem Shneor, 'The Context: The Crowdfunding Market and its Recent Developments', in Macchiavello (n 3), 2ff, 15ff.

ing the automatic matching of crowd-lenders' preferences with crowd-borrowers' characteristics and/or offer guarantee funds to (partially) cover clients' losses. Under the 'notary model', a bank originates the loans and then resells the credit rights to a Special Purpose Vehicle (SPV) created by the CSP and issues notes to crowd-lenders, also coping with regulatory restrictions (banking monopoly, Germany and Korea; State-based banking licences, USA). Finally, the CSP might collect resources from crowd-lenders/investors through the issuance of financial instruments (itself or through *ad hoc* SPVs or investment funds) and then lend/invest such resources on its own account to project owners ('balance-sheet' model, USA, Australia and Canada), sometimes guaranteeing a certain return to investors ('guaranteed-return' model). Some platforms, mostly LBC, also offer crowd-lenders the opportunity to re-sell their rights to the platform (early reimbursement) or on P2P marketplaces ('bulletin boards').

Crowdfunding has been regarded as a useful tool to meet the under/unmet financing needs of consumers and businesses (especially, start-ups and small and micro-enterprises, SMEs), as well as investors' need for diversified alternative investments finance and desire for a more 'democratic' and 'disintermediated' financial system, directly connecting financers and finances and reducing the traditional chain of financial intermediation. However, crowdfunding platforms' activities present similarities to traditional financial services, suggesting a 're-intermediation' phenomenon and an at least partial role of crowdfunding platforms as gatekeepers.[5]

Although relevant differences exist among countries, LBC has been associated with credit intermediation, banking/lending and payment services, while IBC has been associated with with investment services, in particular reception and transmission of orders, underwriting without firm commitment (sometimes also investment advice, markets and execution).[6] Nonetheless, some countries, and the EU recently, have underlined the resemblance of LBC to investment services and public investment offerings, facilitating the transfer of financial resources between parties through the reduction of information asymmetries and transaction costs. From an economic point of view, a crowd-loan is very close to a bond,[7] although relevant differences might exist, also from a legal perspective, in terms of transferability and rights attached (making LBC a new asset class).

However, crowdfunding also presents special features, which might influence its legal classification and treatment such as: the expectation also of non-financial rewards (e.g. personal satisfaction from influencing a campaign's outcome with shared principles and sense

---

5 About financial sector's gatekeepers, see: Jennifer Payne, 'The Role of Gatekeepers' in Niamh Moloney, Eilís Ferran and Jennifer Payne (eds), *Oxford Handbook of Financial Regulation* (OUP 2015) 254. On crowdfunding and disintermediation/re-intermediation, see: Eugenia Macchiavello, 'The Licensing Principle and Investment-based Crowdfunding' in Dária M Vicente, Diogo Duarte and Catarina Granadeiro (eds), *Fintech Regulation and the Licensing Principle* (EBI 2023), 46–70; Fatjon Kaja, Edoardo D Martino and Alessio M Pacces, 'Fintech and the Law and Economics of Disintermediation' in Iris Chiu and Gudula Deipenbrock (eds), *Routledge Handbook of Financial Technology and Law* (Routledge 2021), 78ff.

6 Macchiavello (n 3) 44–67; Eugenia Macchiavello, 'Disintermediation in Fund-raising: Marketplace Investing Platforms and EU Financial Regulation', in Chiu and Deipenbrock (n 5), 291–306.

7 Commission, 'Impact Assessment Accompanying the Document Proposal for a Regulation on European Crowdfunding Service Providers (ECSP) for Business' (8 March 2018).

of involvement);[8] the importance assigned by crowd-investors to soft information, 'signals' and non-financial factors, pitches and forums[9] rather than financial statements;[10] alternative risk-mitigation instruments (mandatory diversification, 'all-or-nothing' rule,[11] co-investing).[12]

This chapter analyses the regulatory approaches towards crowdfunding in various countries/regions (EU, UK, USA, Singapore and Australia), comparing the main solutions adopted by each in terms of tools generally deployed in financial regulation (e.g. the main framework, organizational/prudential requirements, investor protection, etc.) to attain the fundamental financial regulation goals (e.g. stability, investor protection, efficiency, etc.), highlighting similarities, differences and the level of relevant interests protected.

2. REGULATORY APPROACH: OVERVIEW OF THE MAIN LEGAL FRAMEWORK, CLASSIFICATION OF THE ACTIVITY/PRODUCTS AND AUTHORIZATION

2.1 The Main Legal Framework: New Special Regulation versus Application of Traditional Financial Regulation, Scope and Different Balance of Regulatory Goals

All of the analysed jurisdictions have decided to address crowdfunding in their regulations with the objective of facilitating SMEs' access to finance while protecting platforms' clients. Nonetheless, in doing so, they also present different approaches which reflect different regulatory priorities: the USA and Singapore show a more 'traditional' approach, introducing limited exemptions within the pre-existing legal framework focused on issuers' duties and thus favouring the level-playing field and, in the USA case, investor protection; on the opposite side, the EU has introduced a special regime for exemption from the mainstream framework and is willing to sacrifice some traditional safeguards to expand SMEs' financing opportunities and favour cross-border competition; the UK and Australia, instead, present a hybrid system, having introduced special rules only for certain crowdfunding models, and focus on platforms' duties.

2.2 The 'Traditional' Approach: Securities Regulation with Limited Exemptions and Main Burden on Issuers (USA and Singapore)

In both the USA and Singapore, a very broad concept of securities is deployed, therefore covering also the notes issued by crowdfunding platforms within a 'notary' business model

---

[8] Anna Lukkarinen, 'Equity Crowdfunding: Principles and Investor Behaviour', in Shneor, Zhao and Flåten, (n 1) 96ff.

[9] Macchiavello (n 6) 49–50.

[10] Lukkarinen (n 8) 99.

[11] I.e. issuers obtain the financing only if the campaign reaches the declared target amount, convincing enough investors.

[12] Eugenia Macchiavello, 'The Crowdfunding Regulation in the Context of the Capital Markets Union' in Pietro Ortolani and Marije Louisse (eds), *The EU Crowdfunding Regulation* (OUP 2021) 25–46.

(USA)[13] and invitations to lend money (Singapore).[14] As a consequence, all crowdfunding offers and issuers as well as platforms as intermediaries are subject – in principle – to the whole set of securities regulation and to supervision (but this appears quite light in Singapore).[15] Crowdfunding issuers might benefit from general exemptions such as 'small offerings' (not above $5 million in the USA; SG$5 million in Singapore) or 'private offerings' (reserved to 'accredited investors', i.e. professional investors and experienced high-net-worth individuals),[16] subject anyway to significant limitations and extensive disclosure obligations.

While Singapore introduced such exemptions only in 2016 and to support in general SMEs and their financing needs,[17] the 2012 USA Jumpstart Our Business Startups Act (JOBS Act), with a dedicated title III (CROWDFUND Act),[18] introduced, in addition, a special exemption from the Securities Act for small offerings of securities and intermediated by regulated brokers[19] or new specialized funding portals,[20] both members of the Financial Industry

13 See *In re Prosper Marketplace, Inc.*, Securities Act Release No 8984, SEC LEXIS 279124 (November 2008) <http://www.sec.gov/litigation/admin/2008/33-8984.pdf>, applying the well-established doctrine *SEC v. W. J. Howey Co.*, 328 U.S. 293 (1946) and *Reves v. Ernst & Young*, 494 U.S. 56 (1990).

14 Debentures offering includes 'any invitation to a person [...] to lend money to an entity' or 'any document [...] issued by an entity acknowledging [...] the indebtedness of the entity in respect of any money [...] lent [...] in response to such an invitation' (except the offer of units in collective investment schemes) (since 2018, Part I, sec 2; 239 SFA).

15 For the USA: Securities Act of 1933, 15 USC §77a ff (2022) on the registration of securities with the SEC and their offering to the public; Securities Exchange Act of 1934, 15 USC §78a ff (2022) on disclosures, secondary markets and intermediaries.

16 In the USA, there is also the 'intrastate offering' exemption (for local offerings). Cf secs 4(a)(2) and 4(a)(5) of the Securities Act and the SEC's Regulation D and Regulation A. In Singapore: Securities and Futures Act §§240, 239(3); §272A, §272B, §274, §275: §4A(1)(a); MAS, 'Securities and futures Act (cap 289) financial advisers Act (cap 110)-FAQs on lendingbased crowdfunding' (2018), A16 <https://www.mas.gov.sg/-/media/mas/regulations-and-financial-stability/regulations-guidance-and-licensing/securities-futures-and-fund-management/regulations-guidance-and-licensing/faqs/faqs-on-lendingbased-crowdfunding-8-oct-18.pdf>; Christian Hofmann, 'Crowdfunding Regulation in Singapore' in Caroline Kleiner (ed.) *Legal Aspects of Crowdfunding* (Springer 2021) 401.

17 Pornchai Wisuttisak, Nguyen Ba Binh and Andrew Terry, 'Regulatory Frameworks of Crowdfunding for Startups in Singapore, Thailand, and Vietnam' in Farhad Taghizadeh-Hesary, Roohallah Aboojafari and Naoyuki Yoshino (eds), *Innovative Finance for Technological Progress* (Routledge 2022) 117; Swee Liang Tan, Yoke W Tok and Chansriniyom Thitipat, 'Financing Singapore's SMEs and the Crowdfunding Industry in Singapore' in Hian T Hoon (ed.), *The Singapore Economy: Dynamism and Inclusion. Research Collection School of Economics* (Singapore, 2021) 22ff. See <https://www.mas.gov.sg/news/parliamentary-replies/2016/reply-to-parliamentary-question-on-the-new-licensing-regime-for-crowdfunding-platforms>.

18 This Act was complemented by the 2015 SEC Crowdfunding Regulation: SEC Rules 80 FR 71387.

19 Authorized under sec 15(b) Exchange Act.

20 Authorized under the new sec 4A(a)(1) Securities Act and rule 400 Crowdfunding Regulation. Härkönen, 'ECSPR versus the United States Crowdfunding Regime', in Macchiavello (n 3), 796–807, 796.

Regulatory Authority (FINRA) and subject to a light regime, stricter for brokers.[21] Such exemption applies to any type of security offerings up to $5 million (as raised in 2021) but only when issued by domestic companies, with the exclusion of certain types of entities[22] and limitations in the use of SPV.[23]

In Singapore, instead, platforms facilitating securities issuance need one of the following authorizations for traditional regulated activities: a Capital Markets Services (CMS) licence under the Singapore's Securities and Futures Act (SFA) from the Monetary Authority of Singapore (MAS), for the service 'dealing in securities'[24] or as an 'adviser on corporate finance' and an 'adviser on securities' (which covers also indirect advice and publication of research analysis).[25] When acting as a professional lender or agent of the same in respect to loans to consumers, the platform needs to obtain a licence as money lender from the Singapore's Registrar of Moneylenders (Ministry of Law).[26] Instead, platforms resorting

---

21 FINRA is a not-for-profit organization overseeing broker-dealers. See Härkönen (n 20) 799. Registration with the SEC consists in simply submitting an online form, disclosing disciplinary history, compensation, client money protection, main shareholders and non-securities activities, and becoming a FINRA member. Brokers present stricter requirements (e.g. professional requirements of associated persons; minimum capital ranging from $5,000 – when not holding clients' funds/ securities- to $250,000): 17 CFR §240.15c3-1. On the other hand, portals are limited intermediaries and cannot hold clients' money/securities or offer other types of services: see 17 CFR §227.402(b); Securities Exchange Act sec 3(a)(80); sec 304(b) JOBS Act; Yanzhe Li, 'The regulation of equity crowdfunding in the US: remaining concerns and lessons from the UK' (2022) 22(2) J Corp Law Stud 265 (online issue 1), 7–8; Härkönen (n 20) 800–801.

22 In particular, investment companies, Special Purpose Acquisition Companies (SPAC), companies having already filed – or failed to provide – reports with the SEC under the Securities Exchange Act and 'bad actors' issuer (i.e. disqualified for business practices violations or felonies): 17 CFR §227.503; Härkönen (n 20) 802.

23 A 2019 review has allowed SPV structures in crowdfunding only when the SPV acts solely as a conduit for investments in an issuer and under certain conditions, such as investors having the same economic exposure, voting power, and disclosures as in case of direct crowdfunding investments: New Investment Company Act Rule 3a-9i; <https://www.sec.gov/corpfin/facilitating-capital-formation-secg>.

24 Under the CMS or the Financial Advisers Act (FAA). Cf Securities and Futures Act §342 Second Schedule, Regulated Activities Part I; MAS 2018; MAS, 'Securities and Futures Act (cap. 289) FAQs on Licensing and Business Conduct (Other than for Fund Management Companies)' (rev. July 2022), No 2 and 4 <https://www.mas.gov.sg/-/media/mas/regulations-and-financial-stability/regulations-guidance-and-licensing/securities-futures-and-fund-management/regulations-guidance-and-licensing/faqs/faqs-on-licensing-and-business-conduct-other-than-for-fund-management-companies_18-jul-22.pdf>. Hofman (n 16) 397, 402; Wisuttisak (n 17) 107. Financial Advisers Act, c. 110, §2, Second Schedule; Hofmann (n 16) 406–407.

25 SFA ibidem; Financial Advisers Act, c 110, §6.

26 Moneylenders Act §5(5)(c), § 2(e)(ii)–(iii), §§2, 5; Tan and others (n 17). The initial minimum capital requirement for moneylenders is a deposit of SG$20,000; for CMA license holders offering IBC: SDG50,000 (since 2016) in case of clients accredited investors and SDG500,000 in case of retail investors. MAS in 2016 removed the SG$100,000 security deposit for CSPs but only when not handling customer monies/assets, not acting as principal in transactions and raising funds only from accredited/institutional investors: Hofmann (n 16) 396ff; Tan and others (n 17) 22–23.

to (alternative) collective investment schemes through limited partnerships remain mostly unregulated.[27]

2.3 In the Middle: Special Rules only for Certain Models and Regulatory Focus on Platforms (UK and Australia)

The UK and Australia show a similar but symmetrical approach to regulating crowdfunding: they both focus on the intermediary role played by platforms and regulate separately IBC and LBC but special rules have been reserved only, in the UK, to LBC and, in Australia, to IBC.

In more detail, the FCA (British financial conduct authority) regards investment-based crowdfunding services as falling within existing investment services,[28] in particular as brokerage-like services ('arranging deals in investments'[29] or 'making arrangements with a view to transactions in investments'[30]) or, depending on the specific model, also operating/managing an unregulated collective investment scheme or alternative investment fund (AIF) or (more rarely) 'advising on investments' or 'managing investments'.[31] Consequently, a relevant bulk of financial regulation applies.[32] On the side of issuers, no special rules exist but the general Prospectus exemption typically applies (total consideration in 12 months not above €8 million).[33] On the contrary, LBC was added in 2014 in the FCA handbook as the new regulated activity of 'operating an electronic system in relation to lending' and, in particular, to P2P agreements of art 36H, which are loans, only facilitated by a platform, where the borrower is an individual[34] and either the loan does not exceed £25,000 or it is not wholly/predominantly for business. Requirements for LBC platforms have grown progressively also following market developments, showing LBC to be more complex and varied models compared with

---

27 Hofmann (n 16) 403.

28 Part 4a FSMA, sec 55A.

29 The Financial Services and Markets Act 2000 (Regulated Activities) Order 2001 (RAO) art 25(1).

30 RAO art 25(2).

31 Respectively, arts 21, 53 and 37 RAO. See Kirstene Baillie, 'Regulation of Crowdfunding in the UK: Past, Present and Future' (2019) 20 Bus L Int'l 148.

32 E.g. the Financial Services and Markets Act (FSMA) 2000, its secondary acts (e.g. RAO) and relative FCA handbooks on principles for businesses (PRIN), senior management arrangements, systems and controls (SYSC), investment conduct of business sourcebook (COBS) (mainly derived from MiFID II), client assets rules (CASS), and, more recently, financial promotions (see §4.4). Minimum capital requirements for FCA licences range from £50,000 (e.g. reception and transmission of orders only and without holding clients' funds/securities) to £730,000 depending on the type of service.

33 FSMA 2000, s 86(1).

34 I.e. a natural person, a partnership or an unincorporated body of persons.

equity-based crowdfunding (EBC).[35] In the case of borrowers who are also consumers, the 1974 Consumer Credit Act and FCS consumer credit rules (CONC) apply too.[36]

Australia, instead, introduced special rules for IBC starting in 2017[37] subjecting small issuers to simplified disclosure obligations. The regime covers the offering of ordinary shares of Australian unlisted public companies with less than A$25 million in assets and annual turnover and proprietary companies with certain characteristics[38] offered to retail investors through an online platform.[39] Such platforms, when offering crowdfunding services related to securities (e.g. shares or debentures), conduct a regulated activity[40] requiring an Australian financial service (AFS) license and the compliance with financial regulation (with specific requirements).[41] LBC is subject to general financial regulation in all respects: since platforms generally use a collective 'managed investment scheme' (MIS) model, they are subject to the relative regime but they must obtain an AFS licence and publish an investment plan/constitution only when the fund presents more than 20 members or is promoted by a professional person among retail investors.[42] In principle, other possible classifications of LBC services, requiring again an AFS licence, are 'financial product advice'[43] in the case of scoring/ranking of borrowers[44] or 'arranging for a person to engage in dealing in financial products' or, when

---

35 See FCA, 'Loan-based ("peer-to-peer") and Investment-based Crowdfunding Platforms: Feedback on our Post-implementation Review and Proposed Changes to the Regulatory Framework' (2018) CP18/20 <www.fca.org.uk/publication/consultation/cp18-20.pdf>; Francesco D Pascalis, 'Crowdlending and Crowdinvesting in Europe: A Comparative Analysis Between the UK and EU Regulatory Frameworks' in Macchiavello (n 3) 650–651.

36 See Gerard McMeel, 'Crowdfunding and UK Law', in Ortolani and Louisse (n 12) 70.

37 cf 2017 Corporations Amendment (Crowd-Sourced Funding) Act (and related Regulations), the following 2018 Corporations Amendment (Crowd-sourced Funding for Proprietary Companies Act) and minor modifications to the Australian Securities and Investments Commission (ASIC) Act 2001. See Andrew A Schwarz, *Investment Crowdfunding* (OUP 2023) ch 6, 143ff; Pelma Rajapakse, 'Regulatory and Policy Reforms in P2P Lending in Australia' in Pelma Rajapakse, Yinxu Huang and Hatsuru Morita, *Law and Practice of Crowdfunding and Peer-to-Peer Lending in Australia, China and Japan* (Springer 2022), 66ff. See <https://asic.gov.au/regulatory-resources/financial-services/crowd-sourced-funding//>.

38 At least two directors, annual financial and directors' reports, compliance with related party transaction rules.

39 738G–738H Corporations Act 2001; ASIC, 'Crowd-sourced Funding: Guide for Companies' (2020), RG 261.6 <https://download.asic.gov.au/media/5702668/rg261-published-19-june-2020-20200727.pdf>.

40 Cf part 6D.3A Corporations Act 2001. See ASIC, 'Crowd-sourced Funding: Guide for Intermediaries' (2018), 262.28 <https://download.asic.gov.au/media/cfxatjf5/rg262-published-18-october-2018-20220328.pdf>.

41 Section 738C Corporations Act.

42 Sections 601ED and 601FA Corporations Act. Investors are presumed retail unless certain conditions apply (e.g. price above A$500,000, non-small business, high net assets or gross income, professional investors; previous experience in using financial services): sec 761G Corporations Act; ASIC 2018 (n 40), RG 262.23; Rajapakse (n 37) 69.

43 Defined as recommendation/statement to influence an investment decision in relation to particular securities/interests in registered/unregistered MIS.

44 ibid 71.

the platform offers an organized market for shares/debentures, as regulated market.[45] When the borrower is a consumer (i.e. a natural person requesting a loan for consumption from a professional lender), the platform directly providing the loan or a credit-related service (e.g. intermediation, right exercise in debt collection) needs a licence as credit provider,[46] with requirements similar to those of the AFS.[47]

2.4 A Separate and Special Regime for Crowdfunding: Simplifying Investment Firms' Framework (EU)

The regulatory treatment of crowdfunding among European Member States has been extremely fragmented for many years.[48] Harmonization has been reached only through the adoption of the EU regulation No 1503/2020 on crowdfunding service providers for business (hereinafter, ECSPR),[49] with the relevant exclusion of P2P consumer lending. The ECSPR introduces a new special EU-wide licence and regime for new intermediaries, in exemption, under certain conditions, from MiFID II and Prospectus Regulation (PR) requirements, assigning the supervision of the activities to the national competent authority (generally, the financial one). It covers the offer of transferable securities (e.g. shares and bonds) and/or admitted instruments for crowdfunding purposes (i.e. shares of private limited companies not considered transferable securities by national law) and business loans (where unconditional and onerous), up to €5 million in total consideration,[50] through a crowdfunding platform. The use of SPV is limited only in the case of indivisible and illiquid assets.[51]

Therefore, ECSPR regulates both the offerings (through issuers' disclosure obligations) and the intermediaries operating such platforms and conducting crowdfunding services, focusing in particular on platforms' requirements inspired by MiFID II but with simplifications and some original instruments. Crowdfunding services are identified with the 'matching of business funding interest of investors and project owners through the use of a crowdfunding platform' and consisting of the facilitation of granting of (business) loans and/or the joint provision of placing without firm commitment and reception and transmission of orders, as identified in MiFID II (art 2(1)(a) ECSPR). The regulation allows and seems to consider as 'core' crowdfunding services the use of filtering systems based on objective factors (e.g. economic sector, risk category, interest rate), while pricing/scoring of offers and, further, portfolio management of loans (even when algorithmic-based) are subjected to additional and

---

45 Section 767A Corporations Act 2001; ASIC 2018 (n 40), RG 262.17; Rajapakse (n 37) 85.

46 Under the National Consumer Credit Protection Act 2009 (sec 6) and its Schedule 1 (National Credit Code).

47 ASIC 2020 (n 39); Rajapakse (n 37) 75–76.

48 Macchiavello (n 6).

49 Regulation (EU) 2020/1503 [...] of 7 October 2020 on European Crowdfunding Service Providers for Business, and Amending Regulation (EU) 2017/1129 and Directive (EU) 2019/1937 [2020] OJ L347/1 [hereinafter ECSPR].

50 For such threshold also offers of the same issuer covered by the PR 'small offers' exemption, up to €1–8 million, are relevant.

51 ECSPR recital 22 and art 3(6); ESMA, 'Questions and Answers on the European Crowdfunding Service Providers for Business Regulation' (updated 8 March 2023) ESMA35-42-1088, sec 1 (ESMA Q&A).

stricter requirements and might be regarded as ancillary services.[52] P2P consumer lending and crowdfunding offered through other types of services (e.g. financial advice, collective investment schemes, trading venues) remain subject to their respective national/EU regimes[53] and authorizations, which might be separately obtained by CSPs.

3. ORGANIZATIONAL AND PRUDENTIAL REQUIREMENTS

3.1 Conflict of Interest Rules

Agency problems are particularly relevant in a crowdfunding context, considering the particular intermediary role played by platforms, screening borrowers/investees without bearing the risks. Therefore, most regimes require CSPs to have systems/measures to deal with conflicts of interest (the UK,[54] the EU[55] and Australia[56]) and limit or prohibit inducements. In particular, platforms cannot obtain compensation for the solicitation/promotion of offers (USA, EU, Australia in case of retail advice)[57] or direct investors to particular offers but can make available for investors search engines or highlight certain offers based on objective criteria. In the UK, the solicitation must be approved by an authorized person but in 2022 monetary/non-monetary benefits incentivizing promotions for high-risk investments were banned.[58]

The EU and USA present additional, although different, restrictions in this area: the US prohibits platform's managers and main shareholders from having financial participation in the offers/issuers, while allowing the CSP itself to invest under certain conditions;[59] the ECSPR, instead, prohibits the CSP from investing in project owners but allows its managers/

---

52 See ESMA 'Q&A', sec 3.2.

53 The ECSPR does not mention crowdfunding of DLT-based financial instruments but these might be covered by ECSPR, DLT-pilot and/or MiFID II. Crowdfunding offered through investment advice or the operation of a trading venue is subject to MiFID II/MiFIR or national law (when the advice is exempted under MiFID II art 3(1)), while through collective investment schemes to AIFMD/national law. See Macchiavello (n 3) 50, 62–67.

54 Principle 8 and SYSC 10.1.3R. The preferential treatment of institutional investors over retail ones is prohibited: FCA, 'Interim Feedback to the Call for Input to the Post-implementation Review of the FCA's Crowdfunding Rules', 16/13, 12 <https://www.fca.org.uk/publication/feedback/fs16-13.pdf>.

55 ECSPR art 4(1) and 8.

56 s912A(1)(aa) Corporations Act 2001.

57 ECSPR art 3(3); 17 CFR §227.402(b); Australian s963A Corporations Act 2001.

58 FCA, 'Strengthening our Financial Promotion Rules for High-risk Investments and Firms Approving Financial Promotions', PS22/10, <https://www.fca.org.uk/publication/policy/ps22-10.pdf>; Li (n 21) 25; Härkönen (n 20) 801.

59 E.g. same conditions as offered to other investors and in exchange for the services provided: 15 USC §77d-1 (a)(11); 17 CFR §227.300(b). See Härkönen (n 20) 801. Beside this, the US does not set a general conflict of interest regime: Li (n 21) 25.

shareholders to do so under certain conditions.[60] Australian CSPs cannot offer to investors financial assistance to buy shares.[61]

3.2 Organizational and Prudential Requirements

In addition to general requirements of adequate organization, most jurisdictions impose on CSPs the requirement of adequate risk management systems and governance arrangements, including outsourcing rules (UK, Singapore, Australia) and continuity arrangements (UK, EU). Nonetheless, additional risk management rules for LBC exist in some countries. The UK has, since 2019, imposed the presence of an independent risk management function and permanent effective independent compliance function (conditional to a proportionality principle), independent internal audit function and rules on credit risk assessment. Additional and stricter rules have been introduced, in the UK, EU and Singapore, for more complex models entailing the provision by the platform of pricing or, further, portfolio management, concerning among other things, money allocation, minimum basis and timing for credit risk assessment, portfolio composition, calculation methods and contingent funds.[62]

Prudential requirements used to be reserved to large and systemic intermediaries, in particular with liquidity/maturity transformation functions. Nonetheless, especially after the global financial crisis, such requirements have been expanded in coverage also to market-based intermediaries with broker-like functions (e.g. Investment Firms Directive/Regulation, IFD/IFR,[63] in Europe). However, crowdfunding platforms might present a low systemic risk relevance, especially in some countries, to justify no or low requirements. In the UK, Australia and Singapore, IBC platforms must comply with investment firms' prudential requirements for operational risks (but Australia adds also crowdfunding-tailored surplus liquid funds and

---

60 E.g. disclosure to clients, investors' equal treatment and access to information. Instead, crowdfunding service providers cannot accept their own managers, relevant shareholders and employees as project owners: ECSPR art 8(1)–(2).

61 RG 262.191.

62 For the ECSPR (very detailed): arts 4(2)–(4) and 6(1)–(2); Macchiavello (n 6) 49. For UK: COBS 18.12.5R–COBS 18.12.10R; COBS 18.12.11R–COBS 18.12.17R; Peter Chapman, 'Crowdfunding', in Jelena Madir (ed.), *Fintech. Law and Regulation* (2nd edn, Edward Elgar Publishing 2021) 64–89, at 75–76; Pascalis (n 35) 653. In Singapore, the use of auto-allocation tools requires platforms, in addition, to 'educate users and warn them about [the] limitations' of such systems: MAS, 'Circular No CMI 27/2018 – Controls and Disclosures to be Implemented by Licensed Securities-based Crowdfunding Operators' (rev. 2021), No 14 <https://www.mas.gov.sg/-/media/mas/regulations-and-financial-stability/regulations-guidance-and-licensing/securities-futures-and-fund-management/regulations-guidance-and-licensing/circulars/cmi-272018-controls-and-disclosures-implemented-by-licensed-sec-based-crowdfunding-operators-210310.pdf>.

63 Directive (EU) 2019/878 of 20 May 2019 amending Directive 2013/36/EU as regards exempted entities, financial holding companies, mixed financial holding companies, remuneration, supervisory measures and powers and capital conservation measures [2019] OJ L 150/253 and Regulation (EU) 2019/876 of 20 May 2019 amending Regulation (EU) No 575/2013 as regards the leverage ratio, the net stable funding ratio, requirements for own funds and eligible liabilities, counterparty credit risk, market risk, exposures to central counterparties, exposures to collective investment undertakings, large exposures, reporting and disclosure requirements and Regulation (EU) No 648/2012 [2019] OJ L 150/1.

cash requirements),[64] while the USA set general net capital requirements only for brokers (not platforms).[65] Special requirements are set for LBC in the UK[66] and for all platforms in the EU (following an IFD/IFR-like approach but lighter than class-3 firms).[67]

4. CLIENT PROTECTION: CONDUCT REQUIREMENTS AND DISCLOSURE

4.1 General Conduct Rules

Considering the typical agency problems affecting crowdfunding, conduct rules and transparency requirements are particularly important, especially to protect investors. Most jurisdictions apply the same general conduct requirements as for investment firms.

EU CSPs are required to act honestly, fairly and professionally in the clients' best interests (art 3 ECSPR; cf. MiFID II). Specific and detailed duties are established for complex models (e.g. loan portfolio management: art 3(4)–(5)). In the UK, IBC and – since 2019 – LBC providers are subject to both the general FCA handbook principles and general conduct requirements specific for CF platforms indicated in Conduct of Business Sourcebook (COBS; the latter actionable in Court and derived from MiFID II), with standards comparable with those of the ECSPR.[68]

US brokers and funding portals, as FINRA intermediaries, must meet 'high standards of commercial honour and just and equitable principles of trade'.[69] Moreover, special requirements apply to CSPs: communications 'must be based on principles of fair dealing and good faith and must be fair and balanced'.[70] Similar general conduct requirements exist in Australia but only for collective investment schemes licensed to offer to retail investors (not for unregistered ones).[71]

---

64 In particular, 5% of projected/actual cash outflow: ASIC, 'AFS Licensing: Financial Requirements' RG166 (2022), 166.365ff; ASIC Corporations (Financial Requirements for CSF Intermediaries) Instrument 2017/339 <https://www.legislation.gov.au/Details/F2017L01215/Html/Text#_Toc493600973>; Corporations Acts 912A; ASIC 2018 (n 40), 262.28ff; Rajapakse (n 37) 73.

65 Exchange Act Rule 15(c)3-1.

66 The higher between £50,000 and a percentage of loaned funds (0.2% for the first £50 million; 0.15% for the next £200 million; 0.1% for the next £250 million; 0.05% of any remaining balance above £500 million): FCA handbook IPRU-INV 12.2; Chapman (n 63) 73.

67 The higher between €25,000 and one-quarter of overheads of the previous year in the form of CET1 or professional insurance or a combination of the two (ECSPR art 11).

68 COBS 2.1.1R and MiFID II art 24(1) (see also FCA Handbook PRIN, 2 and 6); COBS 4.2.1 R; MiFID II arts 24(3) and 30(1) (see FCA Handbook PRIN, 7). See also Chapman (n 62) 75.

69 See FINRA, 'Funding Portal Rules', 200(a) <https://www.finra.org/rules-guidance/rulebooks/funding-portal-rules/200>.

70 Li (n 21) 9.

71 Sect 601FC and 601FD-FE.

4.2 Disclosure Requirements

Disclosure is at the centre of FRC regimes to reduce information asymmetry (particularly high in the case of SMEs) and generally entails exemption from Prospectus or similar requirements, while introducing special (lighter) transparency rules. Particular emphasis is assigned to the clarity and simplicity of language considering the typical retail nature of investors and lack of intermediaries' support. As later explained, some jurisdictions impose disclosure mainly on issuers, others on platforms, and yet others on both.

4.2.1 Issuers' disclosure

Issuers must generally prepare a special document based on a template, with only key information – to focus investors' attention on the most important aspects – and in simple terms (EU, Australian EBC) about the CSP, project, offering and products (price, rights, risks and risk mitigation), including special warnings (EU, USA). In particular, EU project owners must prepare a very short and simple Key Investor Information Sheet (KIIS), then make it available by CSPs to investors (even sophisticated/professional ones) with reference to any particular offer (art 23). Australian EBC issuers must similarly prepare an offer document, including financial statements.[72] If the EU CSP offers portfolio management of loans, it is responsible for preparing itself the KIIS, focusing the information on the selection criteria, portfolio composition methods and diversification strategies (art 24).

The US regime appears one of the strictest for issuers, who must fill a standard format (form C) with specific information about themselves,[73] the offering (e.g. intended use of the proceeds, target amount and price), securities[74] and investors' rights, including reviewed/certified financial statements. Moreover, they must also provide progress updates when reaching 50/100% of the target amount,[75] and ongoing disclosures,[76] which might be expensive while not particularly informative and too complex for unassisted retail investors.[77] Investors have an explicit right of action against issuers for omissions or fraudulent statements (sec 4A(c)). Interestingly, both the USA and Singapore prohibit issuers from advertising the offering, except for directing investors to the funding portal.[78]

Instead, UK issuers are not required by law to prepare alternative documents. Similarly, in Singapore, FRC offers are generally exempted from Prospectus requirements and the offeror,

---

72 Schwarz (n 37) ch 6. ASIC (n39), RG 261.132.

73 In particular: directors and officers, large shareholders, ownership and capital structure, business, number of employees, financial condition of the issuer and particular risks.

74 E.g. terms/rights, including aggregated amount, how valued, risks for minority shareholders, other exempted offerings: 17 CFR §227.203(a).

75 Unless the platform already updates investors in this regard: 17 CFR §227.203 (a)–(a)(3).

76 17 CFR §227.201–203.

77 Li (n 21) 11; Härkönen (n 20), 806.

78 Since 2021, communications with prospective investors are permitted to USA issuers once Form C is filed, under certain circumstances: 17 CFR §227.204. In Singapore, issuers can advertise exempted offers only to pre-identified persons (previous contacts or explicitly interested): MAS FAQ licensing, No 3; Hofmann (n 16) 401, 407. Contrary, EU issuers can market their own projects: ESMA 'Q&A' 5.7.

although not required to prepare another type of document,[79] must explicitly declare that the offer does not entail a prospectus[80] and presents resale restrictions.[81] Investors have anyway access to public company information, business reports and general meeting reports.[82]

4.2.2 CSPs' disclosure

CSPs must generally disclose key information in plain language about themselves, risks, costs, investors' rights, selection criteria and lack of traditional safeguards (the EU, the UK, Australia for EBC). Additional specifications depend on the service offered: European LBC CSPs must also disclose the default rates of the past 36 months (art 20) and, when offering credit scoring/pricing, the calculation method used and whether they use audited financial statements (art 19); if loan portfolio management is offered, a description of systems and procedures deployed for credit risk assessment must be provided, with portfolio composition and several additional items of information required when a contingent fund exists (art 6(2)–(6)); and CSPs operating bulletin boards must disclose their nature, the loan performance and, where present, pricing methodology (art 25).

In the UK, CSPs are only required to provide 'accurate and sufficient' information. However, the FCA, in reaction to inadequate market practices, has more recently specified the provision of information on themselves,[83] authorization, the performance expected, costs and charges, client money safeguards, risks and warnings[84] (including, recently for all high-risk investments, about the risk of losing all sums invested, with a link to further information).[85] While more specific risk disclosure requirements for IBC derive from art 24 MiFID II,[86] the 2019 reform introduced specifications for LBC,[87] such as information about borrowers' selection and loans' assessment/price, portfolio composition, the procedure for late payments/defaults, tax calculation, the lack of compensation schemes (portfolio management) or warnings on the risk of platform failure and, if present, on contingency funds, and ongoing disclosures (basic model), along with a basic written agreement with the essential rights and obligations.[88]

In Australia, there are differentiated duties: LBC platforms structured as unregistered investment funds are not subject to particular disclosure requirements. Instead, registered schemes must provide retail investors with a constitution/compliance plan[89] and a product disclosure statement (PDS), with information on the business structure, loans offered, matching system, interest rate calculation, returns, risks, the process for borrowers' assessment, fees/costs, withdrawal (where possible), protection measures and notion of default.[90] Retail

79 Hofmann (n 16) 415.
80 §272A(1)(b)(i).
81 §§272A(1)(b)(ii), (3), (8).
82 Wisuttisak (n 17) 106.
83 FCA COBS 6 and 2.2 (2023 version); Chapman (n 62) 78.
84 FCA COBS 2.2, 2.2A; 4.5; 4.5A.
85 New COBS 4.12A.11R; FCA, 'Strengthening our Financial Promotion Rules for High-risk Investments and Firms Approving Financial Promotions' (August 2022), PS22/10.
86 See COBS 2.2.A.
87 COBS 18.12.24R.
88 COBS 18.12.12R, 31R, 23R–38R. Baillie (n 31) 154; McMeel (n 36) 80–81.
89 Rajapakse (n 37) 79–80; ASIC (n 39).
90 Part 7.9. Corporations Act.

clients also benefit from ongoing/periodic disclosure and disclosure of material change.[91] If the LBC CSPs provide personal advice, another PDS is needed, with information regarding the characteristics of the financial product, applicable fees, risks and benefits. an EBC platform instead must prominently display only risk warnings, fees by companies or other parties and cooling-off rights.[92]

US CSPs' duties appear lighter, having to disclose information about their compensation and investment promoters and to merely provide investors with educational materials about crowdfunding and its risks.[93] Furthermore, CSPs must transfer to investors all information provided by an issuer no later than 21 days before any securities are sold to the same.[94] Interestingly, the US and Australian regimes require CSPs to establish communication channels between issuers and investors: in the USA, they should assume only a moderating role to protect clients' privacy,[95] while in Australia the communication facility works among companies, investors and the platform.[96]

Finally, Singaporean platforms must only pre-inform the investor about the key risks and obtain acknowledgement of his/her understanding of the specific risks.[97] LBC platforms are required to disclose also defaults and interest rates based on MAS guidelines to ensure comparability.[98] Licensed CSPs are also expected to have procedures to handle issuer's defaults and to disclose different recovery options and costs, obtaining investors' consent in advance.[99]

4.3 Due Diligence and Gatekeeper Role

The level of due diligence imposed on platforms is closely linked to their role as gatekeepers and depends on the interpretation of legal texts and the evolution of supervisory practices. The main consequences of a violation, anyway, appear to be administrative sanctions since private actions/enforcement, even when in principle recognized (USA), seem unlikely considering the diversification and small size of investments.

For instance, in Singapore, MAS expects IBC operators to simply disclose the scope of their due diligence, while LBC operators are expected not to lend to a borrower with past due (saved for reasonable and disclosed justifications).[100] In the UK, although the law requires platforms to simply disclose the level of their due diligence, the FCA has clarified that a violation of the general obligation of care, skill and diligence and best interest has to be assumed when the platform has not carried out enough due diligence. Moreover, LBC platforms must verify project owners' statements on future commercial success.[101]

---

91 Section 1017B–D.
92 ASIC 2018 (n 40), RG 262.147 and RG 262.149.
93 17 CFR §227.302(b).
94 Härkönen (n 20) 801.
95 Härkönen (n 20) 801; Li (n 21) 8–9.
96 ibid RG 262.154.
97 Hofmann (n 16) 405.
98 MAS Circular No CMI 27/2018 No 4.
99 ibid No 5–6.
100 MAS Circular No CMI 27/2018, No 11.
101 Chapman (n 62) 81.

US law only specifies CSPs' duty to ensure systems to reduce the risk of frauds,[102] checking the background/regulatory history of the issuer's officers, directors and main shareholders. Anyway, the platform is liable for the violation of the duty to obtain a reasonable basis for believing that the issuer is in compliance with its relevant rules, being allowed to rely on issuers' representations unless there are reasons to question the reliability (with the consequent duty to remove the offer).[103] The SEC has recently won a case against a platform for failing to check criminal records and reduce the risk of fraud.[104]

EU CSPs are required to simply screen issuers for certain criminal and AML/CT records (art 5 ECSPR). However, they must have systems to verify the completeness, clarity and 'correctness' of the project owner's KIIS, having the power to suspend or even cancel the offer if they identify omissions, mistakes or inaccuracies (art 23(8), (11)–(12)). ESMA has clarified that the project owner is solely responsible for 'inaccurate or misleading information' in the KIIS but 'unless those omissions are the direct result of inadequate procedures' by the CSP 'in the collection of this information made available in the KIIS' or when, during the offer, information comes to light giving 'sufficient reason to believe that the KIIS document might be incomplete, incorrect or unclear',[105] the liability regime established at national level will ultimately set the level and intensity of platforms' gatekeeping role.[106]

At the other extreme of the spectrum, Australian platforms are attributed an explicit role of gatekeepers:[107] in addition to identifying the company and verifying whether eligible, they must reasonably check if the offer document contains the required information and, under a strict liability standard, if this is clear, concise and effective. They have also the duty to remove the offer where they are not satisfied with the identity check or have reasons to believe that the officers/directors do not have good character or the company has knowingly engaged in omissive or misleading/deceptive conduct.[108] In particular, they are liable where no systems/arrangements for conducting the checks are in place or the offer document is deceptive and they had reasons to believe so.[109]

---

[102] 17 CFR §227.301.

[103] 15 USC 77d-1(a); 17 CFR §227.301(a); see also sec 4A(c) investors' right of action towards issuers, extensively interpretated to cover also CSPs as offerors: Li (n 21) 14–15. See also Steven Bradford, 'Shooting the Messenger: The Liability of Crowdfunding Intermediaries for the Fraud of Others' (2014) 83 Univ Cincinnati L Rev 371.

[104] The red flags consisted in the criminal records of issuers: *SEC v Shumake, Civil Action* No 2:21-cv-12193 (ED Mich Filed 20 September 2021), final judgment 23 December 2021 <https://www.sec.gov/litigation/litreleases/2022/judgment25298-trucrowd.pdf>; SEC, 'SEC Obtains Final Judgments Against Crowdfunding Issuer CEO and Registered Funding Portal and Its CEO', Litigation Release No 25298 (January 3, 2022) <https://www.sec.gov/litigation/litreleases/2022/lr25298.htm>. See Härkönen (n 20) 800, 806.

[105] ESMA, 'Q&A', 5.2 and 5.9 (setting a stricter standard).

[106] Macchiavello (n 6) 61.

[107] Reg 6D.3A.08(2)–(4).

[108] ASIC 2018 (n 40), RG 262.130ff; RG262.145; RG262.172.

[109] See ASIC 2018 (n 40), RG262.192.

4.4 Investor Protection: Special Measures

Some jurisdictions have introduced additional protections, such as investor tests, cancellation rights or caps on investors' commitments. The presence of all or one/some of these instruments and how they are structured show a different balance between the objectives of expanding SME access to funding and investor protection. In particular, different levels of investor self-responsibility or, on the other hand, paternalism are present.

4.4.1 Investor tests

FCA guidelines require CSPs to ensure that the client has sufficient knowledge and experience to understand the risks: for IBC, the assessment is similar to the MiFID appropriateness test, looking at type of services/products, previous investments and education/profession. For LBC, instead, the client should have enough knowledge to understand the nature of the contractual relationship with the borrower and the firm, credit risk exposure, capital at risk and the absence of compensation schemes/protection, the characteristics of the agreement/portfolio, risk diversification measures, contingent fund, illiquidity risk, the role of the platform and platform risk.[110] In 2022, appropriateness rules for high-risk investment like crowdfunding have been reinforced: in case of a negative result, the investor must wait at least 48 hours before re-taking the test.

Similarly, in Singapore, CSPs must assess whether potential investors have, only alternatively, the financial competence/experience or are suitable to invest in crowdfunding given their investment objectives and risk tolerance (mandatory in case of investment advice).[111]

The ECSPR, instead, reserves special measures only to non-sophisticated investors:[112] an entry-knowledge test aimed at assessing investors' knowledge and previous experience with crowdfunding and early-stage companies in general.[113] Moreover, platforms must also make available to investors a system to simulate their ability to bear losses, calculated as 10% of their net worth (NW). Both measures appear quite weak, since negative results do not impede the investment, a simple investor's acknowledgement being sufficient (art 21(5)–(6)).

Lighter requirements exist in the USA and Australia: Australian CF providers must obtain from retail investors an acknowledgement of risks before the investment,[114] while US platforms must also ensure that investors complete a questionnaire after reviewing the relevant educational material.[115] However, US brokers offering investment advice (prohibited to funding portals) are subject to the suitability duty.

---

[110] COBS 10.2.9G.

[111] Hofmann (n 16) 404–406. Financial Advisers Act §25.

[112] For sophisticated investors' criteria, differentiated for legal entities (own funds/turn-over/balance sheet above certain thresholds) and natural persons (income/portfolio, professional/investment experience), see annex II ECSPR.

[113] This appears close to the appropriateness test but more abstract/generic (not in relation to a particular financial instruments) and at a preliminary stage. Moreover, the ECSPR requires platforms to also collect information about investors' investment objectives and financial situation (as under the suitability test) without limiting this to portfolio management services (art 21(1)–(4)), which sounds incoherent (but such information is useful for the loss simulation test).

[114] Reg 6D.3A.07; RG 262.188.

[115] 17 CFR §227.303(b). Härkönen (n 20) 800; Li (n 21) 8.

4.4.2 Reflection period/cancellation right

Online transactions, being faster and easier to make, might be more dangerous: EU law generally allows consumers to have second thoughts. To balance investor protection with SMEs' interest in certain and fast funding, the duration of the reflection period, compared with consumer law, appears to have shrunk.

The FCA had considered the general 14-day cancellation right derived from the Directive on distant financial services[116] applicable to the initial contract with the platform but, since 2023, a special 24 hour cooling-off period applies to all high-risk investments. Similarly, a reflection right is recognized for EU non-sophisticated investors (4 days) and Australian investors (5 days). Instead, US investors have the right to cancel the order until 48 hours before closing.[117]

4.4.3 Maximum offer size and investment limits

The ECSPR sets at €5 million (including all offers exempted from the Prospectus under the small/private offers exemptions) the maximum threshold for crowdfunding offers, while not entailing a single investment limit. However, investments in a single offer above €1,000 or 5% of the investor's NW require the CSP to issue a warning and receive the investor's explicit consent and evidence of understanding (art 21(7)).

Singapore and the UK do not set special maximum offer threshold or investment caps. However, the UK presents restrictions on financial promotions: direct offers of unlisted securities or P2P investments cannot be directed to retail clients unless they are a certified or self-certified sophisticated investor or high NW individual or receive regulated advice or are a restricted investor (i.e. investment not above 10% of their NW in 12 months)[118] and, anyway, only if they pass the required test (see above §4.4.a).[119]

The USA limits instead both issuers' requests (up to US$ 5 million in 12 months – raised in 2021)[120] and investors' commitments. In particular, non-accredited investors[121] cannot invest, depending on their wealth, more than the greater of $2,500 or 5% of (the greater) of the investor's annual income or 10% of NW. CSPs must ensure compliance with these limits, having reasonable basis for relying on investors' representations.[122]

In Australia, retail investors cannot invest more than A$10,000 per year and per company offer and CSPs must have systems and procedures to ensure compliance.[123] However, no limit is placed on the total number of offers in which they can participate.[124]

---

116 FCA, 'The FCA's Regulatory Approach to Crowdfunding Over the Internet, and the Promotion of Non-readily Realisable Securities by Other Media', (2014), PS14/4 <https://www.fca.org.uk/publication/policy/ps14-04.pdf>; Baillie (n 31) 154; Chapman (n 62) 84.

117 With offers open for at least 21 days. See Härkönen (n 20) 804.

118 COBS 4.12A (2022 version).

119 COBS 10-10A; COBS 10.1.2R. McMeel (n 36) 78–79; Baillie (n 31) 154–155.

120 Crowdfunding securities cannot be re-sold for 12 months, unless through registered offerings, to accredited investors or investor family members: 15 USC §77d-1(e); 17 CFR §227.501.

121 Accredited investors, not covered by investment limits, are financial companies and companies or natural persons with assets/net worth/income above certain thresholds or with professional certifications: 17 CFR § 230.501. See Härkönen (n 20) 805; Li (n 21) 6.

122 15 USC §77d(6); 15 USC §77d-1(a)(8); 17 CFR 227.303(b). See Härkönen (n 20) 803.

123 MAS RG 262.190.

124 Schwarz (n 37) ch 6.

4.4.4 Client money protection measures and exclusion from compensation schemes

All regimes tend to entail client money protection measures: the ECSPR does not allow platforms to hold clients' money, unless they also obtain a PSD2, bank or equivalent licence. Similarly, in the UK, client money protection measures apply to LBC platforms, requiring the money to be secured in segregated bank account.[125] Again, US funding portals cannot hold client money, contrary to brokers; moreover, funds must be transferred to the issuer only if and when the target amount is reached or otherwise returned to investors within 5 days.[126] In Singapore and Australia, CSPs must place customers' money and assets into trust/custody accounts.[127]

Crowdfunding, in fact, is generally excluded from the existing compensation scheme: this is the case under the ECSPR, in the UK for LBC (while IBC, being regulated under MiFID II, is covered) and in the USA (while brokers are members of the Securities Investor Protection Corporation[128]). This might be to clearly distinguish crowdfunding from traditional finance and subject it to a lighter regime.

5. CONCLUSIONS

Although all balancing SMEs' access to funding with investor protection, regulatory approaches in the analysed jurisdictions range from the application of traditional financial regulation rules (with small adaptations: the USA and Singapore), to more articulated and hybrid regimes (special rules only for EBC in Australia and for LBC in the UK), to finally, *ad hoc* special regimes (EU), also reflecting different rankings in regulatory goals and different regulatory focus.

In particular, the USA focuses the regulatory attention on issuers' disclosure duties. Instead, the UK puts all the regulatory burden on platforms, while Australia and the EU have introduced special simplified requirements on both issuers and platforms, while looking at platforms as gatekeepers (especially in Australia). Finally, Singapore, while applying general financial regulation, presents a quite light framework.

These differences might be explained by different market structures and regulatory priorities: the British market, the most mature in Europe, has moved towards a prevalence of managed-based crowdfunding models (in part, also in Australia) and their regulation has consequently also moved from principle-based and light touch regulation/supervision to more rule-based and hard-touch ones. In such a context of managed-based models, for investors it is more important how the platform works and how its activity is conducted (in particular, how projects are chosen) than information on each project itself. At the same time, platform activity becomes closer to traditional intermediaries and assimilating the two responds to the objectives of competition and a level-playing field. However, in this perspective, the exclusion of platforms from traditional compensation schemes appears hardly understandable. The USA, instead, assigning more importance to project disclosures in line with the traditional efficient capital market hypothesis and relevance of public disclosures, looks at platforms as

---

125 Chapman (n 62) 82.

126 17 CFR §227, 402(a); Chapman (n 62) 82; Härkönen (n 20) 801, 804.

127 Hofmann (n 16) 407.

128 With a coverage up to $500,000: FINRA's customer protection rules, Rule 4330.

broker-like operators, simply putting in contact issuers and investors. Imposing specialization (only limited crowdfunding services) and neutrality on platforms allows this jurisdiction to subject the same to an even more simplified regime. The EU shows a light approach for EBC basic models, while reserving stricter regulation in case of more complex or riskier (in the ECSPR's perspective, even LBC) models, although platforms' role and potential liability are not clear yet.

Anyway, all jurisdictions introducing through special rules a new intermediary show a prevalent focus on platforms' general conduct duties (inspired to traditional intermediaries' regimes), in particular as regards disclosure and conflict of interest, rather than on prudential or organizational requirements.

Investor protection measures evidence a relevance of warnings and key information documents written in plain and clear language. Nonetheless, we can observe various combinations of such measures reflecting different balances of investor self-responsibility and paternalism: Singapore seems to resort only to traditional instruments such as investor tests, while the UK deploys traditional tests but also limitations on the offering of crowdfunding products to retail clients as risky products. The USA and Australia seem to rely on investor ability to decide based on issuers' disclosure and warnings, but this is counterbalanced by more paternalistic caps on the amount of offers and investments to limit risk size. The ECSPR, instead, trusts more investor self-responsibility, entailing warnings and special lighter investor tests, mostly reserved to unsophisticated investors only. All jurisdictions recognize investor reflection periods but within a limited timeframe to balance investor protection with firms' funding needs. In this regard, a few days seem more reasonable than 24 hours.

PART III

REGULATION OF FINANCIAL INSTITUTIONS

10. Microprudential regulation

Lucrezia Cipriani and Andrea Minto[1]

1. INTRODUCTION: THE RATIONALE FOR MICROPRUDENTIAL REGULATION AND POLICY MAKING

Traditionally, financial regulation and banking supervision were microprudential in nature, in that they sought to limit each financial institution's risk and ensure its soundness and general financial viability in the market.

Microprudential regulation, in fact, is concerned with the structure of each intermediary and its ability, in essence, to operate in the marketplace in a healthy and sound fashion in the long run. In this respect, financial legislation worldwide developed so as to set out the microprudential requirements against which to appraise such ability by financial supervisors. The assessment is conducted in the moment of the 'birth' and throughout the various 'life phases' of the intermediary, thanks to the exercise of the ongoing oversight which aims at ensuring compliance with the prudential requirements considering the possible developments of its business model.

In general, such requirements are related to own funds (capital requirements), liquidity and corporate governance of the regulated and supervised entities. Many rationales exist for focusing on institution-level risk and soundness in this way.

First, financial markets are particularly prone to market failures and credit institutions are inclined to engage in practices – should financial markets be unfettered – that may result in negative externalities, leading to negative economic consequences that are borne by society at large.

Thus, 'the design of financial regulation is ultimately an exercise in economics – applying the analytic tools of economics to determine the legal and regulatory framework best suited to correcting the failures of financial systems'.[2] In this regard, particular features of financial markets make them prone to malfunction, failing to achieve the efficient outcomes which they are theoretically assumed to achieve.[3]

---

1 Andrea Minto is primarily responsible for Sections 1 and 7, whereas Lucrezia Cipriani is primarily responsible for Sections 2–6.

2 John Armour and others, *Principles of Financial Regulation* (Oxford University Press 2016) 51. See also Jacques Pelkmans, *The Economics of Single Market Regulation* (College of Europe 2012) 25, 13, available at <https://www.coleurope.eu/sites/default/files/research-paper/beep25_0.pdf>.

3 John W Cioffi, 'After the Fall: Regulatory Lessons from the Global Financial Crisis' in David Levi-Faur (ed.), *Handbook on the Politics of Regulation, Cheltenham* (Edward Elgar Publishing 2011) 642; Ioannis Glinavos, 'Regulation and the Role of Law in Economic Crisis' (2010) 21 European Business Law Review, 539.

The pre-eminent role of the financial sector in risk allocation exacerbates the manifestation of market failures, raising a host of regulatory issues.[4] Four types of market failures are inherent in the financial system – information failure, principal–agent failure, incentive failure and responsibility failure[5] – and can eventually contribute and lead, individually or in combination, to systemic failures.[6]

Not only are market failures greater or more likely to come about in the financial sector, but the remedial intervention to cope with them is also extremely difficult to devise. Some of the regulatory strategies that were conceived to address market failures turned out to fall short of achieving the desired outcome, or even to exacerbate them.[7] In this respect, financial regulators face potentially severe asymmetries of information and expertise *vis-à-vis* regulated actors.

Second, in the retail banking sector, intermediaries are funded thanks to a quite dispersed group of creditors. Such constituency is likely to respond to warning signals about bank health via disruptive 'runs'.

Third, in many countries and especially in emerging markets the government is a direct stakeholder in the financial sector. Government-sponsored enterprises and state-owned banks (which play an important role in the banking sector of many Asian countries) are primary examples.

Against this backdrop, in the quest to take adequate care of the abovementioned issues, regulators conceived microprudential legislation as a form of risk-based regulatory framework that sets out *ex ante* the regulatory requirements that financial intermediaries must respect to carry out financial services.

As mentioned above, regulation is 'prudential' in nature,[8] as it incapsulates a regulatory approach that is based on the prior identification of the requirements as well as of the principles and criteria underpinning them. Thus, the regulators establish the principles that guide credit institutions in applying those requirements *vis-à-vis* the actual risks they are exposed to.

2. CAPITAL AND LIQUIDITY REQUIREMENTS AS A RESPONSE TO MARKET FAILURES

The financial structure of a bank is fundamentally delicate: unexpected fund withdrawals from short-term lenders can deplete its liquid assets; or misjudgement in assessing borrowers' cred-

---

4 For an analysis of the functions of the financial system, see Dwight B Crane and others (eds), *The Global Financial System: A Functional Perspective* (Harvard Business School Press, 1995); John Armour (n 2) 24.

5 Steven L Schwarcz, 'Regulating Shadows: Financial Regulation and Responsibility Failure' (2013) 70 Washington and Lee Law Review 1781.

6 Steven L Schwarcz, 'Controlling Financial Chaos: The Power and Limits of Law' (2012) 2012 Wisconsin Law Review 815, 816–839.

7 Joel P Trachtman, 'The International Law of Financial Crisis: Spill-overs, Subsidiarity, Fragmentation and Cooperation' (2010) 13, Journal of International Economic Law, 719.

8 Viral V Acharya, 'Adapting Micro-prudential Regulation for Emerging Markets', in Otaviano Canuto and Swati R Ghosh (eds), *Dealing with the Challenges of Macro Financial Linkages in Emerging Markets* (World Bank Publications 2013) 57.

itworthiness can cause the bank's asset value to drop below its liabilities, potentially leading to insolvency. At a prudential level, the failure of one institution can have a cascading effect on the entire economy.

Given the vulnerability of banks and the crucial role they play, regulation and insurance of depositors against potential failures are deemed necessary. However, in designing the regulatory framework, both the nature and degree of any market failure are to be identified (such as asymmetries of information, negative externalities and bias in individual decision-making).

This chapter focuses on two microprudential tools imposed on banks to preserve financial stability.

The first is to impose capital requirements on banks to maintain on-balance sheet reserves, so as to cope with any shortfall in asset value compared with liabilities, ensuring capacity for absorbing losses; the second is to require banks to hold a portion of their assets in a liquid form to meet deposit withdrawals.

Thus, the purpose of capital rules for banks is to increase the chances that a bank will be able to absorb losses on the assets side of its balance sheet without becoming insolvent, thus preventing runs on deposits.[9] Concretely, credit risk – defined as the risk of borrowers failing to fulfil their loan repayment obligations – constitutes the predominant risk necessitating vigilant capital safeguarding measures.[10]

The greater the own funds, the more the chances that banks will withstand losses stemming from their business activity before facing difficulties in meeting its obligations and entering into a crisis. In other terms, the higher the level of the bank's capital, the less the risk of balance sheet insolvency.

However, capital requirements alone do not mitigate the risk of bank runs: even if a bank possesses valuable assets, their illiquid nature poses challenges.[11]

In the attempt to mitigate this concern, liquidity requirements demand to keep some liquid assets, diminishing the possibility of depositors suffering losses during bank runs. In terms of surviving a shock, liquidity regulation has an important part to play, because it responds to a sudden withdrawal of short-term funds.[12]

---

[9] The capital adequacy rules preserve the value of shareholders' ownership stake in the bank. The most basic metric is the bank's net assets, which serve as an asset value and reduce the risk of a bank becoming insolvent.

[10] This is, in fact, the basis upon which Basel I approached this issue.

[11] So long as the bank's losses do not exceed its equity, it will still have positive net assets. The higher the level of liquid assets the bank holds, the easier it will be to meet demands from depositors, thus reducing the risk of liquidity crises. Thus, 'leverage' – the ratio of the bank's debt funding to its funding through equity or capital – is always a central issue in bank regulation.

[12] During the early liquidity phase of the financial crisis starting in 2007, many banks – despite meeting the existing capital requirements – experienced difficulties because they did not prudently manage their liquidity. For example, Northern Rock in the UK, Bear Stearns in the US and Lehman Brothers International were probably balance-sheet solvent in the period immediately before they were bailed out or went into bankruptcy, but they could not continue in the face of liquidity shortages. Caroline Bradley, 'Private International Law Making for the Financial Markets' (2005) 29 Fordham International Law Journal 127; Mads Andenas, 'Harmonising and Regulating Financial Markets' in Mads Andenas and Camilla B Andersen (eds), *Theory and Practice of Harmonisation* (Edward Elgar Publishing 2012), 7–10; Richard A Posner, *Economic Analysis of Law* (7th edn, Aspen Publishers 2007); Richard A Posner, 'Theories of Economic Regulation' (1974) 5 The Bell

As a result, requirements for both capital and liquidity are frequently used *in tandem*; that means it is not possible to use a 'silos-thinking' approach that separates capital regulation (as addressing solely the risks on the asset side of a bank's balance sheet) and liquidity regulation (tackling the risk of an unexpected withdrawal of short-term deposits). Indeed, problems on one side of the balance sheet might quickly spread to the other side and both perspectives (capital and liquidity) are crucial components of sound banks.

3. SHAPING MICROPRUDENTIAL REGULATION: THE ROLE OF THE BASEL COMMITTEE ON BANKING SUPERVISION

Since 1974, date of its establishment, the Basel Committee on Banking Supervision (hereinafter BCBS) played a pivotal role in the policy and regulatory design of micro- (and macro-) prudential regulation and supervision, by elaborating a set of international standards for banking supervision, and especially capital adequacy requirements ('Basel standards').

The first milestone, dated back to 1988 ('Basel I'), adopted quite a 'silos-approach' as it separated assets into categories and gave risk-weights ranging from 0 to 100% to each category. In particular, risk-weighted assets were calculated by multiplying the sum of the assets in each category by these risk-weights. Banks then should hold a minimum ratio of 8% of capita l-to-risk-weighted-assets. The accords' essential purpose was to define the minimum capital requirements for credit institutions, with the primary goal of minimizing credit risk.

In June 1999, the BCBS proposed a revised framework, which culminated in the implementation of a new prudential regulatory framework. This represents an important step forward, as it developed a more sophisticated approach as compared to Basel I approach, since it introduced (i) the internal risk assessment processes, (ii) a more accurate assessment of risks by adding a gradation of risk categories and (iii) the incorporation of value-at-risk-based capital charges for trading books.

Consequently, with the adoption of 'Basel II' in 2004, the BCBS narrowed the gap between prudential standards and market rules, by introducing the so-called 'three pillar approach' for banking supervision.

More specifically, Pillar I established guidelines for qualitative requirements and specified the capital and liquidity requirements that banks must meet as a minimum standard, based on the applicable rules for quantification of risk related to on-balance and off-balance sheet items.

Furthermore, Pillar II defines the supervisory review and evaluation process (SREP), while Pillar III defines the market discipline rules, based on the assumption that disclosure of the risk management approach upheld by the bank and its key prudential ratios will drive banks to benchmark their performance, capital ratios and liquidity management with competitors in the market.

Journal of Economics and Management Science 335; George J Stigler, 'The Theory of Economic Regulation' (1971) 2 The Bell Journal of Economics and Management Science 3; Niamh Moloney, 'EU Financial Market Regulation after the Global Financial Crisis: More Europe or More Risks' (2010) 47 Common Market Law Review 1317.

Yet, when the 2007–2009 financial crisis unfolded, the BCBS intervened as to develop a new proposal for capital adequacy and liquidity requirements, denoted 'Basel III', which came out in 2010.[13]

4. BASEL III: A MORE COMPREHENSIVE FRAMEWORK FOR ENHANCING LIQUIDITY AND CAPITAL REQUIREMENTS

The Basel II approach was all focused on gauging individual bank risk and overlooked systemic risk (the primary rationale for bank regulation). In addition, until the adoption of Basel III, there have been only a few internationally harmonized rules on qualitative capital requirements and trading risk was not considered until the expansion of the investment banking activities of large banks. Moreover, Basel II did not address the liquidity problems associated with the (fragile) bank liability side caused by the increased uninsured wholesale deposit funding. In fact, banks' lack of liquidity proved to be a cause of instability during the global financial crisis. Thus, BCBS has imposed substantial requirements on banks in terms of the levels of liquid assets they hold.

The new framework was mostly projected at overcoming the major shortcomings of the previous framework, that demonstrated some 'blind spots' or 'gaps' concerning the regulatory engagement with the significant financial actors ('too-big-to-fail'). These actors, armed with their funding advantage, easily exploited the conflict of interests of rating agencies and played off external versus internal risk models, while minimizing value-at-risk, although not systemic risk.[14]

Despite remaining at the center of the Basel rules, risk-weighting in Basel III has been supplemented by an unweighted leverage ratio and banks' own rating mechanisms have been subject to greater controls (such as stress tests). In this respect, the race to the bottom in risk-taking and economic leverage led the BCBS to separate the capital risk from liquidity risk.

Besides introducing a minimum leverage ratio and higher capital requirements (possibly countercyclical in nature), Basel III creates liquidity ratios that banks eventually have to abide by, creating a new and harmonized comprehensive set of rules. Still, in addition to credit and trading risk, operational risk has been identified as a third capital-triggering category.

---

[13] The 2007–2008 great financial crisis (GFC) proved the inability of the regulatory and supervisory framework in place back then to address severe externalities. The regulatory fragmentation amounted most certainly to a contributing factor to the crisis. Not only had it opened up to regulatory arbitrage practices in the first place, but, once the crisis unfolded, it prevented supervisors from taking appropriate action to deal with a highly intertwined and interconnected market. Nonetheless, the GFC exerted a profound influence on how to regulate financial markets and institutions.

[14] The adequacy of both micro- and macro-prudential rules came to the forefront during the crisis, which revealed that the current financial system was merely focused on individual intermediaries rather than the system as a whole. For example, the main instrument for measuring risk – known as 'value at risk' – could only capture the risk linked to an individual bank in isolation and, consequently, could not be used to identify systemic risk. See *Financial Stability Oversight Council* (FSOC 2011) Annual Report, 132; Panagiotis Delimatsis, 'Financial Innovation and Prudential Regulation – The New Basel III rules' (2012) TILEC Discussion Paper, 7.

Consequently, the requirements for Common Equity Tier 1 capital have been substantially increased and efforts have been made to reduce the *procyclicality* of the capital rules by introducing of two buffers: the *Capital Conservation Buffer* and the *Countercyclical Capital Buffer* (CCCB).[15] Ultimately, the provision of an additional buffer for systemically important banks shows the recognition of the concept of 'systemic importance'.[16]

Apart from capital regulation, another microprudential element addressed by the BCBS concerns the liquidity constrains imposed on banks: actually, the Basel standards did not contain much information on this subject, so that liquidity requirements were mainly regulated by national authorities. The Basel rules on liquidity, introduced in 2010, contain two liquidity constraints on a bank's portfolio: the *Liquidity Coverage Ratio* ('LCR') and the *Net Stable Funding Ratio* ('NSFR'): the former promotes banks' short-term resilience to liquidity shocks,[17] while the latter gives banks an incentive to fund themselves on an ongoing basis. Moreover, the introduction of *Liquidity Adequacy Assessment Process* (LAAP) requires banks to assess the internal organization and risks of their business and to report on the relevant assessment by the supervisory authority in SREP process.

Therefore, the bank is required to hold sufficient liquid assets at any moment to cope with any scenario that might have a significant impact on the bank. In brief, the idea behind the LCR mechanism is to require that a certain percentage of the bank's assets always consist of instruments that maintain their liquidity in the private markets even in a period of market stress.

5. WHAT DRIVES DIVERGENCE IN THE MICROPRUDENTIAL REGULATION OF BANKS?

Undoubtedly, the formulation of the Basel standards has been a significant source of convergence in the microprudential regulatory framework. Nonetheless, divergence can be observed in how Basel III is being implemented among different jurisdictions, including differences in timing and mode of adoption.

Although the move to stricter requirements has received widespread support, there is concern as to whether the implementation of the Basel III standards could have negative reper-

---

15 The CCCB has been designed to constrain lending by banks during an economic boom and to prepare banks for the economic 'bust'.

16 Before Basel III, the rules assumed that the negative externalities of bank failure were linearly related to the size of the bank's asset. However, Basel III states that, if that relation is non-linear, it might be appropriate to impose a higher capital requirement on those banks.

17 In particular, the LCR demands that banks recalibrate their liquidity reserves in order to take account of tail risks, requiring banks to hold a stock of *High-Quality Liquid Assets* ('HQLA') at least equivalent to the likely net cash outflows from the bank over 30 days in a specified stress scenario. The LCR is not simply a requirement to hold a certain percentage of the bank's assets in liquid form; rather, the liability and asset sides of the balance sheet are linked: the amount of HQLA to be held at any point in time is a function of the expected stability of short-term funding in a stress scenario.

cussions for emerging countries, especially if credit institutions are domestic, small and with a very basic business model.[18]

The incentives to align with international standards are significantly different for domestic banks than for internationally active banks, since the business model of the former focuses on the domestic market, whereas internationally active banks focus their business strategy on global markets and benefit from the use of international standards in terms of reputation.[19] Originally, the Basel standards were only supposed to be applied by internationally active banks represented by the BCBS members, as they were considered to be the ones capable of preserving global financial stability. However, the expression 'internationally active banks' is not widely accepted: banks with the same business model and size may be considered internationally active in one jurisdiction and not in another.

To increase the resilience of the local economy, regulators and national authorities may, nevertheless, apply more stringent prudential standards ('gold-plating') than the relevant international criteria. For these reasons, Basel requirements ought to be adjusted to consider the specific characteristics, as well as the economic priorities, of each jurisdiction.

Another element to consider when assessing the reasons for divergence in microprudential regulation concerns the specific objectives that financial regulation pursues in different countries. Although protecting investors, fostering competition, improving market efficiency, preventing financial crime and ensuring financial stability are all shared significant goals of microprudential regulation, such goals may vary depending on the jurisdiction: this may be caused by the nuances in the concrete interpretation of those objectives, also owing to the different enforcement and supervisory approaches developed across countries (e.g. twin peaks, institutional models, single financial supervisor).[20]

In addition, there are several reasons why domestic microprudential regulation departs from the Basel standards, such as different asset valuation practices in how banks calculate their regulatory capital and variations in the jurisdictional applicability of Pillars 1 and 2.[21]

---

[18] In fact, in a first phase, only internationally active banks were required to fully apply Basel standards, because of the twofold assumption that they were intended to be exclusively used by BCBS members and that, in any case, internationally active banks were sufficient to safeguard global financial stability. To this regard, it is also interesting to underline that the largest banking groups in the EU were 'universal banks': the diversity in the business model was calibrated with the need of realizing the 'Single Rulebook'. See Emily Jones and Peter Knack, 'The Future of Global Financial Regulation' (2017) GEG WP 127.

[19] Emily Jones, *The Political Economy of Bank Regulation in Developing Countries: Risk and Reputation* (OUP 2020).

[20] Actually, the US Securities and Exchange Commission's mandate and the Financial Conduct Authority in the UK do not include financial stability among their objectives, as this is responsibility of other regulatory bodies (the Federal Reserve and the Prudential Regulation Authority, respectively).

[21] Variations in Pillar 1 requirements stem from differences in the timing and substance of the implementation of international standards. The lack of a uniformly agreed definition for an internationally active bank is another cause of discrepancy, as is the adoption of country-specific rules for banks not subject to the Basel framework.

Moreover, the microprudential framework has been recently affected by the development of crypto-assets, thereby increasing the risks for banks.[22]

Given the rapidly evolving nature of these assets, the BCBS has taken initiatives to address these risks, outlining a set of minimum supervisory expectations for banks that are authorized and decide to acquire crypto-assets or provide related services. In June 2022, the BCBS issued a consultation on the prudential treatment of banks' exposures to crypto-assets, thereby finalizing a prudential standard that should be implemented by January 2025. A simplified capital and liquidity treatment will be available to banks with limited crypto-asset exposures.

Another element that should be considered when addressing the topic of convergence in the microprudential framework – at least in Europe – regards the 'Green Deal'.[23] Climate change and environmental degradation are sources of structural change that affect economic activity and, in turn, the financial system.[24] This calls for a better reflection of risks associated with climate and other environmental factors in microprudential regulation.[25]

At an international level, sustainability factors have been incorporated across the microprudential framework thanks to the *Network for Greening the Financial System* (NGFS). According to the NGFS, credit institutions should integrate climate-related risks into internal capital adequacy assessment procedures.[26]

The differences in the implementation of the Basel standards lead to market fragmentation and an unequal playing field for banks operating in various countries.

On the other hand, convergence is encouraged by the full, timely and consistent implementation of the Basel III framework, which strengthens the stability of both national and international financial systems.

---

[22] According to the BIS, the term 'crypto-asset' refers to 'a type of private digital asset that depend on cryptography and distributed ledger technologies (DLT) or similar technologies'. See FSB, *Regulation, Supervision and Oversight of 'Global Stablecoin' Arrangements: Final Report and High-Level Recommendations* (2020) 5, available at <www.fsb.org>.

[23] See COM(2018) 97 final, *Action Plan: Financing Sustainable Growth* (2018), 9. For a distinction between ESG and sustainability see Iain MacNeil and Irene-Marie Esser, 'From a Financial to an Entity Model of ESG' (2022) 23 European Business Organization Law Review 9.

[24] Martin Oehmke and Marcus M Opp, 'Green Capital Requirements' (2022) 22 Swedish House of Finance Research Paper 4; Stefano Giglio, Bryan Kelly and Johannes Stroebel, 'Climate Finance' (2021) 13 Annual Review of Financial Economics 15.

[25] See Council Directive (EU) 2019/878 of 20 May 2019 amending Directive 2013/36/EU as regards exempted entities, financial holding companies, mixed financial holding companies, remuneration, supervisory measures and powers and capital conservation measures [2019] OJ L 150/253 ('CRD5') and Council Regulation (EU) 2019/876 of 20 May 2019 amending Regulation (EU) No 575/2013 as regards the leverage ratio, the net stable funding ratio, requirements for own funds and eligible liabilities, counterparty credit risk, market risk, exposures to central counterparties, exposures to collective investment undertakings, large exposures, reporting and disclosure requirements, and Regulation (EU) No 648/2012 [2019] OJ L 150/1 ('CRR2').

[26] Institutions should take a comprehensive approach to understand how these factors are material to the bank balance sheets and, namely, how the balance sheet can be affected by these potential risk drivers. See ECB, *The State of Climate and Environmental Risk Management in the Banking Sector* (ECB 2021); BCBS, *Principles for the Effective Management and Supervision of Climate-related Financial Risks* (BCBS 2022).

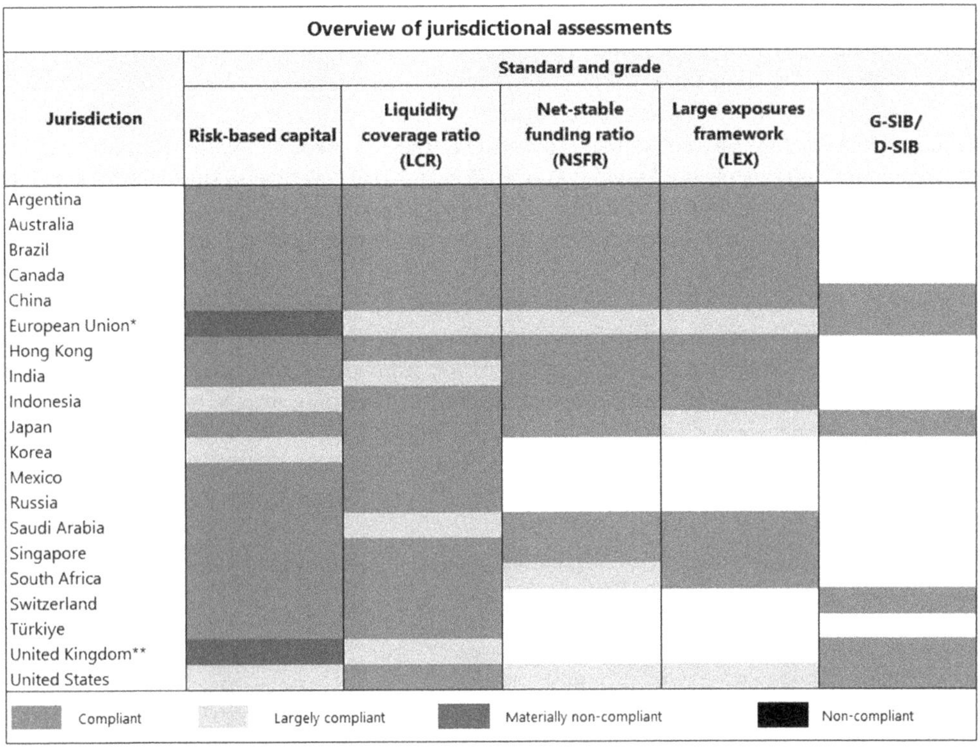

Notes: * Eight EU Member States participate in the Basel Committee: Belgium, France, Germany, Italy, Luxembourg, the Netherlands, Spain and Sweden; ** until the end of 2020, the United Kingdom has been assessed as an EU Member State.
Source: RCAP Jurisdictional assessments: regulatory implementation consistency <https://www.bis.org/bcbs/implementation/rcap_jurisdictional.htm?m=92> accessed on 26 June 2024.

Figure 10.1 *Overview of the Basel III Implementation*

6. OVERVIEW OF MICROPRUDENTIAL REGULATORY FRAMEWORKS

The following subsections zoom-in on four specific jurisdictions, with the aim of assessing how the microprudential requirements, established by the BCBS, have been specifically implemented in those selected countries. The analysis will be confined to capital and liquidity requirements, since governance requirements are dealt with in a different chapter.

6.1 The EU Implementation of the Basel Standards

The 2007/2008 crisis raised questions as to the effectiveness of the Basel II agreements and prompted the BCBS to produce an extensive package of reforms (now referred to as Basel

III). In responding to the crisis, the major jurisdictions worldwide, including the EU, started a process that aimed to impose stricter rules and to encourage harmonization.[27]

As advised by the High-Level Committee chaired by Jacques de Larosière, it was necessary to launch a process 'to remove key-differences stemming from the derogations, exceptions and vague provisions currently contained in some directives'. Consequently, the Basel III capital and liquidity requirements – adopted by the BCBS in 2010 – were promptly implemented in the EU in 2014, throughout the binding legislation constituted by the Capital Requirement Regulation (CRR) – which introduced the Liquidity Coverage Ratio (LCR) – and the Capital Requirement Directive (CRD IV).[28]

Although the formal starting point of the new regulatory system was in 2014, many requirements were gradually introduced up to the beginning of 2019. The CRD IV sets out the market access processes for banks, the organization of the supervisory and review process by the competent authorities, cooperation between authorities regarding groups of banks operating on a cross-border basis and harmonized rules on sanctions and enforcement. Furthermore, it comprises rules for 'Global Systemically Important Institutions' (GSII), other systemically important institutions, the capital conservation buffer, the countercyclical capital buffer and the systemic risk buffer.

More specifically, with regard to 'regulatory capital', this includes three tiers, each of which must be compliant with a set of criteria.[29]

First of all, the 'going-concern capital' is divided into two categories:

1. Common Equity Tier 1 (CET1);[30] and
2. Additional Tier 1.[31]

Secondly, the 'gone-concern capital' is represented by the Tier 2 Capital.[32] According to Basel III, risk-based capital requirements must be fulfilled by all banks. Thus, the Basel standards regulate the entire banking sector regardless of the size or importance of credit institutions.[33]

---

[27] The new standards are also considered the foundation for the substantive rules to be administered by the ECB in supervising the Eurozone's largest banks as part of the newly established Single Supervisory Mechanism ('SSM').

[28] Most of the substantive prudential requirements for banks are contained in the CRR and the secondary regulation adopted by the European Commission. Member states are also required to enact legislation compliant with the principles provided in the CRD IV.

[29] Specifically, CET1 must be at least 4.5% of risk-weighted assets (RWA); secondly, Tier 1 capital must be at least 6% of RWA. Moreover, the total capital must be at least 8% of RWA.

[30] On the components which compose up the Common Equity Tier 1 see BIS, *CAP Definition of Capital*, 2023, p. 3, available at <www.bis.org>.

[31] Additional Tier 1 capital is defined as non-cumulative perpetual preferred stock and related surplus, and qualifying minority interest.

[32] In particular, the Tier 1 capital is the sum of (1) and (2), while the 'total regulatory capital' is the sum of the 'going concern capital' and the 'gone-concern capital' (net of some regulatory adjustments).

[33] In particular, there are more than 8000 banks in the EU and they can be mainly divided into three classes: (1) small local banks, most of which have assets of less than EUR 1 billion; (2) medium-sized banks operating on a country basis with assets ranging from EUR 1 billion to EUR 100 billion; and (3) fewer than 100 large banks with assets exceeding EUR 100 billion, mostly

Implementing Basel III involved replacing existing EU banking directives with the new Basel III-compliant EU banking Directive and Regulation comprising CRD IV. Therefore, Basel III results from a global process in which both the EU institutions and many EU Member States participated (each country was expected to comply with Basel III's requirements but is free to impose higher standards).

6.2 The UK Implementation of the Basel Standards

As a major international financial hub with a financial industry accounting for 8.3% of the UK's GDP in 2020, the UK plays a crucial role in the global financial system.

The UK had an important impact on shaping the post-2008 regulatory framework in the EU and has been instrumental in pushing the idea of a Capital Markets Union. In line with this, the Prudential Regulation Authority (PRA) pursues its objectives through strict alignment with international standards.

As is known, before Brexit the UK–EU frameworks were more than converging: there were harmonized rules (i.e. the Single Rulebook) as well as convergence of practices, with the UK authorities being members of the different supervisory systems (i.e. the European System of Financial Supervision and its European Supervisory Agencies – the European Banking Authority (EBA), the European Insurance and Occupational Pensions Authority (EIOPA), the European Securities and Markets Authority (ESMA), and the European Systemic Risk Board (ESRB)). On 31 January 2020, the UK left the EU and, for a transition period, some EU Law acquis was quickly 'onshored' into UK law.

Many of the reforms addressed through the 2020 Brexit legislation were subsequently developed by the Prudential Regulation Authority.[34] The PRA was actively involved in the negotiations that led to the agreements and published the proposed rules and expectations in the form of a Consultation Paper.[35] This document outlines specific deviations from the BCBS's standards[36] and addresses parts of Basel III that have not been implemented in the UK (the so-called 'Basel 3.1 standards').

More in detail, the proposals mainly concern the measurement of risk-weighted assets (RWAs) – that is, as known, the denominator of capital ratios – and revise its calculation by

---

operating in the EU. Overall, banks range from regional or community-based banks to specialized and global systemically important banks (G-SIBs).

[34] Bank of England, *Implementation of Basel Standards: Final Rules*, Policy Statement (PS) 22/21 (Bank of England 2021) <https://www.bankofengland.co.uk/prudential-regulation/publication/2021/october/implementation-of-basel-standards> accessed 17 December 2023 and *The UK Leverage Ratio Framework*, Policy Statement (PS) 21/21 (Bank of England 2021) <https://www.bankofengland.co.uk/prudential-regulation/publication/2021/june/changes-to-the-uk-leverage-ratio-framework#:~:text=The%20policy%20material%20in%20this,and%20consolidated%20basis%20respectively)%2C%20> accessed 17 December 2023.

[35] See Bank of England, *Implementation of the Basel 3.1 Standards*, CP16/22 (Bank of England 2022) <https://www.bankofengland.co.uk/prudential-regulation/publication/2022/november/implementation-of-the-basel-3-1-standards> accessed 15 December 2023.

[36] Many jurisdictions – Australia, Canada, Hong Kong, Singapore and Switzerland – are further along in their implementations and have stayed true to the BCBS's standards, with only minor deviations.

improving the measurement of risk in internal models and standardized approaches, as well as the comparability of risk measurement across firms.

The global financial crisis, in fact, exposed serious flaws in the methodology used to compute capital ratios and RWAs, and investors lost confidence in Basel I- and Basel II-compliant capital ratios.[37]

Fundamentally, the implementation of the Basel III.1 standards has been carried out in such a way as to strengthen the robustness and risk sensitivity in the standardized approaches, while imposing constraints on the use of internal models and restricting the RWA benefits these models can provide (however, in neither the UK nor Switzerland has the CET1 requirement been raised much beyond about 10% of RWA).

Lastly, in June 2023, the Financial Services and Markets Bill received Royal Assent, becoming law through what is now known as the Financial Services and Markets Act. The Act imposes a new secondary objective on the PRA and Financial Conduct Authority to operate in a way that promotes the international competitiveness of the UK economy and its growth in the long term. The Act also establishes the regulatory architecture pursuant to which the Financial Conduct Authority, Prudential Regulation Authority (PRA) and Bank of England will regulate the UK's financial services. Many of the features of this new regulatory architecture will be familiar to the financial services sector and the Act expressly builds on the established model of regulation set out in the Financial Services and Markets Act 2000.

In particular, the Act seeks to bolster the competitiveness of UK markets, promote the effective use of capital and promoting financial inclusion. Therefore, the UK's rationale behind the will to diverge from the EU could just pertain to broader political and regulatory objectives: flexibility, competitiveness, growth. Overall, across the entire package of proposals, the PRA has been found to be aligned with the Basel III.1 standards, while exercising its judgement to adapt them where appropriate.

6.3 The US Implementation of the Basel Standards

In the United States, the power to regulate and supervise banks is in the hand of the US federal banking agencies: the Office of the Comptroller of the Currency (OCC), the Federal Deposit Insurance Corporation (FDIC) and the Board of Governors of the Federal Reserve System (FRB).

In particular, the USDA has a dual banking system, allowing banks to opt for either federal or State chartering. When a bank is chartered by a State it is supervised not only by the federal supervisors but also from the State, thus having a particular system to implement prudential regulation.[38]

With regard to capital and liquidity requirements established by the BCBS, after the collapse of Lehman Brothers in 2008, the US adopted a 'tiered approach', operating a distinction between small banks (i.e. credit institutions with less than USD 100 billion in total assets) and

---

37 Average risk weights fell from 37% in 2015, at the time of the negotiations of the Basel 3.1 standards, to historically low levels of 25% in 2020. See Bank of England (n 34).

38 For the larger banks, the new regulations introduced by the Dodd–Frank Act, including those on stress tests, represented the main regulatory constraint. See Dodd–Frank Act (2010), par. 115.

large domestic and foreign banks (i.e. credit institutions with USD 100 billion or more in total assets).[39] In more detail, the largest banks have been divided into different categories:

1. the most complex and internationally active banks, the 'global systemically important banks' (G-SIBs);
2. banks with USD 700 billion or more in total consolidated assets or banks with USD 75 billion or more in cross-jurisdictional activity;
3. banks with total consolidated assets of USD 250 billion or more or USD 75 billion or more in weighted short-term wholesale funding, non-bank assets or off-balance sheet exposure.

With the endorsement of Basel agreements by the BCBS in 2010, the US banking agencies have supported the adoption of a comprehensive regulatory framework by specifying a minimum capital ratio and setting minimum liquidity requirements. In particular, the regulation and supervision of large banks with more than USD 50 billion in total consolidated assets had to be compliant with the Dodd–Frank Act which became effective in July 2010.

In June 2012, the above-mentioned banking agencies – OCC, FDIC and FRB – proposed a set of rules to implement the Basel III reforms, with the goal of protecting the financial stability of the banking system and addressing the deficiencies that emerged in the pre-crisis framework.

The US regulators decided to include all banks with total assets under USD 500 million, thus catching also smaller and community banks (which differ from larger banks in terms of capital structure, capacity to access capital markets, systemic importance and other elements).[40]

In further tightening the definition of regulatory capital, the proposed rules changed risk weights for different asset classes and included three additional adjustments not covered in the initial revisions authorized by the BCBS.[41] Then, in 2014 the Federal Reserve Board approved the final rules based on the Dodd–Frank Act.[42]

---

[39] See IMF, *Lessons of the Financial Crisis for Future Regulation of Financial Institutions and Markets and for Liquidity Management* (IMF 2009) <https://www.imf.org/external/np/pp/eng/2009/020409.pdf> accessed 17 December 2023. For a general analysis on how higher capital requirements introduced at the supranational and implemented at the national level affect the regulatory capital of banks see Reint Gropp and others, 'Supranational Rules, National Discretion: Increasing versus Inflating Regulatory Bank Capital?' (2020) 59 Journal of Financial and Quantitative Analysis 831.

[40] Indeed, at first glance it seemed that Basel III was designed only for large, internationally active banks (in response to a crisis primarily attributable to those institutions).

[41] In particular: (1) risk-weights for high volatility commercial real estate exposures increased from 100 to 150%; (2) risk weights for credit unsecured or non-guaranteed loan exposures that were more than 90 days past due or in a non-performing status increased – under Basel II, these risk weights ranged from 50 to 150%, whereas under the proposed rules these risk weights have been set uniformly at 150%; and (3) a new differentiated risk weighting scheme was introduced for residential mortgage exposures, whereby different risk weights were applied to these assets according to key risk factors.

[42] In 2014 the Federal Reserve Board approved the final rules based on the Dodd–Frank Act. See BIS, *Evaluation of the Impact and Efficacy of the Basel III Reforms* (BIS 2022), available at <https://www.bis.org/bcbs/publ/d544.pdf> accessed 17 December 2023.

Following the series of US bank failures in 2023, some requirements for banks with assets between USD 100 billion and USD 250 billion changed. In particular, banks with assets above USD 100 billion will account for market losses in their capital ratios and all banks will increase the amount of capital to be held when regulators determine that the economy is headed for a recession.[43]

Following President Donald Trump's election in 2016, there was a significant change in the approach to financial regulation. The Trump administration openly advocated for reducing regulatory burdens on businesses and banking institutions, on the assumption that strict prudential requirements on banks, such as those under the Dodd–Frank Act, have inevitably hindered lending activity.

Consequently, in 2017 the Financial Choice Act (FCA), a comprehensive piece of legislation passed by the House of Representatives, was proposed, repealing large parts of the Dodd–Frank Act.[44]

The FCA introduces new standards for large banking institutions, while providing them with the opportunity to avoid costly regulatory scrutiny if certain capital requirements are met. For instance, the proposal allows banking organizations maintaining a certain leverage ratio to be exempt from numerous regulatory capital and liquidity requirements and even the largest banks can opt out of some of the Dodd–Frank Act provisions (e.g. prudential standards imposed by Section 165).[45]

The heart of the FCA approach to monetary policy is the specification of the 'Taylor rule', introduced by John Taylor in 1993 for determining the appropriate level of the Fed's target interest rate. In particular, the FCA enshrines the Taylor rule within the legislation as the 'reference rule' for assessing Fed policy setting. Additionally, it mandates the Federal Reserve to issue a 'directive policy rule' outlining its plans to adjust the policy instrument.[46]

6.4 The Chinese Implementation of the Basel Standards

The core business of the Chinese banking industry remains relatively traditional, predominantly being concentrated in domestic lending. In 2018, for instance, most of the banks were small independent rural banks. However, the banking system is growing rapidly, and the

---

43 See Colby Smith and Stephen Gandel, 'Regulators Announce "Basel III Endgame" Rules for large US Banks' *Financial Times* (New York, 27 July 2023) <https://www.ft.com/content/d4d15a2a-1568-47db-bd29-937a478dc768> accessed 17 December 2023.

44 H.R. 10 – 115th Congress (2017–2018), available at <https://www.congress.gov/bill/115th-congress/house-bill/10> accessed 29 April 2024. See also Paul Wachtel, 'Monetary Policy and the Financial CHOICE Act' in Matthew P Richardson and others (eds), *Regulating Wall Street: CHOICE Act vs. Dodd–Frank* (2017) 142, available at <https://www.stern.nyu.edu/sites/default/files/assets/documents/STERN%20White%20Paper%202017-03%20withcover%20%281%29_0.pdf> accessed 29 April 2024.

45 If the bank maintains a leverage ratio of 10% – which is only a modest increase over the 6–8% leverage ratios that large banks maintain – it can choose not to comply with risk-based capital and liquidity requirements.

46 See H.R.10, §1001, available at <https://www.congress.gov/bill/115th-congress/house-bill/10> accessed 29 April 2024.

banks' structures have become more complex on both the liability and asset sides, while their off-balance sheet activities have risen significantly.[47]

As one of the more emerging economies, China has opted for a stringent approach in implementing the global regulatory standards provided by the BCBS.[48]

When the first Basel Accord was released in 1988, the central bank in China had existed for a mere four years and banks were state-owned. A commercial banking law was not in place until 1995. Since the 1990s, in order to achieve business growth and management improvements, the Chinese government has attempted to reduce bank ownership, but government still has a controlling interest in Chinese banks.[49] It is thus not surprising that domestic authorities did not engage with Basel standards until 2003.

In fact, the China Banking Regulatory Commission – a politically centralized government regulatory authority established in 2003 – was primarily tasked with developing prudential regulations, and one of its first acts was to implement Basel I standards domestically.

In 2014, the *China Banking and Insurance Regulatory Commission* – which has been considered the main regulatory body in China along with the People's Bank of China (PBOC) – issued the 'Rules on Liquidity Risk Management of Commercial Banks', which are built precisely on the Basel III benchmark, showing the China's intent to ensure a timely implementation of Basel III in order to strengthen the financial system.

China's new banking standards are not only stricter than Basel III, but they were also implemented ahead of the internationally agreed schedule.[50] In 2015 the China Banking Regulatory Commission issued the 'Rules on Information Disclosure of Liquidity Coverage Ratio of Commercial Banks', characterized for a wider scope of application compared to the Basel provisions. In line with this perspective, in 2018 it issued the 'Rules on Large Exposure of Commercial Banks', which correspond to the large exposures Basel standards applied to all commercial banks.[51]

---

[47] According to the information released by the *China Banking and Insurance Regulatory Commission*, as of the end of December 2022, the total assets of the Chinese banking industry stood at 3720.86 trillion yuan.

[48] The introduction of Basel I in China was opposed by powerful factional elements within the party-state apparatus that benefited from the politically directed credit allocation, and implementation only began in earnest after the Asian financial crisis alerted the leadership to the risks associated with an unreformed financial sector. See Andrew Walter, 'Chinese Attitudes Towards Global Financial Regulatory Co-operation: Revisionist or Status Quo?' in Eric Helleiner, Stefano Pagliari and Hubert Zimmermann (eds), *Global Finance in Crisis: The Politics of International Regulatory Change* (Routledge 2010); Hyoung-Kyu Chey, *International Harmonization of Financial Regulation? The Politics of Global Diffusion of the Basel Capital Accord* (Routledge 2014).

[49] According to the official list of banking institutions in 2022, the six large state-owned commercial bank are: the Industrial and Commercial Bank of China (ICBC), the China Construction Bank, the Agricultural Bank of China (ABC), the Bank of China (BOC), Bank of Communications (BoCom) and the Postal Savings Bank of China (PSBC); see www.cbirc.gov.cn.

[50] The Chinese schedule stipulates full compliance by the end of 2016, two years before the global deadline.

[51] See BIS, Regulatory Consistency Assessment Programme (RCAP), Assessment of Basel III LCR regulations – China (BIS 2017) <https://www.bis.org/bcbs/publ/d411.pdf> accessed 15 December 2023.

Domestic rules are stricter than the international standards in several categories.[52] Overall, the LCR regulations are considered as compliant with the LCR standards and there exist no gaps between the Basel LCR standards and the Chinese regulatory framework. Yet, the Chinese LCR framework is even stricter than the Basel standards, in particular with regard to the high-quality liquidity assets.[53] Furthermore, the requirements for the capital adequacy ratio of commercial banks are aligned with those stipulated under Basel III.

Over-compliance with the Basel standards can be justified as a consequence of the post-GFC credit boom in the context of China's regulatory state model.[54] Both the PBOC and the State Council favor a gradual liberalization of the capital account, but authorities are concerned that further reform may increase risk and volatility of domestic financial markets.

7. CONCLUDING REMARKS

This chapter examines the role played by microprudential regulation and the major developments in international standard-setting from Basel I to Basel III. The analysis found that the global financial crisis of 2007–2008 marked a turning point in terms of microprudential requirements and regulatory tools adopted. Against this backdrop, the chapter studies factors of possible convergence and divergence in microprudential regulation, accounting for the challenges arising from financial innovation and sustainability.

In the EU, Member States have been implementing the Basel standards through various reforms, 'packaged' in the CRD/CRR (through the various phases of updates); in the UK,

---

52 The following three rules stand out:

1. Basel III raised the common equity capital ratio from 2 to 7%, but China's minimum ratio is set at 7.5%.
2. Chinese authorities require a leverage ratio that is one percentage point higher than the international standard.
3. China's regulators do not impose a fixed provisions rate or coverage rate on banks. However, they promote a model of dynamic provisions regulation with the goal of loan-loss provisions equal to 2.5% of total loans, and a 150% coverage rate of these loans.

53 There are also other areas in which the Chinese authorities have adopted a stricter approach than the minimum standards prescribed by the BCBS. For example, the definition of 'large exposure' in China is about 2,5% of Tier 1 (instead of 10%). Still, the Basel standard permits central bank reserves to be included in Level 1 HQLA, to the extent that the central bank policies allow them to be drawn down in times of stress, while Chinese banks can use only excess central bank reserves as Level 1 HQLA. The CBRC's implementation is thus stricter than the Basel standard. See BIS (n 51) 26.

54 Peter Knaack, 'An Unlikely Champion of Global Finance: Why is China Exceeding International Banking Standards' (2017) 46 Journal of Current Chinese Affairs 41; David Bach and Abraham L Newman, 'The European Regulatory State and Global Public Policy: Micro-Institutions, Macro-Influence' (2007) 14 Journal of European Public Policy 827; David Bach, Abraham L Newman and Steven Weber, 'The International Implications of China's Fledgling Regulatory State: From Product Maker to Rule Maker' (2006) 11 New Political Economy 499; Wei Ping He, 'Banking Regulation in China: What, Why, and How?' (2012) 20 Journal of Financial Regulation and Compliance 367.

the PRA has been found to be aligned with the Basel III.1 standards, while exercising its judgement to adapt them where appropriate. The US, instead, has supported the adoption of a comprehensive regulatory framework through its banking agencies, opting for a 'tiered approach', while microprudential regulation in China proved to be overcompliant with the new global standards.

11. Macroprudential regulation

Luca Amorello

1. INTRODUCTION

The last two decades have witnessed national and supranational regulators scrambling to define new reforms aimed at countering the negative spillover effects caused by a deterioration of financial stability on real economies. In this respect little was understood in respect of how macroeconomic shocks could amplify in the financial sector following the build-up of system-wide risks prior to the 2007–2008 global financial crisis. Despite the economic literature being aware of potential threats posed by aggregate excessive risk-taking behaviors of financial institutions,[1] supranational and regional policy frameworks were not generally armed with institutional arrangements and tools devoted to restricting or countering systemic events arising from euphoric financial institutions' conducts.

Macroeconomic analysis and policy actions were mainly focused on central banks' ability to maintain price stability through a defined set of rule-based monetary policy instruments. From a microeconomic standpoint, financial supervisors were solely concerned with safeguarding financial institutions and markets from idiosyncratic risks leading to failures. For banks this idiosyncratic approach was translated in micro-prudential regulations having their prudent and sound management on a going-concern basis as its primary objective.

The intellectual shake-up triggered by the events of 2007–2008 caused policymakers to reassess the foundations of the available policy institutions and regulatory tools to 'fill the gap' between central banks' monetary policies and microprudential financial supervision. Global fora such as the Financial Stability Board (FSB), the International Monetary Fund (IMF) and the Basel Committee on Banking Supervision (BCBS) – supported by a growing trend of data analysis – began to advocate for dedicated 'macroprudential policies' aiming at mitigating systemic risks posed by collective behaviors of financial institutions to ultimately safeguard the financial stability of global economies at large.[2] Since then, macroprudential frameworks –

---

1 For a review, see Olivier de Bandt and Philipp Hartmann, 'Systemic risk: A survey' (2000) European Central Bank Working Paper Series 35, <https://ssrn.com/abstract=258430> accessed 1 July 2023. For examples of studies on systemic risks before the 2007–2008 financial crisis, see *inter alia*: Philip Bartholomew and Gary Whalen, 'Fundamentals of Systemic Risk' in George G Kaufman (ed.) *Research in Financial Services* vol 7 (JAI Press 1995), pp. 3–18; George G Kaufman and Kenneth E Scott, 'What Is Systemic Risk, and Do Bank Regulators Retard or Contribute to It?' (2003) 7 The Independent Review 371; Martin Schüler, 'The Threat of Systemic Risk in European Banking' (2002) 41 Quarterly Journal of Business and Economics 145.

2 Among others, see Financial Stability Board, International Monetary Fund and Bank for International Settlements, *Guidance to Assess the Systemic Importance of Financial Institutions, Markets, and Instruments: Initial Consideration Report to the G-20 Finance Ministers and Central Bank Governors* (IMF, FSB and BIS 2009) <https://www.imf.org/external/np/g20/pdf/100109.pdf> accessed 1 July 2023; IMF, FSB and BIS, *Macroprudential Policy Tools and Frameworks*

comprising dedicated institutions, tools and strategies – have been institutionalized at national and international levels while the realm of global financial regulations has been enhanced to incorporate this new macroeconomic dimension.

This chapter provides a comparative analysis of the main regulatory and policy components setting up the macroprudential architecture in different jurisdictions, including the US, UK, EU, and selected Asia-Pacific countries. In doing so, this chapter will delve into common theoretical foundations of macroprudential regulations globally and different policy tools and governance models implemented across numerous jurisdictions. Some concluding remarks on the effectiveness of macroprudential policies will be also provided.

2. FINANCIAL STABILITY AND GLOBAL PUBLIC GOODS

Looking back at the last two decades it is not a surprise that central banks and supervisory authorities across the globe have been entrusted with a financial stability mandate in their founding statutes, commonly defined as protecting the efficient functioning of the financial systems at large. Various sectoral regulations and policies have been developed over time to contribute to financial stability, including frameworks relating to (i) the protection of depositors, (ii) the recovery and resolution of financial institutions, (iii) the operational resilience of financial market infrastructures, and (iv) the functioning of markets in derivative.[3]

In this respect we have witnessed a growing debate about what the term 'financial stability' means.[4] While several definitions have been provided in the economic literature, policymakers are generally in agreement that financial stability should be understood as the ultimate objective of macroprudential policies. These macroprudential frameworks are formed and developed with the aim of ensuring, contributing and promoting the stability of the financial markets and its actors. In simple terms macroprudential policies seek to achieve this objective by preventing and mitigating the excessive build-up of risk deemed 'systemic' owing to its capacity to disrupt the smooth functioning of the financial system and negatively affect the real economy.

In this light financial stability is instrumental to maintain the general good functioning of developed economies and prevent negative shocks that may ultimately affect GDP growth, general consumption, public and private investments, and economic welfare. It is no surprise

---

Progress Report to G20 (IMF, FSB and BIS 2011) <https://www.imf.org/external/np/g20/pdf/102711.pdf> accessed 1 July 2023; FSB, IMF and BIS, *Macroprudential Policy Tools and Frameworks: Update to G20 Finance Ministers and Central Bank Governors* (FSB, IMF and BIS 2011) <https://www.imf.org/external/np/g20/pdf/021411.pdf> accessed 1 July 2023.

[3] Luca Amorello, *Macroprudential Banking Supervision & Monetary Policy: Legal Interaction in the European Union* (Palgrave Macmillan 2018), p. 30.

[4] Among others, see: William Allen and Geoffrey Wood, 'Defining and Achieving Financial Stability' (2006) 2 Journal of Financial Stability 152; Garry J Schinasi 'Defining Financial Stability' (2004) IMF Working Paper No. 04/187; Hilary J Allen, 'What is "Financial Stability" – The Need for Some Common Language in International Financial Regulation' (2014) 45 Georgetown Journal of International Law 929.

that financial stability has been recognized among the 'global public goods'[5] embedded – at least in some jurisdictions – in constitutional and primary legislations.[6]

The legal and economic literature on the notion of global public goods is extensive.[7] In short, they represent those facilities or services needed for the global economy to function properly. These goods are generally scarce and prone to risk of being misallocated across citizens. While the societal benefits generated by these goods are overall extensive, each individual shares just a small portion of them. Moreover, benefits are normally reaped only in the future while citizens are to bear their costs immediately.[8]

Because of these features there is a strong argument for having the sovereigns (along with national and international organizations) playing a dominant role in the provision of global public goods,[9] also ensuring the maximum level of protection via the foundational provisions of the national and international orders. The need to preserve and promote financial stability as a particular global public good represents for legislatures and financial supervisors across the globe the constitutional basis for implementing macroprudential regulations.

3. ECONOMIC FOUNDATIONS OF MACROPRUDENTIAL REGULATION

As the ultimate objective of macroprudential regulation is related to the maintenance of financial stability, now questions arise on (i) how macroprudential policy and regulation is intended to achieve this objective and (ii) what are the key components that make the macroprudential regulatory architecture in different jurisdictions. In this respect it is particularly important to lay down the economic rationale of setting up an independent macroprudential policy along with its transmission channels and intended macroeconomic outcomes and effects.

---

5 For a discussion of the topic, see Rosa M Lastra, 'Systemic Risk and Macro-Prudential Supervision' in Niamh Moloney, Eilís Ferran and Jennifer Payne (eds), *The Oxford Handbook of Financial Regulation* (OUP 2017), 313–314.

6 By way of example, in the European Union financial stability is recognized in Article 127(5) of the Treaty of the Functioning of the European Union. Section 2A of the Bank of England Act 1988 mandates the Bank of England to protect and enhance the stability of the UK financial system. Discussing financial stability as global public good, see Bram van der Eem, 'Financial Stability as a Global Public Good and Private International Law as an Instrument for its Transnational Governance—Some Basic Thoughts' in Horatia M Watt and Diego P Fernández Arroyo (eds) *Private International Law and Global Governance* (OUP 2014), 294–301.

7 For example, see: Inge Kaul 'Global Public Goods: Concepts, Policies and Strategies' in Inge Kaul, Isabelle Grunberg and Marc Stern (eds), *Global Public Goods; International Cooperation in the 21st Century* (OUP 1999), 450–508; Wolfgang Buchholz and Todd Sandler, 'Global Public Goods: A Survey' (2021) 59 Journal of Economic Literature 488.

8 See Moya Chin 'What Are Global Public Goods?' (December 2021) IMF Finance & Development 62.

9 Joseph E Stiglitz 'Knowledge as a Global Public Good' in Inge Kaul, Isabelle Grundberg, and Marc Stern (eds) *Public Goods; International Cooperation in the 21st Century* (OUP 1999), 311.

3.1 Financial Cycles and Inherent Instability

The theoretical milestone in the development of macroprudential policy can be traced back to the scholarship of Hyman Minsky, an American economist and professor of Economics at Washington University in St Louis. His seminal 'Financial Instability Hypothesis'[10] provided the analytical foundation for a supervisory policy devoted to overseeing systemic events arising along the financial cycles. Minsky argues that capitalist economies are inherently fragile as investment and financing process in good times eventually lead to destabilizing events.

When market actors become overoptimistic owing to positive economic trends, they tend to accumulate debts, over-invest and fuel asset prices. This accrual leads to unsustainable levels of risk-taking, consumption and indebtedness. When the breaking-point is reached a destabilizing debt-deleveraging event will follow, triggering asset price crashes, bank runs and output contraction. The inherent nature of boom-and-bust cycles requires a more peculiar type of financial supervision and examination focused on understanding the negative externalities arising in upswing and downswing phases.

Minsky recognizes the need to move away from a microprudential approach to supervision heavily dependent on assessing individual bank's balance sheet robustness. As a preferable alternative to forecast the likelihood of financial instability and systemic events, he proposed a 'cash flow approach' focusing on the interrelationship of banks' balance sheets and liquidity positions.[11] Minsky's ideas undoubtedly previewed the need of such macroeconomic dimension to financial supervision (and regulation) and the theoretical underpinnings of what years later will become macroprudential policy. The events of 2007–2008 proved him correct.

3.2 Transmission Channels

Since instability is as an inherent characteristic of the financial system, we should determine how systemic events may originate and spread across the markets to ultimately pop up in financial crisis. Prior to describing the strictly legal components of macroprudential regulation, the reader should in fact delve into the 'transmission channels' that may eventually lead to macroeconomic disruption.[12] Such analysis allows us to better understand how macroprudential provisions are set and what tools and frameworks are envisioned by regulators to mitigate systemic risks and safeguard financial stability.

---

[10] Hyman P Minsky, 'The Financial Instability Hypothesis' (1992) Levy Economics Institute of Bard College, Working Paper No. 74 <https://www.levyinstitute.org/pubs/wp74.pdf> accessed 1 July 2023. For a review of Minsky's scholarship, see Perry Mehrling, 'The Vision of Hyman P. Minsky' (1999) 39 Journal of Economic Behavior and Organisation 129.

[11] Hyman P Minsky, 'Suggestions for a Cash Flow Oriented Bank Examination' (1967) Hyman P. Minsky Archive Paper 175. See also: Ronnie J Phillips 'Rethinking Bank Examinations: A Minsky Approach' (1997) 31 Journal of Economic Issues 509.

[12] For a general discussion of the topic, see Howell E Jackson, 'Thinking Hard About Systemic Risk', in Douglas W Arner and others (eds), *Systemic Risk in the Financial Sector: Ten Years After the Great Crash* (CIGI Press 2019) where the author provides not only a careful analysis of the concept of systemic risk, but also a summary of the principal transmission channels through which systemic risk propagates.

An ever-growing economic literature is today dedicated to qualifying these transmission channels and quantifying the negative spillover effects resulting from severity and scope of the crisis.[13] As the financial system becomes increasingly more complex and interrelated, progressive economic analysis is deemed necessary to fully capture new transmission mechanisms or recontextualize old transmission scenarios. A summary of the most relevant transmission channels is provided below.

(a) *Risk-taking:* This channel operates when financial agents are incentivized to increase their leverage or assume riskier investments over the financial cycle's upswings. For banks this channel is particularly prominent as in good times they may increase their risk appetite and fuel lending supply. Aggregate risk-taking behaviors of banking institutions and other financial intermediaries may exacerbate procyclicality. In the long run financial imbalances may build up because of distortion in the allocation of credit. Should these financial imbalances amplify over time systemic risk may eventually arise triggering a credit burst. A downturn period will follow.

(b) *Asset price:* This transmission channel operates through movements in asset prices. Macroeconomic variables, such as changes in underlying interest rates, may affect agents' decisions on borrowing and spending. In financial cycles' upswings excessive levels of borrowing and spending may rapidly inflate the prices of stocks, bonds, real estate and commodities. Asset prices greatly exceeding their underlying intrinsic values may lead to systemic risks. Should asset prices become unsustainable a sharp correction usually follows with serious macroeconomic consequences to the whole economy.

(c) *Liquidity and maturity transformation:* The liquidity channel operates based on potential overreliance and/or under-pricing of liquidity by multiple financial intermediaries in the financial cycle's upswings. Periods of abundant market funding and liquidity may incentivize financial institutions to undervalue liquidity risk. As the perceived risk is low, institutions may be willing to rely on (less stable) short-term wholesale funding to finance their long-term activities. On the asset side, institutions may be incentivized to hold illiquid assets owing to their perceived higher liquidity risk-bearing capacity. As the liquidity conditions tighten, financial institutions are rushed to increase their liquidity reserves and seek new long-term funding. A fire sale of illiquid assets to meet short-term obligations could follow. As the crisis deteriorates a sudden dry-up of liquidity flows may trigger systemic risk to the financial system.

(d) *Financial interconnectedness:* Interconnectedness among financial institutions is another channel of instability. The financial system can be rationalized as a complex dynamic network where economic agents are highly interrelated through their balance

[13] By way of example, see: Nikos Paltalidis and others, 'Channels of Systemic Risk and Contagion in the European Financial Network' (2015) 61 Journal of Banking and Finance 36; Guojin Chen and others, 'Stock Price Bubbles, Leverage and Systemic Risk' (2021) 74 International Review of Economics & Finance 405; Markus Brunnermeier, Simon Rother and Isabel Schnabel, 'Asset Price Bubbles and Systemic Risk' (2020) 33 The Review of Financial Studies 4272. For a general review of the topic, see also Amorello (n 3) 25–28.

sheet exposures and liabilities. Direct and indirect linkages among these entities may amplify systemic risks through financial contagion.[14]

These channels of instability allow systemic risk to emerge and propagate across the financial networks. Yet they also allow supervisors and policymakers to locate market actors' position in the financial cycle by monitoring their aggregate behaviors. Finally – as noted in the next sections – these channels can help outline a definition of macroprudential policy and a taxonomy of systemic risk categories based on which the basic building blocks of macroprudential regulation come to be constructed.

3.3 Macroprudential Policymaking vs Regulation

Having identified the channels of financial instability, a simple operating rationale of macroprudential policymaking can now be provided. Macroprudential policy is primarily intended to mitigate the extremes of the financial cycles.[15] To do so tools are designed to operate along the transmission channels and mitigate risks of systemic nature that may arise during upswing and downswing phases.

Because the financial cycle is inherently dynamic and requires targeted intervention along its different phases to operate effectively, macroprudential instruments should not be set according to fixed rules.[16] Effective policymaking should be given a certain degree of discretion by the legal framework and macroprudential tools should be designed in a flexible dynamic fashion, meaning that authorities should be able to tighten or ease these tools depending on the boom–bust cycle.[17]

Against this backdrop, macroprudential regulatory frameworks just set out legal constraints within which dedicated macroprudential authorities can exercise their discretionary counter-cyclical actions to reduce the inherent systemic risks in the financial system and mitigate its negative spillover effects.

Despite some variance in the institutional settings, these legal constraints are present in all jurisdictions having a macroprudential framework and are intended to: (i) enlist a pre-defined set of policy tools and indicators that can be used depending on different macroeconomic

---

[14] For a brief introduction to the systemic risk transmission arising from complex financial interconnectedness, *inter alia* see: Jackson (n 12) 5–6. As an example of economic analysis of this transmission channel, see: Alan Roncoroni and others, 'Interconnected banks and systemically important exposures' (2021) 133 Journal of Economic Dynamics and Control, Issue C, 104266.

[15] See: Group of Thirty, *Enhancing Financial Stability and Resilience: Macroprudential Policy, Tools and Systems for the Future* (Group of Thirty Washington DC 2010) 20.

[16] Bank of England, *The Role of Macroprudential Policy* (BOI 2009) 4. However, the debate on the matter is not settled. A different view is provided in Jeremy Kress and Metthew Turk, 'Rethinking Countercyclical Financial Regulation' (2022) 56 Georgia Law Review 495, where the authors argue in favor of embedding 'automatic triggers' in macroprudential tools.

[17] See: Itai Agur and Sunil Sharma, 'Rules, Discretion, and Macro-Prudential Policy' (2013) IMF Working Paper, No. 2013/065; Lien Laureys and Roland Meeks, 'Monetary and Macroprudential Policies Under Rules and Discretion' (2017) Bank of England Staff Working Paper No. 702.

scenarios; (ii) ensure the predictability of the policy strategies and actions; and (iii) promote accountability and transparency of macroprudential authorities.[18]

4. COMPONENTS OF MACROPRUDENTIAL REGULATORY FRAMEWORKS

Having identified the economic underpinnings of macroprudential policies, the analysis can now delve into the actual macroprudential regulatory regimes, particularly exploring the existing commonalities and divergences across jurisdictions.

It must be reiterated that origin and development of macroprudential regulatory frameworks have been primarily led in the aftermath of the 2007–2008 financial crisis by international organizations, such as the FSB, IMF and BCBS. These fora have provided the intellectual high ground for the refined set of principles and arrangements governing the most notable macroprudential regimes, laying down a homogenous theoretical backdrop replicated and implemented across most G-20 jurisdictions.[19]

Looking at the foundational work undertaken by these global organizations, it can be argued that the main components of a functioning macroprudential regulatory regime are: (i) a taxonomy of 'intermediate objectives'; (ii) an array of relevant indicators; (iii) a pre-defined set of macroprudential instruments; and (iv) clear governance models. The law of macroprudential policy is therefore calibrated to ensure all these components are clearly spelled out in the financial architecture of different jurisdictions.

4.1 Intermediate Objectives

In the previous sections the maintenance and promotion of financial stability has been identified as the ultimate objective of macroprudential regulation. In this context preserving financial stability means mitigating the excessive build-up of risks which may 'systemically' spread across the financial system via transmission channels.

While multiple definitions of 'systemic risk' exist depending on features and criticalities,[20] suffice it to say that systemic risk is characterized by a multifaceted nature and may take different forms depending on how it propagates through the channels of instability. Regulators and policymakers have identified common taxonomies of systemic risk categories which are instrumental in shaping and developing tools and indicators.[21] Albeit non-exhaustive, the

---

18 See: IMF, *Macroprudential Policy: An Organizing Framework* (IMF 2011). On this topic, see also Anat Keller, *Legal Foundations of Macroprudential Policy, An Interdisciplinary Approach* (Intersentia 2020) 177–216.

19 See n 3. See also FSB, IMF and BIS, *Elements of Effective Macroprudential Policies Lessons from International Experience* (FSB, IMD and BIS 2016).

20 For a literature review on systemic risk, see Sylvain Benoit and others, 'Where the Risks Lie: A Survey on Systemic Risk' (2017) 21 Review of Finance 109. For a debate on the legal definition of systemic risk, see: Steven L Schwarcz, 'Systemic Risk' (2008) 97 Georgetown Law Journal 193.

21 In this respect, see for example, the *ESRB Handbook on Operationalising Macroprudential Policy in the Banking Sector*, where a taxonomy of systemic risks that may affect the EU banking sector is clearly defined.

following systemic risk categories are particularly noteworthy for the purposes of this chapter and are widely shared among all G-20 jurisdictions.

(a) *Cyclical/structural risk:* This category relates to the risk of excessive leverage and credit growth which may spread via the risk-taking and asset price channels. This systemic risk particularly arises when financial institutions are incentivized to assume excessive risks in the upswings of the financial cycle. In downswing periods, the risk is associated with financial institutions becoming excessively risk averse, hoarding credit supply and triggering an output contraction to the economy as a result.

(b) *Systemic liquidity and funding risk:* This systemic risk category is due to the disruption of the liquidity and maturity transformation channel. On the liability side (*funding*) of financial institutions' balance sheets, funding risk would arise because of a sudden liquidity dry-up owing to a shock or negative expectations. On the asset side (*liquidity*) this risk stems from fire sales of illiquid assets and/or mismatches between asset and liabilities.

(c) *Exposure-based risk:* This risk arises from interconnectedness and common exposures of financial institutions and is basically associated with contagion risk within the market. Financial institutions can act as both risk receiver and risk driver in a crisis and can propagate losses from both sides of the balance sheets to other connected institutions.

(d) *Risk posed by systemically important institutions:* This risk category may affect all transmission channels and is fundamentally due to collective moral hazard of financial institutions deemed systemically important (SIIs) or too big to fail.

(e) *Other (emerging) systemic risks:* This category is broad and may encompass a wide range of different risks or events. Some particularly notable examples include systemic cyber-risk, climate risk and risks associated with crypto currencies and decentralized finance.[22] Another well-known systemic risk relates to the 'bank–sovereign nexus' and the financial institutions' sovereign overexposures to highly indebted countries.[23]

The systemic risk categories identified through this taxonomy can be understood as 'intermediate objectives' of macroprudential regulations. While the ultimate objective describes the aim which the policy action should focus on, intermediate objectives allow policymakers and regulators to actively operationalize macroprudential policy via tools, indicators and governance models. It follows that macroprudential regulation provides for each systemic risk type a specific set of indicators and tools especially designed to mitigate its extremes.

[22] These represent the most recent systemic risks identified in the EU. For details, see: European Systemic Risk Board, *Systemic Cyber Risk* (ESRB 2020); *Crypto-assets and Decentralised Finance, Systemic Implications and Policy Options* (ESRB 2023).

[23] For a general overview of the topic, see: Giovanni Dell'Ariccia and others, 'Managing the Sovereign–Bank Nexus' (2018) 2018 IMF Departmental Papers.

4.2 Indicators

Quantitative and qualitative indicators are used by authorities to monitor the evolution of systemic risks across the financial cycles and measure risk levels on financial stability.[24] These indicators can also be leveraged as 'triggers'. Should entities breach certain risk thresholds, this may compel macroprudential authorities to consider adopting a specific action. Automatism however is generally discouraged: the regulatory regimes even in these cases grant a certain degree of discretion to the authorities in setting their final decisions.[25] This ensures comprehensive analysis of all the variables and prevent excessive reliance on decontextualized data. Indicators are always looked at holistically, and their primary function is to support authorities' expert judgement.[26]

More importantly, there is a clear linkage between intermediate objectives and indicators. For any systemic risk category, a dedicated set of indicators is developed and calibrated. These risk-specific indicators are intended to monitor each phase of the financial cycle, including the build-up of risk, the materialization of shocks and the propagation of negative spillover effects.

Finally, it must be noted that the predictive and monitoring power of the indicators is heavily dependent upon the quality of data and information gathered and aggregated by relevant authorities. While this is true for all public policy areas, this is particularly important for macroprudential frameworks owing to the ever-evolving nature of systemic risks and the volume of granular information required to make meaningful policy decisions. Against this backdrop, macroprudential authorities have made multiple efforts over the years to close any data gaps along with designing and collecting new sophisticated datasets for reporting and statistical purposes.[27]

4.3 Toolkits and Policy Instruments

Central to macroprudential regulatory frameworks is the creation of 'toolkits', namely a wide range of policy instruments that can be applied by relevant authorities to different classes of financial institutions. Each tool is designed to target a specific systemic risk category and operate within a specific transmission channel. A clear linkage is thus established between intermediate objectives, indicators and policy instruments.

The first category of macroprudential instruments is characterized by a 'dynamic nature', meaning that they can be flexibly adjusted during upswing and downswing phases to mitigate negative externalities. Policymakers have typically leveraged microprudential policies to build these instruments, adding countercyclical features to well-known capital and liquidity pruden-

---

[24] Among others, see Claudio Borio and Mathias Drehmann, 'Towards an Operational Framework for Financial Stability: Fuzzy Measurement and its Consequences' (2009) BIS Working Paper No. 284; Mencia Javier and Jesus S Salas, 'Macroprudential Policy: Objectives, Instruments and Indicators' (2016) 1601 Banco de Espana Occasional Paper 14.

[25] For a counterargument in support of automatism, see n 15.

[26] For details, see: Ellen Ryan, 'The Role of Macroprudential Indicators in Monitoring Systemic Risk and Setting Policy' (2017) Central Bank of Ireland Quarterly Bulletin Articles 62.

[27] In this respect, see for example the G20 Data Gaps Initiative launched in 2009 by the G20 Finance Ministers and Central Bank Governors to close the policy-relevant data gaps identified during the 2007–2008 global financial crisis.

tial requirements.[28] By way of example, during period of excessive credit growth supervisory authorities can tighten banks' capital buffers to help reduce credit supply by making it more expensive. In downturns capital buffers may be relaxed to sustain credit supply to a weakened economy.

A few other macroprudential tools are structural in nature and are mainly intended to (i) either increase the overall resilience of financial institutions or (ii) influence market participants' behaviors. For example, capital and liquidity surcharges can be applied to systemically important institutions to strengthen their loss-absorbing capacity. Limits on borrowers – such as caps on loan-to-value or loan-to-income ratios – can be imposed to dampen borrowing incentives or reduce excessive loan creation.

Additional instruments may belong to other public policy areas – e.g. fiscal, monetary, or administrative – but can be strategically used to mitigate systemic risks. For example, real estate taxes may be utilized to slow down periods of excessive asset price growth. These tools are typically in the hands of independent fiscal and monetary authorities rather than financial supervisors. As a result, it is important to deploy them in coordination with macroprudential authorities to avoid policy conflicts or sub-optimal outcomes.[29]

4.3.1 Tools for banking institutions

The most developed macroprudential regulatory instruments apply to banking institutions. Over the last 15 years G-20 countries have particularly designed macroprudential instruments to increase the resilience of the financial systems against shocks generated by banking organization of different sizes. Table 11.1 summarizes the main macroprudential tools for banks linking each of them to its intermediate objective and transmission channel.

Countercyclical capital buffers are capital cushions of common equity that banks must hold specifically designed to (i) protect against periods of excessive aggregate credit growth and (ii) help banks supply credit in downturns. These buffers can be flexibly adjusted by the relevant authorities: in the upswing periods authorities may increase the countercyclical capital buffer rate to incentivize banks to curb their credit supply; in downswings these buffers can be eased, making it cheaper for banks to extend credit to the economy. Generally, the regulatory framework allows the buffer rates to be set between 0 and 2.5% of bank's risk-weighted assets (although a value in excess of this can be envisioned under certain circumstances). A dedicated early warning indicator (i.e. the so-called credit-to-GDP gap[30]) is mainly used as a guide for the setting the buffer rates.

Sectoral capital requirements are instruments designed to mitigate risks arising in specific sectors of the economy and are represented by extra capital cushions that banks must hold

28 For an interesting perspective on this microprudential basis for macroprudential tools, see Jeremy C Kress and Jeffery Y Zhang, 'The Macroprudential Myth' (2024) 112 Georgetown Law Journal, where the authors assess the shortcomings and economic consequences of these policy construction.

29 See Stijn Claessens, 'An Overview of Macroprudential Policy Tools' (2014) IMF Working Paper No. 14/214 10. For an analytical study on the coordination benefits, see *inter alia* Malmierca, María (2023) *Optimal Macroprudential and Fiscal Policy in a Monetary Union*, Economic Modelling, vol 122.

30 For details, see Mathias Drehmann and Kostas Tsatsaronis, 'The Credit-to-GDP Gap and Countercyclical Capital Buffers: Questions and Answers' (2014) March BIS Quarterly Review 55.

Table 11.1 Overview of the available macroprudential tools

Transmission channel	Intermediate objective	Macroprudential tool
Risk-taking	Cyclical risk	Countercyclical capital buffers
Risk-taking/asset prices	Structural risk	Sectoral capital requirements
Risk-taking	SIIs risk	Capital surcharges
Risk-taking	Cyclical/structural risk	Leverage ratio
Financial interconnectedness	Exposure-based risk	Large exposures limits
Liquidity and maturity transformation	Liquidity and funding risk	Liquidity requirements
Asset prices	Cyclical risk	LTV, LTD and LTI caps
All channels	All systemic risks	Stress testing
All channels	All systemic risks	Reporting and disclosure requirements

Source: Author's own.

vis-à-vis their exposure to the specific economic sectors. For example, should the real estate sector in a specific jurisdiction heat up, banks may be required to build an add-on capital reserve against their exposures to the affected real estate segment. This should moderate the aggregate bank supply of mortgage loans and, ultimately, ease real estate asset prices. Sectoral indicators (such as real estate valuations and lending terms) are commonly used to support the adoption of these capital requirements.

The SII capital surcharges represent additional common equity buffers imposed on systemically important banks in addition to their minimum risk-based capital requirements. Their rate usually follows the size and complexity of the affected banking institution, meaning that the more systemic the bank the higher the capital surcharge is likely to be. The policy rationale of these instruments is to increase the loss absorption capacity of significant institutions and reduce their incentives to become even bigger or more complex.

Leverage ratios are intended to limit excessive bank leverage. They require institutions to hold a certain percentage of equity irrespective of their risk exposures and, because of this, are generally considered as a backstop to risk-weighted capital instruments. Leverage ratios can be construed as macroprudential tools by calibrating them in accordance with the boom/bust phases of the financial cycle (i.e. higher ratios can be applied in periods of market exuberance; ratios can be eased in downturns).

Large exposures limits are microprudential instruments that prevent banks from having exposures to a specific entity or group that are equal or above a certain percentage of their equity. By limiting exposures towards a single counterparty, these instruments help banks withstand losses resulting from the failure of the counterparty or connected counterparties and prevent the risk of contagion. Depending on the systemic nature of the risks perceived in the financial system, authorities generally have the power to tighten or ease these exposure limits vis-à-vis certain risk exposures. As a result, these limits can be tailored in a macroprudential fashion to counter systemic exposure-based risks.

Liquidity tools, such as the liquidity coverage ratio (LCR) and the net stable funding requirements (NSFR), can also be utilized macroprudentially. The LCR requires banks to hold enough high-quality liquidity assets to ensure that in the event of a liquidity shock they can maintain the ability to meet their short-term obligations over a 30-day period. The NSFR reduces incentives to heavily rely on unstable short-term wholesale funding by requiring banks to maintain a certain percentage of stable long-term funding sources on an ongoing basis. Authorities generally have the power to add a dynamic cyclical component to these liquidity tools by increasing/reducing the relevant ratios in accordance with the conditions of the financial cycles. In doing so, liquidity tools can operate through the liquidity and maturity transformation channel targeting systemic funding and liquidity risks.

Loan-to-value (LTV)/loan-to-deposit (LTD) caps are aggressive macroprudential tools designed to curb booms driven by excessive housing credit growth and inflated real estate price. These tools consist of limits imposed by the authorities on the size of loans that banks can offer based on (i) the value of the underlying collateral or (ii) the deposit amount provided by the borrower. Other macroprudential borrowers' limits, such as the loan-to-income (LTI) and the debt service-to-income (DSTI) ratio caps, are also widely adopted. These limits may heavily reduce mortgage loan creation as banks would be no longer able to extend credit without the required collateral, borrower's income, or equity. This in turn may negatively affect borrowers' housing choices and prevent entire segments of the society to become houseowners.

Stress testing has become quite a common macroprudential tool among banking supervisors. In this respect, stress tests are organized to assess and test the resilience of the banking sector at large, rather than single credit institutions. This macroprudential testing helps authorities better understand how shocks can propagate across the banking sector and the financial system and monitor adverse effects to the real economy. Macroprudential testing is also used to inform policymakers on the banking sector's ability to withstand shocks and assess the efficiency of deploying certain macroprudential instruments under pre-defined scenarios.

Reporting and disclosure requirements allow supervisors to collect, aggregate and publish banking sector data that is instrumental to macroprudential policy analysis and decision-making. Enhanced reporting and disclosure requirements may also be imposed by the authorities (where necessary) to improve the quality, granularity and frequency of information deemed essential to monitor emerging systemic risks.

4.3.2 Tools for non-bank financial institutions

While developed macroprudential regulations primarily focus on systemic risks arising in the banking sector, global and local policymakers have over the last few years sought to expand international and national macroprudential frameworks to target other non-bank financial institutions, such as insurance companies, money market funds (MMFs) and investment funds. Policy proposals have been put forward to this purpose and a few macroprudential tools have been implemented in the regulatory regime of few G-20 countries.

The array of non-bank macroprudential instruments is not systemically organized and is still subject to debate regarding scope and efficacy. The overall contribution of these tools to general financial stability is small at present owing to their infancy status and lack of proper regulatory rationalization. Yet the understanding (and awareness) of non-bank vulnerabilities affecting financial stability is rapidly growing and forcing policymakers to leverage non-bank microprudential instruments to address macroprudential concerns.[31] Without attempting to

---

[31] For a discussion of the topic, see: Agustín Carstens, 'Non-bank Financial Sector: Systemic Regulation Needed' (2021) December BIS Quarterly Review 1.

be comprehensive, we provide here below a summary of some of the most relevant non-bank macroprudential tools as envisioned today.

In several jurisdictions ongoing supervisory requirements deemed macroprudential in nature apply to insurance companies. Higher capital requirements for global systemically important insurers proportionate to their systemic risk profiles have been developed by the International Association of Insurance Supervisors and are now subject to national implementation. Symmetrical adjustments of the equity capital charge are used to mitigate procyclicality in the insurance sector by making equity more or less expensive in market upwards or downwards. System-wide solvency stress testing is also widely implemented.

For MMFs and investment funds macroprudential liquidity requirements have been envisioned by regulatory frameworks. These entities may be prone to significant liquidity issues in times of crisis as investors may rush to exercise their redemption rights to safeguard their investments. Large volumes of sudden redemptions may affect the liability side of balance sheets. As a result, these entities may find it difficult to obtain new liquidity owing to negative money markets conditions. Simultaneously, it may be particularly expensive to sell illiquid assets, generally representing a large portion of the assets side of their balance sheets. Owing to interconnectedness with other financial institutions (especially banks) these systemic liquidity risks may quickly spread across the financial markets, causing significant instability.

A few jurisdictions (particularly the European Union) have therefore introduced cyclical liquidity requirements for MMFs aiming at (i) ensuring entities have sufficient liquidity to meet investors' redemption requirements and (ii) demanding a certain degree of portfolio diversification with minimum amounts of daily and weekly liquid assets holdings. Additional provisions have been envisioned in the regulatory frameworks to allow for the temporary suspensions of redemptions to deal with liquidity constraints during stress.

Leverage requirements applicable to investments funds are also considered by some jurisdictions. Hedge funds and other pooled investments vehicles may amplify shocks during financial turmoil owing to their use of leverage and the absolute size of their exposures. As these funds are generally very interconnected to the wider financial system (especially pension funds and banks), contagion risk may ensue. Leverage limits have therefore been adopted in number of countries to mitigate the build-up of these systemic risks.

Finally, as for the case of banks, reporting and disclosure requirements applicable to non-bank financial institutions are a fundamental source of data for macroprudential policy analyses and decision-making. Numerous provisions have been embedded in national regulatory frameworks applicable to insurance companies, MMFs and investment funds providing for macroprudential data collection and disclosure.

4.3.3 Market-wide tools

Additional market-wide macroprudential instruments are currently subject to policy discussion across several jurisdictions and proposals have been put forward for their implementation. These tools are designed to mitigate systemic risks arising from targeted financial transactions in wholesale financial markets rather than financial intermediaries. A prominent example in this respect is the development of countercyclical margining requirements for derivatives and secured financing transactions to tackle the procyclical nature of margin and haircut-setting practices of market participants and the build-up of leverage and liquidity risk.

5. SELECTED INSTITUTIONAL MODELS

The last component of macroprudential regulatory frameworks is represented by their institutional governance. Specialized authorities are generally set up with a clear macroprudential mandate and pre-defined powers and responsibilities. These authorities are then provided with (and may develop) the relevant indicators to monitor systemic risks and determine the best course of action. In addition, they are entrusted with the adoption of the regulatory instruments based on their informed discretion.[32]

In other words, while the regulatory framework sets out the array of macroprudential tools that can be utilized, it is the responsibility of the macroprudential authority to implement them based on the specific circumstances. The regulatory framework is to ensure transparency of the policy actions and accountability of the policy outcomes.[33] Considering the far-reaching (and sometime burdensome) consequences of these policies, public scrutiny and oversight are vital.[34]

The biggest differentiation across jurisdictions with a macroprudential framework lies in the large variety of governance models set up to address systemic risks. While macroprudential instruments are in fact replicated across jurisdictions depending on the specific needs and features of national financial cycles, the institutional variance is driven by the level of independence granted to the macroprudential authority and its proximity to other public bodies, such as the central bank and the treasury.

In this respect the economic and policy literature has identified three main institutional models underpinning the construction of the governance architectures.[35] First, under the so-called 'full integration model'[36] the macroprudential authority is either the national central bank or the treasury. This is pursued by giving a financial stability mandate to one of these bodies. This model better ensures coordination with other public policies (such as monetary or fiscal policies) but may negatively affect the necessary independence of the macroprudential policy action.

Second, a 'partial integration model'[37] exists where the macroprudential mandate is entrusted to an independent committee with systemic risk monitoring responsibilities. This committee is generally composed of members of the central bank, treasury and national supervisory authorities and – disregarding national specificities – its function is to provide policy recommendations to other public bodies to adopt and implement macroprudential instruments.

---

[32] For a seminal description of the optimal institutional arrangements for macroprudential frameworks see FSB, IMF and BIS, *Macroprudential Policy Tools and Frameworks, Progress Report to G20* (FSB, IMF and BIS, 27 October 2011). See also: IMF, 'Macroprudential Policy: An Organizing Framework' (2011) IMF Policy Papers.

[33] See n 18.

[34] For a discussion of this topic, see among others IMF, 'Key Aspects of Macroprudential Policy' (2013) IMF Policy Papers, 28–29.

[35] For more insights on the institutional models for macroprudential policy see Erlend W Nier and others, 'Institutional Models for Macroprudential Policy' (2011) IMF Discussion Note 11/18; Erlend W Nier and others, 'Towards Effective Macroprudential Policy Frameworks: An Assessment of Stylized Institutional Models' (2011) IMF Working Paper 11/250.

[36] ibid, p. 9, where this model is first described.

[37] ibid., p. 11.

Having a separate committee ensures greater independence of the policy action, although external or political pressure can still be exercised by the committee members. This model is not the most efficient as the actual implementation of the macroprudential tools is separate from the committee's decision-making.

Third, a 'full separation model'[38] exists where the macroprudential authority is a fully independent body with assigned powers and responsibilities. In such a case the macroprudential authority is responsible for both decision-making and actual policy implementation with a large degree of autonomy and discretion.

To provide a comparative analysis of these regulatory regimes, the following sections are intended to provide a description of the macroprudential governance models as implemented in selected jurisdictions.

5.1 The US Macroprudential Oversight Experience

Following the implementation of the Dodd–Frank Act in 2010, the US have adopted a partial integration model by establishing the 'Financial Stability Oversight Council' (FSOC). The FSOC's statutory responsibility is primarily the monitoring and oversight of risks to financial stability in the US. It is chaired by the Secretary of State and comprises 10 voting members and five non-voting members. These members are representatives from financial regulators, state regulators and an independent member with insurance expertise.[39]

It is noteworthy that the FSOC does not have the power to impose macroprudential tools directly.[40] Its mandate is to identify, monitor and assess potential systemic risks emerging in the US financial system following a clearly defined analytical framework. Additionally, the committee helps facilitate communication and cooperation across all represented US supervisory agencies. Key risks currently identified by the FSOC are (i) the risks arising from non-bank financial intermediation, (ii) climate-related financial risk, Treasury market vulnerabilities and (iii) risks related to digital assets.[41]

Moreover, the Dodd–Frank Act gives the FSOC the power to determine that a non-bank financial institution may pose a material threat to US financial stability owing to its nature, scope, size, concentration or activities.[42] Designated non-bank financial institutions are to be subject to consolidated supervision by the Federal Reserve and enhanced prudential standards. A similar power exists in respect of financial market utilities that may create significant liquidity or credit risks. Financial market utilities identified as systemically important are to be subject to enhanced prudential and supervisory requirements.

---

[38] ibid., p. 15.

[39] For a general description of the FSOC, see Edward V Murphy and Michael B Bernier, 'Financial Stability Oversight Council: A Framework to Mitigate Systemic Risk' (2011) Congressional Research Service Report for Congress.

[40] For a critical analysis of the FSOC (including the lack of autonomous regulatory powers), see Paolo Saguato, 'Rethinking the Financial Stability Oversight Council' (2022) 16 Virginia Law & Business Review 505.

[41] See FSOC 2022 Annual Report.

[42] For a critical review of this mandate, see: Jeremy C Kress, Patricia A McCoy, and Daniel Schwarcz, 'Regulating Entities and Activities: Complementary Approaches to Nonbank Systemic Risk' (2018) 92 Southern California Law Review 1455.

The power to adopt macroprudential instruments is generally allocated to prudential supervisors but it must be noted that the US macroprudential toolkit (and its use) is relatively limited at present. Only a few macroprudential tools have been embedded in the regulatory regime. In this respect, the Federal Reserve has played a prominent role as it applies SII capital charges to systemically important banks and has the power to set the countercyclical capital buffer rates. The Federal Reserve also conducts annual bank stress testing exercises with macroprudential components, such as system-wide scenarios and associated risks.

5.2 Macroprudential Supervision in EU and UK

The EU is characterized by a more layered macroprudential governance. Following a partial integration model, the European Systemic Risk Board (ESRB) has been established in 2010 with the responsibility of macroprudential oversight of the EU financial system.[43] The ESRB is tasked with gathering relevant data and information relevant to financial stability along with the identification, prioritization, and analysis of systemic risks across the EU.

The ESRB General Board is chaired by the Governor of the European Central Bank (ECB) and is composed of representatives of the national central banks of EU countries and the chairs of the European supervisory authorities. A representative of the European Commission also attends the Board meetings.

The ESRB does not have the power to adopt macroprudential instruments directly. This power is generally allocated to designated national authorities in the EU Member States. Depending on the national institutional arrangements and model preferences, these designated authorities can be (i) the national central bank (with a full integration model), (ii) the national financial supervisors or (ii) an independent macroprudential committee (reflecting the full separation model).

These peculiar organizational settings reflect and ensure the retention of macroprudential powers at national level as EU Member States are considered better able to cope with local externalities arising out of the financial cycles. As the EU financial system is not fully integrated and the financial cycle may differ across Member States, national authorities are better positioned to proactively target systemic risk and adopt macroprudential tools that are more closely tailored to the characteristics of their respective national economies.[44] In view of this, a full centralization of macroprudential powers and full harmonization of macroprudential tools at EU level would not seem desirable as this would probably produce sub-optimal policy outcomes.

The ESRB can influence the implementation of national macroprudential policies by issuing (non-binding) warnings and recommendations addressed to Member States, European supervisory authorities, or national supervisory authorities. This is particularly the case when

---

[43] For a general description of the ESRB, see *inter alia*: Luis G de Rozas, 'The First Ten Years of the European Systemic Risk Board (2011–2021)' (2022) 42 Banco de España Financial Stability Review 121. See also: Thierry Tressel 'Macroprudential Oversight and the Role of the European Systemic Risk Board' in Charles Enoch and others (eds), *From Fragmentation to Financial Integration in Europe* (IMF 2013).

[44] For details, see the ESRB, *ESRB Handbook on Operationalising Macroprudential Policy in the Banking Sector* (ESRB 2018), describing the divergence of financial cycles in the EU and the need to apply tools at national level to target country-specific systemic risks.

systemic risk is identified in a specific jurisdiction and remedial action is considered necessary to mitigate negative externalities. A comply-or-explain process is provided allowing the ESRB to monitor the recipients' compliance status.[45]

A different model has been adopted in the UK where the Financial Policy Committee (FPC) – the UK body established in 2013 with responsibilities for macroprudential oversight – has broader powers. The FPC can issue binding directions and instructions to the Prudential Regulation Authority and Financial Conduct Authority (FCA), requiring them to apply macroprudential tools to financial institutions. Similar to the ESRB, the FPC can also issue recommendations under a comply-or-explain regime. The FPC is composed of six members from the Bank of England, the Chairperson of the FCA and five external independent members. A non-voting Treasury representative also attends its meetings.[46]

5.3 Macroprudential Models in Asia-Pacific Economies

Asia-Pacific countries are generally characterized by fully integrated macroprudential governance models where macroprudential policy is conducted by the national central bank alongside monetary policy.

This is the case in China where macroprudential policy is responsibility of the People's Bank of China in line with its financial stability mandate. Since the 2009 financial crisis a sophisticated macroprudential policy framework has been established in the country including a wide range of macroprudential tools.[47] Particularly noteworthy is the widespread use of LTV ratio caps on property lending and countercyclical reserve requirements for liquidity risk management. An advanced macroprudential assessment system was introduced in 2016 which includes indicators for capital and leverage, asset and debt, liquidity, pricing, asset quality and cross-border risks.

A similar institutions model exists in Indonesia where the Indonesian central bank is mandated with macroprudential responsibilities alongside monetary and payment system policies. Its macroprudential supervision extends to banks and non-banks financial institutions alike. Since 2011 several macroprudential tools have been implemented in the country, including LTV ratio caps, reserves requirements and counter-cyclical capital buffers. A country-specific macroprudential intermediation ratio and a Sharia macroprudential intermediation ratio have also been adopted to reduce procyclical behaviours in the banking industry.[48]

---

[45] For a detailed description of the ESRB's 'soft law' powers, see the ESRB, *ESRB Handbook on the Assessment of Compliance with ESRB Recommendations* (ESRB 2016).

[46] For a detailed analysis of the UK macroprudential framework, see Kosmas Kaprinis, *The Institutional Structure of Macroprudential Policy in the UK* (Springer 2023).

[47] For a review of the Chinese macroprudential framework, see: Kerry Liu, 'China's Macroprudential Policies: Framework, Implementations and Implications' (2020) 3 Journal of Financial Compliance, Henry Stewart Publications, 273. See also: The People's Bank of China, 'Macroprudential Goals, Implementation and Cross-border Communication' (2017) 94 BIS Papers 99.

[48] For an overview of the Indonesian macroprudential framework, see: Perry Warjiyo, 'Indonesia: The Macroprudential Framework and the Central Bank's Policy Mix' (2017) 94 BIS Papers 189.

Slightly more complex is the institutional framework in India. As regulator of banks and non-bank financial institutions and being tasked with a financial stability mandate, the Reserve Bank of India (RBI) conducts macroprudential policy in respect of these financial institutions. Since 2004 the RBI has applied numerous macroprudential instruments, such as countercyclical capital buffers, sectoral capital requirements, LTV ratio caps and large exposure limits. Macro-financial stress tests and a wide range of indicators provide for a robust analytical framework for the identification and monitoring of systemic risks.[49]

In addition, separate supervisory agencies for capital markets, insurance and pension funds also play a role in macroprudential policy as they are entrusted with targeting systemic risks arising in these specific markets. Interagency coordination is ensured by the Financial Stability and Development Council (FSDC). Established in 2020, the FSDC has the explicit mandate to safeguard financial stability, supervising the implementation of macroprudential policies in the country and acting as a single inter-institutional forum for policy discussion and information sharing.

6. ARE MACROPRUDENTIAL REGULATIONS EFFECTIVE? SOME CONCLUDING REMARKS

This chapter has described the economic foundations of macroprudential policy along with the regulatory building blocks of what constitutes a macroprudential regulatory architecture. Additionally, we have summarized the most common governance models by looking at selected jurisdictional regimes across the globe. Despite the multifaceted nature of systemic risks and the variance in the institutional governance, substantial harmonization exists globally with respect to scope, objectives, and policy toolkits.

In concluding this chapter a few words are to be said on how effective macroprudential policies are in achieving their intermediate and ultimate objectives. Considering the public significance of this topic, it is no surprise that a growing economic literature is seeking to theoretically and empirically quantify the level of effectiveness of macroprudential tools along with any externalities arising from their implementation.[50] Without attempting to be comprehensive, a few important considerations in this respect can be drawn from the bulk of this economic scholarship and institutional literature.

First, macroprudential policies are relatively effective in increasing the resilience of financial institutions and borrowers.[51] They are particularly successful in limiting the build-up of systemic risks in the financial cycle's upswings and mitigating excessive leverage. Second,

---

[49] A review of the Indian macroprudential framework is provided in Reserve Bank of India, 'Macroprudential Frameworks, Implementation, and Relationship with Other Policies' (2017) 94 BIS Papers 179.

[50] For a critical review of the literature, see Gabriele Galati and Richhild Moessner, 'What Do We Know About the Effects of Macroprudential Policy?' (2017) 85 Economica, 735.

[51] Miguel Ampudia and others, 'On the Effectiveness of Macroprudential Policy' (2021) 2559 ECB Discussion Paper. See also: Kristin J Forbes, 'The International Aspects of Macroprudential Policy' (2021) 13 Annual Review of Economics 203.

macroprudential policies are less effective in downturns.[52] Relaxing policy instruments in downswing phases is not seen as helpful in supporting credit growth and, more generally, economic expansion. Third, the effectiveness of macroprudential policies is largely dependent on the economic openness and development of the jurisdictions.[53] The more open or developed the economy is, the less likely are macroprudential policies to be successful. Lastly, macroprudential policies are more effective when are complementary to other public policies, particularly monetary policy.[54] Policy coordination in fact provides better outcomes for financial stability and macroeconomic growth.

---

52 For example, see Carlos Cantú, Leonardo Gambacorta and Ilhyock Carlos, 'How Effective are Macroprudential Policies in Asia Pacific? Evidence from a Meta-analysis' (2020) BIS Paper No 110; Leonardo Gambacorta Giovanni Lombardo and Luiz A P da Silva, 'What are the Effects of Macroprudential Policies on Macroeconomic Performance?' (2017) September BIS Quarterly Review. See also Juliana Araujo and others, 'Effects of Macroprudential Policy: Evidence from over 6,000 Estimates' (2020) IMF Working Paper 20/67.

53 Among others, see Eugenio Cerutti and Stijn Claessens, Luc Laeven, 'The Use and Effectiveness of Macroprudential Policies: New Evidence' (2017) 28 Journal of Financial Stability 203.

54 See Longmei Zhang and Edda Zoli, 'Leaning Against the Wind: Macroprudential Policy in Asia' (2014) IMF Working Paper 14/22; Leonardo Gambacorta and Andrés M Pabón, 'The Impact of Macroprudential Policies and Their Interaction with Monetary Policy: An Empirical Analysis Using Credit Registry Data' (2017) BIS Working Paper No 636.

12. Corporate governance of banks

Katrien Morbee

1. INTRODUCTION

The 2007–2008 financial crisis focused attention on the problems with the corporate governance of systemically important banks, leading to the introduction of corporate governance rules specifically designed for banks.[1] The most recent banking crisis – which began with a bank run on Silicon Valley Bank and spread globally affecting major European Banks such as Credit Suisse and Deutsche Bank – highlighted again the importance of good bank governance. An analysis by the *Financial Times*, for example, showed that executives at Silicon Valley Bank received generous pay after the bank changed its investment strategy and started investing in riskier assets,[2] a strategy that would eventually result in the bank's collapse.

Corporate governance refers to the system[3] by which firms are directed and controlled.[4] The chapter takes an agency perspective on corporate governance.[5] More specifically, it starts from the premise that firms delegate the management of their business to a manager ('the agent'), who is in charge of the decision-making in the interest of the firm and its constituencies ('the principal').[6] Traditionally, it was accepted – according to the predominant view in the Anglo-American corporate governance scholarship[7] – that a firm (including banks) should be

---

1 European Banking Authority, *EBA Guidelines on Internal Governance* (EBA, 2011); Organisation for Economic Co-operation and Development, *Corporate Governance and the Financial Crisis: Key Findings and Main Messages* (OECD, 2009).

2 Antoine Gara, Patrick Temple-West and Tabby Kinder, 'Executive Pay at Silicon Valley Bank Soared after Big Bet on Riskier Assets' *Financial Times* (New York and San Francisco, 24 March 2023) <https://www.ft.com/content/02ff2860-2d5b-4e21-96af-cef596bff58e> accessed 6 May 2024.

3 There is no canonical definition of corporate governance in the literature or policy documents; however, most definitions focus on the internal processes related to the power balance between shareholders, board and managers, such as board independence, board composition and shareholder empowerment, see Mariana Pargendler, 'The Corporate Governance Obsession' (2016) 42 The Journal of Corporation Law 359, 361–362.

4 Adrian Cadbury, *Report of the Committee on the Financial Aspects of Corporate Governance* (Gee 1992) <https://media.frc.org.uk/documents/Cadbury_Code_-_The_Financial_Aspects_of_Corporate_Governance.pdf> accessed 6 May 2024.

5 The agency perspective on corporate governance is widely used, see Jonathan R Macey, *Corporate Governance: Promises Kept, Promises Broken* (Princeton University Press 2008); Andrei Shleifer and Robert W Vishny, 'A Survey of Corporate Governance' (1997) 52 The Journal of Finance 737.

6 Michael C Jensen and William H Meckling, 'Theory of the Firm: Managerial Behavior, Agency Costs and Ownership Structure' (1976) 3 Journal of Financial Economics 305.

7 In the comparative literature, the standard narrative is that corporate governance in continental Europe, Japan and China tends more towards the stakeholder-oriented model, while the

run in the interests of its shareholders, within the boundaries of the applicable law and prior agreements with other stakeholders.[8] However, studies conducted in the aftermath of the 2007–2008 financial crisis showed that the banks that adhered to 'good' corporate governance practices, as defined pre-crisis, also encountered the most losses.[9] Today, the emerging consensus is that the activities of (large) banks may generate systemic losses, which are not considered by shareholders when making discretionary decisions and distort decision-making from a financial stability point of view.[10] Therefore, the literature argues for a retreat from the shareholder maximization model in banks.[11] In this chapter, we will first discuss why bank governance should be different from 'general' corporate governance. We will argue that bank governance should be an integral part of an effective prudential framework. Secondly, we will analyze the approaches taken by regulators in the EU and US to tackle the identified problems.

2. THE CORPORATE GOVERNANCE OF BANKS: WHY ARE BANKS DIFFERENT?

This section introduces the governance debate with respect to systemically important banks. First, we discuss the systemic nature of the business model of banks. Second, we argue that the current 'external' prudential regulation and supervision – in place to address systemic issues in banks – is likely to have significant loopholes. Finally, we argue that governance interventions can help gain traction to address systemic issues in banks and are therefore a key part of an effective prudential framework.

---

corporate governance in the UK and US is focused on shareholder value, see M Gelter, 'The Dark Side of Shareholder Influence: Managerial Autonomy and Stakeholder Orientation in Comparative Corporate Governance' (2009) 50 Harvard International Law Journal 129, 131; Mathias M Siems, *Convergence in Shareholder Law* (Cambridge University Press 2008) 176–178.

8 Frank H Easterbrook and Daniel R Fischel, *The Economic Structure of Corporate Law* (Harvard University Press 1991) 38; Milton Friedman, 'The Social Responsibility of Business is to Increase its Profits' *The New York Times* (New York, 13 September1970) <https://www.nytimes.com/1970/09/13/archives/a-friedman-doctrine-the-social-responsibility-of-business-is-to.html> accessed 6 May 2024; Macey (n 5).

9 Marco Becht, Patrick Bolton and Ailsa Röell, 'Why Bank Governance is Different' (2011) 27 Oxford Review of Economic Policy 437; Andrea Beltratti and René M Stulz, 'The Credit Crisis around the Globe: Why Did Some Banks Perform Better?' (2012) 105 Journal of Financial Economics 1; David H Erkens, Mingyi Hung and Pedro Matos, 'Corporate Governance in the 2007–2008 Financial Crisis: Evidence from Financial Institutions Worldwide' (2012) 18 Journal of Corporate Finance 389.

10 John Armour and Jeffrey N Gordon, 'Systemic Harms and Shareholder Value' (2014) 6 Journal of Legal Analysis 35; Lucian A Bebchuk and Holger Spamann, 'Regulating Bankers' Pay' (2009) 98 Georgetown Law Journal 247, 251–252; Jonathan R Macey and Maureen O'Hara, 'The Corporate Governance of Banks' (2003) 9 Economic Policy Review 91, 97–98; Joel Shapiro, Alan Morrison and Hamid Mehran, 'Corporate Governance and Banks: What Have We Learned from the Financial Crisis?' in Mathias Dewatripont and Xavier Freixas (eds), *The Crisis Aftermath: New Regulatory Paradigms* (Centre for Economic Policy Research 2012) 37.

11 John Armour and others, *Principles of Financial Regulation* (Oxford University Press 2016) 371; Armour and Gordon (n 10); Macey and O'Hara (n 10); Shapiro, Morrison and Mehran (n 10).

2.1 The Systemic Nature of the Bank's Business Model

First, we determine why the business model of a bank can create systemic risk and therefore is different from other corporations. We start by determining the business model of banks. Next, we look for features of the business model that could pose a threat to financial stability. Finally, we determine whether the pursuit of profit under the business model encourages the presence and severity of these systemic features.

2.1.1 The bank's business model

In banks, the business model consists of earning profits from the transformation of deposits into loans, i.e. through the spread between the interests on deposits (liabilities) and the interests on loans (assets). In other words, banks earn profits by performing a 'transformation function'.[12] The literature identifies three transformation functions of banks.[13] First, banks engage in liquidity transformation. They provide depositors with liquidity by offering to pay back a 'sum certain' whenever depositors need cash. Banks then invest these deposits into assets – i.e. loans – which cannot be quickly converted into cash by the bank. The bank can perform such liquidity transformation because only a fraction of the depositors will actually use the option to withdraw their deposits.[14] Second, banks engage in maturity transformation. They transform short-term deposits into long-term loans. Third, they engage in credit transformation. Loans are risky investments, which might not accord with the risk-appetite of risk-averse undiversified depositors. A bank is better placed to take on such risk, if only because the pooling of funds allows banks to better diversify the risks involved than individual investors.

2.1.2 The systemic nature of bank activities

It is generally accepted that the activities of (large) banks, can have a significant impact on financial stability and the functioning of the real economy. The transformation function performed by banks makes a bank's balance sheet structurally fragile. The transformation of short-term liquid deposits into long-term illiquid loans makes banks particularly vulnerable to liquidity problems.[15] Such transformation creates multiple equilibria. If confidence in the operations of the bank is maintained, banks provide efficient risk-sharing between depositors by insuring for liquidity shocks of depositors. If confidence is lost, investors will want to withdraw deposits before the bank runs out of assets. Early withdrawals are more likely to be fully repaid, creating a dominant strategy for investors to run on the bank. Such a dynamic could even result in the failure of financially healthy banks, as banks will be forced to sell off illiquid loans at fire sale prices in order to meet withdrawals.[16]

These difficulties can constitute a local shock or 'trigger' event and affect the entire financial system through a variety of 'contagion channels', i.e. interconnections within the

---

[12] Armour and others (n 11) 277–279; Xavier Freixas and Jean-Charles Rochet, *Microeconomics of Banking* (2nd edn, MIT Press 2008).

[13] For a more detailed discussion of these three transformation functions, see Armour and others (n 11) 277–279.

[14] Douglas Diamond and Philip Dybvig, 'Bank Runs, Deposit Insurance, and Liquidity' (1983) 91 The Journal of Political Economy 401.

[15] Armour and Gordon (n 10) 40.

[16] Diamond and Dybvig (n 14).

financial system that allow for a local shock to spread and 'contaminate' a significant part of the financial system.[17] First of all, spillovers can happen through direct counterparty exposure, namely the 'counterparty channel'. Banks and other financial institutions are closely linked through trade activities amongst each other. For example, bank A takes out an unsecured loan from bank B and C. As a result, the failure of bank A could lead to difficulties at banks B and C because they most likely will not get repaid on the loan contracts. This might lead to cascading failures and take down a substantial part of the banking sector. Furthermore, even without direct counterparty exposure, other financial institutions could be exposed to a failing institution through the 'asset liquidation channel'. Imagine bank A having similar investments to bank D and E. Banks A, D and E have no direct contractual relationship. Bank A might encounter liquidity problems and be forced to quickly sell the correlated assets in fire sales, depressing the market value of the assets. This will result in losses for banks D and E if their holdings of those assets are marked-to-market.[18] In addition, imperfect information might lead to overreaction by market participants who incorrectly fear that other institutions are directly or indirectly exposed to the failing bank.[19] The bigger the bank the more likely it is that distress will spread through the financial system via the counterparty and asset liquidation channel.

Finally, systemic risk is characterized by its consequences for the real economy. Bank failures – and distress in the financial system more generally – are systemic because of the costs the difficulties pose for the real economy. More specifically, bank failures impose a cost on society owing to the critical role of banks in the real economy. Banks perform an essential function by reducing the cost of credit intermediation by developing expertise in identifying good borrowers, establishing long-term customer relationships and writing loan conditions.[20] Moreover, banks provide critical payment services.[21] Disruptions in the banking system, therefore, lead to efficiency losses in the credit allocation process – leaving good business projects unfunded – and interruptions in the payment system.

2.1.3 The perverse incentives under the bank business model

Given the systemic nature of the business model, the question remains whether the business benefits from the presence of these systemic features and, therefore, will actively pursue business strategies that increase systemic risk. If the answer is positive, the trade-offs made by the business model will not consider the system-level costs resulting from systemic features, as these costs can be externalized to third parties.

---

[17] The discussion is based on the more detailed account of systemic externalities generated by financial institutions in Markus Brunnermeier and others, *The Fundamental Principles of Financial Regulation: Geneva Reports on the World Economy 11* (International Center for Monetary and Banking Studies 2009) 3–5.

[18] For example, derivatives instruments are marked-to-market under both IAS 39 and its replacement IFRS 9. Generally speaking, IFRS 9 has reduced marked-to-market of assets compared with IAS 39.

[19] Armour and Gordon (n 10) 40–41.

[20] Ben S Bernanke, 'Nonmonetary Effects of the Financial Crisis in the Propagation of the Great Depression' (1983) 73 The American Economic Review 257, 263.

[21] Independent Commission on Banking, 'Final Report' (ICB, September 2011) <http://webarchive.nationalarchives.gov.uk/20131003105424/https:/hmt-sanctions.s3.amazonaws.com/icb%20final%20report/icb%2520final%2520report%5B1%5D.pdf> accessed 25 July 2018, 35.

In banks, the business does not bear a huge part of the potential systemic downside of risky business decisions. This is so because banks are highly levered relative to other firms, which allows banks to take a huge bet on the firm's balance sheet. Consider a bank with a leveraged loan portfolio of £10 financed by £1 of equity and £9 of debt in the form of deposits. Leverage allows the shareholders to increase their exposure to value changes in the loan portfolio from £1 to £10. When the portfolio generates gains, the bank benefits from the upside of the entire portfolio net the costs of the deposits. Leverage also increases the exposure of the bank to decreases in the value of the portfolio. Losses on the loan portfolio beyond the initial equity investment of £1 will result in the inability of the bank to pay back its depositors. However, this is of little concern to the bank's constituencies – and the shareholders and creditors in particular – owing to the presence of externalities. Shareholders, on the one hand, are protected through limited liability. Shareholders do not bear the losses beyond the shareholders' capital investment of £1, making the bet on the firm's balance sheet asymmetric from the vantage point of the shareholders.[22]

The bank creditors, on the other hand, are thought to have reduced incentives compared with creditors of regular firms to police risky behaviour by banks by increasing the price of credit, including restrictive covenants, or monitoring the behaviour of the bank.[23] This is largely because much of the bank's debt consists of deposits. Depositors are widely dispersed which leads to coordination and free-riding problems with regard to monitoring. More importantly, the systemic importance of the bank's activities has induced the government to provide deposit insurance in order to prevent bank runs. Such insurance further discourages depositors from monitoring the bank's behaviour as their claims are (partly) guaranteed by the state.[24] In addition, in previous times of crisis, governments have decided to bail out systemically important banks in difficulties in order to prevent a bankruptcy, and this could happen again in the future. Such bail-outs shield even the long-term creditors (e.g. bondholders) – who cannot run on the bank – from the consequences of a bankruptcy.[25] These creditors might therefore also have reduced incentives to increase the price of credit, include restrictive covenants and/or monitor the bank, insofar as they expect a government bail-out of the bank. This is because in the case of a bail-out, they will not bear the full costs of default either.[26] This implicit government guarantee for systemically important banks gives banks incentives to become 'too big to fail', as this will reduce their costs of credit.[27] In other words, state guarantees, explicit or implicit, turn the creditors' problem into a problem for the government and its taxpayers. The contractual problem turns into a regulatory problem.

---

[22] Bebchuk and Spamann (n 10).

[23] Armour and Gordon (n 10) 45; Bebchuk and Spamann (n 10) 251 and 257.

[24] Bebchuk and Spamann (n 10) 257; Macey and O'Hara (n 10) 98; Shapiro, Morrison and Mehran (n 10) 14.

[25] Armour and others (n 11) 342.

[26] Bebchuk and Spamann (n 10) 266–267.

[27] Armour and others (n 11) 374; Mark J Roe, 'Structural Corporate Degradation Due to Too-Big-to-Fail Finance' (2014) 162 University of Pennsylvania Law Review 1419.

2.2 Gaps in the 'External' Prudential Regulation and Supervision

Prior to the crisis, 'external' prudential regulation and supervision were considered sufficient to prevent banks from taking excessive risk. There is a substantial body of 'external' prudential regulation that constrains banks in taking certain decisions (e.g. structural regulation prevents banks from engaging in proprietary trading) or encourages or even requires banks to take certain precautionary measures (e.g. bank capital and liquidity requirements).[28]

However, 'external' regulation is inevitably incomplete, as it is impossible – ex ante – to unambiguously specify for all future contingencies.[29] In the context of systemic risk, this problem is especially pertinent, if only because the fast pace of innovation leaves regulators always one step behind market developments.[30] Financial innovations can create systemic problems in a short period of time, which ex-ante rules are unable to anticipate. The issues surrounding the calculation of risk-based bank capital requirements or the premium paid for deposit guarantee systems are illustrative examples in this context.

Supervision by the prudential authorities can – to some extent – fill in the gaps left by incomplete external prudential norms. Traditionally, bank supervision focused on ensuring compliance with prudential regulation. In the mid-1990s the Federal Reserve started implementing a 'risk-based' approach to supervision. In risk-based supervision the focus lies on the discretionary assessment of the supervisor regarding the bank's risk management and quality of its assets, rather than compliance with specific rules.[31] Risk-based supervision is based on a conversation between supervisors and the firm and provides supervisors with the ability to adjust the behavior of banks – ex post – in the case it is deemed necessary for financial stability. In recent years there has been a trend to limit – to some extent – the discretion of the prudential authorities within the supervisory process of banks.[32]

However, supervision – as a solution to the incompleteness of external prudential norms – has significant flaws, if only because financial innovation and complexity create an information asymmetry between market participants and supervisors. Moreover, even in the presence of complete information, the limited public resources put significant constraints on the ability of prudential supervisors to understand the functioning of the market and timely identify risks.[33]

---

28 Bebchuk and Spamann (n 10).

29 Katharina Pistor and Chenggang Xu, 'Incomplete Law' (2003) 35 New York University Journal of International Law and Politics 931.

30 Dan Awrey, 'Regulating Financial Innovation: A More Principles-Based Alternative?' (2011) 5 Brooklyn Journal of Corporate, Financial and Commercial Law 273.

31 Eric J Pan, 'Understanding Financial Regulation' [2012] Utah L. Rev. 1897.

32 An example in this context is the introduction of CAMELS, i.e. a rating system used by prudential authorities to rate banks based on six factors, namely capital adequacy, asset quality, management, earnings, liquidity and sensitivity.

33 Armour and others (n 11) 82–84.

2.3 The Role of Corporate Governance

In light of the analysis above, we argue that governance interventions are an important part of an effective prudential framework.[34] In this context, we need to determine how governance interventions can help gain traction to address the systemic concerns identified. Prior to the financial crisis, the governance mechanisms used in banking did not differ significantly from those used in the general corporate governance framework. Bank governance relied on board oversight and independence, stock-based compensation, and strong shareholder rights in order to manage agency costs between managers and shareholders.[35] Stock-based compensation in particular was widely used to align the incentives of managers with the bank's business model by using the share price as proxy for bank performance.

The financial crisis has focused attention on the problems with the corporate governance of banks. There are at least two stances in the literature related to the failure of bank governance. On the one hand, it is argued that governance practices did not properly align the incentives of managers and shareholders. Boards did not have the necessary knowledge and independence to properly oversee the operations of the bank business in the interests of the shareholders. The complexity of a bank's business makes such oversight more difficult for bank boards than boards in non-financial firms. In non-financial firms, board oversight consists of ensuring that the firm's strategy is properly operationalized. However, in banks, such oversight demands an assessment of the risks involved in financial assets, which requires highly specialized knowledge. For example, in order to determine the value of an asset, the liquidity of the underlying market should be considered.[36] Moreover, if it has already proven difficult to correctly calibrate performance-based compensation in non-financial firms, the complexity of the bank's business model makes such calibration issues even more pertinent in banks. Performance depends on an assessment of the state of the financial assets (e.g. the creditworthiness of the borrower), which is difficult to translate into performance benchmarks. In this context, Bebchuk, Cohen and Spamann argue that the pre-crisis bank executive compensation gave incentives to increase short-term profits in order to receive large amounts of performance compensation, even though this increased the probability of large losses for shareholders in the long term.[37] However, an empirical study by Fahlenbrach and Stultz[38] found no evidence

---

[34] This idea is confirmed by changes made to the post-crisis regulatory landscape to strengthen governance. Bank governance for example has a prominent role in the Supervisory Review and Evaluation Process (Pillar 2 of the Basel Framework).

[35] For a detailed discussion of why bank governance is different and an overview of the post-crisis reforms, see John Armour and others, *Principles of Financial Regulation* (Oxford University Press 2016), 370–390.

[36] ibid 378; Paul Davies and Klaus J Hopt, 'Non-Shareholder Voice in Bank Governance' in Danny Busch, Guido Ferrarini and Gerard van Solinge (eds), *Governance of Financial Institutions* (Oxford University Press 2019).

[37] Lucian Bebchuk, Alma Cohen and Holger Spamann, 'The Wages of Failure: Executive Compensation at Bear Stearns and Lehman 2000–2008' (2010) 27 Yale Journal on Regulation 257.

[38] Rüdiger Fahlenbrach and René M Stulz, 'Bank CEO Incentives and the Credit Crisis' (2011) 99 Journal of Financial Economics 11.

that greater sensitivity of CEO pay to stock volatility was related to worse stock returns during the crisis.[39]

Another stance in the literature holds that shareholders benefitted from the excessive risk-taking by managers and therefore the governance failure did not occur in the manager–shareholder relationship, but in the manager–society relationship. As discussed above, limited liability entails that shareholders enjoy unlimited upside, but capped downside. In other words, corporate governance constraints increased the manager's incentives to create systemic externalities in line with the principal-level incentives. It is argued that where 'general' corporate governance measures should (mainly) be calculated to prevent abuse in the shareholder–manager relationship, bank corporate governance additionally needs to consider the conflict of interests between shareholders and society as a whole. Schwarcz, for example, argues for including bondholders' interests in the corporate governance of systemically important firms[40] through representation of bondholders on the board or through making managers accountable to both shareholders and bondholders. Although the incentives of bondholders are not perfectly aligned with the incentives of the public in general, Schwarcz argues that the pursuit of the interests of creditors will indirectly improve systemic stability by reducing the incentives to take risk.[41] Others argue for altering the compensation structure of the bank's executives to better align their interests with the interests of the creditors and/or the public. For example, Bebchuk and Spamann advocate tying executive compensation to a broader basket of securities than stocks and stock options.[42] Other authors advocate for an increased liability structure for bank officers and directors.[43] Omarova proposes an even more radical reconfiguration by giving the federal government – as holder of a 'golden share' – a seat on the board of each systemically important banking organization with direct but conditional management rights. At all times, such directors should have certain 'dormant' rights, e.g. to approve risk policies. When there is a higher likelihood of increasing systemic risk, the special director gets more intrusive rights to, for example, veto or slow down certain activities.[44] These proposals aim to change the interaction between the governance framework and the systemic concerns identified for banks. More specifically, the proposals want to make the interaction beneficial for systemic stability by reducing the agent's incentives to create systemic externalities more than would be desirable based on the principal-level – or shareholders' – incentives.

39 'A plausible explanation for these findings is that CEOs focused on the interests of their shareholders in the buildup to the crisis and took actions that they believed the market would welcome. Ex post, these actions were costly to their banks and to themselves when the results turned out to be poor.' See ibid 12.

40 Where the literature discusses the problem from a broader perspective and includes other financial institutions, it abstains from engaging in a detailed analysis of the characteristics of these non-bank financial institutions.

41 Steven L Schwarcz, 'Rethinking Corporate Governance for a Bondholder Financed, Systemically Risky World' (2017) 58 William & Mary Law Review 1345.

42 Bebchuk and Spamann (n 10).

43 Armour and Gordon (n 10); Claire A Hill and Richard W Painter, *Better Bankers, Better Banks: Promoting Good Business through Contractual Commitment* (The University of Chicago Press 2015).

44 Saule T Omarova, 'Bank Governance and Systemic Stability: The'Golden Share'Approach' (2017) 68 Alabama Law Review 1029.

3. THE REGULATORY FRAMEWORK IN THE EU AND THE US

In this section, we discuss the approaches taken in the EU and the US to tackle the problems identified in the previous section. Most company laws identify two distinct bodies which govern the companies' affairs: the general meeting of shareholders and the board of directors. Increasingly, the board of directors in 'general' corporate governance frameworks is being made responsible for monitoring managerial behaviour on behalf of the shareholders in addition to managing the companies' business.[45] The shareholders in a general meeting – especially in the case of publicly traded companies with dispersed ownership – can face significant information and coordination costs to monitor managers themselves and, therefore, are given voting rights to elect directors to do so on their behalf, whether based on pre-nomination by the board or not. Directors are subject to legal duties of loyalty and care towards their corporation and shareholders. In addition, corporate governance codes generally require boards to have a number of directors that fulfil specific independence requirements in order to ensure that the directors will represent the shareholders instead of the managers. Independent directors are typically required to participate in the board committees in order to encourage shareholder accountability in the committees' decisions.[46] Below, we will evaluate to what extent regulators have 'de-linked' the incentives of decision-makers or 'agents' in bank corporate governance from the perverse incentives of shareholders. We will organize the discussion along three important levers used in corporate governance: the board of directors and their independence, remuneration and shareholder rights.

3.1 The Board of Directors and their Independence

The regulators in the EU and the US have both intervened in the operations of the board of directors. The discussion below will focus on the presence of 'independent' directors on bank boards. Indeed, post-crisis reforms have relied to a greater or lesser extent on independent directors to act as buffer between the senior managers and a robust risk management framework.[47]

In the EU, the Capital Requirements Directive (CRD) emphasizes the role of the board of directors to approve and review the 'policies for taking up, managing, monitoring and mitigating the risks the institution is or might be exposed to'.[48] The CRD does not impose a minimum number of independent directors on the board, although having both independent

---

[45] OECD, 'G20/OECD Principles of Corporate Governance' (2015) 45 <https://www.oecd-ilibrary.org/governance/g20-oecd-principles-of-corporate-governance-2015_9789264236882-en> accessed 6 May 2024.

[46] John Armour and others, *The Anatomy of Corporate Law: A Comparative and Functional Approach* (Oxford University Press 2017) 63–64.

[47] Christopher M Bruner, 'Corporate Governance Reform in Post-Crisis Financial Firms: Two Fundamental Tensions' (2018) 60 Arizona Law Review 959, 976.

[48] Council Directive 2013/36/EU of 26 June 2013 on access to the activity of credit institutions and the prudential supervision of credit institutions and investment firms, amending Directive 2002/87/EC and repealing Directives 2006/48/EC and 2006/49/EC [2013] OJ L 176/338 [hereinafter CRD], art 76.

and non-independent board members is considered good practice. Proportionality should be considered when determining the sufficient number of independent directors.[49] The CRD does require the separation of the functions of chairman of the board and the chief executive officer.[50] It also requires that board members should commit sufficient time to perform their function.[51] They should also be of good repute and possess sufficient knowledge and skills and experience to perform their duties;[52] they should act with honesty, integrity and 'independence of mind'.[53] Moreover, the CRD requires that institutions that are significant – considering their size, internal organization and the nature, scope and complexity of the activities – establish a risk committee,[54] a nomination committee[55] and a remuneration committee,[56] composed of non-executive – 'independent' – directives.[57] Joint European Securities and Market Authority (ESMA) and European Banking Authority (EBA) guidelines identify the situations where it is presumed that a member is not 'being independent'.[58] Important for the present purpose is that only independence of a controlling shareholders is required, not of the shareholders as a class. Being a shareholder should not lead to non-independence within 'an appropriate de minimis threshold'.[59]

In the US, the post-crisis reforms added special independence requirements at the level of the compensation committee and risk committees. The Dodd–Frank Act introduces the requirement that certain publicly traded systemically important financial institutions and bank

---

49 ESMA and EBA, 'Joint ESMA and EBA Guidelines on the assessment of the suitability of members of the management body and key function holders under Directive 2013/36/EU and Directive 2014/65/EU' (EMSA and EBA, July 2021) 39.

50 CRD IV art 88 (1) (e).

51 CRD art 91 (2).

52 CRD art 91 (1).

53 CRD art 91 (8).

54 CRD art 76 (3).

55 CRD art 88 (2).

56 CRD art 95 (2).

57 The EBA guidelines on internal governance determine that the risk and nomination committees should be composed of non-executive members. According to the EBA guidelines on sound remuneration policies, the remuneration committee should be composed of non-executive members. In Global Systemically Important Institutions (G-SIIs) and Other Systemically Important Institutions (O-SIIs), the remuneration committee should include a *majority* of members who are independent. The chair should always be an independent member. In other significant institutions – as determined by competent authorities or national law – the remuneration committee should include a *sufficient number* of independent members, see EBA, 'Guidelines on Internal Governance Under Directive 2013/36/EU' (EBA, July 2021) <https://www.eba.europa.eu/sites/default/files/document_library/Publications/Guidelines/2021/1016721/Final%20report%20on%20Guidelines%20on%20internal%20governance%20under%20CRD.pdf> accessed 6 May 2024, 24–25; EBA, 'Guidelines on Sound Remuneration Policies under Directive 2013/36/EU' (EBA, July 2021) <https://www.eba.europa.eu/sites/default/files/document_library/Publications/Guidelines/2021/1016720/Draft%20Final%20report%20on%20GL%20on%20remuneration%20policies%20under%20CRD.pdf> accessed 6 May 2024, 33.

58 ESMA and EBA, 'Joint ESMA and EBA Guidelines on the Assessment of the Suitability of Members of the Management Body and Key Function Holders under Directive 2013/36/EU and Directive 2014/65/EU', EBA/GL/2017/12, 40–41.

59 ESMA and EBA (n 49) 42.

holding companies establish risk committees. These should include a number of independent directors, as determined appropriate by the Federal Reserve Board of Governors based on 'the nature of operations, size of assets, and other appropriate criteria' related to institution.[60] The Federal Reserve requires that at least one director has 'experience in identifying, assessing, and managing risk exposures of large, complex financial firms'. The chair should be independent. More specifically, the chair should not be (or not have been during the previous three years) an officer or employee of the institution, or an immediate family member of an executive officer.[61] Moreover, the chair should be (or qualify as) 'independent' under the listing standards of a national securities exchange.[62]

Regarding remuneration committees, Section 952 of the Dodd–Frank Act requires the SEC to adopt rules directing the national securities exchanges to prohibit the listing of securities unless issuers follow the requirements regarding compensation committee independence. More specifically, each member of the compensation committee must be a member of the board of directors and should be independent. Subject to SEC approval, the exchanges should develop their own definition of independence considering relevant factors, including the factors determined by Section 952: 'the source of compensation of a member of the board of directors of an issuer' and 'whether a member of the board of directors of an issuer is affiliated with the issuer, a subsidiary of the issuer, or an affiliate of a subsidiary of the issuer'.[63]

In others words, we need consider the specific listing standards of the national securities exchanges in order to determine what is considered 'independent' in the US. For example, the New York Stock Exchange Listed Company Manual specifies an 'independence test'. Regarding the independence from shareholders' incentives, the manual determines that 'no director qualifies as "independent" unless the board of directors affirmatively determines that the director has no material relationship with the listed company (either directly or as a partner, shareholder or officer of an organization that has a relationship with the company)'.[64] The NYSE independence test therefore does not allow the director to have a relationship with the company as a shareholder, if such relationship can be considered 'material'. However, the commentary clarifies that 'the concern is independence from management' and that ownership of a significant amount of stock, by itself, does not bar a qualification as independent.

Overall, the discussion makes clear that requiring 'independent' directors in the board composition is an important tool in the EU and US bank governance framework. However, considering the perverse incentives of shareholder, such independence requirements should not only ensure the independence from management, but also from shareholders. The discussion of the EU and US regulatory framework makes it clear that this is not guaranteed through the independence tests adopted. Indeed, independence of shareholders as 'a class' is not required. In sum, the independence of board members introduced does not de-link the directors' incentives

---

[60] Section 165 (h) Dodd–Frank Act.

[61] 12 CFR § 252.33 for bank holding companies with total consolidated assets of at least $100 billion and 12 CFR § 252.22 for bank holding companies with total consolidated assets of at least $50 billion and less than $100 billion.

[62] 12 CFR § 252.33 for bank holding companies with total consolidated assets of at least $100 billion and 12 CFR § 252.22 for bank holding companies with total consolidated assets of at least $50 billion and less than $100 billion.

[63] §952 Dodd–Frank Act.

[64] New York Stock Exchange Listed Company Manual § 303A.02.

from shareholders' incentives. This is unsurprising as board independence has traditionally been adopted as a means to ensure directors are independent from managers' influence to the benefit of shareholders.[65]

3.2 Remuneration

After the 2007–2008 financial crisis, regulators in the EU and US also intervened in the remuneration packages offered in banks (and other institutions) in order to align them with prudent risk management. Traditionally, compensation was considered an important tool to encourage the company's officers to pursue the economic interests of shareholders.[66] Payment through bonuses, shares and options can link compensation to the performance of the firm. Holding periods and clawbacks can ensure that executives do not pursue short-term goals.[67] In this section, we will compare the post-crisis interventions in the types of compensation allowed in banks in the EU and the US, in light of the analysis above. We will consider the substance of the remuneration packages and not the interventions in the 'procedure' of setting remuneration.

In the EU, the CRD adopts a detailed set of requirements related to remuneration in credit institutions and investment firms. The requirements are applicable to the remuneration of staff whose professional activities have a material impact on the institution's risk profile.[68] The requirements set a cap on the 'variable' – i.e. performance-based – component of the remuneration package. More specifically, the variable component cannot exceed 100% of the fixed component. Member States can set a lower maximum percentage. Moreover, Member States can allow a higher maximum level of the ratio between the fixed and variable components of remuneration with shareholder approval by supermajority, provided that the overall level of the variable component does not exceed 200% of the fixed component of the total remuneration.[69] When calculating the ratio between the variable and fixed component of the remuneration, Member States may allow a discount rate of maximum 25% of the variable

---

[65] In practice, it is difficult to prevent independence requirements from being a box ticking exercise, as an inability of shareholders to monitor managers themselves is likely to correlate with an inability to actively engage in the election process and ensure the true independence of the directors from managers' influence. Moreover, directors will generally need to rely on the managers to provide them with the information necessary to monitor these same managers. Hopt and Leyens state that in publicly traded companies in Germany the management board often just picks the supervisory board, see Klaus J Hopt and Patrick C Leyens, 'Board Models in Europe – Recent Developments of Internal Corporate Governance Structures in Germany, the United Kingdom, France, and Italy' (2004) 1 European Company and Financial Law Review 135, 141.

[66] European Commission, 'Action Plan: European Company Law and Corporate Governance – a Modern Legal Framework for More Engaged Shareholders and Sustainable Companies' (EC, December 2012) <https://eur-lex.europa.eu/legal-content/EN/TXT/PDF/?uri=CELEX:52012DC0740&from=EN> accessed 25 July 2018, 9; Financial Reporting Council, 'The UK Corporate Governance Code' (FRC, 2018) 14.

[67] Financial Reporting Council (n 66) 14; OECD (n 45) 48.

[68] CRD art 92.

[69] CRD art 94 (1)(g).

remuneration, provided the variable component is paid in instruments that are deferred over a period of not less than 5 years.[70]

At least 50% of the variable remuneration must consist of a balance of shares, equivalent ownership rights, share-linked or equivalent non-cash instruments and certain other defined eligible instruments. These instruments shall be subjected to an appropriate retention policy 'designed to align incentives with the longer-term interests of the institution'.[71]

Moreover, at least 40% of the variable remuneration must be deferred over a period which is not less than four to five years and correctly aligns with 'the nature of the business, its risks and the activities of the staff member concerned'. The deferral period should be not less than five years for members of the management body and senior management of institutions that are significant in terms of their size, internal organization and the nature, scope and complexity of their activities.[72]

The CRD also includes a 'clawback' provision. In particular, the variable remuneration should be paid or vest only if it is 'sustainable according to the financial situation of the institution as a whole, and justified on the basis of the performance of the institution, the business unit and the individual concerned'. Moreover, the variable remuneration 'shall generally be considerably contracted where subdued or negative financial performance of the institution occurs'.[73]

In the US, the Dodd–Frank Act specifies principles for executive compensation of both financial and non-financial firms in Sections 951–957. The provisions are less prescriptive than in the EU. They require implementation by the competent agencies. Some rules – such as the rules on compensation committees as discussed above – have been implemented by the relevant agencies. Others have remained on regulatory hold. Relevant in this context for example is Section 956 of the Dodd–Frank Act, which requires agencies to prescribe regulations and guidelines that 'prohibit any types of incentive-based payment arrangement, or any feature of any such arrangement, that the regulators determine encourages inappropriate risks by covered financial institutions (1) by providing an executive officer, employee, director, or principal shareholder of the covered financial institution with excessive compensation, fees, or benefits; or (2) that could lead to material financial loss to the covered financial institution'. The proposed inter-agency rule was released in 2016 determining substantive requirements for remuneration packages, including rules on deferral of variable pay and downward adjustment in the case of losses for larger institutions. The proposed rules do not impose a ceiling on overall incentive compensation, in contrast to the EU.[74] At the end of 2022, the SEC adopted – after reopening the comment period – the final rule implementing Section 954 imposing a change in the listing standards on national securities exchanges requiring companies to recoup incentive-based compensation received by (current or former) executive officers, in the event of a required accounting restatement, 'where that compensation is based on the erroneously reported financial information'.[75]

---

[70] CRD art 94 (1)(g).
[71] CRD art 94 (1)(l).
[72] CRD art 94 (1)(m).
[73] CRD art 94 (1)(n).
[74] Incentive-based Compensation Arrangements, 81 Fed. Reg. 37669 (proposed July 22 2016).
[75] Listing Standards for Recovery of Erroneously Awarded Compensation , 87 Fed. Reg. 73076 (Nov. 28, 2022) (revising 17 CFR 229, 17 CFR 232, 17 CFR 240, 17 CFR 249, 17 CFR 270, 17 CFR 274).

In sum, both regimes aim to tailor incentive-based compensation in banks, using holding periods and clawbacks to align compensation with long-term risks and ex-post risk adjustments.[76] These interventions aim to prevent managers profiting from short-term gains to the detriment of long-term profits. In others, these measures aim to align compensation arrangements with the long-term interests of shareholders, rather than de-link managers' incentives from shareholders' interests altogether.

The EU – in contrast to the US – also imposes a cap on variable remuneration in banks. In other words, where shareholders' profits are uncapped, the EU regulation does limit the variable component in the compensation package of banks. The cap is highly controversial. This is exemplified by the proposals in the UK to abandon the cap post Brexit. It is argued that the cap will lead to an increase in the amount of fixed remuneration, a reduction of the incentives to take 'good' risk and create value, and the loss of talented bankers to financial firms without such pay caps.[77] The reduction of shareholder value owing to interventions in the governance framework in the interest of financial stability – away from the traditional shareholder value paradigm – seems an inevitable consequence in the presence of systemic externalities. More important for the present purposes, however, is that the impact of the cap on risk-taking is not at all obvious. It is argued that the pre-crisis fixed component already included a discount to the competitive rate on the employment market and, therefore, incorporated a penalty for poor performance. The decrease in variable pay – and likely increase in fixed pay – could therefore lead to more incentives to take risk with significant downside, as managers bear less of the cost. Moreover, it is argued that the cap also provides less incentives to take risk with a significant upside, as the variable performance pay is capped.[78] In addition, it is claimed that the cap on variable pay will be detrimental to financial stability, because the fixed component of the pay package will be higher and – unlike the variable component – will need to be paid out even in a downturn.[79] However, a study by the EBA does not find an indication that bonus caps decrease the stability of the financial institution.[80] A study by Hakenes and Schnabel,[81] moreover, finds that ceilings on bank bonuses are desirable to mitigate excessive risk-taking when the probability of a bank bailout is likely, i.e. in the case of systemically important financial institutions. In sum, the effect of the cap on variable pay on managerial risk-taking is not straightforward and is likely to depend on the context in which these caps operate. Further research on the exact impact on risk-taking of the introduced bonus caps in banks is necessary to determine whether such interventions mitigate risk-taking by banks.

---

76 Financial Reporting Council (n 66) 14; OECD (n 45) 48.

77 Kevin J Murphy, 'Regulating Banking Bonuses in the European Union: A Case Study in Unintended Consequences' (2013) 19 European Financial Management 631.

78 ibid 645–648.

79 Murphy (n 77).

80 EBA, 'Benchmarking of Remuneration Practices at the European Union Level and Data on High Earners' (EBA, 2016] <https://www.eba.europa.eu/sites/default/files/document_library/Publications/Reports/2022/1037293/Report%20on%20Remuneration%20benchmarking%202019%20and%202020%20and%20High%20Earners%202020.pdf> accessed 6 May 2024.

81 Hendrik Hakenes and Isabel Schnabel, 'Bank Bonuses and Bailouts' (2014) 46 Journal of Money, Credit and Banking 259.

3.3 Shareholders' Rights

Finally, a series of post-crisis interventions aim to enhance shareholders' rights. The idea behind these interventions is that lack of shareholder oversight led to problems with bank governance. The EU Shareholder Rights Directive, for instance, aims to encourage long-term shareholder engagement and applies to listed companies – independent of their sector of activities. For example, it introduces a 'say on pay' for shareholders.[82] Another example of the focus on shareholder rights can be found in the provisions on variable pay in the CRD, as discussed above. Where the CRD in principle does limit the variable component of packages of credit institutions and investment firms to 100% of the fixed component of the total remuneration package for each individual, it allows shareholders to increase this ratio up to 200%.[83] In the US, Section 951 of the Dodd–Frank Act requires advisory votes by shareholders about executive compensation and golden parachutes. The SEC adopted the necessary measures implementing these provisions.[84] Given the analysis of the perverse shareholders incentives discussed above, it is highly unclear whether such measures are desirable from a systemic risk perspective.

4. CONCLUSION

This chapter discussed the corporate governance of banks. More specifically, it introduced the governance debate with respect to systemically important banks. We argued that the systemic nature of the business model of banks – combined with the incompleteness of 'external' prudential regulation and supervision – justify a 'special' regime for bank corporate governance. Indeed, governance interventions are a key part of an effective prudential framework. We then showed that both in the EU and the US regulators have intervened in the governance of banks. While the emerging consensus in the post-crisis literature on bank governance is that shareholders have perverse incentives, the regulatory frameworks in the EU and US are less focused on de-linking bank corporate governance from shareholders. Some reforms do aim to detach decisions in banks from shareholder value. The cap on variable compensation in the EU is the clearest example of such intervention. Yet other measures seem to actively encourage more shareholder involvement and point fingers at corporate governance mechanisms – such as short-term performance-based compensation packages – that encourage decision-makers to increase short-term gains to the detriment of long-term shareholder value.

---

[82] European Commission, 'Press Release – Shareholders' Rights Directive Q&A' <http://europa.eu/rapid/press-release_MEMO-17-592_en.htm> accessed 26 May 2017.

[83] CRD art 94.

[84] Shareholder Approval of Executive Compensation and Golden Parachute Compensation, 76 Fed. Reg. 6009 (Feb. 2, 2011) (revising 17 CFR 229, 17 CFR 240, 17 CFR 249).

13. Recovery and resolution of banks

Shuai Guo

1. INTRODUCTION

The year 2023 witnessed a new round of banking failures starting with Silicon Valley Bank, then Signature Bank, Credit Suisse in March, First Republic Bank in May and Heartland Tri-State Bank in July.[1] The resurgence has once again brought crisis management in the banking sector into sharp focus, 15 years after the global financial crisis (GFC) in 2008. The GFC had shown the inadequacy of tools to address failing banks. Back at the time before 2008, only limited instruments were available for authorities, such as national bailout by recourse to taxpayers' money or normal insolvency proceedings.[2] Neither of these instruments can ensure an orderly resolution of banks. Therefore, world leaders called for the development of 'resolution tools and frameworks for the effective resolution of financial groups to help mitigate the disruption of financial institution failures and reduce moral hazard in future'.[3] Subsequently, international standards were formulated, including the benchmark document *Key Attributes of Effective Resolution Regimes for Financial Institutions* (Key Attributes, or KAs) formulated by the Financial Stability Board (FSB).

According to the FSB's latest resolution report, quite a few jurisdictions have adopted a comprehensive resolution regime while a number of others are in the process of legal

---

1 See Federal Deposit Insurance Corporation, 'FDIC Creates a Deposit Insurance National Bank of Santa Clara to Protect Insured Depositors of Silicon Valley Bank, Santa Clara, California' (FDIC, 10 March 2023) <https://www.fdic.gov/news/press-releases/2023/pr23016.html> accessed 1 November 2023; FDIC, 'FDIC Establishes Signature Bridge Bank, N.A., as Successor to Signature Bank, New York, NY' (FDIC, 12 March 2023) <https://www.fdic.gov/news/press-releases/2023/pr23018.html> accessed 1 November 2023; Swiss Financial Market Supervisory Authority, 'FINMA approves merger of UBS and Credit Suisse' (FINMA, 19 March 2023) <https://www.finma.ch/en/news/2023/03/20230319-mm-cs-ubs/> accessed 1 November 2023; FDIC, 'JPMorgan Chase Bank, National Association, Columbus, Ohio Assumes All the Deposits of First Republic Bank, San Francisco, California' (FDIC, 1 May 2023) <https://www.fdic.gov/news/press-releases/2023/pr23034.html> accessed 1 November 2023; FDIC, 'Dream First Bank, National Association, of Syracuse, Kansas, Assumes All of the Deposits of Heartland Tri-State Bank of Elkhart, Kansas' (FDIC, 28 July 2023) <https://www.fdic.gov/news/press-releases/2023/pr23058.html> accessed 1 November 2023.

2 See, e.g. Andrew R Sorkin, *Too Big to Fail: The Inside Story of How Wall Street and Washington Fought to Save the Financial System – and Themselves* (Penguin 2010); David A Skeel Jr, *The New Financial Deal: Understanding the Dodd–Frank Act And Its (Unintended) Consequences* (John Wiley & Sons 2010).

3 G20, 'G20 Leaders Statement: The Pittsburgh Summit' (24 September 2009) <http://www.g20.utoronto.ca/2009/2009communique0925.html> accessed 1 November 2023.

reforms.[4] This chapter compares home jurisdictions to all Global Systemically Important Banks[5] (G-SIBs), i.e. Canada, China,[6] EU Member States (France, Germany, Italy, the Netherlands and Spain), Japan, Switzerland, the UK, the US and two key host jurisdictions: Hong Kong and Singapore.

This chapter finds that all jurisdictions have embraced the concept of resolution as a legitimate form of government intervention. Convergence is thus evident within the realm of recovery and resolution, aimed at effectively addressing bank failures. However, jurisdictions are at varying stages of incorporating the regime and have adopted diverse rules due to the distinct characteristics of legal and financial traditions. For the rest of the chapter, Section 2 introduces the rationale and international standards of the special regimes of bank recovery and resolution. Section 3 examines national legislation and practices, and Section 4 further investigates specific recovery and resolution measures. Section 5 concludes.

2. SPECIAL TREATMENT OF BANKS IN DISTRESS

The first question examined is why banks need a special crisis management regime. Banks act as financial intermediaries and hold 'highly liquid liabilities in the form of deposits' and 'long-term loans that may be difficult to sell or borrow against on short notice'.[7] As a result, banks are highly vulnerable to delayed loan repayment, and, given a large number of creditors, banks cannot be quickly restructured or wound up swiftly in normal corporate insolvency proceedings. Once a bank is in trouble, public confidence in the financial system may be lost given the interconnectedness of banking and financial systems, and it may easily lead to the so-called contagion effect, such as mass withdrawal of deposits (bank runs) or the discontinuation of other financial services.[8] With the expansionary business of investment banks, runs can also happen to other investors apart from depositors, for example, money market fund investors during the failure of Lehman Brothers.[9] Banks perform additional fundamental 'public service' functions, such as the payment and settlement system.[10] Any cessation or

---

4 Financial Stability Board, '2022 Resolution Report: "Completing the Agenda and Sustaining Progress"' (FSB, 8 December 2022) <https://www.fsb.org/2022/12/2022-resolution-report-completing-the-agenda-and-sustaining-progress/> accessed 1 November 2023.

5 FSB, '2022 List of Global Systemically Important Banks (G-SIBs)' (21 November 2022) <https://www.fsb.org/2022/11/2022-list-of-global-systemically-important-banks-g-sibs/> accessed 1 November 2023.

6 In this chapter, China refers to the mainland part of the Peoples' Republic of China.

7 Eva H G Hüpkes, *The Legal Aspects of Bank Insolvency: A Comparative Analysis of Western Europe, the United States, and Canada* (Kluwer Law International 2000), 8; Eva H G Hüpkes, 'Insolvency – Why a Special Regime for Banks?' (2005) 3 Current Developments in Monetary and Financial Law), 3.

8 See, e.g. Andrew D Crockett, 'Why is Financial Stability a Goal of Public Policy?' (1997) 82 Proceedings – Economic Policy Symposium – Jackson Hole, Federal Reserve Bank of Kansas City 7, 7–12; Andrew Campbell and Peter Cardwright, 'Deposit Insurance: Consumer Protection, Banks Safety and Moral Hazard' (1999) 10 European Business Law Review 96; Hal S Scott, *Connectedness and Contagion: Protecting the Financial System from Panics* (MIT Press 2016).

9 At that time, the Reserve Fund was the largest commercial paper holder of Lehman Brothers.

10 See, e.g. Hüpkes, 'Insolvency – Why a Special Regime for Banks?' (n 7) 472.

reduction of banking services would cause great difficulties in the provision of these social functions and interrupt economic activities and social operations.[11] Moreover, central banks implement their monetary policies through banks, primarily by influencing the money supply, interest rates and overall financial conditions in an economy.[12] The aim of insolvency law is to maximize debtors' assets for the distribution among creditors or granting second chances for debtors under the 'rescue' culture;[13] it does not address public interests such as financial stability and systemic risk,[14] and, therefore, cannot resolve bank failures in an orderly manner. These reasons explain why banks need a separate insolvency regime from other companies.

Prior to the GFC, there had been debates about how to address bank failures, and national legislators were choosing from general corporate insolvency regimes, or special regimes designed exclusively for banks.[15] A large number of jurisdictions relied on their traditional corporate insolvency laws, with additional requirements and modifications such as appointing banking authorities as liquidators or administrative approval in judicial proceedings. It was criticized that normal insolvency proceedings are led by courts and cannot ensure an expedited market-exit process without causing systemic risks.[16] Meanwhile, some other jurisdictions adopt special regimes tailored to banks for timely intervention and consistency between insolvency and supervisory frameworks.[17] At that time, government bailout was frequently applied, i.e. using taxpayers' money, which can easily lead to moral hazard issues.[18]

Against this background, the post-GFC financial reform introduced a 'recovery and resolution' regime, which aims to resolve failing banks in an orderly manner and minimize the usage of taxpayers' money. Two stages are distinguished. Recovery measures are implemented before placing a bank into resolution with a reasonable prospect of restoration, including measures to reduce the risk profile of a bank and conserve capital, as well as considering

---

[11] See, e.g. Steven L Schwarcz, 'Systemic Risk' (2008) 97 Geo LJ 193; Rosa M Lastra, 'Systemic Risk, SIFIs and Financial Stability' (2011) 6 Capital Markets Law Journal 197.

[12] Ronald Davis and others, *Financial Institutions in Distress: Recovery, Resolution, and Recognition* (OUP 2023) 22–25.

[13] Bob Wessels, Hon Bruce A Markell, and Jason Kilborn, *International Cooperation in Bankruptcy and Insolvency Matters* (3rd edn, OUP 2009) 14–16. See also, e.g. Philip R Wood, *Principles of International Insolvency* (Sweet & Maxwell 2007); Roy M Goode, *Principles of Corporate Insolvency Law* (5th edn, Sweet & Maxwell 2011).

[14] Lynette Janssen, 'EU Bank Resolution Framework: A Comparative Study on the Relation with National Private Law' (Thesis, Leiden University 2019).

[15] IMF and World Bank, 'An Overview of the Legal, Institutional, and Regulatory Framework for Bank Insolvency' (International Monetary Fund and World Bank 2009).

[16] Martin Čihák and Erlend W Nier, 'The Need for Special Resolution Regimes for Financial Institutions – The Case of the European Union' (2012) 2 Harvard Business Law Review 395.

[17] See, e.g. the US, discussed in below Section 3.

[18] Čihák and Nier (n 16). This term 'moral hazard' usually refers to the situation where financial institutions engaged in over-risky investments (such as subprime mortgages), knowing that they could shift the potential losses to taxpayers or central banks if their risky bets failed. For instance, in the US, the Capital Purchase Program injected $204.9 billion of preferred equity into 709 banking organizations; in the EU, between 2008 and 2016, the European Commission approved a total of about €5 trillion of state aid. See a general overview, Allen N Berger and Raluca A Roman, *TARP and Other Bank Bailouts and Bail-Ins Around the World: Connecting Wall Street, Main Street, and the Financial System* (Elsevier 2020) 7–13.

strategic options, such as divestiture of business lines and restructuring of liabilities.[19] Unlike resolution, recovery measures are taken by banks in distress and usually only involve a change in a bank's business strategy.

In contrast, resolution measures are taken by administrative resolution authorities and may substantively alter the debtor–creditor relationship. This chapter follows the FSB's approach and defines resolution as 'the exercise of resolution powers ... by a resolution authority in respect of a bank that meets the conditions for entry into resolution, with or without private sector involvement, with the aim of achieving the statutory objectives of resolution'.[20] It excludes judicial insolvency proceedings. Resolution is initiated 'when a firm is no longer viable or likely to be no longer viable, and has no reasonable prospect of becoming so'.[21] Upon entering into resolution, resolution authorities generally have the powers to: (i) control and operate a firm, or to conduct resolution through an administrator; (ii) remove and replace management; (iii) ensure continuity of services and functions in resolution; (iv) transfer assets and liabilities, and establish and operate temporary bridge banks and asset management vehicles; (v) impose temporary stays on the exercise of early termination rights; and (vi) write and convert liabilities (bail-in).[22]

Resolution encompasses three features. First, resolution serves the purpose of maintaining financial stability and avoiding using taxpayers' money to bail out failing financial institutions. This addresses the shortcomings of pre-GFC bank insolvency regimes.[23] Second, resolution is an administrative action directly taken by administrative resolution authorities, which are designated to decide and implement resolution measures.[24] This feature distinguishes resolution from normal corporate insolvency proceedings where courts play a central role. Third, resolution actions can be exercised directly by resolution authorities, without obtaining consent from creditors. This marks a significant departure from normal corporate insolvency proceedings where a reorganization plan or a liquidation plan must be approved by creditors. There is a consensus on the paradigm shift to such an administrative regime, and jurisdictions are adopting reforms largely in line with international standards.[25]

---

[19] FSB KA I-Annex 4, para 1.5.

[20] FSB, 'Key Attributes Assessment Methodology for the Banking Sector' (FSB, 19 October 2016) <https:// www .fsb .org/ 2016/ 10/ key -attributes -assessment -methodology -for -the -banking -sector/> accessed 1 November 2023.

[21] FSB KA 3.1.

[22] FSB KA 3.2. The summary version is drawn from FSB's resolution peer review report. FSB, 'Second Thematic Review on Resolution Regimes' (FSB, 18 March 2016) 20 <https://www.fsb .org/2016/03/second-thematic-review-on-resolution-regimes/> accessed 1 November 2023.

[23] FSB KA 2.3.

[24] See, e.g. Thomas F Huertas, 'Too Big To Fail: A Policy's Beginning, Middle and End (?)' in Matthias Haentjens and Bob Wessels (eds), *Research Handbook on Crisis Management in the Banking Sector* (Edward Elgar Publishing 2015) 11; Matthias Haentjens and Bob Wessels, 'Three Paradigm Shifts in Recent Bank Insolvency Law' (2016) 31 Journal of International Banking Law and Regulation 396, 398–399; Gabriel Moss, Bob Wessels and Matthias Haentjens, *EU Banking and Insurance Insolvency* (2nd OUP 2017) vi.

[25] Haentjens and Wessels (n 24) 398–399.

3. NATIONAL RECOVERY AND RESOLUTION REGIMES

3.1 National Legislation and Practices

Despite the general doctrinal consensus on adopting recovery and resolution reforms, specific national regimes differ in various jurisdictions. Prior to the GFC, administrative insolvency regimes had been in place in several jurisdictions, quite similar to the present regime of resolution. A typical example is the US, in which the Federal Deposit Insurance Corporation (FDIC) is designated by the Banking Act of 1933/1935 and later the Federal Deposit Insurance Act of 1950 as the resolution authority for all FDIC insured depository institutions.[26] The FDIC has the capacity to directly interfere with the process of resolving failing institutions, without the approval of courts, by either receivership or conservatorship.[27] Receivership is with the purpose of liquidating banks in distress (gone-concern), ending with market exit; conservatorship is with the purpose of restructuring banks to restore them to normal operation (going-concern).[28] However, prior to the GFC, such a mechanism was only applicable to depository institutions but no other financial (holding) companies, which later proved to be insufficient.[29] The 2010 Dodd–Frank Wall Street Reform and Consumer Protection Act established the Orderly Liquidation Authority to address the gap, empowering the FDIC to exercise resolution powers. However, only institutions that may impose systemic risks can be subject to such mechanism.[30] The factors to commence such proceedings include: (i) the institution is 'in default or in danger of default'; (ii) the failure of the institution 'would have serious adverse effects on financial stability in the United States'; (iii) 'no viable private sector alternative is available'; (iv) actions that may affect stakeholders' interest should be appropriate, for the purpose of maintaining financial stability; (v) resolution actions take into consideration 'the effectiveness of the action in mitigating potential adverse effects on the financial system, the cost to the general fund of the Treasury, and the potential to increase excessive risk taking on the part of creditors, counterparties, and shareholders'; and (vi) convertible debt instruments have been converted first subject to the regulatory order.[31] Non-depository institutions that do not meet these criteria are still subject to the US Bankruptcy Code.

---

26 FDIC, 'History of FDIC' <https://www.fdic.gov/about/history/> accessed 1 November 2023. See also, e.g. Robert R Bliss and George G Kaufman, 'A Comparison of U.S. Corporate and Bank Insolvency Resolution' (2006) 30 Economic Perspectives 44; Heidi M Schooner, 'US Bank Resolution Reform: Then and Again' in Rosa M Lastra (ed.), *Cross-border Bank Insolvency* (OUP 2011) 403–425.

27 12 US Code §1821(c)(1).

28 Richard Scott Carnell, Jonathan R Macey and Geoffrey P Miller, *The Law of Financial Institutions* (2nd edn, Wolters Kluwer 2013) 497.

29 For example, the insolvency of Lehman Brothers. See, e.g. James Bromley and Tim Phillips, 'International Lessons from Lehman's Failure: A Cross-border No Man's Land' in Rosa M Lastra (ed.), *Cross-border Bank Insolvency* (OUP 2011); Dennis Faber and Niels Vermunt, *Bank Failure: Lessons from Lehman Brothers* (OUP 2017).

30 12 US Code §5382(a)(1)(A)(i).

31 12 US Code §5383(b).

Similarly, Canada[32] follows the US and promulgated the 1967 Canada Deposit Insurance Corporation Act (CDICA). This Act was most recently amended by the Budget Implementation Act 2021. Accordingly, the Canada Deposit Insurance Corporation (CDIC) was vested with resolution powers for all of its member institutions. The Office of the Superintendent of the Financial Institutions decides that a bank has ceased or is about the cease to be viable and viability cannot be restored.[33] A variety of factors should be considered: excessive dependence on financial assistance such as loans or guarantees; loss of depositor or public confidence; actual or likely substantial deficiencies in regulatory capital; and actual or likely failure to pay liabilities as they fall due. Having met these standards, a failing bank can be put into resolution directly managed by the CDIC. Alternatively, the CDIC can also be appointed as liquidator by a court when a bank is insolvent.[34]

Japan also established the Deposit Insurance Corporation of Japan as the deposit insurance managing authority and resolution authority. The Deposit Insurance Act was first introduced in 1971 and was amended several times in the following years. The 2000 amendment permanently introduced administrative bank resolution measures such as financial administrators and bridge banks, and the 2013 amendment introduced the present orderly resolution regime.[35] There are three types of resolution options in Japan:[36] (i) failure resolution under limited coverage applies to deposit-taking institutions with no systemic risk by simply paying out insured deposits; (ii) measures against financial crisis apply to deposit-taking institutions whose failure would cause systemic risks and include recapitalization, financial assistance and temporary nationalization measures; and (iii) measures for orderly resolution apply to all types of financial institutions that may cause systemic risks, leading to either capital support for solvent institutions or resolution measures for insolvent institutions. In other situations, banks are subject to normal corporate insolvency proceedings.

Switzerland amended its Banking Act in 2003 and replaced the traditional corporate insolvency regime with an administrative regime.[37] Instead of vesting the resolution powers in the deposit insurance managing institution, Switzerland authorized its financial regulator the Swiss Federal Banking Commission, which became the Swiss Financial Market Supervisory Authority (FINMA) in 2009, as the resolution authority. FINMA can either restructure or liquidate a bank (through a liquidation agent).[38] In 2011 and 2012, the Swiss Banking Act was amended to introduce the new resolution regime in line with the FSB Key Attributes. To be

32 Janis P Sarra, 'A Bridge Over Troubled Waters – Resolving Bank Financial Distress in Canada' in Janis P Sarra and Barbara Romaine (eds), *Annual Review of Insolvency Law 2017* (Carswell 2018).

33 CDICA, s 39.1(1).

34 The Winding Up and Restructuring Act, art 23.

35 FSB, 'Peer Review of Japan' (*FSB*, 21 December 2016) 25 <https://www.fsb.org/2016/12/peer-review-of-japan/> accessed 1 November 2023.

36 ibid 25–26.

37 Eva H G Hüpkes, 'Learning Lessons and Implementing a New Approach to Bank Insolvency Resolution in Switzerland' in David G Mayes and others (eds), *Who Pays for Bank Insolvency?* (Palgrave Macmillan UK 2004).

38 FINMA, 'Resolution of Banks' (Eidgenössische Finanzmarktaufsicht FINMA) <https://www.finma.ch/en/enforcement/recovery-and-resolution/finma-as-a-resolution-authority/resolution-of-banks/> accessed 1 November 2023.

put into resolution, a bank must be over-indebted, have serious liquidity problems or no longer fulfil the capital-adequacy provisions after the expiry of a deadline set by FINMA.[39]

In other jurisdictions, failing banks were traditionally subject to judicial insolvency management in the pre-GFC era.[40] Among them, the UK amended its Banking Act in 2009, introducing special regimes for distressed banks and empowering the Bank of England (BOE) to take measures.[41] The EU promulgated the Bank Recovery and Resolution Directive (BRRD)[42] and the Single Resolution Mechanism Regulation (SRMR)[43] in 2014, harmonizing resolution laws across the EU Member States and establishing the Single Resolution Board as the resolution authority for large and cross-border institutions in the Banking Union.[44] It is clarified that the UK has implemented the BRRD while it was still an EU Member State. After Brexit, most rules transposing the BRRD are still in place.[45] The BRRD prescribes three conditions that must be met for a resolution authority to take a resolution action: (i) the institution is 'failing or is likely to fail'; (ii) 'there is no reasonable prospect that any alternative private sector measures ... would prevent the failure of the institution within a reasonable timeframe'; and (iii) a resolution action is 'necessary in the public interest'.[46]

---

39 Swiss Banking Act, art 25.

40 Eva H G Hüpkes, *The Legal Aspects of Bank Insolvency, A Comparative Analysis of Western Europe, the United States and Canada* (Kluwer Law International 2000).

41 BOE, 'Resolution' <https://www.bankofengland.co.uk/financial-stability/resolution> accessed 1 November 2023.

42 Directive 2014/59/EU of 15 May 2014 establishing a framework for the recovery and resolution of credit institutions and investment firms and amending Council Directive 82/891/EEC, and Directives 2001/24/EC, 2002/47/EC, 2004/25/EC, 2005/56/EC, 2007/36/EC, 2011/35/EU, 2012/30/EU and 2013/36/EU, and Regulations (EU) No 1093/2010 and (EU) No 648/2012, of the European Parliament and of the Council [2014] OJ L 173/190, amended by Directive (EU) 2019/879 of 20 May 2019 amending Directive 2014/59/EU as regards the loss-absorbing and recapitalization capacity of credit institutions and investment firms and Directive 98/26/EC [2019] OJ L 150/296, or known as BRRD II.

43 Regulation (EU) No 806/2014 of 15 July 2014 establishing uniform rules and a uniform procedure for the resolution of credit institutions and certain investment firms in the framework of a Single Resolution Mechanism and a Single Resolution Fund and amending Regulation (EU) No 1093/2010 [2014] OJ L 225/1, amended by Regulation (EU) 2019/877 of 20 May 2019 amending Regulation (EU) No 806/2014 as regards the loss-absorbing and recapitalization capacity of credit institutions and investment firms [2019] OJ L 150/226, or known as SRMR II.

44 Jeffrey N Gordon and Wolf-Georg Ringe, 'Bank Resolution in the European Banking Union: A Transatlantic Perspective on What it Would Take Essay' (2015) 115 Columbia Law Review 1297.

45 EU Exit Instrument: The Technical Standards (Bank Recovery and Resolution) (Amendment Etc.) (EU Exit) (No 1) Instrument 2019; EU Exit Instrument: The Technical Standards (Bank Recovery and Resolution Directive) (EU Exit) (No 2) Instrument 2019. See BOE, 'The Bank of England's Amendments to Financial Services Legislation under the European Union (Withdrawal) Act 2018' <https:// www .bankofengland .co .uk/ paper/ 2019/ the -boes -amendments -to -financial -services-legislation-under-the-eu-withdrawal-act-2018> accessed 1 November 2023.

46 BRRD art 32(1); see also SRMR art 18(1).

China is the only G-SIB home jurisdiction that does not have a comprehensive bank resolution law at the moment.[47] The new National Financial Regulatory Administration, established in March 2023, replaced the previous China Banking and Insurance Regulatory Commission as the new resolution authority. It has limited administrative powers to temporarily assume control over commercial banks that have suffered or are likely to suffer a credit crisis, thereby seriously affecting the interests of depositors and other customers.[48] The authority can also apply to the court to commence insolvency proceedings for banks.[49] The 2015 Deposit Insurance Regulation established the Chinese deposit insurance agency, which is vested with deposit payout powers. A most significant reform took place in 2022. The People's Bank of China, China's central bank, published the draft Financial Stability Law for public consultation and later submitted to the National People's Congress, China's highest legislative body.[50] The main section of the draft legislation is resolution, which is largely compatible with the FSB Key Attributes.

Two of the financial hubs and key host jurisdictions – Hong Kong and Singapore – both adopted resolution rules in line with FSB Key Attributes, respectively through the Hong Kong 2017 Financial Institutions (Resolution) Ordinance (FIRO) and the amended Monetary Authority of Singapore Act (MASA) 2017. The Hong Kong Monetary Authority is the resolution authority for banks and other financial institutions designated on the financial stability grounds. Three conditions have to be met to put a bank into resolution: (i) the bank 'has ceased, or is likely to cease, to be viable'; (ii) there is no reasonable prospect that private sector action would restore the viability; and (iii) the non-viability of the bank 'poses risks to the stability and effective working of the financial system of Hong Kong', and 'resolution will avoid or mitigate those risks'.[51] The Monetary Authority of Singapore (MAS) is the designated resolution authority for all financial institutions, irrespective of whether they are systemically important. Resolution measures are taken if one of the followings is met: (i) 'a failure of the pertinent financial institution would have a widespread adverse effect on the financial system in Singapore or the economy of Singapore, or both'; (ii) 'it is in the public interest to do so'; and (iii) 'any other matter that the Authority considers relevant'.[52] Other institutions are subject to ordinary insolvency proceedings initiated by the MAS under the supervision of courts.[53]

---

[47] Matthias Haentjens, Shuai Guo and Bob Wessels, *New Bank Insolvency for China and Europe Volume 3: Comparative Analysis* (Eleven International 2021).

[48] Commercial Banks Law of China, art 64. See the Baoshang Bank Case, Shuai Guo, 'Bank Resolution in China: The Case of Baoshang Bank' (2021) 18 International Corporate Rescue 357.

[49] Enterprise Bankruptcy Law of China, art 134.

[50] Shuai Guo, 'Comment on the Financial Stability Law Draft for Consultation – Improving Financial Risk Prevention, Mitigation and Resolution Regimes' (《金融稳定法 (草案征求意见稿) 》评析——健全金融风险防范化解和处置机制) (Tiantonglaw, 28 April 2022) <http://www.tiantonglaw.com/Content/2022/09-17/2017182133.html> accessed 1 November 2023.

[51] FIRO, s 25.

[52] MASA, s 50.

[53] MASA, s 54.

3.2 Divergent Mechanisms toward International Convergence

As summarized above, jurisdictions have adopted or are in the process of implementing comprehensive resolution regimes. Some maintained their pre-GFC administrative practices but expanded or clarified the scope of resolution, while others completely shifted to the administrative regime from the previous judicial regime, generally in line with the FSB Key Attributes. Such international standards establish best practices for national legislators, providing both internal incentives to effectively managing bank failures and external incentives to keep up with international counterparts.[54]

Nonetheless, given the soft-law nature of international standards,[55] such as the FSB Key Attributes, national legislators can adopt their own recovery and resolution regimes. Several differences persist. First, there is variation in the scope of institutions covered. On the one end of the spectrum, the US puts all deposit-taking institutions, regardless of their systemic importance, under the resolution regime, alongside with Switzerland, China and Singapore. In between, Canada and Japan also adopt resolution regimes for all institutions; however, different measures could be adopted based on each institution's systemic importance. On the other hand, the EU and Hong Kong only focus on banks that may cause systemic risks. For other banks not subject to resolution, they would enter normal corporate insolvency proceedings.[56]

Second, the scope of resolution may or may not cover (administrative) liquidation. Under the European regime, resolution authorities only have powers within the scope of reorganization measures,[57] same as China and Hong Kong. In contrast, the US FDIC has additional powers to liquidate institutions, as does the Swiss FINMA. It is worth noting that the EU is considering adopting such administrative liquidation powers.[58] In Canada, Japan and Singapore, resolution authorities have liquidation powers but need to be appointed by courts as liquidators or get judicial approval.

Third, the decision to put a bank into resolution needs to satisfy three conditions: (i) the bank is failing or likely to fail; (ii) the public interest is at stake; and (iii) the use of resolution powers is necessary and proportionate. However, not all jurisdictions adopt all three criteria and there is a difference between cumulative and alternative approaches.[59] The former means that all three conditions need to be met, while the latter only requires the fulfilment of one of them. Given the vagueness of these expressions, each jurisdiction may adopt different methods, combining both quantitative and qualitative indicators. For example, with regard

---

54 Eric A Posner and Alan O Sykes, 'International Law and the Limits of Macroeconomic Cooperation' (2012) 86 Southern California Law Review 1025, 1037.

55 Chris Brummer, Soft Law and the Global Financial System: Rule Making in the 21st Century (CUP 2015).

56 Matthias Haentjens, Lynette Janssen and Bob Wessels, *New Bank Insolvency for China and Europe Volume 2: European Union* (Eleven International 2017) 12–13.

57 BRRD, art 117.

58 European Parliament, 'Liquidation of Banks: Towards an "FDIC" for the Banking Union?' (February 2019) <http://www.europarl.europa.eu/RegData/etudes/IDAN/2019/634385/IPOL_IDA(2019)634385_EN.pdf> accessed 1 November 2023.

59 FSB, 'Second Thematic Review on Resolution Regimes' (n 22) 46. G-SIB home jurisdictions, i.e. Canada, China, EU Member States, Japan, Switzerland, UK and US, adopt the cumulative approach, while key host jurisdictions, Hong Kong and Singapore, adopt the alternative approach.

to the viability of a bank, normal insolvency indicators such as balance sheet insolvency (i.e. liabilities exceeding assets) or cash flow insolvency (i.e. inability to meet debts as they fall due) and prudential regulatory indicators such as capital adequacy ratio are both factors to be considered.

These differences may give rise to new concerns. For instance, as exemplified in the SVB case, it sparks a debate over the 'systemic risk exception', questioning whether special treatment of smaller banks can be justified by systemic risk considerations.[60] It stems from the divergence in understanding whether systemic importance pertains to a large institution that is 'too-big-to-fail' or to the potential contagious effects that may result from the failure of a smaller bank.[61] Futhermore, there is ambiguity regarding how non-systemically important banks should be treated. To bridge these gaps, the International Institute for the Unification of Private Law (UNIDROIT), together with the Financial Stability Institute under the Bank for International Settlement, are formulating an international legislative guide for bank liquidation, favouring an administrative approach.[62] This legislative guide aims to address the nuances surrounding the scope and triggering events for crisis management measure, providing more concrete international guidance on resolving bank failures and contributing to greater convergence in this field.

4. SPECIFIC RECOVERY AND RESOLUTION MEASURES

The preceding section has shed light on the existing fragmented national practices, which may result in discrepancies in exercising resolution powers and in particular may impede cross-border bank resolution if different authorities hold conflicting opinions regarding whether and how to impose resolution actions.[63] It is imperative to delve into the variations at the more detailed implementation level.

4.1 Recovery and Resolution Plans

In the post-GFC reforms, a significant change is for banks to formulate recovery and resolution plans (RRPs). The FSB requires that recovery plans should be developed, maintained and executed by the firm's senior management, serving as a guide for recovery business strate-

---

60 See, e.g. Anna Gelpern, 'Silicon Rhymes with Savings and Loan (and It's a Ratchet)' (*Yale Journal on Regulation*, 29 March 2023) <https://www.yalejreg.com/nc/silicon-rhymes-with-savings-and-loan-and-its-a-ratchet-by-anna-gelpern/> accessed 1 November 2023.

61 It also reflects the regulatory approach of micro and macro prudence. See Davis and others (n 12) 30–31.

62 See Unidroit, 'Bank Insolvency' <https://www.unidroit.org/work-in-progress/bank-insolvency/#1637156948432-1d04168e-7a08> accessed 1 November 2023.

63 FSB, 'Second Thematic Review on Resolution Regimes' (n 22) 22. See also Shuai Guo, *Recognition of Foreign Bank Resolution Actions* (Edward Elgar Publishing 2022).

gies.[64] In contrast, for resolution, a plan is formulated by the resolution authorities, laying out potential resolution measures.[65]

Some support the idea and maintain that preparation is necessary for risk prevention and can guarantee a smooth transition in the times of crisis.[66] In particular, RRPs may facilitate cross-border cooperation which is a main obstacle at the global level, by the way of planning the crisis management strategies in advance.[67] In contrast, some argue that RRPs add extra burden on banks and increase the operational costs,[68] and even question the feasibility of RRPs since their formulation largely depends on envisaged valuation and does not necessarily reflect the realities including group structures and counterparty reactions.[69] Nevertheless, in practice, RRPs have been in place for all the jurisdictions compared.[70] Periodically, resolution authorities undertake resolvability assessments for at least G-SIBs, evaluating the feasibility of resolution strategies and their creditability.[71] RRPs are expected to be a cornerstone for risk preparedness in the banking sector.

4.2 Transfer Tools

Transfer is one of the most accepted resolution tools across jurisdictions. According to the FSB, transfer tools include the actions of transferring assets and liabilities to either an existing third institution or a newly established bridge institution/asset management vehicle.[72] Such transfer helps segregate impaired assets (bad bank) from other healthy parts of a bank (good bank) or assist the bank to go through a transition period.[73] Resolution authorities in all compared jurisdictions have the powers to transfer or sell assets and liabilities. Most authorities

---

64 FSB KA 11 and I-Annex 4, para 1.6.

65 FSB KA 11 and I-Annex 4, paras 1.8–1.9. It is worth noting that in the US, resolution plans are also formulated by banks, together with recovery plans also known as 'living wills'. See 12 US Code §5365(d).

66 Costanza A Russo, 'Resolution Plans and Resolution Strategies: Do They Make G-SIBs Resolvable and Avoid Ring Fence?' (2019) 20 European Business Organization Law Review 735.

67 Emilios Avgouleas, Charles Goodhart and Dirk Schoenmaker, 'Bank Resolution Plans as a Catalyst for Global Financial Reform' (2013) 9 Journal of Financial Stability 210.

68 In response, for instance, the Bank of England introduced simplified obligations. See BOE, 'Simplified Obligations for Recovery Planning' (BOE, 30 June 2023) <https://www.bankofengland.co.uk/prudential-regulation/publication/2020/simplified-obligations-recovery-planning> accessed 1 November 2023.

69 Alexander Lehmann, 'Impediments to Resolvability of Banks' (Bruegel, 29 November 2022) <https://www.bruegel.org/report/impediments-resolvability-banks> accessed 1 November 2023.

70 FSB, '2022 Resolution Report' (n 4) 28–29.

71 FSB KA 10.

72 FSB KA 3.2 (vi)–(viii). In the EU, transfer tools encompass three forms: the sale of business tool, the bridge institution tool and the asset separation tool. BRRD, arts 38–42.

73 See e.g. Stephan Madaus, 'Bank Failure and Pre-emptive Planning' in Matthias Haentjens and Bob Wessels (eds), *Bank Recovery and Resolution: A Conference Book* (Eleven International 2014); Michael Schillig, 'The EU Resolution Toolbox' in Matthias Haentjens and Bob Wessels (eds), *Research Handbook on Crisis Management in the Banking Sector* (Edward Elgar Publishing 2015) 91–95; Michael Schillig, 'Private Sector Transfer, Bridge Bank and Asset Separation' in Michael Schillig *Resolution and Insolvency of Banks and Financial Institutions* (OUP 2016).

in the compared jurisdictions have the powers to establish a temporary bridge institution,[74] except China, although the draft Financial Stability Law includes a specific provision on bridge banks.[75]

When exercising transfer tools, a substantive concern is about the partial transfer. In this context, certain liabilities might be transferred to another entity, thus unaffected, but the remaining liabilities entering into liquidation would suffer losses. Creditors left behind might be treated less favourably than those whose claims are transferred. The authorities have discretionary powers to determine which liabilities are transferred to a solvent institution and which liabilities are left behind for loss-absorbing. In the US, resolution authorities would follow a loss-absorption rule that the statutory priority should be respected in the sequence of equity, subordinated debt and senior unsecured debt,[76] while the EU does not have a similar explicit provision. The reason is speculated to be that the US treats the transfer tool as a mechanism for loss absorption and thus respects the insolvency hierarchy, while in the EU, the transfer tool does not serve a similar function, which is assigned to a sperate tool of bail-in. However, the general principle of 'no worse off than in liquidation'[77] still applies and thus can ensure the ranking of claims in the insolvency law is respected.

Safeguard measures are also in place for the purpose of balancing different interests, for instance, to avoid adverse impact on the financial market. In the EU, special protection is provided for liabilities arising out of security arrangements, title transfer financial collateral arrangements, set-off arrangements, netting arrangements, covered bonds and structured finance arrangements,[78] in order to 'preserve legitimate capital market arrangements' and to 'prevent the splitting of linked liabilities, rights and contracts'.[79] Similarly, the US provides protection for 'qualified financial contracts', which should be transferred either altogether or not at all.[80] It can be concluded that transfer tools have been largely harmonized across the jurisdictions.

4.3 Bail-In

Bail-in is the most controversial tool in the new resolution regime, which is to achieve or help achieve continuity of essential functions either by recapitalizing the entity in resolution or a newly established entity or bridge institution.[81] Bail-in in the FSB context has two forms: write-down and conversion, targeting both shareholder's equity and creditors' claims. In principle, 'equity should absorb losses first, and no loss should be imposed on senior debt holders until subordinated debt (including all regulatory capital instruments) has been written-off

---

74 FSB, '2022 Resolution Report' (n 4) 28–29.

75 Financial Stability Law of China (draft), art 30(3).

76 78 Fed. Reg. 76614, 76616.

77 BRRD, art 74.

78 BRRD, art 76. Also Commission Delegated Regulation (EU) 2017/867 of 7 February 2017 on classes of arrangements to be protected in a partial property transfer under Article 76 of Directive 2014/59/EU of the European Parliament and of the Council [2017] OJ L 131/15.

79 BRRD, recital (95).

80 12 US Code §5390 (c)(9).

81 KA 3.2(ix) and 3.5.

entirely'.[82] Bail-in should respect the hierarchy of claims, and any departure from the equal (*pari passu*) treatment of creditors principle should be stated in the law and meet the necessity either to contain potential systemic risk or to maximize the bank's value for all of the creditors.

When introduced in the first place, bail-in was advocated as an alternative to bail-out and perceived as means to avoid using public funds and to prevent moral hazard,[83] whereas more recent opinions reflect that bail-in may encounter many practical issues. The triggers for bail-in are quite strict given the impact on private rights and the process may need liquidity support using public funds, thus authorities may be hesitant to take action.[84] Also, there are ambiguities regarding bail-inable liabilities and such uncertainty may impede the efficiency of resolution.[85] Other issues involve the provision of sufficient information and data, amendments to relevant securities laws, and cross-border issues including valuation difference between home and host jurisdictions.[86]

In spite of these debates, most jurisdictions have adopted bail-in. The EU has a typical bail-in tool, which is either to 'recapitalise an institution or an entity' or 'to convert to equity or reduce the principal amount of claims or debt instruments that are transferred (i) to a bridge institution with a view to providing capital for that bridge institution; or (ii) under the sale of business tool or the assets separation tool'.[87] Bail-in in the EU can be exercised independently on the distressed bank through an 'open bank' approach.[88] Accordingly, shareholders and subordinated creditors are supposed to absorb losses first. Certain liabilities are excluded from the coverage of the bail-inable liabilities, such as covered deposits, secured liabilities and client assets or client money.[89] Also, there are exceptional circumstances in which the resolution authority can exclude certain liabilities from bail-in.[90] Similarly, Canada, Switzerland, Hong Kong and Singapore[91] also included explicit bail-in provisions, subject to specific national

---

82 KA 5.1.

83 Chris Bates and Simon Gleeson, 'Legal Aspects of Bank Bail-Ins Perspective' (2011) 5 Law and Financial Markets Review 264.

84 Wolf-Georg Ringe, 'Bank Bail-in between Liquidity and Solvency' (2018) 92 American Bankruptcy Law Journal 299.

85 Jens-Hinrich Binder, 'Bank Bail-in and Disputed Claims: Can it Cope? The Case for and against a Vis Attractiva Resolutionis' (2020) 21 Journal of Banking Regulation 54.

86 FSB, 'Principles on Bail-in Execution: Overview of Responses to the Public Consultation' (FSB, 21 June 2018) <https://www.fsb.org/2018/06/principles-on-bail-in-execution-overview-of-responses-to-the-public-consultation/> accessed 1 November 2023.

87 BRRD, art 43(2).

88 FSB, 'Principles on Bail-in Execution' (FSB, 21 June 2018) 5 <https://www.fsb.org/2018/06/principles-on-bail-in-execution-2/> accessed 1 November 2023.

89 BRRD, art 44(2).

90 ibid art 44(3); Commission Delegated Regulation (EU) 2016/860 of 4 February 2016 specifying further the circumstance where exclusion from the application of write-down or conversion powers is necessary under Article 44(3) of Directive 2014/59/EU of the European Parliament and of the Council establishing a framework for the recovery and resolution of credit institutions and investment firms [2016] OJ L 144/11.

91 Canada only adopts bail-in for large D-SIBs. Singapore's scope of bail-in covers unsecured subordinated debt and unsecured subordinated loans, but excludes senior debt (except for senior debt instruments that are contingently convertible into equity or which contain contractual bail-in clauses). MAS reported that this strikes an appropriate balance between ensuring that banks have

conditions.[92] In China, the new draft Financial Stability Law also regulates bail-in in a special provision.[93]

Another model is the US which does not mention bail-in in the statutory laws. The Treasury stated that 'the FDIC has taken several critical steps to address these concerns, including through the development of [the single point of entry (SPE)] strategy that would involve "bail-in" of long-term creditors of the holding company'.[94] The bail-in mechanism is believed to be carried out by implementing the SPE strategy. Simply put, the holding company of the financial group in distress would be put into resolution with the aim of absorbing the losses, while the operating subsidiaries, including the deposit-taking subsidiaries, would continue their normal businesses.[95] The bail-in is exercised together with the transfer tools, through a 'closed bank' approach.[96] Under the SPE strategy, assets of the holding company, mainly the investments and loans to the subsidiaries, would be transferred to a bridge financial company,[97] and the remaining liabilities, including equity, subordinated debt and senior unsecured debt of the holding company, would be either partly repaid or, worse, not repaid at all.[98] The resolution authority can also apply a 'securities-for-claims exchange' tool, by which the claims of creditors could be converted to the new debt, equity or contingent securities of the 'new holding company or new holding companies (NewCo or NewCos)'.[99]

In Japan, the authorities thought 'they are able to achieve the economic objectives of bail-in by capitalizing a bridge institution to which functions have been transferred and by liquidating the residual firm via powers to separate assets and liabilities of a failed institution'; however, the FSB disagrees because 'it is not clear that the recapitalization is achieved by converting claims of creditors of the failed institution into equity of that institution or of any successor in resolution'.[100] It seems that Japan follows the US approach but there may be some discrepancies in implementation. It thus can be observed that bail-in has been widely adopted, either through explicit legal provisions or indirect transfer tools.

4.4 Treatment of Financial Contracts

In the resolution process, financial contracts are often granted special treatment. The FSB Key Attributes advocate the power to '[t]emporarily stay the exercise of early termination rights'.[101]

---

sufficient loss-absorbing capacity and minimizing the risk of contagion to the financial system and broader economy in the event of a bail-in. See FSB, '2022 Resolution Report' (n 4) 30.

[92] ibid 28–30.

[93] Financial Stability Law of China (draft), art 32.

[94] Treasury, 'Orderly Liquidation Authority and Bankruptcy Reform', February 21, 2018. See also FDIC, 'Resolution of Systemically Important Financial Institutions: The Single Point of Entry Strategy' (FDIC, 2013) 78 Fed. Reg. 76614. See Thomas H Jackson and David A Skeel, 'Dynamic Resolution of Large Financial Institutions' (2012) 2 Harv Bus L Rev 435.

[95] 78 Fed Reg 76614, 77616.

[96] FSB, 'Principles on Bail-in Execution' (n 88) 5.

[97] 12 US Code §5381 (a)(3).

[98] 78 Fed Reg 76614, 77616.

[99] ibid.

[100] FSB, '2022 Resolution Report' (n 4) 30.

[101] KA 3.2(x).

In insolvency, there is the *ipso facto* clause that grants an automatic effect that a contract is terminated when a party enters into insolvency.[102] The rationale behind such a clause is that insolvency is an anticipatory default event and the other party in an insolvency proceeding is presumed incapable of performing the contract. Financial contracts contain provisions for any party to accelerate, terminate or close-out contractual rights in the case of insolvency of the other party. These are collectively referred to as 'early termination rights'.[103] Some jurisdictions however nullify the *ipso facto* clause, which jeopardizes the collective nature of insolvency proceedings, but with the exception that financial contracts are under special protection through a so-called safe harbour mechanism. This is because of the need to avoid market risk and systemic risk, since the incapability of exercising these financial contractual terms may lead to contagious effects on the whole financial market.[104]

The GFC, however, indicated that exercising these early termination rights may have negative effects on the market. The BCBS explains that the exercise of these early termination rights upon resolution 'could destabilise markets and undermine orderly resolutions of failing institutions' because of the way that '[c]ounterparties may be required to use the asset values determined in the closing out of financial contracts to establish market prices for similar assets subject to contracts with third parties', and thus 'transmit the debtor's instability far beyond its counterparties'.[105] The FSB confirms that 'the termination of large volumes of financial contracts upon entry into resolution could result in a disorderly rush for the exits that creates further market instability and frustrates the implementation of resolution measures aimed at achieving continuity'.[106] Some scholars questioned the legality and practicability of safe harbour provisions[107] and even argued for repealing these provisions for financial contracts.[108]

---

[102] Philip Wood, *Principles of International Insolvency* (Sweet & Maxwell 2007) 75. See also UNCITRAL, UNCITRAL Legislative Guide on Insolvency Law, Parts One and Two (2004), 122.

[103] KA Appendix I-Annex 5, para 1.1. See, e.g. Francisco Garcimartín and Maria I Saez, 'Set-off, Netting and Close-out Netting' in Matthias Haentjens and Bob Wessels (eds), *Research Handbook on Crisis Management in the Banking Sector* (Edward Elgar Publishing 2015) 332; Edward Janger, 'Symposium Introduction: Treatment of Financial Contracts in Bankruptcy and Bank Resolution' (2015) 10 Brooklyn Journal of Corporate, Financial & Commercial Law 1.

[104] See, e.g. Stephen J Lubben, 'Repeal the Safe Harbors' (2010) 18 American Bankruptcy Institute Law Review 319, 322–326; Edward J Janger and John A E Pottow, 'Implementing Symmetric Treatment of Financial Contracts in Bankruptcy and Bank Resolution' (2015) 10 Brooklyn Journal of Corporate, Financial & Commercial Law 155, 163–168; Mark J Roe and Stephens D Adams, 'Restructuring Failed Financial Firms in Bankruptcy: Selling Lehman's Derivatives Portfolio' (2015) 32 Yale J on Reg 363, 377–380.

[105] BCBS, 'Report and Recommendations of the Cross-Border Bank Resolution Group' (BCBS, March 2010) 40 <https://www.bis.org/publ/bcbs162.htm> accessed 1 November 2023.

[106] KA Appendix I-Annex 5, para 1.1.

[107] See, e.g. Rizwaan J Mokal, 'Liquidity, Systemic Risk, and the Bankruptcy Treatment of Financial Contracts' (2015) 10 Brooklyn Journal of Corporate, Financial & Commercial Law 15; Anna Gelpern and Erik F Gerding, 'Private and Public Ordering in Safe Asset Markets' (2015) 10 Brooklyn Journal of Corporate, Financial & Commercial Law 97; Janger and Pottow (n 104); Roe and Adams (n 104).

[108] See, e.g. Lubben (n 104). cf David A Skeel and Thomas H Jackson, 'Transaction Consistency and the New Finance in Bankruptcy' (2012) 112 Columbia Law Review 152; Darrell Duffie and David A Skeel, 'A Dialogue on the Costs and Benefits of Automatic Stays for Derivatives and

The US, for instance, has taken this approach.[109] Resolution is no longer an automatic trigger for early termination rights.[110] The authority explains the policy document that this rule is 'intended to facilitate the orderly resolution of the most systemically important banking firms – the GSIBs – by limiting the ability of the firm's counterparties to terminate QFCs upon the entry of the GSIB or one or more of its affiliates into resolution'.[111] There are two types of restrictions: first, a stay shall only be temporary.[112] Second, a stay could also be imposed 'after the person has received notice that the contract has been transferred',[113] then the temporary stay becomes a permanent prohibition.

All the other jurisdictions follow the US approach,[114] with the only exception being China. However, a significant change has been spotted. After the GFC, China was on the track of embracing early termination rights. The National Association of Financial Market Institutional Investors (NAFMII) put forward a standardized set of documents for derivatives, which in the 2009 version adopted the close-out netting mechanism for onshore derivatives transactions.[115] Also, the NAFMII Bond Repurchase Master Agreement (2013 version) recognized the application of close-out netting in Outright Transfer Repos.[116] According to the International Swaps and Derivatives Association (ISDA) 2017 Memorandum on Enforceability of Close-out Netting in China, in general, close-out netting is not prohibited under any circumstances.[117] However, in the draft Financial Stability Law, a new provision is added on temporary stay on close-out netting.[118] These changes demonstrated the general trend across the globe to impose such temporary stays on early termination rights.

5. CONCLUDING REMARKS

This chapter offers a broad overview of bank recovery and resolution regimes. Discussions regarding the reform of crisis management measures in the banking sector have been the central topic of financial regulation in the post-GFC era and most recently in 2023. Thanks

Repurchase Agreements' in Kenneth E Scott and John B Taylor (eds), *Bankruptcy Not Bailout: A Special Chapter 14* (Hoover Institution Press 2012).

[109] See, e.g. Douglas G Baird and Edward E Morrison, 'Dodd–Frank for Bankruptcy Lawyers' (2011) 19 American Bankruptcy Institute Law Review 287; Roe and Adams (n 104) 373–377.

[110] 12 US Code §5390(c)(10)(B)(i). See also 12 US Code §1821(e)(10)(B)(i).

[111] Fed, 'Restrictions on Qualified Financial Contracts of Systemically Important U.S. Banking Organizations and the U.S. operations of Systemically Important Foreign Banking Organizations; Revisions to the Definition of Qualifying Master Netting Agreement and Related Definitions' (2017), 82 Fed Reg 42882, 42899. See also 12 CFR §252.81.

[112] 12 US Code §5390(c)(10)(B)(i)(I). See also 12 US Code §1821(e)(10)(B)(i)(I).

[113] 12 US Code §5390(c)(10)(B)(i)(II). See also 12 US Code §1821(e)(10)(B)(i)(II).

[114] FSB, '2022 Resolution Report' (n 4) 28–30.

[115] NAFMII Master Agreement (2009 version), Section 9. See also Qingjiang Kong and others, *New Bank Insolvency Law for China and Europe Volume 1: China* (Eleven International 2017) 73.

[116] NAFMII Bond Repurchase Master Agreement (2013 version), Special Provisions of Outright Transfer Repo, Section 3(V).

[117] ISDA, Memorandum on Enforceability of Close-out Netting in China (2017).

[118] Financial Stability Law of China (draft), art 30(4).

to the endeavours of international standard setting bodies, national laws have been largely harmonized in this field.

However, variations exist in national frameworks. Different types of resolution authorities are appointed, such as deposit insurance agents, central banks, financial regulators or supervisors, or special resolution authorities. The coverage of banks subject to resolution ranges from all banks to only systemically important ones. A resolution process is decided on a case-by-case basis and can be determined on several factors such as the viability of a bank, public interest, and/or necessity and proportionality. For specific resolution tools such as bail-in, transfer tools and temporary stay on early termination rights, there are also implementation disparities.

Given the thematic focus on comparative financial regulation in this book, this chapter underscores the importance of identifying these differences across jurisdictions. On the one hand, national legislators and regulators can glean valuable insights from their counterparts, through either statutory laws or case management experiences. Many jurisdictions have been significantly influenced by the US and EU, two of the largest financial markets in the world. On the other hand, understanding the basic position of each jurisdiction is vital for effectively addressing failing banks with international presence that pose global systemic risks. Similar effects may be achieved through different implementation rules under distinct national regimes, forming a solid foundation for cooperation. In today's era of economic integration, a comparative study serves to establish the common baseline for comprehending the legal and regulatory regimes, thereby fostering collective progress and stability in the financial sector.

14. Regulation of financial collateral

Hossein Nabilou

1. INTRODUCTION

Financial collateral sits at the heart of the modern financial markets and plays an indispensable role in the functioning of the financial and monetary systems. Repurchase agreements (repo), securities lending, margin accounts, and many forms of derivatives all rely on the security provided by financial collateral. As the collateral in such transactions reduces information asymmetries between parties, it transforms information-sensitive financial relationships into information-insensitive ones.[1] Depending on the quality of the collateral and the maturity of the instrument, financial collateral further transforms financial instruments into monetary instruments in the financial markets. Needless to say, such collateralized transactions play an indispensable role in the well-functioning of the financial markets and their infrastructure. For example, monetary policy in its modern form is partly conducted through repo transactions under which central banks engage with their select counterparties (primary dealers) to either lend them cash (thereby expanding broader money supply) or borrow cash from them (thereby contracting broader money supply in the economy). As these collateralized transactions underpin our financial and monetary systems, the law and regulation of financial collateral play a pivotal role in the overall functioning of financial markets.[2]

Despite the benefits of such collateralized transactions in terms of liquidity and their contribution to the allocational efficiency in financial markets, such transactions have been criticized for their potential role in systemic instability and financial crises. Indeed, one of the main catalysts or culprits of the global financial crisis of 2007–2009 (GFC) is believed to have been a 'run on repo' – a paradigmatic example of a collateralized transaction in financial markets – which is comparable with a traditional bank run in modern securitized banking with repo as

1 Bengt Holmstrom, 'Understanding the Role of Debt in the Financial System' (2015) BIS Working Paper No 479; Tri V Dang, Gary Gorton and Bengt Holmström, 'Ignorance, Debt and Financial Crises' (2020) Yale University and Massachusetts Institute of Technology, working paper <https://spinup-000d1a-wp-offload-media.s3.amazonaws.com/faculty/wp-content/uploads/sites/20/2021/02/Ignorance-Debt-and-Financial-Crises.pdf> accessed 2 July 2024; Hossein Nabilou and André Prüm, 'Ignorance, Debt and Cryptocurrencies: The Old and the New in the Law and Economics of Concurrent Currencies' (2019) 5 Journal of Financial Regulation 1; Gary B Gorton and Guillermo L Ordoñez, *Macroeconomics and Financial Crises: Bound Together by Information Dynamics* (Princeton University Press 2023) Chapter 2.

2 For a discussion on the similarities between the money creation by collateral reuse and deposit taking, see: Hossein Nabilou, 'The Law and Macroeconomics of Custody and Asset Segregation Rules: Defining the Perimeters of Crypto-Banking' (2022) Amsterdam Law School Research Paper.

a funding source.[3] Gorton and Metrick show that during the GFC, the average haircut of structured securities peaked, which rendered some of them unacceptable as collateral (i.e. a 100% haircut) in repo markets. Although the impact of repos on the GFC might be overstated,[4] since repos allow for leveraged maturity and liquidity transformation without access to government safety nets, they lie at the heart of the fragility of the (shadow) banking system.[5] In addition, it is argued that the reuse of financial collateral creates systemic risk. The criticism alleges that since in collateralized financial contracts the collateral provided by the collateral provider could be reused or rehypothecated, complex collateral chains (between the banking and the shadow banking system) could be created which could then contribute to financial instability.[6]

Given this high level of controversy as well as the importance of such contracts, this chapter investigates the legal underpinnings of financial collateral, with a special focus on repo transactions by taking a comparative law and economics perspective. The aim of this chapter is to shed light on some major differences in the legal structure of collateralized transactions in financial markets. This chapter first defines and describes the mechanics of collateralized transactions by highlighting their importance in the financial markets. Second, it sketches out the legal underpinnings of such transactions and the regulatory and legal frameworks applicable to financial collateral on both sides of the Atlantic. Third, it focuses on a paradigmatic example of a collateralized transaction – repo – and compares the most relevant aspects of the treatment of financial collateral across the Atlantic, i.e. the differences in legal construction, applicable law, special insolvency treatment, and the legal and regulatory treatment of the right of use. The last part concludes.

---

3 Gary B Gorton and Andrew Metrick, 'Securitized Banking and the Run on Repo' (2012) 104 Journal of Financial Economics 425, 1; Gary B Gorton, *Slapped by the Invisible Hand: The Panic of 2007* (Oxford University Press 2010); Gary B Gorton, *Shadow Banking* (Federal Reserve Bank of Minneapolis December 2010).

4 For a critique of this view, see Arvind Krishnamurthy, Stefan Nagel and Dmitry Orlov, 'Sizing Up Repo' (2014) 69 The Journal of Finance 2381; International Capital Market Association, 'Frequently Asked Questions on Repo' (ICMA, 2024) <https://www.icmagroup.org/market-practice-and-regulatory-policy/repo-and-collateral-markets/icma-ercc-publications/frequently-asked-questions-on-repo/> accessed 2 July 2024.

5 Financial Stability Board, 'Securities Lending and Repos: Market Overview and Financial Stability Issues- Interim Report of the FSB Workstream on Securities Lending and Repos' (FSB, 2012), 8.

6 For example, recital 21 of the Securities Financing Transactions Regulation (SFTR) reads: 'Reuse of collateral provides liquidity and enables counterparties to reduce funding costs. However, it tends to create complex collateral chains between traditional banking and shadow banking, giving rise to financial stability risks. The lack of transparency on the extent to which financial instruments provided as collateral have been reused and the respective risks in the case of bankruptcy can undermine confidence in counterparties and magnify risks to financial stability'. Regulation (EU) 2015/2365 of the European Parliament and of the Council of 25 November 2015 on transparency of securities financing transactions and of reuse and amending Regulation (EU) No 648/2012 (Text with EEA relevance), OJ L 337, 23 December 2015, 1–34. The recital acknowledges the benefits of collateral reuse in terms of providing liquidity and reducing funding costs. However, it seems that the recital goes astray in stating that the reuse of collateral creates complex collateral chains between traditional banking and shadow banking which increases the financial stability risks.

2. THE STRUCTURE OF COLLATERALIZED TRANSACTIONS

Collateralization in finance may take many forms. However, there are two main methods for collateralizing financial contracts. Collateralization could either be conducted through creating security interest in the collateral (a security financial collateral arrangement, SFCA) or through transfer of title of the collateral to the secured party (a title-transfer financial collateral arrangement, TTCA). In other words, the debate about financial collateral is a sub-category of a general topic of secured transactions as well as title finance, which is itself a subcategory of lending and borrowing or credit relationships.

The contractual framework for most collateralized financial contracts such as derivatives, repurchase agreements and securities lending agreements id provided by various standard Master Agreements drafted by industry associations. In the case of repo, the 2011 version Global Master Repurchase Agreement (GMRA) issued by the Securities Industry and Financial Markets Association (SIFMA) and the International Capital Market Association (ICMA) provides the current contractual framework. Likewise, the Global Master Securities Lending Agreement (GMSLA 2010 Agreement) issued by the International Securities Lending Association (ISLA) provides the standard contractual framework for securities lending agreements. By the same token, over-the-counter derivatives collateralization is mainly governed by the standard credit support annexes (CSAs) of the ISDA Master Agreements drafted by the International Swaps and Derivatives Association (ISDA).

The regulatory framework for financial collateral arrangements in Europe is mainly provided by the Financial Collateral Directive (FCD).[7] The main aim of the FCD is to harmonize the regime applicable to financial collateral arrangements. The FCD governs the collateral provided using title transfer or the grant of a security interest.[8] The main provisions include the prohibition of the recharacterization of title transfer as grant of security interests,[9] right of use for collateral taker,[10] a mechanism for rapid enforcements including close-out netting[11] and

---

[7] Council Directive 2002/47/EC of June 2002 on financial collateral arrangements [2002] OJ L168/43 (Directive 2002/47/EC), as amended by Council Directive 2009/44/EC of 6 May 2009 amending Directive 98/26/EC on settlement finality in payment and securities settlement systems and Directive 2002/47/EC on financial collateral arrangements as regards linked systems and credit claims [2009] OJ L146/37 and Directive 2014/59/EU of 15 May 2014 establishing a framework for the recovery and resolution of credit institutions and investment firms and amending Council Directive 82/891/EEC, and Directives 2001/24/EC, 2002/47/EC, 2004/25/EC, 2005/56/EC, 2007/36/EC, 2011/35/EU, 2012/30/EU and 2013/36/EU, and Regulations (EU) No 1093/2010 and (EU) No 648/2012, of the European Parliament and of the Council [2014] OJ L173/190. In addition, Chapter V of the UNIDROIT Convention on Substantive Rules for Intermediated Securities (Geneva Securities Convention or GSC) has also provisions governing financial collateral arrangements and reuse. However, this convention is far from being signed and adopted in the near future. See UNIDROIT Convention on Substantive Rules for Intermediated Securities <http://www.unidroit.org/english/conventions/2009intermediatedsecurities/convention.pdf> accessed 31 May 2014. It was adopted in 2009.

[8] For the distinction between the title transfer financial collateral arrangement and security financial collateral arrangement, see: Directive 2002/47/EC, art 2(1)(a), (b), and (c).

[9] Directive 2002/47/EC, art 6.

[10] Directive 2002/47/EC art 5.

[11] Directive 2002/47/EC arts 4 and 7.

the protections in insolvency (bankruptcy safe harbors).[12] The FCD generally strengthens the position of collateral takers vis-à-vis collateral providers.[13]

In the US, various private and public law provisions at the state as well as federal level regulate financial collateral; these laws and regulations range from the Uniform Commercial Code to state laws such as that of the New York Law, to federal regulations, such as those issued by the Securities and Exchange Commission (SEC), the Commodity Futures Trading Commission and the Federal Reserve.

2.1 Security Financial Collateral Arrangement

Normally in any debt or credit relationship, the creditor has two main concerns: first, whether the debtor will be able to repay the principal and the interest at the maturity of the transaction or based on an agreed upon schedule, and if not, whether the repayment through the (re)possession and sale of the collateral is possible or not. Such concerns are often addressed by the creation of security interest on the collateral posted by the debtor.[14] The second main concern of the creditor is whether the creditor will have priority over any other creditors having rights in the same collateral. Such a concern is often addressed by various methods of perfection of security interests. Perfection of a security is the legal process by which secured parties protect themselves against the claims of third parties who want to be repaid by selling the same collateral. There are two main methods of perfection of security interest: perfection by filing and perfection without filing. Perfection without filing can take the form of either perfection by possession or perfection on attachment (i.e. perfection without filing and without possession). In the former, the collateral is transferred into the possession of the secured party. In the latter, security interests are automatically perfected at the time of creation. For example, in the UK, a purchase-money security interest in consumer goods is perfected upon creation.

In the US, financial collateral arrangements are mainly based on security arrangements. Although in most European jurisdictions, financial collateral arrangements are based on title transfer, where title transfer is not used in the EU, the perfection of security interest over the collateral does not require registration or filing. Mere possession or *control* by the collateral taker would suffice for the perfection of such security interests. Indeed, under FCD, any requirements other than possession or control for the perfection of security interests in financial collateral are prohibited.[15] If perfection requirements other than possession or control were permitted, they would be detrimental to the liquidity of collateralized transactions such as repos and would hamper the reuse of collateral.

---

[12] Directive 2002/47/EC art 8.

[13] Such a provision is based on the ground that providing such a special treatment would improve market liquidity, lead to inexpensive credit and contribute to financial stability by preventing domino effects originating from individual insolvencies.

[14] For example, under the US UCC, there are three requirements for the creation of an enforceable security interest: possession, otherwise, a written or authenticated security agreement clearly describing the collateral; the secured party must give the debtor something of value; or the debtor must have rights in the collateral. Once these requirements are met, the creditor's rights attach to the collateral. Upon the attachment, an enforceable security interest in the collateral for the creditor is created.

[15] Directive 2002/47/EC, art 3(1).

2.2 Title-Transfer Financial Collateral Arrangement

A TTCA is a subcategory of title finance or title-based finance.[16] In essence and economic substance, title finance is a security substitute with very similar commercial effects. Owing to its functional similarity with security arrangements, sometimes it is called quasi-security.[17] Title finance arrangements are financial mechanisms that perform a very similar function to security interests but under the laws of some jurisdictions, such as English law, are not considered security.[18] There are two types of title finance: title-retention finance and title-transfer finance. In the former, the creditor's exposure (payment or other obligations) is secured by retaining the title by the seller while the possession is transferred to the purchaser. This is not a true 'security'.[19] However, the TTCA, as the name suggests, belongs to the second category whereby title of the good or asset is transferred to the lender along with the possession or control of the asset.

In Europe, most repos, securities lending and receivable financing are conducted through title transfer. A TTCA is an arrangement under which financial collateral is transferred outright from the collateral provider to the collateral taker. The most salient advantage of this type of finance over security is that because title transfer does not need registration or other formalities, it gives better protection to the creditor in the insolvency of the debtor. However, there is a major risk of recharacterization, where the title transfer finance could be recharacterized as security interest. This is particularly risky for the lender because if recharacterization risk realizes, the title transfer finance would be considered as security interest. As creating security interest often requires certain formalities without which the validity of the security interest could be questioned, the lender may find itself an unsecured creditor if he has not followed the required procedures for the creation and perfection of security interests. Nonetheless, under the relevant laws of major jurisdictions, recharacterization risks have become minimal by specific regulations prohibiting recharacterization.[20]

3. A PARADIGMATIC EXAMPLE: REPURCHASE AGREEMENTS (REPOS)

The number and types of collateralized transactions in finance may not know any boundaries. However, a few of them stand out, such as repurchase agreements (repo), securities lending (and similar transactions), margin lending and (collateralization of exposures in) derivatives. Owing to the limitations of space in this article, only repo is discussed. From an economic point of view, a repo is equivalent to a secured loan. The lender or buyer in a repo receives the

---

16 Vendor/lessor security, asset-based finance, title financing, quasi-security. For more, see: Philip R Wood, *Law and Practice of International Finance* (Sweet & Maxwell 2008), 292.

17 This sometimes gives rise to recharacterization risk, where such an arrangement risk being recharacterized as a security arrangement.

18 Hugh Beale and others, *The Law of Security and Title-based Financing* (3rd edn, Oxford University Press 2018).

19 Supply agreements, conditional sales, hire purchase, finance lease.

20 This recharacterization risk is dealt with in Directive 2002/47/EC art 2(2) in the European Union.

underlying securities as collateral while the borrower or seller commits to buy the same asset back in the future. Under normal circumstances, the buyer will earn a return (pricing rate or repo rate) after reselling the asset back to the repo seller in the closing leg at a higher price. Owing to its simple legal structure, repos are widely accepted across common-law as well as civil-law jurisdictions.

A typical repo transaction can be chronologically divided into multiple steps. The first step, which is referred to as 'trading', involves the parties reaching an agreement as to the key terms and conditions. The parties will then each examine their remaining obligation to deliver cash in the same currency and/or the same security to each other and work out a net volume on a daily basis. They may also be bound by a legal obligation to clear this transaction multilaterally. After this 'clearing' stage, the seller keeps the security on its book while adding a loan to its liabilities and the received cash as an asset. The purchased asset does not appear on the balance sheet of the buyer since the seller agrees to buy it back. Finally, the parties or a third-party agent will manage the collateral.[21]

Despite repo transactions being ubiquitous in the financial markets worldwide, their legal underpinnings show considerable divergences across the Atlantic. In what follows, the chapter briefly discusses three main aspects of the repo transaction, two of which have proven to be most controversial. The investigation of these three aspects is of great functional comparative-law value as they manifest the dynamics of convergence and divergence in financial markets. Those three aspects relate to the contractual and private law underpinning of repo transactions and applicable law, the special insolvency treatment of repo transaction and the right of (re)use or rehypothecation of collateral.

3.1 Differences in Legal Construction and Applicable Law

In Europe, a repurchase agreement transfers legal title to collateral from the seller to the buyer. In other words, a repo in Europe is a true sale; hence the name 'title transfer (financial) collateral arrangement'.[22] This renders repo a cheap source of funding and liquidity for repo market participants because the repo seller can use the cash it has borrowed to buy the same or similar assets in the market (i.e. to finance its long positions), meanwhile, the repo buyer can reuse the collateral to refinance itself in a similar fashion during the life of the repo (e.g. to cover its short positions). Theoretically, this process could repeat several times until profitability is exhausted by initial margining or credit limits.

However, in the US, under the New York State law, since transferring title to collateral is difficult, the collateral is pledged, but it is exempt from certain provisions of the US Bankruptcy Code such as automatic stays that apply to pledges. Nonetheless, the pledgee is

---

21 As will be explained in this chapter, one of the most significant differences between the European and the US Repo markets lies in this 'collateral management' stage.

22 In Europe, there are both 'title transfer financial collateral arrangements' and 'security financial collateral arrangements' (Directive 2002/47/EC, art 2), but it seems that the majority of repos are in the form of TTCAs. For a difference between traditional collateralized lending and TTCAs, see; Joanna Benjamin, Guy Morton and Michael Raffan, 'The Future of Securities Financing' (2013) 7 Law and Financial Markets Review 4, 5.

given a general right of use of collateral, which is also known as rehypothecation.[23] In spite of this legal nuance, this arrangement effectively – and in economic terms – is equivalent to an outright sale. Under the New York State law, repos include a fall-back provision; namely, if the buyer's right to collateral proves to be unenforceable, the repo will be recharacterized as secured lending. However, English law, and by the same token the EU law,[24] does not allow such recharacterization.

Efforts to standardize and harmonize repo transactions at the international level have been underway well before the GFC. For example, industry initiatives through self-regulatory organizations, such as the ICMA, SIFMA and ISDA, have been relatively successful in achieving certain degrees of standardization in the design, governance and legal framework of collateralized transactions including repos.[25] For instance, the ICMA (and its predecessor institutions) played a significant role in pushing governments to adopt bankruptcy safe harbors for repos and certain types of derivatives transactions with financial counterparties.

Despite such efforts towards standardization, the repo markets in Europe and in the US operate differently in various aspects and many repo transactions are subject to local rules and regulations of specific jurisdictions. This is the case especially in Europe where those transactions are still governed and regulated by the Member State laws, subject to varying degrees of harmonization at the EU level. In addition, there are still frictions in the legal regime for repos even within the international self-regulatory frameworks. For example, the choice of different master agreements amounts to different governing laws across the Atlantic. In Europe, the GMRA drafted and continuously updated by the ICMA is often executed between the lender and the borrower, the governing law of which is English law.[26] This master agreement also has a major impact on the US repo market when the repo transaction involves an international counterparty. However, for US domestic repos, the SIFMA Master Agreement, which is governed by New York State law,[27] is prevalent.

3.2 Special Bankruptcy Treatment

One of the most controversial aspects of collateralized financial contracts and in particular repos is their special bankruptcy treatment. Under the New York State law, which governs the SIFMA Master Repo Agreement (MRA), the collateralization is based on a SFCA.[28] However, the US Bankruptcy Code has special provisions for Qualified Financial Contracts (QFCs) – which include repos – by exempting them from the 'automatic stay' and allowing counterparties to terminate these contracts by closing out, netting or setting off their net exposures.[29]

---

23 For the subtleties of the right of rehypothecation, see: Kettering KC, 'Repledge Deconstructed' (1999) 61 *University of Pittsburgh Law Review* 45.

24 Directive 2002/47/EC art 6.

25 This has played a major role in liquidity in the market for such instruments.

26 GMRA Version 2011, para. 17.

27 SIFMA's MRA, Version 1996, para. 16.

28 ICMA, 'Frequently Asked Questions on Repo' (n 4).

29 The Safe Harbor Provisions are embedded in the following provisions: 11 U.S.C. (2018) §§ 362 (b)(6), 362(b)(7), 362(b)(17), 546, 556, 559, 560 & 561 (2012). In Europe, such safe harbors are granted in the Financial Collateral Directive. See: FCD, art 8. See also Adam Copeland and others, 'Key Mechanics of the US Tri-party Repo Market' (2012) 18 Federal Reserve Bank of New

In the EU, the TTCA-based repo transactions do not per se necessitate the use of bankruptcy safe harbors because such transactions are already concluded as a true sale transaction (title transfer) rather than a secured transaction. However, it seems that owing to the differential treatments of such transactions in different Member States and potential conflicts stemming from such frictions, bankruptcy safe harbors have been included in the FCD[30] and Settlement Finality Directive.[31]

In addition to the benefits that these bankruptcy safe harbors provide in terms of enhanced market and funding liquidity,[32] they may strengthen financial stability. The underlying rationale for these safe harbors for derivatives and repos was that the derivatives markets can be a source of systemic risk and this exemption would be necessary to prevent the risks of contagion and systemic risk.[33] Exempting such contracts from bankruptcy stays would increase market confidence provided by guaranteeing the lenders their right to the collateral, thereby mitigating the possibility of a debtor's bankruptcy resulting in systematic failure.

However, repo runs, as one of the main contagion channels in the GFC, ignited a contentious debate on the special bankruptcy regime for repos.[34] It is argued that such safe harbors increase the likelihood of fire sales and collateral crises.[35] Further evidence suggests that the role of closeout netting in reducing systemic risk is far from straightforward.[36] In other words, although this exemption produces numerous benefits and is necessary for the well-functioning of financial markets,[37] it encourages the run on financial institutions by incenting counterparties to close-out or net derivatives contracts at the first signals of insolvency of a financial firm.

An additional downside to bankruptcy safe harbors is that they amplify the moral hazard risk by undermining the parties' incentive to closely monitor their debtors' financial condition by giving the counterparty the guarantee to their collateral.[38] Furthermore, if lenders believe

---

York Economic Policy Review 17 5; Darrell Duffie and David A Skeel, 'A Dialogue on the Costs and Benefits of Automatic Stays for Derivatives and Repurchase Agreements' (2012) 2. See 11 U.S.C. (2018) § 362 (a).

30 Directive 2002/47/EC of the European Parliament and of the Council of 6 June 2002 on financial collateral arrangements.

31 Directive 98/26/EC of the European Parliament and of the Council of 19 May 1998 on settlement finality in payment and securities settlement systems, OJ L 166, 11 June 1998, 45–50.

32 See Philipp Paech, 'The Value of Insolvency Safe Harbours' (2015) LSE Legal Studies Working Paper No 9/2015; Nathan Goralnik, 'Bankruptcy-proof Finance and the Supply of Liquidity' (2012) 122 Yale Law Journal 460.

33 See for example, René M. Stulz, 'Should We Fear Derivatives?' (2004) 18 The Journal of Economic Perspectives 173 188.

34 Gorton and Metrick, 'Securitized Banking and the Run on Repo' (n 3).

35 Carolyn Sissoko, 'The Legal Foundations of Financial Collapse' (2010) 2 Journal of Financial Economic Policy 5. See also Steven L. Schwarcz, 'Derivatives and Collateral: Balancing Remedies and Systemic Risk' (2015) 2015 University of Illinois Law Review 699.

36 Robert R. Bliss and George G. Kaufman, 'Derivatives and Systemic Risk: Netting, Collateral, and Closeout' (2006) 2 Journal of Financial Stability 55.

37 For why the derivatives contracts should be treated differently on efficiency-based grounds, see Franklin R Edwards and Edward R Morrison, 'Derivatives and the Bankruptcy Code: Why the Special Treatment' (2005) 22 Yale Journal on Regulation 91.

38 Duffie and Skeel, 'A Dialogue on the Costs and Benefits of Automatic Stays for Derivatives and Repurchase Agreements' (n 29), see also its fn. 10.

that the government would bail out their debtors in the event of distress or default, a safe harbor clause will almost certainly encourage lenders to take advantage of their counterparties' too-big-to-fail status, further contributing to moral hazard. In addition, repo transactions in the US are mostly overnight and short term. Since the law recognizes repo as a QFC, it would incentivize lenders to concentrate their funds in this method of funding, decreasing the incentive to use more traditional financing methods (e.g. long-term and unsecured loans). This would amount to a decrease in market discipline as the unsecured creditors are believed to be the watchdogs of market discipline.[39]

Therefore, it is argued that safe harbors do not reduce systemic contagion, because some intricate complexities, interconnectedness and interactions among financial institutions are overlooked. The safe harbors are also considered responsible for the failure of Lehman Brothers, especially accounting for the fact that the exemptions from the automatic stay failed to prevent a run on Lehman.[40] It is documented that just before the collapse of Lehman Brothers, JP Morgan seized $17 billion in Lehman's collateral and demanded an additional $5 billion payment.[41]

Scholars are also divided on a wide spectrum on this contested issue. Some believe that the safe harbors should be totally repealed.[42] Others believe that they should be maintained in their entirety. A third group believes in narrowing down the scope of such safe harbors.[43] In general,

---

39 Such concerns have been paramount in the case of covered bonds, which are another form of secured lending. See European Banking Authority, *EBA Report on EU Covered Bond Frameworks and Capital Treatment: Response to the Commission's call for advice of December 2013 related to Article 503 of the Regulation (EU) No 575/2013 and to the ESRB Recommendation E on the funding of credit institutions of December 2012 (ESRB/12/2)*, 1 July 2014, 138.

40 Schwarcz, 'Derivatives and Collateral: Balancing Remedies and Systemic Risk' (n 35).

41 See Darrell Duffie, 'The Failure Mechanics of Dealer Banks' (2010) 24 Journal of Economic Perspectives 51. In addition, this safe harbor also encourages systemically risky market concentration on the conviction that on the default of a counterparty, the dealer would simply seize the collateral, making the dealer care less about the amount of its concentrated exposure to one counterparty. Schwarcz, 'Derivatives and Collateral: Balancing Remedies and Systemic Risk' (n 35).

42 Stephen J Lubben, 'Repeal the Safe Harbors' (2010) 18 American Bankruptcy Institute Law Review 319; Stephen J Lubben, 'Derivatives and Bankruptcy: The Flawed Case for Special Treatment' (2009) 12 University of Pennsylvania Journal of Business Law 61; Stephen J Lubben, 'The Bankruptcy Code Without Safe Harbors' (2010) 84 American Bankruptcy Law Journal 123; Charles W. Mooney, 'The Bankruptcy Code's Safe Harbors for Settlement Payments and Securities Contracts: When is Safe Too Safe?' (2014) 49 Texas International Law Journal 245. Antinolfi et al. also find that the bankruptcy safe harbors had contributed to the growth and development of repo markers, but also this may increase the likelihood of fire sales and hence reduce the real investment in the economy. Therefore, bankruptcy policy makes face a trade-off between the reduction of the risk to the investment activities in the real economy and better liquidity of repo markets. See G. Antinolfi and others, 'Repos, Fire Sales, and Bankruptcy Policy' (2015) 18 Review of Economic Dynamics 21. Sissoko, 'The Legal Foundations of Financial Collapse' (n 35). However, given the benefits of this safe harbor, it is argued that abolishing them would so more harm than good and it would adversely affect the liquidity of financial markets. See Goralnik, 'Bankruptcy-Proof Finance and the Supply of Liquidity' (n 32).

43 Bryan G. Faubus, 'Narrowing the Bankruptcy Safe Harbor for Derivatives to Combat Systemic Risk' (2010) 59 Duke Law Journal 801. David Skeel and Thomas Jackson also explore the effects of transaction consistency (or 'equivalent treatment of similar transactions') in bank-

removing the automatic stay exemption would act as a curb on repos by reducing the liquidity of the collateral, particularly in tri-party markets.[44] This can be viewed as a sensible regulatory measure to reduce the reliance on lower-quality collateral, akin to setting minimum haircuts. However, removing this exemption would probably be unwarranted for higher-quality collateral, such as most government-guaranteed securities.[45]

In the US, as a response to the concerns of run on repo giving rise to disorderly resolution of banks, the exemption from automatic stay no longer entirely applies to banks being taken over by the Federal Deposit Insurance Corporation (FDIC).[46] Similarly, under the Dodd–Frank Act, counterparties to a 'covered financial company'[47] may not be able to terminate contracts after the institution is put under the FDIC's receivership.[48] Under the EU FCD, holders of instruments involving financial institutions whereby cash or securities are transferred by way of security financial collateral arrangement (as opposed to title transfer financial collateral arrangement) are protected from the application of the insolvency laws or other measures that could hinder the enforcement of their close-out netting.[49] Since such protections may result in the erosion of the financial institutions' goodwill, they were viewed as posing major challenges to insolvency procedures and successful resolutions. To address this problem, the FCD was revised by the Bank Recovery and Resolution Directive (BRRD)[50] to allow for a stay on close-out netting and enforcement provision until midnight at the end of the next business day.[51] This new rule is intended to afford resolution authorities with adequate time for an

ruptcy and conclude that imposing transaction consistency on repos would have limited impact. They also have a nuanced approach to removing safe harbors. David A. Skeel and Thomas H. Jackson, 'Transaction Consistency and the New Finance in Bankruptcy' (2012) 112 Columbia Law Review 152.

44 Goralnik, 'Bankruptcy-Proof Finance and the Supply of Liquidity' (n 32).

45 See Hossein Nabilou and Alessio Pacces, 'The Law and Economics of Shadow Banking' in Iris H. Chiu (ed.), *Research Handbook in Shadow Banking* (Edward Elgar Publishing 2018).

46 For the operation of FDIC after receivership of the regulated bank, see Duffie and Skeel, 'A Dialogue on the Costs and Benefits of Automatic Stays for Derivatives and Repurchase Agreements' (n 29) see also 12 U.S.C. (2018) § 1821 (e)(9), (10)(B), (13)(C)(i), which provides for a general prohibition to exercise certain contractual rights without consent.

47 Defined in 12 U.S.C. (2018) § 5381(a)(8) which does not include insured depository institution.

48 See 12 U.S.C. (2018) § 5390 (e)(9), (b)(10)(B), (13)(C)(i); see also Duffie and Skeel, 'A Dialogue on the Costs and Benefits of Automatic Stays for Derivatives and Repurchase Agreements' (n 29), 4.

49 Directive 2002/47/EC arts 4 and 8.

50 Directive 2014/59/EU of the European Parliament and of the Council of 15 May 2014 establishing a framework for the recovery and resolution of credit institutions and investment firms and amending Council Directive 82/891/EEC, and Directives 2001/24/EC, 2002/47/EC, 2004/25/EC, 2005/56/EC, 2007/36/EC, 2011/35/EU, 2012/30/EU and 2013/36/EU, and Regulations (EU) No 1093/2010 and (EU) No 648/2012, of the European Parliament and of the Council, OJ L 173, 12 June 2014, 190–348.

51 See, BBRD, arts 70–71 and 118 that revises the FCD by inserting a new article 1(6) to that directive.

orderly resolution. Any modification beyond that has not gained considerable traction.[52] It is noteworthy to mention that the limited scope of the BRRD applies to such provisions, meaning that contracts in which one counterparty is a bank (credit institution) to which BBRD resolution tools are applicable only enjoys such a privileged treatment. The exposures to financial market infrastructures such as central clearing counterparties are also exempt from automatic early termination rights under the special treatment afforded by the BRRD.[53]

3.3 Right of Use

Another controversial aspect of collateralized financial contracts including repos is rehypothecation or reuse of collateral.[54] Article 2(1)(m) FCD defines the right of use as the right of the collateral taker to use and dispose of financial collateral provided under a SFCA as its owner in accordance with the terms of the SFCA. Such a right is an exception to the general rule that the provided collateral could not be used by the collateral taker. Rehypothecation is often practiced in the relationship between broker-dealers and their clients and it provides an inexpensive source of financing for financial institutions, especially broker-dealers.[55] For example, in repo financing, the broker-dealer often hypothecates the collateral provided by its client so that it can procure financing for it from another client on a matched-book basis.[56] Rehypothecation plays an important role in providing liquidity to markets. However, it is believed to pose risks to financial stability, particularly if one looks at how the GFC manifested itself, namely, as withdrawals of collateral from investment banks such as Lehman Brothers.[57]

---

52 Philipp Paech, *Shadow Banking: Legal Issues of Collateral Assets and Insolvency Law* (European Parliament; Directorate General for Internal Policies 2013) 5. See also Skeel and Jackson, 'Transaction Consistency and the New Finance in Bankruptcy' (n 43), 166–168. Although Skeel and Jackson argue that the most bankruptcy safe harbor should be eliminated, they argue that there should still be automatic stay safe harbors for repos collateralized by cash like instruments (cash like collateral used in repo transactions.) See, Skeel and Jackson, 'Transaction consistency and the new finance in bankruptcy' (n 43), 156–157. Other commentators believe that the safe harbors should be removed even for such instruments. See Norbert J. Michel, *Fixing the Regulatory Framework for Derivatives* (The Heritage Foundation 2016) <https://www.heritage.org/government-regulation/report/fixing-the-regulatory-framework-derivatives>.

53 Arts 68–71 BRRD.

54 It appears that the term rehypothecation would be confusing term in English law because its commercial use is different from its legal use. The word reuse could be a better and more precise term than rehypothecation. For more details See Daniel Harris, 'Use of Customer Securities by UK Prime Brokers: The Road Ahead' (2013) 7 Law and Financial Markets Review 107. Reuse sometimes is also called repledge. For the difference between rehypothecation and reuse, see Manmohan Singh, 'Velocity of Pledged Collateral: Analysis and Implications' (2011) IMF Working Paper WP/11/256 9.

55 Christian A. Johnson, 'Derivatives and Rehypothecation Failure: It's 3:00 pm, Do You Know Where Your Collateral Is?' (1997) 30 Arizona Law Review 949 969.

56 See Zoltan Pozsar, 'Shadow Banking: The Money View' (2014) Office of Financial Research Working Paper.

57 Darrell Duffie, 'The Failure Mechanics of Dealer Banks' (n 41). Steven L. Schwarcz, 'Distorting Legal Principles' (2010) 35 Journal of Corporation Law 697 700. See also: James Aitken and Manmohan Singh, *Deleveraging After Lehman – Evidence from Reduced Rehypothecation*

Unless there are exceptions to the contrary, the reuse of collateral is permitted not only under repo transactions, but also under many other collateralized financial contracts such as derivatives. The contractual basis for the right of use in derivatives transactions could be found in the 1994 CSA to the Schedules to the ISDA Master Agreement subject to New York Law, which creates SFCAs. Under paragraph 6(c), the secured party has the right to 'sell, pledge, rehypothecate, assign, invest, use, commingle or otherwise dispose of, or otherwise use in its business any Posted Collateral it holds, free from any claim or right of any nature whatsoever of the Pledgor, including any equity or right of redemption by the Pledgor'.[58] Such a right of rehypothecation does not apply to the 1995 CSA to the Schedules to the ISDA Master Agreement subject to English Law because the English law CSA provides for a TTCA whereby the collateral taker becomes the owner of the collateral and can freely dispose of it.[59]

In addition, reuse of collateral under repo transactions is permitted because under the standard documentation for repo transactions 'all right, title and interest in and to Securities and money transferred or paid under [the ...] Agreement shall pass to the transferee upon transfer or payment, the obligation of the party receiving Purchased Securities or Margin Securities being an obligation to transfer Equivalent Securities or Equivalent Margin Securities'.[60] Therefore, the borrower (in economic terms) can freely use and dispose of the borrowed securities and the lender (again, in economic terms) can use and dispose of the collateral. In other words, as TTCAs involve the transfer of title, a right of reuse or rehypothecation is not technically applicable. As under the securities lending arrangements, the borrower should return the *equivalent* securities to the lender and the lender should return *equivalent* collateral, it is presumed that the borrower and the lender can use the securities received on loan or the securities received as collateral.[61] Accordingly article 5(1) of the FCD, the collateral taker is entitled to exercise a right of use in relation to financial collateral provided under a SFCA.

(EPub), vol 9 (International Monetary Fund 2009) (showing that after the Lehman bankruptcy there was a significant reduction in rehypothecation by broker dealers; although this reduced counterparty risks in the system, it comes at the cost of having less liquid markets.) Singh finds that the decline in the source of pledgeable collateral, and the subsequent reduction in the liquidity of the markets had an effect on the conduct of monetary policy. See Singh, 'Velocity of Pledged Collateral: Analysis and Implications' (n 54).

58 In this sense, 'rehypothecation' involves the collateral taker's use of financial collateral in which a security interest has been vested. This practice, rather than being a rule, is an exception to the general rule and only applies to *financial* collateral in security financial collateral arrangements.

59 Paragraph 5 of the 1995 Credit Support Annex to the Schedules to the ISDA Master Agreement subject to English Law. Paragraph 5(a) stipulates: 'Each party agrees that all right, title and interest in and to any Eligible Credit Support, Equivalent Credit Support, Equivalent Distributions or Interest Amount which it transfers to the other party under the terms of this Annex shall vest in the recipient free and clear of any liens, claims, charges or encumbrances or any other interest of the transferring party or of any third person (other than a lien routinely imposed on all securities in a relevant clearance system)'. Furthermore, paragraph 5(b) provides: 'No Security Interest. Nothing in this Annex is intended to create or does create in favour of either party any mortgage, charge, lien, pledge, encumbrance or other security interest in any cash or other property transferred by one party to the other party under the terms of this Annex'.

60 Section 6(f) GMRA.

61 See GMSLA, paragraphs 1(1.1) and 8(3) and 8(4).

Although the reuse of collateral can take place in various contexts in the collateralized transactions such as in margin accounts, derivatives collateralization, and repo and securities lending, the reuse of collateral in margin accounts has been subject to restrictions in terms of the ratio of the collateral that could be reused or even outright prohibition of the reuse of collateral.[62] The regulatory developments in the aftermath of the financial crisis put strict restrictions on the reuse of collateral in the derivatives transactions, especially a ban on the reuse of initial margin.[63] It seems that currently, the most important transactions under which reuse of collateral happens without much restriction are repo and securities lending transactions.

There are important exceptions and limitations to the right of use. First, the reuse or rehypothecation is permitted only in *financial* collateral arrangements (i.e. (TTCAs and SFCAs), where there are restrictions on the type of collateral. In the EU, for instance, only cash, securities and credit claims can be provided as financial collateral and treated as such.[64] Second, there are restrictions on the parties that can enter into financial collateral arrangements. For example, investment firms are prohibited from concluding TTCAs with retail clients for the purpose of securing or covering present or future, actual or contingent or prospective obligations of clients.[65] Therefore, the FCD is not applicable to natural persons,[66] which implies that the reuse of collateral is only permitted among institutions. Third, *certain types of collateral cannot be reused*. For example, credit claims (sums owed to the banks) cannot be subject to a right of use.[67] In addition, the collateral provided as initial margin to secure non-centrally cleared derivatives should be segregated and cannot be reused.[68] Fourth, certain requirements

---

62 Charles W Mooney Jr, 'The Truth About Shortfall of Intermediated Securities – Perspectives Under the Geneva Securities Convention, United States Law, and the Future EU Legislation' in Pierre-Henri Conac, Ulrich Segna and Luc Thévenoz (eds), *Intermediated Securities: The Impact of the Geneva Securities Convention and the Future European Legislation* (Cambridge University Press 2013).

63 Commission Delegated Regulation (EU) 2016/2251 of 4 October 2016 supplementing Regulation (EU) No 648/2012 of the European Parliament and of the Council on OTC derivatives, central counterparties and trade repositories with regard to regulatory technical standards for risk-mitigation techniques for OTC derivative contracts not cleared by a central counterparty, C/2016/6329, art 20.

64 See, for example, Art. 1(4)(a) Directive 2002/47/EC.

65 Art. 16(10) MiFID II. There are also limitations on the scope of the FCD, for example, FDC does not apply to financial collateral arrangements when a party is a natural person and where both parties belong to one of the categories listed in the article 1(2)(e) such as non-financial enterprises, unincorporated firms, and partnerships. For more details, see Thomas Keijser, Maria Kyrkousi and Andreas Bakanos, 'Financial Collateral: The Legal Framework of the European Union and Unidroit Compared' (2014) 19 Uniform Law Review 429.

66 Art. 1(2)(e) Directive 2002/47/EC.

67 Art. 5(7) Directive 2002/47/EC.

68 BCBS, Margin Requirements for Non-centrally Cleared Derivatives. See also art 11(3) Regulation (EU) No 648/2012 of the European Parliament and of the Council of 4 July 2012 on OTC derivatives, central counterparties and trade repositories, OJ L 201, 27 July 2012, 1–59 (hereinafter EMIR).

such as information provision, prior express consent and signature apply to the right of use.[69] In other words, the collateral provider must be duly informed in writing by the collateral taker of the risks of granting consent to a right of use.[70] The collateral provider must grant its prior express consent for reuse of collateral, and the express consent must be evidenced by a signature in writing. Such safeguards are in place because the exercise of right of use transforms the collateral provider's secured claim to the collateral to an unsecured claim against the collateral taker for the return of equivalent collateral.[71] In other words, the collateral provider accepts an insolvency risk in respect to the collateral taker, although it retained an ownership right when it agreed to a security collateral transaction.

Another important instance of financial collateral is the margin account agreements,[72] which often authorize the custodian or the broker-dealer to take security interest against customer assets to secure the anticipated or unanticipated credit extension by the custodian (broker-dealer) to the customer. As for margin accounts, in the US, according to Uniform Commercial Code (UCC) Section 8-504,[73] an intermediary has a duty to have on hand sufficient securities to cover the credits that the intermediary has made to the securities accounts of its account holder. To complement this rule, SEC Rule 15c3-3(1)(b) requires that '[a] broker or dealer shall promptly obtain and shall thereafter maintain the physical possession or control of all fully paid securities and excess margin securities carried by a broker or dealer for the account of customers'. Therefore, fully paid securities, i.e. '[s]ecurities credited to a securities account for which the account holder has made full payment and in which the broker-dealer does not have a security interest' are subject to possession or control requirement. Excess margin securities, namely, margin securities with a market value in excess of 140% of the account holder's secured obligation to the broker dealer, are also subject to possession or control requirement. However, margin securities or non-excess margin securities,[74] namely, securities other than fully paid securities which are credited to a securities account (margin account), are not subject to the possession or control requirement. Therefore, the broker dealer can have a securities interest in margin securities to secure the account holder's debt to the intermediary (broker-dealer). Therefore, non-excess margin securities may be pleaded, repledge or loaned. In other words, the amount of a client's assets that can be rehypothecated

---

69 Art 38(7) CSD regulation provides that 'A CSD shall not use for any purpose securities that do not belong to it. A CSD may however use securities of a participant where it has obtained that participant's prior express consent. The CSD shall require its participants to obtain any necessary prior consent from their clients'.

70 Art. 15 Regulation (EU) 2015/2365.

71 Matthias Haentjens, *Financial Collateral: Law and Practice* (Oxford University Press 2020) 233. Furthermore, upon the reuse of the collateral, the collateral provider will not be entitled to exercise voting rights and reuse may prevent the collateral provider's right of substitution, 'that is the collateral provider's right to demand substitution of the securities collateral for other eligible securities collateral'; ibid.

72 Margin accounts are account held by a broker dealer which makes it possible for the customer to obtain credit secured by the funds and securities of the customer to enable the customer to finance his investments.

73 Similar requirement can be found in the Geneva Securities Convention art. 28(2).

74 In other words, margin securities in a customer account are those securities with a market value equal to or less than 140% of the customer's debit balance (the amount the customer owes the broker-dealer for the purchase of the securities).

by a prime broker or a broker dealer is capped to the equivalent of 140% of the client's liability to the prime broker or dealer.[75]

In addition, in the US, according to Section 724 of the Dodd–Frank Act,[76] parties accepting money, securities or property to margin, guarantee or secure a swap cleared by a derivatives clearing organization should register as Futures Commission Merchants (FCMs). The FCMs should treat all money, securities, and property of any swaps customer as belonging to the swap customer. They are also required to separately account for and not commingle the customer's funds with the funds of the FCM.

In addition, Section 724 requires the segregation of margin for uncleared swaps. According to this requirement, a swap dealer or a Major Swap Participant (MSP) should notify the party wishing to enter a swap transaction at the beginning of the swap transaction that it has 'the right to require the segregation of the funds or other property supplied to margin, guarantee, or secure the obligations of the counterparty'. The aim of this provision is to prevent the swap dealers or an MSPs from using customers' assets posted with them as collateral to be used as margin, guarantee or security for any of its trades.[77]

Therefore, one of the significant divergences in the regulatory treatment of collateralized transactions across the Atlantic is the limit or cap on the rehypothecation of collateral in the US as opposed to many other markets including the EU markets. At the EU level, there is no cap on the reuse, as opposed to the 140% cap in the US.[78] However, individual member states, such as France, have established similar limitations (140% cap). Although in the UK there is no 140% cap on rehypothecation, it seems that the percentage used in the US has created anchoring effect, and in fact many hedge funds are using the 140% cap as a benchmark in negotiating prime brokerage agreements with their banks.[79]

4. CONCLUSION

This chapter studied financial collateral from a comparative law perspective by focusing on the EU and US legal and regulatory frameworks. In doing so, it briefly sketched the regulation of financial collateral across the Atlantic by investigating its contractual framework, its private law underpinnings, and its regulatory treatment. This chapter focused on a paradigmatic example of a collateralized financial transactions, i.e. repo and on other transactions only when necessary. The chapter highlighted three most important legal and economic issues of financial collateral: the divergences in the legal construction and applicable law across the Atlantic, the special bankruptcy treatment for financial collateral, and the right of reuse or rehypothecation of collateral. The study finds that despite the existence of various divergences in the private law underpinnings of financial collateral there has been considerable convergence in the reg-

---

[75] Federal Reserve Regulation T (12 CFR §220) and SEC Rule 15c3-3.

[76] 7 U.S.C. (2018) § 6d.

[77] Lloyd Dixon, Noreen Clancy and Krishna B. Kumar, *Hedge Funds and Systemic Risk* (RAND Corporation), pp. 77–79.

[78] Autorité des Marchés Financiers, 'The Reuse of Assets: Regulatory and Economic Issues' (9 November 2016).

[79] Manmohan Singh and James Aitken, 'The (Sizable) Role of Rehypothecation in the Shadow Banking System' (2010) 10/172 IMF Working Paper 12.

ulatory treatment of financial collateral. Such convergences were driven both by the harmonization efforts initiated by the industry associations mainly targeted at reducing market frictions and transaction costs and by financial regulatory agencies aiming at containing systemic risk spillovers.

15. Regulation of clearing and settlement

Paolo Saguato[1]

1. INTRODUCTION

Financial infrastructures are the backbone of financial markets. Once a trade is executed on a trading venue or over-the-counter (OTC) between parties, financial market infrastructures (FMIs) come into play.[2] They confirm the terms of the trade, reconcile the obligations of buyer and seller, manage the risks of the transaction, guarantee its performance, and discharge the final contractual obligations of each party.[3] These clearing and settlement (C&S) functions are commonly referred to as post-trade services and are traditionally performed by two FMIs, central counterparties (CCPs) clearinghouses – firms that interpose themselves between parties to a contract, becoming the buyer to every seller and the seller to every buyer and committing to guarantee the performance of open contracts[4] – and central securities depositories (CSDs)[5] – entities that support the settlement, i.e. the performance of the legal obligations, of a trade.[6]

Over the past forty years, FMIs have garnered growing attention from policymakers and commentators. Structural changes in global finance, financial crises and the disruptive force of innovation have contributed to a fast evolution of the industry and its regulatory framework. International standard-setting bodies, in particular the Committee on Payment and Settlement Systems (CPSS) (now the Committee on Payments and Market Infrastructures, CPMI)[7] and the International Organization of Securities Commissions (IOSCO)[8] have worked on promoting and adopting recommendations, common principles, and standards to support cross-border coordination and harmonization in clearing and settlement arrangements that enhance safety and efficiency in the markets.[9]

---

1 Thanks to the participants at the 2023 ACLE-EY Workshop on Comparative Financial Regulation for their feedback. In addition, I would like to thank Andrea Gentilini, Alessio Pacces, Hossein Nabilou, Pietro Stecconi, and an anonymous reviewer for their useful comments. Sam Katulich provided excellent research assistance.

2 CPSS-IOSCO, 'Principles for Financial Market Infrastructures' (2012) <https://www.bis.org/press/p120416.htm> accessed 16 January 2023 (hereinafter PFMI). FMIs are defined as 'multilateral system[s] among participating institutions, including the operator of the system, used for the purposes of clearing, settling, or recording payments, securities, derivatives, or other financial transactions'.

3 Tina P Hasenpusch, *Clearing Services for Global Markets* (1st edn, CUP 2009) 17–49.

4 PFMI (n 2) 9.

5 PFMI (n 2) 8.

6 Demort Turing, *Clearing and Settlement* (3rd edn, Bloomsbury Professional 2021).

7 CPMI, 'About the CPMI' <https://www.bis.org/cpmi/about.htm?m=2029> accessed 16 January 2023.

8 IOSCO <https://www.iosco.org/> accessed 16 January 2023.

9 Bank for International Settlements, 'Principles for Financial Market Infrastructures (PFMI)' <https://www.bis.org/cpmi/info_pfmi.htm?m=118> accessed 3 November 2023 (listing all the standard-setting initiatives of CPMI and IOSCO for FMIs).

After the 2008 financial crisis, policymakers embarked on structural reforms of the financial markets and special attention was given to the role of post-trading FMIs. In the aftermath of the collapse of Lehman Brothers and AIG,[10] the Group of Twenty (G20), an international forum for finance ministers and central bank governors representing the largest twenty global economies, recommended that all its member states adopt central clearing for standardized OTC derivatives through the use of a CCP and reporting of all OTC derivatives transactions to trade repositories. This policy decision reignited an interest in the resilience and effectiveness of these critical FMIs.[11] More recently, events in the derivatives markets – like Brexit[12] and the London Metal Exchange's nickel crisis[13] – and in the securities markets – like the meme stock frenzy and the Robinhood events in the US[14] – have been keeping the debate around clearing and settlement active and central in the policy discourse.[15] Policymakers now face the issue of assessing the impact of innovation on current post-trading services market structure and the impact of cross-border markets on regulatory dynamics.[16] Two recent examples illustrate how derivatives and securities C&S have become prominent issues for the policy and regulatory agenda in the EU and in the US.

The EU derivatives markets faced – and continue to face – interesting challenges following the formal withdrawal of the UK from the EU on 31 January 2020. The most recent data show that around 80% of the total notional outstanding on euro-denominated interest rate swaps is cleared outside the EU, and more precisely by UK-based CCP, LCH Ltd (LCH),[17] and around 50% of EU clients active in euro-denominated interest swaps do not clear these trades in

---

10 *The Financial Crisis Inquiry Report* (Official Government Edition 2011) 324, 344.

11 G20, 'Leaders' Statement: The Pittsburgh Summit' <https://2009-2017.state.gov/e/eb/ecosum/pittsburgh2009/resources/165081.htm> accessed 3 November 2023; 'Improving over-the-counter derivatives markets: All standardized OTC derivative contracts should be traded on exchanges or electronic trading platforms, where appropriate, and cleared through central counterparties by end-2012 at the latest. OTC derivative contracts should be reported to trade repositories. Non-centrally cleared contracts should be subject to higher capital requirements. We ask the FSB and its relevant members to assess regularly implementation and whether it is sufficient to improve transparency in the derivatives markets, mitigate systemic risk, and protect against market abuse'.

12 Dermot Turing, 'Clearing Away After Brexit' (2021) 9(3) Journal of Financial Market Infrastructures 1; Paolo Saguato, Guido Ferrarini and Eric Pan, 'Financial Market Infrastructures', in Jens-Hinrich Binder and Paolo Saguato (eds), *Financial Market Infrastructures – Law and Regulation* 55 (OUP 2021).

13 Philipp Stafford, 'Traders in Uproar over the LME', *Financial Times* (19 March 2022); LME, 'Independent Nickel Marker Review' <https://www.lme.com/en/Trading/Initiatives/Nickel-market-independent-review> accessed 16 June 2023.

14 Paolo Saguato, 'Behind the Stock Market' (2023) (working paper on file with the author); Alexander Osipovich, 'Robinhood's GameStop Debacle Spurs Calls to Modernize Stock Clearing' *Wall Street Journal* (8 February 2021) accessed 16 June 2023.

15 E.g. Securities and Exchange Commission, Shortening the Securities Transaction Settlement Cycle, 88 F.R. 13872, 13873 (6 March 2023).

16 E.g. European Securities and Markets Authority, 'Call for Evidence on Shortening the Settlement Cycle' <https://www.esma.europa.eu/press-news/esma-news/esma-consults-potential-impact-shortening-standard-settlement-cycle> accessed 3 November 2023.

17 LCH Ltd <https://www.lch.com/services/swapclear/what-we-clear> accessed 3 November 2023.

the EU.[18] In the immediate aftermath of the 2008 financial crisis, in fact, the London Stock Exchange Group and its clearing subsidiary LCH have grown to become the primary clearinghouse for derivatives in Europe, processing transactions denominated in multiple currencies, including the euro and dollar. Brexit, and the loss of direct access to the EU internal market for UK financial services firms, set the future of euro-denominated derivatives markets in London on a bumpy road.[19] Until 30 June 2025, LCH will be permitted to offer its services to European counterparties as a result of (i) the EU Commission's decision to deem the post-Brexit UK regulatory and supervisory framework for clearinghouses as 'equivalent' to the EU one and (ii) the decision of the European Securities and Markets Authority (ESMA) to recognize UK clearinghouses, thus granting them access to the EU internal market and EU clients. However, past that date, post-trading markets will look different. On 24 April 2024, in fact, the EU Parliament adopted in its plenary session the final text of a new set of amendments to the European Financial Market Infrastructure Regulation (EMIR),[20] the legislative framework for mandatory central clearing of derivatives and CCPs regulation in the EU. These changes, which are known as 'EMIR 3.0', are meant to reduce the reliance on systemically important third country CCP (currently LCH and ICE Clear Europe Ltd). They require EU clearing members and clients subject to the clearing mandate to hold an active account with EU CCPs.[21] This yet not fully solved and critical issue about the future of cross-border clearing is going to have interesting effects on the EU derivatives market structures and ultimately EU FMIs.

In the US, on 15 February 2023, the Securities and Exchange Commission (SEC) adopted a structural reform for the securities post-trading markets and the way certain securities are cleared and settled.[22] Following the events of the meme stock frenzy in January 2021, when Robinhood, a retail-oriented broker-dealer, was caught unprepared in meeting its contractual obligations with the National Securities Clearing Corporation (NSCC) – the US securities CCP – the SEC decided to shorten the settlement cycle for most routine securities trades from two business days after the trade date to one day after the trade date, or using the finance jargon, moving from 'T+2' to 'T+1'.[23] The decision to shorten the securities settlement cycle, while it applies only to US securities market, has already influenced the EU financial policy

---

[18] Fabio Panetta, 'Central Clearing in Turbulent Times: Frontiers in Regulation and Oversight', Keynote speech at the Fifth Joint Deutsche Bundesbank, European Central Bank and Federal Reserve Bank of Chicago Conference on CCP Risk Management (22 June 2023) <https://www.ecb.europa.eu/press/key/date/2023/html/ecb.sp230622~e1a8c64758.en.html> accessed 3 November 2023.

[19] Niamh Moloney, 'Brexit and Financial Services: (Yet) Another Re-ordering of Institutional Governance for the EU Financial System' (2018) 55 Common Market Law Review 175.

[20] See European Market Infrastructure Regulation (EMIR), Regulation (EU) No 648/2012 [2012] OJ L201/1.

[21] Proposal for a Regulation of the European Parliament and of the Council amending Regulations (EU) No 648/2012, (EU) No 575/2013 and (EU) 2017/1131 as regards measures to mitigate excessive exposures to third-country central counterparties and improve the efficiency of Union clearing markets <https://eur-lex.europa.eu/legal-content/EN/TXT/?uri=celex%3A52022PC0697>.

[22] SEC (n 15).

[23] See Paolo Saguato, 'Behind the Stock Market', on file with the author.

discourse,[24] with industry participants and policymakers starting to discuss the move to single-day settlement in the EU as well.[25] The transition to T+1 in the EU might be a necessary step for EU markets and regulators to keep EU markets competitive, but at the same time, it poses interesting challenges to EU policymakers given the different (and more complex) market structure of securities clearing and settlement in the EU. In the US, in fact, there is currently one securities CCP, NSCC,[26] and one CSD, the Depository Trust Corporation (DTC).[27] And both are wholly owned subsidiaries of the Depository Trust & Clearing Corporation (DTCC), a holding company that provides the whole securities post-trading market plumbing services. The EU post-trading market landscape, on the other hand, is very fragmented with 14 authorized CCPs[28] and 29 authorized CSDs.[29]

These two developments in the clearing and settlement environment offer insights into the effects of different market structures on regulatory dynamics and set challenging foundations for a functional comparative analysis of these markets.[30] After a brief description of the structure and economic functions of clearing and settlement, this chapter provides a three-level discussion of post-trading infrastructures. First, it examines the role of the Principles for Financial Market Infrastructures (PFMI) adopted by CPMI-IOSCO in 2012 in guiding policy initiatives and reform in the C&S space.[31] Second, it offers two examples on how the PFMIs are applied in the US and the EU. A comparison of the market structure of securities and derivatives clearing (and settlement) shows how the EU and the US markets have evolved onto distinct paths in the securities markets, yet similar approaches have developed in the derivatives markets. Finally, the chapter concludes with a brief discussion on a few future challenges for cross-border C&S and the impact and role that technology might play in (re-)shaping clearing and settlement markets and infrastructures.[32]

---

24 ESMA (n 16); Christine Lagarde, 'A Kantian Shift for the Capital Markets Union', Speech by Christine Lagarde, President of the ECB, at the European Banking Congress (4 November 2023) <https://www.ecb.europa.eu/press/key/date/2023/html/ecb.sp231117~88389f194b.en.html> accessed 1 December 2023 'a truly European capital market needs consolidated market infrastructures – and this is where the private sector can show its determination, too'.

25 Nikou Asgari, 'European Banks Explore Shift to Single-day Trade Settlement' *Financial Times* (2 March 2023) <https://www.ft.com/content/7e236ad9-1ef0-48ff-906a-c4d831347bf0> accessed 26 March 2023.

26 NSCC <https://www.dtcc.com/about/businesses-and-subsidiaries/nscc>.

27 DTC, <https://www.dtcc.com/about/businesses-and-subsidiaries/dtc>.

28 ESMA, List of Central Counterparties Authorised to Offer Services and Activities in the Union (last updated 10 November 2022) <https://www.esma.europa.eu/sites/default/files/library/ccps_authorised_under_emir.pdf> accessed 26 March 2023.

29 ESMA, CSD Register <https://www.esma.europa.eu/sites/default/files/library/esma70-155-11635_csds_register_-_art_21.pdf> accessed 26 March 2023.

30 Edoardo D Martino, Hossein Nabilou and Alessio M Pacces, 'Comparative Financial Regulation: The Analytical Framework' in Edoardo D Martino, Hossein Nabilou and Alessio M Pacces (eds), *Research Handbook of Comparative Financial Regulation* (Edward Elgar Publishing forthcoming 2024).

31 PFMI (n 2).

32 CPMI, 'Distributed Ledger Technology in Payment, Clearing and Settlement – An Analytical Framework' (2017) <https://www.bis.org/cpmi/publ/d157.pdf> accessed 23 March 2023.

2. A BRIEF LOOK AT CLEARING AND SETTLEMENT

The lifecycle of a financial transaction is made up of a trading and a post-trading phase. During trading, a buyer and seller agree on the quantity and price of a security or on the characteristic of a derivative contract. The trade then is executed, and the parties agree to make mutual transfers. In the case of a security trade, the buyer agrees to transfer money to the seller in exchange for securities. In the case of a derivative contract, for instance a swap, the parties agree to exchange payments linked to the fluctuation in the value of an underlying reference for a set period of time.

After this first trading phase, which can occur on a trading platform or bilaterally OTC,[33] the post-trading phase begins. The executed trade is first cleared and then settled.[34] Once a trade is executed, it is then transferred to a clearinghouse that acts as CCP for its clearing members.[35] During the process of clearing, the CCP reconciles and confirms the terms of the trade, and records and novates the transaction – becoming the buyer to the original seller and the seller to the original buyer.[36] By acting as a central counterparty, the clearinghouse commits to support and guarantee the settlement of the cleared trade. The clearinghouse is a special type of financial intermediary that acts as a risk manager.[37] By acting as CCP, the clearinghouse centralizes and bears certain risks of the processed transactions, the biggest being counterparty or credit risk,[38] and contributes to the mitigation of systemic risk.[39] A CCP manages counterparty risk

---

[33] Guido Ferrarini and Paolo Saguato, 'Governance and Organization of Trading Venues: The Role of Financial Market Infrastructures Groups' in Danny Busch and Guido Ferrarini (eds), *Regulation of the EU Financial Markets: MiFID II and MiFIR* (OUP 2015) 285.

[34] Securities transactions settle in no more than two business days, while the maturity of a derivative contract can vary, which means the final settlements of the contractual obligations resulting from a derivative can occur days, weeks or months after the trade is executed.

[35] When referring to clearinghouses, this chapter refers to clearinghouses that act as central counterparties; see Paolo Saguato, 'Financial Regulation, Corporate Governance, and the Hidden Costs of Clearinghouses' (2021) 72 Ohio St. L. Rev. 1071 (hereinafter 'Hidden Costs of Clearinghouses'); Paolo Saguato, 'The Unfinished Business of Regulating Clearinghouses' (2020) 2 Columb. Bus. L. Rev. 450; Paolo Saguato, 'The Ownership of Clearinghouses: When "Skin in the Game" is Not Enough, the Remutualization of Clearinghouses' (2017) 34 Yale J. on Regulation 601.

[36] Novation is a contractual agreement between two contracting parties to allow for the substitution of a new party for an existing one. By novation, for instance, A and B agree to substitute each other as contractual parties with a single counterparty, the clearinghouse. By force of novation, the clearinghouse becomes the central counterparty, and the original contract between A and B is substituted by a new contract between A and the CCP, and between B and the CCP. Turing (n 6) 27.

[37] CPSS, 'Recommendations for Central Clearing' (November 2004) at 1 available at <https://www.bis.org/cpmi/publ/d64.pdf>.

[38] Counterparty or credit risk is 'the risk that a counterparty, whether a participant or other entity, will be unable to meet fully its financial obligations when due, or at any time in the future', PFMI (n 2) 19.

[39] Systemic risk defines the contagion and cascade effects that 'the inability of one or more participants to perform as expected could cause other participants to be unable to meet their obligations when due', PFMI (n 2) 19.

by virtue of netting arrangements,[40] and by adopting different layers of financial resources to guarantee the performance of each cleared trade.[41] The CCP commits to guarantee the obligations under the terms of the cleared contract if one counterparty defaults and to internalize – and ultimately mutualize – the residual losses of the defaulted contractual party among all other clearing members, thus preventing the fallout from spilling over into the markets.[42]

After clearing follows the settlement of the trade. CSDs are the FMIs that support the functioning of settlement services. Settlement occurs when the contractual obligations under the contract are performed and cash and/or securities are exchanged, and in the specific case of a securities trade, delivery of the securities occurs versus payment, and the transfer of securities is ultimately recorded by a CSD.

A CSD operates in the settlement phase of cash/securities transactions by holding the securities of listed entities either in certificate form or dematerialized, managing the legal transfer of securities from the seller to the buyer against the payment from the buyer to the seller (generally referred to as a DvP – delivery versus payment), and ultimately recording the final transaction in formal ledgers.

Both CCPs and CSDs are market responses to mitigate transaction costs and risk in securities and derivatives markets.[43] Through different practices and mechanisms, each of these intermediaries allows transactions to be fully finalized, provides market participants with

---

40 Netting is the process of offsetting multiple financial obligations into a single net obligation amount; Hasenpusch (n 3) 24–27.

41 Id. CCPs have in place multiple layers of financial resources. First, CCPs set membership requirements for financial institutions that intend to access their services. These requirements encompass prudential and conduct standards, obligation to regular monitoring and disclosure obligations, etc. A clearing member, once admitted to a CCP is not just subject to the self-regulatory and supervisory authority of the CCP, but it is also bound by risk management obligations contained in each CCP's rulebook. Each clearing member needs to post margin for all transactions submitted to the CCP. Margin can be distinguished between initial margin, collateral collected by the CCP at the time the member enters into a trade, and variation margin, collected by the CCP throughout the lifespan of a cleared trade. In addition to margin, clearing members agree to contribute to what is generally referred to as a guaranty fund. A guaranty fund is a cushion of prefunded resources each member contributes to in proportion to the risk exposure that its cleared portfolio presents to the CCP. The function of the guaranty fund is to mutualize the remaining losses triggered by the default of one of the members in case the posted collateral of the defaulted member has been ineffective to contain the cost of the default. Clearing members are contractually required to replenish the guaranty fund through assessment rights if more resources are needed to cover the costs associated to manage the default of one or more clearing member. In addition to members contributions, the CCP itself contribute to its 'default waterfall' – the industry and policy jargon for the ensemble of financial resources a CCP can deploy to contain default losses – with a set amount of capital contribution called 'skin in the game'.

42 Saguato, 'Hidden Costs of Clearinghouses' (n 35) 1087–1098.

43 In addition to mitigate counterparty risk, CCPs and, in particular, CSDs, also contribute to the mitigation of operational risk. Operational risk is 'is the risk that deficiencies in information systems or internal processes, human errors, management failures, or disruptions from external events will result in the reduction, deterioration, or breakdown of services provided by an FMI', PFMI (n 2) 20.

arrangements to reduce the risk of failed trades and ultimately supports liquidity and market stability.

3. THE PFMI AND CROSS-BORDER COORDINATION

Since the 1990s, international coordination efforts and work-streams in standard-setting bodies have come to focus on the clearing and settlement space.[44] The growth of cross-border capital flows and investments, the increase in volume of cross-border financial transactions and the expansion of cross-border operations of financial institutions resulted in a steady industry demand for policymakers to coordinate the regulatory approach to clearing and settlement (and also payment system), reduce cross-border friction and facilitate capital flows.

The major international public initiatives driven by the IOSCO, BIS and CPSS (now CPMI) were preceded by two reports published by the Group of Thirty (G-30), a financial industry policy forum. In a 1988 report and, more recently, in a 2003 report on global clearing and settlement, the financial industry acknowledged the expansion of global financial markets and recommended policymakers to adopt and implement global standards and to harmonize the legal and regulatory environment for clearing and settlement.[45] The three pillars of the reports were: (i) creating a strengthened, more effective, and interoperable global network of clearing and settlement services providers;[46] (ii) ensuring clearing and settlement system resilience and supporting effective risk management practices; and (iii) improving the governance of clearing and settlement firms, taking into account the interests of the firms' stakeholders.[47]

The G-30 Global Clearing and Settlement Plan of Action came out around the same time the Giovannini Reports were published by the European Commission (EC) in the early 2000s. In the late 1990s, the EC established a group of financial market experts to advise on issues relating to EU financial integration and the efficiency of EU financial markets. The Group, named the 'Giovannini Group' after its chairman Alberto Giovannini, published in total five reports. The last two focus on cross-border clearing and settlement arrangements in the EU securities markets in the context of completing the internal market for financial services in the EU. The first Giovannini Report, published in 2001, diagnosed the problems of cross-border clearing and settlement in the EU. It built on responses to a questionnaire shared with financial institutions, offered a taxonomy of clearing and settlement arrangements in the EU members states at that time and identified a total of fifteen barriers to efficient of cross-border clearing and settlement. The barriers were grouped into (i) barriers relating to national differences in technical requirements and market practice; (ii) barriers related to taxation of securities; and (iii) barriers related to legal certainty, i.e. legal barriers that relate to the presence of different

---

[44] Hal S Scott and Anna Gelpern, *International Finance – Transactions, Policy, and Regulation* (24th ed. Foundation Press 2022) 814.

[45] Group of Thirty, 'Global Clearing and Settlement – A Plan for Action' <https://group30.org/images/uploads/publications/G30_GlobalClearingSettlement.pdf>.

[46] Among the twenty recommendations, recommendation 6 encourages the use of central counterparties in unserved markets as risk mitigation mechanism. Id at 32.

[47] Recommendation 19 emphasizes the importance for clearing and settlement firms to ensure equitable and effective attention to stakeholders interests. Id at 54.

private law regimes for intermediated securities.[48] The second Giovannini Report, published in 2003, attempted to provide a strategy to remove the barriers to efficient clearing and settlement arrangements and addressed the costs connected to the fragmentation of post-trading markets.[49] The Report acknowledged that some form of consolidation among EU clearing and settlement providers is necessary to achieve more efficient markets.[50]

More recently, a major international initiative in the clearing and settlement space was the publication of the PFMI in 2012. The twenty-four principles constitute the 'commandments' given by the international financial standard-setters to the financial community to strengthen and enhance financial stability in the post-trading FMI landscape. The PFMI set the foundations of the risk-management regulation of CCPs, CSDs and FMIs in general. The PFMI acknowledge the systemic and critical role of FMIs in fostering financial stability and efficiency in financial markets. In building this new architecture and by concentrating risk in FMIs, the drafters were aware that if FMIs were not properly managed, they could become a source of financial shock and a major vector for financial contagion across domestic and international markets. To address these issues, CPMI-IOSCO advised domestic regulators in implementing the PFMI in their legal systems to consider two sets of principles to enhance the safety, soundness and robustness of FMIs.

The first set of principles targets organizational risk management and stresses the importance of setting well-founded, clear, transparent and enforceable legal bases for FMIs' activities. This translates into clear governance arrangements that should include the ownership structure of FMIs, their internal governance policies (i.e. composition and responsibilities of the board of directors), the design of robust risk management and internal controls (i.e. audit, risk-management policies, procedures and systems). The second set of principles addresses the business of managing risk and focuses on transaction and hybrid risk management. It called on regulators to: (i) ensure that FMIs have in place effective risk-management mechanisms aimed at measuring, monitoring, and managing credit and liquidity,[51] operational and business risk;[52] and (ii) require FMIs to maintain sufficient financial resources to cover their credit exposure to their member-counterparties (i.e. collateral, margin, default management strategies), limit the procyclicality of their risk-management practices and maintain the liquidity of their risk-mitigation financial resources.

The relevance of the PFMI is at least three-fold. First, the document has its roots in the systemic importance that post-trading FMIs play in the financial markets in the post 2008

48 European Commission Giovannini Group (2001) <https://ec.europa.eu/info/publications/giovannini-reports_en>.

49 European Commission Giovannini Group (2003) <https://ec.europa.eu/info/publications/giovannini-reports_en>.

50 In a recent speech, ECB President Christine Lagarde noted that 'a truly European capital market needs consolidated market infrastructures', reiterating what the Giovannini Reports had already concluded; see Lagarde (n 24).

51 Liquidity risk is 'the risk that a counterparty, whether a participant or other entity, will have insufficient funds to meet its financial obligations as and when expected, although it may be able to do so in the future', PFMI (n 2) 19.

52 Business risk is 'the risks related to the administration and operation of an FMI as a business enterprise, excluding those related to the default of a participant or another entity, such as a settlement bank, global custodian, or another FMI', PFMI (n 2) 19.

financial crisis world. The PFMI identify the critical role that FMIs play as a source of strength and as an element of trust and confidence in the modern markets, acknowledge the necessity of having shared standards and put in place clear principles for the regulation of FMIs. The PFMI framework also aims at supporting and achieving two main public policy objectives: promoting financial stability in the markets and enhancing the efficiency and resilience of FMIs and their operations.[53]

Second, the PFMI have proved to be one of the most successful sets of international principles to coordinate regulatory actions across multiple jurisdictions over different critical aspects of the business and organization of FMIs. The principles-based approach adopted by CPMI-IOSCO has facilitated the domestic implementation of the PFMI by jurisdictions around the world. The PFMI accommodate jurisdictional differences in regulatory approaches to markets by setting clear goals and principles and leaving national regulators the ultimate authority to choose the most appropriate regulatory tool to implement the principles into local laws. Furthermore, they are drafted in such a way that they are adaptable to the challenges posed by financial innovation and technological advancement. In drafting the principles, the standard setters crafted a general and adaptable framework capable of supporting and fostering efficient and stable FMIs, while preserving the jurisdictional autonomy of member states. While CPMI and IOSCO do not have a formal authority to impose or force compliance with the PFMI nor the authority to sanction noncompliance, they nevertheless do run monitoring rounds to assess the implementation of the principles in each member state, and the publicity of the self-assessments and the disclosure of the peer review evaluation intend to create compliance incentives in member states.[54]

Finally, the PFMI have expanded their application and relevance beyond what the drafters envisioned. The PFMI have in fact grown to become a critical document in building cross-border bridges and facilitating and guiding equivalence and comparability determinations and negotiations. PFMI are used by EU regulators to assess and eventually grant equivalence and mutual recognition of foreign regulation to EU law and, in the US context, financial regulators have been looking at PFMI compliance as basis to make comparability and substituted compliance determination.[55] More broadly, the PFMI can be seen as a benchmark to

---

[53] CPMI-IOSCO also published a series of ancillary documents that are meant to offer guidance on how to implement the PFMI and that, in particular, have supported and informed domestic regulation in the implementation of rules on the resilience and resolution of FMIs and other critical risk clearing and settlement infrastructure plays; see e.g. CPMI-IOSCO, 'Recovery of Financial Market Infrastructures – Revised Report' (2017) accessed 10 March 2023; CPMI-IOSCO, 'Resilience of Central Counterparties (CCPs): Further Guidance on the PFMI – Final Report' (2017) accessed 10 March 2023; CPMI-IOSCO, 'Guidance on Cyber Resilience for Financial Market Infrastructures' (2016) <https://www.bis.org/cpmi/publ/d146.pdf> accessed 10 March 2023.

[54] CPMI published all reports of the monitoring mechanisms established to ensure the implementation of PFMI in all jurisdictions with systemically important FMIs. CPMI and IOSCO member states committed to adopt the principles and responsibilities and agreed to self-assess the status of the adoption of the PFMI domestically and to be subject to a peer review by other member states to assess the consistency and completeness of the adoption of the PFMI. See CPMI-IOSCO, 'Principles for Financial Market Infrastructures: Disclosure Framework and Assessment Methodology' (2012); CPMI, 'Monitoring Implementation of the PFMI' <https://www.bis.org/cpmi/info_mios.htm> accessed 10 March 2023.

[55] Saguato, Ferrarini and Pan (n 12) 58–72.

then comparatively evaluate how jurisdictions domestically approach the regulation of FMIs, and accordingly, the International Monetary Fund (IMF) has used the PFMI in conducting its assessment of its members' financial sectors.[56]

The PFMI represent a particularly successful story of cross-border cooperation in financial regulation because they acknowledge different market structures and legal regimes for clearing and settlement (and payments systems) in different jurisdictions and create flexible and malleable principles that can result in coordination of different national regimes built on an outcome-based assessment of the regulatory frameworks.

4. CLEARING AND SETTLEMENT IN THE EU AND IN THE US: TWO CASE STUDIES

The EU and US financial markets are strongly connected with policymakers and market forces playing a strong role in modernizing the infrastructures of their markets. This section analyzes two case studies on how the US and EU markets and regulation have diverged in some parts and converged in others in their construction of post-trading ecosystems. The development of post-trading markets in the EU and in the US is quite unique – with securities markets organized in structurally different ways on each side of the Atlantic and derivatives markets more recently developed embracing similar structures. Structural regulatory frameworks in the US and in the EU have also conditioned this parallel development. In the US, financial markets' regulatory and supervisory jurisdiction has historically been allocated to two distinct market regulators: the SEC, which has jurisdiction over the securities markets,[57] and the Commodity Futures Trading Commission (CFTC), whose jurisdiction covers the derivatives markets.[58] This jurisdictional split between the CFTC and the SEC reflects also the two different market structures for securities and derivatives markets. Today, the derivatives markets, under the CFTC jurisdiction, are generally characterized by vertically integrated FMIs, with trading and post-trading services offered by firms that belong to the same corporate group. Meanwhile securities markets, under the SEC jurisdiction, operate with a horizontal market structure with

---

56 See *e.g.* IMF, 'United States: Financial Sector Assessment Program – Technical Note – Supervision of Financial Market Infrastructures, Resilience of Central Counterparties and Innovative Technologies', 10 August 2020, <https://www.imf.org/en/Publications/CR/Issues/2020/08/07/United-States-Financial-Sector-Assessment-Program-Technical-Note-Supervision-of-Financial-49658>.

57 See 15 U.S.C. § 77b, defining 'securities' as 'note, stock, treasury stock, security future, security-based swap, bond, debenture, … any put, call, straddle, option, or privilege on any security, certificate of deposit, or group or index of securities (including any interest therein or based on the value thereof), or any put, call, straddle, option, or privilege entered into on a national securities exchange relating to foreign currency'.

58 See 7 U.S.C. § 2, setting the 'exclusive jurisdiction … with respect to accounts, agreements (including any transaction which is of the character of, or is commonly known to the trade as, an "option," "privilege," "indemnity," "bid," "offer," "put," "call," "advance guaranty," or "decline guaranty") and transactions involving swaps or contracts of sale of a commodity for future delivery …, traded or executed on a contract market … or a swap execution facility … or any other board of trade, exchange, or market'.

a stand-alone member-owned clearinghouse and CSD that offer their post-trading services to multiple trading venues.[59]

In the EU and in the vast majority of EU member states, jurisdiction over financial markets has been traditionally allocated to a single market regulator and supervisor.[60] This common feature reflects a similar development in market structure for both derivatives and securities markets, which have historically developed as vertically integrated FMI groups.[61]

4.1 The Diverged Paths in Clearing and Settlement Market Structures in Securities Markets

The US securities markets adopted a unique market structure following the market distress caused by the paperwork crisis in the late 1960s. That crisis revealed structural fragilities of the fragmented post-trading securities markets environment – where each stock exchange had its own clearinghouse, and where trades executed on different exchanges needed to be reconciled across multiple FMIs at the end of the trading day.[62] The response of the industry and the regulator was to encourage competition at the trading level and support stability and resilience in the post-trading infrastructures. This resulted in the adoption of the Securities Act Amendments of 1975, which required post-trading FMIs to register as clearing agencies and adopt interoperability arrangements to support the smooth reconciliation of executed trades.[63] While keeping the door open to vertically integrated securities exchanges with their own clearing and settlement firms, the SEC, in practice, encouraged consolidation of clearinghouses and securities depositories focusing on the cost saving connected to the network nature and scale economies of the clearing business.[64]

The market structure that resulted from the post-paperwork crisis reform was one built around a consolidated securities clearinghouse and one securities depository. The NSCC was created in 1976 with the merger of the clearing subsidiaries of the New York Stock Exchange, the American Stock Exchange and the National Association of Securities Dealers.[65] Since 1976, the NSCC, by virtue of market and ownership structure synergies and benefit of scale

---

[59] The Federal Reserve Board maintains some residual regulatory and supervisory authority over systemically important financial market utilities – i.e. derivatives CCPs, and securities CCPs and CSD – under Title VIII of the Dodd–Frank Act.

[60] Some jurisdictions like France, the Netherlands and Italy allocate to the central banks some regulatory and supervisory authority of FMIs.

[61] Ferrarini and Saguato (n 33).

[62] Peter Norman, The Risk Controllers, Central Counterparty Clearing in Globalized Financial Markets (Wiley, 2011).

[63] See Dan Awrey and Joshua Macey, 'Open Access, Interoperability, and the DTCC's Unexpected Path to Monopoly' (2022) 132 Yale. L. J. 96.

[64] Study of Unsafe and Unsound Practices of Broker-Dealers, H.R. Doc No 231, 92nd Cong., 1st Sess. 13 (1971); Ruben Lee, *Running The World's Markets – The Governance of Financial Infrastructure* (Princeton University Press 2011).

[65] See DTCC History, <https://www.dtcc.com/annuals/museum/index.html>; see also DTCC's Businesses, Subsidiaries and Joint Ventures, Depository Trust & Clearing Corporation, <https://www.dtcc.com/about/businesses-and-subsidiaries> (describing the DTCC group's structure).

economies and network effects, has consolidated its role as market-wide clearing agency for the equity securities markets.[66]

The NSCC is virtually the only equity securities markets clearinghouse serving the US markets and operates as a stand-alone specialized infrastructure in a horizontal market structure. The NSCC provides clearing services in a non-discriminatory way to multiple trading venues and supports the post-trading of virtually all broker-to-broker transactions involving equities.[67] Over the years, the regulatory approach adopted by the US legislature and implemented by the SEC has embraced a vision of post-trading service providers as 'utility-like' firms and entrusted them with self-regulatory authority.

Today, the NSCC is one of three wholly owned FMI subsidiaries of the DTCC, a holding company that resulted from the affiliation of different post-trading infrastructure firms: the NSCC, a CCP, DTC, a CSD and the Fixed Income Clearing Corporation (a clearing and settlement provider operating in the fixed income markets – US treasuries and mortgage backs securities). The DTCC is a unique post-trading FMI holding company because of its peculiar ownership structure. It is not affiliated or directly controlled by any trading venues nor is it a subsidiary of any exchange group. The DTCC is a private corporation and is directly owned by its members. Its common shareholders are the users of one or more of the DTCC's clearing agencies.[68]

Both the unique market structure and the singular ownership model adopted by the DTCC have influenced the recent market and regulatory dynamics in the US securities post-trading markets.[69] The 2021 events of high volatility in meme stocks resulted in market turmoil and catalyzed a structural reform of the US securities markets. The SEC adopted new rules that shorten the securities settlement cycle to T + 1.[70] This structural change in market structures, which has required substantial operational changes in the industry, was supported by the DTCC and its members. The central role of the DTCC and its subsidiaries in providing post-trading services for US securities market has facilitated and smoothed the implementation of the reform.

In the EU, in the early 2000s, the Giovannini Reports identified the highly fragmented securities clearing and settlement as one of the major barriers to a full market integration and argued for a consolidation of post-trading services. Almost twenty years after the publi-

---

66 In the 1980s, the Boston Stock Exchange, the Pacific Stock Exchange, the Midwest Clearing Corporation and the Chicago Stock Exchange closed their clearing subsidiaries, with their transactions migrating to NSCC, and in 1997, the Philadelphia Stock Exchange transferred its securities clearing businesses to DTCC.

67 Paolo Saguato, 'Securities and Derivatives Central Counterparties in the United States', in Jens-Hinrich Binder and Paolo Saguato (eds) *Financial Market Infrastructures: Law and Regulation* (Oxford University Press, 2021).

68 See Depository Trust & Clearing Corporation, CCP Resiliency and Resources 2 (2015), <http://www.dtcc.com/news/2015/june/01/ccp-resiliency-and-resources>.

69 See Paolo Saguato, 'Behind the Stock Market' (on file with the author) (discussing the political economy of the reform, and noting that the reform was not driven by a failure of NSCC in the operation of the clearing process – NSCC actually applied its own Rulebook, specifically Rule 15, to its member Robinhood – but rather by a market-wide decision of reduce credit risk in securities C&S).

70 SEC (n 15).

cation of the reports, the European securities clearing and settlement market structure is still very fragmented, with 14 authorized EU-based CCPs and 29 authorized EU-based CSDs.[71] While US lawmakers and regulators decided to simplify and consolidate the landscape of post-trading infrastructure to reduce transaction costs in securities markets, the EU is still facing the challenges of a market environment with at least one CSD per member state and 14 CCPs serving multiple trading venues. LCH S.A.,[72] Cboe Clear Europe,[73] Eurex Clearing[74] and Euronext Clearing (previously Cassa di Compensazione and Garanzia)[75] have emerged as the largest EU CCPs. In recent months, the Euronext Group has moved to consolidate the clearing services for six Euronext cash markets in its CCP, Euronext Clearing, in an effort to support a more unified European financial market and ecosystem, necessary backbone of the Capital Market Union. At the same time, Eurex Clear continues to be the CCP for the vertically integrated Deutsche Börse Group. Yet complexity and fragmentation re-emerge in the settlement environment, where national CSDs dominate the markets, particularly in smaller EU member states. Three CSDs, Euroclear, Euronext Securities and Clearstream, are becoming the major international CSDs.[76]

The issue of the high fragmentation of clearing and settlement infrastructures in the EU was also addressed in a recent Report published by former ECB President, Mario Draghi. The Report, commissioned by the EC, elaborates a policy agenda to unlock competition in the EU and to complete the EU's Capital Market Union project. Interestingly, the Report calls for fostering the centralization of clearing and settlement firms as an important step towards the integration of securities markets in the EU. As a possible practical pathway towards consolidation, the Report imagines the largest CCPs and CDSs starting the process, and then, the smaller ones following.[77]

To reduce complexity in cross-border settlement procedure the European Central Bank (ECB) introduced the pan-European real-time gross settlement system T2S settlement platform that supports CSD settlement in central bank money. At the time of writing, 24 of the 29 authorized CSDs are connected to the T2S settlement platform.[78]

---

71 Regulation (EU) No 909/2014 of the European Parliament and of the Council of 23 July 2014 on improving securities settlement in the European Union and on central securities depositories and amending Directives 98/26/EC and 2014/65/EU and Regulation (EU) No 236/2012, [2014] OJ L257/1 (CSDR).

72 LCH S.A. <https://www.lch.com/about-us/our-clearing-houses>.

73 Cboe Clear <https://clear.cboe.com>.

74 Eurex Clear <https://www.eurex.com/ec-en/>.

75 Euronext Clearing <https://www.euronext.com/it/post-trade>.

76 Eilis Ferran and Eleanore Hickman, 'Central Securities Depositories in the EU', in Jens-Hinrich Binder and Paolo Saguato (eds) *Financial Market Infrastructures: Law and Regulation* (Oxford University Press, 2021).

77 European Commission Draghi Report (2024) <https:// commission .europa .eu/ topics/ strengthening-european-competitiveness/eu-competitiveness-looking-ahead_en>.

78 ECB, What is TARGET2-Securities (T2S)?, <https://www.ecb.europa.eu/paym/target/t2s/html/index.en.html> accessed 3 April 2024.

4.2 Converging Paths in Derivatives Markets: Risk Management Practices and Market Structures

Derivatives post-trading infrastructures have converged towards a more shared path in the aftermath of the 2008 financial crisis. The international responses adopted by the G-20 and FSB have encouraged jurisdictions to implement a clearing mandate for standardized derivatives and create a robust regulatory and supervisory framework to guarantee the safety and soundness of CCPs.

Derivatives clearing markets have developed into vertically integrated silos on both sides of the Atlantic, with clearinghouses being either direct subsidiaries of a listed FMI group holding company or business units of a trading platform which is itself a subsidiary of a listed firm. They operate as open or partially open vertical silos, which means that while a group's clearinghouse clears all transactions executed on the group's venues, it also offers its services and clears trades executed on other venues that have been deemed clearable by the firm itself.[79]

In the USA, two of the major derivatives clearinghouses operate under the CFTC jurisdiction as derivatives clearing organizations, the Chicago Mercantile Exchange (CME Inc.) with its clearing division (CME Clearing), which is a subsidiary of the CME Group, and ICE Clear Credit, a subsidiary of the Intercontinental Exchange Group. Both FMI groups, and indirectly their clearinghouses, transitioned at different points in time in the last twenty years from being owned by their members or by a mutual exchange to being investor-owned (or, more precisely, owned by a demutualized and investor-owned trading platform or holding company).[80]

In a unique position is the Options Clearing Corporation (OCC). The OCC is the only clearinghouse registered as clearing agency with the SEC and as a derivative clearing organization with the CFTC. The OCC is the predominant provider of clearing and settlement services for equity derivatives – options and futures. The OCC has a unique ownership structure, being owned by the five participant exchanges for which it provides clearing services. The OCC, while owned by exchanges, relies on clearing members for contributions and gives them a central role in the governance of the firm.

The European derivatives clearing markets have developed around three major market champions, Eurex Clearing, LCH and Ice Clear Europe – the latter two being systemically important third country CCPs (based in the UK) – and four smaller (yet growing) players, Euronext Derivatives (formally Cassa di Compensazione e Garanzia S.p.A.), CBOE Europe (formally European Central Counterparty N.V.), LCH S.A. and LME.

What is particularly interesting about the structure of derivatives clearing markets is the convergence in market structure and risk management practices that market participants have adopted in the aftermath of the 2008 financial crisis. Derivatives clearinghouses are virtually always part (the exception being the OCC) of a vertically integrated group that offers trading and post-trading services to its members. In addition, they are also part of investor-owned firms, where ownership and control rights are allocated to capital providers – i.e. shareholders – and clearing members, the users of the clearing services are contractually bound to mutualize the losses of default of other cleating members.

---

79 Ferrarini and Saguato (n 33).

80 See Paolo Saguato, 'Securities and Derivatives Central Counterparties in the United States', in Jens-Hinrich Binder and Paolo Saguato (eds) *Financial Market Infrastructures: Law and Regulation* (Oxford University Press, 2021).

Aware of the systemic importance of clearinghouses in the post-crisis landscape, international standard setters, in addition to publishing the PFMI, have published multiple guidelines and principles on the resilience, recovery and resolution of derivatives clearinghouses,[81] and while the enhanced prudential requirements and risk-management standards set by EU and US lawmakers both preceded the adoption of these international principles, regulators on both sides of the Atlantic have worked to create a regulatory framework for clearinghouses that, while incorporating national regulatory preferences, also takes into account the importance of qualifying as potentially equivalent to or comparable with its peer jurisdiction to guarantee access to deeper cross-border markets. Detailed rules cover the operations of the default waterfall and both the transactional and mutualization defenses that a clearinghouse deploys to handle the failure of its members.

5. FUTURE CHALLENGES

The evolution of clearing and settlement infrastructures in the US and the EU over the past thirty years shows how innovation and crises have contributed to the shaping of securities and derivatives markets.

Securities market structures in the US and in the EU have been shaped structurally differently. In the US, policy and market preferences shaped the market with a clear demarcation between trading and post-trading infrastructures. Competition was encouraged at a trading level, but in the post-trading segment, policymakers embraced the outcome of scale and scope economies, supported consolidation and legitimized the creation of a monopolistic player in the securities clearing and settlement markets. An interesting feature of this monopolistic player, DTCC, is its member-owned ownership structure, where market participants in the securities clearing and settlement markets are also shareholders of the infrastructure.

In the EU, the fragmented reality of clearing and settlement infrastructures has been a challenge for policymakers. In the 2000s, the two Giovannini Reports saw in the fracture post-trading ecosystem an obstacle to achieving further integration in the European internal market. In 2023, the ECB President Christine Lagarde observed that 'a truly European capital market needs consolidated market infrastructures'.[82] More recently, in the Fall of 2024, in its Report former ECB President Mario Draghi echoed the importance of the consolidation of post-trading servicing onto few – if not one – market infrastructure service providers for both efficiency and financial stability rationales and identified it as a necessary step to complete the Capital Markert Union Project.

The EU seems to have started to look more closely at the US consolidated post-trading market structure as a successful feature to support efficient capital markets, and EU policymakers have considered the opportunity of bringing the EU market to a more converging path with the US model. Nevertheless, in the 2020s, as in the early 2000s, policymakers still face the same barriers to integration and consolidation in post-trading securities markets, in particular the divergences in private law and national regulatory framework, that call for a deeper functional comparative dialogue among jurisdictions to be overcome.

---

81 See e.g. (n 53).

82 See (n 24).

On the derivatives market front, equivalence and comparative assessments have become of the essence for the very existence of the delicate cross-border architecture deployed to assure market access in 'comparable' jurisdictions. The mechanisms of equivalence and substituted compliance, coupled with the cooperative supervisory framework for cross-border activities sponsored by IOSCO since the early 2000s, have been adopted to create cross-border linkages between derivatives clearinghouses and market participants. And since 2012, after EMIR was adopted, regulators across the globe have entertained deep comparative discussion to assess the equivalence of their respective regulatory framework for derivatives post-trading markets. An outcome-based and functional comparative assessment, even though in some instances deviated by pure political preferences, has been the driver of cross-border dialogue among financial regulators.

16. Regulation of payment services

Phoebus L. Athanassiou[1]

1. INTRODUCTION

The pivotal role of payment services for the operation and stability of modern economies, and the risks accompanying their provision create ample space for regulatory intervention. In essence, the regulation of payment services is a two-pronged public interest-driven exercise, seeking to preserve the socio-economic benefits to be had from the provision of safe, competitive and affordable payment services and to rein in the risks incidental to their provision.

This chapter provides an outline of the law and regulation governing the provision of (non-cash) payment services by payment service providers (PSPs)[2] in select jurisdictions. For the purposes of this chapter, the term 'payment services' denotes the sum total of retail[3] electronic fund transfer activities[4] that PSPs render by way of business to their customers (payment service users – PSUs).

The focus of this chapter is on the main payment services-related rules applicable in the EU. For comparative reasons, the rules applicable in the UK and the US will also be touched on, but at a higher level of abstraction, for lack of space. Significantly, the purview of our analysis, below, overlaps, in part, with the regulatory analysis, in the above jurisdictions, of *payment systems*, a term denoting any organized, multi-lateral, rules-based arrangement for the settlement of financial transactions through monetary value transfers.[5]

---

1 The author is most grateful to Jessie Cheng, Christopher K. Odinet, Tom Coates, David Geen and an anonymous reviewer for their comments and input. All remaining errors are those of the author.

2 These are market intermediaries that hold client funds and offer payment and ancillary services to their customers. PSPs will either be credit institutions or non-banks, such as E-money institutions, payment institutions and payment initiation service providers.

3 *Wholesale* payment services, such are corporate and inter-bank payments, are beyond the scope of this chapter.

4 The reference is mainly to money transfers and remittances, merchant acquiring and card payments.

5 For more comprehensive overviews of EU payment systems regulation see, *ex multi*, John Casanova, Max Savoie and Abit Twist, 'Regulation of Payment Systems' in John Casanova and Max Savoie (eds), *Payment Services – Law and Practice* (Edward Elgar Publishing, 2022), 101–127; and Phoebus L Athanassiou, 'Payment Systems' in Amtenbrink and Herrmann (eds), *The EU Law of Economic and Monetary Union* (Oxford University Press, 2020) 711–736.

2. AIMS AND CATEGORIZATION OF EU OF PAYMENT SERVICES REGULATION

The EU payment services regulatory regime pursues a three-pronged objective. A *first* objective is to promote *payments market integration* through regulatory harmonization, while at the same time enhancing *competition* in the provision of payment services. Regulatory measures falling within this category (hereinafter, 'Category I measures') include (but are not limited to) (i) the Second Payment Services Directive,[6] (ii) the Single Euro Payments Area (SEPA) Regulation[7] and (iii) the Second E-money Directive.[8] A *second* objective is to protect *market integrity*. Regulatory measures falling within this category (hereinafter, 'Category II measures') include (iv) the Fourth Anti-Money Laundering Directive,[9] as amended,[10] and (v) the Regulation on information accompanying transfers of funds,[11] as amended. A *third* objective is to safeguard *financial stability*. Regulatory measures falling in this category (hereinafter, 'Category III measures') include (vi) the Settlement Finality Directive (SFD),[12] as amended, and the Financial Collateral Directive (FCD).[13] What follows is an account of some of the above measures, and an assessment of the extent to which they appear to have achieved those objectives. Elements of payment services regulation in the UK and the US will also be provided, where relevant and helpful for the reader's understanding of some of the core regulatory policy themes in the payment services field.

---

6 Council Directive (EU) 2015/2366 of 25 November 2015 on payment services in the internal market, amending Directives 2002/65/EC, 2009/110/EC and 2013/36/EU and Regulation (EU) No 1093/2010, and repealing Directive 2007/64/EC [2015] OJ L 337/35 (PSD2).

7 Council Regulation (EU) 260/2012 of 14 March 2012 establishing technical and business requirements for credit transfers and direct debits in euro and amending Regulation (EC) No 924/2009 [2012] OJ L 94/22.

8 Council Directive (EC) 2009/110 of 16 September 2009 on the taking up, pursuit and prudential supervision of the business of electronic money institutions amending Directives 2005/60/EC and 2006/48/EC and repealing Directive 2000/46/EC [2009] OJ L 267/7 (EMD2).

9 Council Directive (EU) 2015/849 of 20 May 2015 on the prevention of the use of the financial system for the purposes of money laundering or terrorist financing, amending Regulation (EU) No 648/2012 of the European Parliament and of the Council, and repealing Directive 2005/60/EC of the European Parliament and of the Council and Commission Directive 2006/70/EC [2015] OJ L 141/73 (AMLD4).

10 Notably, by Directive (EU) 2018/843 on the prevention of the use of the financial system for the purposes of money laundering or terrorist financing, and amending Directives 2009/138/EC and 2013/36/EU [2018] OJ L 156/43 (AMLD5).

11 Council Regulation (EU) 2015/847 of 20 May 2015 on information accompanying transfers of funds and repealing Regulation (EC) No 1781/2006 [2015] OJ L 141/1, as amended.

12 Council Directive (EC) 98/26 of 19 May 1998 on settlement finality in payment and securities settlement systems [1998] OJ L 166/45 (SFD).

13 Directive 2002/47/EC on financial collateral arrangements [2002] OJ L 168/43 (FCD).

2.1 Category I Measures: The EU's PSD2

The entry into effect, on 13 January 2018, of PSD2 signalled the repeal of the original Payment Services Directive (PSD),[14] only a decade after its adoption. What prompted the enactment of PSD2 was the policy makers' recognition that the substantial technical innovations that had seen the light of day since 2007 had the potential to reshape retail payment markets, and that regulatory intervention was necessary to help realize that potential by enabling novel electronic and mobile payment channels operated by new, non-bank payment service providers. These innovations, which included cloud technology and networking services, were deemed to call for regulatory changes to govern the controlled access of innovative players to existing (bank-dominated) payment infrastructures but, also, to customer data. An accessory (but related) regulatory concern behind PSD2 was to improve the safety and efficiency of digital payment services across the EU by reinforcing security standards for electronic/online payments.

PSD2 distinguishes between PSPs and 'payment institutions' (PIs), with the latter being a subset of the former. Unlike other types of PSPs (notably, credit institutions, non-bank E-money institutions, and the Eurosystem central banks, including the European Central Bank – ECB), PIs require an authorization to provide payment services, and they are not covered by the SFD, meaning that they cannot participate in SFD-designated securities settlement systems (SSSs). Authorized PIs may 'passport out' to other EU Member States. PSD2 mandates the European Banking Authority (EBA) to develop, in close co-operation with the ECB, regulatory technical standards and guidelines for *all* PSPs.[15]

To improve economies of scale and to complement the SEPA (see *infra*), PSD2 harmonizes the law governing electronic retail payments throughout the internal market. Significantly, PSD2 covers payments in *all EU/EEA Member State currencies*, provided the PSP is in the EU or in the European Economic Area (EEA).[16] In common with the PSD, PSD2 captures both 'one leg' transactions (i.e. those where the payor, the payee or their respective PSPs are located outside of the EU) and 'two leg' transactions (i.e. those where both parties and their payment processors are located outside the EU).

To increase consumer choice, enhance competition between PSPs, cater for the growing trend towards customer relationships with multiple account providers, and support the growth of e-commerce activities and mobile payments, PSD2 expands the regulatory payment services universe to encompass non-bank 'third party providers' (TPPs) (typically, FinTechs, such as 'payment initiation service providers' and 'account information service providers').[17] Starting in September 2019, players already active in the provision, within the EU, of payment services (referred to, in PSD2, as Account Service PSPs or ASPSPs) were to offer application

---

[14] Directive (EC) 2007/64 of 13 November 2007 on payment services in the internal market amending Directives 97/7/EC [2007] OJ L 319/1.

[15] For a recent example see EBA/RTS/2022/03 amending Commission Delegated Regulation (EU) 2018/389 supplementing Directive (EU) 2015/2366 with regard to regulatory technical standards for strong customer authentication and common and secure open standards of communication.

[16] In that respect, PSD2 is far wider in scope compared to the SEPA Regulation, which, as explained later in this chapter, only covers euro-denominated payments.

[17] Jane K Winn, 'Reengineering European Payment Law' in Edward A Morse (ed.), *Electronic Payments in the 21st Century* (American Bar Association 2017).

programming interfaces (APIs) to TPPs, granting them access to customer payment data – i.e. account, product and services data, including transactions and payment history – subject to the data subject's consent. It is through recourse to APIs that banks and TPPs can exchange data with one another and initiate payments. It is also through APIs that TPPs can build new applications and provide innovative services to their customers (such as personal financial management tools and automated payment initiation services).[18]

To enhance consumer protection, PSD2 requires PSPs operating within the EU to provide customers with transparent information on the charges and conditions applicable to domestic and cross-border payments alike, while at the same time introducing a liability regime for failed and unauthorized payments and requiring the institution, by PSPs, of dispute resolution procedures. In the same spirit, PSD2 also introduces fraud prevention security requirements for electronic payments (including so-called 'strong customer authentication' – SCA – requirements) as well as consumer financial data protection guarantees, including reduced liability for non-authorized payments, and an unconditional, time-bound customer right of refund for direct debits in euro. Finally, to ensure client funds protection, PSD2 requires PIs to safeguard all funds they receive from PSUs or through another PI for the execution of payment transactions, either through segregation or through an insurance policy or another comparable guarantee from an insurance company or bank not belonging to the same group as the PI itself.

Opinions are divided on the success of PSD2 in meeting its triple objectives of promoting innovation, encouraging competition and improving the general level of security of payment transactions. The consensus is that PSD2 reinforced the security of payments and curtailed payment fraud, increased the rights of PSUs and helped to open the European payment services market to more innovation and competition, to the benefit of consumers. At the same time, the respondents to a public consultation launched by the European Commission (EC) in the summer of 2022 expressed several concerns. Prominent amongst them were concerns with: (i) the considerable divergence in its national interpretation and implementation (notably reflected in the fragmented implementation of SCA rules), the asymmetry in the obligations of ASPSPs compared with those of PIs (to the detriment of the former) and the lack of API standardization; (ii) legal uncertainty regarding the scope of the rights and obligations of TPPs, the regulatory treatment of online marketplaces (large merchants) and payment facilitators (Big Tech and other online platforms) and the interplay between PSD2 and other examples of EU legislation (including the EMD2) as well as with PSD2's own Level 2 measures; and (iii) doubts regarding the adequacy of the compliance framework and controls of PIs, and the practical efficiency of the PSD2's liability regime for unauthorized payments. Several of the respondents expressed a preference for the recast of PSD2 into a Regulation (a *prima facie* legitimate preference, given the discrepancies in its national implementation), and against an expansion of its scope of application.

Having launched the PSD2 review process in 2022, the EC published, on 28 June 2023, a proposal for a directive on payment services and electronic money services in the Internal Market amending the SFD, and repealing PSD2 and EMD2 (the Proposed Directive).[19] The Proposed Directive was part of a 'Payments Package', which also included a proposal

---

[18] One of the aims of PSD2 is to promote so-called 'open-banking'. Pioneered in the UK, this consists in the sharing, by established market players, of customer data with new players, to promote competition and improve PSUs' experience.

[19] COM(2023) 366 final.

for a regulation on payment services in the internal market.[20] If adopted as published, the Proposed Directive would, amongst others, lead to a merger of the regimes applicable to PIs and non-bank E-money institutions (see *infra*), an extension of payment fraud protection measures, a clarification of the PSD2's SCA rules and enhanced transparency on costs and charges for remittances to non-EU countries and ATM withdrawals. Although it is premature to assess its implications, if adopted as published the Proposed Directive would probably mark an evolution (rather than a revolution) for Europe's payment services landscape, which, however welcome, may not adequately address all of the PSD2's many shortcomings.

2.2 Comparative Perspective: Payment Services Regulation in the UK and the US

At the time of writing, the UK boasted the highest number of registered TPPs, and the most mature 'open banking' environment in Europe. The provision of payment services in the UK is governed by the Payment Services Regulations 2017 (PSRs),[21] which came into effect on 13 January 2018, implementing PSD2. In view of the UK's withdrawal from the EU, the PSRs were amended by the Electronic Money, Payment Services and Payment Systems (Amendment and Transitional Provisions) (EU Exit) Regulations 2018 (the EPPRs). Following the UK's withdrawal from the EU, the UK's Financial Conduct Authority (FCA) produced technical standards on strong customer authentication and common and secure methods of communication (SCA-RTS), as well as adjustments to the FCA Handbook, with the relevant EU regulatory technical standards being simultaneously revoked. However, even following the UK's exit from the EU, UK businesses continue to apply the EBA Guidelines, where relevant.

One of the UK's peculiarities in the payment services space is the co-existence of a healthy number of payment sector regulators, supervisors and overseers, with partly overlapping mandates. These include, amongst others, the FCA, which is co-responsible for promoting open banking and for monitoring and enforcing compliance with most of the PSRs, the Bank of England, which oversees systemically important payment systems and designates them for the purposes of the Settlement Finality Regulations, and the Payment Systems Regulator, whose mission is to foster innovation and competition in the national payments markets (inter alia, by supporting open banking), protect consumer interests and monitor compliance with some of the PSRs. The complexity of the UK's payment services and systems' governance landscape calls for considerable coordination efforts to avert duplication of work, regulatory misalignments, and legal uncertainty.[22]

In the US, PSPs (referred to, locally, as 'money transmitters') that are not insured depository institutions (i.e. companies that are not licensed as fully-fledged banks), are, by law, to hold a State-level license (where state law so requires) to engage in the business of facilitating fund

---

[20] COM(2023) 367 final. The Proposed Directive seeks to deal with the authorization and supervision of PSPs, including PIs, while the proposed Regulation aims to govern other issues.

[21] UK SI 2017/752.

[22] At the time of writing there was an MoU in place between all payment authorities under the Financial Services (Banking Reform) Act 2013 (the PSR, the FCA, the Bank of England and the Prudential Regulation Authority), providing a coordination framework.

transfers ('money transmissions'),[23] and be registered with the Federal Government. Most US States have enacted their own, distinct money transmission laws to govern the activities of non-bank money transmitters. Money transmitters engaging in business beyond State borders are to comply with the money transmission laws applicable in the US jurisdictions where they conduct their business (there is, in other words, no US equivalent to the 'passport' that PSPs and PIs enjoy under PSD2).[24] Attempts at harmonization, including the Uniform Money Services Act (UMSA),[25] which lays down licensing and compliance standards for Money Transmitters, have not, so far, proven very successful (at the time of writing, the UMSA had only been enacted into law in a handful of US States).

As in thc UK, also in the US the regulation of payment services is divided between several regulators, with the resulting patchwork being challenging to navigate through. At the Federal level, the number of agencies responsible for the regulation and oversight of PSPs include, amongst others, the Federal Reserve Board (FRB), the Federal Deposit Insurance Corp (FDIC), the Office of the Comptroller of the Currency and the Consumer Financial Protection Bureau (CFPB). Differently from the EU and the UK, the US had yet to formalize, at the time of writing, a dedicated open banking legal framework. That said, in a July 2021 Executive Order mandating the promotion of competition across the US economy, the US administration urged the Consumer Financial Protection Bureau (CFPB) to establish rules and regulations facilitating the portability of customer banking data. Provided data privacy concerns can be overcome, data portability could pave the way for FinTechs and other non-depository institution PSPs to become more actively involved in the provision of (more affordable) retail payment services, ringing in far-reaching changes in the provision of payment services and the processing of retail payments in the US.

3. CATEGORY I MEASURES: THE EU'S SEPA REGULATION

Adopted in March 2012, the SEPA Regulation lays down common rules for the initiation and processing of euro-denominated credit transfers and direct debits. The adoption of the SEPA Regulation signalled the culmination of the SEPA Project, a regional payments scheme initiated in 2002, with the European banking industry's political backing. The aim of the SEPA Project was to achieve European integration in the field of euro retail payments as a precondition for Europe's closer economic unification. The goal of a more integrated European retail payments market was to be attained by introducing and implementing common payment schemes and standards for different types of retail payments in euro (launched virtually on 1 January 1999 and physically on 1 January 2002), helping to transform the various national

---

23 Federal anti-money laundering law provides that, '[W]hoever knowingly conducts, controls, manages, supervises, directs, or owns all or part of an unlicensed money transmitting business, shall be fined in accordance with this title or imprisoned not more than 5 years, or both' (see 18 USC § 1960(a)).

24 There existed, at the time of writing, a Model Money Transmission Modernization Act that would standardize licensing requirements across states and a Uniform Interstate Application being developed that would create a common licensing application for multiple states to use for a single license (neither of which were widely adopted).

25 See UMSA, Sections 201–502.

payment markets into a single, 'SEPA' market. Already in 2001, banks and other PSPs were prohibited from levying higher charges for cross-border euro payments (including credit transfers) within the EU than for corresponding domestic ones in the national currency.[26]

Concretely, SEPA allows customers in 45 European countries and territories (most of them in the euro area) to make electronic euro payments in the form of direct debits and credit transfers (including instant credit transfers) but *not* credit card payments, through use of certain pan-European SEPA schemes, which replaced the corresponding national schemes. Under the aegis and guidance of the Eurosystem and the EC, the European Payments Council (EPC)[27] defined new rules and procedures for euro payments, eventually adopted by euro area and non-euro area (EU/EEA) stakeholders alike. For direct debits, standardization was achieved through the EPC's SEPA Direct Debit (SDD) scheme. With the support of the PSD and PSD2, the EPC's SEPA Credit Transfer (SCT) scheme rendered cross-border credit transfers within the EEA as uncomplicated, efficient and secure as national payments. Since 1 August 2014, all euro-denominated credit transfers and direct debits have migrated to the SEPA DD and the SEPA CT schemes. Regarding instant credit transfers, the Euro Retail Payments Board (ERPB)[28] identified, as early as 2014, the need for a pan-European instant payment solution in euro. This was followed, in November 2016, by the publication, by the EPC, of the SCT Inst rulebook, with the EPC's SCT Inst scheme itself becoming operational in November 2017.

Notwithstanding Brexit, the UK continues to be part of SEPA, with the EPC having approved the application of UK Finance for the continued participation of UK-based PSPs in the SEPA schemes after 29 March 2019. As a result, provided they continue to adhere to SEPA's standardized set of rules, UK-based parties can keep sending and receiving euro payments through direct debits or credit transfers to and from other SEPA-participating countries.

4. CATEGORY I MEASURES: REGULATION OF E-MONEY INSTITUTIONS

In the jurisdictions under consideration in this chapter, E-money institutions (ELMIs) are to be understood as specialized, non-bank financial institutions whose business is to issue electronic money ('E-money') and to provide E-money payment accounts and services to enable their customers to send or accept E-money payments. For its part, E-money is, in essence, a prepaid payment instrument (whether card-based or account/server-based), intended for use as a digital alternative to cash.[29] Importantly, the issuance of E-money is not *reserved* to ELMIs:

---

[26] See Regulation (EU) 2021/1230 of 14 July 2021 on cross border payments in the Union (codification) [2021] OJ L 274/20.

[27] The EPC was founded in 2002 as the 'decision-making and co-ordination body of the European banking industry in relation to payments' (see <http://www.europeanpaymentscouncil.eu>).

[28] The ERPB was created (and is chaired) by the ECB, to replace the SEPA Council, and to foster an integrated, innovative and competitive market for retail payments in euro. Its composition is broader than that of its predecessor, with representatives from the demand and the supply sides as well all EU national central banks.

[29] The CPSS has defined E-money as 'value stored electronically in a device such as a chip card or a hard drive in a personal computer' (Commission on Payment and Settlement Systems,

banks may also issue E-money (even if subject, in some jurisdictions, to a separate regulatory authorization). What follows is a concise account of the regulation of ELMIs in the EU, as well as elements of the corresponding rules applicable in the UK and the US.

4.1 The EU's Second E-Money Directive

In the EU, the issuance of E-money is a regulated activity. At the time of writing, the legal framework for the licensing and operation of ELMIs was laid down in EMD2, which repealed and replaced, with effect from April 2011, the original EMD.[30] EMD2 defines e-money as 'electronically, including magnetically, stored monetary value as represented by a claim on the issuer which is issued on receipt of funds for the purpose of making payment transactions ... and which is accepted by a natural or legal person other than the electronic money issuer'.[31] In addition to issuing E-money, ELMIs qualify as PSPs, under PSD2, and can engage in the provision of payment services, within its meaning, subject to compliance with the EU's AML/CFT framework. EMD2 lowered the original market entry barriers for ELMIs and expanded the scope of permissible financial services that ELMIs can provide to their customers. Apart from the issuance of E-money, those services include the provision of all payment services that PIs can provide under Annex 1 to PSD2, the granting of credit related to those payment services, the provision of operational and closely related ancillary services (such as the execution of payment transactions, currency exchange and safekeeping services as well as the storage and processing of data) and the operation of payment systems. Significantly, ELMIs may not accept deposits or other repayable funds from the public, within the meaning of the EU prudential banking framework, and they are to exchange, without delay, for E-money, any funds they receive from the E-money holder, on the understanding that these funds do not legally constitute deposits or other repayable funds from the public. Significantly, ELMIs no longer qualify as 'credit institutions' under EU law, as the case had been under the original EMD.[32]

The EMD2 requires ELMIs to protect the sums that customers pay to them, and which ELMIs hold for the issuance of E-money and the provision of related payment services. The purpose of the EMD2's so-called 'safeguarding requirements' (which are visibly borrowed from the PSD, and which include, but are not limited to, segregation of client funds) is to ensure that an ELMI's insolvency will not lead to customer losses. Other than its safeguarding requirements, which are central to the regulatory duties to which ELMIs are subject, the EMD2

'A glossary of terms used in payments and settlement systems' (Bank for International Settlement, 2003).

[30] Directive (EC) 2000/46 on the taking up, pursuit of and prudential supervision of the business of electronic money institutions [2000] OJ L 275/39. On the EMD see, *ex multi*, Phoebus Athanassiou, 'When is E-money not E-money? Reflections on the Revision of the E-money Directive' (2006) 3–4 European Banking and Financial Law Journal 321.

[31] E-money is not, *stricto sensu*, money but, rather, evidence of a debt of the E-money issuer to the E-money holder, in return for the provision, by the former, of certain (mostly payment) services, to the latter. If this interpretation is correct, then the issuance of E-money is a specialized payment service, for possible inclusion in a revised PSD2.

[32] EMD2 art 20(1) changed the definition of 'credit institutions' in CRD art 4(1) to remove ELMIS from the scope of that definition, reclassifying ELMIS as 'financial institutions', within the meaning of (revised) CRD art 4(5).

sets out regulatory requirements that are, in many respects, similar to but less cumbersome than those applicable to banks (notably, lower initial capital and own funds requirements) and provides for a narrower spectrum of permissible financial services.

Until the start of the Covid-19 pandemic, demand for the services of ELMIs in the EU was modest. Following the outbreak of the Covid-19 pandemic, demand for E-money products and services spiked.[33] However, ELMI penetration continues to differ markedly from one country to another. At the time of writing, the UK boasted the largest number of registered ELMIs in Europe, followed, at a distance, by Lithuania. European micro-states were leaders by their number of ELMIs per inhabitants, while Malta scored highly in both metrics. ELMIs' penetration was at its lowest in Hungary, the Czech Republic and Denmark.

One can only speculate on whether the modest take up of E-money is attributable to the EMD2's shortcomings as opposed to the inherent weaknesses of E-money itself, and the legal uncertainties surrounding it,[34] which appear to warrant the EMD2's overhaul (and more). E-money suffers from certain drawbacks that constrain its attractiveness and explain its relatively modest popularity with PSUs.[35] Interestingly, the Proposed Directive of 28 June 2023 (*supra*, §2.1) advocates the EMD2's repeal, and the absorption of E-money services into a revamped PSD2. The adoption into law of the Proposed Directive would, therefore, spell the end of ELMIs as specialized financial institutions and the abolition of their hitherto dedicated regulatory regime, with E-money services becoming one of a range of services that PIs will be authorized to provide, putting an end to a framework that did not, with hindsight, meet its goals.

4.2 Comparative Perspective: E-Money Regulation in the UK and the US

As in the EU, the issuance of E-money is a regulated activity also in the UK. The legal framework for the licensing and operation of ELMIs, and for the issuance of E-money, is provided by the Electronic Money Regulations of 2011 (EMRs), as amended by the EPPRs, read in conjunction with the PSRs. The EMRs are very similar, in substance, to EMD2, of which they were the UK implementation, and they remain in place even post-Brexit. Both legal frameworks define E-money as an electronic store of monetary value on a technical device that can be widely used for making payments to entities other than the e-money issuer, both of them treat it as a prepaid digital alternative to cash, and both of them treat ELMIs as specialized entities that are in many ways similar to but, also, different from banks,[36] and which may, amongst others, engage in the provision of payment services, not unlike PIs under the

[33] At the time of writing, both the outstanding E-money balances, and the volume of E-money transactions remained relatively small, and the same was true of the value of daily transactions.

[34] The key point of uncertainty concerns the question of the fundamental legal nature of E-money, which spills over to those of its definition and proper regulatory treatment, either as a money-issuance service, with certain payment and other services attached, or, alternatively, as a specialized payment service.

[35] For instance, E-money is not legal tender, and, despite its redeemability and convertibility in cash, it generally affords consumers and merchants alike less protection compared with several other means of payment.

[36] It bears noting that UK banks (regulated, at the time of writing, under the Financial Services and Markets Act 2000) wishing to issue e-money must hold a specific authorization.

PSRs. That said, as reflected in the parallelism between E-money rules with those applicable to payment systems and payment services, the UK's approach to E-money is that this is, fundamentally, the means to the provision of a payment service, with ELMIs being viewed as specialized PSPs.

In the US there was, at the time of writing, no federal level equivalent to the EMD2 to specifically cover the business of non-depository institutions as issuers of prepaid cards or other types of stored value instruments, and the provision of payment services around them. This, however, is not to say that E-money and the attendant payment services are 'unregulated' in the US. To start with, prepaid cards (irrespective of the legal status of their issuer) were, at the time of writing, governed by the Electronic Funds Transfer Act and Regulation E, both administered by the CFPB. Moreover, in the US, the focus of regulatory attention was on E-money as a (regulated) payment service, which different entities may provide in the course of business. The likelihood that a non-depository institution would issue an E-money instrument is small, at least for cards intended for use through the large card scheme networks, whose rules required, at the time of writing, that card issuers be FDIC-insured banks. Be that as it may, non-bank issuers of prepaid cards may well be subject to State-level money transmitter laws, typically requiring non-bank money transmitters to obtain a State-level license and to comply with several regulatory, including prudential and reporting, requirements as a precondition for the provision of payment services. Similarly, if a money transmitter were to offer E-money payment services over E-money products linked to an account, it could be regarded as engaging in banking business, subject to State banking laws. Interestingly, the UMSA introduces the notion of 'stored value' (the US equivalent of E-money), which it defines as 'monetary value that is evidenced by an electronic record', with 'monetary value' being defined as 'a medium of exchange, whether or not redeemable in money'.

5. CATEGORY II MEASURES: AML/CFT REGULATION

Preventing the diversion of the financial system into a conduit for the pursuit of money laundering, terrorist financing and other illicit activities features high on the agenda of policy makers and regulators the world over. According to estimates, up to 5% of the global gross domestic product results from money laundering activities. Amongst the financial intermediaries subject to anti-money laundering (AML) regulation and supervision are PSPs, including PIs. What follows is the briefest of outlines of the AML/CFT regime applicable in the EU but, also, elements of the corresponding regime in the UK and the US.

5.1 AML/CFT Regulation in the EU

The adoption, in May 2015, of AMLD4 signaled the EU's resolve to modernize its AML/CFT framework, which, by that time, was already a decade old. In a bid to improve on the EU's collective ability to combat money laundering connected to criminal activities and to curtail the financing of terrorism, the drafters of AMLD4 drew heavily on the Recommendations of the Financial Action Task Force (FATF), which they sought to carry over into Europe's new AML/CFT framework.[37]

The EU's AML/CFT framework applies to 'obliged entities', a term that is defined to include, apart from credit institutions, also auditors, external accountants, tax advisors, notaries and other independent legal professionals and 'financial institutions'.[38] Entities providing 'payment services' under the PSD will qualify as 'financial institutions' (hence, they will also amount to 'obliged entities'). Finally, AMLD4 applies to natural persons storing, trading or acting in goods involving cash transactions of EUR 10,000 or more. The centerpiece of the AMLD4 is the customer due diligence (CDD) measures that obliged entities are to apply when establishing a business relationship or carrying out occasional transactions that fulfil certain statutory requirements.[39] These transactions include 'transfers of funds' within the meaning of Regulation (EU) 2015/847 (see *infra*, Part 6).[40] AMLD4 elaborates[41] on the CDD measures, which include the need to identify the customer and the beneficial owner and to verify their identity based on documents, data or information gathered from a reliable and independent source, as well as the need to obtain information on, and to assess, the purpose and intended nature of the legal relationship.

AMLD4 mandates Member States to ensure that obliged entities can be held liable for breaches of national provisions transposing it.[42] It also recognizes the Member States' discretion to provide for and impose criminal sanctions while at the same time mandating them to lay down rules on administrative sanctions and measures, ensuring that their competent authorities can enforce national AML-related provisions and their accompanying sanctions.[43] Member States are to also ensure that their competent authorities report, in a timely manner, to their law enforcement authorities any breaches they have identified that are subject to criminal sanctions.

June 2018 saw the publication of Directive 2018/843 (AMLD5), which amended AMLD4 to, inter alia, limit the anonymity of transactions in virtual currencies and pre-paid cards, enhance the powers of EU Member State Financial Intelligence Units and improve their access to information, improve cooperation and information exchanges between AML supervisors and between them and prudential supervisors and the ECB, and promote transparency through the establishment of publicly available registers for companies, trusts and other legal arrangements. Further refinements were made to the EU's AML/CFT framework through the

---

37 Financial Action Task Force, 'The 2012 FATF Recommendations' (*FATF*, 2022) <https://www.fatf-gafi.org/publications/fatfrecommendations/documents/fatf-recommendations.html> accessed 14 May 2024.

38 See AMLD4 art 2.

39 ibid art 11. These requirements include situations where there is a suspicion of money laundering or terrorist financing, or of any doubts as to the veracity of a prior CDD effort.

40 Council Regulation (EU) 2015/847 of 20 May 2015 on information accompanying transfers of funds and repealing Regulation (EC) No 1781/2006 [2015] OJ L 141/1, art 3(9) defines 'transfer of funds' to mean 'any transaction at least partially carried out by electronic means on behalf of a payer through a payment service provider [emphasis is ours], with a view to making funds available to a payee through a payment service provider'.

41 AMLD4 art 13.

42 ibid art 58(1).

43 ibid art 58(2).

adoption of Directive (EU) 2018/1673 (AMLD 6), which, inter alia, harmonizes the definition of money laundering across the EU with a common list of 22 'predicate offences' (thereby also paving the way for greater cooperation among EU Member States), lists cybercrime and environmental crime as predicate offences, reinforces sanctions for violators in money laundering cases, and extends criminal liability to legal entities.

5.2 Comparative Perspective: AML/CFT Regulation in the UK and the US

Prior to Brexit, the UK had transposed into its national law both AMLD4 and AMLD5. At the time of writing, there were no plans for a departure from the resulting AML regime. The UK had, nonetheless, opted out of transposing AMLD6, mostly because UK already covered many of its requirements. Brexit has not had an impact on the UK's (long-standing) membership of the FATF.

The origins of the anti-money laundering legal framework in the US lie in the Banking Secrecy Act of 1970 (BSA).[44] Since then, a spate of other laws and regulations have been introduced on top of the BSA, to reinforce the hand of law enforcement agencies and regulatory authorities in the struggle against money laundering.[45] Amongst others, the BSA requires financial institutions, including those active in the provision of payment services, to develop and implement AML compliance programs. Depending on the nature of their activities, financial firms may also come within the scope of sectoral AML rules (for instance, firms active in the provision of securities service are also subject to the anti-money laundering provisions in FINRA Rule 3310).

6. CATEGORY II MEASURES: THE EU'S REGULATION ON INFORMATION ACCOMPANYING TRANSFERS OF FUNDS

Regulation (EU) 2015/847 is part of a package of EU measures aimed at preventing money laundering and terrorist financing. That package includes, notably, AMLD4.

The Regulation applies to transfers of funds, in any currency, sent or received by an EU-established PSP. The payor's PSP is required to provide certain information, both on the payor and on the payee (including their names and account numbers) as well as check the accuracy of that information. Similarly, the payee's PSP is required to have in place effective procedures to detect missing or incomplete information, as well as risk-based procedures based on which to decide whether to execute, reject or suspend the relevant fund transfer. Any personal data obtained by the PSPs should only be used to prevent money laundering and terrorist financing, with PSPs required to ensure its confidentiality, and to retain it, in principle, for no more than 5 years.

---

44 31 USC § 5311 et seq., 12 USC.

45 One notable example is the Money Laundering Suppression Act (1994), which sought to encourage banks to improve the AML training of their staff, develop AML examination procedures and improve in terms of their suspicious activities reporting to law enforcement agencies.

7. CATEGORY III MEASURES: FINALITY AND COLLATERAL

The SFD seeks to harmonize Member State laws by immunizing the operation of, amongst others, eligible payment and SSSs against the risk of the insolvency of their participants. Alongside the FCD (see *infra*), it is amongst the earliest examples of EU financial markets legislation still in force, but also amongst the most important, given the pivotal role of the *legal* concept of *finality* for the protection of payment and SSS participants from the disruptive consequences of the opening of insolvency proceedings against other participants, and for the reduction of the attendant systemic risks. Central to the operation of the SFD is the concept of the 'moment of entry into the system' of a transfer (or netting) order: under the SFD, transfer orders entered into a 'system' (a payment system, a central securities depository – CSD – an SSS or a central counterparty – CCP – governed by the law of an EU Member State and duly designated as a 'system'), as of the moment defined in the system rules, are *irrevocable* and *final*, i.e. legally enforceable *erga omnes*, even in case of insolvency of a 'participant' (i.e. a credit institution, a settlement agent, a CCP or the system operator of a system, e.g. a CSD, in the case of an SSS).

The SFD is closely connected to other financial market-related legislative instruments, such as the Financial Collateral Directive,[46] as amended, which creates a Community-wide uniform legal framework for the provision of securities and cash deposits as collateral in the form of a limited right *in rem* or by way of an outright transfer of ownership and which, since 2009, has also covered the security assignment of credit claims.

8. INNOVATION IN PAYMENT SERVICES

The significant advances over the last decade in information, communication and digital technology have also had an impact on payment services. These advances have signaled a widening in the pool of entities involved in payments' processing, beyond traditional PSPs, and a growth in consumer appetite for E-commerce transactions, where settlement in innovative payment services (broadly defined as those involving payments other than through credit or debit cards) has been on the rise. There are several facets to innovation in payment services, such as instant payments (IPs), the use of distributed ledger technology (DLT)-based payment platforms and recourse to innovative payment media, such as virtual currencies and stablecoins. In the remainder of this chapter we explore IPs, and how they are supported by EU regulation. Readers interested in the use, in the field of payments, of DLTs and innovative payment media are referred to other publications of this author.[47]

---

46 Council Directive (EC) 2002/47 on financial collateral [2016] OJ L 168/43 (FCD).

47 See, *ex multi*, Athanassiou (n 5) 711–736; Phoebus L Athanassiou, *Digital Innovation in Financial Services – Legal Challenges and Regulatory Policy Issues* (Kluwer 2018); Phoebus L Athanassiou, 'Impact of digital innovation on the processing of electronic payments and contracting: an overview of legal risks' (2017) ECB Legal Working Papers Series 16.

8.1 Instant Payments: Definition, Advantages and Challenges

Instant payments can be defined as electronic, retail payment solutions available 24/7/365 that allow for the real-time (i.e. immediate/close-to-immediate) processing of the relevant payment and for the crediting, within seconds of the payment initiation, of funds to the payee's account, with confirmation to the payer. As a form of credit transfer, IPs are to be distinguished from 'slow' payments (those taking up to two days between their initiation and the crediting of funds to the payee's account) and fast(er) payments (those that are faster than slow payments, but not instant).

As mentioned earlier in this chapter, already in 2014, the ERPB identified the need for *at least one* pan-European (cross-border) IP solution in euro. This came at a time when market participants in several EU Member States were in the process of developing *national* instant payment solutions. These solutions had the potential to fragment the market, for lack of interoperability. The ERPB invited the EPC to develop such a solution, in the form of a pan-European instant payment scheme based on the EPC's SEPA credit transfer (SCT) scheme. In November 2016, the EPC published the SEPA Instant Credit Transfer (SCT Inst) rulebook, with the SCT Inst scheme itself becoming operational in November 2017. Despite the launch of SCT Inst, IPs had yet to become, at the time of writing, the 'new normal' in the EU. We explore the reasons why below.

Instant payments hold certain promises compared to slower or fast(er) payments, accounting for the policy makers' interest in them. Because of their real-time processing, IPs make incoming liquidity immediately available, rendering them an attractive option for certain payments, including time-critical ones. Linked to the foregoing, because of their very low processing latency, IPs release for re-use funds that would otherwise remain 'locked' for the duration of the processing cycle of slow(er) payments, allowing them to increment their beneficiaries' working capital. What is more, the automated nature of IPs renders the manual processes typically used for many slow(er) payments redundant, averting errors (and their attendant costs). Finally, specifically in the case of the EU, IPs hold the promise of increasing Europe's strategic autonomy in the field of payments and reducing its reliance on foreign payment schemes (notably in the field of card payments).

Promising as they are, IPs are not devoid of certain, mostly operational and legal, challenges. Because of the low level of interoperability between domestic IP solutions, their level of coverage is lower than that of competing types of payments (notably, card payments), making them unsuitable for cross-border payments. The absence of cross-border rails for IPs is unlikely to be overcome by the market alone, without public sector involvement and encouragement, including through *regulatory* means. Moreover, because of their speed and irreversibility, IPs can be vulnerable to external threats (notably, cyber-threats and fraud – with or without end-user involvement) and are apt to become money-laundering instruments. Unless tailor-made security and validation processes, consistent with the applicable AML/CFT rules and the local know-your-customer regulations, can be developed and applied, such money-laundering can go undetected.[48] Legal and operational challenges aside, IPs also come

---

[48] AML checks consist in tracking and assessing the legitimacy of financial transactions. In the case of IPs, these checks must take place within a fraction of the time available for slower payments.

with extra costs (including those necessary to develop their supporting infrastructure), which risks making them less attractive than other existing types of payment (card payments are popular with PSUs despite being notoriously costly, mostly for merchants).

8.2 Instant Payments: Overview of EU Initiatives and Regulation

As a credit transfer variant, IPs are subject both to PSD2 and to the Regulation on cross-border payments. It is not, therefore, the case, that, in the EU, IPs are unchartered regulatory territory. That said, both the ECB and the European Commission have, in recent years, taken a keen interest in IPs, reflected in some of their initiatives. These initiatives are further explored below.

In a bid to simultaneously promote European integration in the field of instant payments, and to extend the availability of settlement in CeBM on a 24/7/365 basis, the Eurosystem developed and operationalized the TARGET Instant Payment Settlement (TIPS) service. This is, in a nutshell, a Eurosystem-owned instant payment solution, offering real-time, final and irrevocable IPs in CeBM. The decision to develop and offer TIPS dates to June 2017. The Governing Council of the ECB adopted the TIPS legal framework in August 2018, while the TIPS service itself became operational in November 2018. The main focus of TIPS is on credit institution PSPs,[49] and on the provision to the latter of a 'front-to-end' IP service (i.e. one that does not include a separate clearing stage as part of the process for executing instant payments), with immediate settlement in CeBM. With TIPS, the Eurosystem aims to meet demand for IPs through the safe and efficient infrastructure of TARGET, which serves as the technical platform of the TIPS service.[50] Although the market take-up of TIPS was relatively limited at the time of writing, it was expected to increase, inter alia following the conclusion, in April 2020, of an agreement, between the ECB and the Central Bank of Sweden, under the terms of which the latter would connect to TIPS, as of 2023, for the processing of domestic IPs (in Swedish Krona).

The strongest manifestation, to date, of the EU policy maker's interest in the promotion of IPs was the adoption, on 26 February 2024, of a Regulation on instant credit transfers in euro.[51] In a nutshell, this amends the earlier Regulation on cross-border payments in the Union and the SEPA Regulation, adding to the latter's general provisions on credit transfers in euro several provisions specifically targeting euro-denominated instant credit transfers. The centrepiece of the Regulation is the obligation it imposes on all EU-based PSPs offering credit transfer services in euro to also *offer* to all PSUs (as opposed to merely *receiving*) IPs in euro (defined as those where the payee's payment account is credited with the amount transferred within 10 seconds after the receipt of the payment order), for a fee that is no higher than the one that the

---

[49] Although it is mainly credit institution PSPs that are eligible to directly participate in TIPS as holders of settlement accounts for instant payments ('TIPS Dedicated Cash Accounts'), TIPS applies a flexible access structure, under which PSPs may also connect to TIPS as 'reachable parties'. The latter can settle their IP orders on the TIPS DCA of a direct participant, i.e. without an own-TIPS DCA.

[50] In TIPS, instant payments are processed on a technically separate platform, which, from a legal point of view, is part of TARGET. Being incorporated in TARGET, TIPS is not a 'system' within the meaning of the SFD.

[51] Not published on the Official Gazette of the EU at the time of writing.

same PSP charges for non-IPs in euro. Under the Regulation, euro area PSPs would have to receive IPs within 6 months after the date of entry into force of the proposed Regulation and offer them within 12 months of that date. Although the ECB welcomed[52] the Commission Proposal,[53] market actors criticized its scope (which covers all EU-based PSPs, not just those in the euro area), its ambitious timelines and the significant infrastructure-level economic costs that its implementation would impose on credit institution PSPs.

8.3 What Future for Instant Payments?

At the start of 2022 only two-thirds of banks in the EU offered IPs, with only 11% of all credit transfers made in the EU being instant.[54] A future generalization of IPs would mark a significant technological step forward for EU payment markets and could considerably weaken the incentives to explore the use of alternative payment media (such as virtual currencies) or the application to payments of new technologies (such as DLTs). At the same time, IPs are no panacea: leaving aside their challenges, which have yet to be overcome, IPs need not always be the most desirable payment method (depending on the use case, regular credit transfers may be preferable). Significantly, their take-up will depend not only on their roll-out by PSPs but also on PSUs' *preferences* and on their *costs*. The introduction of legislative incentives, and the (seemingly inexorable) move towards central bank digital currencies could accelerate the move towards IPs. Whether these will also encourage consumers to take them up remains to be seen: the adoption by the public of new payment methods depends more on the level of confidence that these inspire and less on legal prescriptions.

9. CONCLUDING REMARKS

The need to create a single payments market – reinforced by the introduction of the single currency – was to motivate multiple legislative initiatives, during the last two decades, in the field of payment services regulation. The EU legal framework in this field was to evolve gradually, by allowing an ever-growing number of actors to compete with incumbents for the provision of payment services, once the near-exclusive preserve of credit institutions. Starting with the adoption of the EMD, the EU legislator was to gradually open the market for the provision of payment services to a wider range of providers, a trend that was to be reaffirmed with the adoption of the PSD and then of PSD2. After twenty years of intense regulatory activity, the EU regulatory landscape for the provision of payment services remains fragmented, and difficult to navigate through. The proposed consolidation of EMD2 and PSD2 looks set to reverse the trend of the proliferation of dedicated legal frameworks in the field of payment services.

---

52 See ECB, 'Opinion of the ECB of 1 February 2023 on a proposal for a regulation amending Regulations (EU) No 260/2012 and (EU) 2021/1230 as regards instant credit transfers in euro (CON/2023/4).

53 Proposal for a Regulation of the European Parliament and of the Council amending Regulations (EU) No 260/2012 and (EU) 2021/1230 as regards instant credit transfers in euro (Brussels, 26.10.2022 COM (2022) 546 final).

54 ibid, Explanatory Memorandum to the Proposal for a Regulation on instant credit transfers in euro.

With the advent of instant payments, and the emergence of innovative means of payment, including virtual currencies and stablecoins, payment services, both in the EU and beyond, look set to undergo further changes, making this area of the law one that is both constantly evolving and exciting to follow.

17. The law of central banking

Rosa Lastra[1]

1. INTRODUCTION

The law of Central Banking is an expanding area of research and scholarship[2] which encompasses a significant number of substantive and procedural issues. In this chapter, I first discuss briefly the impact of the law on Central Banking and the development of the narrow model of Central Banking, which safeguarded independence and facilitated accountability. Secondly, I explore the expanded mandate of Central Banks as crisis managers in the aftermath of the Global Financial crisis (2007–2009), during the COVID pandemic (2020–2021) and now in the context of the challenges that the fight against climate change and, more broadly, sustainability poses for Central Banks. This expanding role can create tensions between objectives, compromise the independence of Central Banks and complicate accountability. The fourth and final section considers the role of Central Banks in the provision of digital money, which has the potential to alter the design of our existing monetary and financial framework.

2. THE ROLE OF LAW IN CENTRAL BANKING AND THE 'NARROW' MODEL

The development of Central Banking law sits between administrative law, commercial law, banking law, regulation and the interaction between law and economics.[3] And politics has

1 I would like to thank Marina Estato Apsan Frediani for research assistance. During 2023 I acted as Specialist Adviser to the House of Lords Economic Affairs Committee in its inquiry into *The Bank of England: How is Independence Working?* The final evidence-based report 'Making an independent Bank of England work better' was published in November 2023 and is available at <https://publications.parliament.uk/pa/ld5804/ldselect/ldeconaf/10/10.pdf>. Appendix 3 of the Report (pp. 61–63) provides an overview of the Bank of England remit, with the evolution of statutory objectives and functions.

2 My work on central banking law, stemming over three decades, is considered seminal in the subject, in particular with regard to central bank independence. See inter alia: Rosa M Lastra, 'The Independence of the European System of Central Banks' (1992) 33 Harvard International Law Journal 475; Rosa M Lastra, *Central Banking and Banking Regulation* (LSE, FMG, 1996), chap 1; Rosa M Lastra, 'Accountability Mechanisms of the Bank of England and of the European Central Bank' (European Parliament, 2020) <https://www.europarl.europa.eu/cmsdata/211623/1_LASTRA-final.pdf>; Rosa M Lastra and Charles A E Goodhart, 'The Changing and Growing Roles of Independent Central Banks now do require a Reconsideration of their Mandate' Accounting, Economics and the Law: A Convivium (27 February 2023); <https://eprints.lse.ac.uk/118448/1/10.1515_ael_2022_0097.pdf>.

3 See generally Thomas Cottier and others, *The Rule of Law in Monetary Affairs World Trade Forum* (Cambridge University Press 2014).

always played an essential role in Central Banking. The law, with its procedural and substantive guarantees, provides predictability and certainty, which are essential for the functioning and constitutional position of Central Banks. Like Gulliver tied up by the chains that the Lilliputians placed around to restrain him, the Central Bank needs to be increasingly tied by the law and by adequate mechanisms of accountability.[4] Back in 1992 I developed the model of 'accountable independence' of Central Banks, to explain why independence and accountability go hand in hand.[5] Independence without accountability would be like freedom without responsibility. How can giving freedom (i.e. independence) to unelected officials be reconciled with a society remaining democratic? The answer is: through accountability. With power comes responsibility; with extended powers there should be commensurate measures of accountability. This was one of the main conclusions and recommendations of the House of Lords Report 'Making an independent Bank of England work better' in which I had the privilege of acting as Specialist Adviser.[6] Accountability and transparency are essential to reconnect normative legitimacy with societal legitimacy.[7] Leaving aside the early history of Central Banking,[8] a consensus developed in the 1990s arguing that Central Banks should be independent from political instruction in order to maintain price stability. This was based on the one hand on the theory of time inconsistency, political business cycles (as well as rational expectations) and vertical Philipps curve and on the other hand on the empirical evidence provided by inflation targeting in New Zealand, as well as the Bundesbank record.[9] This consensus influenced a wave of legislation around the world granting independence to the

[4] I have dealt with the concept of central bank accountability extensively in my publication, see Lastra (n 2). See also Rosa M Lastra, *Legal Foundations of International Monetary Stability* (OUP, 2006) ch. 2 and ch. 7 and Rosa M Lastra, *International Financial and Monetary Law* (OUP 2015), ch. 2 and ch. 7; Rosa M Lastra and Heba Shams, 'Public Accountability in the Financial Sector' in Eilis Ferrán and Charles A E Goodhart (eds), *Regulating Financial Services and Markets in the 21st Century* (Hart Publishing 2001), 165–188; Rosa M Lastra and Geoffrey P Miller, 'Central Bank Independence in Ordinary and Extraordinary Times' in Jan Kleineman (ed.), *Central Bank Independence. The Economic Foundations, the Constitutional Implications and Democratic Accountability* (The Hague: Kluwer Law International 2001), 31–50; Rosa M Lastra and Fabian Amtenbrink 'Securing Democratic Accountability of Financial Regulatory Agencies – A Theoretical Framework' in Richard V de Mulder (ed.) *Mitigating Risk in the Context of Safety and Security. How Relevant is a Rational Approach?* (Rotterdam: Erasmus School of Law & Research School for Safety and Security (OMV) 2008), 115–132; Rosa M Lastra and Luis Garicano 'Towards a new Architecture for Financial Stability: Seven Principles' (2010) 13 Journal of International Economic Law, 597; Rosa M Lastra and Charles A E Goodhart, 'Populism and Central Bank Independence' (2017) 29 Open Economies Review 49.

[5] Lastra (n 2).

[6] See House of Lords Report, Economic Affairs Committee, 'Making an Independent Bank of England Work Better' (House of Lords 2023) <https://publications.parliament.uk/pa/ld5804/ldselect/ldeconaf/10/1002.htm>.

[7] See Amaryllis Verhoeven, *The European Union in Search of a Democratic and Constitutional Theory* (The Hague: Kluwer Law International 2002) 10–11.

[8] See Lastra (1996) (n 2) appendix and ch 1.

[9] See Lastra (1996) (n 2) ch 1.

Central Bank. Thus, a narrow 'Central Banking model' in line with the Tinbergen rule[10] with one agency (the Central Bank), one primary objective (price stability) and one main instrument (interest rate policy) became embedded in Central Bank laws around the world, including the Maastricht Treaty. It is important to put independence in context. Most Central Banks do not have goal independence. The goal or goals are set in the law (statute, Treaty, constitutions). The European Central Bank (ECB) has only one primary objective: price stability and a range of secondary objectives. The Bank of England has price stability and financial stability as primary objectives and other secondary objectives. The US Federal Reserve System has a 'dual mandate' of price stability and employment. Independence thus constitutes an instrument in the pursuit of price stability (or other statutory objectives delegated to the Central Bank).[11]

3. WIDENING OF THE MANDATE

The last 15 years have witnessed a change in the understanding of Central Banks, bringing new objectives, tasks and an expanded range of instruments and, consequently, new challenges. A new mode or model of Central Banking is emerging; yet, it is not crystallized.[12] The consensus around the narrow *model* or *mode* of Central Banking started to splinter with the Global Financial Crisis (GFC) – a Black swan event in the words of Nassim Taleb[13] – that led to a renewed emphasis on financial stability and triggered legislative changes that expanded the role of Central Banks around the world in the areas of macro and micro prudential supervision and resolution. The law relating to the supervisory role of central banks diverges across jurisdictions and changes over time, with the pendulum shifting, bringing supervision in and out of the central bank depending on economic and political circumstances. Post GFC the pendulum has now shifted toward keeping supervision in, with the Bank of England being the most significant example given the range and scope of its responsibilities in the areas of micro and macro prudential supervision, supervision of Financial Markets Infrastructures (FMIs) and resolution. Price stability has been the primary objective of the Bank of England since 1998 according to Section 11 of the Bank of England Act 1998. Financial stability was added as an objective of the Bank in 2013, according to Section 2A of the Bank of England Act 1998, as amended. In the case of the US Federal Reserve System, although the Fed has always been in charge of supervising depository institutions, its role in the pursuit of financial stability is implied and the role of macro-prudential policy is entrusted to the Financial Stability Oversight Council, set up by the Dodd–Frank Act 2010.[14] In the case of the ECB, the activation of Article 127 (6) of the Treaty for the Functioning of the European Union (TFEU)[15]

---

10 Jan Tinbergen, *On the Theory of Economic Policy* (New York: North-Holland 1952); and Jan Tinbergen, *Economic Policy: Principles and Design* (New York: North-Holland 1956).

11 Rosa M Lastra and Christina Skinner, 'Sustainable Central Banking' (2023) 63 Virginia Journal of International Law 397.

12 Lastra and Goodhart (n 2).

13 Nassim N Taleb, *The Black Swan: The Impact of the Highly Improbable* (Random House 2007).

14 Dodd–Frank Wall Street Reform and Consumer Protection Act, Pub. L. No. 111–203 (2010).

15 See Rosa M Lastra and Georgios Psaroudakis, 'Prudential supervisory tasks (art. 127(6) TFEU, monetary policy vs. prudential supervision). Kissing awake the Sleeping Beauty provision'

transferred responsibility for the micro-prudential supervision of significant credit institutions from the national competent authorities to the ECB/Single Supervisory Mechanism (SSM) via the Single Supervisory Mechanism Regulation, which was adopted in 2013 and entered into force in November 2014.[16]

Monetary independence is not the same as supervisory independence (nor is monetary accountability the same as supervisory accountability) given the closer links with the political authorities that central banks have in the management of banking and financial crises (and the potential role of the Government in the resolution of a crisis if it is called to provide guarantees or to recapitalize troubled institutions).[17]

The role of Central Banks as crisis managers further expanded and acquired new contours in the context of the COVID crisis, which led to very close cooperation between the Central Banks and the fiscal authorities and to further expansion of quantitative easing (QE). Furlough schemes and fiscal largesse together with loose monetary policy were an extraordinary response to an extraordinary set of circumstances. Yet the challenge is how to move back from the extraordinary to the ordinary, from the exceptional to the regular, in particular when the solutions to the problems implied a large debt overhang, with acute problems for many developing countries currently experiencing sovereign debt problems. The cooperation and consistency between fiscal and monetary policy has now been questioned in the context of desired 'region of stability', that is 'the region that maps the constellation of the two policies that foster sustainable macroeconomic and financial stability, keeping the inevitable tensions between the policies manageable'.[18] The image of 'steering the boat through the storm' is one that can be applied to Central Banking in their expanded crisis management mode.

> It could be said that crisis management involves both good steering of the boat through the storm as well as any due diligence or preventive measures, aimed at devising mechanisms that can strengthen or defend the boat against any negative contingencies.[19]

In a study coordinated by Caroline Kleiner (of which I was part) for the 150th anniversary of the establishment of the International Law Association we considered the following challenges in particular:[20]

---

in Fabian Amtenbrink and Christoph Hermann (eds) *Handbook on European Monetary Union* (Oxford University Press 2020).

16 Council Regulation (EU) No 1024/2013 of 15 October 2013 conferring specific tasks on the European Central Bank concerning policies relating to the prudential supervision of credit institutions OJ L 287/63.

17 On the differences between monetary and supervisory independence and corresponding accountability, see Lastra (n 2), ch 2 of both the first and second edition of my OUP treatises on *Legal Foundations of International Monetary Stability* and *International Financial and Monetary Law*.

18 See BIS, BIS Annual Economic Report 2023 (*BIS*, 2023) <https://www.bis.org/publ/arpdf/ar2023e.htm> accessed 20 December 2023.

19 Rosa M Lastra, 'Central Banks as Lenders of Last Resort: Lessons from the Asian Contagion' (1999) 7 Journal of Financial Regulation and Compliance 234.

20 Caroline Kleiner and others, 'International Financial Law in the Next Decades' (ILA/ADI Paris 2023) Whitepaper 11 <https://www.ilaparis2023.org/wp-content/uploads/2023/08/ADI-ILA-finances-internationales-V02-EN.pdf>, 48–49.

(1) Climate Change – the protection of the environment and reduction of carbon emissions are the main concerns for the financial industry and governments. In order to address those issues, it has been recognized that massive investments will need to be made to reduce carbon emissions and to achieve the goals defined in the Paris Agreement and many of the signatories will have difficulties in providing those investments.
(2) Wave of new rules – in addition to the need for investments to tackle climate change, new rules need to be created, considering this new era of sustainability. The principal rules are issued and, most of the times, this leads to the creation of derivatives rules and policies.
(3) Lack of common nomenclatures – because of the different jurisdictions and laws, it has been difficult to define common grounds in relation to environmental, social, governance (ESG) terminology that is accepted by every government. The same struggle is seen when trying to set the standards for climate disclosure.[21]
(4) The existence of non-binding initiatives – one of the positive actions from the Central Banks in tackling climate change is the creation of initiatives, such as the Network for Greening the Financial System (NGFS), that promote the role of the financial system in dealing with the ESG agenda.
(5) Central Banks are also recognizing that risks related to climate change are relevant factors to consider in their supervisory function and are considering it essential to include climate risks factors into the financial risks categories and stress tests.
(6) Instruments such as green bonds, green loans and derivatives based on sustainability factors are becoming more popular within the financial sector. Those instruments are created focusing on monitoring compliance with ESG goals and end up fostering practices that are climate oriented.[22]

With regard to climate change, Mark Carney referred it as the 'tragedy on the horizon' in a speech in 2015, lamenting that it fell outside 'the horizon of technocratic authorities, like Central Banks, who are bound by their mandates'.[23] That speech also established the nomenclature to refer to climate-related risks: physical risk, transition risk and liability risk. These categories together with mitigation and adaptation strategies form the template under which Central Banks look at climate risk.[24]

As discussed in the paper on *Sustainable Central Banking* co-authored with Christina Skinner, the question arises: what should the role of Central Banks in climate change be? What is the best distribution of tasks between political authorities (in charge of taxation,

---

21 Lastra and Skinner (n 11) 407.

22 Kleiner (n 20) 48–56.

23 Mark Carney, Address at the Bank of England: Breaking the Tragedy of the Horizon – Climate Change and Financial Stability (29 September 2015), <https://www.bankofengland.co.uk/-/media/boe/files/speech/2015/breaking-the-tragedy-of-the-horizon-climate-change-and-financial-stability.pdf?la=en&hash=7C67E785651862457D99511147C7424FF5EA0C1A>.

24 See Frank Elderson, Chair, Cent. Banks & Supervisors Network for Greening the Fin. Sys., Member, Exec. Bd. of the ECB & Vice-Chair, Supervisory Bd. of the ECB, The Embrace of the Horizon: Forcefully Moving with the Changing Tide for Climate Action in Financial Sector Policies (June 3, 2021), <https://www.ecb.europa.eu/press/key/date/2021/html/ecb.sp210603~2da57607e2.en.html>.

expenditure, legislation and regulation) and depoliticized independent agencies with narrower mandates and more limited tools? And how to guard against the dangers of politicization and conflicting mandates? The answer varies depending on the different statutory mandates of Central Banks. Indeed we examine in our paper the divergent approaches taken by the US Federal Reserve System (rather skeptical with the Fed Chair Jay Powell stating that it is not the role of the Fed to be a climate fighter[25]) and the more sympathetic approaches adopted by the European Central Bank and the Bank of England.[26]

What is clear is that a broader Central Banking agenda is more susceptible to politicization. Otmar Issing told the Economic Affairs Committee during the House of Lords QE inquiry that 'Central Banks have come closer to political decisions during the financial crisis and now in the context of the pandemic'.[27] The return of inflation in 2021 signified a readjustment of the broadened mode or model of central banking, given that the pursuit of different objectives can create tensions or inconsistencies between goals and threaten their independence and credibility in the pursuit of price stability. For example, in the UK, the support by the Financial Policy Committee of the Bank of England of the pension fund industry, in response to the dysfunction in the gilt market following the mini-Budget announced by the then Chancellor Kwasi Kwarteng in September 2022, was the first time that the Bank had intervened via QE in the financial markets for reasons of financial stability. The Bank was purchasing gilts at the same time as the Monetary Policy Committee was setting out the importance of Quantitative Tightening on the monetary policy side for price stability considerations.[28]

---

[25] See Colby Smith and Delphine Strauss, 'Fed will not Become a "Climate Policymaker", says Jay Powell', *Financial Times* (Washington and London, 10 January 2023) <https://www.ft.com/content/6abb5562-59a0-49a7-8cc0-8fb48e5d6fe9> accessed 20 December 2023.

[26] Lastra and Skinner (n 11) 12. I have also discussed the need for adequate accountability in greening central banking, with emphasis on the ECB in an article co-authored with Sara Dietz, entitled 'Accountability of Greening the ECB' forthcoming in the Maastricht Journal of European and Comparative Law (2024).

[27] See House of Lords Economic Affairs Committee, 'Quantitative Easing: A Dangerous Addiction?' (Authority of the House of Lords, 2021) <https://committees.parliament.uk/publications/6725/documents/71894/default/>.

[28] See the Report of the House of Commons Treasury Select Committee of January 2024 on Quantitative Tightening <https://committees.parliament.uk/publications/43233/documents/215145/default/> stating at §52: 'For most of the history of QE this has been profitable for the Treasury, but from 2022 the Bank began incurring losses (QT)' and then at §62: 'Annual losses in each of 2023 and 2024 will amount to £40 billion, eroding the cumulative £124 billion positive cashflow that was generated up until September 2022. Subsequent further losses bring the current "highly uncertain" estimate of the total cumulative lifetime net present value of QE cashflows to between −£50 billion and −£130 billion' <https://committees.parliament.uk/committee/158/treasury-committee/news/199797/bank-of-england-has-taken-a-leap-in-the-dark-on-quantitative-tightening-treasury-committee-concludes/>.

4. DIGITALIZATION HAS REACHED THE SHORES OF CENTRAL BANKING[29]

While unbacked cryptocurrencies and 'stablecoins' are examples of private digital money (together with 'tokenized deposits' or commercial bank digital money), central bank digital currencies (CBDCs) are a manifestation of the power of the state in the provision or issuance of money.[30] Notwithstanding the private or the public origin of money, money is or becomes a public good. This means that the public authorities should have a role both in the issuance of public digital money, CBDCs, and – as ultimate guarantors – in the regulation and supervision of private digital money and the payment systems associated with it. The SVB (Silicon Valley Bank) crisis and subsequent saga of banking troubles in 2023 evidence that 'there are few libertarians in a financial foxhole'.[31] Charles Goodhart explains in his book 'The Evolution of Central Banks' (1988) how competing banks had a natural tendency to centralize reserves and how this competition and centralization of reserves led to the emergence of a Central Bank as a non-competitive, non-profit maximizing institution. Arguably, in the FinTech universe, we can already observe a gravitation toward the centre in the concept of stablecoins, which gravitate around fiat currency and safe assets. The legal frameworks of money and Central Banking around the world were drafted well before the digital revolution. Central Bank laws therefore speak about coins, banknotes and reserves, but not of digital currencies, tokens or ledger systems. In a paper with Jason Allen entitled *Lex Chryptographia Financiera*[32] we confront some of these issues and we link the idea of 'code as law' (borrowing from Lawrence Lessig's seminal contribution[33] – the concept of embedded norms) with the medieval *lex mercatoria* (a non-state legal system that evolved within trading networks across the complex, fragmented, political geography of medieval Europe). Central Banks were skeptical of virtual currencies till Libra arrived. Central Banks had watched the arrival of Bitcoin as a niche experiment for exoteric libertarian techno aficionados in California or, worse, for money launderers around the world; in a word they had watched the advent of virtual currencies not with a great deal of sympathy, but not with a great deal of concern either. They did not feel threatened. However, the announcement by Meta/Facebook (with 2.9 billion users) of a digital currency: Libra (which then became Diem and was ultimately discarded in 2022) was a turning point. Central Banks, which were reluctantly dragged into the digital provision of money, started

---

[29] See Rosa M Lastra, 'En Defensa del Dinero Digital' (2022) 89 El Trimestre Económico 1007. See the keynote speeches on the subject of public digital money (CBDCs) delivered in 2022 in Edinburgh University at the School event page and <https://media.ed.ac.uk/media/t/1_blfdmpwv>, in the Dominican Republic and in the Erasmus University in Rotterdam <https://www.eur.nl/en/ese/events/witteveen-lecture-keynote-rosa-lastra-2022-11-16>.

[30] See generally Rosa M Lastra, ch 1 of *International Financial and Monetary Law* (3rd edition, OUP, forthcoming). See also Rosa M Lastra, 'En Defensa del Dinero Digital' (2022) 89 El Trimestre Económico, 1007.

[31] See John Thornhill, 'SVB Shows There are Few Libertarians in a Financial Foxhole' *Financial Times* (13 March 2023).

[32] See Rosa M Lastra and Jason Allen, 'Lex Financiera Cryptographia' in William Blair, Christos Gortsos and Chiara Ziliolo (eds), *International Monetary and Banking Law post Covid-19* (OUP 2023).

[33] Lawrence Lessig, *Code and Other Laws of Cyberspace* (Basic Books 1999).

experiencing some form of FOMO (fear of missing out, like teenagers …). Although they do not want to let the system of *fiat money*, independent Central Banks pursuing a monetary policy based on the reserves of the banking system and financial stability, derail because of private virtual currencies and shadow payments,[34] they are aware that digitalization has indeed reached the shores of Central Banking. China and Sweden went first with their proposals and they are at an advanced stage of development. Around 90 countries are exploring the introduction of CBDCs according to the Atlantic Council 'Central Bank Digital Currency Tracker'.[35] Successful launches include the Bahamas' Sand Dollar, Nigeria's e-Naira and Cambodian Bakong. The ECB published in October 2020 a report on the digital euro and the European Commission launched on 5 April 2022 a targeted consultation on the introduction of a digital euro[36] and on 28 June 2023 the Commission unveiled a comprehensive legislative package on the potential establishment of the digital euro. This 'single currency package' comprises a Proposal for a Regulation on the establishment of the digital euro (based on art. 133 TFEU),[37] a Proposal for a regulation on the legal tender of euro banknotes and coins (based on art. 133 TFEU) and a Proposal for a Regulation on the provision of digital euro services by payment services providers incorporated in Member States whose currency is not the euro (based on art. 114 TFEU).[38]

On 31 October 2023[39] the ECB issued an opinion on the digital euro where it emphasizes that the proposed regulations must respect the principle of central bank independence enshrined in Article 130 TFEU and other Treaty provision. After a two-year investigation phase, the ECB's Governing Council decided to proceed to the preparation phase, starting on 1 November 2023. The preparation phase will comprise two stages: the first stage will last for two years. Based on the results of the first stage (in terms of the design of the digital euro and developments in the legislative process), the Governing Council will then decide whether to move to a second

---

[34] See, e.g. Dan Awrey and Kristin van Zwieten, 'The Shadow Payment System' (2018) 43 *Journal of Corporation Law* 775; Daniela Gabor and Jakob Vestergard, 'Towards a Theory of Shadow Money', Institute for New Economic Thinking (14 April 2016) <https://www.ineteconomics.org/perspectives/blog/towards-a-theory-of-shadow-money/> accessed 20 November 2023. See also Simon Gleeson, *The Legal Concept of Money* (OUP 2018), ch 1.

[35] The Atlantic Council 'Central Bank Digital Currency Tracker' is available at <https://www.atlanticcouncil.org/cbdctracker>.

[36] European Commission, 'Targeted Consultation on a Digital Euro' (European Commission) <https://ec.europa.eu/info/consultations/finance-2022-digital-euro_en> accessed 23 December 2023.

[37] Article 133: Without prejudice to the powers of the European Central Bank, the European Parliament and the Council, acting in accordance with the ordinary legislative procedure, shall lay down the measures necessary for the use of the euro as the single currency. Such measures shall be adopted after consultation of the European Central Bank.

[38] Article 114 (1): The European Parliament and the Council shall, acting in accordance with the ordinary legislative procedure and after consulting the Economic and Social Committee, adopt the measures for the approximation of the provisions laid down by law, regulation or administrative action in Member States which have as their object the establishment and functioning of the internal market.

[39] ECB, 'Opinion of the European Central Bank of 31 October 2023 on the digital euro (CON/2023/34)' (ECB, 2023) <https://www.ecb.europa.eu/pub/pdf/legal/ecb.leg_con_2023_34.en.pdf> accessed 23 December 2023.

stage, and define its scope and duration. As stated in the ECB website,[40] the preparation phase will allow extensive analysis, testing, experimentation and stakeholder consultation to take place, ensuring that the digital euro meets the highest standards of quality, security and usability. The start of the preparation phase marks a significant step, but it does not pre-empt any decision by the Governing Council on the issuance of a digital euro. That decision can only be considered after the relevant legislation has been adopted. In the UK, the Bank of England and His Majesty's Treasury (HMT) announced the creation of a taskforce in 2021 to explore CBDCs, though the House of Lords published a sceptical report entitled: 'Central Bank Digital Currencies: A Solution in Search of a Problem?'[41] in January 2022, raising a number of important issues that ought to be debated before the adoption of a CBDC. In April 2022, the UK government announced plans that would recognize stablecoins as a valid form of payment, as part of a wider agenda to make Britain a global hub for cryptoasset technology and investment.[42] In February 2023 HMT and the Bank of England published the Digital Pound Consultation Paper[43] on the potential adoption of a digital pound. This was accompanied by a Technology Working Paper[44] published by the Bank of England. On 25 January 2024 the Bank of England and HMT published their response to the consultation on a digital pound that was launched in February 2023.[45] The Financial Markets and Services Act 2023, which received Royal Assent on 29 June, classifies crypto as a regulated financial activity and stablecoins as a means of payment under existing laws. The Act also introduces new secondary objectives for the Financial Conduct Authority and the Prudential Regulation Authority – to facilitate the growth and international competitiveness of the UK economy. The Act is central to the Government's vision to grow the economy and create an open, sustainable, and technologically advanced financial services sector. In the US in early 2022 the Federal Reserve System (a reluctant latecomer when it comes to CBDCs) also published a report on the US dollar in the digital age, and in March 2022, US President Biden signed an executive order requiring the government to assess the risks and benefits of creating, evidencing the increasing pressure from politicians to regulatory agencies to modernize the financial regulatory framework and make it fit for the

---

40 ECB, 'Eurosystem Proceeds to Next Phase of Digital Euro Project' <https://www.ecb.europa.eu/press/pr/date/2023/html/ecb.pr231018~111a014ae7.en.html> accessed 23 December 2023.

41 See Economic Affairs Committee, 'Central Bank Digital Currencies: A Solution in Search of a Problem?' (Economic Affairs Committee, 13 January 2022) <https://publications.parliament.uk/pa/ld5802/ldselect/ldeconaf/131/131.pdf> accessed 23 December 2023.

42 See HM Treasury, 'Government Sets Out Plan to Make UK a Global Cryptoasset Technology Hub' (HM Treasury 2022) <https://www.gov.uk/government/news/government-sets-out-plan-to-make-uk-a-global-cryptoasset-technology-hub> accessed 23 December 2023.

43 See Bank of England, 'Consultation Paper – The Digital Pound: A New Form of Money for Households and Businesses?' (Bank of England 2023) <https://www.bankofengland.co.uk/paper/2023/the-digital-pound-consultation-paper> accessed 23 December 2023.

44 See Bank of England, 'The Digital Pound: Technology Working Paper' (Bank of England 2023) <https://www.bankofengland.co.uk/paper/2023/the-digital-pound-technology-working-paper> accessed 23 December 2023. See also Bank of England, 'The Digital Pound' (Bank of England) <https://www.bankofengland.co.uk/the-digital-pound> accessed 23 December 2023.

45 See Bank of England, 'Bank of England and HM Treasury Respond to Digital Pound Consultation' (Bank of England, 2024) <https://www.bankofengland.co.uk/news/2024/january/boe-hmt-respond-to-digital-pound-consultation> accessed 23 December 2023.

digital and decentralized finance age.[46] In 2023 two stablecoin draft bills were published: the Democratic Compromise Draft – 'To provide requirements for payment stablecoin issuers, research on a digital dollar, and for other purposes'[47] – and the Republicans' bill – 'To provide for the regulation of payment stablecoins, and for other purposes'.[48]

Alhough in this contribution I do not discuss private digital money in any depth, it is important to realize that the name stablecoin (which borrows from the functions of money as store of value) is a bit of a misnomer. This was evidenced by the events in 2022 (Terra/Luna, FTX) which tarnished the image of crypto markets. Suffice is to say that stablecoins are cryptocurrencies that peg their market value to some external reference for the purpose of maintaining stability over time, and that despite their common name, stablecoins have different operational structures and reserve compositions.[49] Generally, stablecoins are backed by either a fiat currency like the US Dollar, or a basket of commodities; some are backed only by another crypto-token (often issued by the same or a related entity) in ratios controlled by an algorithm. Of course, 'digital money' has been with us for some time since bank deposits are accounted for and transferred using online systems. However, the competition between public virtual currencies (CBDCs) and private virtual currencies (such as Bitcoin or stablecoins) adds a new dimension to the old debate between the state theory of money and societal theories of money[50] as well as the notion of sovereignty.[51]

---

46 Decentralized finance aims to replicate the dynamics of the provision of financial products and services but in a decentralized and fully automated environment, thus removing the need for intermediaries.

47 Ranking Member Waters. See <https://docs.house.gov/meetings/BA/BA21/20230518/115973/BILLS-118pih-Toprovidefortheregulationofpaymentstablecoinsandforotherpurposes.pdf> accessed 23 December 2023.

48 Chairman McHenry. See <https://docs.house.gov/meetings/BA/BA21/20230518/115973/BILLS-118pih-Thediscussiondraftdefinesp.pdf> accessed 23 December 2023.

49 International Monetary Fund (IMF), *Global Financial Stability Report* (IMF October 2021).

50 See Rosa M Lastra, 'Monetary Sovereignty', ch 2 of *International Financial and Monetary Law* (3rd edn, OUP, forthcoming). In that chapter I discuss the traditional and modern versions of sovereignty (including cyber sovereignty). The societal theories of money, anchored in Savigny and influencing a number of scholars from Nussbaum to Morgan Ricks (and many others), argue that it is not the state but ultimately society and custom that decided what money is.

51 ibid. For recent thoughts on monetary sovereignty see Katharina Pistor, 'From Territorial to Monetary Sovereignty' (2018) 18 Theoretical Inquiries in Law 491. Pistor argues that control over money and finance determines *actual* sovereignty and that the system is hierarchical. She writes: 'Countries that adopt a foreign currency (by dollarizing their economies) or join forces with others to adopt a new, common, currency (the euro) give up more than control over interest rate policy. They also relinquish their ability to address financial crises that are endogenous to a financial system built on credit' (page 3). And she adds: 'At the heart of the problem lies the fact that the world has embraced the free flow of capital but has not created mechanisms for sharing the costs of crises that will inevitably erupt from time to time' (page 10). See also Christine Desan, 'Strange New Music: The Monetary Composition Made by the Enlightenment Quartet' (2018) Harvard Public Law Working Paper No. 18-49. Desan argues that modern money worked synergistically with circulating public debt, capital markets and commercial banking and that together these four innovations (the quartet) made the monetary composition of the modern world. At page 30 she notes: 'Circulating public debt became an indispensable instrument of sovereignty'.

4.1 Legal Authority and Competence to Issue CBDCs

The limits or contours of the legal concept of money delineate regulatory perimeters. For example, in 2018 the then President of the ECB Mario Draghi stated his position on the classification of 'virtual currencies'. An Estonian proposal for a CBDC ('Estcoin') had been deemed to be a proposal for a new form of 'money' thereby inconsistent with Article 128 of the Treaty on the Functioning of the European Union.[52] Privately issued virtual currencies were dismissed as money candidates and were held to fall outside the oversight remit of the ECB. In consequence, regulation occurred at the national level, leading to a proliferation of regulations with the potential for undesirable regulatory arbitrage.[53] However the adoption of the EU Regulation on Markets in Crypto-assets (MICA) in May 2023 establishes a harmonized regulatory framework and a common supervisory architecture to both issuers and providers of crypto-asset services.[54]

A key question in the adoption of public digital money concerns the legal mandate to issue CBDCs. Broadly speaking, the provisions authorizing a Central Bank to issue notes can provide a legal basis for token-based CBDC and the provisions in Central Bank laws to open accounts at the Central Bank for their counterparties (which are currently exclusively commercial banks) can serve as a legal basis regard for account-based CBDCs. Note issue is considered to be part of the exclusive competence of the European Union in the area of

---

[52] See Rosa M Lastra and Jason Allen, 'Virtual Currencies in the Eurosystem: Challenges Ahead' (2019) 53 The International Lawyer 177.

[53] ibid.

[54] Council Regulation (EU) 2023/1114 of 31 May 2023 on markets in crypto-assets, and amending Regulations (EU) No 1093/2010 and (EU) No 1095/2010 and Directives 2013/36/EU and (EU) 2019/1937 [2023] OJ L 150/40 (MICA). MICA regulates crypto-assets, crypto-assets issuers and crypto-asset service providers under a harmonized regulatory framework. MICA however only covers some assets or tokens. The new rules cover issuers of utility tokens, asset referenced tokens and 'stablecoins'. It also covers service providers such as trading venues and the wallets where crypto-assets are held. MICA does not cover NFTs (non-fungible tokens) including digital art and collectibles nor crypto-assets representing services or physical assets that are unique and non-fungible, such as product guarantees or real estate nor DeFi (decentralized finance). MICA does not apply to CBDCs. Digital assets issued by Central Banks acting in their monetary authority capacity, including Central Bank money in digital form, or crypto-assets issued by other public authorities, including central, regional and local administrations, should not be subject to the Union framework for markets in crypto-assets. Nor should related services provided by such Central Banks when acting in their monetary authority capacity or other public authorities be subject to that Union framework. MICA distinguishes between three types of crypto-assets governed under this regulation:

1. Crypto-Assets, other than asset-referenced tokens or e-money tokens (utility tokens). These are the tokens that do not constitute financial instruments nor stablecoins.
2. Asset-referenced tokens (ARTs). These are stablecoins that are pegged to a reference by using asset reserves, with a peg to more underlying assets. There are significant and non-significant issuers of ARTs, whereby the first are subject to additional comprehensive prudential requirements and to centralized supervision by the European Banking Authority.
3. E-Money tokens. These are tokenized bank deposits that have a hard peg with a single fiat money.

monetary policy for the Member States whose currency is the euro according to Article 3(1) TFEU and Article 128 TFEU, which provides a legal basis for the ECB and the national central banks to issue a digital euro in the form of a digital equivalent and complement to tangible cash. Interestingly the proposed Regulation[55] does not mention Article 17 of the ESCB statute, which deals with accounts with the ECB and the national central banks.[56]

4.2 Legal Tender and Design Issues

Legal tender status is the power to validly and definitely extinguish monetary obligations which must be accepted by the state as well as by all private individuals as final settlement.[57] Features of legal tender are therefore: (1) mandatory acceptance, (2) at full face value, (3) with the power to discharge payment obligations. Whether it is legally possible to attribute legal tender status to a currency (defined as the power to extinguish monetary obligations which must be accepted by the state as well as by all private individuals as final settlement) depends also on the relevant enabling provisions. The EU Treaty is clear in this regard. Indeed, Article 128 TFEU introduces the concept of legal tender, although it does not elaborate on its scope and legal effects. The digital euro (if adopted according to the proposed Regulations) is to be granted legal tender status, which entails mandatory acceptance by payees, and this is confirmed by the legal tender proposed Regulation.[58] Article 4 of such Regulation says: 'the legal tender status of euro banknotes and coins shall entail their mandatory acceptance, at full face value, with the power to discharge from a payment obligation. In accordance with the mandatory acceptance of cash, the payee shall not refuse euro banknotes and/or coins tendered in payment to comply with that obligation'. Article 15 states: 'Euro banknotes and coins and the digital euro shall be convertible into each other at par'. 'A digital euro would provide an anchor of stability for our money in the digital age'.[59] According to the proposals, the digital euro shall be a liability of the central bank[60] which will exist as a complement to existing notes

---

55 Commission, Proposal for a Regulation on the establishment of the digital euro COM(2023) 369 final.

56 Rosa M Lastra and Sara Dietz, 'Central Bank Digital Currencies' (2021) Butterworth Journal of International Banking and Financial Law 700.

57 Interestingly, the adoption of Bitcoin (a private currency) in El Salvador as legal tender raises issues about the confluence between the private and the public domain in the provision of money. It also provides a new gloss to the concept, even though 'cryptoization' is unlikely to beat dollarization (at least for the time being).

58 Commission, Proposal for a Regulation on the legal tender of euro banknotes and coins, COM (2023) 364 final.

59 ECB, 'Digital Euro' (ECB) <https://www.ecb.europa.eu/paym/digital_euro/html/index.en.html> accessed 23 January 2024.

60 In Michael Kumhof and others, 'Central Bank Money: Liability, Asset, or Equity of the Nation?' (2020) Cornell Legal Studies Research Paper 20, we question the characterization of money as a liability of the Central Bank and suggest that a different interpretation is needed (that of money as 'social equity'). The widespread treatment of Central Bank Money (CBM) as a Central Bank liability goes back to the gold standard, and uses analogies with commercial bank balance sheets. However, CBM is *sui generis* and legally not comparable with commercial bank money. In modern economies, CBM holders cannot demand repayment of CBM in anything other than CBM. CBM is not an asset of Central Banks either, and it is not Central Bank shareholder equity because

and reserves. The digital euro shall be a retail CBDC (not wholesale) and will not bear interest. By going for a retail CBDC, the EU takes a different path from other jurisdictions. The Swiss National Bank, for example is interested in a wholesale CBDC that could be used to facilitate interbank settlements.

A controversial issue in the proposed regulation for the establishment of a digital euro is that of holding limits. Article 16[61] introduces limits on the use of the digital euro as a store of value, including holding limits. The reason for doing this is financial stability in line with Article 127 (5) TFEU since it is feared that an unrestricted use of digital euro could have adverse effects on credit provision to the economy by credit institutions. This is the fear of 'disintermediation', given that some banks have expressed the worry that too attractive a digital euro could lead savers to withdraw their money from bank deposits and store it in safer digital euro accounts backed by the Central Bank. If such move happened too quickly, this could pose a risk to financial stability in the euro area. Depending on their design, CBDCs can alter the patterns of access to credit and payment intermediation offered by the formal regulated commercial banking sector and, in turn, affect its profitability. If every citizen can open an account with the Central Bank and make transfers of Central Bank money via an electronic wallet and a token directly with each other without intermediaries, banks could lose their role as gateways to high powered money. And the potentially unlimited, easy access to Central Bank money could backfire in the case of a 'digital run'.[62]

However, also during normal times, disintermediation could have negative side effects for financial stability and monetary policy. If commercial banks are faced with the Central Bank as a competitor providing retail CBDC, their business vis-à-vis private retail customers might decline, shifting their focus toward the wholesale side. There is also the concern about excessive power – and consequently the need for adequate mechanisms of accountability. With expanded mandates we need commensurate measures of accountability. As stated above, this legitimizes the existence and operations of Central Banks as independent entities.

---

it does not confer the same ownership rights as regular shareholder equity. Based on comparisons across a number of legal characteristics of financial instruments, we suggest that an appropriate characterization of CBM is as 'social equity' that confers rights of participation in the economy's payment system and thereby its economy.

[61] Commission, Proposal for a Regulation on the establishment of the digital euro COM(2023) 369 final. In terms of distribution 'All credit institutions providing payment account services would be required to provide basic digital euro payment services upon request of their clients'. The Commission wants to ensure that 'basic digital euro services' are 'offered for free to natural persons', even if they are not consumers of credit institutions. In addition, public institutions like postal offices or local and regional authorities would be able to distribute the digital euro, helping to make its use independent from banks. Payment services providers would also have to offer the transactions free of charge for natural persons. There are provisions on interoperability and integration in the European Digital Identity Wallets, and of course, on anti-money laundering and data protection.

[62] See Gillian Tett, 'Wake up to the Danger of Digital Bank Runs' *Financial Times* (20 April 2023). 'When SVB failed it was dubbed the first "Twitter-fuelled bank run" by Patrick McHenry, House Financial Services Committee chair.'

5. CONCLUSION

This chapter examined selected aspects of law related to the objectives, functions and status of Central Banks in light of the overarching theme of the book: convergence or divergence in financial regulation. The chapter traced the evolution from a narrow model or mode of Central Banking focused on keeping inflation under control to a broader model or mode of Central Banking. Central banks have become 'crisis managers' in the context of the global financial crisis, the COVID-19 pandemic and now even climate change and sustainability in general. With expanded mandates, independent Central Banks need commensurate measures of accountability. The chapter also explored succinctly some issues concerning the digitalization of money with the advent of central bank digital currencies and how traditional legal categories, such as legal tender, are adapting to the digital space. Money is a public good and this justifies the public ordering of the monetary and payment system via supervision and regulation.

Postscript: the appointment of Donald Trump as 47th US President may unleash a new era in the development of private digital money.

PART IV

NEW FRONTIERS IN FINANCIAL REGULATION

18. Sustainability and securities market regulation

Youcef Rahmani

1. INTRODUCTION

The term 'sustainability' has witnessed varied interpretations. At its core, it traces back to the globally recognized definition from the 1987 Brundtland Report,[1] which envisions sustainability as ensuring that current needs are met without jeopardizing the prospects of future generations. This report emphasized not just ecological sustainability but a broader concept encompassing economic and social pillars, striving for a holistic global balance. Within the financial realm, however, sustainability often narrows down to align with concepts such as corporate social responsibility (CSR), environmental, social and governance (ESG) factors, and climate-related risks and opportunities. The 2021 IPCC Reports underscored the intertwined nature of climate, ecosystems and human societies, reinforcing the importance of this broader perspective.[2] Nevertheless, jurisdictions like the European Union (EU) have made strides in proposing a mandatory sustainability disclosure framework that transcends mere climate disclosures.

Mandatory disclosure is generally costly for both companies and regulators. As a result, the case for mandatory disclosure is often justified on the grounds of enhanced social welfare. In other words, the private costs of producing and monitoring information disclosure must be exceeded by the social benefits that mandatory disclosure can generate for wider society. Disclosures are usually mandated under a securities law framework to enhance the price accuracy of securities, thereby ensuring a better allocation of resources and, ultimately, greater market efficiency.[3]

The aim of this chapter is to explore whether mandating sustainability disclosure under a securities law framework pursues traditional market efficiency objectives. The chapter is divided into three parts. Section 2 examines traditional securities law justifications for mandatory disclosure. Section 3 assesses, from a theoretical viewpoint, whether mandatory sustainability disclosure can be supported using these traditional justifications, or whether an additional, corporate accountability objective has been introduced. Section 4 reviews how the US, the UK and the EU, which have each mandated, or intend to mandate, some form of sustainability disclosure under a securities law framework, justify this mandate.

---

1 World Commission on Environment and Development, *Our Common Future* (Oxford University Press 1987).

2 See Intergovernmental Panel on Climate Change, Climate Change 2022 Mitigation of Climate Change – Summary for Policymakers, 2022.

3 Paul Davies and others, *Principles of Financial Regulation* (1st edn, Oxford University Press 2016), 165–167.

2. OBJECTIVES, RATIONALES AND COST–BENEFITS OF MANDATING DISCLOSURE IN SECURITIES MARKETS

When analysing mandatory disclosure on securities markets, we should distinguish between (i) the objectives of disclosure, irrespective of whether such disclosure is mandatory or voluntary, (ii) the rationales for mandating disclosure, which will depend on whether it is desirable for disclosure to happen and what market failures might exist to restrain voluntary disclosure and (iii) how to ensure mandating disclosure strikes the right balance between costs and benefits for market players, given these objectives and market failures.

We first turn to the objectives of disclosure on securities markets. One of the key functions of securities markets is to produce and aggregate information about the fundamental value of an asset.[4] A stock's price is said to be accurate when its market price approximates its fundamental value, understood as the sum of all discounted future cash flows of the stock.[5] The more prices are accurate, the more they are informative to traders regarding future expected cash flows of an asset, thereby ensuring an efficient allocation of capital to the most deserving assets. This makes informative prices a function of market efficiency and therefore socially desirable. Price accuracy critically depends on the amount and quality of information made available to the market in the first place. Therefore, the main objective of disclosure is to drive accurate prices. Two additional objectives are often brought up: investor protection and agency cost reduction.[6] The investor protection objective is in fact only a reformulation of the benefits of accurate prices, thanks to which all investors are in theory guaranteed assets at fair prices. In this sense, unsophisticated investors can simply free ride on the analysis of sophisticated investors driving price accuracy. Moreover, disclosure allows investors to more easily monitor corporate managers' behaviour, reducing overall agency costs. However, this objective is weak in that dishonest managers concealing their actions would have no incentive to disclose truthful information. In this sense, mandatory disclosure is a necessary but insufficient condition for meeting the agency cost objective.[7]

Satisfying the main objective of price accuracy depends on how costly information is to acquire, produce or verify. Information about an asset is usually either held by the owner of

---

4 While the efficient market hypothesis is a useful foundation for understanding price accuracy and the policy-driven role of disclosures in this chapter, it is essential to recognize its assumptions and limitations, especially in the context of sustainability. Behavioural finance research suggests that investor decisions often deviate from strict rationality, influenced by cognitive biases and emotions. While investor sustainability preferences are addressed later, this chapter does not address general issues in the dynamics of information dissemination, such as information overload. For more on the limits of disclosure using a behavioural finance approach, see Ben-shahar Omri and E. Schneider Carl, 'The Failure of Mandated Disclosure' (2011) 159 University of Pennsylvania Law Review 647.

5 Marcel Kahan, 'Securities Laws and the Social Costs of "Inaccurate" Stock Prices' (1992) 41 Duke Law Journal 977, 979.

6 Luca Enriques and Sergio Gilotta, 'Disclosure and Financial Market Regulation' in Niamh Moloney, Eilís Ferran and Jennifer Payne (eds), *The Oxford Handbook of Financial Regulation* (Oxford Handbooks in Law, 1st edn, Oxford University Press 2015).

7 ibid.

such asset or available through other means and costly to access for most traders.[8] The fact that information is a public good benefitting all traders once it is leaked through trading weakens incentives for traders to bear the costs of producing information. Traders might prefer to free ride on leaked information other traders have paid for. As such, if no one has an incentive to produce information, we are in the presence of a collective action problem. Furthermore, even if issuers disclose their information at no cost to attract capital, markets cannot verify whether this information is complete and accurate. This is an asymmetric information problem. These two forms of market failures affecting the voluntary production of information form the rationales for mandating disclosure.[9] It is because market participants are incapable of voluntarily producing the optimal amount of information to ensure price accuracy that regulators mandate information disclosure.

Understanding what an 'optimal' amount of information amounts to is key when discussing mandatory disclosure, as both over- and under-disclosure generate costs for markets. Under-disclosure leads to less accurate prices and occurs when information asymmetry and collective action problems hamper the production of information. However, over-disclosure is also costly for wider market participants. Mandatory disclosure produces important externalities for competitors and wider stakeholders. The issuer's competitors can use disclosed information to benchmark their performance against their peers, to the detriment of the disclosing entity's competitive edge. Wider stakeholders, such as employees or suppliers, also use disclosed information to obtain useful information allowing them to potentially bargain for respectively higher salaries or higher prices for supplied goods. In both cases, these externalities, known as 'interfirm costs', are redistributive in nature. This means that disclosure confers private benefits to competitors and stakeholders, to the issuer's detriment.[10] As such, over-disclose, i.e. disclosing information that is not necessary to achieve an acceptable level of price accuracy, would prove extremely costly and encourage companies to avoid disclosure triggers under securities laws. Companies would choose not to list their securities, entailing the end of public markets. Therefore, the supply of information is 'optimal' only if the private costs borne by companies for disclosing information are offset by wider societal gains, leading to a Pareto improvement of social welfare, usually expressed through market efficiency.[11]

To achieve such market efficiency, securities laws define a balance between over-disclosure and under-disclosure by assessing the trade-offs of each. Disclosure requirements are usually determined by entrusting the disclosing entity with the responsibility of determining the sig-

---

[8] Typically, so-called 'alternative datasets' providing insight into an asset's value, obtained through such means as satellite images or mass surveys, are costly to obtain, but are not automatically in the possession of the asset's owner by virtue of such ownership. This relates to the problem of aggregating and structuring relevant raw data points in the first place.

[9] Luca Enriques and Sergio Gilotta, 'Disclosure and Financial Market Regulation' in Niamh Moloney, Eilís Ferran and Jennifer Payne (eds), *The Oxford Handbook of Financial Regulation* (Oxford Handbooks in Law, 1st edn, Oxford University Press 2015).

[10] Merritt B Fox, 'Retaining Mandatory Securities Disclosure: Why Issuer Choice Is Not Investor Empowerment' (1999) 85 Virginia Law Review 1335, 1345–1346.

[11] Theoretically, the gains made by the market could be used to compensate the loss by companies, such that the net effect on companies is zero and the market is still better off. Under this assumption, Hicks efficiency and Pareto efficiency are the same, where distribution issues are solved through lump-sum taxation.

nificance of the information it holds, hinging on a legal definition of 'materiality'. In the US, materiality is characterized by case law and the Security and Exchange Commission (SEC) as information that would be deemed pivotal by a 'reasonable' investor when making investment choices.[12] In the EU, the Market Abuse Regulation adopts a materiality-based approach to general disclosure obligations for listed entities. Here, materiality is determined by whether the information would be likely to have a significant impact on the price of the financial instrument if it were made public. The focus in the EU is therefore on the impact of the information on the market price, rather than on the impact of the information on a reasonable investor's decision-making process, as per the US approach.[13]

Under both approaches to materiality, also known as single materiality, the notions of 'reasonable investor' and 'likelihood' of impact on prices are key. Until recently, a 'reasonable investor' was deemed as being mainly interested in the risk and return profiles of companies. Yet in the context of sustainability disclosures, if sustainability issues broadly are not considered financially relevant for companies, but still regarded as a topic of public interest, these sustainability issues could potentially start being considered as material under both US and EU conceptions.

3. THE OBJECTIVES OF SUSTAINABILITY DISCLOSURES IN SECURITIES MARKETS

Mandatory sustainability disclosure could pursue three general objectives. Firstly, if sustainability information is considered price-relevant, it would contribute to price accuracy on securities markets. Secondly, the disclosure of sustainability information allows investors to better match their funds with their personal sustainability preferences. Finally, sustainability disclosure enhances corporate accountability towards stakeholders in cases where sustainability-related impacts on wider society must be reported.[14] Where sustainability disclosure can be justified through enhancing price accuracy and investor protection objectives, the rationales for mandating sustainability disclosure would be the same as for mandating financial disclosure. Corporate accountability appears to be an additional objective that is not usually pursued under securities law regulations.

---

12 *Basic Inc. v. Levinson*, 485 U.S. 224, 231–232 (1988).

13 Council Regulation (EU) No 596/2014 of 16 April 2014 on market abuse (market abuse regulation) and repealing Directive 2003/6/EC of the European Parliament and of the Council and Commission Directives 2003/124/EC, 2003/125/EC and 2004/72/EC [2014] OJ L 173/1, arts 7(1)(a) and 17(1).

14 Company-level disclosures may also serve as a cornerstone for information production to satisfy the disclosure needs of other financial market participants. For instance, in the EU, CSRD disclosures equip other financial market participants with vital data to meet their SFDR and Taxonomy Regulation obligations. This transparency aims to ensure that capital is steered towards truly sustainable projects. The chapter does not explore the regulatory ecosystem's disclosure interdependency. However, this objective remains very similar to that of allowing investors to better match their funds with their personal preferences. It is simply once-removed, given that end investors will select funds based on SFDR information, which are themselves generally based on CSRD information.

3.1 Sustainability Disclosure to Enhance Price Accuracy on Financial Markets

The relationship between a firm's sustainability-related strategies and its value is still widely debated.[15] Theoretically, any sustainability-related issue relating to firm value must present either a risk or an opportunity for the firm to increase its revenues and/or reduce its costs. Therefore, insofar as a sustainability-related issue relates to costs that can be externalized by a firm with no further consequence (monetary or otherwise), such an issue will only be price relevant if there is a risk that such externalization could represent a cost at some point in time. This is typically the case when disclosing direct emissions, if there is legally no cost imposed on the company for emitting.

Despite the theory, empirical studies have struggled to establish any causal link between sustainability performance and firm performance.[16] At least two methodological approaches are possible to answer this question. One approach is to ask whether 'sustainable' firms create more value than 'non-sustainable' firms. This requires examination of whether a specific sustainability-related policy adopted by a firm can be causally linked to the firm's increase in profitability. Another approach is to ask whether 'sustainable' firms are priced higher by financial markets than 'non-sustainable' firms. This approach requires a definition of 'sustainable companies', before examining whether they are priced higher than their non-sustainable peers. The issue with this approach is that establishing any causal link between the sustainable element of these firms and the higher price is challenging. Because of this lack of robust empirical evidence linking sustainability performance and firm value, it is difficult to conduct a cost–benefit analysis to determine whether the costs of imposing sustainability disclosures on companies are offset by wider market efficiency gains, which remains the main justification for mandating disclosures under securities regulations.

Accordingly, many jurisdictions decided to focus on mandating the disclosure of one sub-topic within sustainability issues: climate risks. Climate risks are often deemed to be directly price-relevant owing to physical, transition, and liability risks. Physical risks, i.e. direct effects of climate-related events on company assets such as extreme weather events, rising sea levels and temperature changes, appear to be a straightforward case of material information. For instance, the knowledge that key internet infrastructure could be submerged in fifteen years is certainly financially material for investors, given that this represents a direct cost for the relevant internet infrastructure companies.[17] Transition risks represent an organization's failure to adapt to a changing regulatory environment linked to the economy's

---

[15] See Alex Edmans, *Grow the Pie: How Great Companies Deliver Both Purpose and Profit* (Cambridge University Press 2021); Bradford Cornell and Aswath Damodaran, 'Valuing ESG: Doing Good or Sounding Good?' (2020) NYU Stern School of Business.

[16] Mozaffar Khan, George Serafeim and Aaron Yoon, 'Corporate Sustainability: First Evidence on Materiality' (2016) 91 The Accounting Review 1697 is often cited as an authoritative empirical study assessing how industry-specific SASB classifications of materiality identify ESG information that is value-relevant and predictive of companies' future financial performance. However, this study was replicated and its methodology has been criticized as weak by Luca Berchicci and Andrew A King, 'Corporate Sustainability: A Model Uncertainty Analysis of Materiality' (2022) 7(2) Journal of Financial Reporting (Sarasota, FL) 43–74.

[17] See Ramakrishnan Durairajan, Carol Barford and Paul Barford, 'Lights Out: Climate Change Risk to Internet Infrastructure' (2018) ANRW 9.

transition to a low carbon economy. These risks are difficult to estimate because they require some level of anticipation of future regulation around emissions and climate-related activities. Given the importance of climate change in the public debate, most investors have taken an interest in climate risks, meaning that assets are gradually starting to reflect climate risks in their pricing.[18] A typical example is the risk of stranded assets. If fossil fuels are suddenly impacted by highly restrictive forms of regulation, fossil fuel assets would lose much of their market value. This could have a significant impact on market actors that are highly exposed to fossil fuel assets, with potentially systemic consequences on the financial system.[19] Investors should therefore be pricing such risk into fossil fuel asset prices. Finally, liability risks represent the risk that organizations that have or are currently contributing to climate change may have to compensate individuals or other organizations for the harm caused.[20] Climate litigation is on the rise, and while no court has yet dished out important damages to be paid by corporations, proceedings are far from over and could lead to the imposition of damages with important financial consequences on companies. Again, it would make sense for investors to price such risk.[21] Overall, given the importance of climate change issues in the public debate, and the backing of scientific research on increasing physical risks across the globe, mandating the disclosure of climate risk appears to be justified under securities laws disclosures. Note, however, that it would be tenuous to call this 'sustainability' disclosure, given that such disclosure would essentially fulfil the same role as normal financial disclosures, i.e. providing price-sensitive information to markets.

The categories of physical, transition and liability risks can arguably be expanded to other categories of sustainability issues. For instance, the loss of biodiversity can lead to physical risks (fewer fish in the ocean means lower fish harvests for fisheries), enhanced public scrutiny on the sale of products presenting health issues to consumers could lead to enhanced transition risks for an industry (new regulations on cigarettes or alcohol could lower sales or make them even more costly) and poor management of local communities' values could lead to liability risks (associations could challenge the building permit of a local infrastructure project that could lead to significant delays for the project). So, it may be argued that it makes sense to

---

[18] Patrick Bolton and Marcin Kacperczyk, 'Do Investors Care about Carbon Risk?' (2021) 142(2) Journal of Financial Economics 517–549.

[19] For instance, a study has shown that in 2021, eleven leading banks in the Eurozone collectively held over €530 billion in fossil fuel-related assets, amounting to 95% of their total equity. In a scenario where there is an 80% loss in the value of fossil fuel assets, the equity of Crédit Agricole and Société Générale, the third and fourth largest banks studied, would fall into deficit, while Deutsche Bank and Commerzbank would nearly deplete their equity. In the worst-case scenario, where these fossil fuel assets become worthless, five banks, including three of the top five, would lack sufficient equity to absorb their losses, inducing important systemic risk to the financial system. See Christian Nicol and others, *Actifs Fossiles, Les Nouveaux Subprimes? Quand Financer la Crise Climatique Peut Mener à la Crise Financière* (Institut Rousseau, June 2021).

[20] Madison Condon, 'Market Myopia's Climate Bubble' (2021) SSRN Electronic Journal, 70–71.

[21] However, studies argue that investors are in fact mispricing assets by not taking climate risks into account, see John Armour, Luca Enriques and Thom Wetzer, 'Mandatory Corporate Climate Disclosures: Now, but How?' (2021) European Corporate Governance Institute-Law Working Paper and Condon (n 20), 'Market Myopia's Climate Bubble'.

enhance disclosure around sustainability issues, given that it can theoretically contribute to a better pricing of assets, even if this is not yet empirically demonstrated.

3.2 Sustainability Disclosure to Protect Investors with Sustainability Preferences

The market for sustainable investing could grow to 53 trillion dollars by 2025.[22] This rise indicates that investors are developing an additional preference in their investment choices that appears sufficiently homogenous to be considered as a potential market-swaying force. This holds true whether sustainable investing is viewed as a smart financial decision to reduce risks, a purely impact-driven preference, or both. As a result, institutional investors are demanding the disclosure of better-quality sustainability information to guide their investment decisions. The aim is to provide end investors with investment products that match their preferences.[23] This apparent shift in investor preferences[24] is explained principally by the transfer of wealth to the millennial generation, who appear ready to trade off financial returns for more sustainable investments.[25] In this sense, because sustainability-related issues are not necessarily price-relevant, unsophisticated investors with sustainability-related preferences are not protected by informed trading mechanics as underlined in Section 2. So, one objective sought by sustainability disclosure is to protect investors by ensuring that their investments match their sustainability preferences. Sustainability disclosure therefore allows, in theory, for the elimination of informational asymmetries by allowing investors to better distinguish between sustainable and unsustainable securities. This ensures capital is allocated to what sustainability investors deem to be sustainable investments.

Sustainable investment preferences could have an impact on market prices. Indeed, setting aside the debate on the price-sensitivity of sustainability information per se, if enough investors hold the same sustainability preferences, these preferences will influence the price of an asset.[26] Sustainability disclosure could therefore be an important driver in reaching a new

---

22 Adeline Diab and Gina Martin Adams, 'ESG Assets May Hit $53 Trillion by 2025, a Third of Global AUM', *Bloomberg Intelligence* (23 February 2021) <https://www.bloomberg.com/professional/insights/trading/esg-assets-may-hit-53-trillion-by-2025-a-third-of-global-aum/> accessed 18 May 2024.

23 And one of the reasons why the EU Sustainable Finance Disclosure Regulation exists: to ensure that institutional investors are not mis-selling their products to end investors.

24 Wolf-Georg Ringe, 'Investor-led Sustainability in Corporate Governance' (2021) European Corporate Governance Institute-Law Working Paper, 20–23.

25 Michal Barzuza, Quinn Curtis and David H Webber, 'Shareholder Value(s): Index Fund ESG Activism and the New Millenial Corporate Governance' (2020) 93 Southern California Law Review 1243; it should be noted that investors also believe that ESG information, defined broadly, has an impact on corporate financial performance, see United States Government Accountability Office, *Disclosure of Environmental, Social and Governance Factors and Options to Enhance Them*, July 2020.

26 Bradford Cornell and Aswath Damodaran, 'Valuing ESG: Doing Good or Sounding Good?' (2020) NYU Stern School of Business; see also Eugene F Fama, 'Efficient Capital Markets: A Review of Theory and Empirical Work' (1970) 25 The Journal of Finance (New York) 383. While multiple pricing models have been developed to understand how sustainability-related investing could impact asset prices, an in-depth examination falls outside the scope of this chapter. See for example Itay Goldstein and others, 'On ESG Investing: Heterogeneous Preferences,

market price equilibrium for assets that incorporates sustainability as an additional dimension to risk and return.[27] Furthermore, as examined in Section 2, disclosure is also an effective governance tool that allows principals (investors) to better monitor their agents (company executives) so as to ensure that prior commitments made by the agents are held. With this traditional governance function in mind, sustainability information monitoring can help investors monitor the effectiveness of sustainability policies firms have committed to.[28]

3.3 Sustainability Disclosure to Hold Companies Accountable towards Wider Affected Stakeholders

Beyond protecting investor sustainability preferences, sustainability disclosure is useful for informing wider stakeholder groups, such as citizens, interest groups and governments, of corporate social impacts. These groups have an interest in curtailing sustainability-related negative externalities generated by companies for which society bears the costs.

Conceptually, an externality results from the absence of a transaction over a cost or benefit generated through an activity. The absence of transaction means that the cost or benefit is not reflected in the price of a good or service resulting from the externality-generating activity. Contrary to common belief, externalities are a problem of a reciprocal nature. Through its activities, party A inflicts harm on party B. Yet if party A were to avoid this harm, such avoidance would then inflict harm on party A. So, for instance, if we assume that a factory's pollution negatively impacts fish in the local river, the question from a social welfare perspective is whether the value of the fish loss is greater than the value of the product which necessitates the contamination of the stream. Obviously, many factors come into the calculation of this cost, such as the cost of the factory shifting to less polluting facilities, or the trade-off this might create vis-à-vis the quality of the product being produced.

Information, and Asset Prices' (National Bureau of Economic Research, Working Paper No w29839, 2022).

[27] For instance, investors with sustainability preferences can construct a portfolio delivering the maximal risk-adjusted financial return while holding a sustainability-related preference constant. This would drive a different price equilibrium to one set by purely financial considerations, assuming that the sustainability-related preference is homogenous across a large number of investors. For a formal model advocating this risk-adjusted trade-off approach to sustainability and financial performance, see Lasse Heje Pedersen, Shaun Fitzgibbons and Lukasz Pomorski, 'Responsible Investing: The ESG-efficient Frontier' (2021) 142 Journal of Financial Economics 572; see also regarding the conditions that could bring about new market price equilibria incorporating ESG factors: Itay Goldstein and others, 'On ESG Investing: Heterogeneous Preferences, Information, and Asset Prices' (National Bureau of Economic Research, Working Paper No w29839, 2022).

[28] Some reserves can be emitted regarding this function. Disclosures often involve forward-looking statements that are not strongly enforced, while other traditional governance mechanisms, like board structure and executive compensation, lack sufficient constraints on shareholder decision-making. For instance, even when sustainability goals are included in variable compensation metrics, the goals can be ambiguous and subject to change. This variability makes it easier for executives to meet financial targets while sidelining more challenging sustainability goals. See John Armour, Luca Enriques and Thom Wetzer, 'Green Pills: Making Corporate Climate Commitments Credible' (2023) 65 Ariz L Rev 285, 311–313.

The Coase theorem implies that absent transaction costs, and assuming property rights are well defined, all self-interested economic agents would bargain to achieve Pareto optimal transactions where all costs and benefits are appropriately internalized.[29] In this sense, transaction costs and unclear property rights generate externalities. Coase's definition of transaction costs can be summarized into three categories: search costs (identifying items/opportunities), bargaining costs (negotiating trade conditions) and monitoring and enforcement costs (verifying agreement compliance).[30] In addition, strategic interactions can occur between parties in the presence of contract incompleteness. Contract incompleteness occurs when contracts cannot specify every possible outcome or action, allowing parties to exploit these gaps and thereby increasing the costs of bargaining, enforcement and monitoring efforts.[31]

In the presence of externalities, regulation has a role to play. Transaction costs are explained by a lack of information (hampering search and monitoring costs) and a lack of clearly defined property rights (hampering bargaining and enforcement costs). If parties have access to all material information, and if property rights pertaining to the issues around such information are clearly defined ex ante, externalities would be priced in these arrangements. So, by reducing or eliminating transaction costs insurmountable for the market, regulation plays a role in tackling the externality problem. Regulation could therefore contribute to better internalizing sustainability-related externalities in two ways. Firstly, it could define ex ante property rights around sustainability issues. This is usually achieved by setting clear liability rules relating to sustainability issues.[32] A second, complementary approach is by mandating corporate sustainability disclosure, to achieve optimal information flow and reduce monitoring and enforcement costs in cases where property rights are not being respected.

Having said this, it is important to state that not all externalities are worth addressing. If addressing an externality is more costly than the overall benefit gained, this represents a net loss for society. As discussed earlier in this chapter, disclosure is costly for companies because of administrative and competitive costs that are associated with it. Furthermore, regulation itself can be subject to failures. First, the limitation of measurability means that governments can only usually regulate quantifiable factors, potentially overlooking significant but less measurable externalities. For instance, taxing companies based on pay ratios to address social inequality may neglect other crucial elements such as flexible working hours or cor-

---

[29] Ronald H Coase, 'The Problem of Social Cost' (2013) 56 The Journal of Law & Economics 837.

[30] Carl J Dahlman, 'The Problem of Externality' (1979) 22 The Journal of Law & Economics 141, 147–148.

[31] See Lea-Rachel Kosnik, 'Determinants of Contract Completeness: An Environmental Regulatory Application' (2014) 37 International Review of Law and Economics 198–208.

[32] A typical example would be the setting of a carbon price, or a cap-and-trade carbon market up to an acceptable threshold of carbon emissions, effectively forcing market participants to price and gradually reduce emissions, like the EU Emissions Trading Scheme. Another example is the EU Corporate Sustainability Due Diligence Directive, which will hold in-scope companies liable for upstream (and depending on the company, downstream) sustainability-related harms, including human rights abuses, caused by their global value chain partners, thus forcing companies to contractually allocate risk relating to sustainability issues and providing third party stakeholders with clear avenues for redress in cases where sustainability harms arise, regardless of the physical location of such harms.

porate culture, leading to increased pay but decreased investment in these areas. Secondly, one-size-fits-all regulations may not accommodate the unique circumstances of all companies. While diversity quotas might enhance performance in companies with biased selection processes, they could detract from those with optimized boards, as evidenced by negative outcomes from gender quotas in Norway and California.[33] Intervention is thus justifiable only when the cost of the externality outweighs the associated market and regulatory costs.

Sustainability disclosure could help stakeholders hold companies to account. Even where liability rules and property rights are not clearly defined, generating uncertainty around the bargaining terms and ultimate liability before a court of law, sustainability disclosure nevertheless creates transition risk that needs to be priced in by companies.[34] This is because stakeholders can exert various forms of pressure on companies to force a change in their approach to sustainability issues. While shareholders can voice their opinion through activist campaigns or by simply selling their shares,[35] other stakeholders can engage through consumer boycotts, employee strikes and sit-ins, revocation of legal agreements,[36] and even stakeholder litigation.[37]

Mandating stakeholder-oriented information under a securities law disclosure framework has been viewed as problematic by some critics.[38] Disclosure under a securities law framework is required to be investor-centric in many jurisdictions to fall under the securities regulator's mandate. As such, disclosures blatantly pursuing stakeholder-oriented objectives expose themselves to legal challenges. For instance, companies were required to determine whether their products contained conflict minerals by carrying out supply chain due diligence under US securities law. This mandate, known as the 'conflicts mineral' disclosure obligation, was challenged before courts. The regulation could not be defended by the SEC under its traditional investor-oriented role, given that it was primarily intended for wider stakeholder awareness. It

---

[33] Alex Edmans, 'Applying Economics – Not Gut Feel – To ESG' (2023) 79(4) Financial Analysts Journal 16–29, 27–28.

[34] For instance, for a study examining how, in the context of hydraulic fracturing activities, the introduction of related disclosure mandates led to operators polluting less per unit of production, using fewer toxic chemicals and causing fewer spills and leaks of fluids and wastewater, see Pietro Bonetti, Christian Leuz and Giovanna Michelon, 'Internalizing Externalities: Disclosure Regulation for Hydraulic Fracturing, Drilling Activity and Water Quality' (National Bureau of Economic Research, Working Paper No w30842, 2023).

[35] Various NGOs have been involved in shareholder activism to further their cause, for instance the Dutch NGO 'Follow This' bought shares in BP, Shell, ExxonMobil and Chevron to file shareholder resolutions calling for these companies to cut emissions more aggressively, see Myles McCormick and Tom Wilson, 'Activist Group Follow This Launches Climate Campaign Against Big Oil' *Financial Times* (New York and London, 18 December 2022).

[36] For instance, for a study finding that consumer boycott announcements were followed by statistically significant decreases in stock prices, see Stephen W Pruitt and Monroe Friedman, 'Determining the Effectiveness of Consumer Boycotts: A Stock Price Analysis of Their Impact on Corporate Targets' (1986) 9(4) Journal of Consumer Policy 375–387.

[37] For an account on how legal action shifts or amplifies physical and transition risk exposures and creates additional climate risk exposures, see Thom Wetzer, Rupert Stuart-Smith and Arjuna Dibley, 'Climate Risk Assessments Must Engage with the Law' (2024) 383(6679) Science 152–154.

[38] For instance, see Ann M Lipton, 'Not Everything is About Investors: The Case for Mandatory Stakeholder Disclosure' (2020) 37 Yale J on Reg 499.

was ultimately struck down.[39] Additionally, stakeholder-oriented disclosures mandated under securities laws are often limited because their scope is restricted to listed corporations, which are the only entities usually within the scope of securities laws. Yet stakeholder information needs are likely to require disclosures from any companies large enough to do some harm to society, irrespective of whether they are listed or not. As a result, stakeholder disclosures unnecessarily burden securities law disclosures while failing to deliver on stakeholder disclosure objectives. Ultimately, listed companies can escape mandatory disclosures by spinning off certain business lines or 'going dark', i.e. delisting and slipping entirely out of regulatory and public scrutiny.[40] Stakeholder-oriented securities disclosures could therefore be viewed as ineffective while also undermining the attractiveness of public markets from a company's point of view. These criticisms lie at the core of the difference in the approach to mandatory sustainability disclosures in the US and the UK, and the approach taken by the EU.

4. COMPARATIVE ANALYSIS OF APPROACHES TO MANDATORY CORPORATE SUSTAINABILITY DISCLOSURE

Having set out the traditional justifications for mandating disclosure, and having mapped sustainability disclosure objectives onto financial disclosure objectives, we now turn to a comparative overview of how the US, the EU and the UK justify sustainability disclosure mandates.

4.1 The US

The SEC adopted new climate disclosure rules in March 2024, effective on 28 May 2024. These require securities markets participants 'to provide certain climate-related information in their registration statements and annual reports' and 'require information about [an exchange] registrant's climate-related risks that have materially impacted, or are reasonably likely to have a material impact on, its business strategy, results of operations, or financial condition. In addition, under the final rules, certain disclosures related to severe weather events and other natural conditions will be required in a registrant's audited financial statements.'[41] The SEC

---

[39] See Brief of Respondent, *Nat'l Ass'n of Mfrs. v. SEC*, No 13-5252, 2014 WL 6901084 (D.C. Cir. Dec. 8, 2014); Brief of Respondent, *Nat'l Ass'n of Mfrs. v. SEC*, No 13-5252, 2013 WL 5756165 (D.C. Cir. Oct. 23, 2013). The Court ruled: '[The Commission's rule] violate[s] the First Amendment to the extent the statute and rule require regulated entities to report to the Commission and to state on their website that any of their products have "not been found to be 'DRC conflict free'".' When issuing its regulations, the SEC admitted that the statute's objectives 'appear to be directed at achieving overall social benefits and are not necessarily intended to generate measurable, direct economic benefits to investors or issuers specifically. Additionally, the social benefits are quite different from the economic or investor protection benefits that our rules ordinarily strive to achieve.' Conflict Minerals, Exchange Act Release No 34-67716, 77 Fed. Reg. 56,350 (12 September 2012).

[40] On this topic, see Alperen A Gözlügöl and Wolf-Georg Ringe, 'Private Companies: The Missing Link on the Path to Net Zero' (2022) 22(2) Journal of Corporate Law Studies 887–929.

[41] Securities and Exchange Commission, *The Enhancement and Standardization of Climate-Related Disclosures for Investors* (Final Rule, 6 March 2024) <https://www.sec.gov/rules/2022/

has thus limited mandatory sustainability disclosure to climate disclosures. The SEC justified this rulemaking through the traditional securities law framework lens, invoking how both the objectives of price accuracy and investor protection can be better met if climate-related physical and transition risks are disclosed in a consistent, standardized and reliable manner.[42]

There is current debate as to whether the SEC's climate disclosure rule will survive legal challenges initiated by various stakeholders in the US.[43] This debate is of interest here because it explains why the SEC may have strategically angled its proposed rule towards single materiality as opposed to also mandating impact-oriented disclosures. The legal challenges revolve around the fundamental argument that the SEC's proposed rule could be construed as overstepping the SEC's mandate and in breach of US constitutional law, statutes and rules.[44] This mandate is to protect the financial integrity of securities exchanges and protect investors from financial fraud. So, if the policy objective underlying mandatory climate disclosures were clearly formulated as holding issuers accountable for their emissions and impact on climate, this would be outside of the SEC's mandate. Indeed, the SEC has no mandate to be an environmental watchdog. However, if the SEC can credibly argue that climate risks are merely an additional category of financially material information that investors require, the SEC could provide a reasonable legal defence for its proposed rule. Here we see that the stakeholder disclosure criticisms explored above are at play and central to the survival of climate disclosures in the US.

4.2 The UK

In October 2021, the UK's HM Treasury department published its 'Greening Finance: a Roadmap to Sustainable Investing' report, setting out its policy objectives for integrating sustainability issues into financial regulation. In 2019, the UK had already expressed its ambition to move towards a net zero economy by 2050, underpinned by green finance. The Government's roadmap sets out three stages to achieving what it calls a 'green financial system': (i) informing consumers and markets on corporate environmental sustainability; (ii) acting on the information through encouraging investor stewardship; and (iii) shifting financial flows towards net zero-compatible activities.[45]

Following this roadmap, the Financial Conduct Authority (FCA) required issuers to make disclosures against the Task Force on Climate-Related Financial Disclosures (TCFD) recom-

03/enhancement-and-standardization-climate-related-disclosures-investors> accessed 19 May 2024, 1.

[42] ibid., 19–24.

[43] Some of the main ongoing cases: *State of Iowa, et al v. US Securities and Exchange Commission* (8th Cir, No 24-1522, Dkt No 1); *Petition for Rev, Energy Company Litigation* (5th Cir, No 24-60109); *State of West Virginia, et al v. US Securities and Exchange Commission* (11th Cir, No 24-10679, Dkt No 1); *Sierra Club, et al v. US Securities and Exchange Commission, et al* (DC Cir, No 24-1067, Dkt No 1).

[44] More specifically, the SEC faces four legal challenges: (i) ultra vires, (ii) major questions doctrine, (iii) first amendment violation through compelled speech and (iv) arbitrary and capricious action under the Administrative Procedure Act.

[45] HM Treasury, Greening Finance: A Roadmap to Sustainable Investing (HM Treasury, 18 October 2021).

mendations and recommended disclosures on a 'comply or explain basis'. This was closely followed by UK-wide mandatory climate-related financial disclosure requirements on all publicly listed companies under the Companies and LLPs Regulations 2022 in January 2022.[46] It should be noted that the TCFD focuses on climate risks, i.e. how climate change impacts the value of a business. The UK's climate disclosures are thus very similar in approach to the SEC's, both having drawn from the TCFD's approach to climate-related risk disclosures.

However, the Government's roadmap states that this disclosure framework will be built out through additional disclosure requirements that will include environmental impact reporting.[47] In October 2022, the FCA published its consultation paper on the Sustainability Disclosure Requirements (SDR) and investment labels.[48] The SDR aim at expanding mandatory corporate sustainability disclosures, through 'entity-level disclosure requirements', beyond the climate risk disclosure framework. The exact sub-categories of sustainability issues will be contained in the UK-endorsed ISSB standards, expected to be made available by the UK Government in early 2025.[49] The FCA has indicated four recommendations it would follow regarding these: (i) governance around sustainability-related risks and opportunities; (ii) actual and potential impacts of sustainability-related risks and opportunities on their businesses, strategy and financial planning, where such information is material; (iii) how the firm identifies, assesses and manages sustainability-related risks; and (iv) the metrics and targets used to assess and manage relevant sustainability-related risks, where such information is material.[50]

However, while the SDR appear set to expand sustainability-related disclosures beyond purely climate risk-related disclosures, the materiality assessment remains focused on single materiality, in line with the ISSB's approach. In this sense, the SDR focuses on how sustainability-related issues impact a firm's bottom line, similarly to the TCFD's approach. The SDR's cost–benefit analysis provides further insight into this chosen materiality approach. For the FCA, the development of the SDR is clearly made necessary by shifting investor preferences for sustainable assets and companies. In this sense, the FCA seeks to mandate sustainability-related disclosures to ensure that investors can better identify investments that resonate with their sustainability preferences. In this sense, the SDR appear to be defending the investor protection objective, whereby investors with sustainability preferences should be provided sufficient sustainability information to make an investment decision.

4.3 The EU

The European Commission's eighth climate action plan published on 8 March 2018, known as the 'Sustainable Finance Action Plan', formulated an arguably new financial regulation

---

46 Department for Energy Security and Net Zero and Department for Business, Energy & Industrial Strategy, *Climate-related Financial Disclosures for Companies and Limited Liability Partnerships (LLPs)* (Guidance, 21 February 2022).

47 HM Treasury, 'Policy Paper Greening Finance: A Roadmap to Sustainable Investing' (HM Treasury, 18 October 2021).

48 Financial Conduct Authority, 'Consultation Paper CP22/20 Sustainability Disclosure Requirements (SDR) and investment labels' (FCA, 25 October 2022).

49 HM Treasury, 'Sustainability Disclosure Requirements: Implementation Update 2024' (HM Treasury, 16 May 2024).

50 ibid 5.97.

policy objective of reorienting capital flows towards sustainable investments. Under this new objective, the EU is amending the Non-financial Reporting Directive to make it the first fully fledged mandatory sustainability disclosure framework. This amendment, known as the Corporate Sustainability Reporting Directive (CSRD), appears to extend securities regulation mandated disclosures beyond its traditional objectives of protecting investors and pursuing market efficiency. Indeed, the preamble of the CSRD states that transparency around sustainability performance, in addition to meeting investor needs, should allow 'civil society actors, including non-governmental organisations and social partners, [...] to better hold undertakings to account for their impacts on people and the environment'.[51] The CSRD mandated the European Financial Reporting Advisory Group to develop a set of sustainability accounting standards, the European Sustainability Reporting Standards (ESRS), to be used by firms reporting under the CSRD. In this sense, the EU has chosen to diverge from other major jurisdictions like the US and the UK financial markets, because the EU will not directly incorporate the International Sustainability Standards Board (ISSB) standards into the CSRD reporting requirements.

Contrary to the ISSB standards, the ESRS adopts a 'double materiality' approach. This means that disclosures under CSRD must be made if the information meets at least one of either 'impact materiality' or 'financial materiality'. On the one hand, a sustainability matter is deemed to be financially material 'if it triggers or may trigger material financial effects on the undertaking's development, performance, and position in the short-, medium- or long-term. This is the case, in particular, when it generates or may generate risks or opportunities that influence or are likely to influence significantly its future cash flows.'[52] Sustainability information meeting the financial materiality threshold under the ESRS matches the single materiality approach adopted by the US and the UK. On the other hand, a sustainability matter is deemed to be impact material 'when it pertains to the undertaking's material actual or potential, positive or negative impacts on people or the environment over the short, medium or long-term. A material sustainability matter from an impact perspective also includes impacts caused or contributed to by the undertaking and impacts which are directly linked to the undertaking's operations, products, and services through its business relationships.'[53] While impact materiality could interest some impact-focused investors, as discussed previously, it is also clearly oriented towards a wider stakeholder audience.[54] The ESRS approach to materiality is therefore very different from the ISSB and the TCFD, which adopt only a financial materiality position for reporting sustainability matters. In this sense, the EU has taken a bolder

---

[51] Council Directive (EU) 2022/2464 14 December 2022 amending Regulation (EU) No 537/2014, Directive 2004/109/EC, Directive 2006/43/EC and Directive 2013/34/EU as regards corporate sustainability reporting [2022] OJ L 322/15 (Directive (EU) 2022/2464), Preamble 9.

[52] EFRAG, *ESRS 1 General Principles* (Exposure Draft, April 2022), AR8 to AR10.

[53] EFRAG, *ESRS 1 General Principles* (Exposure Draft, April 2022), Appendix A.

[54] Directive (EU) 2022/2464, 'the sustainability information disclosed in the annual reports of undertakings first has to reach two primary groups of users. The first group of users consists of investors, including asset managers, who want to better understand the risks and opportunities that sustainability issues pose for their investments and the impacts of those investments on people and the environment. The second group of users consists of civil society actors, including non-governmental organisations and social partners, which wish to better hold undertakings to account for their impacts on people and the environment' [Preamble 9].

step towards mandatory sustainability disclosure because it appears to include information that does not fall within the scope of traditional securities law objectives. Indeed, by publishing 'impact materiality' assessments, companies will effectively be disclosing the negative externalities they are producing, irrespective of whether such externalities are relevant to the company's financial prospects.

5. CONCLUSION

The chapter has proceeded to first examine the traditional objectives of mandatory disclosure under a securities law framework. It has then sought to map sustainability disclosure onto these traditional objectives, to assess whether sustainability disclosure is simply an extension of conventional financial disclosures. Evidently, sustainability disclosure appears to also be geared towards wider stakeholder groups that wish to be better informed about a company's social impacts. In this sense, sustainability disclosure has an inherent wider corporate accountability objective, although this is not traditionally within the scope of securities laws. The chapter then reviews how the US, the UK and the EU have justified their mandatory sustainability disclosure rules, and whether the rules effectively pursue these objectives. While the US and the UK seek to justify sustainability disclosure using traditional securities law objectives, the EU has explicitly stated that corporate accountability towards wider stakeholder groups is a clear objective of such regulation. The EU has thus introduced a new objective for corporate disclosures.

19. Sustainability and prudential banking regulation

Seraina Grünewald

1. INTRODUCTION

Sustainability represents one of the major overarching themes that banking regulators around the globe – at times reluctantly – are starting to tackle. As economies and societies are increasingly facing the multidimensional consequences of climate change, biodiversity loss, migration, inequality and other environmental and social concerns, banks are seen by many as a major force in driving the transition to a more sustainable economy. In their capacity as intermediators, banks allocate capital and are thus uniquely positioned to reward those that move ahead and punish those that lag behind. This is particularly evident for climate change, where the Paris Agreement obliges its signatories to bring finance flows in line 'with a pathway towards low greenhouse gas emissions and climate-resilient development'.[1] By redirecting funding to 'green' economic activities (e.g. renewable energy infrastructure and technology) and supporting the transformation of carbon-intensive industries into more sustainable businesses, banks could contribute to the goal of a swift and orderly transition.

However, there are few issues in banking regulation that are discussed so ambivalently as sustainability. A fundamental controversy is whether and to what extent sustainability aspects are indeed a matter that falls within the prudential mandate of banking regulators.[2] The remarkable growth in membership of the Network for Greening the Financial System (NGFS)[3] shows that sustainability has become more mainstream in supervisory and central banking circles – at least when it comes to environmental factors. It remains, however, a politically contentious issue. As this chapter will show, there are fundamental differences in ideology in different parts of the world that have a crucial bearing on the degree of regulatory activism regarding sustainability factors and risks. While banking regulators in the European Union (EU) and Asia have expressly embraced sustainability as a prudential issue, US regulators are more hesitant to openly do so given the strong anti-environmental, social, governance

1 Paris Agreement 2015, art 2(1)(c).

2 See, e.g. Agnieszka Smolenska and Jens van 't Klooster, 'A risky bet: Climate change and the EU's microprudential framework for banks' (2022) 8 JFR 51; Dimitri Demekas and Pierpaolo Grippa, 'Walking a tightrope: Financial regulation, climate change, and the transition to a low-carbon economy' (2022) 8 JFR 203; Antonio Luca Riso, 'Which role for the prudential supervision of banks in sustainable finance?' in Danny Busch, Guido Ferrarini and Seraina Grünewald (eds), *Sustainable Finance in Europe* (Palgrave Macmillan 2021), 275.

3 The NGFS is a self-proclaimed group of central banks and supervisors that contributes to the development of climate-related and environmental risk management in the financial sector and to the mobilization of finance to support the sustainability transition. See <https://www.ngfs.net/en> accessed 20 May 2024.

(ESG) sentiment prevailing in the country. While the chair of the Federal Reserve (Fed) Jerome Powell acknowledges the Fed's 'narrow, but important, responsibilities regarding climate-related financial risks', he does not view the use of supervisory tools to facilitate the transition as appropriate 'without explicit congressional legislation'.[4]

By ensuring that banks adequately manage sustainability risks, prudential regulation will contribute to an orderly transition. However, the main objective of prudential regulation is to safeguard the safety and soundness of banks and the stability of the financial system overall. Any adjustment to the prudential framework should be motivated by stability concerns and thus aim at correcting deficiencies in the framework to fully tackle the risks unsustainable business practices pose for banks.

The aim of this chapter is twofold. Section 2 first substantiates the normative claim that prudential banking regulation ought to consider sustainability and explores the analytical and methodological challenges associated with doing so. Sections 3–5 then provide a comparative analysis of how key financial centers – including the US, the UK, the EU, Switzerland, and Singapore – integrate sustainability within prudential considerations. This bottom-up methodological approach is commensurate to the reality that accounting for sustainability issues in prudential banking regulation constitutes a process of mutual learning between banks, supervisors, regulators and central banks in different jurisdictions. Section 6 concludes.

2. SUSTAINABILITY AS A PRUDENTIAL CONCERN

The fundamental question that this chapter seeks to explore is whether and to what extent sustainability – or rather the lack of it – qualifies as a prudential concern. This section starts by discussing the objectives of prudential banking regulation and the framework to address bank risk-taking. It then turns to how sustainability factors can be framed as drivers of traditional risk categories. The section concludes with a conceptual discussion of why sustainability risk needs special consideration in prudential banking regulation.

2.1 Prudential Banking Regulation: Objectives and Framework

Banks play an important economic role as they mobilize savings, allocate funds to those providing goods and services and facilitate payments. Accordingly, the failure of banks can create social costs that by far exceed the losses incurred by their shareholders and creditors. Their intermediary function renders banks inherently risky in that they borrow short term (by taking deposits and through the interbank market) and lend long term to households and businesses. Moreover, many banks operate with a high leverage. These externalities and banks' propensity to risk-taking constitute the main justifications for prudential banking regulation, which aims to make banks more stable, while ensuring that they can finance economic activity and growth.[5] To prevent bank failures and their potential systemic implications, prudential require-

---

4 Jerome H Powell, Panel on 'Central bank independence and the mandate – Evolving views', speech (10 January 2023) <https://www.federalreserve.gov/newsevents/speech/powell20230110a.htm> accessed 20 May 2024.

5 Amongst many others, Kern Alexander, *Principles of Banking Regulation* (Cambridge University Press 2019), 42–50.

ments safeguard that banks hold sufficient capital against unexpected losses and adequately manage all material risk.

The Basel Committee on Banking Supervision (BCBS) sets the standard for international prudential banking regulation – Basel III in its latest version[6] – that has been implemented and is applied in most jurisdictions. The Basel Framework is based on three mutually reinforcing pillars. Pillar 1 defines regulatory capital requirements to address credit risk, market risk and operational risk that apply to banks across the board. These requirements are calculated using either a 'standardized' approach based on fixed risk weights or an 'internal ratings based' approach based on parameters estimated by banks' internal models. Pillar 2 links capital requirements to the supervisory process and is more principles based. It allows supervisors to impose pillar 2 minimum capital requirements (pillar 2A) to address risks that are not (fully) captured under pillar 1, ensuring that banks are capitalized against all material risks. Moreover, supervisors can impose capital add-ons (pillar 2B) on individual banks as part of the supervisory review process to mitigate against external factors or where they assess a bank's governance and/or risk management processes as significantly weak. Finally, pillar 3 promotes market discipline through prudential disclosure requirements. Banks must publicly disclose certain qualitative and quantitative data on their risk exposure, appetite and management processes on a regular basis, either as part of their financial reporting or in dedicated pillar 3 reports.

2.2 Sustainability Factors and Sustainability Risk

Sustainability affects banks in two different ways. Through their lending and investment decisions, banks have a profound impact on sustainability factors (inside-out or impact perspective). For example, as banks continue to finance fossil fuel extraction, they undermine efforts to align emissions with the goals of the Paris Agreement. On the other hand, unsustainable business practices may affect banks' balance sheet and create material risks for banks (outside-in or risk perspective). This latter perspective is what international standard-setters have focused on.

Over the years, they have come to agree on a basic analytical framework to capture sustainability factors and risks from a prudential point of view.[7] This framework treats sustainability factors, in particular climate-related and environmental factors, largely as drivers of traditional categories of financial risk. Climate change has become widely acknowledged to create financial risks for banks – a development that goes back to Mark Carney's famous speech in 2015 on breaking the tragedy of the horizon.[8] Carney highlighted three broad channels, through

---

6 See <https://www.bis.org/basel_framework/index.htm> accessed 20 May 2024.

7 In particular, BCBS, 'Climate-related risk drivers and their transmission channels' (April 2021) <https://www.bis.org/bcbs/publ/d517.pdf> accessed 20 May 2024; Financial Stability Board, 'Supervisory and regulatory approaches to climate-related risks. Final report' (13 October 2022) <https://www.fsb.org/wp-content/uploads/P131022-1.pdf> accessed 20 May 2024.

8 Mark Carney, 'Breaking the tragedy of the horizon – Climate change and financial stability', speech (London, 29 September 2015) <https://www.bis.org/review/r151009a.pdf> accessed 20 May 2024.

which climate change can affect financial stability.[9] These channels are now commonly used to frame climate-related, but increasingly also other environmental risks:[10]

1. *Physical risks* through the financial impact caused by the more frequent and severe acute as well as chronic physical manifestations of climate change, such as droughts, floods and rising sea levels;
2. *Liability risks* arising from compensation claims from those who have suffered loss or damage from the effects of climate change; and
3. *Transition risks* capturing the financial losses from the process of transitioning to a low-carbon economy, including changes in policy, social behavior and technological development.

Within this basic framing, regulators and supervisors seek to understand how environmental factors are material to banks' balance sheets. Most of them focus largely on immediate financial materiality, namely how traditional risk categories will be affected by environmental factors ('single materiality'). *Credit risks* may increase if the solvency of bank customers is under threat or if collateral loses value owing to climate disasters or business practices misaligned with the transition. *Market risks* may arise from a sudden repricing due to changing climate risk perceptions, leading to 'stranded assets'. Large-impact climate disasters and misalignment of banks' balance sheets with the transition may lead to large outflows and, hence, *liquidity risk*. And finally, banks may face *operational risk* if directly affected by physical risks (e.g. a crucial bank IT service center flooded) or through increasing climate litigation.[11]

Some regulators and supervisors, however, recognize that the contribution of banks to climate-related and environmental risk through their lending and investments must also be considered, at least over the medium and long term. This 'double materiality' approach, albeit not supported in all jurisdictions, has gained traction over the last years, in particular with respect to new (corporate) sustainability disclosure requirements. While difficult to operationalize, a conceptual case can also be made for double materiality within the prudential framework.[12]

---

[9] Besides clearly being a microprudential concern, climate-related risks are bound to affect all banks in one way or another and must thus be tackled also from a macroprudential point of view. See, e.g. Seraina Grünewald, 'Climate change as a systemic risk in finance: Are macroprudential authorities up to the task?' in Danny Busch, Guido Ferrarini and Seraina Grünewald (eds), *Sustainable Finance in Europe* (Palgrave Macmillan 2024), 265.

[10] E.g. NGFS, 'Nature-related financial risks: A conceptual framework to guide action by central banks and supervisors' (July 2024) <https://www.ngfs.net/sites/default/files/medias/documents/ngfs-conceptual-framework-nature-risks.pdf> accessed 15 November 2024.

[11] On climate litigation specifically, NGFS, 'Report on micro-prudential supervision of climate-related litigation risks' (September 2023) <https://www.ngfs.net/sites/default/files/medias/documents/ngfs_report-on-microprudential-supervision-of-climate-related-litigation-risks.pdf> accessed 20 May 2024. For the climate case of Milieudefensie against ING, see <https://climatecasechart.com/non-us-case/milieudefensie-v-ing-bank/#:~:text=According%20to%20Milieudefensie%2C%20the%20scope,of%20all%20of%20the%20Netherlands%27> accessed 20 May 2024.

[12] Jean Boissinot and others, 'Aligning financial and monetary policies with the concept of double materiality: Rationales, proposals and challenges', The INSPIRE Sustainable Central Banking Toolbox, Policy Briefing Paper 05 (June 2022); Matthias Täger, '"Double materiality":

Clearly, negative sustainability impacts can translate into financial risks, through climate litigation, legal liabilities or reputational damage. For example, significant exposures of a bank to borrowers with large climate footprints might impact the bank's turnover, market value and credit rating. The intersection between environmental materiality and financial materiality is set to grow over time, as policies evolve and strategic litigation increases. Anticipating these risks according to a double materiality approach will thus require that banks bring their strategies and balance sheets in alignment with the sustainability transition in the medium to long term. While a risk-based framework, the Basel Framework is accommodative of a broad spectrum of supervisory action under both single and double materiality approaches.

The framework to capture risks from social factors, on the other hand, has remained far less developed and largely revolves around factors such as diversity and inclusiveness as well as compliance with labor rights. The drivers of social risk are conceptually different from those of environmental risk. Social risk may materialize from environmental risk, changes in social policy and an evolving market sentiment regarding social factors.[13] Following the approach of regulators, this chapter focuses on the integration of climate and environmental factors in the prudential framework. However, as the comparative analysis below will show, some jurisdictions are more open to including social factors within their prudential frameworks as well.

2.3 Challenges Associated with Integrating Sustainability Risk in the Prudential Framework

While they may ultimately manifest themselves as traditional financial risks, sustainability risks have unique features rendering it challenging to monitor, manage and mitigate them with conventional risk management approaches and capital requirements. Accordingly, to ensure that banks adequately manage all material risk from environmental (and social) factors, there is a need to adapt the existing prudential framework to the specificities of these risks.

As far as climate-related risks are concerned, the biggest challenge for banks and supervisors lies in the forward-looking nature of these risks.[14] The long-term nature of climate change requires banks and their regulators to consider horizons that can extend significantly beyond the one-year horizon they commonly consider for setting capital requirements. There is little past record from which banks could extrapolate in the future. Moreover, modelling uncertainty is much higher, owing to the sheer complexity of climate events as well as non-linearities and tipping points in their evolution. Accordingly, the traditional approach to risk analysis and management based on historical data and loss experience needs to be replaced by

---

What is it and why does it matter?', LSE Grantham Research Institute on Climate Change and the Environment, commentary (21 April 2021) <https://www.lse.ac.uk/granthaminstitute/news/double-materiality-what-is-it-and-why-does-it-matter/> accessed 20 May 2024.

13 Seminal European Banking Authority, 'EBA report on management and supervision of ESG risks for credit institutions and investment firms' (28 June 2021) <https://www.eba.europa.eu/sites/default/documents/files/document_library/Publications/Reports/2021/1015656/EBA%20Report%20on%20ESG%20risks%20management%20and%20supervision.pdf> accessed 20 May 2024, 43–47.

14 See, e.g. Seraina Grünewald, 'Macroprudential policies and climate risks', EBI Working Paper No. 133 (18 January 2023).

a forward-looking assessment of risk outcomes to adequately capture climate-related risk.[15] Otherwise, regulators risk that banks systematically underestimate such risk in the longer term.

Another key challenge are persistent data limitations. For banks and supervisors to assess the climate-related and environmental risk that banks might be exposed to, information on the exposures of their counterparties and invested assets to physical and transition risk, including their alignment with transition pathways, would be necessary. However, as meaningful, comparable and consistent data to that end is not yet available, banks often work with approximations. In many jurisdictions, legislators and regulators are working on obliging (large) companies to publish sustainability-relevant information to fill that void.[16]

Banking regulators have gathered in international standard-setting bodies, including the BCBS, the Financial Stability Board (FSB), and the NGFS, to tackle these methodological challenges and to discuss ways to integrate climate-related financial risk (CRFR) in existing regulatory frameworks. Potential adjustments could in principle pertain to all three pillars of the existing Basel Framework. Their aim would be to ensure that banks effectively manage climate-related (and potentially other sustainability) risk and can absorb losses from such risks should they materialize in the future. However, as the following analysis will show, not all pillars are equally flexible to accommodate the unique features of CRFR and the methodological challenges they are associated with.

3. PILLAR 1: ADJUSTING REGULATORY REQUIREMENTS WITH A GREEN SUPPORTING OR BROWN PENALIZING FACTOR?

Pillar 1 capital requirements are designed to ensure that banks hold sufficient loss-absorbing capacity to withstand unexpected losses.[17] They are calibrated based on banks' historical loss experience over a time horizon of one year in most cases. Banks measure their losses from specific exposures in contingent scenarios occurring with a pre-determined probability. This approach is a bad fit for CRFR, which requires a forward-looking assessment over longer time horizons and for which a probability distribution is inherently difficult to estimate. Moreover,

---

[15] See, e.g. BCBS, 'Climate-related financial risks – Measurement methodologies' (April 2021) <https://www.bis.org/bcbs/publ/d518.pdf> accessed 20 May 2024.

[16] Directive (EU) 2022/2464 of 14 December 2022 amending Regulation (EU) No 537/2014, Directive 2004/109/EC and Directive 2013/34/EU, as regards corporate sustainability reporting [2022] OJ L 322, 15 ('CSRD') obliges most listed companies in the EU to disclose the risks and opportunities arising from social and environmental issues (outside-in perspective) as well as the impact of their activities on people and the environment (inside-out perspective). In March 2024, the Securities and Exchange Commission (SEC) adopted new climate-related disclosure requirements for public issuers, facing strong opposition from both political exponents and the industry. See SEC, 'The enhancement and standardization of climate-related disclosures for investors', Final rule (6 March 2024), <https://www.sec.gov/files/rules/final/2024/33-11275.pdf> accessed 20 May 2024.

[17] It is important to note that prudential capital requirements do not cover those losses that banks *expect* to bear owing to the materialization of known risks. It is mostly for the accounting framework to capture expected losses through provisioning, impairments, write-downs and the appropriate valuation of financial assets.

the high-level 'bucketing' of assets under the pillar 1 framework fails to capture CRFR that specifically impact certain sectors (e.g. fossil fuel energy) and/or regions (e.g. coastal areas).

One the one hand, pillar 1 capital requirements may provide the biggest regulatory leverage to safeguard against CRFR materialization, as they prescribe the calculation of the required minimum level of own funds applicable to all banks at all times. On the other hand, the rigidity of this rules-based approach renders the inclusion of the specific features of CRFR in pillar 1 requirements particularly challenging. Bank regulators have thus far focused on assessing the extent to which CRFR are already captured by the prudential framework. Any amendment to the pillar 1 requirements would have to be designed so as to avoid double counting and ensure consistency within the framework. The BCBS Taskforce on Climate-related Financial Risks has produced a set of answers to frequently asked questions intended to facilitate the consistent interpretation of pillar 1 standards given the unique features of CRFR.[18] The pillar 1 framework already contains some selective mechanisms that allow new types of risk drivers to be addressed, including internal models, external credit ratings and valuations of collateral and financial instruments.[19]

An alternative to recognizing CRFR within the existing framework would entail a fundamental review of pillar 1 requirements, including the introduction of a forward-looking estimation of probability of default and loss given default measures and prescribed adjustments of risk weights to account for CRFR. Under pillar 1, banks are asked to assign a risk weight to each asset representing the risk attached to it. The higher the risk weight of an asset, the more capital the bank must hold against it. In particular, the banking sector itself as well as academics and some NGOs have discussed the possibility of introducing climate-specific risk weights.[20] This could be done in two fundamentally different ways. A 'brown penalizing factor' (BPF) would raise capital requirements for (certain) carbon-intensive assets, while a 'green supporting factor' (GSF) would lower capital requirements for (certain) climate-friendly investments. In both cases, changes to risk weights would impact the marginal cost of financing for the affected activities, thus incentivizing banks to support the transition to a low-carbon economy.

Most banking regulators and academic commentators, however, view the use of climate-specific risk weights as too rigid and too crude given our current understanding of CRFR, as they would generally assume that brown assets are associated with more risk and green assets with less. The fact that an investment might be labeled as climate-friendly, for example, by a taxonomy,[21] does not render that investment low risk. In fact, the classical

---

[18] See BCBS, 'Frequently asked questions on climate-related financial risks' (8 December 2022) <https://www.bis.org/bcbs/publ/d543.htm> accessed 20 May 2024.

[19] See European Banking Authority, 'Report on the role of environmental and social risks in the prudential framework' (October 2023) <https://www.eba.europa.eu/sites/default/documents/files/document_library/Publications/Reports/2023/1062711/Report%20on%20the%20role%20of%20environmental%20and%20social%20risks%20in%20the%20prudential%20framework.pdf> accessed 20 May 2024.

[20] See, e.g. the proposal by Finance Watch that new fossil fuel projects be assigned a 1250% risk weight ('one-for-one rule'), requiring these projects to be entirely funded by shareholder equity: <https://www.finance-watch.org/publication/a-safer-transition-for-fossil-banking/> accessed 20 May 2024.

[21] The EU Taxonomy, for example, represents a classification system of economic activities that make a substantial contribution to the environmental objectives of the EU.

example is that start-ups active in developing novel green technologies will often represent high-risk investments for reasons unrelated to the climate friendliness of their economic activities. A GSF could thus create funding incentives that run counter to what would be warranted from a prudential point of view. A BPF, on the other hand, is more aligned with the risk-based, prudential logic of bank capital requirements. It would increase bank capital requirements and thus the resilience of those banks that are most exposed to transition risk. Opponents of a BPF, however, often point to the lack of a common understanding of what represents a 'brown' asset that should be subject to a BPF, question the need to impose such risk weight adjustment across the board and raise the concern that it may lead to double counting of climate risk (especially due to interactions with the accounting framework), amongst other challenges.

Owing to the difficulty of identifying clear-cut risk differentials, none of the jurisdictions studied in this chapter have introduced a BPF or GSF.[22] In the EU, the co-legislators mandated the European Banking Authority (EBA) to produce a report assessing 'the potential effects of a dedicated prudential treatment of exposures related to assets and activities which are associated substantially with environmental and/or social objectives on financial stability and bank lending in the Union'.[23] In its report published in October 2023, the EBA refrained from recommending specific risk-weighted adjustment factors, as for the time being 'the most consistent way forward from a prudential risk-based perspective is to address environmental risks through effective use of and targeted amendments to the existing prudential regime'.[24]

The UK Prudential Regulation Authority (PRA) cautions against the costs of fundamentally reviewing pillar 1 requirements compared with alternative options (e.g. adjustments in pillar 2). Based on a review of the existing literature, a 2021 PRA report rejected the idea of a GSF as ineffective and potentially even running counter to prudential objectives.[25] In an update published on 13 March 2023, the PRA expressly dismissed the idea of a BPF for assets exposed to carbon-intensive energy sources by stating: 'The PRA does not believe that such an intervention is currently supportable on prudential grounds as risks of individual assets will be correlated with the economic viability of the assets, and this will in turn be influenced as the detail of countries' transition and energy strategies becomes clear. In addition, the assets in

---

22 Policy documents of both the US bank regulators and the Monetary Authority of Singapore (MAS) remain silent on potential adjustments to pillar 1 requirements.

23 Regulation (EU) No 575/2013 of 26 June 2013 on prudential requirements for credit institutions and investment firms and amending Regulation (EU) No 648/2012 [2013] OJ L 176/1 (CRR), art 501c.

24 EBA, 'Report on the role of environmental and social risks in the prudential framework' (October 2023) <https://www.eba.europa.eu/sites/default/documents/files/document_library/Publications/Reports/2023/1062711/Report%20on%20the%20role%20of%20environmental%20and%20social%20risks%20in%20the%20prudential%20framework.pdf> accessed 20 May 2024, 9. The introduction of a BPF for lending towards the instigation or expansion of fossil fuel projects was discussed by the responsible ECON committee of the European Parliament (EP) in the context of discussions on the '2021 Banking Package', but later dropped.

25 PRA, 'Climate-related financial risk management and the role of capital requirements', Climate change adaptation report (28 October 2021) <https://www.bankofengland.co.uk/-/media/boe/files/prudential-regulation/publication/2021/october/climate-change-adaptation-report-2021.pdf?la=en&hash=FF4A0C618471462E10BC704D4AA58727EC8F8720> accessed 20 May 2024, 50.

question might only become more risky beyond the time horizons currently used for regulatory capital setting'.[26]

Similarly, the Swiss government concluded in a position paper of 2020 that it does not currently view climate-differentiating capital requirements under pillar 1 as 'sensible'. If not motivated by risk considerations, such requirements would create skewed incentives and reduce the competitiveness of Swiss banks globally. Any adjustments to capital requirements are thus to be coordinated within the BCBS.[27]

These observations show that banking regulators are generally hesitant to introduce any climate-specific pillar 1 requirements without prior international coordination. Divergence of individual jurisdictions from the global standard would indeed risk fragmentation and harm regulatory cooperation. Adjustments to pillar 1 requirements, as a rules-based framework, are a protracted process. More timely prudential measures against the build-up of CRFR can be taken under the broader and more flexible pillars 2 and 3.

4. PILLAR 2: CLIMATE/SUSTAINABILITY RISKS IN BANK RISK MANAGEMENT AND SUPERVISORY PROCESSES

Determining principles rather than across-the-board rules in terms of how banks must manage their risks, pillar 2 provides the largest flexibility to integrate CRFR in prudential banking regulation. Through the supervisory review process of the Basel Framework, banking supervisors can influence how banks identify, monitor, measure and control their risks. The supervisory review process is meant not only to ensure that banks hold adequate capital against all the risks associated with their business, but also 'to encourage banks to develop and use better risk management techniques in monitoring and managing their risks'.[28]

Supervisors expect banks to consider all risks that could be material to their business. Pillar 2 specifically addresses risks that are not at all or not fully captured by the pillar 1 process, including business risks, interest rate risks and concentration risks. The supervisory review process enables supervisors to evaluate banks' assessment of their capital needs relative to their risk profiles and to intervene, if necessary. It establishes an active dialogue between the supervisor and the supervised banks and allows for corrective action to reduce risk or restore capital. Corrective actions by supervisors may include qualitative requirements to strengthen risk management and potentially limit certain lines of business as well as quantitative requirements in the form of capital add-ons. The latter in particular differ across jurisdictions.

Pillar 2 thus allows supervisors to assess banks' exposures to CRFR and to seek changes in how banks identify, monitor, measure and control these risks. In June 2022, the BCBS

---

[26] PRA, 'Bank of England report on climate-related risks and the regulatory capital frameworks' (13 March 2023) <https://www.bankofengland.co.uk/prudential-regulation/publication/2023/report-on-climate-related-risks-and-the-regulatory-capital-frameworks> accessed 20 May 2024, para. 44.

[27] Der Bundesrat, 'Nachhaltigkeit im Finanzsektor Schweiz, Eine Auslegeordnung und Positionierung mit Fokus auf Umweltaspekte' (24 June 2020), 47–48.

[28] BCBS, 'Overview of pillar 2 supervisory review practices and approaches' (June 2019) <https://www.bis.org/bcbs/publ/d465.pdf> accessed 20 May 2024, 2.

released principles for the effective management and supervision of CRFR.[29] These principles seek to improve banks' risk management and supervisors' practices with a view to CRFR, spanning the whole spectrum of governance, internal control, capital and liquidity adequacy, risk management, monitoring and reporting as well as scenario analysis. In many jurisdictions, banking supervisors have taken steps to include CRFR in their supervisory processes by issuing supervisory expectations, at times with follow-up measures, and conducting scenario analysis exercises.

4.1 Supervisory Expectations on Sustainability Risks

All banking supervisors studied in this chapter have issued (draft) principles-based supervisory expectations or guidance on CRFR and partially other sustainability risk. Structured around governance, strategy, risk management and disclosure, these supervisory expectations are – explicitly or implicitly – based on the recommendations by the Task Force on Climate-related Financial Disclosures (TCFD),[30] an industry-led group established in 2015 by the FSB. The TCFD recommendations provide a global standard for voluntary and consistent climate-related financial disclosures that are decision-useful for investors, lenders and insurance underwriters in understanding material CRFR.

In a first step, these supervisory expectations are meant to raise awareness and support banks' efforts in including CRFR in their internal processes. By outlining to banks what supervisors expect of them, they structure the supervisory dialogue between supervisors and banks. Some authorities have followed up or indicated that they will follow up with supervisory measures in case banks persistently fail to meet the expectations.

The PRA was the first banking supervisor to publish a set of expectations for banks on their management of CRFR in April 2019,[31] based on an earlier review of the preexisting industry practice.[32] In particular, the PRA asked banks to identify their material exposures to CRFR and demonstrate that they hold adequate capital against them. In its 2021 climate change adaptation report, the PRA described the progress made by banks and its future supervisory strategy.[33]

The ECB published in November 2020 a guide on climate-related and environmental risks, outlining its supervisory expectations in terms of banks' business strategy, governance, risk

---

29 BCBS, 'Principles for the effective management and supervision of climate-related financial risks' (15 June 2022) <https://www.bis.org/bcbs/publ/d532.pdf> accessed 20 May 2024.

30 Task Force on Climate-related Financial Disclosures, 'Recommendations of the Task Force on Climate-relate Financial Disclosures: Final report' (June 2017) <https://assets.bbhub.io/company/sites/60/2021/10/FINAL-2017-TCFD-Report.pdf> accessed 20 May 2024. In October 2023, the TCFD was disbanded, and its work taken over by the IFRS Foundation.

31 PRA, 'Enhancing banks' and insurers' approaches to managing the financial risks from climate change', Supervisory statement SS3/19 (April 2019) <https://www.bankofengland.co.uk/-/media/boe/files/prudential-regulation/supervisory-statement/2019/ss319> accessed 20 May 2024.

32 PRA, 'Transition in thinking: The impact of climate change on the UK banking sector' (26 September 2018) <https://www.bankofengland.co.uk/-/media/boe/files/prudential-regulation/report/ transition -in -thinking -the -impact -of -climate -change -on -the -uk -banking -sector .pdf> accessed 20 May 2024.

33 PRA (n 25).

management frameworks and disclosures.[34] In early 2021, it requested banks to perform a self-assessment of their practices against these expectations and set out how they intend to implement the expectations in the future. An ECB report published in November 2021 summarized the outcome of the assessment.[35] In 2022, the ECB conducted a thematic review, with further deep dives into banks' climate-related and environmental risk strategies, governance and risk management. It communicated the results of this review in a report of November 2022.[36] Based on this review, the ECB also identified a set of good practices across different banks to illustrate practicable ways in which banks can align their practices with its supervisory expectations.[37]

Singapore was also among the early movers in setting out environmental risk management expectations for banks.[38] In May 2022, the Monetary Authority of Singapore (MAS) followed up with a publication on the progress made with the implementation of these supervisory expectations and the development of good practices.[39] It also convened the so-called Green Finance Industry Taskforce (GFIT) with the task of enhancing environmental risk management practices of financial institutions and improving disclosures, amongst others. The GFIT issued a handbook on environmental risk management and disclosure in January 2021,[40] complementing MAS's supervisory expectations from the perspective of industry practice.

Prima facie, things moved more slowly in Switzerland and the US. The Swiss Financial Market Supervisory Authority (FINMA) published laconic guidance on the management of

---

34 ECB, 'Guide on climate-related and environmental risks: Supervisory expectations relating to risk management and disclosure' (November 2020) <https://www.bankingsupervision.europa.eu/ecb/pub/pdf/ssm.202011finalguideonclimate-relatedandenvironmentalrisks~58213f6564.en.pdf> accessed 20 May 2024.

35 ECB, 'The state of climate and environmental risk management in the banking sector: Report on the supervisory review of banks' approaches to manage climate and environmental risks' (November 2021) <https://www.bankingsupervision.europa.eu/ecb/pub/pdf/ssm.202111guideonclimate-relatedandenvironmentalrisks%7E4b25454055.en.pdf> accessed 20 May 2024.

36 ECB, 'Walking the talk: Banks gearing up to manage risks from climate change and environmental degradation' (November 2022) <https://www.bankingsupervision.europa.eu/ecb/pub/pdf/ssm.thematicreviewcerreport112022~2eb322a79c.en.pdf> accessed 20 May 2024.

37 ECB, 'Good practices for climate-related and environmental risk management: Observations from the 2022 thematic review' (November 2022) <https://www.bankingsupervision.europa.eu/ecb/pub/pdf/ssm.thematicreviewcercompendiumgoodpractices112022~b474fb8ed0.en.pdf> accessed 20 May 2024.

38 MAS, 'Guidelines on environmental risk management (banks)' (December 2020) <https://www.mas.gov.sg/-/media/mas/regulations-and-financial-stability/regulations-guidance-and-licensing/commercial-banks/regulations-guidance-and-licensing/guidelines/guidelines-on-environmental-risk---banks/guidelines-on-environmental-risk-management-f> accessed 20 May 2024.

39 MAS, 'Information paper on environmental risk management (banks)' (May 2022) <https://www.mas.gov.sg/-/media/mas-media-library/publications/monographs-or-information-paper/bd/2022/information-paper-on-environmental-risk-management-banks.pdf> accessed 20 May 2024.

40 GFIT, 'Handbook on implementing environmental risk management for asset managers, banks and insurers' (January 2021) <https://abs.org.sg/docs/library/handbook-on-implementing-environmental-risk-management> accessed 20 May 2024.

CRFR by banks, outlining its expectations and supervisory approach only in January 2023.[41] However, it had previously prepared a qualitative assessment of CRFR at Swiss banks in the form of heat maps, which have formed the basis of FINMA's supervisory dialogue with banks.[42]

The Fed indicated in its 2020 Financial Stability Report that 'Federal Reserve supervisors expect banks to have systems in place that appropriately identify, measure, control and monitor all of their material risks, which for many banks are likely to extend to climate risks'.[43] Following similar initiatives by the Office of the Comptroller of the Currency (OCC)[44] and the Federal Deposit Insurance Corporation (FDIC)[45] in December 2021 and March 2022, respectively, it published draft principles for CRFR management in December 2022.[46] To promote consistency across supervision of large financial institutions, the three sets of (draft) principles were merged into final interagency guidance in October 2023.[47]

4.1.1 Scope of application

The approaches taken by the various banking supervisors in formulating supervisory expectations on CRFR differ substantially. Some supervisory expectations are more principles based, others more prescriptive. Benchmarking exercises, identifying good practices, enable banks to learn from each other and to establish who is best in class (and who is not). At the same time, they serve as an indication to the supervisors of what they can reasonably expect from

---

41 FINMA, 'FINMA Guidance 01/2023: Developments with regard to the management of climate risks' (24 January 2023) <https://www.finma.ch/en/~/media/finma/dokumente/dokumentencenter/myfinma/4dokumentation/finma-aufsichtsmitteilungen/20230124-finma-aufsichtsmitteilung-01-2023.pdf?sc_lang=en&hash=AE5AC34C3A564F4CF9FBD08557A3D124> accessed 20 May 2024.

42 FINMA, 'Annual report 2020' <https://www.finma.ch/~/media/finma/dokumente/dokumentencenter/myfinma/finma-publikationen/geschaeftsbericht/20200325-finma-jahresbericht-2020.pdf> accessed 20 May 2024, 37–39. By January 2025, new supervisory guidance on nature-related financial risks is set to enter into force: <https://www.finma.ch/en/documentation/archiv/completed-consultations/2024/> accessed 15 November 2024.

43 Federal Reserve Board of Governors, 'Financial Stability Report' (November 2020) <https://www.federalreserve.gov/publications/files/financial-stability-report-20201109.pdf> accessed 20 May 2024, 59.

44 OCC, 'Principles for climate-related financial risk management for large banks' (16 December 2021) <https://www.occ.gov/news-issuances/bulletins/2021/bulletin-2021-62a.pdf> accessed 20 May 2024.

45 FDIC, 'Statement of principles for climate-related financial risk management for large financial institutions', Notice of proposed policy statement and request for comment, Federal Register, Vol. 87(64) (4 April 2022) <https://www.fdic.gov/news/board-matters/2022/2022-03-29-notational-fr.pdf> accessed 20 May 2024.

46 Federal Reserve Board of Governors, 'Principles for climate-related financial risk management for large financial institutions', Notice and request for comment (2 December 2022) <https://www.federalreserve.gov/newsevents/pressreleases/files/other20221202b1.pdf> accessed 20 May 2024.

47 Department of the Treasury, Federal Reserve System and Federal Deposit Insurance Corporation, 'Principles for climate-related financial risk management for large financial institutions', Final interagency guidance (23 October 2023) <https://www.govinfo.gov/content/pkg/FR-2023-10-30/pdf/2023-23844.pdf> accessed 20 May 2024.

banks considering current data and methodological limitations. There are also differences in the amount of information that is shared with the public on the performance of the aggregate banking sector against the expectations of supervisors. Supervisors have not shared information on the performance of individual banks.

Supervisory expectations and the identification of best practices are not intended to serve as a one-size-fits-all roadmap. In their application, banks and supervisors need to consider individual banks' size, business model and risk profile. In some jurisdictions, supervisory expectations regarding CRFR are *a priori* confined to a subset of larger banks. Compliance with these expectations is costly for banks and may burden smaller banks disproportionally. The final guidance issued by US supervisors, for example, targets the largest financial institutions only, i.e. those with over USD 100 billion in total consolidated assets. FINMA's supervisory expectations focus on the global and domestic systemically important banks. However, FINMA has announced that it intends to address also smaller banks in the future, 'while always having due regard to the principle of proportionality'.[48]

While a proportional application of supervisory expectations on CRFR is in line with the risk-based approach of the Basel Framework, the impact of CRFR on medium-size and smaller banks must not be underestimated, especially if they have more concentrated portfolios in terms of geographic or sector exposures. For that reason, supervisory expectations have a broader scope in the UK, Singapore and the euro area. All banks, building societies and PRA-designated investment firms must observe the PRA's supervisory expectations in principle, while the PRA applies the expectations proportionally based on banks' size, complexity, exposures to CRFR and different business models.[49] The guidelines issued by MAS also apply to all banks, merchant banks and finance companies in Singapore on a group basis and must be implemented by banks 'in a way that is commensurate with the size and nature of [their] activities as well as [their] risk profile'.[50]

The ECB's supervisory expectations cover all banks under the direct supervisory remit of the ECB (the so-called 'significant institutions'[51]).[52] National supervisors are recommended to apply the ECB's supervisory expectations in their supervision of less significant institutions 'in a manner that is proportionate to the nature, scale and complexity of the activities of the institution concerned'.[53] Some national supervisors have issued similar supervisory expec-

---

48 FINMA (n 41) 6. A new circular on nature-related risks implements this proportionality approach: <https://www.finma.ch/en/~/media/finma/dokumente/dokumentencenter/anhoerungen/laufende-anhoerungen/20240201-naturbezogene-finanzrisiken/20240201_rs_naturbezogenerisiken_anhoerung_rs.pdf?sc_lang=en&hash=CCA38C5620B9E010D4EAB56C7AFD2FDE> accessed 15 November 2023.

49 PRA (n 25) 10.

50 MAS (n 38) 1.

51 These are institutions that meet at least one of the following thresholds: (1) total value of assets exceeding EUR 30 billion; (2) total assets exceeding 20% of national GDP in the Member State in which the bank is established; (3) total value of assets exceeding EUR 5 billion and ratio of cross-border assets/liabilities in more than one other participating Member State to total assets/liabilities is above 20%; (4) request for or receipt of direct public financial assistance from the European Stability Mechanism; or (5) bank is one of the three most significant credit institutions in a participating Member State.

52 ECB (n 34) 6–7.

53 ibid 7.

tations for the less significant banks within their supervisory remit, including the German BaFin,[54] the Austrian FMA[55] and the Dutch DNB.[56]

4.1.2 Sustainability risks covered

As previously discussed, there is broad international agreement that climate change and the transition to a low-carbon economy can give rise to material financial risks for banks. For other forms of environmental degradation, the potential financial impacts on banks are less well understood. Accordingly, supervisory authorities have so far focused on CRFR. The guidance issued by the PRA and the US supervisors does not refer to environmental risks other than climate change. As of January 2025, FINMA is broadening the scope of its guidance to include a wider set of nature-related risks such as climate change, biodiversity loss and impairments of ecosystem services. MAS refers to environmental issues more broadly, including besides climate change also the loss of biodiversity, pollution and changes in land use.[57] It finds, however, that '[a]part from climate-related risks, banks have yet to make meaningful progress to address other environmental risk factors, such as biodiversity loss'[58] and stresses that further work is required by banks to adequately account for the financial impact of environmental degradation beyond climate-related risk factors.[59]

The ECB's supervisory expectations cover both climate-related and other environmental risks ('C&E risks').[60] Environmental (physical) risk drivers highlighted by the ECB include water stress, resource scarcity, biodiversity loss and pollution, amongst others. The ECB guide also stresses the interconnection between climate change and other environmental risks and their potentially combined effects. In its assessments, the ECB has paid special attention to banks' progress in targeting environmental risks beyond CRFR.[61] It finds that many banks are successfully re-using the concepts and methods developed for CRFR, but that banks are more advanced in assessing the materiality of CRFR compared with other environmental risks.

Only the guidance issued by the US banking supervisors mentions social aspects of sustainability, albeit tangentially. The guidance acknowledges that 'both climate change and the actions that financial institutions may take to manage climate-related financial risks could potentially have a disproportionate impact on [low- to moderate income] and other underserved consumers and communities'.[62] As a social safeguard, banks are expected to apply

---

54 Bundesanstalt für Finanzdienstleistungsaufsicht, 'Merkblatt zum Umgang mit Nachhaltigkeitsrisiken' (13 January 2020) <https://www.bafin.de/SharedDocs/Downloads/DE/Merkblatt/dl_mb_Nachhaltigkeitsrisiken.pdf?__blob=publicationFile&v=9> accessed 20 May 2024.

55 Österreichische Finanzmarktaufsicht, 'FMA-Leitfaden zum Umgang mit Nachhaltigkeitsrisiken' (2 July 2020) <https://www.fma.gv.at/fma/fma-leitfaeden/> accessed 20 May 2024.

56 De Nederlandsche Bank, 'Good practice: Integration of climate-related risk considerations into banks' risk management' (1 April 2020) <https://www.dnb.nl/media/jwtjyvfn/definitieve-versie-gp-en-qa-klimaatrisico-s-banken.pdf> accessed 20 May 2024.

57 MAS (n 38) 1.

58 MAS (n 39) 3.

59 ibid 15–16.

60 ECB (n 34) 10–13.

61 See ECB (n 36) 39–41; ECB (n 37) 55–59.

62 Department of the Treasury, Federal Reserve System and Federal Deposit Insurance Corporation (n 47) 8–9.

a proportionality assessment to ensure that the reduction of CRFR on their balance sheets does not unduly affect more vulnerable groups of society.[63]

4.1.3 Follow-up measures in case of material misalignment with supervisory expectations

Approaches taken in different jurisdictions vary strongly regarding the extent to which supervisory expectations are followed up by supervisory measures other than dialogue with the affected banks. Perhaps unsurprisingly given the prevailing politization of climate-related action by banking regulators in the US, the guidance published by the Fed, OCC and FDIC does not mention any potential supervisory follow-up measures. MAS's approach has also rested on supervisory dialogue with banks. In its information paper issued in 2022, MAS announced that it 'will continue to partner with banks to accelerate their efforts' in meeting supervisory expectations,[64] without setting any hard deadlines for banks' compliance that could be enforced with supervisory measures.

FINMA's 2023 guidance highlighted that it is deploying 'tools such as supervisory discussions, surveys and also, where necessary, on-site supervisory reviews' to ensure that banks take appropriate measures to address CRFR.[65] With the entry into force of the new circular on nature-related risks in January 2025, FINMA now also has the option of harder supervisory measures, such as capital add-ons.

The ECB and PRA, on the other hand, have already taken additional steps in supervisory engagement. Banks under the ECB's direct supervisory remit received comprehensive feedback letters indicating (on average) around 25 shortcomings and with institution-specific remediation timelines for full alignment with all ECB supervisory expectations by the end of 2024. The ECB incorporated the outcome of the 2022 thematic review in the Supervisory Review and Evaluation Process (SREP). To address severe weaknesses, it imposed case-by-case binding *qualitative* SREP requirements on more than 30 banks. It has refrained from imposing *quantitative* SREP requirements so far but indicated that it may enforce compliance with its expectations, where appropriate, also with quantitative requirements in 2023 and beyond.[66] According to media reports, the ECB had warned 20 banks that they would be fined if they failed to address their climate risk shortcomings at end-2023 and imposed such periodical penalty payments on as many as four banks in 2024.[67]

---

63 ibid 18.

64 MAS (n 39) 4.

65 FINMA (n 41) 6.

66 See ECB (n 36) 7.

67 'ECB threatens 20 banks with fines after climate-risk warning' (22 November 2023) <https://www.bloomberg.com/news/articles/2023-11-22/ecb-threatens-20-banks-with-fines-for-mismanaging-climate-risk?sref=gPAG2MJ8&leadSource=uverify%20wall> accessed 20 May 2024; 'ECB warns banks of yet more fines over climate risk management' (4 October 2024) <https://www.bnnbloomberg.ca/business/2024/10/04/ecb-warns-banks-of-yet-more-fines-over-climate-risk-management/> accessed 17 November 2024.

The PRA also addressed letters to bank CEOs in July 2020[68] and October 2022,[69] following up on its supervisory expectations and progress assessments. Unlike in the case of the ECB, however, these letters contained feedback on industry-wide, rather than bank-specific, progress. They also set out observations on effective and less effective industry practices. From 2022, the PRA moved from assessing implementation of its supervisory expectations by banks to actively supervising against them.[70] The management of CRFR has thus become part of banks' formal supervisory assessments, including their plans for meeting the PRA's supervisory expectations, climate-related capital adequacy assessments and climate-related disclosures. Banks judged to have not made sufficient progress in complying with the PRA's expectations must 'provide a roadmap to explain how they intend to overcome the gaps', while the PRA is ready to respond with its wider supervisory toolkit, including capital scalars or add-ons, if failure to meet its expectations is persistent.[71] Overall, the BoE has trimmed back its work in climate change in 2024 in response to the fact that the Chancellor removed climate change from his annual remit letter to the Bank's Financial Policy Committee.

4.2 Climate-Related Scenario Analysis and Stress Testing

The unique features of CRFR enhance the need for banks and supervisors to deploy forward-looking measurement methodologies such as scenario analyses and stress testing.[72] By definition, stress tests are hypothetical exercises, aiming at identifying the implications of severe but plausible scenarios on the resilience of individual banks and the financial system at large. The uncertainties associated with CRFR and the potentially longer time horizons for them to manifest remain key challenges. As their results are preliminary and subject to data and modelling limitations, climate stress tests represent joint learning exercises. At this early stage, they aim to incentivize banks to put preconditions in place to be able to identify and measure CRFR and to enhance their risk management frameworks. The first pilot climate stress tests conducted in the jurisdictions studied in this chapter have primarily served the purpose of acting as a catalyst for banks to improve their collection of climate-relevant data breakdowns and data infrastructures. Except for some banks under the ECB's direct supervision,[73] they have not had any direct implications for capital requirements.

Compared with traditional stress tests, institutionalized by the Basel Framework in the aftermath of the global financial crisis, CRFR-specific stress tests target much longer time

---

[68] PRA, 'Managing climate-related financial risk – Thematic feedback from the PRA's review of firms' SS3/19 plans and clarifications of expectations', Letter from Sam Woods (1 July 2020) <https://www.bankofengland.co.uk/-/media/boe/files/prudential-regulation/letter/2020/managing-the-financial-risks-from-climate-change.pdf> accessed 20 May 2024.

[69] PRA, 'Thematic feedback on the PRA's supervision of climate-related financial risk and the Bank of England's climate biennial exploratory scenario exercise', Letter from Sam Woods (21 October 2022) <https://www.bankofengland.co.uk/-/media/boe/files/prudential-regulation/letter/2022/october/managing-climate-related-financial-risks.pdf> accessed 20 May 2024.

[70] See PRA (n 25) 20–22.

[71] ibid 21.

[72] See BCBS (n 15).

[73] The outcomes of the ECB's 2022 climate stress test were incorporated into banks' annual SREP assessment in a qualitative manner.

horizons of up to 30 years. In all the jurisdictions examined in this chapter, these stress tests were based on a set of scenarios developed by the NGFS,[74] although adapted to the specificities of the jurisdictions at hand. The conducted stress testing exercises reach similar conclusions: estimated credit losses are lower under an 'orderly transition' scenario, compared with a 'disorderly transition' with a sudden increase of carbon prices. Even higher are the estimated losses under a 'hot house world' scenario of unabated climate change.

In May 2022, the Bank of England published the results of its first exploratory scenario analysis exercise on CRFR, run with the UK's largest banks and insurers during 2021.[75] The bank-specific findings from the exercise inform the supervisory dialogue of the PRA with participating banks and helps the PRA assess banks' progress against its supervisory expectations in this area.

In 2020, the Swiss National Bank (SNB) and FINMA conducted a pilot climate stress test aimed at obtaining an initial picture of transition risk concentrations at Switzerland's globally systemically important banks, UBS and Credit Suisse.[76] In line with its general practice for stress tests, SNB did not share any detailed results of the exercise. The results of the analysis 'will flow into (...) FINMA's supervisory dialogue with the banks', without any further follow-up supervisory measures expected at this stage.[77]

In 2023, the Fed conducted a pilot climate scenario analysis exercise, pursuing two objectives: (1) learning about banks' climate risk management practices and challenges; and (2) enhancing the ability of both banks and supervisors to identify, measure, monitor and manage CRFR. Like in other jurisdictions, the exercise is of an exploratory nature, with consequences for bank capital or other supervisory follow-up measures expressly excluded.[78] Six bank holding companies[79] participated in the exercise and submitted data templates, supporting documentation and responses to qualitative questions. The Fed disclosed aggregated information about how the six banks incorporate CRFR into their risk management frameworks, but no

---

74 For the fifth and latest vintage of these scenarios see NGFS, 'NGFS long-term scenarios for central banks and supervisors' (November 2024) <https://www.ngfs.net/sites/default/files/medias/documents/ngfs_scenarios_main_presentation.pdf> accessed 17 November 2024.

75 Bank of England, 'Results of the 2021 Climate Biennial Exploratory Scenario (CBES)' (24 May 2022) <https://www.bankofengland.co.uk/stress-testing/2022/results-of-the-2021-climate-biennial-exploratory-scenario> accessed 20 May 2024.

76 SNB, '2022 Financial Stability Report' <https://www.snb.ch/en/mmr/reference/stabrep_2022/source/stabrep_2022.en.pdf> accessed 20 May 2024, 14.

77 Swiss Financial Market Supervisory Authority, '2021 Annual Report' <https://www.finma.ch/~/media/finma/dokumente/dokumentencenter/myfinma/finma-publikationen/geschaeftsbericht/20220405-finma_jahresbericht_2021.pdf?sc_lang=en&hash=39D0EED3823CAE735B128E31DE0FDAD1> accessed 20 May 2024, 30.

78 Federal Reserve Board of Governors, 'Pilot climate scenario analysis exercise: Participant instructions' (January 2023) <https://www.federalreserve.gov/publications/files/csa-instructions-20230117.pdf> accessed 20 May 2024, iii: 'The Board views climate scenario analyses as distinct and separate from regulatory stress tests. (...). The pilot [climate scenario analysis] exercise, on the other hand, is exploratory in nature and does not have consequences for bank capital or supervisory implications.'

79 Bank of America; Citigroup; Goldman Sachs; JPMorgan Chase; Morgan Stanley; and Wells Fargo.

quantitative estimates of potential losses resulting from the scenarios included in the exercise, nor any firm-specific information.[80]

In 2022, MAS conducted a climate scenario analysis exercise for selected banks as part of its industry-wide stress test.[81] The exercise was meant to raise awareness of the potential economic and financial implications of CRFR and to further develop capabilities both at MAS and within the industry. MAS published aggregate findings from the exercise, without disclosing any bank-specific information nor which (subset of) banks participated in the exercise.

The ECB's 2022 climate risk stress test of the banks under its direct supervision aimed at exploring the level of banks' preparedness for tackling and managing CRFR, taking into account both qualitative and quantitative elements.[82] The ECB provided participating banks with institution-specific assessments of their climate risk stress-testing capabilities and with benchmarked results in relation to relevant peers.

5. PILLAR 3: DISCLOSURE OF CLIMATE/SUSTAINABILITY RISKS

Under pillar 3 of the Basel Framework, banks are required to disclose information on their risk exposures and internal processes to manage and control these risks. Pillar 3 disclosures are key for market discipline to operate effectively. They ensure that market actors gain a good understanding of the risk exposures and capital adequacy of banks.

The Basel Framework does not currently provide for distinct information on how climate risk could impact individual banks or the banking sector. In November 2023, the BCBS published a preliminary proposal for a pillar 3 disclosure framework for CRFR with the aim of promoting the comparability of banks' risk profiles and give (potential) investors and other market participants access to key information regarding banks' exposures to CRFR.[83] The proposal is meant to complement regulatory initiatives on sustainability reporting standards that have a broader circle of target addressees[84] with bank-specific prudential disclosure requirements. These requirements include both qualitative information (on governance, strategy, risk management and concentration risk) as well as quantitative targets and metrics (including financed emissions and exposure by sector) and will be partially mandatory and partially subject to national discretion.

---

80 Federal Reserve Board of Governors, 'Pilot climate scenario analysis exercise – Summary of participants' risk-management practices and estimates' (May 2024) <https://www.federalreserve.gov/publications/files/csa-exercise-summary-20240509.pdf> accessed 20 May 2024.

81 See MAS, 'Financial stability review' (November 2022) <https://www.mas.gov.sg/-/media/mas-media-library/publications/financial-stability-review/2022/financial-stability-review-2022.pdf> accessed 20 May 2024, 73–84.

82 ECB, '2022 climate risk stress test' (July 2022) <https://www.bankingsupervision.europa.eu/ecb/pub/pdf/ssm.climate_stress_test_report.20220708~2e3cc0999f.en.pdf> accessed 20 May 2024.

83 BCBS, 'Consultative document – Disclosure of climate-related financial risks' (29 November 2023) <https://www.bis.org/bcbs/publ/d560.pdf> accessed 20 May 2024.

84 E.g. the standards issued by the International Sustainability Standards Board (ISSB).

Many jurisdictions have already developed prudential disclosure requirements for CRFR (and at times other sustainability risks) as part of the expectations formulated by bank supervisors. In line with the TCFD Recommendations, supervisors ask banks to describe and regularly disclose their material CRFR and the impact of these risks on their business strategy, business model and financial planning. Typically, this includes information on the process for identifying, measuring and addressing CRFR (risk management) and quantitative data (measures and targets), as well as a description of the methodology used to collect that data. Often, banks are also required to describe the core characteristics of their governance structure regarding CRFR and disclose the criteria and assessment methods used to evaluate the materiality of these risks.

The PRA's supervisory expectations published in 2019 require banks to develop appropriate climate-related disclosures in their pillar 3 reports and from 2022, the PRA has started reviewing disclosures of material CRFR.[85] The ECB's supervisory guidance also expects banks 'to publish meaningful information and key metrics on climate-related and environmental risks that they deem to be material'.[86] Since June 2022, MAS requests banks to make CRFR disclosures in accordance with well-regarded international reporting frameworks, such as the TCFD Recommendations.[87] FINMA specified principle-based disclosure rules for CRFR in its existing supervisory guidance on disclosures by banks.[88] The most significant Swiss banks included the first CRFR disclosures in their annual reporting on the financial year 2021.

However, in the absence of international standards and as the quality of climate-related data is still evolving, these supervisory expectations on disclosure have produced limited results. Supervisors view banks' CRFR disclosures as too general so far and see limited usefulness of the disclosed information for investors to judge banks' exposure to and handling of CRFR. Perhaps expectedly, they have identified the largest gaps regarding quantitative information (targets and key data) and the evaluation of the materiality of CRFR. Moreover, banks often explain with insufficient detail how they are affected by CRFR in terms of their business strategy and risk profile and fail to distinguish appropriately between short-, medium- and long-term horizons.[89]

Some jurisdictions are introducing or contemplating to introduce mandatory CRFR disclosures on a statutory basis. In the EU, a pre-existing legal obligation for large listed banks to disclose information on ESG risks, including physical and transition risks, was extended to

---

[85] See PRA (n 25) 19, 21.

[86] ECB (n 34) expectation 13.

[87] MAS (n 38) 9–10. GFIT (n 40) 62–70, also offers guidance to banks on best practices regarding disclosures.

[88] FINMA, 'Circular 2016/1 "Disclosure – banks"' (update of 8 December 2021) <https://www.finma.ch/en/~/media/finma/dokumente/dokumentencenter/myfinma/rundschreiben/finma-rs-2016-01.pdf?sc_lang=en&hash=D411DB5EE94E16A385AA2A689D94AF94> accessed 20 May 2024, para. 14.2 and Annex 5.

[89] See FINMA, 'FINMA Guidance 03/2022: Implementation of climate-related risk disclosures by category 1–2 institutions' (29 November 2022) <https://www.finma.ch/en/~/media/finma/dokumente/dokumentencenter/myfinma/4dokumentation/finma-aufsichtsmitteilungen/20221129-finma-aufsichtsmitteilung-03-2022.pdf?sc_lang=en&hash=76D53FE0BCE81FEAC2C25077BD69D190> accessed 20 May 2024; ECB, 'Supervisory assessment of institutions' climate-related and environmental risks disclosures' (March 2022) <https://www.bankingsupervision.europa.eu/ecb/pub/pdf/ssm.ECB_Report_on_climate_and_environmental_disclosures_202203~4ae33f2a70.en.pdf> accessed 20 May 2024.

include all banks.[90] Revised Implementing Technical Standards (ITS) detail the quantitative and qualitative information banks have to provide on their transition risk and physical risk exposures.[91] MAS has also announced that it will consult on mandatory disclosure requirements for banks (and other financial institutions), referencing the standards of the International Sustainability Standards Board (ISSB).[92]

Less tangible progress has been made in the US, where the debate has been more about what information investors are demanding, rather than what is necessary and appropriate from a prudential point of view. In an Executive Order of 2021, the former administration of President Biden declared a new federal policy of 'advanc[ing] consistent, clear, intelligible, comparable, and accurate disclosure of climate-related financial risk'.[93] Currently, US bank disclosure requirements do not contain targeted requirements related to CRFR and their management. However, large banks often disclose climate-related information on a voluntary basis (e.g. according to the TCFD framework).[94] Because the existing regulatory requirements and voluntary frameworks 'do not result in disclosures that are consistent, comparable, and decision-useful' across US banks, the Financial Stability Oversight Council (FSOC) 'recommends that federal banking regulators … continue to review banks' public regulatory reporting requirements to assess whether enhancements are needed to provide market participants with information on institutions' CRFR, taking into account a bank's size, complexity, and activities'.[95] However, the Fed, OCC and FDIC have not followed up with proposals for revised reporting requirements.

6. CONCLUSIONS

This chapter advanced the argument that sustainability issues can create both material financial risks and opportunities for banks and are thus of prudential concern. It attempted to identify the specific challenges that bank regulators face when including sustainability factors and risk in prudential frameworks. Doing so remains a process based on mutual learning between the industry, supervisors, regulators and central banks, but also between different jurisdictions. This is where the comparative analysis of this chapter provides some important insights.

---

90 CRR art 449a. In addition, banks are required to report the ESG-related risk exposure to their supervisor.

91 Commission Implementing Regulation (EU) 2022/2453 of 30 November 2022 amending the implementing technical standards laid down in Implementing Regulation (EU) 2021/637 as regards the disclosure of environmental, social and governance risks [2022] OJ L 324/1, 1. The ITS also cover information on the alignment of banks' portfolios with the EU Taxonomy, which testifies to the 'double materiality' approach that the EU pursues.

92 See <https://www.mas.gov.sg/development/sustainable-finance/regulatory-and-supervisory-approach> accessed 20 May 2024.

93 Executive Order 14030 on climate-related financial risk, 87 Federal Register 27067 (20 May 2021) <https://www.whitehouse.gov/briefing-room/presidential-actions/2021/05/20/executive-order-on-climate-related-financial-risk/> accessed 20 May 2024.

94 FSOC, 'Report on climate-related financial risk' (October 2021) <https://home.treasury.gov/system/files/261/FSOC-Climate-Report.pdf> accessed 20 May 2024, 73–74.

95 ibid 84, 123.

By comparing the regulatory frameworks of the US, the UK, Switzerland, Singapore and the EU, the chapter revealed that not all pillars of the Basel Framework are equally flexible to accommodate the specificities of CRFR. Action in most jurisdictions has so far focused on pillar 2, i.e. 'supervisory dialogue' with banks on their identification, measurement, and management of CRFR. In all jurisdictions analyzed in this chapter, bank supervisors have issued supervisory expectations, based on which they evaluate banks' progress in incorporating CRFR in their risk management and internal control frameworks, but also their strategy and governance. Large differences exist regarding the supervisory follow-up measures in case of persistent failure by banks to comply with these expectations. Only for banks under the remit of the ECB has such failure had implications in terms of capital requirements.

While disclosure can play a crucial role in incentivizing banks to improve their management of CRFR, approaches differ across jurisdictions. Some regulators are in the process of introducing mandatory pillar 3 disclosure requirements regarding CRFR, while others rely on supervisory expectations also in that regard. International standards on CRFR disclosures, as proposed by the BCBS, would crucially improve the global comparability of banks' efforts to address CRFR.

Owing to its rigidity, CRFR are most difficult to reflect in pillar 1. Quite naturally, the BCBS has taken a leading role in the discussion on potential amendments to the pillar 1 framework. Only in the EU have policymakers contemplated further-reaching measures than those taken or planned by the BCBS.

20. Cryptocurrencies and stablecoins regulation

Edoardo D. Martino[1]

1. INTRODUCTION

The advent of the blockchain technology, more than 15 years ago, spurred a countless number of applications and experimentations that can be labelled as 'crypto economy'.[2] The financial applications of the blockchain technology have always been at the forefront of the debate.[3] This chapter focuses on those financial applications, 'crypto finance'. Within crypto finance, the chapter focuses on the comparative regulation of its two key instruments, cryptocurrencies and stablecoins. This adds to the literature on the regulation of crypto finance as it provides a functional framework to approach an area whose regulation is quickly evolving. Moreover, it also adds to the comparative law literature, looking at the sources and dynamics of divergence in the regulation of innovative technologies.

The first-ever blockchain application, the Bitcoin protocol, aimed at creating 'purely peer-to-peer version of electronic cash [that] would allow online payments to be sent directly from one party to another without going through a financial institution'.[4]

As the Bitcoin White Paper proudly stated, the vision of Bitcoin, and many other cryptocurrencies that followed, was to build a financial system without intermediaries; hence, to completely revolutionize finance. Steering away from the debate about the classification of some cryptocurrencies as 'financial instruments', at a more conceptual level it is crucial to highlight that eliminating, or perhaps substituting, traditional intermediaries carrying out financial activities in the blockchain has massive implications for legislators and policymakers. Regulating intermediaries is, indeed, the most common and simple approach to regulating financial activities.[5] From a regulatory perspective, this means that fostering market efficiency, protecting investors, safeguarding financial stability and any other regulatory goal become much more complicated when confronted with crypto finance.[6]

---

[1] Thanks to Ugo Malvagna and the participants to the ACLE-EY Workshop on Comparative Financial Regulation of their feedback and insights. I am grateful to Melek Redzheb for the outstanding research assistance. Usual disclaimers apply.

[2] Iris HY Chiu, *Regulating the Crypto Economy: Business Transformations and Financialisation* (Bloomsbury Publishing 2021).

[3] Arguably, because of the growth of the technology and the various financial scandals, the non-financial applications of the blockchain technology, such as smart contracts, DAOs and Asset Tokenization are getting more and more traction. See, for instance, Lin W Cong and Zhiguo He, 'Blockchain Disruption and Smart Contracts' (2019) 32 The Review of Financial Studies 1754.

[4] Satoshi Nakamoto, 'Bitcoin: A Peer-to-Peer Electronic Cash System' <https://bitcoin.org/bitcoin.pdf> 1.

[5] See Chapter 1 in this volume, p. 6.

[6] John Armour and others, *Principles of Financial Regulation* (Oxford University Press 2016) 52.

The counternarrative promoted by the early proponents of crypto finance is that getting rid of intermediaries and relying on trustless protocols to validate transactions is the real way to empower the people and have a free and efficient financial system.[7]

After 15 years, we can safely say that the promises of the early crypto enthusiast did not stand the test of time. However, these radically different positions lead to a heterogeneous and at times polarized policy debate whose focus has repeatedly changed in different jurisdictions and across time, alternating moments of crypto hype with moments of crypto winter, depending on the performance and the reliability of the crypto economy compared with the 'traditional' financial sector. A functional approach also allows abstraction from the contingencies of the current, ongoing and fast evolving policy debate, making sense of the divergent approaches.

Accordingly, this chapter maps and analyses the main regulatory approaches to crypto finance in different jurisdictions, primarily but not exclusively the EU, the UK and the US. The scope of the analysis is delimited even further, as it only looks at the traditional regulatory tools used in financial regulation applicable to cryptocurrencies and stablecoins: conditions to operate, obligations on the issuers, crisis management tools and so forth.[8]

The chapter unfolds as follows. Section 2 sets out the key functional difference between crypto and stablecoins. Section 3 discusses the main dimensions that it is crucial to regulate, respectively, for cryptocurrencies and stablecoins. Based on the functional analysis, Section 4 presents different regulatory models for cryptocurrencies and stablecoins, both with respect to 'corner solutions' as exemplified by China and El Salvador, and with regard to 'interior' solutions, with a focus on the EU, UK and US regimes. Section 5 provides insights into the key regulatory features of the EU and UK, as these are the jurisdictions with the most advanced regulatory projects and they offer a perfect example of the source, dynamics and implications of regulatory divergences.

2. FINANCIAL (DIS)INTERMEDIATION AND REGULATORY GOALS

The first step to build a functional framework for comparative analysis is to look at how different blockchain applications, namely cryptocurrencies and stablecoins, aim at disrupting traditional finance.[9]

This allows a functional comparison to be drawn between blockchain finance and traditional finance. Specifically, cryptocurrencies functionally resemble financial activities in the capital

---

7 See, for instance, Aaron Wright and Primavera De Filippi, 'Decentralized Blockchain Technology and the Rise of Lex Cryptographia' (2015) <https://papers.ssrn.com/sol3/papers.cfm?abstract_id=2580664>.

8 However, it is worth stressing that the legal and regulatory perimeter is much wider including the areas of AI regulation, privacy regulation, money laundering and terrorism financing regulation. See, for instance, Qi Feng and others, 'A Survey on Privacy Protection in Blockchain System' (2019) 126 Journal of Network and Computer Applications 45; Daniel Dupuis and Kimberly Gleason, 'Money Laundering with Cryptocurrency: Open Doors and the Regulatory Dialectic' (2020) 28 Journal of Financial Crime 60.

9 Dirk A Zetzsche, Douglas W Arner and Ross P Buckley, 'Decentralized Finance (Defi)' (2020) 6 Journal of Financial Regulation 172.

market, as they offer investment opportunities characterized by high upside potential and high volatility. On the other hand, stablecoins aim at promising safety and liquidity in the crypto economy, gearing more towards (shadow) banking.

This section details why these functional comparisons hold and what can be inferred from a regulatory perspective. As a first approximation, it is important to notice that different financial activities bring about different regulatory priorities. Namely, capital market activities traditionally need a regulatory framework protecting investors and fostering market efficiency; whereas banking activities should be subject to preventive regulation whose main purpose is to safeguard financial stability.

Delving into the specific regulatory goals for cryptocurrencies and stablecoins provides an understanding of the dynamics underpinning law-making in such a new and fast-evolving area. Before doing so, one additional caveat needs to be spelled out. Policymakers and regulators may not act purely following financial and legal rationales, but they are likely to be influenced by the willingness to engage in regulatory competition, so attracting crypto activities into their jurisdiction. Moreover, lobbying by influential figures in industry also has an impact on the timing and content of law-making. These two tendencies would advise a lenient regulatory approach. Two examples suffice to substantiate this claim.

Soon after being appointed as the new Prime Minister of the UK, Rishi Sunak publicly stated his intention to turn the country into a global hub for crypto.[10] This would imply, among other things, an effort to increase legal and regulatory certainty around the crypto economy and promote regulation that does not hamper growth and innovation in the sector.[11] This approach is likely to alter the previous, harsher, positions of independent regulators.

Another relevant example is provided by the peculiar trajectory of Sam Bankman-Fried, the former CEO of FTX, the second largest crypto exchange in the world, currently awaiting trial for his responsibility for the collapse of FTX, for which he faces charges that may lead to up to 155 years of jail time.[12] Interestingly, before FTX went bankrupt, Bankman-Fried was considered a reliable industry leader with whom federal agencies and the US legislator often discussed the most desirable regulatory approach to the growing crypto industry. For instance, in a testimony to the House of Representatives given on December 2021, less than a year before the FTX collapse, Bankman-Fried stated that 'an appropriate policy framework for market regulation of crypto assets should remain market-structure neutral and expressly allow non-intermediated markets'.[13]

---

[10] Sandali Handagama, 'Now That He Has the Power to Make His Crypto Dreams Come True, Will He?' (CoinDesk, 5 December 2022) <https://www.coindesk.com/consensus-magazine/2022/12/05/rishi-sunak-most-influential-2022/> accessed 9 June 2023.

[11] Lyllah Ledesma, 'UK Crypto-Focused Parliament Group Calls on New PM Sunak to Clarify Crypto Policies' (CoinDesk, 25 October 2022) <https://www.coindesk.com/policy/2022/10/25/uk-crypto-focused-parliament-group-calls-on-new-pm-sunak-to-clarify-crypto-policies/> accessed 17 April 2023.

[12] Associated Press, 'FTX Founder Sam Bankman-Fried Facing up to 155 Years in Jail after New Fraud Charges Announced' (Euronews, 24 February 2023) <https://www.euronews.com/next/2023/02/24/ftx-founder-sam-bankman-fried-facing-up-to-155-years-in-jail-after-new-fraud-charges-annou> accessed 9 June 2023.

[13] Committee on Financial Services, 'Digital Assets and the Future of Finance: Understanding the Challenges and Benefits of Financial Innovation in the United States' (House of Representatives

Lobbying and regulatory competition are invariant in the regulation of financial activities,[14] and their impact in new, fast-growing, sectors characterized by a high degree of uncertainty can be massive and single-handedly explain the divergence in regulatory regimes. Against this background, a functional framework to analyse the key regulatory goals of cryptocurrencies and stablecoins is ever more necessary. A fruitful starting point is to provide a clear functional definition of the two categories of crypto assets.

Cryptocurrencies are digitally scarce units of value, the properties and circulation of which are prescribed via computer code.[15] This broad definition includes currencies that were designed as a means of payment and alternative investment opportunities, such as Bitcoins, native currencies supporting wider blockchain platforms such as Ethereum as well as crowd-funding schemes based on blockchain protocols, such as the thousands of initial coin offerings (ICOs) that flourished as of 2017.[16] All of these assets are highly volatile by design and are traded in centralized or decentralized crypto exchanges.[17]

Stablecoins are a subset of cryptocurrencies whose aim is to maintain stable value referencing physical, financial or crypto-assets (asset-linked stablecoins) or via specific protocols adjusting supply in response to a change in demand (algorithmic stablecoins).[18] The stabilization mechanism is the key feature differentiating stablecoins from other cryptocurrencies as it generates an expectation of safety and liquidity in stablecoin holders.[19] The existence of crypto assets promising safety and liquidity is a key feature of any financial system characterized by some level of complexity.[20] Therefore, the rise of stablecoins does not simply represent an innovation in the crypto landscape, rather a stepping stone towards the development of the crypto finance and the crypto economy at large.[21]

The overarching goal of a regulatory regime for cryptocurrencies is to make sure that, in the presence of frictions and market failures, the 'digitally scarce units' representing the cur-

---

2021) Congressional Hearings 117–63, 107 <https://www.govinfo.gov/app/details/CHRG-117hhrg46302/CHRG-117hhrg46302/summary> accessed 9 June 2023.

[14] Deniz Igan, Prachi Mishra and Thierry Tressel, 'A Fistful of Dollars: Lobbying and the Financial Crisis' (2012) 26 NBER Macroeconomics Annual 195; Jonathan R Macey, 'Regulatory Globalization as a Response to Regulatory Competition' (2003) 52 Emory LJ 1353.

[15] Valeria Ferrari, 'The Regulation of Crypto-Assets in the EU – Investment and Payment Tokens under the Radar' (2020) 27 Maastricht Journal of European and Comparative Law 325, 327.

[16] Wulf A Kaal, 'Initial Coin Offerings: The Top 25 Jurisdictions and Their Comparative Regulatory Responses (as of May 2018)' (2018) 1 Stan. J. Blockchain L. & Pol'y 41.

[17] Evgeny Lyandres, Berardino Palazzo and Daniel Rabetti, 'Initial Coin Offering (ICO) Success and Post-ICO Performance' (2022) 68 Management Science 8658.

[18] Financial Stability Board (FSB), *Regulation, Supervision and Oversight of 'Global Stablecoin' Arrangements: Final Report and High-Level Recommendations* (Financial Stability Board 2020) 5.

[19] Edoardo D Martino, 'Regulating Stablecoins as Private Money between Liquidity and Safety. The Case of the EU "Market in Crypto Asset" (MiCA) Regulation' [2022] Amsterdam Center for Law & Economics Working Paper No. 2022-07 26.

[20] Gary B Gorton, 'The History and Economics of Safe Assets' (2017) 9 Annual Review of Economics 547.

[21] Sirio Aramonte, Wenqian Huang and Andreas Schrimpf, 'DeFi Risks and the Decentralisation Illusion' (2021) BIS Quarterly Review 21, 26.

rency are allocated efficiently, i.e. to who values them the most. The blockchain technology promise is that such an efficient application directly descends from the algorithmic set-up of the blockchain so that regulation is unnecessary since the 'code' regulates party transactions.[22] However, this promise has been repeatedly frustrated by the numerous frauds and manipulations in the market for cryptocurrencies.

Consequently, the role of 'traditional' state regulation seems unavoidable and should follow the 'traditional' approach of financial market regulation: preventing fraud and manipulation and making sure that the market participants have all the relevant information to correctly price the tokens.

This does not necessarily have immediate normative repercussions, since at this point of the analysis I steer away from the debate of the legal classification of crypto assets as 'financial instruments', which will be further discussed in Sections 4 and 5. However, irrespective of the specific legal classification that different jurisdictions may provide, financial instruments and cryptocurrencies share some functional characteristics largely aligning their regulatory goals.

Stablecoins are different. Despite being a 'sub-category' of cryptocurrencies, their 'liquidity' and 'safety' promise to completely subvert the regulatory priorities as they add financial stability concerns. This implicit promise of liquidity and safety is not necessarily matched by the liquid and safe management of the issuer's reserves.[23] On the contrary, the issuer's incentives will be to use reserves to invest in relatively illiquid and risky projects to maximize their return, hence performing qualitative asset transformation – an activity that is proper for (shadow) banks. Such mismatch between assets and liabilities, if not well managed and regulated, generates incentives to run when the trust in the solvency of the issuer sways.[24] Therefore, preventing runs and panics should be the quintessential regulatory goal for stablecoins. This implies the necessity to regulate more carefully the legal rights of stablecoins holders and the requirements of stablecoin issuers in using and investing reserves, to make sure the mismatch is correctly managed.[25]

So far, the stability concerns are mainly within the crypto economy as evidenced by the 'crypto winter' triggered by the collapse of the Terra stablecoin in May 2022.[26] However, wider spillovers to the real economy cannot be ruled out should the industry grow and become more interconnected with the rest of the financial system. Some signals of the possibility of generating wider spillovers were recently observed in the failure of Signature Bank, a 'crypto friendly' bank that was shut down by the Federal Deposit Insurance Corporation in March 2023.[27] However, this has to be attributed mainly to a reckless management of Signature and

---

22 Wright and De Filippi (n 7) 11.

23 Martino (n 19) 38.

24 Douglas W Diamond and Philip H Dybvig, 'Bank Runs, Deposit Insurance, and Liquidity' (1983) 91 Journal of Political Economy 401.

25 Martino (n 19) 31.

26 Antonio Briola and others, 'Anatomy of a Stablecoin's Failure: The Terra-Luna Case' (2023) 51 Finance Research Letters 103358.

27 Gary B Gorton and Jeffery Y Zhang, 'Bank Runs During Crypto Winter' (2024) 14 Harvard Business Law Review 297.

this concerns can be better handled indirectly, through better regulation and supervision of banks.[28]

3. FINANCIAL (DIS)INTERMEDIATION AND REGULATORY STRATEGIES

The second step of this comparative functional analysis is to look at the regulatory strategies and tools to achieve this goal as these are key drivers of divergence across jurisdictions. This section looks at four key aspects of the regulatory regime for intermediaries applied to the regulation of cryptocurrencies and stablecoins. Namely, this section discusses the regulatory point of entry, the obligations imposed on issuers, the supervisory powers and the specific crisis management tools.

Broadly speaking, regulators could attract crypto-related financial activities within the regulatory perimeter in two ways: first regulating the activities of issuing and trading cryptocurrencies and/or stablecoins in themselves, also called an activity-based regulatory approach. Second, regulators may prefer to target the entities who issue and trade cryptocurrencies and/or stablecoins, also called an entity-based regulatory approach. Both approaches have positive and problematic aspects and relate to goals pursued by the regulation.[29]

An activity-based approach, as the name suggests, applies to the activity, irrespective of the entity carrying it on. This approach has the benefit of decreasing the scope for regulatory arbitrage and forum shopping, as it can apply to any activity carried out in a given jurisdiction. It also seems to better capture the nature of the blockchain activities in so far as it does cryptocurrencies and stablecoins can be issued by decentralized protocols that are difficult to trace back to a traditional 'entity'. Moreover, an activity-based regulation is more conducive to innovation as it does not strive to standardize the type of entities that can carry out a certain activity according to a rather homogeneous organizational structure.

On the other hand, and in close connection with the latter observation, under an activity-based regulation cryptocurrencies and/or stablecoins would be more difficult to supervise and rules would be more difficult to enforce. Moreover, to capture heterogeneity, standards most likely dominate rules as a regulatory technique, which can allow for more innovation but also prevents the imposition of tailored-based obligations when needed.[30] A pure activity-based regulation does not seem possible. However, regulators may decide to pursue a hybrid approach whereby issuers are regulated according to the activities carried out and gatekeepers, such as custodians, trading platforms and so forth, are regulated according to an entity-based regulation and are used as an indirect point of entry to discipline the activities in the cryptocurrency market.

An entity-based approach has several advantages revolving around the simplicity in the regulatory design, supervision and enforcement. In a nutshell, any entity aiming at carrying out a certain activity, such as issuing cryptocurrencies and/or stablecoins, must first obtain

---

28 Basel Committee on Banking Supervision (BCBS), 'Prudential Treatment of Cryptoasset Exposures' (BCBS, December 2022) <https://www.bis.org/bcbs/publ/d545.htm>.

29 Fernando Restoy, *Fintech Regulation: How to Achieve a Level Playing Field* (Financial Stability Institute, Bank for International Settlements, 2021).

30 Louis Kaplow, 'Rules versus Standards: An Economic Analysis' (1992) 42 Duke LJ 557.

a licence from the relevant authority. All and only the licensed entities can carry out a certain activity and are, consequently, subject to the relevant regulatory regime. This ensures a more preventive approach, as 'bad apples' can be prevented from entering the market in the first place. The harmonization and standardization reduce regulatory costs and empower regulators and supervisors, but may not capture the heterogeneity of the actors acting in the crypto economy, especially when activities are carried out through decentralized, non-incorporated, protocols. Moreover, this approach is prone to regulatory arbitrage, as non-licensed entities may try to carry out functionally equivalent operations to escape the tighter regulatory regime.[31]

The second key aspect relates to the obligations imposed on the issues of cryptocurrencies and/or stablecoins. This is the aspect is tightly related to the regulatory goals discussed in Section 2. Regulation prioritizing different policy goals should resort to different, non-mutually exclusive, tools. To guarantee investor protection and foster market efficiency, regulators should focus on disclosure duties, the conduct of business rules and civil liability regimes for wrongdoings of material risk takers.[32] Disclosure duties aim at providing the necessary, high-quality information to decrease the information asymmetry between the issuer and the investors. In turn, this should allow the investors to price the instruments correctly.[33] Conduct of business rules want to make sure that the issuer and its management body are prevented from acting opportunistically.[34] The effectiveness of such rules must be guaranteed by an appropriate liability regime for the management body of the issuer. On top of these rules, market efficiency must be supported by another set of rules prohibiting the abuse of inside information and market manipulations. Based on the framework proposed in Section 2, this set of rules should be the main focus for cryptocurrency regulation.[35]

In contrast, the obligations imposed on (the issuers of) stablecoins should go beyond investor protection and market efficiency, prioritizing stability. This does not mean that rules protecting stablecoin holders and the efficiency of the market for stablecoins should not be enacted. It means that further, stricter, rules should apply to stablecoins and that when a trade-off between investor protection, market efficiency and financial stability exists, financial stability considerations should prevail.[36] Specifically, preserving financial stability may require tighter authorization requirements; hence, entity-based regulation should be preferred. Beyond authorization requirements, regulators should make sure that the regulatory design minimizes the risk of a run even if stablecoin holders are not insured by any form of deposit guarantee.[37] This should look at two inter-related components: first, the risk management regime on the issuer's reserves; and second, the legal rights conferred upon stablecoins holders

---

31 Victor Fleischer, 'Regulatory Arbitrage' (2010) 89 Tex. L. Rev. 227, 277.

32 Stephen J Choi, 'A Framework for the Regulation of Securities Market Intermediaries' (2004) 1 Berkeley Bus. LJ 45.

33 Luca Enriques and Sergio Gilotta, 'Disclosure and Financial Market Regulation' in Niamh Moloney, Eilís Ferran and Payne, Jennifer (eds), *The Oxford Handbook of Financial Regulation* (Oxford University Press 2015).

34 Alessio M Pacces, 'Financial Intermediation in the Securities Markets Law and Economics of Conduct of Business Regulation' (2000) 20 International Review of Law and Economics 479.

35 Text to note 21.

36 Text to note 22.

37 Gary B Gorton and Jeffery Zhang, 'Taming Wildcat Stablecoins' (2023) 90 University of Chicago Law Review 909.

in terms of withdrawal. In other terms, the regulator should limit the ability of stablecoins issuers to perform maturity and liquidity transformation. It can do so by limiting the activities that the stablecoin issuer can undertake, for instance limiting the assets it can invest in, or on the other hand, by limiting the possibility to withdraw on demand or setting accounting rules for the valuation of the market value of stablecoins that curb the incentive to run in case of turmoil.[38]

The third regulatory dimension to consider relates to ongoing supervision. The key is the design of the power of the competent authority. Again, a broad distinction can be drawn between supervisory powers aiming at protecting investors and preserving market efficiency on the one hand, and supervisory powers aiming at preserving financial stability on the other hand. In protecting investors and preserving market efficiency supervisors should be empowered to require information and mandate additional disclosure related to the regulated activities. Moreover, supervisors should have the power to bring to an end potential infringement of the applicable regulation. This is particularly relevant in cases of activity-based regulation, where issuers do not need to preventively acquire a licence. On the other hand, safeguarding financial stability requires more intrusive, preventive, powers in the hands of the competent authority. For instance, the supervisor can impose additional requirements on issuers to cover for additional risks not covered in primary regulation, stress-test the relevant market players and adapt their requirements and supervision accordingly, and so forth.

Finally, the last key regulatory element is the provision of special crisis management tools. This latter element exclusively relates to instances when normal insolvency and liquidation procedures are considered unfit; hence, financial stability considerations must have some level of priority. There are two main categories of crisis management tools: first, tools that apply before the failure of the issuer, such as redemption gates or liquidity fees imposed on the holders of liquid claims in times of liquidity stress; and second, special resolution procedures that apply instead of normal insolvency procedures to avoid market disruption.

Finally, it is important to mention that the specific regulation of cryptocurrencies and stablecoins is part of a more complex regulatory framework, beyond the scope of the analysis. Therefore, the regulation of key intermediaries in crypto finance, such as crypto exchanges and custodians, also has a considerable impact on the regulatory regime of cryptocurrencies and stablecoins.[39]

4. REGULATING CRYPTO: *UBI IRE*?

The last task to complete the framework for a comparative analysis of cryptocurrencies and stablecoins regulation is to look at the possible rule-making strategies pursued by different jurisdictions. Chronologically, the first regulatory approach tried to attract the new instruments within the realm of traditional financial regulation.[40] The US Securities and Exchange

---

38 Martino (n 19) 39.

39 On the role of intermediaries and their regulation in fintech, see Fatjon Kaja, Edoardo D Martino and Alessio M Pacces, 'FinTech and the Law and Economics of Disintermediation', *Routledge Handbook of Financial Technology and Law* (Routledge 2021).

40 Ferrari (n 15) 330.

Commission (SEC) was the first to propose such approach in the 'DAO Report'.[41] The SEC applied the Howey Test as developed by the US Supreme Court in 1946.[42] According to the Howey test, a contract is to be considered an 'investment contract' in the scope of the Securities Exchange Act of 1934 if it entails (1) an investment of money (2) in a common enterprise (3) with a reasonable expectation of profits (4) deriving from the effort of the promoter or a third party. Soon after, a similar approach was followed in the EU, enquiring whether cryptocurrencies fell within the definition of 'transferable securities'.[43]

Beyond this initial and reactive approach, this section analyses three different approaches: designing and implementing a completely new regime, expressly referring to an existing regime and an agency-driven enforcement of the existing regime based on legal interpretation. These approaches loosely describe the rule-making strategies pursued by, respectively, the EU, the UK and the US. This section also consider 'corner solutions' whereby some countries gave cryptocurrencies – mainly Bitcoin – legal tender status. In contrast, other countries – chiefly China – enacted some sort of ban on cryptocurrencies.

The EU is the front-runner in the design and implementation of a dedicated regime for cryptocurrencies and stablecoins. On 31 May 2023, the European Parliament finally approved the 'Market in Crypto Asset' (MiCA) Regulation.[44] MiCA will apply to cryptocurrencies and stablecoins that are not considered 'financial instruments' according to EU law.[45] MiCA also expressly exempts potential issuance of Central Bank Digital Currency.[46]

This proactive rule-making approach has some clear advantages. The European Regulator aims at having a first-mover advantage and setting the tone of the international debate over crypto finance regulation. Moreover, enacting a completely new and independent regulatory framework allows the regime to be tailored to the specific risks and opportunities that relate to cryptocurrencies and stablecoins, in terms of both regulatory requirements and supervisory oversight. Finally, a dedicated regime is relatively easy to adjust over time, tracking the developments of the industry.

However, this approach also has negative implications. It generates an un-level playing field between crypto and traditional financial activity. This can go both ways: traditional financial activities can be advantaged because of a more efficient or laxer regulatory framework or the other way around. Additionally, a dedicated regime, especially if stringent, runs into the risk of crystalizing the industry and discouraging innovation. From a public finance perspective, a dedicated regime for regulation and supervision is more costly to design, implement and enforce.

---

41 Securities and Exchange Commission, 'Report of Investigation Pursuant to Section 21(a) of the Securities Exchange Act of 1934: The DAO' (2017) Release No. 81207.

42 *SEC v. W. J. Howey Co.*, 328 U.S. 293 (1946).

43 Article 4(1)(44) Directive 2014/65/EU of the European Parliament and of the Council of 15 May 2014 on markets in financial instruments (MiFID II) [2014] OJ L 173/349. See also European Securities and Market Authority, 'Initial Coin Offerings and Crypto-Assets' (2019) 37 <https://www.esma.europa.eu/sites/default/files/library/esma50-157-1391_crypto_advice.pdf> accessed 9 June 2023.

44 Regulation (EU) 2023/1114 of the European Parliament and of the Council of 31 May 2023 on markets in crypto-asset [2023] OJ L 150/40. hereinafter MiCA.

45 Article 2(4)(a) MiCA.

46 Article 2(2)(c) MiCA.

The UK decided to regulate cryptocurrencies and stablecoins following a 'staged' approach in the Financial Service and Market Bill (FSMB), in stark contrast with the EU's approach to MiCA, which aims to comprehensively regulate crypto finance.[47] The FSMB is a key post-Brexit piece of legislation approved in October 2022 by the House of Common and currently waiting for the final approval of the House of Lords. The UK decided to include stablecoins within the scope of existing legislations, namely the regulation of payment systems. On the other hand, it provides a wide regulatory power to the Treasury for the regulation of cryptocurrencies.[48]

This rule-making approach, especially compared with the EU MiCA, has the appeal of being easy to design and implement, as it does not require a whole new regulatory infrastructure to be built. Moreover, this approach ensures a level playing field between blockchain-based and other instruments. This is a crucial point in the British approach, as confirmed by Andrew Griffith, the Economic Secretary to the Treasurer: 'The substance here is to treat [crypto] like other forms of financial assets and not to prefer them, but also to bring them within the scope of regulation for the first time'.[49] In turn, this approach is in line with the manifesto of the Prime Minister Rishi Sunak, who pledged to make the UK the crypto hub of the world.[50] Such a light, wait-and-see approach, where a wide regulatory power is allocated on the HM Treasury, clearly looks at promoting innovation and experimentation in the crypto industry. On the other hand, this approach may prove unfit to handle crypto-specific risks from both a regulatory and a supervisory perspective.

The third example of rule-making strategy is the US. Perhaps, it would be more accurate to say that the US is, so far, an example of the lack of a clear rule-making strategy. At Federal level, there is still no comprehensive regulation of cryptocurrencies and stablecoins, whereas the several attempts to pass a comprehensive or sectoral regulation have, so far, failed. Therefore, the regulatory and supervisory debate has been driven by the activism of agencies, mainly the SEC and the Commodity Future Trading Commission (CFTC).[51] These agencies widened the scope of their mandate, interpreting it in a way that includes the oversight and enforcement of cryptocurrencies.[52] On the one hand, this activism is trying to compensate for the lack of coherent federal legislation but, on the other hand, it generated considerable uncertainty and confusions.[53]

In contrast, individual states undertook specific regulatory initiatives for regulating crypto assets and stablecoins. It is difficult to summarize many different state legislative initiatives.[54]

---

[47] Financial Services and Markets HC Bill (2022–2023) [124], hereinafter FSMB.

[48] See art 21 FSMB.

[49] Sandali Handagama, 'UK Lawmakers Vote to Recognize Crypto as Regulated Financial Instruments' (Yahoo Finance, 25 October 2022) <https://finance.yahoo.com/news/uk-lawmakers-vote-recognize-crypto-153128469.html> accessed 9 June 2023.

[50] Text to note 9.

[51] Chris Brummer, Yesha Yadav and David T Zaring, 'Regulation by Enforcement' (2022) University of Southern California Law Review, 1297.

[52] Taylor Anne Moffett, 'CFTC & SEC: The Wild West of Cryptocurrency Regulation' (2022) 57 U. Rich. L. Rev. 713.

[53] ibid 720.

[54] For an overview 'Cryptocurrency Laws and Regulations by State' (Bloomberg Law) <https://pro.bloomberglaw.com/brief/cryptocurrency-laws-and-regulations-by-state/> accessed 9 June 2023.

However the most far-reaching of these seem to engage in regulatory competition, trying to create a 'crypto-friendly' environment to attract crypto activities.[55]

Finally, it is interesting to briefly look at 'corner solutions', meaning extreme legislative approaches to cryptocurrencies and stablecoins that either fully embrace or radically ban them.

The first 'benevolent' corner solution is to adopt cryptocurrencies as legal tender. This radical choice was made only by two countries: El Salvador and the Central African Republic. Both jurisdictions adopted Bitcoin as legal tender. In particular, El Salvador's 'Bitcoin Law' requires both the government and businesses to accept Bitcoins as a means of payment and launched a State-backed wallet, Chivo.[56] There are two main reasons for this choice: first, the government wanted to promote financial inclusion, giving access to crypto wallets also to unbanked citizens and facilitating remittances from abroad; and second, El Salvador lacks monetary sovereignty, and it has used the Dollar since 2001.[57] The volatility in the value of Bitcoin has put this experiment under pressure, especially considering the sharp decrease in value experienced by Bitcoin since the first half of 2022.

The second, opposite, corner solution is a ban on crypto activities. Several countries have adopted some form of ban. The most famous and relevant case is the ban on crypto activities enacted by China as of 2017.[58] At first, such prohibition was directed at ICOs, cryptocurrency mining and the trading of other currencies, such as Bitcoin and Ether.[59] In 2018, the Chinese government banned all offshore cryptocurrency trading platforms to completely eradicate trading.[60]

However, the stance of the Chinese government against cryptocurrencies seems stronger on paper than in practice. In 2019, the Hangzhou Internet Court became the first Chinese court to recognize Bitcoin as virtual property according to the 'General Civil Law', stating that digital currencies possess the value, scarcity and dominance required of property as an object of rights.[61] In 2020, the Shanghai No. 1 Intermediate People's Court held that Bitcoin was legal property and deserved protection under Chinese law.[62] Moreover, research shows that the

---

55 Pierluigi Matera, 'Delaware's Dominance, Wyoming's Dare: New Challenge, Same Outcome?' (2022) 27 Fordham J. Corp. & Fin. L. 73.

56 Pwc, 'El Salvador's Law: A Meaningful Test for Bitcoin' (2021) <https://www.pwc.com/gx/en/financial-services/pdf/el-salvadors-law-a-meaningful-test-for-bitcoin.pdf>.

57 On sovereignty and digital money, see Edoardo D Martino, 'Monetary Sovereignty in the Digital Era' (2023) 141 European Banking Institute Working Paper Series <https://papers.ssrn.com/sol3/papers.cfm?abstract_id=4437723>.

58 Hui Deng, Robin Hui Huang and Qingran Wu, 'The Regulation of Initial Coin Offerings in China: Problems, Prognoses and Prospects' (2018) 19 European Business Organization Law Review 465, 471.

59 ibid 472.

60 John Riley, 'The Current Status of Cryptocurrency Regulation in China and its Effect around the World' (2021) 7 China and WTO Review 135, 141.

61 Mitchell Moss, 'Chinese Court Upholds Legality of Bitcoin Ownership, BTC Protected by China's Property Laws' (Cryptoslate, 7 November 2019) <https://cryptoslate.com/chinese-court-upholds-legal-bitcoin-ownership-btc-protected-china-property-law/> accessed 17 April 2023.

62 Riley (n 60) 144.

level of adoption of crypto assets in China is still very high, concluding that the ban has been either ineffective or loosely enforced.[63]

5. DIVERGENT REGULATORY REGIMES

This section looks at the current legislative actions for the regulation of cryptocurrencies and stablecoins. Specifically, it will look at the Market in Crypto Asset Regulation for the EU and the Financial Service and Market Bill for the UK. A comparison between only two jurisdictions has limitations from a comparative perspective; however, comparing the EU and UK approaches perfectly fits the functional approach of this chapter as it perfectly highlights the source, dynamics and implications of regulatory divergences.

At the time of writing, these two legislative initiatives are the most advanced comprehensive approaches to cryptocurrency and stablecoin regulation. Therefore, the analysis focuses on the key functional choices related to the regulatory goals and strategies, rather than on legal details that may be amended or modified. This section looks first at cryptocurrencies and then at stablecoins.

5.1 Cryptocurrencies: Different Path to Protect Investors

When regulating cryptocurrencies, all of the analysed jurisdictions aim at protecting investors. However, they do so by adopting different legal strategies and tools as well as pursuing partially divergent goals.

In the EU, cryptocurrencies belong to the broader category of crypto assets defined as 'a digital representation of value or rights which may be transferred and stored electronically, using distributed ledger technology'.[64]

The key regulatory tool is the 'crypto asset white paper'. Issuers of cryptocurrencies are not required to seek ex-ante authorization from the relevant authority. Rather they must draft the white paper, notify it to the competent authority and publish it on their website.[65] Only after the notification and publication can the cryptocurrency seek admission to a crypto trading platform. Therefore, MiCA takes an activity-based approach to cryptocurrency regulation, coupled with an entity-based regulation of the relevant gatekeepers, mainly the crypto-trading platform.[66] These platforms shall not admit for trading cryptocurrencies whose white paper was not duly published and shall assess the quality and reliability of the cryptocurrency

63 'The 2022 Global Crypto Adoption Index: Emerging Markets Lead in Grassroots Adoption, China Remains Active Despite Ban, and Crypto Fundamentals Appear Healthy' (Chainalysis 2022) 10 <https://blog.chainalysis.com/reports/2022-global-crypto-adoption-index/> accessed 9 June 2023.

64 Art 3(2) MiCA.

65 Respectively, arts 5, 6 and 7 MiCA.

66 Trading platforms must be authorized as Crypto Asset Service Providers pursuant arts 53 and 54 MiCA.

according to their operating rules, including due diligence procedure, requirements for fair and orderly trading and so forth.[67]

MiCA chiefly aims at protecting investors by putting in place a comprehensive framework centred on disclosure duties and rules of conduct. The white paper, a sort of simplified prospectus, is again the key tool which allows investors to make informed choices. In the white paper, the issuer must provide, among other things, a detailed description of the project, the main participants involved, the rights and obligations attached to the crypto asset and of the risks related to it.[68] These transparency requirements are complemented by rules of conduct for the issuer of crypto assets, which should act honestly, fairly and professionally; provide clear and non-misleading communication; prevent, identify, manage and disclose any conflicts of interest that may arise; and maintain their systems and security access protocols to appropriate standards.[69] The violation of these obligations results in civil liability for the issuer of cryptocurrency.[70] Consistent with the regulatory design, the supervisory powers are focused on ensuring the effectiveness of these disclosure duties and suspend, or require the gatekeepers to suspend, trading shall the issuer materially infringe the regulation.[71]

In contrast to the European approach, the UK FSMB has lower protective ambitions, at least in primary regulation. The key focus is on the regulatory scope, namely whether a crypto asset can be used for the settlements of payment obligations. In this case, crypto assets are considered payment services and are regulated according to the Electronic Money Regulations and Payment Service Regulations.[72] These instruments are discussed in Section 5.2.

'Other' crypto assets are defined as 'cryptographically secured digital representation of value or contractual rights that (a) can be transferred, stored or traded electronically, and (b) that uses technology supporting the recording or storage of data'.[73]

As discussed in Section 4, the HM Treasury retains a wide and crucial regulatory power to determine the actual regulatory regime applicable to different cryptocurrencies, as it can amend by regulation the definition itself of crypto assets to expand or tighten the regulatory scope.[74] The only clear regulatory regime applicable to all crypto assets is the restrictions on financial promotions.[75] This aims at protecting naive and unexperienced investors from the most aggressive marketing activities. Beyond financial promotion, crypto assets can be included as 'designated activity' among the 'financial instruments, financial products and financial investments' as disciplined by the Financial Service and Market Act of 2000.[76] The inclusion of crypto assets in this category depends by the HM Treasury determination through

---

67 Article 58. The operating rules are part of the documents needed to receive the relevant authorization.

68 Article 5(1) MiCA.

69 Article 13(1) MiCA.

70 Article 14 MiCA.

71 See, respectively, art 82(1)(t) and art 82(1)(q) and (r) MiCA.

72 Article 21 FSMB.

73 Article 65 FSMB.

74 Article 65(4)(b) FSMB.

75 Amendment to Financial Service and Market Act (FSMA) 2000, Section 21 explicitly including cryptoassets.

76 Article 71K (7) FSMA 2000, as amended by the FSMB.

regulation, leaving the Treasury with the widest regulatory discretion.[77] Should cryptocurrencies be included among the designated activities, it would be subject to the oversight of the Financial Conduct Authority.

5.2 Stablecoins and Financial Stability: Between Stable Value and Payment Services

Stablecoins are crypto assets that aim to maintain a stable value relative to a specified asset or a pool or basket of assets.[78] Broadly speaking, stablecoins can be distinguished into two broad categories according to the nature of reserve assets: first, those with reserve assets made almost exclusively of fiat currencies, government bonds and other very liquid money market instruments, hence functioning as tokenized electric money; and second, those with reserves composed of a wider range of assets, allowing for a more pronounced qualitative asset transformation activity, hence posing more stability risks. While the first category poses little risk and is almost unanimously regulated similarly to electric money, the second category is potentially more cumbersome and its regulatory regime more divergent. Therefore, this section mainly focuses on this second category.

In the EU, MiCA labels these stablecoins as 'Asset Referenced Tokens' (ART), defining them as 'crypto-asset that purports to maintain a stable value by referring to the value of several fiat currencies that are legal tender, one or several commodities or one or several crypto-assets, or a combination of such assets'.[79]

The key regulatory tool is the authorization that is granted by the competent authority upon the request of the ART issuer. To be authorized, the issuer must submit the crypto asset white paper together with other documents proving the operational resilience of the ART project and the fact that the main participants in the project possess the necessary fit and proper qualifications.[80] The authorization is refused if the management is not fit and proper; the applicant issuer fails to meet or is likely to fail to meet the relevant requirement; and most notably, if the business model of the applicant issuer may pose a serious threat to financial stability, monetary policy transmission or monetary sovereignty.[81] This signals the focus of the European regulator on the crypto-specific issues related to financial stability.

The regime applicable to the ART is more stringent than that applicable to general crypto assets in terms of obligations on the issuer. The rules on transparency and conduct of business are adapted and reinforced. On top of those, the issuers shall establish, maintain and implement sound governance arrangements related to all the relevant aspects of their business model: from the treatment of reserve assets to the ways to handle conflict of interests passing through the protocols for validating the transactions, and so forth.[82]

---

[77] Article 8 FSMB.

[78] Financial Stability Board (FSB) (n 18) 5. This leaves 'algorithmic stablecoins' out of this working definition.

[79] Article 3(3) MiCA. The difference between ART and eMoney Tokens is that the latter can only refer to the value of a fiat currency that is legal tender.

[80] Article 16 MiCA.

[81] Article 19 MiCA.

[82] Article 30 MiCA; see article 28 Regulation (EU) No 575/2013 of the European Parliament and of the Council of 26 June 2013 on prudential requirements for credit institutions and investment firms [2013] OJ L 176/1, hereinafter CRR.

However, the most relevant and distinctive regulatory tool consists of the substantive restrictions on the ART issuer business model, specifically on the treatment of reserve assets and redemption. First, ART issuers must have in place own funds equal to 2% of the average amount of reserve assets, 3% for significant ART. Own funds must be of the same quality required for Common Equity Tier 1 in banking.[83] This guarantees that ART issuers have an equity buffer to withstand losses. Moreover, MiCA regulated reserve assets and token withdrawal/redemption in an attempt to limit maturity and liquidity transformation. On the asset side, issuers of ART must at all times maintain a reserve of assets that matches the amount of issued tokens, and the management body must ensure the effective and prudent management of the reserve assets.[84] The issuers shall ensure that the creation and destruction of asset-referenced tokens are always matched by a corresponding increase or decrease in the reserve of assets and that such increase or decrease is adequately managed to avoid any adverse impacts on the market of the reserve assets. The ART issuer can invest the reserve assets only in instruments considered as 'High-Quality Liquid Assets' under the bank regulation.[85] On the other hand, on the liability side, the holders of ARTs have a general right to liquidity and issuer shall at all times grant redemption.[86] These provisions are supported by more intrusive supervisory powers, with the possibility to adopting supervisory measures similar to those granted for banking supervision.[87]

Finally, in terms of crisis management provisions, the issuers of ART must draw up and maintain a 'living will', which is a plan with prearranged state contingent measures in case of a sudden deterioration of the issuers' financial condition. Crucially, the plan must 'include appropriate conditions and procedures to ensure the timely implementation of recovery actions as well as a wide range of recovery options', including (1) the imposition of liquidity fee on redemption; (2) a cap on maximum day redemption; and (3) the possibility of suspending redemption.[88]

The European approach looks at regulating stablecoins mainly looking at the promise of value stability as the main problematic issue for institutions that are not backed by deposit insurance and a fiscal backstop. While imperfect, this approach seems to match, at least in principle, the framework depicted in Section 2 in terms of regulatory goals.

In contrast, the UK model diverges from this approach, mainly looking at the regulation of stablecoins as a payment service. As previously discussed, the FSMB defines digital settlement assets (stablecoins) as crypto assets that can be used for the settlements of payment obligations. The regulatory regime follows accordingly. Article 21 of the FSMB provides that the regime for payments services is extended to Digital Settlement Assets (DSA).[89] This implies that issuers of in-scope stablecoins will have to seek a licence as an 'Electronic Money Institution' (EMI) as detailed in the Electronic Money Regulation 2011.[90] The stablecoin

---

[83] Article 31 MiCA.

[84] Article 32 MiCA.

[85] Article 34 MiCA; see art 412 CRR.

[86] Article 35 MiCA.

[87] Article 112 MiCA.

[88] Article 41a(1) MiCA. For comparison, see art 34 MMF regulation.

[89] See Schedule 6 of the FSMB for the specific amendments needed to the Part V of the Banking Act 2009 and to the Financial Services (Banking Reform) Act 2013.

[90] Electronic Money Regulation 2011, hereinafter EMR.

issuer applies for the licence to the Financial Conduct Authority (FCA), submitting a business plan that identifies the main activities of the issuer and the type of payment services to be provided.[91] The issuer must set up appropriate governance arrangements, internal controls, risk management and money laundering controls.[92] Fit and proper requirements for relevant participants also apply.[93]

In terms of prudential regulation, EMIs must at all times comply with minimum capital regulation of 2% average outstanding e-money.[94] Moreover, EMIs must segregate the client's funds.[95]

The FCA generally has oversight and enforcement power over e-money, and issuers of in-scope stablecoins will also be supervised by the FCA. The specific supervision regime is yet to be established by the Treasury.[96] Issuers that are deemed systemic will become subject to the supervision of the Bank of England.[97]

In terms of crisis management, the FSMB grants HM Treasury the regulatory power to design insolvency arrangements in relation to payment systems that include arrangements using DSA.[98] HM Treasury has issued a public consultation on the possibility of extending to DSAs the 'Special Administration Regime' applicable to Central Counterparties. This would provide a proper resolution regime for distressed stablecoins, in contrast to the MiCA approach that only relies on early intervention measures designed after the Money Market Funds Regulation.

This is a brief overview of the baseline applicable regulation to UK stablecoin issuers. However, the actual regulatory regime is as yet uncertain. First, the regulatory scope is as yet uncertain, meaning that stablecoin will be considered 'for the settlements of payment obligations'. While it is clear that eMoney tokens will be in-scope, the scope determination is particularly relevant for stablecoins that do not simply retain reserves in money market instruments and fiat currencies, that is that the EU MiCA categorizes as 'Asset Referenced Tokens'. This uncertainty is not accidental; rather, it seems to perfectly fit the UK 'staged' regulatory strategy. Indeed, the FSMB provides impressive regulatory powers to HM Treasury to re-define the regulatory scope of DSA and, even more far-fetched, HM Treasury also retains the regulatory power to amend primary legislation to design a tailored regime for DSA.[99] Practically speaking, it may well be that risky stablecoin issuers engaging in considerable qualitative asset transformation may be completely exempted from the EMI regulation and only subject to the very light regime on crypto assets.

This stark divergence between the EU and UK approach to stablecoin regulation can be explained also, and perhaps chiefly, by the post-Brexit regulatory competition approach. Indeed, the FSMB is considered one of the key post-Brexit pieces of legislation. This raises concerns in terms of the relationship between the UK and EU financial regulation in the

---

91 Schedule 1, EMR 2011.
92 Reg. 6(5) and (7), paras 5 and 6 of Schedule 1, EMR.
93 Reg. 6(6)(b), para 9 of Schedule 1, EMR.
94 Reg. 19 EMR.
95 Reg. 20 EMR.
96 See art 22(13) FSMB.
97 Schedule 6 to the FSMB, Parts 1, 11 and 20.
98 See art 22 FSMB.
99 Article 22 FSMB.

post-Brexit era that is consistent with the framework depicted in Section 2 but whose detailed analysis goes beyond the scope of this contribution.[100]

6. CONCLUDING REMARKS

This chapter proposed an analytical framework to approach the (financial) regulation of cryptocurrencies and stablecoins from a comparative perspective. It links the regulatory goals pursued by different policymakers to different, possibly divergent, regulatory strategies, focusing on the regulatory point of entry, the substantive obligations imposed on the issuers, the role and powers of the supervisors and the existence of crisis management tools.

Building on this framework, the chapter reviews the divergent regulatory approaches of several jurisdictions, differentiating between 'corner' and 'interior' regulatory solutions and highlighting the sources and effects of regulatory divergence. Finally, the chapter zooms in the comparison between the EU and UK regulatory regimes, as these jurisdictions have the most advanced regulatory projects, and they offer a perfect example of the source, dynamics and implications of regulatory divergence.

[100] For initial considerations and current practices, see Christy Ann Petit and Thorsten Beck, 'Recent Trends in UK Financial Sector Regulation and Possible Implications for the EU, Including its Approach to Equivalence' (European Parliament 2023).

21. Regulatory policies for crypto-asset offerings

Iris H.-Y. Chiu

1. INTRODUCTION

Unregulated offerings of 'crypto-assets' on permissionless blockchain platforms such as Ethereum have, since 2017, attracted regulatory attention. Regulatory debates and discussions revolve around how best to treat crypto-asset offerings, which do not neatly fit into many jurisdictions' existing financial regulation categories.[1] Crypto-asset offers are often offers of tokens that would become developed[2] to embed future rights in a variety of forms.[3] Such rights include: rights to participate in decentralized applications that facilitate peer-to-peer services or digital goods transactions (utility rights); rights to transfer value (payment, usually denoted in the native cryptocurrency, such as ether for the Ethereum blockchain); mining (which is a process for the operation of consensus mechanisms programmed in the network's protocols for validation of transactions and writing to the single distributed ledger); and even governance, such as voting on protocol changes or development. In some cases, rights include distribution or profit-sharing based on the levels of crypto-asset (or token) ownership. Crypto-assets offer largely involve early-stage digital tokens with a variety of yet-to-be-developed functions. They provide, uniquely, an early-stage form of financing for business developers in the permissionless blockchain space.[4]

Before regulators made moves to clarify or act in this space, there had already been self-regulating developments to meet the supply- and demand-side needs for crypto-asset offers. Supply-side issuers generally offer information signalling of some form, such as in a White Paper, social media communications,[5] and engagement with ICO rating analysts,[6] to

1 Jonathan Rohr and Aaron Wright, 'Blockchain-based Token Sales, Initial Coin Offerings, and the Democratization of Public Capital Markets' (2019) 70 Hastings Law Journal 463 on the characterization debates in the US; Philipp Hacker and Chris Thomale, 'Crypto-Securities Regulation: ICOs, Token Sales and Cryptocurrencies under EU Financial Law' (2018) 15 European Company and Financial Law Review 645 on the EU.

2 Saman Adhami, Giancarlo Giudici and Stefano Martinazzi, 'Why do Businesses Go Crypto? An Empirical Analysis of Initial Coin Offerings' (2018) 100 Journal of Economics and Business 64.

3 Carol Goforth, 'Securities Treatment of Tokenized Offerings under U.S. Law' (2018) 46 Pepperdine Law Review 405.

4 Iris H-Y Chiu, *Regulating the Crypto-economy* (Oxford: Hart Publishing 2022), ch 5.

5 Sabrina T Howell, Marina Niessner and David Yermack, 'Initial Coin Offerings: Financing Growth with Cryptocurrency Token Sales' (2020) 33 Review of Financial Studies 3925.

6 Jongsub Lee, Tao Li and Donghwa Shin, 'The Wisdom of Crowds in FinTech: Evidence from Initial Coin Offerings' (2022) 11 Review of Corporate Finance Studies 1.

provide visibility for attracting demand. The demand side relies on these relatively selective[7] and even hazardous information signals,[8] as well as wisdom of the crowd,[9] to decide whether or not to subscribe for tokens. There is some evidence of investors being able to protect themselves by limiting outlays,[10] as well as by diversifying their purchases.[11] Further, if a token is subsequently listed for secondary trading, investor protection is generally ensured by the wisdom of the crowd feeding into price signals[12] and the ability of investors to exit. The documented significant margins of return[13] may to an extent compensate for the self-regulatory space with limited investor protection.

However, regulators remain concerned about retail investors being scammed and defrauded, even if empirical research shows that a minority of unregulated crypto-offerings worldwide are scams.[14] Further, regulators are concerned with regulatory arbitrage, as crypto-asset offers achieve the same aim as securities offers to raise funds for businesses,[15] and yet appear to be spared from securities regulatory governance which imposes significant cost on issuers. The US Securities and Exchange Commission (SEC) has therefore embarked on capturing many crypto-asset offers into the 'security' definition based on many crypto-asset holders' investment appreciation expectation.[16] Further, in the EU, some commentators support the extension of the 'transferable security' definition to crypto-assets as many of them are secondarily

---

[7] Anca Mirela Toma and Paola Cerchiello, 'Initial Coin Offering: Risk or Opportunity?' (2020) 3 Frontiers in Artificial Intelligence Article 18, doi: 10.3389/frai.2020.00018 discuss differences in the amount and quality of crypto-asset issuers' communications.

[8] David Florysiak and Alexander Schandlbauer, 'Experts or Charlatans? ICO Analysts and White Paper Informativeness' (2022) 139 Journal of Banking and Finance 106476.

[9] Toma and Cerchiello (n 7) on social media discussions, Lee et al. (n 6) on analyst ratings on competitive platforms like ICOBench.

[10] Many investors do not invest more than $1200 in one crypto-asset offering; Rüdiger Fahlenbrach and Marc Frattaroli, 'ICO Investors' (2021) 35 Financial Markets and Portfolio Management 1.

[11] ibid; Dmitri Boreiko and Dimche Risteski, 'Serial and Large Investors in Initial Coin Offerings' (2021) 57 Small Business Economy 1053.

[12] Paul Momtaz, 'Entrepreneurial Finance and Moral Hazard: Evidence from Token Offerings' (2021) 36 Journal of Business Venturing 106001.

[13] Hugo Benedetti and Leonard Kostovetsky, 'Digital Tulips? Returns to Investors in Initial Coin Offerings' (2021) 66 Journal of Corporate Finance 101786. But see caution in Francesco Cappa and Michele Pinelli, 'Collecting Money Through Blockchain Technologies: First Insights on the Determinants of the Return on Initial Coin Offerings' (2021) 27 Information Technology for Development 561, finding gains attributable mostly to general price hikes in cryptocurrency like ether.

[14] Toma and Cerchiello (n 7).

[15] Houman B Shadab, 'Regulation of Blockchain Token Sales in the United States' in Ioannis Lianos, Philipp Hacker, Stefan Eich and Georgios Dimitropoulos (eds), *Regulating Blockchain* (Oxford: OUP 2019), ch 13; Usha Rodrigues, 'Semi-Public Offerings? Pushing the Boundaries of Securities Law' (2018) University of Georgia School of Law Research Paper Series Paper No 2018-30 <https://ssrn.com/abstract=3242205> accessed 5 May 2024.

[16] US Securities and Exchange Commission, 'Framework for "Investment Contract" Analysis of Digital Assets' (SEC, 2023) <https://www.sec.gov/corpfin/framework-investment-contract-analysis-digital-assets> accessed 5 May 2024.

traded and such liquidity forms an essential part of investors' participation and expectations.[17] However, some crypto-assets are not listed on secondary crypto-asset markets for trading, and these trading systems do not meet the Markets in Financial Instruments Regulation's definition.[18] Early commentary argued that crypto-asset offers do not fairly and squarely fall within the existing definitions of the EU's regulated suite of financial instruments.[19] The Swiss regulator introduced three categories of crypto-assets, i.e. the 'payment', 'security' or 'utility' crypto-assets in order to clarify that those digital assets that function no differently from existing payment or security instruments should be treated as such.[20] However, there is a large category of 'utility' crypto-assets which embed various developmental rights. These have drawn debates in terms of which aspects resemble what existing category of regulated financial instruments. However, the three-fold classification has not definitively provided answers for regulators grappling with the innovations that have come to fore.

Some aspects of the innovative qualities in crypto-assets make them distinguishable from securities regulated in many jurisdictions. One difference concerns the types of rights to be developed for crypto-asset-holders, and these do not always include the conventional rights associated with securities, i.e. voting and corporate governance rights, as well as profit-sharing rights.[21] Another difference concerns the range of different 'organizational' arrangements for crypto-asset holders as a community, as crypto-asset holders are not clearly shareholders within the organizational framework of a company. Some crypto-asset issuers wish to develop a decentralized network such as the Decentralized Autonomous Organization (DAO) where crypto-asset holders are bound by certain conventions that would be executed by automated code, but are otherwise largely autonomous.[22] Arguably, the initial 'fund-raising' similarity between securities and crypto-asset offers dissipates once one considers that the former is for general business purposes while the latter is project-based. The initial developers of the project for which the crypto-assets are offered may also retreat from development and governance so as to hand the project over to the community in due course. Their intentions seem different from corporate directors stewarding corporate assets for shareholders as residual claimants.

That is not to say that crypto-asset offers, as a form of fund-raising, should be unregulated if they are not treated as securities. It may be efficient for regulators to leverage upon existing regulatory categories. Regulatory differences can be based on different regulators' perceptions of what the key defining indicia are for crypto-assets, but these perceptions are also shaped

---

17 Philipp Maume and Matthias Fromberger, 'Regulation of Initial Coin Offerings: Reconciling US and EU Securities Laws' (2019) 19 Chicago Journal of International Law 548.

18 Filippo Annunziata, 'Speak, If You Can: What Are You? An Alternative Approach to the Qualification of Tokens and Initial Coin Offerings' (2020) 17 European Company and Financial Law Review 129.

19 Niels Vandezande, 'Regulating Initial Coin Offerings and DAO Tokens under the EU's Financial Instruments Framework' (2020) 14 Law and Financial Markets Review 33.

20 See <https://www.finma.ch/en/~/media/finma/dokumente/dokumentencenter/myfinma/1bewilligung/fintech/wegleitung-ico.pdf> accessed 5 May 2024.

21 Fahlenbrach and Frattaroli (n 10).

22 António Garcia Rolo, 'Challenges in the Legal Qualification of Decentralised Autonomous Organisations (DAOs): The Rise of the Crypto-Partnership?' (2019) 1 Revista de Direito e Tecnologia 33; Ori Oren, 'ICO's, DAO'S, and the SEC: A Partnership Solution' (2018) 2018 Columbia Business Law Review 617.

by regulatory priorities in terms of the competing needs to support innovation, protect retail investors, foster credible and reputable financial markets and engage in worthwhile regulatory competition.[23]

This chapter discusses how the balance of these competing policies shape different regulators' approaches to crypto-asset offers. However, with the introduction of the EU's Markets in Crypto-assets Regulation (MiCAR), a policy benchmark is arguably set for other regulators to consider. This chapter compares the pre-MiCAR landscape for regulatory differences, with the post-MiCAR landscape for regulatory development. It argues that MiCAR forges a certain policy balance that sets a benchmark, *viz.* crypto-assets are innovative but should be governed for meeting the established investor protection and financial stability objectives. In early 2023, however, it is clear that the collapse of FTX, a significant but unregulated crypto-exchange, may be the 'market failure' excuse needed by most regulators to embark on explicit forms of regulatory governance for crypto-finance. This looks increasingly subject to international convergence led by international bodies forging a narrative of common interests and solutions.

Section 2 provides an overview of pre-MiCAR differences in key regulatory approaches and how these reflect regulators' different priorities. Section 3 discusses the introduction of MiCAR and how it sets a policy benchmark for crypto-asset regulation. Section 4 predicts broad policy convergence in key jurisdictions although with continued differences in regulatory detail amongst regulators. Section 5 concludes.

2. MAPPING REGULATORS' APPROACHES TO CRYPTO-ASSETS: PRE-MICAR

This section provides a brief survey of different approaches that regulators in many jurisdictions have taken in response to the innovative challenges posed by crypto-assets. Regulators' different competing policy interests arguably shape their approaches pre-MiCAR.

The suite of competing policy interests for regulators are: promoting innovation, often seen to benefit economic development and competition;[24] protecting investors, theorized and empirically shown to be important for capital markets development;[25] as well as what this chapter calls 'other protective interests', i.e. protecting economic, social or political institutions against disruption by technological revolutions (seen perhaps as a threat by authorities in power). These protective interests arguably underpin decisions taken by jurisdictions such as China, Turkey, India and Indonesia, amongst others, to ban the use of cryptocurrency.[26]

---

[23] An overview of the forces driving regulatory divergences or convergence for the same issue area in finance is provided in Chapter 1 of this volume.

[24] Maarten J Arentsen, Wouter van Rossum and Albert E Steenge (eds), *Governance of Innovation* (Cheltenham, UK and Northampton, MA, USA: Edward Elgar Publishing, 2010).

[25] Rafael La Porta and others, 'Law and Finance' (1998) 106 Journal of Political Economy 1113; Rafael La Porta, Florencio Lopez-de-Silanes and Andrei Shleifer 'What Works in Securities Laws' (2006) 61 Journal of Finance 1.

[26] Chloe Orji, 'Bitcoin Ban: These are the Countries Where Crypto is Restricted or Illegal' (Euronews, 25 August 2022) <https://www.euronews.com/next/2022/08/25/bitcoin-ban-these-are-the-countries-where-crypto-is-restricted-or-illegal2> accessed 5 May 2024.

In jurisdictions where the pro-innovation preference is dominant, one group of jurisdictions has adopted a slow/incremental approach to policy reform, therefore leaving unregulated crypto-asset offers (that do not fall squarely within the definitions of existing regulated financial instruments) to be indirectly permitted to be offered. Another group of jurisdictions has adopted regulatory innovation to legitimize crypto-asset offers, so as to attract issuers to their jurisdictions. Broadly, this category comprising the two groups is called 'pro-innovation jurisdictions'.

2.1 Regulatory Approaches in Pro-Innovation Jurisdictions

This chapter discusses the UK as the leading example in the first-mentioned group, and Switzerland and Singapore adopt similar approaches. The UK regulator, the Financial Conduct Authority (FCA) adopted the three-fold classification of crypto-assets as being payment, security or utility tokens. Its regulatory perimeter would be extended over payment and security tokens but not utility tokens.[27] Legitimately unregulated, crypto-asset offers for utility tokens have been quietly permitted to be made. This section argues that the UK's approach, followed by its subsequent gestures to protect consumers by issuing warnings[28] and to ban retail participation in crypto-derivatives,[29] reflected a pro-innovation approach while attempting to minimize harm to naive retail consumers. A similar tenor in regulatory policy was observed in Switzerland[30] and Singapore.[31] The UK, Switzerland and Singapore remain popular jurisdictions for crypto-asset offers, although not having the most significant market shares. These jurisdictions have, however, been under pressure to consider more regulatory governance since revelations of consumer harm and after the scandal of the collapse of FTX.

There are jurisdictions which have undertaken regulatory innovation to promote technological innovation in finance. An early proactive regime that has already passed legislation is Thailand. Thailand offers an authorization regime[32] for digital token offers for those crypto-assets that are utility tokens (i.e. conferring rights in respect of future goods or ser-

27 FCA, *Guidance on Crypto-assets Policy Statement* (July 2019) <https://www.fca.org.uk/publication/policy/ps19-22.pdf> accessed 5 May 2024.

28 FCA, 'FCA Reminds Consumers of the Risks of Investing in Cryptoassets' (11 May 2022) <https://www.fca.org.uk/news/statements/fca-reminds-consumers-risks-investing-cryptoassets> accessed 5 May 2024.

29 FCA, 'FCA Bans the Sale of Crypto-derivatives to Retail Consumers' (6 October 2020) <https://www.fca.org.uk/news/press-releases/fca-bans-sale-crypto-derivatives-retail-consumers> accessed 5 May 2024.

30 FINMA, 'FINMA Publishes ICO Guidelines' (16 Feb 2018) <https://www.finma.ch/en/news/2018/02/20180216-mm-ico-wegleitung/> accessed 5 May 2024.

31 Where it is clarified that token offerings subject to regulation effectively have characteristics of regulated financial instruments, such as shares, debentures, units in collective investment schemes, payment instrument; MAS, *A Guide to Digital Token Offerings* (2020) <https://www.mas.gov.sg/-/media/MAS/Sectors/Guidance/Guide-to-Digital-Token-Offerings-26-May-2020.pdf> accessed 5 May 2024.

32 Baker and McKenzie, 'A Complete Guide to Cryptocurrencies and ICOs in Thailand' <https://www.bakermckenzie.com/-/media/files/insight/guides/2023/guide-to-regulation-on-cryptocurrency-and-digital-token.pdf?sc_lang=en&hash=964D4E24866C240B691FC95B484B5265> accessed 5 May 2024.

vices). These offerings must be made via approved digital token offering portals (i.e. the platforms used for conducting token offers). Digital tokens can also be created for assets such as real estate or other debt instruments and special rules apply to them. The authorization regime also extends to digital asset exchanges, brokers, dealers fund managers, advisors and custodial wallet providers. The Thai authorization regime seems to be a pared down version of the securities regulation model, appealing to attract crypto-businesses. Registered digital asset entities that are incorporated in Thailand are subject to 'lite' versions of regulatory regimes adapted from their functional equivalents. To date Thailand has registered about 13 crypto-asset exchanges, and one approved ICO portal in 2019. The first ICO happened in 2021[33] but was based an offering of digitalized real estate tokens. It seems that digitalized tokens in the style of utility tokens for permissionless blockchains have not taken off there.

Malta offers a tailor-made regulatory regime for blockchain-based businesses under the Innovative Technological Arrangements and Services Act (ITASA)[34] and virtual assets under the Virtual Financial Assets Act.[35] This offers broader thinking than a financially focused regime, as the ITASA caters for recognition of blockchain-based enterprises as legitimate registered enterprises in Malta subject to certain standards of governance and accountability. However, the ITASA's bid to boost credibility in the new organizational form has resulted in rather cumbersome legislation imposing responsibilities on systems and technical administrators of distributed ledger arrangements, as well as introducing a third-party technological auditing system, which has taken time to get underway. In 2020, 20 virtual asset offerings were registered with the Maltese regulator but this does not seem to be a significant market share.[36]

The Liechtenstein Token Act 2020[37] takes a different approach by enabling a tokenized economy and the making of liquid markets using the distributed ledger infrastructure. Crypto-asset offers are also proportionately regulated, and principles-based conduct regulation is introduced for issuers, to ensure that DLT arrangements adopted are suitable for users. Principles-based regulation would connect investor protection to *ex post* remedies in general civil law.

It is interesting to compare the endeavours by the pro-innovation jurisdictions that have engaged in regulatory innovation with the pro-innovation jurisdictions that have refrained from regulatory innovation but operate an indirectly permissive regime. The latter group comprises reputable financial jurisdictions, and their refrain from regulatory innovation

---

[33] Paul D Volodarsky, 'Thailand's First Initial Coin Offering Using Real Estate Backed Security Tokens Approved by the Thai Securities and Exchange Commission Expected to Raise THB 2.4 Billion', <https://www.dfdl.com/resources/legal-and-tax-updates/thailands-first-initial-coin-offering-using-real-estate-backed-security-tokens-approved-by-the-thai-securities-and-exchange-commission-expected-to-raise-thb-2-4-billion/> accessed 5 May 2024.

[34] See <https://legislation.mt/eli/cap/592/eng/pdf> accessed 5 May 2024.

[35] Grant Thornton, 'Malta Introduced New Regulations Governing Virtual Financial Assets' <https://www.grantthornton.com.mt/industry/fintech-and-innovation/The-Malta-Virtual-Financial-Asset-Act/> accessed 5 May 2024.

[36] Asia Blockchain Review, 'Malta: A Blockchain Island and Cryptocurrency Wonderland?' (2 March 2020), <https://www.asiablockchainreview.com/malta-a-blockchain-island-and-cryptocurrency-wonderland/> accessed 5 May 2024.

[37] Philipp G. Sandner, Agata Ferreira and Thomas Dunser. 'Crypto Regulation and the case for Europe'. In *Handbook on Blockchain* (Springer 2022) 661–693.

could be motivated by their perception that the already-popular status quo and reputational capital should not be unduly disturbed. Further, if the status quo has already been attracting crypto-asset issuers, then did more need to be done? Hence, these jurisdictions maintained their stance by introducing appropriate balances in consumer protection, such as warnings and bans, but not comprehensive regulatory regimes. They have, however, extended anti-money laundering and financial crime regulation to crypto-asset service providers in order maintain their reputations. On the other hand, jurisdictions engaged in regulatory innovation have ironically been less spectacularly successful in this bid for regulatory competition, as perhaps their existing reputational capital and market size did not sufficiently attract crypto-asset issuers.

2.2 Regulatory Approaches in Pro-Investor Protection Jurisdictions

Jurisdictions where the investor protection objective is dominant have generally developed that way owing to social and institutional pressures. These 'pro-investor jurisdictions' comprise two groups, with the key example of the US in its own 'group', owing to its institutional architecture which has driven a mixture of federal and state approaches. On the other hand, South Korea, Japan and Canada form a group in relation to their similar responses to high-profile scandals. This is not to say these are not pro-innovation jurisdictions, but the chapter's categorization indicates a relative leaning in the face of competing priorities for regulators.

The US features a mixture of state-based and federal approaches to the crypto-economy reflecting the dilemmas in its enabling as well as protective policy orientations. This may also be attributed to its sectoral regulatory system that introduces a multiplicity of goals for financial regulation stewarded by each agency.[38] Nevertheless, it is home to the oldest cryptocurrency exchange, Coinbase, and at the height of 2017 was the top crypto-asset offering jurisdiction. Regulatory policy in the US is very much crafted along the lines of established sectoral delineations. The regulatory regime for money service businesses is applicable to cryptocurrency, the regulatory regime for securities offers is applicable to crypto-asset offers and the regulatory regime for commodities, futures and derivatives trading is applicable to cryptocurrency and crypto-derivatives. State-level policies have been relatively welcoming to innovation in the crypto-economy.[39] However, federal regulators, i.e. the SEC and the Commodities and Futures Trading Commission (CFTC), signal tougher stances against regulatory arbitrage and have taken actions to secure investor protection and market integrity. These stances are perceived as necessary to address high profile scams and frauds, such as the AriseCoin scam.[40]

The SEC and CFTC have interpreted their regulatory perimeters broadly in order to engage in enforcement against unregulated activity,[41] therefore defending their mandates. However,

---

[38] Howell E Jackson, 'Regulation in a Multi-sectored Financial Services Industry' (1999) 77 Washington University Law Quarterly 319.

[39] Over money service businesses, e.g. NY's Bitlicense.

[40] Milind Tiwari, Adrian Gepp and Kuldeep Kumar, 'The Future of Raising Finance – A New Opportunity to Commit Fraud: A Review of Initial Coin Offering (ICOs) Scams' (2020) 73 Crime, Law and Social Change 417.

[41] E.g. SEC's cease and desist order against Munchee Inc. <https://www.sec.gov/litigation/admin/2017/33-10445.pdf>; against Paragoin Coin <https://www.sec.gov/litigation/admin/2018/33-10574.pdf> accessed 5 May 2024; 'SEC Charges Ripple and Two Executives with Conducting

their actions have not provided clarity in terms of what activity or crypto-financial instrument falls within whose regulatory perimeter,[42] and a holistic approach to the financial innovations posed by the crypto-economy is still lacking in the US. The agencies' enforcement actions and their extension of jurisdiction to crypto-financial instruments have culminated in an absolute fall in the issuances of crypto-asset offers in the US.[43] In the alternative some issuers opt only to target accredited investors to avoid securities regulation, and make 'securities token offerings' instead.[44] Empirical research has mixed findings regarding the quality and performance of such offerings.[45] Further, the idea that decentralized applications on permissionless blockchains should only be funded by accredited investors can itself be damaging for the future mass appeal of such applications.[46] The delineation of jurisdiction between the SEC and CFTC also makes it difficult to generate holistic policy and coherent regulatory innovation. Policymakers in the US acknowledge this, especially in view of the passing of the EU's MiCAR. We discuss in Section 4 to what extent the challenge from MiCAR may galvanize choices in US policy regarding the balance of pro-innovation and investor protection.

Jurisdictions such as Canada, Japan and South Korea have also faced challenges in making choices between pro-innovation and investor protection policy objectives. Japan was an early welcomer of crypto innovations and the now-defunct Mt Gox was one of the earliest cryptocurrency exchanges in the world. In response to the failure of Mt Gox and the security hack at crypto-exchange Coincheck which lost customers' cryptocurrency holdings, the Japanese have introduced regulation for crypto-exchanges[47] and have introduced regulation

---

$1.3 Billion Unregistered Securities Offering' (22 December 2020), <https://www.sec.gov/news/press-release/2020-338> accessed 5 May 2024; and CFTC's enforcement against My Big Coin, CFTC v My Big Coin Pay Inc (26 September 2018), <https://www.cftc.gov/sites/default/files/2018-10/enfmybigcoinpayincmemorandum092618.pdf> accessed 5 May 2024.

42 Carol R Goforth, 'U.S. Law: Crypto is Money, Property, a Commodity, and a Security, all at the Same Time' (2019) Journal of Financial Transformation <https://papers.ssrn.com/sol3/papers.cfm?abstract_id=3272975> accessed 5 May 2024.

43 Cristiano Bellavitis, Christian Fisch and Johan Wiklund, 'A Comprehensive Review of the Global Development of Initial Coin Offerings (ICOs) and Their Regulation' (2021) 15 Journal of Business Venturing Insights.

44 Y Guseva, 'When the Means Undermine the End: The Leviathan of Securities Law and Enforcement in Digital-Asset Markets' (Stanford Journal of Blockchain Law and Policy, 2022) <https://papers.ssrn.com/sol3/papers.cfm?abstract_id=3694709> accessed 5 May 2024.

45 Lennart Ante and Ingo Fiedler, 'Cheap Signals in Security Token Offerings' (2020) 4 Quantitative Finance and Economics 608; Jingxing (Rowena) Gan, Gerry Tsoukalas and Serguei Netessine, 'Initial Coin Offerings, Speculation, and Asset Tokenization' (2022) 67 Management Science 914.

46 Chiu (n 4) ch 2; Christian Schaefer and Steffen Stresse, 'Beyond Fundraising – Token Dispersion and Venture Performance in Initial Coin Offerings' (2021) Academy of Management Annual Meeting Proceedings; Evgeny Lyandres, Berardino Palazzo and Daniel Rabetti, 'Initial Coin Offering (ICO) Success and Post-ICO Performance' (2022) Management Science <https://doi.org/10.1287/mnsc.2022.4312> accessed 5 May 2024.

47 Japan has since 2016 regulated crypto-exchanges' custodial responsibilities under its Payment Services Act; Takeshi Nagase, Takato Fukui, and Keisuko Hatano, 'Blockchain & Cryptocurrency Laws and Regulations 2024' (Global Legal Insights) <https://www.globallegalinsights.com/practice-areas/blockchain-laws-and-regulations/japan> accessed 5 May 2024.

for stablecoin issuance by limiting such issuance to be carried out by regulated banks and trust companies.[48] Retail-level activity in cryptocurrency and crypto-assets was also rife in South Korea[49] until crypto-exchange scandals and the collapse of stablecoins Terra and Luna prompted increasingly intensive regulation.[50] South Korea has also banned the issuance of crypto-asset offers since 2019.[51] Canada has also introduced regulation for crypto-exchanges that take custody of their customers' cryptocurrency or asset holdings,[52] arguably in response to the Quadriga CX fiasco. Customers were locked out of their funds held by the exchange, as private keys to customer accounts were stored in the founder's computer which could not be accessed after his sudden demise.

In sum, high-profile scandals and social discontent can feature prominently in the protective choices made in financial regulatory policy. This is because the need for an immediate response is often pressing. Regulators and policy makers facing scandal-driven pressures often choose to tilt in favour of stronger investor protection and concomitantly, restrictions upon crypto-asset or service activities. Restrictive regulatory choices, often leveraging existing regulatory tenets, can be perceived to be able to deliver investor protection. This position is understandable as existing regulation reflects what is forged in the social contract between financial citizens and regulators with state-given mandates. However, the result of such regulatory interventions is that the enabling aspects of regulation tend to be marginalized.

2.3 Prohibitive Jurisdictions

Finally, some jurisdictions have introduced highly restrictive and defensive stances against cryptocurrency or crypto-assets arguably because of the perceived threats to political, social or institutional stability. China has been an early mover that has banned crypto-asset commercial activity, i.e. purchasing, trading, intermediating crypto-asset investments and exchange

---

48 Helen Partz, 'Japan Passes Bill to Limit Stablecoin Issuance to Banks and Trust Companies' (Cointelegraph, 3 June 2022), <https://cointelegraph.com/news/japan-passes-bill-to-limit-stablecoin-issuance-to-banks-and-trust-companies> accessed 5 May 2024.

49 Jung Min-kyung, 'S. Korea's Crypto Assets Exceed W55tr' (The Korean Herald, 1 March 2022), <http://www.koreaherald.com/view.php?ud=20220301000232> accessed 5 May 2024.

50 Danny Park, 'Guilty Verdicts Handed Down in S. Korea's Biggest Crypto Scam' (Forkast News, 11 February 2022) <https://forkast.news/guilty-verdicts-crypto-scam-south-korea/> accessed 5 May 2024; Bruno Invernizzi, 'In the Wake of Terra's Collapse, South Korea Plans New Crypto Oversight Committee: Report' (Cointelegraph, 31 May 2022) <https://cointelegraph.com/news/in-wake-of-terra-collapse-south-korea-plans-new-crypto-oversight-committee-report> accessed 5 May 2024.

51 Joseph Young, 'Why South Korea had to Ban Crypto-ICOs' (CCN, 2 March 2019), <https://www.ccn.com/why-south-korea-ban-crypto-ico-risk-billion-dollars> accessed 5 May 2024.

52 Canadian Securities Administrators, 'CSA Staff Notice 21-327 Guidance on the Application of Securities Legislation to Entities Facilitating the Trading of Crypto Assets' (CSA, 16 January 2020), <https://www.bcsc.bc.ca/Securities_Law/Policies/Policy2/PDF/21-327__CSA_Staff_Notice__-_January_16__2020/> accessed 5 May 2024.

between fiat and cryptocurrency.[53] The Chinese ban[54] has been attributed to policymakers' concerns that crypto-asset investment and payment systems would facilitate the transfer of Chinese capital to overseas markets and evade capital controls put in place by the government. Further, this ban is also in line with China's crackdown on shadow banking in general, where financial activity has been shifting away from mainstream regulated institutions that are perceived to be too restrictive or expensive.[55] Bans are also in place in jurisdictions such as Bolivia,[56] Bangladesh[57] and Turkey, where the use of cryptocurrency and crypto-assets and making payment or facilitation of transfer or investment in them are prohibited. These jurisdictions seem to be motivated by the need to protect the status of their national currency, especially in view of wider contexts of institutional instability. In 2021, India has moved to ban cryptocurrency and provided a transition period for users to cash out.[58] These protective interests are rooted in contextual issues regarding the nature of authority in political regimes and perceived existential and institutional threats. These objectives are hence different in nature from investor protection priorities discussed above. It is predicted that these regimes would probably see no need to respond to MiCAR's lead in regulatory innovation, and the rest of the chapter will be based on a comparison between jurisdictions that largely pursue economically based objectives in dealing with the challenges posed by the crypto-asset market.

Section 3 posits that MiCAR establishes a new policy benchmark for regulators worldwide who recognize the economic phenomena on permissionless blockchains and the creation of crypto-assets, but have been grappling with different policy priorities. It arguably provides a benchmark in terms of a sound policy balance, being enabling and pro-innovation in nature, while providing investor protection in proportionate terms. The key features of MiCAR are sketched below in order to flesh out the 'policy balance' struck in MiCAR.

53 'China's Top Regulators Ban Crypto Trading and Mining, Sending Bitcoin Tumbling' (Reuters 24 Sep 2021) <https://www.reuters.com/world/china/china-central-bank-vows-crackdown-cryptocurrency-trading-2021-09-24/> accessed 5 May 2024.

54 Bhushan Akolkar, 'China Officially Bans All Crypto-Related Commercial Activities' (Bitcoinist, August 2018) <https://bitcoinist.com/china-officially-bans-crypto-activities/> accessed 5 May 2024.

55 See W Shen, *Shadow Banking in China: Risk, Regulation and Policy* (Cheltenham, UK and Northampton, MA, USA: Edward Elgar Publishing 2016) chs 5–9.

56 Pete Rizzo, 'Bolivia's Central Bank Bans Bitcoin' (Coindesk, 19 June 2014) <https://www.coindesk.com/markets/2014/06/19/bolivias-central-bank-bans-bitcoin> accessed 5 May 2024.

57 Golam Mowla, 'Central Bank Issues Notice Banning Bitcoin in Bangladesh' (Dhaka Tribune, 27 December 2017) <https://www.dhakatribune.com/business/banks/133954/central-bank-issues-notice-banning-bitcoin-in> accessed 5 May 2024.

58 Sebastian Sinclair, 'India Grants Crypto Holders Reprieve Ahead of Likely Ban: Report' (Coindesk, 12 February 2021) <https://www.coindesk.com/markets/2021/02/12/india-grants-crypto-holders-reprieve-ahead-of-likely-ban-report> accessed 5 May 2024.

3. MICAR AND ITS POLICY ACHIEVEMENTS

The European Commission's proposal for a Market in Cryptoassets Regulation (MiCAR) finally became law on 31 May 2023.[59] This establishes a regulatory policy for crypto-asset offers, utility tokens, asset-referenced stablecoins, electronic money tokens and crypto-asset service providers. MiCAR is situated against the broader context of the EU's digital finance strategy.[60] This strategy encompasses the need to address new risks emanating from Fintech, digitalization of financial businesses and interfaces as well as crypto-financial developments, while harnessing the benefits of innovation and financial inclusion. In this manner, MiCAR strikes a policy balance that encourages innovation while subjecting risks to appropriate governance.

MiCAR provides an enabling regulatory framework for crypto-asset offers, allowing compliant issuers to benefit from a European passport. These do not include asset-referenced and electronic money tokens, as issuers of asset-referenced tokens must be either an existing regulated credit institution or be authorized, and issuers of electronic money tokens would be regulated electronic money institutions under the Electronic Money Directive. There is however an exemption threshold for offers under 1 million euros over a period of 12 months or targeted at less than 150 investors or exclusively to qualified investors.

The general crypto-asset offer regime caters for pre-developmental fund-raising for tokens that would embed future rights. The regulatory regime requires issuers to make mandatory disclosure in a white paper and is flanked by certain investor protection measures. The disclosure requirements are far less demanding than under prospectus regulation for securities, and in view of the speculative and early-development nature of projects, disclosure items are rather broadly framed. It may be argued that such open-endedness, such as requiring the broad disclosure of 'underlying technologies' or 'information on risks', allows issuers to provide their own narratives, and is less imposing as not being overly prescriptive. But on the other hand, issuers' legal risks may be uncertain since technologies may be in development and may change, so issuers are left to determine what extent of disclosure mitigates their legal risk of compliance. Further, how do issuers disclose matters like risks to investors, that may change in nature owing to the developmental state of the project? If issuers have not finalized their technological programming, it is also uncertain if they can give definite disclosure regarding principal adverse impact on the environment and climate, a mandatory matter for disclosure. Can a crypto-asset issuer developing an application on Ethereum, for example, assume that the proof-of-stake consensus mechanisms do not generate adverse climate impact? Although principles-based disclosure requirements may seem less imposing, issuers may be left to figure out their legal risks.

The regime also provides for a summary to be provided accompanying the white paper. This seems derivative of the prospectus regime for securities. It is questioned if this adds much to

---

59 Commission Implementing Regulation (EU) 2023/1104 of 6 June 2023 amending Regulation (EC) No 1238/95 as regards the fees payable to the Community Plant Variety Office [2023] OJ L 147/65.

60 Directorate-General for Financial Stability, Financial Services and Capital Markets Union, 'FinTech Action Plan: For a More Competitive and Innovative European Financial Sector' (European Commission, 8 March 2018) <https://finance.ec.europa.eu/publications/fintech-action-plan-more-competitive-and-innovative-european-financial-sector_en> accessed 5 May 2024.

retail investor understanding given the already high-level qualitative nature of the white paper and the lack of civil remedy for the summary on a stand-alone basis.

There is no merit vetting of white papers by national securities regulators, but mandatory warnings to retail investors about the speculative and illiquid nature of these tokens must be made. Investors are also protected by the general disclosure standards of 'fair, clear and not misleading' which can entail civil actions otherwise. Investor protection is not exclusively sought in transparency and certain protective measures are in place. Investors have an *ex post* cooling off period of up to 14 days. In order to protect investors, issuers must place raised funds in custody so that withdrawal rights can be expeditiously met.

MiCAR arguably strikes a balance between enabling crypto-asset offers to be made of utility tokens, while providing a governance regime for investor protection that is proportionate. The proportionality lies in relatively less demanding disclosure on the part of issuers while giving investors an opportunity to consider their decisions in a cooling off period, therefore nudging investors to take responsibility for their decisions to engage with a speculative and illiquid investment. Given the empirical evidence on spectacular gains with some ICOs,[61] MiCAR arguably takes a liberal position for investors to determine if such investment opportunities are worth their while.

The regulation of asset-referenced stablecoins is in contrast more protective as these assets are intertwined with conventional financial assets or fiat currency. Regulators would assess the white papers for such offers, involving also the ECB for opinions, and can consider permitting or refusing the offer to be made based on grounds relating to prudence, or the reputation and quality of the issuer's management and shareholders. Continuing regulation for asset-referenced stablecoin issuers is introduced in relation to their conduct, for investor protection[62] as well as other regulatory objectives.

An obligation is placed on issuers with large circulations to ensure that there is a daily cap on transaction value. This is intended to prevent tokens' attainment of systemic or monetary importance that may be disruptive for the functioning of public institutions. Further, prudential requirements, the regulation of issuers' governance and the regulation of reserve maintenance, custodial arrangements, liquidity management and recovery planning are all targeted towards mitigating financial stability risks with respect to these tokens. Regulators' right to vet the potential acquisition of asset-referenced stablecoin issuers pertain to the same objective. Significant tokens with a market cap of 5 billion euros or with over 10 million holders are regulated more stringently for prudential risk management. However, compared with the regulation of money market funds' compositions and liquidity management, it may be argued that the overall regime for asset-referenced stablecoins is relatively less detailed. This is arguably a fair position given that the attraction of stablecoins as near cash-like vehicles still remains to be seen, while the looming context of bank regulation and risk or liquidity management frameworks signal regulators' preparedness to deal with stablecoins' financial stability risks. There is however a general prohibition for asset-referenced and electronic money token issuers to offer interest to investors so as to prevent backdoor competition to deposit-takers.

What may be most significant in MiCAR's policy choice is that asset-referenced stablecoin issues are limited to existing regulated banks or other otherwise authorized issuers whose

---

[61] See n 13.

[62] Such as redemption rights and custody arrangements.

authorization processes resemble the ones applicable to banks and investment firms. In this manner the asset-referenced stablecoin market is skewed in favour of incumbent financial institutions familiar with regulatory demands. On the one hand it can be argued that such institutions would more likely be able to accommodate compliance for stablecoins. In this manner, issues of stablecoins can be made safely for efficient cross-border peer-to-peer payment purposes, such as envisaged in the JPM Coin introduced by JP Morgan.[63] This may however pose high barriers to entry for other, especially non-financial, competitors, such as the now-relegated Diem project started by Meta.[64] Regulators' perception of financial stability risks from the possibility of payment disruption by BigTech has led to a conservative approach relating to asset-referenced stablecoins. This approach is however similarly considered in the US, as discussed shortly.

MiCAR also provides for a regulatory regime for crypto-asset service providers. In so doing, it makes provisions towards the elimination of regulatory arbitrage between established regulated intermediaries subject to conduct regulation regimes (such as the Markets in Financial Instruments regime) and those involved in crypto-asset intermediation. The extension of market abuse regulation to crypto-asset trading also achieves the same effect. Crypto-asset service providers need to be authorized upon meeting organizational, governance (including technological governance), risk management and operational conditions such as those relating to client money/asset custody and business continuity. They are subject to ongoing regulation of their internal governance, prudential requirements, business continuity, conflict of interest management and protective obligations with respect to custody of client monies and assets. These standardizations arguably seem all the more imperative after the fall of FTX. Principles-based regulation is also deployed to subject all crypto-asset service providers across-the-board to conduct of honesty and fairness, reflecting an emerging regime where problems are yet to be fully detected. Principles-based regulation can also more elastically be extended to intermediaries whose nature may be partially decentralized. Providers of Decentralized Finance (DeFi) protocols should not be certain that they fall outside of MiCAR's definition for crypto-asset service providers as arguably only high levels of peer level autonomy or decentralization would suffice. Partially centralized protocols can still be regarded, for example, as 'crypto-asset service providers' that 'exchange crypto-assets against funds', therefore needing authorization and subject to conduct regulation. This potential elasticity, which concomitantly creates legal risk for DeFi arrangements, can also be important for regulators to take swift actions on the basis of investor and consumer protection.

There are certain specialized rules for crypto-asset intermediaries engaged in relatively developed forms of services. Centralized trading crypto-exchanges are subject to specific rules regarding their admissions and maintenance of an orderly marketplace, and an equivalent of the best execution rule for securities trading is introduced for service providers that intermedi-

63 ONYX, 'Digital Solutions Enabling Instant Transfer and Clearing of Multi-bank, Multi-currency Assets on a Permissioned Distributed Ledger' <https://www.jpmorgan.com/onyx/coin-system.htm> accessed 5 May 2024. This token allows cross-border transfers within the vast and global JP Morgan branch network.

64 BBC, 'Facebook-funded Cryptocurrency Diem Winds Down' (BBC News, 1 February 2022), <https://www.bbc.co.uk/news/technology-60156682> accessed 5 May 2024. Diem was envisaged to be a token empowering cross-border transfers across the Facebook platform amongst users.

ate others' trading or exchanges involving crypto-assets. There are also specific conduct obligations for crypto-asset advisors. These are poised to eliminate regulatory arbitrage between crypto and conventional intermediaries engaged in equivalently functional business models.

The MiCAR is a starting point and may need further adjustment as crypto innovations change. However, it does provide broad contours of the balance between enabling and governing aspects in regulation, employing a significant berth of principles-based regulation for conduct while imposing conservatism while financial stability risks matter. Further it has established the preferred policy balance in addressing regulatory arbitrage, fleshing out policymakers' broad preference for 'same activity, same risks, same rules'. Nevertheless, gaps remain, such as there being no specific treatment of algorithmic stablecoins.[65] But it can be argued that offers of these crypto-assets would fall under the general offer regime and their specific 'monetary' policy should be disclosed in the white paper. MiCAR's main drawback may however lie in national implementation as it remains to be seen if national fragmentation can be exacerbated owing to Member States' different agendas in courting the crypto industry.[66] The next section argues that MiCAR has set a benchmark in terms of policy objectives and their balance, whether or not critique of its details remains.[67] This is especially relevant to the US, which is shaping a federal regime. However, by end 2022, the key driver that is spurring many jurisdictions to consider explicit crypto regulation is the scandal regarding FTX, whose narrative, seized upon by international bodies, can forge a path towards convergence of key jurisdictions' regulatory policies.

4. POST-MICAR REGULATORY INITIATIVES

The formalization of MiCAR in the EU as law has most observably galvanized endeavours of regulatory innovation in the US. Further, MiCAR's introduction on the world stage reflects the possibility of achieving a bespoke regulatory regime for crypto-assets. Hence, the debate between whether to fit into an existing regulatory regime or to forge a new one seems resolved in favour of the latter. International financial bodies which have led global standards in convergence also leverage upon MiCAR's framework and principles in order to forge paths towards regulatory convergence.

One of the biggest hurdles to regulatory clarity and coherence in the US is the sectorally delineated regulatory agency structure which comes under test in the face of innovative

65 Ryan Clements, 'Built to Fail: The Inherent Fragility of Algorithmic Stablecoins' (2022) 11 The Wake Forest Law Review Online 131 <https://papers.ssrn.com/sol3/papers.cfm?abstract_id=3952045> accessed 5 May 2024.

66 E.g. Binance, 'France's Courting of Binance, "Binance is Now a Fully Regulated Digital Asset Service Provider in France"' (5 May 2022) <https://www.binance.com/en/blog/markets/binance-is-now-a-fully-regulated-digital-asset-service-provider-in-france-421499824684903809> accessed 5 May 2024.

67 Tina van der Linden and Tina Shirazi, 'Markets in Crypto-Assets Regulation: Does it Provide Legal Certainty and Increase Adoption of Crypto-Assets?' (2022) 9 Financial Innovation 22; David Florysiak, 'Utility Tokens, Markets in Crypto Assets Regulation (MiCAR), and the Costs of Being Public' (2023), <https://papers.ssrn.com/sol3/papers.cfm?abstract_id=4295913> accessed 5 May 2024. (With a more positive view.)

finance that disrupts sectoral boundaries. Although this financial architecture is situated within a rich historical policy context, there is significant need to ensure dynamism and responsiveness to innovations. In June 2022, senators Lummis and Gillibrand introduced the bipartisan Responsible Financial Innovation Act,[68] hoping to deliver coherent regulatory policy in the US despite the institutional barriers. This Bill is being refined for unveiling in the middle of 2023 but other endeavours such as the Republican-sponsored McHenry et al. draft is also being discussed.

Given the existing sectorally delineated regulatory agency structure, determining the appropriate federal regulator is not straightforward. The Lummis–Gillibrand Act chooses the CFTC to be the main regulator while the McHenry et al. draft sees both the SEC and CFTC as having possible jurisdiction over different types of intermediaries for digital assets and commodities.

Under both drafts, the regulation of crypto-assets (termed 'ancillary assets' as a subset of digital assets in the Lummis–Gillibrand Act and as 'digital assets' in the McHenry et al. draft), seems proportionate, bearing in mind the need for investor protection. As is the tradition in the US, investor protection is reliant on mandatory transparency by the issuer. The McHenry draft contains requirements for a registration document that is not too demanding, in similar vein to the MiCAR. The Lummis–Gillibrand Act relies, however, on semi-annual continuing disclosure to the market by the issuer 180 days after the initial offer, if the market capitalization of the issuer is USD5 million or above. Continuing disclosure relates to a list of key information which seems pared down from conventional securities disclosure. This approach is different from that of MiCAR, which places emphasis on initial transparency as well as broad conduct regulation on the part of issuers. The continuing transparency approach can arguably be superior as continuing transparency is more relevant to investors who invest in a pre-development project, as is the case with most crypto-asset offers. Investors would rely on ex post litigation for misleading transparency in the continuing disclosure framework. Both Acts compel disclosure of source code and the McHenry Act has given some thought to pre-development projects and the need to disclose developmental plans as well as the blockchain economics for the crypto-asset offer.

The Lummis–Gillibrand Act subjects digital asset exchanges to voluntary registration and oversight but the McHenry et al. draft covers a wider range of crypto intermediaries and envisages compulsory registration for the relevant intermediary with either the SEC or CFTC. This position has ultimately been supported. The McHenry Act, subject to some modifications which see the SEC and CFTC joint committee as the main overseers of the crypto industry, passed Congress at the end of 2023 with bipartisan support, with its legislative fate still to be determined at the time of writing.[69] Voluntary registration may be untenable after the fall of FTX, although that would reflect a more enabling regulatory framework in nature as it incentivizes the bonding of digital asset exchanges to high standards, while recognizing the international mobility of digital asset exchanges. However, given the need for customer protection such as custodial protections and adequate governance, MiCAR's policy benchmark of mandatory regulation for crypto-asset exchanges seems to have been preferred. Further, as

---

[68] S. 4356, 117th Congress, 2d session, introduced in the Senate, 7 June 2022 <https://www.congress.gov/bill/117th-congress/senate-bill/4356/text#toc-idc9eee73973994df0a374639e54ad8a1f> accessed 5 May 2024.

[69] See <https://www.congress.gov/118/bills/hr4763/BILLS-118hr4763ih.pdf> accessed 5 May 2024.

customers can be attracted to unregulated venues by the promise of low or no fees,[70] market discipline may be lacking where registration of exchanges remains voluntary.

The leadership of the MiCAR has influenced the US response to crypto-regulation[71] as a bespoke regulatory framework seems increasingly likely. This moves away from the current approaches of the SEC and CFTC enforcement actions which can only fit crypto developments into existing frameworks, risking misfit and the lack of clarity.[72] Nevertheless, MiCAR may suffer from fragmented national regulatory administration which affects law in action. Authorization, supervision and enforcement will be largely at a Member State level except where asset-referenced stablecoins are involved with bank supervisors and the ECB. There is, however, a high-level vision for the crypto-asset industry in the US,[73] whose policy balance shares a similar tenor with that of the EU.

By the end of 2022, the crypto universe has been dogged by a significant scandal – the fall of FTX,[74] a large crypto-exchange fronted by charismatic founder and CEO Sam Bankman-Fried. The exchange is incorporated and domiciled in the Bahamas and suffered a liquidity run after story broke regarding concentrated investments made by the exchange in Alameda Research, Bankman-Fried's hedge fund, and missing unaccountable monies from FTX. FTX suffered withdrawals to the point of being unable to honour customers' requests, and has since filed for bankruptcy protection. Revelations of fund misappropriations have now culminated in criminal charges filed against Bankman-Fried.[75] Mainstream investors such as Blackrock and Singapore wealth fund Temasek Holdings nursed significant losses.

The power of a major scandal to drive regulation is an enduring one, as financial regulators are often hesitant to act unless there is incontrovertible evidence of market failure. The UK, which has long refrained from comprehensive MiCAR-like regulation, has now changed its tune and has introduced in its Financial Services and Markets act 2023 a new power for the FCA to regulate the crypto-assets. A blueprint for comprehensive regulation, including

---

[70] Such as Zero-fee trading introduced by Binance, for Bitcoin and Ether; Binance, 'Binance Launches Zero-Fee Bitcoin Trading' (6 July 2022) <https://www.binance.com/en/support/announcement/10435147c55d4a40b64fcbf43cb46329> accessed 5 May 2024.

[71] Amitoj Singh, 'U.S. House Will Have Crypto Bill in 2 Months: Rep. McHenry' (Coindesk, 28 Apr 2023) <https://www.coindesk.com/policy/2023/04/28/us-house-will-have-crypto-bill-in-2-months-mchenry/> accessed 5 May 2024.

[72] For example, the NY district court's indeterminate ruling on whether crypto-assets are securities, *SEC vs Ripple* 13 July 2023 <https://www.nysd.uscourts.gov/sites/default/files/2023-07/SEC%20vs%20Ripple%207-13-23.pdf> accessed 5 May 2024.

[73] The White House, 'FACT SHEET: President Biden to Sign Executive Order on Ensuring Responsible Development of Digital Assets' (9 March 2022) <https://www.whitehouse.gov/briefing-room/statements-releases/2022/03/09/fact-sheet-president-biden-to-sign-executive-order-on-ensuring-responsible-innovation-in-digital-assets/> accessed 5 May 2024.

[74] Kenneth Rapoza, 'FTX Debacle: Is There Anyway To Calm Crypto Investors Down?' (22 November 2022) <https://www.forbes.com/sites/kenrapoza/2022/11/22/ftx-debacle-is-there-anyway-to-calm-crypto-investors-down/> accessed 5 May 2024.

[75] *The Guardian*, 'FTX Founder Sam Bankman-Fried Charged with Defrauding Investors' (*The Guardian*, 13 December 2022) <https://www.theguardian.com/technology/2022/dec/13/sam-bankman-fried-ftx-charged-sec-crypto-exchange> accessed 5 May 2024.

crypto-asset offers, the regulation of centralized crypto-exchanges and other service providers, as well as approaches to stablecoins, has been unveiled.[76]

There is imminent movement that many jurisdictions worldwide are considering crypto regulation more explicitly and comprehensively in the wake of the FTX scandal. Hong Kong is considering regulating crypto-exchanges explicitly,[77] and Singapore has considered more specific consumer protection rules in the wake of the failure of Three Arrows, a Singapore-based hedge fund that suffered significant losses owing to the collapse of algorithmic stablecoins Terra and Luna.[78] With these articulations, it is also opportune that international financial bodies such as the FSB and IOSCO have now made clearer regulatory recommendations for crypto-finance, leading a path towards policy convergence.

IOSCO has unveiled a consultation[79] on regulatory standards for crypto and digital asset markets, focusing on centralized crypto-exchanges and crypto-service providers. These policy recommendations are highly aligned with MiCAR, and respond clearly to the fall of FTX. Market operators and service providers intermediating crypto-assets are to be brought within the same conduct and governance frameworks including customer protection and custodial responsibility, conflict of interest management and operating a fair, orderly and transparent marketplace as well as combatting market abuse and manipulation. Further, the FSB will, building on its early endeavours to warn of stablecoin risks, unveil concrete recommendations for international policy convergence for crypto-assets and stablecoins.[80] It is perhaps no coincidence that the FSB European group's announcement came on the same day as the IOSCO consultation. International coordination seems more orchestrated than was observed pre-MiCAR.

This chapter perceives MiCAR's policy benchmark as a turning point that entails a need for response, especially from key jurisdictions like the US. International financial bodies where European Member States are well represented also provide fora for MiCAR's policy benchmark to become more influential, overcoming the earlier ambiguities in international bodies' narratives. There is potential for convergent policy recommendations to be made, even if regulatory details may differ to an extent. Such convergence is remarkable given the starting point of major differences in terms of how crypto-asset offers, stablecoins and crypto-intermediaries are conceptualized and risk-assessed in terms of regulatory objectives and approaches.

---

76 HM Treasury, 'Future Financial Services Regulatory Regime for Cryptoassets' (1 February 2023) <https://www.gov.uk/government/consultations/future-financial-services-regulatory-regime-for-cryptoassets> accessed 5 May 2024.

77 Prashant Jha, 'Hong Kong to Subject Crypto Exchanges to the Same Laws Governing TradFi' (Coindesk, 8 December 2022) <https://cointelegraph.com/news/hong-kong-to-subject-crypto-exchanges-to-the-same-laws-governing-tradfi> accessed 5 May 2024.

78 Iris H-Y Chiu, 'Singapore Proposes Crypto Rules to Bolster Consumer Protection', *Financial Times* (26 October 2022) <https://www.ft.com/content/9074c158-bd38-4355-92dc-30e3d4ea0c01> accessed 5 May 2024, although predating FTX, was in response to the failure of Three Arrows.

79 OICU-IOSCO, 'Policy Recommendations for Crypto and Digital Asset Markets: Consultation Report' (May 2023) <https://www.iosco.org/library/pubdocs/pdf/IOSCOPD734.pdf> accessed 5 May 2024.

80 Financial Stability Board, 'FSB Europe Group Discusses Risks to Financial Stability, Including Recent Banking Sector Stress, DeFi and Climate Change' (FSB, 23 May 2023) <https://www.fsb.org/2023/05/fsb-europe-group-discusses-risks-to-financial-stability-including-recent-banking-sector-stress-defi-and-climate-change/> accessed 5 May 2024.

5. CONCLUSION

This chapter discusses regulatory approaches to crypto-asset offers, a phenomenon that exploded in 2017–2018, as a form of unregulated fund-raising. Initial different policy approaches were taken by regulators owing to different priorities for pro-innovation, investor protection or other protective interests. The EU has now introduced the MiCAR which offers a policy balance between enabling regulation and proportionate governance for the crypto-asset market. This has led to accelerated regulatory policy in the US as well as the start of international policy convergence. International convergence has also been driven by the fall of large unregulated exchange FTX which provides a culminating market failure moment for regulators worldwide. This chapter offers two key takeaways in policy development comparison. One, policy and regulatory divergences often emerge amongst jurisdictions in the face of a new phenomenon, but these divergences and priorities may be forged towards convergence if narratives of a global and common problem arise and capture regulators' imaginations. Two, the leadership of a pioneering policy in a key jurisdiction, such as the EU in the form of MiCAR, can provide a benchmark effect for other regulators' considerations, although on its own (without the global driver of FTX's failure), the convergence persuasion as such may be mixed.

Index